POLICIES OF THATCHERISM

POLICIES OF THATCHERISM

Thoughts from a London Thinktank

Edited by

DR. RICHARD HAAS & OLIVER KNOX

UNIVERSITY
PRESS OF
AMERICA

Lanham • New York • London

C·P·S·

University Press of America®, Inc.
4720 Boston Way
Lanham, Maryland 20706

3 Henrietta Street
London WC2E 8LU England

Co-published by arrangement with the Centre for Policy Studies

"Victorian Values and Twentieth-Century Condescension"
is copyrighted by the author, Gertrude Himmelfarb

All other essays are copyrighted by the Centre for Policy Studies

Library of Congress Cataloging-in-Publication Data

Policies of Thatcherism : thoughts from a London thinktank
/ edited by Richard Haas & Oliver Knox.
p.   cm.
Includes index.
1. Great Britain—Politics and government—1979-
2. Great Britain—Economic policy—1945-
3. Great Britain—Social policy—1979-
4. Conservatism—Great Britain.
I. Haas, Richard, Dr.   II. Knox, Oliver.
JN237 1991.P65   1991
320.5'2'0941—dc20   90-22861 CIP

ISBN 0-8191-8119-6
ISBN 0-8191-8120-X (pbk.)

 The paper used in this publication meets the minimum requirements of
American National Standard for Information Sciences—Permanence
of Paper for Printed Library Materials, ANSI Z39.48–1984.

Contents

Part Five: The Years of Privatisation

1O DOWNING STREET

LONDON SW1A 2AA

THE PRIME MINISTER

I am delighted that the University Press of America is publishing
this collection of pamphlets by the Centre for Policy Studies
in Britain.

In the 15 years since the Centre was founded by Sir Keith Joseph
and myself, it has provided inspiration for many of the policies
which our Conservative Government has put into practice. A
number of these policy ideas, which were often accused of being
impractical when they were first put forward, are now universally
accepted and are being implemented by governments across the
world. I am very pleased, therefore, that people in America will
have a chance to read these pamphlets. Although the recommendations
they make are for policies in Britain, the principles that underlie
them are universal.

Margaret Thatcher

June, 1989

Introduction

No. 8 Wilfred Street is a modest 18th century house, spared both by the bombs of war and the developers after the war, standing about half way between the Houses of Parliament and Buckingham Palace. Upon entering, the visitor—and let us suppose he is a distinguished academic from the United States, for there are many such who have visited us—will have his eye caught by the placard which hangs above the fireplace of the room serving to receive guests:—

I do think we have accomplished the revival of the philosophy and principles of a free society, and the acceptance of it. And that is absolutely the thing that I live for. History will accord a very great place to Keith Joseph in that accomplishment. A tremendous place. Because he was imbued by this passion too. We set up the Centre for Policy Studies, and it has propagated those ideas, and they have been accepted.

That is the statement by Mrs. Thatcher, quoted in *The Observer* of 24 February 1979. And it speaks for itself. During the fifteen years of its existence, the Centre has remained true to the political hopes of its two founders: hopes founded on giving freedom to individual enterprise, and to the workings of choice and competition within a framework of law: the hopes, indeed, on which the moral case for capitalism rests.

At least three threads are common to the pamphlets which are published in this collection. The first might be said to derive from the tenets of classical liberalism: that it is idle, and often intolerable, to attempt to control most of the activities of the private person, whose energies create the wealth of the nation. The second concerns the vigilance, which must be sleepless, against the encroachments of State power; this underlies the work which the Centre has done from its early days to promote the privatisation of organisations so long shackled by state ownership and control. And the third is the conviction that where the State must act—for example to preserve the honesty of its currency, the integrity of its institutions, the welfare of the unfortunate—it must do so with immediacy, unabashedness, strength.

To these threads let me add scepticism about the collectivism and corporatism which characterised the British political landscape for so much of the thirty years after the last Great War; and which spelt the antithesis of freedom.

But if the mood of these papers is constant, the burden of their recommendations varies; the Centre has never sought to straitjacket its authors, always asking them only to search for new ideas to resolve the political problems of the day; and, in that search, to follow the argument where it leads.

A word about the way in which the Centre pursues its tasks. We are fortunate in having Directors with intimate knowledge of, and free access to, many of the most imaginative and able brains in Westminster, Whitehall, the Universities and the media. The Centre is their meeting ground. Through dinners, study groups and working parties set up to tackle the problems of the day—through informal conversations of every kind and at almost every hour of the day and night—ideas can be discussed without any feeling of grim or onerous responsibility.

No doubt many of these ideas fall to the ground, dissolve under the heat of discussion; that is in the nature of things. But, as I hope this selection demonstrates, what is liveliest and best comes through all the necessary and critical examination; and, both in pamphlet form and in the conferences which we regularly hold after the publication of our pamphlets, helps to form policies designed to be tomorrow's engines of capitalism, of freedom and of enterprise.

I have been privileged to be the Chairman of the Centre for Policy Studies over the last ten years. During that time I have often stood surprised by the fecundity of the ideas which issue, as from some beneficent volcano, from our authors and colleagues. But few things have given me more pleasure than this invitation by the University Press of America to share some of the productions of those years with a far wider range of American readers than we have been able to reach hitherto. The Prime Minister's preface endorses this sentiment.

Lord Thomas of Swynnerton

Part One

The New Conservatism—
Friends and Enemies

The Local Left and Its National Pretensions

David Regan

Labour party traditions and local government

There are three main intellectual traditions in the British Labour Party—the Fabian, the Guild Socialist and the Marxist. They represent respectively the pragmatic, the romantic and the harshly doctrinal emphases in socialism. These three traditions, together with lesser ones, have shaped the development of the party and its policies. The traditions have not of course followed entirely discrete paths. They have interacted with one another. Some Labour policies have been syntheses of elements from two or more of them. Nevertheless the thrust of the three main traditions is different, not least in respect of local government.

The Fabian tradition

The Fabian Society was founded in January 1884 to work for the reconstruction of society on a non-competitive basis. It was an off-shoot of the Fellowship of the New Life, one of the many Utopian groups which bred in the nineteenth century. It had been established a few months earlier, to create a community of superior people who would subordinate the material to the spiritual, and would demonstrate by exceptional moral behaviour how a higher life might be led. One of those initially involved with this Fellowship, Frank Podmore, proposed an organisation to focus on political and economic change, rather than on moral. Hence was born the Fabian Society to follow the path of practical reform, leaving the Fellowship to operate on a higher plane promoting simple life styles, humanitarianism, education, community living, an ethical church and like matters. For a time, the future Labour Prime Minister James Ramsay Macdonald was a leading figure in the Fellowship of the New Life. It was eventually wound up in 1898.

By contrast the Fabian Society is still with us. Its critique of existing society and its proposals for change were essentially socialist from its inception, although at first even its own members did not altogether appreciate this. In Fabian Tract No. 3 published in June 1885 the Society committed itself to 'the advance of Socialism in England'.

George Bernard Shaw was an early recruit; and it was he who edited the *Fabian Essays in Socialism* published by the Society in 1889. The seven essayists included, besides Shaw himself, Annie Besant, Graham Wallas and Sidney Webb—who was to become the leading Fabian theorist for more than half a century. The *Essays* had an astonishing success, going through numerous reprints and translations. They made the Society, which then had only some one hundred and fifty members, famous throughout the world. The approach of the Fabian Society was and is characterised by a stress on gradualism and reason. The name of the Society was suggested by Frank Podmore, an allusion to the Roman general Quintus Fabius Maximus dubbed 'Cunctator' ('the Delayer'). Just as he won his campaign by nibbling away at Hannibal's army rather than set-piece confrontation, so socialism could be achieved in Britain more effectively step by step within the country's constitutional traditions than by violent political upheaval. In a preface to the 1908 edition of the *Essays* Shaw contrasted the Fabian approach with that of the 'catastrophists'. On the one hand there were the Liberal radicals whose 'plan was to cut off the King's head, and leave the rest to nature which was supposed to gravitate towards economic harmonies when not restrained by tyrannical governments'. On the other hand there were the Socialist radicals who 'were quite disposed to believe that if you cut off the head of King Capital you might expect to see things come right more or less spontaneously'. Shaw rejected Marx's espousal of revolution—'did he not say that force is the midwife of progress without reminding us that force is equally the midwife of chaos, and chaos the midwife of martial law?' Edward Pease, historian of the Fabian Society and for many years its General Secretary claimed that the success of the *Fabian Essays in Socialism* was because for the first time they offered a credible alternative to revolutionary socialism[1]. Writing in 1916 Pease went so far as to claim that the first achievement of the Fabian Society 'was to break the spell of Marxism in England'[2]. Indeed Pease made a similar claim in respect of Germany since Eduard Bernstein's critique of Marx owed much to the years of exile he spent in Britain associated with the Fabian Society[3].

The Fabian commitment to gradualism was, and is, matched by a stress on the primacy of reason for solving society's problems. In this characteristic of theirs the Fabians were and are reaching back to pre-socialist tradition, that of Utilitarianism and before that of the Enlightenment. Just as the enormous advances in the natural and applied sciences in the second half of the seventeenth century demonstrated the power of man's reason so, Enlightenment philosophers thought, economic, social and political problems would be equally soluble by rational analysis. Jeremy Bentham developed this approach with rigour in the doctrine of Utilitarianism. He and his disciples believed that human happiness could be maximised by discarding sentiment, tradition and custom, by subjecting all institutions to the stern test of utility and by applying cool reason to the conduct of affairs. Utilitarianism was the most practical of doctrines and helped to shape many of the reforms of the nineteenth century in poor relief, public health, education and local government. The Fabians, for all their commitment to socialism, are inheritors of this tradition. G D H Cole explained their approach in a Second World War pamphlet in the following terms:

> The Fabian Society consists, to a quite remarkable extent, of reasonable people—by which I mean people who believe in using their reason and in not allowing themselves to be the victims either of prejudice or of intellectual dilettantism or of muddled goodwill. It is bound to make fairly high demands of its members in these respects, in order to be true to its essential function . . . It calls, not for high educational attainments, but for a positive state of mind which refuses to be satisfied with phrases or to take things for granted, and insists on having everything carefully examined again and again, in order to find out whether what once held good holds good still, and to seek new ways of dealing with changing situations instead of trying to meet them by the application of ancient formulae that no longer fit the facts[4].

Jeremy Bentham could not have put it better.

How did the Fabians promote their beliefs in gradualist socialism and rational improvement of human affairs? The Society was always a group not a party. For instance it did not adopt a party's methods and sponsor candidates in local or national elections, although individual Fabians stood under other party labels (for instance several Liberal MPs were members of the Fabian Society until well into the twentieth century). Instead their approach was what they called 'permeation'. They set out to persuade the public in general but especially the leaders of society in the political parties, civil service, trade unions and universities of the correctness of their prescriptions. Some Fabians like Sidney Webb believed that the tide of history was on their side and that all sensible people would eventually agree with them. Others like George Bernard Shaw were more sceptical and thought that it would be a mammoth task to win converts. All Fabians agreed on the top priority of persuasion, propaganda, education and 'permeation'. There was always a tinge of élitism about the Fabians, with their stress on people with highly developed powers of reasoning, and on the leaders of society. H G Wells who had a stormy four year membership of the Fabian Society accused it of seeking to create a class of Samurai. The Independent Labour Party founded in 1893 was at first largely Fabian in orientation and had strong links with the Society, but was nevertheless a separate entity. The Labour Representation Committee set up in 1900 by a combination of trade unions and socialist societies included a Fabian representative. When the LRC became the Labour Party six years later this representative was transferred to the Party's executive committee. Nevertheless at first the Society did not focus its attention on the Labour Party. For instance the Society supported the Conservative education legislation of 1902 and 1903, to the irritation of both Labour and Liberal Parties. It was not until the First World War that the Society finally decided that the principal vehicle for implementing its programme should be the Labour Party. Henceforth although the Society has retained its identity it has been closely associated with the Labour Party and for most of the Party's existence Fabian ideas have been predominant.

The Fabian tradition and local government

Local government has always had a key rôle in Fabian prescriptions. From the earliest years of the Society it was envisaged that muncipal public services should be greatly extended to form an essential component of a socialist Britain. One of the Society's early publications, *Facts For Londoners*[5] set out a mass of statistics and proposals for the newly established London County Council—'the raw material of Municipal Socialism'[6]. Ever since, numerous Fabian publications, lectures, conferences and proposals have been devoted to local government. Some eminent people have written Fabian pamphlets on local government subjects—including George Bernard Shaw, Clement Attlee, Professor William Robson—but the foremost exponents of the Fabian school of municipal socialism were undoubtedly Sidney Webb and his wife Beatrice. The Webbs were not content simply to engage in contemporary local government issues, although they certain did that. Thus when the Local Government Act 1929 was passed Sidney Webb wrote a Fabian pamphlet, issued the same year, to urge its fullest use[7], concluding 'the new Local Government Act offers almost endless scope to progressive Councils'. The Webbs also steeped themselves in the whole history and development of municipal services. Their history of local government in England is the standard work[8].

Above all the Webbs had a vision for the future of local government, a vision set out most comprehensively in *A Constitution for the Socialist Commonwealth of Great Britain*[9]. In this book they envisage a structurally reorganised local government, with elected councillors full time and salaried. This system would be responsible for a vast range of industries and services. Apart from those needing to be operated nationally (like banking, railways, coal, Post Office) and the household commodities best supplied by the Co-operative Movement, the scope for municipal socialism would be almost limitless:—

It is of course easy to contemplate the universal provision by our Local Authorities of water, gas and (so far as its distribution is concerned) electricity; of such local transport as tramways, omnibuses, ferries and river services, of the provision of houses of all sorts, of public baths and washhouses, and burial grounds and crematoria; of complete sanitary services, from paving, cleansing and lighting the thoroughfares up to every kind of preventive and remedial treatment for the sick, at home and in institutions; of a complete provision for the special needs of maternity and infancy, infirmity and old age; of education of every kind and grade from nursery schools to postgraduate courses available for students of any age; of parks and open spaces, woodlands and mountainsides with holiday homes of all sorts. With a revival of civic patriotism, the Local Authorities will find themselves undertaking the responsibility for the whole mental and physical environment of the population which they serve—in town planning, in joint organisation of the rapidly dwindling spaces between the towns, in the elimination of hideous advertisements and the prevention of defilement of the ground and streams. Above and beyond all this is the provision of art, music and the drama . . . It may well prove to be the case that, in a Socialist Commonwealth, as much as one half of the whole of the industries and services would fall within the sphere of Local Government[10].

The Fabian policy of a massively expanded rôle for local government must be seen in the context of their utilitarian approach and of their belief in a strong national government. The Fabians did not have a *romantic* attachment to local government. They simply believed that municipal socialism worked.

In the 1870s, even before the Fabian Society was founded, Joseph Chamberlain and his Liberal machine in Birmingham had shown what could be achieved by municipal public works and municipal services. Other cities followed suit and the last decades of the nineteenth century and the first of the twentieth came to be called the era of 'gas and water socialism'. These developments were encouraged—in some cases helped—by the Fabians. But they would have occurred anyway. Nevertheless they confirmed the Fabian belief that municipal socialism was a fair and effective way of providing public services. As Labour representation in local government grew, especially after the First World War, the influence of the Fabian Society became of direct importance in stimulating the growth of municipal enterprise.

But the Fabians also believed in strong *national* government. They did not advocate a decentralised political system. The Webbs might bemoan what they saw as the decay of civic patriotism since the middle ages—'a communal consciousness which claimed the right of self determination in resistance to the autocratic fiat of King or Lord'[11]. Nevertheless they would not permit such defiance in their socialist commonwealth. Their local governments although wide-ranging in responsibilities were to be subject to minimum standards laid down by the central authorities, open to their inspection and subject to their veto on certain matters. As Rodney Barker has pointed out 'The socialist commonwealth which they envisaged in 1920 was, despite the stress on the benefits of municipal enterprise and involvement, a recognizably centralised state[12]'. At most local government was to be a counterbalance to excessive centralisation.

Thus the Fabian view of local government was of a vitally important and powerful institution but a *subordinate* one. Local government had a crucial part to play in the creation of socialism simply because it was considered an effective instrument for providing a wide range of public services.

The Guild Socialist tradition

Guild socialism was a peculiarly British creation, a marriage of French syndicalism with the Fabian collective state. Many of its supporters, notably its leading theorists, S G Hobson and G D H Cole, had close connections with the Fabian Society. Nevertheless its ideas led in a distinctive direction. Cole himself resigned from the Executive Committee of the Fabian Society no less than four times but died its president. At certain periods, Guild Socialists were a powerful force within the Fabian Society although a separate National Guilds League was formed in 1915.

In late Victorian and Edwardian times syndicalist teaching began to attract some support in Britain. 'Syndicat' is, of course, French for 'trade union' and the syndicalists preached the violent overthrow of existing political regimes and the devolving of all economic and political power onto trade unions. They would run all the industries and services and also co-operate together to run the political system. Syndicalism directly appealed to some radical British trade unionists. Its critique of the centralising state even had some appeal to those from all points of the political spectrum who at this time attacked the growth of governmental power. Hilaire Belloc's *The Servile State*[13] is perhaps the most famous of these onslaughts.

More important for present purposes, syndicalism helped to boost the *decentralist* tradition in British socialism. This has an ancestry extending back at least as far as anarchists like William Godwin and utopians like Robert Owen, with his penchant for founding small socialist communities. The seminal figure in Victorian Britain was undoubtedly, however, William Morris who even set up his own organisation, the Socialist League, to promote his brand of political change. This involved a mixture of Marxism and Mediaevalism. Morris abhorred the scale of modern industrial cities and the mechanisation of production. In his fantasy novel *News From Nowhere*[14] he envisaged a future in which the political and economic system had been overthrown and people had reverted to living in small self-governing rural communities. Art was restored to the place which

Morris believed it had occupied in the Middle Ages, namely pleasurable handcrafted labour for everyone rather than a hobby for a leisured minority. The hard headed Fabians dismissed Morris's ideas as impractical but they appealed to the more utopian minded socialists.

William Morris made the sixteen year old G D H Cole into a socialist. 'I was converted, quite simply, by reading William Morris's *News from Nowhere*, which made me feel, suddenly and irrevocably, that there was nothing except a Socialist that it was possible for me to be'[15]. At first, however, Cole embraced Fabianism, not appreciating its inconsistency with the decentralised communalism of William Morris. It was not until syndicalism became an issue in Britain that he began to rethink his position. The Fabians, typically, rejected syndicalism but the idea of the self-governing workshop struck a chord with Cole. He became the foremost exponent of an alternative creed to Fabianism, a paler British version of syndicalism called 'guild socialism'.

Cole invented neither the term nor the concept. They were first set out in the pages of a socialist weekly called *New Age* in the years immediately preceding the First World War. The editor, A R Orage, and S G Hobson, another erstwhile Fabian, were the principal formulators. They in turn owed an intellectual debt to a whimsical architect, A J Penty who, to assist the arts and crafts movement, proposed the revival of the mediaeval guilds as associations of self-governing producers. Nevertheless Cole developed the most sophisticated and coherent version of guild socialism and became its most effective promoter. His fullest account of the doctrine is in *Guild Socialism Re-Stated* published in 1920[16].

The essence of guild socialism was to try to create a system balancing the interests of producers and of society at large:—

> It is absurd to deny the common interest which all the members of the community have, as consumers and users, in the vital industries, or as sharers of a common culture and code in such a service as education; but it is no less futile to deny the special, and even more intense, concern which the miners have in the organisation of their industry, or the teachers in the conduct of the educational system[17].

So the Guildsmen proposed that the production of goods and services be the responsibility of democratic associations of workers by hand and brain; associations which would be transformed versions of trade unions approximating in spirit to the mediaeval guilds. At the same time the guilds would be subject to the co-ordination, adjudication and financing of local, regional and national 'communal' authorities—who would also own the productive capital.

On the one hand, therefore, the Guild Socialists rejected the violence of the syndicalists and their abolition of the state. On the other hand the Guild Socialists differed in important respects from the Fabians. Their political and economic system was less centralised than the Fabian arrangements. They favoured maximum citizen participation in all political and economic institutions as opposed to the Fabians' pragmatic reliance on experts and administrators. And not least they rejected the cool, intellectual rationality of the Fabians which seemed to deprive socialism of its emotional charge.

Wright has suggested a comparison between Cole's rejection of Fabianism and John Stuart Mill's rejection of his father's Utilitarianism:—

> For Mill orthodox utilitarianism could properly apply to the 'merely business part of the social arrangements'; whilst for Cole, orthodox Fabianism was now restricted in scope to the homely world of 'kitchens and offices'. In both cases what was alleged was a failure of imagination, a spiritual void, at the heart of an intellectual system; and in both cases the allegation came from a leading youthful disciple attracted by the pull of the spirit. . . . In both cases the challenge came from a new romanticism, whether in the form of a Coleridgean conservatism or a William Morris socialism[18].

For G D H Cole and other Guildsmen, socialism should be about the liberation of the human personality not about the best municipal arrangements for disposing of sewage.

Guild Socialism and local government

The Fabians wanted local government to be a more powerful and effective version of the existing system. The Guild Socialists envisaged more profound changes—differing in two main respects from the Fabians.

First the Guild Socialists as decentralists wanted as much autonomy and initiative as possible for the smallest local group. Secondly they rejected the principle of *general* representation under which an elector chooses a representative to act on his behalf in respect of all matters. They preferred *functional* representation under which different representative bodies would act in respect of particular purposes or groups of purposes. Thus at the local level instead of the traditional multi-purpose units of local government there would be a radical restructuring.

On the one hand there would be the various kinds of producers' guilds responsible for the supply of goods and services both of an individual kind (like clothing), a collective kind (like electricity) and a civic kind (like education). These would be matched by equivalent elected bodies to represent the interests of consumers of these services—co-operative councils for individual items, utilities councils for the collective, and cultural and health councils for the civic. These producers' and consumers' organisations in each locality would send representatives to form a commune. The commune would allocate local resources, adjudicate in any disputes between the various producers' and consumers' bodies, take initiatives in respect of the locality as a whole and run the coercive services like the police which it would not be appropriate for any single functional body to control. These local arrangements would be replicated at the regional and national level.

Since the Guild Socialists never achieved political power their intricate proposals for local government may seem of only historical interest. Their particular emphases, however, (decentralisation, participation, the romantic concept of self governing communities only loosely set in regional and national political systems) have endured, and at times have played an important part in the thinking of the Labour Party.

The guilds set up in the building, clothing, engineering, furniture and printing industries at the end of the First World War, with the encouragement of Cole and Hobson and other Guildsmen, did not last long. Cole himself returned somewhat reluctantly to Fabian reformism. When he died in 1959 Guild Socialism may have seemed as defunct as the Fellowship of the New Life. Yet two decades later Rodney Barker was pointing to Anthony Wedgwood Benn's encouragement of workers' co-operatives and to the formation of council tenants' groups and claimants' unions as evidence of a resurgent Guild Socialist tradition[19].

The Marxist tradition

Karl Marx's theories of the irreconcilable conflict between social classes, of the inevitable collapse of the political and economic system which he called 'capitalism' and of its ultimate replacement throughout the world by 'communism', are too well known to be set out here. Marx's writings were not for some years translated into English, and only in the 1880s did they begin to be widely read in Britain.

The first major figure in British socialism to espouse Marxism was H M Hyndman. He was founder and leader of the Democratic Federation in 1881, later to become the Social Democratic Federation and later still the Social Democratic Party. Confusing though it is to supporters of Dr. David Owen MP a century later, these Social Democrats were essentially Marxist. Hyndman was both authoritarian and eccentric and his Marxism was not entirely orthodox. Nevertheless his Social Democrats formed the principal Marxist grouping in British Socialism for three decades. They were involved in the formation of the Labour Party but their main object came to be the establishment of a united *socialist* party. Eventually at a conference in Salford in 1911 involving the Social Democrats and other socialist groups, a revolutionary Marxist party called the British Socialist Party was set up—with Hyndman as President.

The British Socialist Party never achieved mass support and indeed split over attitudes to the First World War. Nevertheless it still had a substantial membership when it decided to affiliate to the Labour Party in 1917. The Bolshevik Revolution stimulated demands for the creation of a British communist party. Eventually in July 1920, at a meeting organised by the British Socialist Party and composed mainly of its own members there was established a 'Communist Party of Great Britain' on the model of the Soviet system, the dictatorship of the proletariat and affiliation to the third International[20].

The British Socialist Party was wound up and the Communist Party of Great Britain applied immediately for affiliation to the Labour Party. It was refused. Thereafter it applied repeatedly. The issue became a hardy perennial on the agenda of annual conferences of the Labour Party. The result was always the same, a refusal. It took some years, however, to expel all individual Communist Party members from the Labour Party.

Their exclusion did not of course mean the exclusion of Marxist *influence* from the Labour Party. There have always been substantial numbers of Marxists, covert or overt, in the Labour Party. Many more while not accepting the whole creed have found some aspects of Marxism appealing. It is ironic, for instance, that although Pease claimed that the Fabians broke the spell of Marxism in Britain, some Fabians were deeply impressed by the Bolshevik revolution. Margaret

Cole claimed that the Webbs 'fell in love with Soviet Communism'[21]. Certainly the Webbs produced some particularly unattractive apologetics for Stalin.

In any case Marxism has always been the most fissiparous of creeds. Throughout this century, and indeed before, there has been a bewildering kaleidoscope of parties, groups, sects and tendencies all claiming to represent the one true faith of Marxism and quarrelling bitterly among themselves. There have always been Marxists inside and outside the Labour Party who were not pro-Moscow.

The Labour Party could not prevent people with Marxist *convictions* from joining its ranks, provided they fulfilled other membership requirements. The Party could, however, prevent those who belonged to Marxist *organisations* from becoming members since their aims and activities could be seen as incompatible with Labour's. For many years the Party had a list of proscribed organisations membership of which was forbidden to Labour Party members. Nevertheless Marxist entryism was always a problem, and the abolition of the proscribed list in 1973 enormously boosted such entryism. A notorious example is the penetration of the Labour Party by a Trotskyist organisation called Militant, also the name of the organisation's newspaper. In 1973 Militant was already well ensconced in the Labour Party. It had for instance captured control of the Party's youth wing three years earlier. 'In effect the Labour Party Young Socialists became a section not of the Labour Party but of the Militant Tendency'[22]. The lifting of the proscribed list, while it did not directly affect Militant, flung the door even wider open to its activities. Although from time to time other tendencies in the Labour Party have campaigned against Militant, and a few of the more prominent activists have been expelled, their supporters are too numerous and too deeply embedded in the Party to be dislodged. According to Crick 'There is little the Labour Party can do about it now; Militant is here to stay'[23].

Partly because of the activities of Militant and other Marxist entryist groups, partly because of disappointment at the achievements of the Wilson and Callaghan Labour governments, and partly because of growing sympathy anyway for Marxism within its ranks, the Labour Party has lurched heavily to the left in the 1980s. This has affected structure as well as policy. The 1980 conference which decided on compulsory reselection of parliamentary candidates and on a new electoral college for electing the leader, was the last straw for a substantial group of moderate Labour MPs. They split off to form the Social Democratic Party, an essentially Fabian party in contrast to its

Hyndman namesake. While the Labour Party still embraces all three main intellectual traditions, the Marxist, or at least Marxisant, tendencies are stronger than ever before in its history.

The Marxist tradition and local government

Orthodox Marxism has no distinctive theory of local government. The Marxist view of local government in the West is that it is simply part of the capitalist state. Nor does local government have a special role in the Soviet Union or other Marxist regimes. There it is part of a highly centralised administrative apparatus in which all power and authority flow from above. Of course Marxist regimes claim only to be at a 'socialist' stage of development and that when they attain full 'communism' their centralised apparatus will wither away, leaving highly decentralised political arrangements. All except Marxists are sceptical of the likelihood of any such transition. Moreover, neither Karl Marx himself nor any of his disciples has analysed in detail how a Communist Utopia might work. The implication seems to be that there would be self-governing communities but their form and organisation is obscure.

It is true that some Marxist sects, notably those of a Trotskyite persuasion, argue that more decentralised arrangements could be introduced immediately capitalism is overthrown. In practice their ideas are close to syndicalism or even guild socialism with workers' soviets controlling the industries and services. When George Orwell joined the Trotskyite forces (POUM) in the Spanish civil war he found that their extreme egalitarianism contrasted with the disciplined, hierarchical pro-Moscow Communists (PSUC)—though the characteristic was shared with the anarchists[24]. What distinguishes Marxists is their acceptance of the analyses of history and society advanced by Karl Marx, and their commitment to the complete overthrow of Western economic and political systems—not their centralist or decentralist sympathies. The Marxist sects which oppose centralised arrangements after the revolution are in this respect simply part of the same camp as anarchists, syndicalists, guild socialists and other left-wing decentralists.

Marxists are not really interested in local government as such. In contrast the Fabians and the Guild Socialists in their different ways see local government as an essential building block in the construction of the socialist state. At most the Trotskyite Marxists share the emphasis of the Guild Socialists on decentralisation and participation but add nothing distinctive.

While Marxists are not interested in local government they are interested in using local government as an instrument for their main task: the overthrow of the political and economic system. Marxists use local government in three main ways—as an instrument for achieving national office, as an instrument for propaganda and disaffection and as an instrument for disruption and chaos.

In the Western democracies local government is a useful stepping-stone to national office for politicians of every shade of the political spectrum. Experience in local government gives those aspiring to national office political insight, contacts and perhaps public prominence. In Britain a majority of Members of Parliament have local government experience[25]. Marxists use this springboard like anyone else. But they use it in a distinctive way. Where Marxists can achieve local office as avowed Marxists (not as members of some democratic party) then by their behaviour they might be able to assuage public fear about giving them national office. This is a technique most developed in Italy, and to some extent in Greece, France, Portugal and Spain. Where Communist parties control cities they often seek to achieve a reputation for efficiency, moderation and lack of corruption (Bologna is a well-known example) in the hope that the public will be encouraged to elect them to national power. This technique has not been used in Britain simply because the Communist Party has been singularly unsuccessful in local government. While some Communist councillors have been elected they have never been in sufficient numbers to take control of any British city.

British Marxists, whether inside or outside the Labour Party, have however used local government in the other two ways—to spread disaffection and to cause disruption. Local government offers enormous scope for fomenting public hostility to the political system—through education, publicity, subsidies to subversive groups and much else. Finally local government can be used to bring about a breakdown of public services with the intention of provoking the collapse of the whole political and economic system. Again, as is explained below, this apocalyptic scenario is one which attracts some Marxists in British local government.

The Labour Party in local government 1900 to 1970: the Fabian perspective adopted

The first seventy years of the Labour Party's activities in local government are characterised, first, by the enormous spread of Labour control and influence and, secondly, by the overwhelming dominance of the Fabian tradition in municipal activities.

Even before the formal establishment of the Labour Party, socialist and trade unionist candidates had begun to stand in local elections. Thus the Fabians Mrs Annie Besant and the Rev Stewart Headlam were elected to the London School Board in 1888, and Sidney Webb and five other Fabians to the London County Council in 1892 under the Progressives label. At the Trades Union Congress in 1890 it was reported that there were at least seventy 'Labour' representatives on town councils[1]. When the Independent Labour Party (ILP) was formed in 1893 it straightaway began to promote candidates in local elections, although some 'Labour' candidates continued to stand under other designations. By 1900 when the Labour Representation Committee (LRC) was founded the ILP claimed to have one hundred and twenty-two borough, district, county and parish councillors besides one hundred and seventeen members of school boards or boards of guardians and eight elected citizens' auditors[2]. At first the LRC (subsequently the Labour Party) focused mainly on national elections leaving local government largely to the ILP which continued its municipal advance. The Labour Party itself, however, gradually increased its own involvement. At the borough council elections of 1913 there were 494 Labour candidates, 228 of them ILP; 196 were elected, 109 of them ILP. In the same year there were 353 Labour candidates for district and parish councils and 196 were successful. Before the First World War Labour rarely controlled a council. There were fleeting Labour majorities in West Ham in 1898 and Woolwich in 1903. Immediately after the First World War, however, Labour enjoyed sweeping municipal victories. At the local elections of 1919 Labour captured control of twelve metropolitan boroughs, three counties and the major provincial city of Bradford. Thereafter Labour's fortunes fluctuated in individual municipal elections but as a long term trend the Party continued to gain ground. By 1939 Labour controlled forty-two English and Welsh provincial boroughs, seventeen metropolitan boroughs, fourteen Scottish burghs, the London County Council and three other counties. In 1946 these numbers leapt to one hundred and twenty-five provincial boroughs, twenty-three metropolitan boroughs, forty-three Scottish burghs and sixteen English, Scots and Welsh counties (including London)[3]. In 1971 a survey revealed Labour to be in control of six English, Scots and Welsh counties, twenty-one London boroughs, sixty provincial county and non-county boroughs, one hundred and forty-five urban districts, twenty-two rural districts and thirty-four Scottish burghs.

Moreover this represents some undercounting since some survey forms were not returned and in some councils while Labour had no overall majority it exercised *de facto* control as the biggest party[4].

The Labour approach in local government

Over this seventy-year period of widespread municipal success Labour councillors everywhere tended to follow similar policies. This is surprising because the Party's central co-ordinating machinery for local government matters was generally weak. It is true that from their earliest days the Fabian Society and the ILP produced advice and information for their sympathisers in local government but of course they were not obliged to follow or use it. The Labour Party itself began this advisory activity after the First World War. Its *Handbook of Local Government* appeared in 1920 and was followed occasionally by other published guidance to Labour councillors. It was not, however, until 1936 that a Local Government Department was created at Party headquarters to provide national co-ordination and initiative on local government affairs. Even then their guidance was usually more effective on organisational than on policy issues.

In 1930 and 1931 the Party's annual conference agreed model standing orders which Labour groups in local government were recommended to adopt. Subsequently the model standing orders were made mandatory. Such clarity and force were rarely apparent on policy matters. Even where they were it was not easy to ensure that all Labour councillors toed the line. Thus comprehensive secondary schools became official Party policy at the 1951 annual conference and in principle this bound all local Labour groups. In practice some were slow to adhere to this policy.

There were, of course, some divergencies between local Labour groups, especially in the short-term (as with comprehensive schools). In the long term, despite the rudimentary co-ordinating machinery, the frequently weak policy guidance and the difficulty of enforcing decisions there was a strong tendency to policy convergence during this period. One must seek an explanation for this paradox largely in the predominance of one intellectual tradition—the Fabian.

The tendency to follow a common Fabian line was evident even before the First World War, when Labour's municipal power was small. Labour sympathisers in local government everywhere supported improved pay and conditions of service for local government employees, the increased provision of municipal utilities and the development of the municipal education service. For instance Labour councillor F W Jowett was instrumental in persuading Bradford to introduce school meals for its pupils (using powers conferred by Jowett's own Act of 1906)[5].

After the First World War with Labour enjoying much greater power in local government, broadly the same policies were followed. A new stress on electricity and passenger transport replaced the pre-war one on gas and water, and a new priority given to public housing and slum clearance at least equalled the earlier one on education. Nevertheless the approach was very much still a Fabian one, namely in the wide extension of municipal provision as a more effective way of delivering public services than private enterprise, combined with a ready reliance on experts to achieve this.

Between the wars the best known local Labour politician was Herbert Morrison—secretary and principal creator of the London Labour Party. His achievements first on the metropolitan borough of Hackney and then on the London County Council (LCC) which he led from 1934 to 1940 were a powerful demonstration of applied Fabianism. When Labour won control of the LCC in March 1934 under Morrison's leadership, Beatrice Webb noted in her diary 'He is a Fabian of Fabians; a direct disciple of Sidney Webb . . .'[6]. Under his leadership Labour improved the pay of municipal employees and undertook major programmes of house building, school building, road improvements, public utility development, public health provision and created the Green Belt to check London's outward sprawl.

After the Second World War Labour's course in local government remained essentially the same. It is true that post-war Labour governments deprived local government of some important responsibilities. Municipal gas and electricity undertakings were transferred to new national public corporations, municipal hospitals to new *ad hoc* health authorities. This too was typically Fabian; where they thought it more efficient the Fabians were always prepared to contemplate national rather than municipal provision. Even Herbert Morrison, champion of local government, was also an advocate of public corporations (although he opposed the removal of hospitals from local government). In any case local government was still left with a mass of existing and new responsibilities. Throughout the length and breadth of the Kingdom, Labour controlled local governments threw themselves into major new public housing programmes, slum clearance and redevelopment, an enormous expansion of public education (following the 1944 Butler Act), road building and road improvement schemes on an unheard-of scale, the development of the social services and the new responsibilities for land use planning, and much else. Fabianism was triumphant for another generation.

This picture of Labour local government during the first seventy years of the twentieth century needs a little qualification. While Fabianism was dominant the Guild Socialist and Marxist traditions were not entirely absent and there were sporadic occasions when they rose to the surface. One such episode was 'Poplarism' in the 1920s.

In 1921 the metropolitan borough of Poplar under the leadership of George Lansbury (subsequently leader of the Labour Party) refused to collect any rates on behalf of the LCC, as they were legally obliged to, but only for Poplar's own use. This was a protest at the burden of financing unemployment relief. The boroughs of Stepney and Bethnal Green followed suit—but not, significantly, Hackney under Herbert Morrison. He would not condone illegal behaviour even though he sympathised with the problem of financing unemployment relief and led a famous delegation to Prime Minister Lloyd George, then on holiday in Scotland, to argue for a change in the law. George Lansbury and some of his fellow councillors subsequently spent some weeks in Brixton jail for contempt of court but the Government introduced legislation to equalise rate burdens and in effect Lansbury won. The following year a government-appointed auditor decided that the Poplar Poor Law Guardians were paying relief on too high a scale and Poplar borough councillors were paying too high wages to their employees. Both were ordered to reduce the sums and the councillors and guardians were surcharged (viz ordered to pay for past overspending from their own pockets). Lansbury and his colleagues ignored the auditor, continued to spend at the old levels and declined to be surcharged. The Labour Government of 1924 repealed the order and the Courts anyway decided that the auditor had exceeded his powers. Lansbury had won again.

The details of the disputes are of only historical interest but they clearly reflect a challenge to the Fabian view of the rôle of local government. Lansbury had been for a time a Marxist and a leading member of the Social Democratic Federation, but he subsequently left it and joined first the ILP and then the Labour Party. In the SDF he had professed himself an atheist but he returned to the Church of England. He was primarily a Christian-Socialist-Pacifist, an epitome of the socialist romantic, rather than a Marxist ideologue (although he was another naive apologist for the Soviet Union). Unsurprisingly he was also much attracted to Guild Socialism. In contrast to the Fabians with their insistence on gradualism, reason and legality, Lansbury and Poplarism represented the use of local government to provoke dramatic confrontations to further the socialist cause. Lansbury and Poplarism also implied that the local community was in some sense equal with, not subordinate to, the national community—romantic socialist decentralisation of a Guild Socialist type[7].

Lansbury's victories inspired another flourish of Poplarism a few years later. In 1929 the separate, elected bodies for administering poor relief, the boards of guardians, were abolished and their responsibilities transferred to local government. This transfer coincided with the onset of the slump. Some score of local governments, not all of them Labour controlled, followed Poplar's earlier example and paid higher rates of assistance than the Government prescribed. This time, however, the Government was determined not to be defeated. The rebels were forced to comply. In 1934 the Minister of Health, Neville Chamberlain, transferred poor relief to a new national body, the Unemployment Assistance Board, and henceforth this paid assistance at a uniform rate throughout the country.

The term 'Poplarism' to describe such local government defiance of central authority fell into disuse after the 1930s and instances of it were uncommon in the 1940s and 1950s—but not unknown. Coventry in 1954 and St. Pancras in 1957 (both Labour controlled) refused to carry out their mandatory civil defence responsibilities as a protest against national defence policy, notably against its reliance on the nuclear deterrent. The Government invoked default powers and the rebellion was overcome. It was nevertheless a harbinger of what was to come in the 1970s and 1980s.

There is little or no evidence of Marxist exploitation of British local government during the first seventy years of this century. There were never more than a handful of successful Communist candidates in local elections and Marxists within the Labour Party were more concerned with international and industrial issues. Given orthodox Marxism's lack of interest in local government it is understandable that Marxists should dismiss it as a field for Fabian reformers and Guild Socialist utopians. Nevertheless it is somewhat surprising that for most of this period British Marxists did not recognise the exploitative potential of local government to serve their ends.

Thus, with Marxism muted and Guild Socialist tendencies only sporadically significant, Labour's record during this period when it obtained so much local government power was overwhelmingly Fabian. Experts and administrators were given their head, under Labour supervision, to expand municipal services. The process reached an apogee in the 1950s and 1960s. Despite 'stop-go' macro-economic policies it was a time of continually increasing local government expenditure. Statistical analyses like those of Noel Boaden and Bleddyn Davies clearly demonstrated that Labour municipal control meant much higher levels of expenditure than control by Conservatives or other political groups[8].

The Labour Party in local government after 1970: Fabianism derided

Historical changes can rarely be dated with precision but around the year 1970 a number of factors came together to set in train a decline in the Fabian tradition amongst Labour councillors. Four were particularly important: major changes in local government personnel, widespread criticism of the results of local Fabianism, a new interest in local government on the part of the Marxists and the growing power of the Left in the Labour Party.

New Labour councillors

In the late 1960s the Conservative Party had sweeping successes in municipal elections. The British electorate tends to use local elections to register approval or disapproval of the national government. The unpopularity of Harold Wilson's second Government (1966 to 1970) was largely responsible for these local Conservative victories. A number of formerly impregnable Labour municipal strongholds fell—like Derby, Sheffield, Crawley and Islington. This drove from power many old style Labour municipal leaders who had ruled for decades, sometimes in an authoritarian way. When Labour regained control a few years later, the leadership had often been taken over by younger councillors, less wedded to Fabianism, interested in new approaches and some of them schooled in left-wing radicalism by experience of British higher education in the 1960s.

This shake out of long service councillors and influx of new ones was made severer by local government reorganisation. In England,

Scotland and Wales (outside Greater London) a major restructuring of local government came into force in 1974 creating generally fewer and larger units of local government—and reducing the number of council places. Some of the older generation of councillors either withdrew voluntarily in the face of such change or were unable to obtain one of the smaller number of places.

Criticism of municipal Fabianism

In true Fabian fashion, the older municipal Labour leaders had been confident that the experts and the administrators could bring about continually improving conditions if given enough resources. The architects, the land use planners, the highway engineers and the educationalists had been given free rein and ever increasing budgets. The building of houses and flats, the expansion of educational provision, the clearance and redevelopment of slums, and the increased expenditure on other municipal services had been at first highly popular amongst Labour Party members and supporters, but disenchantment gradually set in.

By the end of the 1960s the volume of public criticism of the effects of some of these policies had become too great to be ignored. The first disappointment was with municipal housing, especially the high rise, prefabricated schemes which had come to dominate the skylines of most of our larger towns. To architects trained in the modernist school, building high seemed exciting, progressive and consonant with modern technology. The 1951 Festival of Britain heralded the promise that new building techniques would transform our cities for the better. The experience of living in such blocks disproved the promise. The problems of noise, lift breakdown, supervision of children, vandalism and crime became the common lot of their inhabitants. It took many years for cities to abandon all new high rise building and even longer to begin to demolish existing blocks; but by the early 1970s professional and political confidence was shaken. Criticism of planning and redevelopment became if anything more bitter. The promise was that the slums would be cleared away, road systems improved and cities made more pleasant, convenient and accessible. In practice, this often meant that areas of solid Victorian or Edwardian housing were ruthlessly bulldozed when they might have been retained and improved at less cost, and with the advantage of maintaining existing communities. Moreover some urban road schemes were not only enormously destructive and expensive but, because they generated more traffic, failed to unclog the jams.

Public hostility was fuelled by two other factors—planning blight and corruption. Where an area of a town was planned for clearance and redevelopment, or for a new road scheme, naturally owners were reluctant to spend money on their properties. Such areas rapidly deteriorated yet it often took many years for enough funds to be raised to implement the plans. Finally confidence was sapped by a series of trials for corruption which generally, though not exclusively, concerned areas with long histories of Labour rule. The most spectacular case involved the conviction and jailing of the Labour leader of Newcastle-upon-Tyne, Councillor T. Dan Smith, in 1974 for accepting bribes to award contracts to a firm of architects.

Education, too, became a subject of growing concern. The results of introducing comprehensive secondary schools, new teaching methods and innovation in the curriculum were increasingly challenged not just from the political right but from the ranks of Labour supporters. The belief waned that educational experts could be trusted to deliver improvements if given sufficient public funds. An archetypal scandal concerned the William Tyndale school in London in 1974 where the extreme 'progressive' methods of a headmaster led to a parental revolt. Two years later public concern had reached such a height that Labour Prime Minister James Callaghan launched a 'great educational debate' in a speech at Ruskin College, Oxford. Later, union leader Hugh Scanlon announced that it was 'no longer reactionary' to believe that educational standards were falling.

Of course, local government also had considerable achievements to its credit, and in any case the policy failures and misdemeanours were not confined to Labour controlled local authorities. Still, the collapse of high hopes and expectations in so many key areas of municipal provision was widely seen as a massive defeat for traditional Labour local government. There were three main consequences. First a large number of books and other publications appeared criticising these policies[1]. Secondly, various pressure groups and community associations were formed to fight such policies (like the 'Homes Before Roads' campaign in London) and they achieved some success. Thirdly, traditional municipal Fabianism was discredited in the Labour Party, leading to a search for new approaches.

New Marxist interest in local government

The classical Marxist view of the State as just an instrument operated by the bourgeoisie to serve their own interests, began to be sophisticated in the 1960s by neo-Marxists like Milliband, Poulantzas, Althusser and Habermas. They argued that although the state fundamentally served the interests of capital, it was a complex and differentiated phenomenon and contained internal tensions and contradictions. Such arguments in turn led French Marxist sociologists, notably Manuel Castells, to suggest that local government should not simply be seen as part of the capitalist state but as a subject worthy of analysis in its own right. According to Castells, local government is a part of the state characterised by 'collective consumption' (broadly the provision of public services) and therefore by its role in 'labour reproduction' (Marxist jargon for producing trained, healthy, well-housed and willing workers). Due to Castells, therefore, local government in general and local politics in particular became respectable subjects for Marxist scholars to study[2]. Marxist writers in many countries began to follow the lead set by Castells and to produce work on local government. In Britain one of the earliest and most influential was by Cynthia Cockburn[3]. This is a study of corporate planning and public participation in the London borough of Lambeth. Following Marxist analysis both activities are seen as contributing to 'capitalist reproduction'—corporate planning by improving resource management and policy co-ordination, public participation by neutralising and incorporating potentially disruptive forces. Public participation *can*, however, awaken and strengthen such disruptive forces and this happened in some measure in Lambeth. The message of the book is that local government possesses great potential for exploitation in the interests of class warfare, especially for disrupting 'labour reproduction' (e.g. by the kind of collective action which public participation sometimes produced in Lambeth).

Thus Marxist study of local government quickly became exhortation to Marxist activity in local government. Marxists had always been prepared to exploit local government but, as was explained above, there was little evidence of it before the 1970s in Britain. With this new theoretical underpinning, Marxist involvement in local government was sharply stimulated. Evidence of exploitative behaviour is adduced below.

The growth of the Left in the Labour Party

Despite the dominance of Fabian gradualism and moderation in the Labour Party until the 1970s there were always some voices calling for more radical socialism. In the 1950s Aneurin Bevan and his supporters were the main repositories of such sentiments. The Bevanites called for more neutralist foreign policies and more egalitarian internal policies. Nevertheless while they were in some ways inheritors of Guild Socialist romanticism they were not particularly decentralist. The prestige of centralised, expert, Fabian socialism was still untarnished.

Unlike the Bevanites, the New Left which emerged in the late 1950s was not confined to the Labour Party. It was the creation of Marxist intellectuals, disenchanted with the Soviet Union, like E P Thompson, Raymond Williams and Stuart Hall. Like the Bevanites, the New Left had a major concern with foreign affairs, and became closely associated with the Campaign for Nuclear Disarmament and other unilateralist groups. Its stance on internal affairs was, however, much more decentralist. While heavily influenced by Marxism, the New Left rejected the Soviet model and tried to draw upon British radical egalitarian traditions (like the writings of William Morris and the seventeenth century Levellers) to put forward a decentralised, libertarian, British version of socialism. The ideas of the New Left were principally set out in the pages of the *New Left Review* founded in 1960, but they were a minority taste in Labour circles.

The balance of the 'left' (or radical) and 'moderate' (or gradualist) tendencies in the Labour Party was transformed by the disastrous record of the Wilson and Callaghan governments in the 1960s and 1970s. An objective observer might have expected these governmental failures to be taken as evidence of flaws in socialism. On the contrary many Labour activists saw them as evidence of insufficient socialism. A dilute solution of the medicine had made the patient worse; a full-strength solution would effect a cure. This reaction, together with the ideas of the *New Left Review* and with Marxist entryism, combined to produce a new surge of support for radical socialist ideas in the Labour Party during the 1970s and 1980s.

It is least confusing to label this burgeoning tendency as simply 'the Labour Left', as opposed to the Labour moderates or 'Right'. Even though the emergence of the Labour Left to great power and influence in the Party is a recent phenomenon it would be wrong to describe it as 'the New Left' since this is associated with the dissident Marxists of the *New Left Review*. Of course their ideas contributed to the Labour Left.

Essentially the Labour Left of the 1970s and 1980s represents the triumph of what until then were the two minority intellectual traditions of the Labour Party—Marxism and Guild Socialism. Marxism prescribes the rapid destruction of the existing political and economic system, Guild Socialism the adoption of decentralist, participative, utopian socialist measures, and is fired by the idea of 'socialist values' rather than effective administrative arrangements. Hilary Wainwright, a leading proponent of the Labour Left describes its character as '. . . a new transformative movement, allying itself with traditions entirely independent of Labourism-Marxism, feminism, syndicalism, pacifism and ecology'[4]. Note that she puts Marxism first.

The Labour Left is neither a stable nor homogeneous entity, quite the contrary; nevertheless it displays certain abiding and common characteristics which sharply differentiate it from Fabianism. In the first place it is, to use Hilary Wainwright's term, transformative. It seeks a radically different state and society. Fabianism by contrast envisaged only a collectivist version of existing state and society.

Secondly it is extra-Parliamentary in its thrust. The Fabian tradition had placed the highest priority on winning control at Westminster. The Left places equal if not higher priority on achieving power in, and working through, local and factory floor trade unions, environmental pressure groups, tenants' associations, feminist groups, ethnic minority societies and similar organisations, and last but not least local government. In the words of Left activist Peter Hain 'We cannot achieve socialism through Parliamentary channels alone'[5]. Similarly Joan Maynard MP wrote of the Campaign Group of Labour MPs in 1986 that it 'has always rejected the illusion that socialism can be brought into existence by the activity of a small group of Parliamentarians'[6].

Thirdly, in striking contrast to the Fabians, the Left is generally prepared to advance its goals by direct action even where this is constitutionally dubious or downright illegal. To quote Peter Hain again 'Labour Left's task' is 'to ensure that the Party supports struggles on every front . . . and we should do so regardless of arguments over illegality'[7].

Fourthly the Left is decentralist. Of course this is linked to its extra-Parliamentary thrust. The Fabians envisaged a massive role for local government but at the same time a strong central government. And the Fabian-type governments of Attlee, Wilson and Callaghan revealed little interest in decentralisation. The Left on the other hand is heavily preoccupied with workers' co-operatives, tenants' self-management, community participation in local services and many other expressions of decentralisation.

Fifthly, in a sharp departure from Labour moderate traditions, the Labour Left is prepared to consort with, even form joint organisations with, Marxist organisations outside the Labour Party. Marxist entryism into the Party is a big enough phenomenon in itself—especially since the abolition of the proscribed list—but many Left activists do not even wait for Marxists to get into the Labour Party; they link up with them outside. Before the 1970s few Labour activists were prepared to associate with overtly Marxist organisations (like the British Communist Party or the Trotskyite Workers' Revolutionary Party) let alone Soviet front organisations (like the World Federation of Trade Unions and the World Peace Council). Such inhibitions are now shed. For two decades there have been numerous instances of individuals from the Labour Left (including MPs and MEPs) involving themselves with the activities of such organisations. To give just one example Messrs Ken Livingstone and Ted Knight (respectively Labour Leaders of the GLC and Lambeth Borough Council) joined the editorial board of *Labour Herald,* mouthpiece of the Workers Revolutionary Party. Moreover the trend does not stop with individuals. It is increasingly common for umbrella organisations to be set up with the explicit aim of linking the Labour Left with Marxist groups outside the Party. Examples of such umbrella organisations include the Rank and File Mobilising Committee for Labour Democracy founded in 1980 and the Labour Left Liaison founded in 1986[8].

The Fabian tradition still exists but now attracts only minority support. In these five respects the Left is directly antithetical to it.

Divisions in the Labour Left

Despite its five consistent features, the Labour Left is not, as was stressed, a homogeneous or stable grouping. On the contrary it is a bewildering kaleidoscope of individuals and groups promoting numerous brands of Marxism and Guild Socialism in infinite permutations. Individuals and groups continually modify their positions under the stress of external events like strikes or general elections or as part of the internecine struggle for power and influence.

Nevertheless it has become conventional wisdom to divide the complex phenomenon of the Labour Left into two broad factions— 'soft' and 'hard'. It is claimed that the 'soft' Left stresses the importance of building a new national consensus in favour of decentralised, socialist life-styles. The 'hard' Left is more concerned with class conflict and seeks to advance the interests as it sees them of the traditional working class, and supports trade union militancy. According to this analysis the dominant Party faction today is the 'soft' Left as personified by the Labour leader Neil Kinnock and his immediate entourage. The romantic vacuities which were his trademark during the 1987 election campaign indicate his intention of trying to create a new anti-conservative coalition embracing all classes. And this approach was adopted from his election as leader in 1983. Geoffrey Foote, for instance, has described Kinnock's definition of the purpose of the Labour Party as 'vague nostrums and moral platitudes':

> to produce in plenty and distribute in justice. Producing in plenty must clearly mean maximising the efficient use of resources by planning and co-ordinating and investing capital resources and human effort. The short-sighted, speculative market system . . . never will produce the plenty necessary to meet human need[9].

This analysis is misleading. It is true that some on the Labour Left are more doctrinaire and confrontational, others more flexible and concerned with their public image. Nevertheless as Peter Shipley points out 'This [hard versus soft] terminology is useful to those who wish to encourage belief in the myth of moderation or to simplify the complexities of socialist politics'[10].

Even the 'soft' Left is an extreme tendency by historical perspectives. The Tribune Group of Labour MPs who for decades were on the far left of the Party are now mainstream and outflanked on the left by the Campaign Group. Neil Kinnock and his predecessor as Labour leader Michael Foot were both from the Tribune Group. The Labour Party manifesto for the 1987 general election although couched in anodyne language was virulently left wing in content—from the unilateral defence policy to the onslaught on private schools, from the restoration of the privileges of the trade union bosses to the extensions of nationalisation (disguised as social ownership).

In any case the terms 'soft' and 'hard' Left are too imprecise to serve as a useful analytical tool. Where for instance should so crucial a figure as Ken Livingstone be placed? On the one hand as Labour leader of the GLC he was deliberately provocative and his own memoirs reveal the extremism of his vision and the ruthlessness with which he has pursued it[11]. This would place him in the 'hard' Left camp. On the other hand he has always stopped short of the more hot-headed behaviour of, say, Labour controlled Lambeth or Liverpool and even more significantly he has shown a willingness to modify his stance in the light of developments. Does this make him 'soft' Left? Perhaps he is 'cunning' Left as opposed to 'stupid' Left.

Moreover the 'soft' versus 'hard' classification obscures the extent to which Left activists are prepared to shift ground in the light of events. The miners' strike of 1984 to 1985 was an encouragement to many to join the ranks of the confrontationists. The Conservative victory in the 1987 general election seems to have softened the position of many previous hardliners.

In short the Labour Left is too heterogeneous and unstable a phenomenon to be neatly categorised. Overall there is no doubt that it is permeated with Marxism and its adherents envisage radical, some might say cataclysmic, changes to our political, economic and social system. One could justify dividing the Labour Left simply into those with short term perspectives and those with long term. The former constantly seek to exploit circumstances to bring about a speedy downfall of the system. The latter are less precipitous and seek to engineer it more subtly. Nevertheless the distinction is tactical. Like Bryan Gould's 'designer socialism' the 'soft' Left try to tailor their message to achieve public appeal without losing sight of their ultimate goals.

The impact on local government

The influx of new personnel, the failures of municipal Fabianism, the Marxist intervention in municipal affairs, and the ideological transformation of the Labour Party have combined to bring about dramatic changes in the behaviour of some local authorities.

In a number of cases the Labour Left have taken control. Sometimes they have taken over where there was already a Labour majority. Leftist Ted Knight became leader of Lambeth Borough Council in 1978 but most left wing takeovers came in the 1980s. Thus in Sheffield in 1980, Hackney and Southwark in 1982 and Manchester in 1984 moderate, Fabian-type Labour majorities were displaced by the Left. In other cases the Left have come to power when a non-Labour majority was defeated in an election. Thus in 1983 the Liberals lost control of Liverpool to a Labour group dominated by the militant Trotskyites. In 1981 Labour won control of the GLC from the Conservatives; in the campaign the Labour leader was the moderate Andrew

MacIntosh but immediately the election victory was secured he was replaced as Labour leader by Ken Livingstone from the Labour Left.

The Left have established particular municipal strongholds in London and in the industrial cities of Scotland and Northern England. Nevertheless some counties like Derbyshire and some Southern cities like Oxford and Southampton are also heavily Left in their orientation. Moreover even where the Labour Left is not the dominant municipal faction it is often a significant one and in many cases a growing one. Even where a city or county generally behaves with moderation it might occasionally act like a Manchester or a Lambeth.

Given the heterogeneity of the Labour Left it is not surprising that it does not act in exactly the same way wherever it achieves municipal power. The hard line behaviour of Liverpool or Lambeth or Brent contrasts with the more calculated left wing policies of Sheffield and the GLC. Nevertheless as will be explained in the next section there are many similarities between them all.

Moreover there are some attempts to co-ordinate the Labour Left in local government. One of the most well-known is *London Labour Briefing*. This is a journal founded by Ken Livingstone and his entourage on the GLC in 1981 to spread the gospel of the Labour Left in London. It now has municipal subscribers in many other parts of Britain. It has indeed become more than merely a journal. Its adherents are in effect another sect in the Labour Left. The message it propagates is not only on municipal affairs but also on national and international issues.

Labour Left inroads into local government in the late 1970s and 1980s have coincided with Conservative general election victories. Thus the Left have been able to argue that local government is the only arena in which they have the power to try out their ideas. Moreover, since the Conservative Government's macro-economic strategy has involved a stress on limiting local government expenditure and improving its efficiency, there has been more than usual potential for central-local conflict.

All this has combined to produce unprecedented behaviour amongst Labour controlled local government. The old Fabian traditions have been widely derided. In their place what amounts to a new Labour doctrine of local government is increasingly applied.

Local government behaviour in the 70s and 80s: lunacies at work

The factors analysed above have combined to produce sharply increased incidents of conflictual and disruptive behaviour amongst

Labour-controlled local governments since 1970. Before then some types of this behaviour were rare, some unknown. Certain activities have been so bizarre that their perpetrators have attracted the nickname 'the loony left' from the press.

This new behaviour which in effect amounts to a new Labour doctrine of local government has four principal characteristics—a readiness to flout the law, an involvement in issues well beyond the responsibilities of local government, a politicisation of career officials and the use of local government powers as an instrument for radical social engineering.

Illegal activities

There has always been, and will always be, some tension between central and local government. In a pluralist political system like that of Britain a degree of tension can be creative; and in any case could only be entirely resolved by abolishing local government altogether. It is not only Labour controlled cities and counties which sometimes go against the wishes of central government. Provided that they keep within the law this is fair enough. Indeed in some disputes local government has itself resorted to the courts and won—for instance Conservative controlled Tameside was upheld by the courts in 1976 when the Secretary of State for Education Mrs Shirley Williams tried to prevent the Borough withdrawing a scheme for comprehensive reorganisation of its secondary schools. Deliberate breaking of the law is quite another matter, and it is this which has noticeably increased amongst Labour controlled local governments since 1970. Of course 'Poplarism' had set the precedent in the 1920s and 1930s, but that was mild compared to the happenings of the 1980s.

Flouting the law has taken two forms—open defiance and surreptitious evasion. The former has been employed mainly on questions of finance and civil defence. Thus Clay Cross in Derbyshire deliberately and publicly broke the law by refusing to adhere to the provisions of the Conservative Government's Housing Finance Act 1972 which related to council house rents. Subsequently the Labour councillors were surcharged for illegal expenditure and disqualified from office. But the next Labour Government lifted their disqualification.

The Conservatives' election victory of 1979 and their implementation of a monetarist macro-economic policy was the signal for a wave of illegal behaviour by Labour controlled local governments. Limitations on expenditure were imposed first by cutting grants, imposing spending targets and levying grant penalties and, secondly, after 1986 by rate capping—the imposition of a mandatory ceiling on rate rises. These measures aroused fierce resistance. The Labour Governments of 1974 to 1979 had introduced financial restrictions of a severe kind—'the party's over' said Labour Minister Anthony Crosland—and had met only resentment and criticism. Thus the strength of resistance to the Conservative restrictions was partly at least ideological. A number of local governments led by Liverpool and Lothian refused to make a rate, in defiance of their legal obligations. At first the Government made minor financial concessions in order to defuse the rebellion, but this only encouraged others to join it. When a dozen or so tried to defy rate capping, the Government stood firm. Only Liverpool persisted to the bitter end. The city teetered on the brink of bankruptcy. There were extraordinary scenes in 1985 when taxis were despatched with redundancy notices to the city's employees. The unions would not, however, risk their members' jobs and the rebellion collapsed. Subsequently some Labour councillors were surcharged and disqualified from office. There is no doubt that some amongst the Left had hoped that Labour councils would form a united bloc in resisting the Conservative Government's financial measures. Methods of resistance were discussed at a series of Labour local government conferences. The Labour Party nationally flirted with the idea of organising concerted resistance. In the end, however, there were too many differences of opinion between Labour groups in different areas and the resistance fell apart. It should be noted too that the NUM strike in 1984/85 encouraged some Labour controlled authorities to refuse to set a rate or introduce a legal budget. They saw such illegalities as part of a pincer attack on the Government. Ted Knight wrote in 1985 'fighting alongside the miners we can create the conditions for a general strike to defeat the Tory Government'[1].

The defeat of the strike was a setback for such confrontationalists. Nevertheless this did not stop profligate spending. Most Labour controlled local governments ultimately drew back from blatant illegalities, and sought instead ways to evade restrictions on expenditure. Some for instance have raised funds by selling their parking meters or lamp posts to foreign banks and are now leasing them back. The Left organ *Labour Briefing* declared in December 1986 'Labour councils should spend all the money they can lay their hands on NOW . . . And from now on, every battle—over rate capping, over privatisation—is in deadly earnest'. The Audit Commission a month

later condemned financial mismanagement amongst Labour controlled London boroughs, but it is not clear how much this was due
to incompetence and how much to ideologically motivated extrava-
gance. Such financially reckless behaviour is an extraordinary and
novel development itself but if, as was the original intention, a
substantial number of local governments had maintained implacable
non-compliance with the law it would have created a major crisis for
the Government.

This indeed is what transpired with civil defence. In the 1980s a
number of Labour controlled local governments followed the lead set
three decades earlier by Coventry and St Pancras and refused to
undertake their legal obligations in respect of civil defence. Their
non-compliance was most publicly demonstrated by their refusal to
participate in the civil defence exercise Hard Rock in 1982, a refusal
which led to its cancellation. Although requirements have been
tightened by new civil defence regulations issued in 1983 many
Labour controlled local governments are still prevaricating. So far the
Government has not insisted. The result is that in some parts of
Britain civil defence arrangements are in tatters.

More surreptitious illegalities characterise the resistance of some
Labour controlled local governments—for instance, to legislation
requiring them to sell council flats and houses to sitting tenants who
want to purchase. In some cases procedures have been so spun out
that only a few properties were actually transferred. The Government
lost patience in the case of Norwich and sent in commissioners to
administer such sales. New legislation proposes to authorise tenants
to withhold rent if unreasonable delays occur in the purchase of their
dwelling.

There is a new spirit abroad amongst Labour Councillors. Far more
than ever before they are prepared to contemplate breaking or evad-
ing the law in order to cause difficulties or embarrassment to the
Government and to test its resolve.

Intervention in defence and foreign affairs

In every country the national government must be vested with
exclusive responsibility for defence and foreign affairs. The nation as
a whole must decide such matters through its representatives. If any
part of a country can conduct its own defence and foreign policy in
defiance of the national government then this must destroy national

sovereignty. Examples of countries like Lebanon demonstrate this. Local government has no legitimate independent role in defence and foreign affairs. Insofar as defence-related responsibilities are delegated to local government (like civil defence and emergency planning), this is only for administrative convenience and in such cases local government should carry out such responsibilities within national policy.

Similarly, international contacts, where they are allowed between local governments (town twinning, international gatherings of municipal engineers and the like) cannot properly be used to challenge foreign or defence policies.

Labour controlled local government in the 1980s has contradicted these principles and intervened blatantly in defence and foreign affairs. The most dramatic manifestation of this is the so called 'nuclear-free zones' movement in local government. This was launched by Manchester in November 1980. Since then it has been joined by more than one hundred and seventy local governments within Britain and several thousand outside. A 'nuclear-free zone' is a declaration by a local government against the manufacture or deployment of nuclear weapons within its municipal boundaries. Such a declaration cannot be enforced but it provides an excuse for an expensive propaganda campaign against current defence policy and the nuclear deterrent. This is not the place for a detailed account of the 'nuclear-free zones' movement which I have undertaken elsewhere[2], but it has become a determined and well organised local government onslaught on defence policy. The original Manchester resolution spoke of creating a 'European nuclear-free zone'. This has nothing to do with Manchester City Council. If the British people want a European nuclear-free zone they can return a government to Westminster favouring one.

The 'nuclear-free zones' movement may be the most striking example of Labour local government's intervention beyond its proper realm, but it is not the only one. Another instance of such misbehaviour is the exploitation of town twinning. Traditionally this has involved the establishment of friendly links between a British and a foreign town, and the development of intercommunal activities, from the exchange of municipal delegations to arranging for young people to study and work with their twin city contemporaries. But recently Labour councillors have begun to use twinning links to promote their views on foreign and defence policy. Thus Sheffield and its twin Donetsk in Soviet Ukraine have signed a joint 'peace declaration'.

Other Labour controlled cities have engaged in similar political ventures with East European twins or have used twinning with Western cities to promote 'nuclear-free zones' or have twinned with Nicaraguan cities to show support for the Sandinista regime.

Ireland is another topic on which some Labour councillors are now happy to misuse their office. Ken Livingstone, Labour Leader of the GLC, was renowned, before the GLC was abolished, for his support for Sinn Fein—the so-called 'political wing' of the IRA terrorists. It is quite extraordinary that the municipal leader of the nation's capital city should express support for an organisation promoting terrorism in Britain, especially when combined with official invitations and municipal hospitality to Sinn Fein representatives. When Labour-controlled Hackney invited a Sinn Fein delegation in 1986 a Liberal councillor fired blank pistol rounds in protest and was subsequently jailed for his pains. At the annual meeting of the Labour co-ordinating committee (a Labour Left group originally set up to back up Mr Anthony Wedgwood Benn's bid for the Deputy Leadership) at Camden Town Hall on 14 November 1987, Ken Livingstone stormed out when contacts with Sinn Fein were condemned after the IRA atrocity on Remembrance Day in Enniskillen[3]. Of course people like Ken Livingstone can point out that many people of Irish descent live in London, indeed many with Eire passports, but it is disingenuous to claim that this gives municipal leaders in London a right to promote particular solutions to the conflict in Ulster. By the same logic Chinese restaurants in Soho could give the City of Westminster the right to spend municipal funds opposing the Sino-British agreement on Hong Kong.

Politicising local government staff

It has been a fundamental principle of British public administration for more than a century that, in both central and local government, the permanent career staff should impartially serve whatever political masters the electorate choose to place above them. It is true that there are certain differences between the central and local situations—for instance local government staff are predominantly professional specialists rather than generalist administrators. It is true too that in practice the respective responsibilities of politicians and career officials cannot always be easily separated; policy and its implementation may blur into one another; many policy initiatives originate with the career staff. Nevertheless such considerations do not negate the essential principle. The permanent career staff should not be overtly partisan. The politicians should bear ultimate responsibility for the policies. The alternative is to move in the direction of the corruptions and inefficiencies of the 'spoils system' which raged in nineteenth century America. Politicians could appoint their political supporters, friends and relations to all the public jobs.

The Fabians accepted the principle of an impartial public service; indeed they embraced it enthusiastically. They were happy to have politically neutral experts and administrators serving socialist politicians. Herbert Morrison in pre-war London explicitly followed this principle. He encouraged his career officials to give their honest advice and to act according to their professional judgement, while making it clear that he and his fellow councillors would make the final decisions on policy. There were always some voices in the Labour Party calling for 'politically committed' career officials but until the 1970s the Morrisonian view prevailed amongst Labour councillors.

The Labour Left and the Marxists reject the traditional principle. David Blunkett, then Left Leader of Sheffield, was candid:—

> . . . the people who work for local authorities have got to be committed to a new type of politics. They are not expected to be members of the Labour Party, but they should have a commitment not to an isolated individual but to the community itself. These workers should be able to see that they are part of community action, that they are part of the political education with small 'p' . . . Commitment to the broad aims of a socialist council should extend up to the top of the officer hierarchy[4].

In effect Blunkett expects career officials to sympathise with the aims and approaches of the Left even if they are not fully paid up Labour Party members. Bernie Grant, then Labour leader of Haringey, was even cruder in his formulation: 'We need . . . political appointments. The farce of neutral civil servants and local government officers is rubbish . . . We are making political appointments in local authorities, and I expect a Labour government to make political appointments in the Department of the Environment, so we'll have the right people to co-ordinate the progressive initiatives of Labour councils all over the country[5]'. This attitude is now commonly reflected in advertisements for local government jobs placed by Labour controlled councils. Sometimes euphemistic words like 'progressive' are used: thus Haringey sought a Borough Planning Officer to continue its 'progressive work[6]'; Wansbeck District advertised for a Principal Chief Officer emphasising its 'progressive' nature[7]. Sometimes the wording is explicit: thus Waltham Forest Borough advertised for the Head of a Race Relations Unit who would be 'committed to the Council's policies'[9]. There are now numerous examples of both types of advertisement.

Local government advertisements do not even have to be specially worded to attract left wing candidates; they can simply be placed in left wing journals and newspapers where the readership is known to be sympathetic. The Campaign Against Council Corruption, an independent monitoring unit, has published since early 1987 a monthly summary *Abuse Update* reviewing local government job advertisements. This reveals a mass of such advertisements placed in *Labour Weekly* (Labour Party official newspaper), *Marxism Today* (Communist Party monthly), *Morning Star* (Communist daily), *Outwrite* and *Spare Rib* (hard line feminist, pro-Lesbian, left wing monthlies), *Asian Times* and *Caribbean Times* (obviously aimed at the ethnic communities but with far left editorial policies) and other left wing publications. The Campaign Against Council Corruption suggests that some of these newspapers and journals could not survive without the money from this advertising.

The situation is exacerbated by 'twin tracking' (viz people serving as politicians in one local council and employees in another). Of course it has long been forbidden to be an elected politician and a salaried employee of the same local government, but there is nothing to prevent Labour councillors in one area being employees of other local governments; and the suspicion must be that in some cases at least such arrangements are carefully contrived.

Obviously there could be no more committed an employee than an active politician. Charles Goodson-Wickes pointed out in 1984 that of 41 Labour councillors in Lewisham Borough, 15 had local government jobs elsewhere in London, and of Southwark's 53 Labour councillors, 14 were local government employees[10]. He also explained the practice of mutual cross-employment. For instance David Blunkett, Labour Leader of Sheffield City, was at that time employed by neighbouring Labour controlled Barnsley as a lecturer in their college of technology and, moreover, allowed indefinite leave. On the other hand the Labour Leader of Barnsley was employed by Sheffield. Some of the most prominent Labour figures in local government have been or are local government employees. Thus Bernie Grant, now an MP, but formerly Labour leader of Haringey Borough and notorious for his boast that the police had received 'a good hiding' after the 1986 riot in which PC Keith Blakelock was murdered, was employed by the Borough of Newham; Derek Hatton the nattily dressed Militant, ('beau Derek') and deputy leader of Liverpool City, was employed by Knowsley Borough.

When the illegal behaviour of some of the Liverpool Labour councillors led to their disqualification from office in 1987, the City was run by a caretaker administration of Liberals until the next municipal elections. They found that about 1,000 new city posts had been created and many allocated to political sympathisers[11]. Amongst those they sacked, although with considerable severance pay, was Militant supporter Sam Bond who had been appointed the City's Race Relations Officer despite protests from the black community[12]. A good many of the local government jobs filled by Labour councillors are of the 'co-ordinator' or 'adviser' category and it is doubtful whether they have a useful content despite the high salaries they command.

Naturally many career officials regard all these measures of politicisation with alarm. Organisations representing local government staff—like the Society of Local Authority Chief Executives—deplore the trend. A few career officials might gain promotion through flaunting their political sympathies but for the majority life and work is made immeasurably harder by politicisation. For instance career officials find it difficult to resist pressure to resign when the ruling group is determined enough. There can be little doubt that a proportion of the many premature retirements which now characterise local government work is the result of political pressure. In some cases, however, politicisation can backfire on its perpetrators. Lambeth has had difficulty filling the post of director of social services, Brent in recruiting teachers. Working for councillors who demand political allegiance from their employees is not an attractive prospect for many career personnel. Herbert Morrison and the Webbs must be revolving in their graves at such extraordinary developments amongst Labour controlled local governments.

Radical social engineering

Social engineering is the deliberate manipulation of peoples' attitudes and behaviour to produce predetermined types of society as opposed to allowing natural social evolution. Of course it could be argued that all governments indulge in a measure of social engineering. The very laws they pass, the objects on which they spend public funds, encourage approval or disapproval of certain attitudes and behaviour. Nevertheless, there is a world of difference between, say, discouraging theft and encouraging family life on the one hand, and, on the other, seeking to create a radically changed society according to some ideological blueprint. The danger lies in applying mechanical methodology to an organic entity. Socialism has always been divided between evolutionist and social engineering tendencies. Fabians and other moderate socialists believe that the superiority of collective provision of services would lead society gradually to evolve in a socialist direction. Guild Socialists and Marxists want a new kind of society with dramatically different life-styles from the present, perhaps even a new Promethean man, and are prepared to engineer to achieve it. The new predominance of the latter elements in the Labour Party has meant a new stress on social engineering by local government.

Municipal services offer wide scope for social engineering and none more than education. Since 1970 many of the curriculum developments in local government schools and colleges have been clear attempts at such engineering. 'Peace studies' has sought to inculcate young people with pacifist and unilateralist sentiments[13]. 'World Studies' has sought to convince young people that the prosperity of the West is the cause of the poverty of the Third World[14]. 'Womens' Studies' has sought to impart an aggressive feminism; 'multi-cultural studies' has sought to weaken the identity and loyalties of young British people. Subjects like politics and sociology have been taught in an ideologically slanted way[15]. At the same time traditional disciplines like history have tended to be emptied of their factual and narrative content to concentrate on 'ideas' and 'concepts'[16]. There is even 'anti-racist mathematics' and 'anti-sexist physical education'.

It is true that some of these developments have originated with left-wing professional educationalists rather than politicians. Nevertheless, over the last two decades, Labour councillors have been their most enthusiastic backers and have themselves initiated many changes. Whatever the denials, there can be no doubt that these educational developments amount to a project for indoctrinating our young people—seeking to inculcate certain beliefs *irrespective of the evidence*. In February 1986 there was a House of Lords debate on educational indoctrination which revealed a mass of disturbing evidence. Former Prime Minister Lord Home of the Hirsel said during the proceedings 'I am bound to say that this debate—and I have listened to the whole of it—has proved that indoctrination is developing to a point of danger to the nation'[17].

While education offers the most obvious scope for social engineering—other local government activities—employment practice, contracting, grants to voluntary bodies, libraries, arts policy and much else—can also be pressed into service. Perhaps the most distinctive feature of the new approach is an obsession with 'discrimination'— presumably what is meant is 'unfair discrimination'—and a fanaticism (like that of a witch hunt) in stamping out the slightest suspicion of it. Indeed some Labour controlled local governments have shown remarkable ingenuity in discovering new forms of 'discrimination'. A slew of new words has been added to the English language—not just 'classism', 'racism' and 'sexism' but 'heterosexism', 'ageism', even 'able-bodiedism'.

Job advertisements have become a source of much innocent amusement to those who are not acolytes of the Left. For instance in the *Caribbean Times* on 6 March, 1987 Lambeth Borough advertised for a gravedigger favouring persons '. . . capable of bringing an innovative approach to the practical implementation of anti-racist and anti-sexist strategies within their areas of work . . . applications from people with disabilities will be particularly welcome'. This is a genuine advertisement, not a parody. Of course it is this kind of behaviour by Labour controlled local government that has attracted the title the 'loony left'. No doubt the press sometimes reports details of these stories inaccurately, but there is far too much hard evidence of such follies for them to be wholly figments of journalists' imagination. For instance reports that nursery schools in Hackney and Islington were singing 'Baa-Baa White Sheep' or 'Baa-Baa Green Sheep' may have been exaggerated but there was certainly some discouragement of 'Baa-Baa Black Sheep'[18]. In any case much of this behaviour is not denied; it is gloried in.

'Contract compliance' is a growing phenomenon amongst Labour controlled local governments. In practice it is used to penalise contractors who have worked for the Ministry of Defence, who have crossed miners' picket lines, who are suspected of even remote links with South Africa or of supporting the Conservative Party, or who even have directors who are freemasons. It is also used to discriminate against firms which do not employ what is thought to be a sufficient quota (often a continually rising one) of women or ethnic

minorities. The Building Employers Federation in Nottingham complained of tenders being refused by some Labour controlled local
governments where firms could not guarantee jobs for women
bricklayers[19].

In the last few years some Labour local governments have become
notorious for their promotion of 'positive images of homosexuals'.
Thus Camden's Lesbian and Gay Unit has announced plans to try to
stamp out the evils of 'heterosexism in the office,' although in the
same press reports a long-standing Camden employee was quoted as
saying 'The way they are talking you are queer if you are not gay'[20].
Haringey is renowned for the publications favourable to homosexuality which it has made available to even the youngest children—like
Jenny Lives with Eric and Martin and *Jesse's Dream Skirt*[21]. One wonders
what even the most radical socialist pioneers a century ago would
have thought of a Labour controlled municipality promoting transves-
tism amongst toddlers.

Some of these activities have aroused strong opposition. For instance a Parents' Rights Group was formed in Haringey to fight
homosexual teaching in its schools; but its members have been
subjected to abuse and even physical assaults. In Brent, community
leaders representing 20,000 Moslems have proclaimed their opposition to the Borough's policy of promoting favourable images of
homosexuality[22].

This kind of opposition raises doubts about the real purpose of
such social engineering. If it is genuinely designed to change peoples'
attitudes and behaviour then at times it is clearly counterproductive.
If, for instance, social engineering is really to persuade people to
regard homosexuals more benevolently, one wonders why more
cautious and subtle approaches are not employed. Much local government activity in this field cannot but increase hostility to homosexuals. To give another example, Labour controlled Nottingham City
introduced in 1986 a 'homosexuals only' session in one of its municipal swimming pools—although it is not clear how one tells a homosexual from a heterosexual in a swimming costume. This aroused
bitter resentment towards homosexuals amongst surrounding residents. Similarly some of the local government hounding of people
for alleged 'racism' must increase rather than reduce racial tensions.
When headmistress Mrs Maureen McGoldrick was disciplined by
Brent Borough for an allegedly 'racist' remark on the telephone
(which was both uncorroborated and denied) she had to be protected
by the intervention of the Secretary of State for Education. This can

have done nothing for race relations in Brent. The similar cases of headmaster Ray Honeyford in Bradford and teacher Jonathan Savery in Avon must have been equally deleterious to good race relations.

Can it be that the social engineering is not designed to change for the better but to cause disruption, conflict and disorientation? Perhaps the 'loony left' are, as Baroness Cox has suggested, the 'lethal left'. Do the social engineers want to transform our society through the instrument of local government or to destroy it? One answer would be that the Left is divided. Its 'softer' section really believes in the possibilities of transforming society by the inculcation of 'socialist values' while the Marxists want to overthrow the whole political and economic system and are simply using local government to this end.

The trouble with this analysis is that it cannot explain the destructive policies of those who claim to be adherents of the Left and who reject revolutionary Marxism. A clear case to take is that of anti-police propaganda. The attempt to change public attitudes to the police is one of the most prominent features of social engineering by Labour local governments over the last five years. Traditionally of course the British public repose great affection and confidence in the police (and indeed the great majority still do). A growing number of Labour controlled local governments, whether or not they have police responsibilities, have become self appointed critics of the police. Many have set up machinery—unofficial police committees, police monitoring units and the like—to check police activities and publish critiques of it. If the purpose of such activity were genuinely to make the police more responsive, and more accountable, to the needs of the communities they serve, then it would be understandable. Instead the propaganda is overwhelmingly if not exclusively hostile. Every real or imagined police error is exposed and magnified. Outrageous and unfair accounts of police behaviour are produced. For instance the GLC under Ken Livingstone produced a notorious video on the Metropolitan police showing them in as unfavourable a light as possible—harassing black people, unsympathetic to assaulted women, obsequious to the wealthy and so on. This video was deliberately peddled in youth clubs and schools. If believed it can only have provoked feelings of hatred and contempt towards the police.

One can only conclude that the 'softer' elements of the Left are either hypocritical, clumsy or confused. Maybe despite their denials they really agree with the Marxists in wanting to destroy the present system completely? Maybe they *want* enfeeblement of family life, loss of national identity, sexual confusion, increased racial tensions, collapse of police morale, public disaffection and as much disruption as possible to cause a complete national breakdown? If so, their policy is akin to that of the Pol Pot regime in Cambodia. They want to destroy in order to have a *tabula rasa* on which to create anew. The other possibilities are less probable. It does not seem credible that they do not appreciate how damaging some of their activities are. Nor does it seem credible that they are just confused—with their heads rejecting Marxist insurrection having seen what it has produced wherever it has been tried, and with their hearts feeling profound antipathy to present British society and so laying into it with unrestrained zeal.

It is true that Socialists have always found it easier to criticise than to be constructive. They have always been impatient of the messy realities of humanity and wanted to create a golden Utopia. The Left today are to some extent inheritors of the romantic socialist tradition, Guild Socialism and decentralisation. But this tradition is clearly intertwined with Marxism and there can be few who do not understand the implications of their behaviour. If there are some who are naive or confused on the Left then they are all the more dangerous for that.

Conclusions and prospects: the new Labour doctrine of local government and its implications

The new Labour doctrine of local government is a product of Marxism and Guild Socialism. Outright Marxists are now a powerful voice in the Labour Party. Although there are ideological distinctions between the various sects and tendencies they all seek, and expect, the complete replacement of the current political and economic order in Britain. Some elements of the Left, while heavily impregnated with Marxism, stop short of accepting the full Marxist programme. In large measure the Left is also an inheritor of the decentralist utopianism of Guild Socialism. This is reflected in the advocacy of massive redistribution of wealth, new 'social ownership' of industry (although in a more decentralised form than the old public corporations), workers' co-operatives, community participation in public services, and the promotion of 'socialist values'. There is no agreed list of such values, but they include collectivism, egalitarianism and the elimination of all 'discrimination'. This stress on 'values' can distinguish the 'softer' elements of the Labour Left from the more doctrinaire Marxists. Militant Trotskyites for instance are known for their lack of interest in, say, feminism. According to Marxism all exploitation, including that of women, will disappear with the dictatorship of the proletariat. Indeed they sometimes see the wilder behaviour of the 'women's liberation' movement as a distraction from the serious business of class warfare. The picture becomes muddied, however, when Marxists come to see 'discrimination' issues as useful instruments to pursue class warfare, given their potential for provoking discontent and disaffection.

Today Marxists both inside and outside the Labour Party, and the Labour Left generally, have a particular interest in local government—the former because of the new underpinning of 'local state' Marxist theory, the latter because of their combination of Marxist and decentralist inclinations. In any case, since Labour has had little success nationally since 1970, local government has offered the main scope for socialism.

In almost every respect the new Labour doctrine of local government differs from the old Fabian tradition. The new doctrine accepts flouting or evasion of the law, welcomes intervention in defence and other non-local government matters, promotes the politicisation of career officials, and emphasises relentless and unscrupulous social engineering—all in contrast to the old. Unlike the Fabians today's Left do not accept that local government is legitimately subordinate to the centre. Local government is seen as possessing equal if not superior validity. The Left thus represents a sometimes implicit, a sometimes explicit, challenge to national sovereignty. This may seem an exaggerated inference but the logic of its position can only point in this direction.

John Gyford describes the emergence of this new doctrine as a move from 'municipal labourism' to 'municipal socialism' and this is a useful shorthand way of seeing it[1]. Nevertheless the Fabians always thought of themselves as 'socialist'. Thus it is more accurate to see the new doctrine as the product of a surge of popularity for socialist tendencies which were always present, but which until recently appealed to only a minority of Labour municipal activists.

In practice it is difficult to disentangle 'hard' from 'soft' Left behaviour in local government. Doctrinaire Marxists are perhaps more ruthless. Militant controlled Liverpool in 1986, for instance, appeared to want to engineer a complete breakdown in order to take the battle onto the streets. Nevertheless all Labour Left behaviour can be heavily disruptive.

Of course the new doctrine does not enjoy a monopoly of allegiance amongst Labour councillors. Labour controlled local governments vary in their degrees of commitment to the new doctrine; some indeed have barely embraced it at all. But it does account for a very large proportion of local government, being especially evident in London, in the urban centres of the English Midlands and North, and in Scotland. While the declaration of a local 'nuclear-free zone' is not entirely co-terminous with commitment to the new doctrine it is certainly one indication and there are some one hundred and seventy such declarations today.

In any case even where the new doctrine does not prevail it is an influence and a growing one amongst Labour councillors. Gyford quotes a 1982 survey in which 68% of Labour councillors described themselves as on the Left or Left of Centre of the Party[2]. Indeed some elements of the doctrine seem to reach beyond the bounds of the Labour Party. The Liberal Party and the Greens are interested in community involvement and in decentralisation; they too have more than a whiff of the William Morris inheritance. The Liberals, however, have not indulged in illegal or bizarre behaviour in local government and the Greens have had too little success to demonstrate anything. Perhaps most insidiously some elements of the new Labour doctrine of local government seem almost imperceptibly to have been absorbed by councillors of other parties. Even Conservative local governments have at times edged towards some elements, say, of the so called anti-racist programme.

It is true that the Labour Party nationally is aware that some aspects of the new doctrine, especially when it manifests itself in 'loony left' behaviour in local government, damage electoral prospects. The Party seems keen to curb at least its wilder excesses—and a handful of the more blatant Marxists have been expelled. Nevertheless it may be too deeply rooted as a doctrine in local government practice to be eliminated even if the Party were inclined to try. It is also true that some leading figures of the Labour Left in local government have displayed a 'new realism' since the Conservative victory in the 1987 general election. Some have even begun to argue for less confrontation with the Government, although they have been attacked by their erstwhile comrades for doing so. Linda Bellos, Labour left leader of Lambeth likened the Conservative Party to the Nazis in an attack which it is thought was made to regain credibility on the left after making £35 million of cuts to stave off bankruptcy[3]. 'New realism' does not mean that the Left in local government is dead.

Responding to the new doctrine

The appropriate response to the new Labour doctrine of local government must involve both understanding and remedial action. In turn understanding must include not just a grasp of what the doctrine is and how it has emerged but a clear appreciation of why it is pernicious.

The new Labour doctrine of local government seeks to elevate local government to a rôle and status it has never enjoyed (in modern times), and can never enjoy within our present constitutional arrangements. All adherents of the new doctrine are inevitably working towards the destruction of these arrangements even where they do not consciously seek to do so.

Local government is the provision of a range of public services by the elected representatives of local communities enjoying substantial discretion within the law and a measure of financial autonomy. Local government is an important, indeed indispensable, institution in any Western liberal democracy. Its locality permits the administration of public services on a convenient scale; its discretion allows adaptation to local circumstances as well as valuable experimentation and innovation; its electoral basis makes for responsiveness to community wishes and needs; its degree of autonomy makes possible a creative tension with the national government; its democratic constitution can strengthen political understanding amongst both electors and elected. A Conservative would also recognise that the long and proud historical traditions of many of our municipalities contribute to social stability, continuity and accumulated wisdom of an intangible, but nonetheless very important kind. As Edmund Burke said 'it is with infinite caution that any man ought to venture upon pulling down an edifice which has answered in any tolerable degree for ages the common purposes of society'[4].

The alternative to local government is the provision of all public services directly or indirectly by central government. Such arrangements could have intolerable complications—administrative elephantiasis, political overload at the centre, catastrophic decline of innovation and the deeply unsettling effect of radical institutional change which went against the grain of centuries of development.

Local government is in practice indispensable. Nevertheless it is also a subordinate and contingent institution. Local government is not a sovereign institution; it is subject to the sovereignty of Parliament. The wishes of the local community must ultimately defer to the wishes of the national community if it is to remain part of it. For instance few local communities would welcome the siting of a new international airport within their boundaries. After due consultation and appropriate compensation the nation as a whole must have a right to decide, however, that the airport should go ahead. The alternative is for the nation not to enjoy full sovereignty. Local government has a lesser validity than national government.

Similarly local government is in principle contingent. If it were clear that local government were unnecesary, or even harmful, to the nation as a whole it could be swept away without causing fundamental political damage. In practice, as has been stressed, local government in both tangible and intangible ways is indispensable. Nevertheless this is a utilitarian justification.

The new Labour doctrine of local government violates these fundamental principles of subordination and contingency. By their actions and their justifications adherents of the new doctrine demonstrate a pernicious belief in the equal validity of local and national government, if not the primacy of the former[5]. Similarly some at least seem to imply the centrality of local government to the human condition. Even those well outside the ranks of the Labour Left sometimes talk about 'believing' in local government, investing a fundamentally utilitarian institution with a spurious credal significance.

Remedial action

Remedial action must operate at several different levels. In its broadest sense it should encompass all who value our democratic way of life. The inanities and malignancies of the operation of the new doctrine in local government must be exposed and contested. One must not underestimate the courage that this sometimes requires. The atmosphere of menace and intimidation which disfigures local government behaviour in some areas is a particularly heavy indictment of the new doctrine. The disgraceful harassment of the Haringey mothers, the unjustified persecution of Mrs Maureen McGoldrick, the scenes of riot and confusion in Lambeth and Brent council chambers and, alas, many similar events should cause decent people, however far left they may be, to reconsider the cause they are favouring.

Alan Alexander, former leader of the Labour group on Berkshire, admits '. . . there is a degree of public disquiet about the way in which some Labour-controlled authorities are being run . . . in their zeal to implement socialist policies some local politicians may sometimes give crucial democratic values and processes short shrift'[6]. Nevertheless even where the going is tough there is no alternative to bold public resistance to the challenge of the new doctrine.

At another level, however, the Government bears a particular responsibility to confront the new doctrine. Government remedial action may be loosely divided into two kinds, short and long term. In the short run the government must be prepared resolutely to legislate against local government misbehaviour spawned by the new doctrine. It will be an iterative process. Some Labour controlled local governments will remain relentless in their search for legal loopholes and ingenious in their exploitation of the potentialities of their powers.

The Government are right to outlaw the abuses of contract compliance and local government publicity of a party political kind. But some measures will have to be even more tightly drawn. And sooner or later the nettle of civil defence will have to be grasped. Laws have to be enforced as well as passed.

Legislation curbing local government is generally necessary because of breaches of convention. All political arrangements rest partly on the law and partly on long accepted convention. As has been explained one feature of the new doctrine of local government is a readiness to break the law. Breaches of settled convention are equally disruptive. Thus local government intervention in defence, foreign affairs and even macro-economic policy goes against all that has long been accepted as appropriate for local government. Ultimately breaches of convention can only be tackled by new legislation.

Legislation, while necessary, has its own dangers and difficulties. The more that restrictive laws are passed the more they have to be enforced and the less is the discretion of local government. There is a danger of administrative and political overload at the centre. While a framework of laws is necessary, and while abuses have to be checked, in the long run the most satisfactory situation would be of new settled conventions in central-local relations. In turn this could be achieved only by a political defeat of the new Labour doctrine of local government at the local level.

The Government could best foster this by improving the political and financial accountability of local government. While, as has been stressed, local government is a vital institution, in Britain it lacks democratic credibility. Its accountability is suspect. Research for the Widdicombe Committee confirmed a mass of earlier evidence that most people vote in local elections according to 'current national preference'[7]. The minority of people who bother to vote do so mainly to vent their feelings about the national government, not to punish or reward those who have been conducting their municipal affairs. Councillors rarely have to fear local electoral defeat because of their own behaviour, even where it is extreme and irresponsible. This situation is exacerbated by the system whereby only a third of local electors pay full rates; in some areas the proportion is less. Thus even those electors who do choose to vote on local issues can in many cases vote extravagant groups into office knowing that they will not have to pay for their profligacy.

The new Labour doctrine of local government is erected on this base of weak accountability. If the government were to rectify this problem then the new doctrine would have to struggle much harder to survive.

The Government's moves to introduce a community charge in place of domestic rates are welcome. Since this will involve a much higher proportion of the municipal electorate directly as local taxpayers the hope must be that they will think more carefully about casting their votes for groups who embrace the extravagances of the new doctrine. Of course it will take some years to establish the new system and ultimately further changes may be needed. For instance, it is doubtful whether in the long run commerce or industry should be taxed by local government even on a pooled basis. The principle of local accountability would be better served if industry were taxed only by national government.

Changes in municipal taxation, while important, are unlikely alone to achieve a sufficient degree of local accountability. To do this basic changes to the political structure of local government should be contemplated. The complexities of the committee system are difficult for most citizens to grasp and they obfuscate and diffuse political accountability. If municipal leadership were dramatised and clarified people could focus on it more easily. They might then cast their votes more in the light of what local leaders have done or propose to do rather than as a referendum on the national government. It is true that a handful of municipal leaders have become well known because of their gifts for publicity (or their notoriety), Ken Livingstone, David Blunkett, Derek Hatton—but this is despite, not because of, the system. Most municipal leaders and their senior colleagues are not well known amongst their electorates. I have suggested elsewhere[8] how the offices of mayor and sheriff could be made powerful and publicly identifiable municipal executives.

With such changes in local taxation and political structure local elections would have a fair chance of being seen as more important. Of course it might be that some local electorates might deliberately put into power Labour groups committed to the new doctrine. If the electorate were prepared to pay for the consequences then within broad limits one could not object. Naturally the Government would always retain the right to intervene if some extraordinary municipal behaviour threatened the national interest. Given, however, that the tide of socialism is ebbing ('La gauche est révolue' wrote Professor Jean-Marie Benoist of the Collége de France in 1985[9]) the hope is that genuinely accountable local government will rid us before long of the lunacies and viciousness of some of the practitioners of the new Labour doctrine of local government.

Notes

Labour Party traditions and local government

1. E R Pease, *The History of the Fabian Society*, 3rd edition, Frank Cass and Company, London 1963, pp. 90, 91.

2. *ibid* p. 236.

3. *ibid* p.239.

4. G D H Cole, *The Fabian Society Past and Present*, Tract No. 258, The Fabian Society, London, 1942, pp 6,7.

5. Tract No. 8, Fabian Society, London 1890.

6. E R Pease, op.cit. p. 81.

7. Sidney Webb, *The Local Government Act 1929: How to Make the Best of It*, Tract No. 231, Fabian Society, 1929.

8. S & B Webb *English Local Government*, Frank Cass, 11 volumes, London 1963.

9. S & B Webb, Longmans, Green & Co, London, 1920, chapter iv.

10. *ibid* pp. 237,238.

11. *ibid* p. 204.

12. R Barker *Political Ideas in Modern Britain*, Methuen, London, 1978, pp 33, 34.

13. T N Foulis, London, 1912.

14. *News From Nowhere or An Epoch of Rest, being some chapters from a Utopian romance*, Reeves & Turner, London, 1891.

15. *British Labour Movement Retrospect and Prospect*, Ralph Fox Memorial Lecture, Fabian society, 1951 p. 3, quoted in A W Wright *G. D. H. Cole and Socialist Democracy*, Clarendon Press, Oxford 1979, p.14.

16. Leonard Parsons, London.

17. *ibid* p. 35.

18. A W Wright, *G.D.H. Cole and Socialist Democracy*, Clarendon Press, Oxford, 1979, p.27.

19. Guild Socialism Revisited in *Political Quarterly*, No 3, 1975.

20. LJ Macfarlane, *The British Communist Party: its origin and development until 1929*, Macgibbon & Kee, London, 1966, p. 56.

21. Margaret Cole, *The Story of Fabian Socialism*, Heinemann, London, 1961, p. 148.

22. Michael Crick, *Militant*, Faber and Faber, London, 1984, p.58. (A revised 2nd ed. entitled *March of Militant* was published in 1986.)

23. *ibid* p. 212.

24. George Orwell, *Homage to Catalonia*, Secker and Warburg, London, 1938.

25. John Gyford & Mari James, *Central and Local Government*, Allen & Unwin, London, 1980.

The Labour Party in local government 1900–1970: the Fabian perspective adopted

1. GDH Cole *British Working Class Politics 1832–1914*, George Routledge & Sons, London 1941, p.108.

2. *ibid* pp 150, 151.

3. GDH Cole *A History of the Labour Party from 1914*, Routledge & Kegan Paul, London 1948, pp. 458 and 459.

4. *The Municipal Yearbook 1972*, Municipal Journal Ltd., London 1972, pp 1985–1998.

5. GDH Cole op.cit. 1948 p. 447.

6. Quoted in B.Donoughue & G. W. Jones *Herbert Morrison: Portrait of a Politician*, Weidenfeld & Nicolson, London 1973 pp. 190,191.

7. See R Postgate *The Life of George Lansbury*, Longmans, Green & Co., London, 1951, pp.216–225.

8. Noel Boaden, *Urban Policy Making: influences on County Boroughs in England and Wales*, Cambridge University Press, Cambridge 1971 and BP Davies, *Social needs and Resources in Local Services: a study of variations in standards of provision of personal social services between local authority areas*, Michael Joseph, London, 1968.

The Labour Party in local government after 1970: Fabianism derided

1. See JG Davies, *The Evangelistic Bureaucrat*, Tavistock Publications, London 1972; Norman Dennis, *People and Planning: the sociology of housing in Sunderland*, Faber, London 1970; Patrick Dunleavy, *The Politics of Mass Housing in Britain 1945–75*, Clarendon Press, Oxford, 1981.

2. Patrick Dunleavy, *Urban Political Analysis: the politics of collective consumption*, Macmillan, London, pp.42–50.

3. Cynthia Cockburn, *The Local State: management of cities and people*, Pluto Press, London, 1977.

4. Hilary Wainwright, *Labour: a Tale of Two Parties*, Hogarth Press, London, 1987, p.13.

5. Article in *Morning Star* 27 April, 1981.

6. Quoted by Peter Shipley, *More Militant: the future of the Labour Left*, Conservative Political Centre, London, 1986, p.17.

7. *Socialist Action*, 11 May, 1984.

8. For an account of Labour Left-Marxist links see Blake Baker *The Far Left: an expose of the extreme left in Britain*, Weidenfeld and Nicholson, London, esp. ch.10. Also Peter Shipley, op.cit., esp pp.14–16.

9. Interview in *Marxism Today* October 1984, quoted in Geoffrey Foote *The Labour Party's Political Thought: a history*, Croom Helm, London, 2nd edition, 1986.

10. Peter Shipley, op.cit., p.5.

11. See Ken Livingstone, *If Voting Changed Anything, They'd Abolish It*, Collins, London, 1987.

Local Government Behavior in the 70s and 80s: lunacies at work

1. *Labour Herald*, 18 January, 1985.

2. David Regan, *It costs A Bomb: the local government anti-nuclear campaign*, Peace Through NATO, London, 1985. See also, *The New City Republic; municipal intervention in defence*, Institute for European Defence and Strategic Studies, London, 1987.

3. *Independent*, 16 November, 1987.

4. David Blunkett and Geoff Green, *Building from the Bottom: the Sheffield Experience*, Fabian Tract 491, Fabian Society, London 1983, p. 26.

5. Interview in *Chartist magazine*, July–September 1985.

6. *Asian Times*, 13 February, 1987.

7. *News on Sunday*, 17 May, 1987.

8. *Asian Times*, 13 February, 1987.

9. *Asian Times*, 20 February, 1987.

10. Charles Goodson-Wickes, *The New Corruption*, Centre for Policy Studies, London 1984 p.14.

11. *Sunday Times*, 22 March, 1987.

12. *Guardian*, 13 May 1987.

13. See Caroline Cox & Roger Scruton *Peace Studies: A Critical Survey*, Institute for European Defence and Strategic Studies, London 1984; and John Marks, *Peace Studies in our Schools: Propaganda for Defencelessness*, Women and Families for Defence, London 1984.

14. See Roger Scruton *World Studies: education or indoctrination?* Institute for European Defence and Strategic Studies, London, 1985.

15. See DJ O'Keeffe (ed), *The Wayward Curriculum*, Social Affairs Unit, London 1986; David Marsland, *Neglect and Betrayal: War and Violence in Modern Sociology*, Institute for European Defence and Strategic Studies, London, 1985 and *Bias Against Business: Anti-Capitalist Inclinations in Modern Sociology*, Educational Research Trust, London, 1987 respectively.

16. See Alan Beattie, *History in Peril: may parents preserve it.* Centre for Policy Studies, London, 1987.

17. *House of Lords Debates*, 5 February, 1986, vol. 470 No. 39, cols. 1139–1250, reproduced as a monograph under the title *The House of Lords Debate: Educational Indoctrination*, Policy Research Associates, London, 1986.

18. See Francis Beckett in *The Times Educational Supplement*, 5 June 1987.

19. *Daily Telegraph*, 23 February, 1987.

20. *Today*, 26 June, 1987.

21. *Daily Telegraph*, 18 August, 1987.

22. *The Times*, 18 June, 1987.

Conclusions and prospects: the new labour doctrines and its implications

1. John Gyford, *The Politics of Local Socialism*, Allen & Unwin, London, 1985: esp.ch.1.

2. John Gyford, op.cit. p. 14.

3. *Daily Telegraph*, 29 September, 1987.

4. *Reflections on the Revolution in France*, Penguin Books, Harmondsworth, 1983, p. 152.

5. David Blunkett and Keith Jackson, *Democracy in Crisis: the town halls respond*, Hogarth Press, London, 1987.

6. Alan Alexander, *Managing Local Socialism*, Fabian Tract 511, Fabian Society, London, 1986 p. 21.

7. *The Conduct of Local Authority Business*, Report of the Committee of Inquiry, Research Volume III, Cmnd. 9800, 1986.

8. David Regan, *A Headless State: the unaccountable executive in British local government*, University of Nottingham, 1980.

9. *Les outils de la Liberté*, Laffont, Paris, 1985.

2

The Local Right: Enabling Not Providing

Nicholas Ridley

Introduction

For the last 150 years local authorities of various persuasions have represented and served their various communities. They have been responsible for those public services which can best be provided locally under the supervision of democratically elected councillors.

But although this central purpose has remained unchanged, there have been many alterations in their shape, size, functions, procedures and finances. Authorities have been created, reorganised, merged and abolished as communities have grown and altered. New functions have been added and others have been taken away as needs have changed. Standards of provision of service required by the public have evolved all the time. Procedures within local authorities have changed to meet new methods of working.

Throughout its history, local authorities' expenditure and manpower have tended to grow and to consume a larger proportion of total public expenditure and of the gross domestic product. Growth has been particularly marked since 1945 with the expansion of education, social services and other labour-intensive personal services.

This expansion has placed a growing burden upon the sources of finance for local authority expenditure. It has also led to a growing public and political concern with many of the main features and aspects of local authorities,

• what functions should local authorities have? What things are best done locally and what can be better organised nationally? What functions need to be in the public sector and what could be better done privately?

• what standard of services is needed and what can be afforded?

• what areas should local authorities cover? How many people are needed to discharge the various functions? Is there any overlap or conflict between different types of authority?

• how should local authorities be organised to conduct their business efficiently, effectively and with propriety?

• what should be their financial structure? How can authorities obtain finance for their functions on a fair, adequate and accountable basis?

• how can value for money best be obtained? How can the needs of the public (the consumer) best be served? How can undue influence of pressure groups be contained?

• how can the overall burden of local authority expenditure on the economy best be contained and related fairly to other public sector burdens?

• how can members and staff be obtained and retained to run the complex local authorities of today in an efficient and responsive way?

Since 1979 the present Government has had two overriding objectives in relation to local government. First, it has been essential to constrain the growth of local authority expenditure in order to stop it taking an ever-larger proportion of the total national product at the expense of other areas of the economy. Secondly, it has remained as important as ever to maintain and enhance the quality of those local authority services which the public really needs. In order to reconcile these two objectives it is essential for local authorities to concentrate on what is really wanted and needed by local people, to improve accountability, to eliminate waste, duplication and unnecessary functions, and to improve value for money.

We have made some progress towards these objectives since 1979. But it is not yet enough.

The need to eliminate duplication and waste was the main reason for abolishing the Greater London Council and the Metropolitan Counties. This has been successfully carried through with no diminution of services to the public, and very few regrets from anyone.

Abandoning or reducing functions that do not need to be carried out by local authorities at all frees resources to concentrate on those things which must remain local authority functions. For example, the progressive diminution of the local authority housing stock through the operation of the right to buy and other disposals frees resources and brings in capital receipts for other tasks.

Competition is vital to secure value for money. Local authorities have long had excellent and stringent requirements when they let contracts for works and services to the private sector in order to ensure that there is keen competition and the best price is obtained. This Government is progressively extending this principle to the services provided by authorities' own staff. Direct labour organisations have been required to draw up proper accounts, and compete on an equal footing with outside firms. Now under the current Local Government Bill, the same competitive disciplines will be extended much more widely.

The total of central government support to local authorities through the rate support grant has been reduced in order to bring home to them the need to restrain spending. And this financial pressure has been reinforced by targets, grant adjustments and rate limits for individual authorities.

The results of these policies over the last eight years have been mixed. The rate of growth of local authority expenditure slowed down initially but has recently increased again. Total manpower too fell for some years but has been increasing for the last two years.

We need to make further efforts to secure better local government for the future. Two of the keys to success lie in strengthening accountability and extending competition.

To strengthen accountability we need a more direct relationship between payment for local services through local taxation and the service being provided. The community charge will provide this. All adult citizens will be liable and will have a much stronger interest than at present in holding their councils to account through the ballot box.

Competition is a spur to efficiency and value for money wherever it operates. Too much of the public sector has been insulated from it. The spread of competition in education, housing and other local services should do an enormous amount to improve standards of efficiency. Measures to bring this about are already in hand in the Education Bill, the Local Government Bill and the Housing Bill.

Ultimately, however, the future of local government lies with the people who elect their Councils and receive their services. The last eight years have seen an extraordinary divergence of response from local authorities to the opportunities provided by sustained economic growth and to this Government's radical new approach to the country's problems. At one extreme there have been authorities—Labour controlled—which have refused to recognise reality. They have expanded their spending and manpower often and to no very useful purpose. While the country as a whole has woken up and looks to the future with confidence and hope, they have continued to preach a measure of decline and hopelessness, a message which has sapped local enterprise and morale. They have lost touch with the beliefs and attitudes of ordinary people. They have imposed massive rate increases on their long-suffering rate payers. And some of them have now got into financial difficulties.

At the other end of the spectrum there are Conservative authorities which have taken up the challenge of accountability and competition. They have scrutinized every service and introduced competition. They have disposed of unproductive assets to those who can use them better. They have sought out ways to encourage the private sector and to stimulate the local economy. They have kept closely in touch with the needs and wishes of local people, they have improved services and reduced rate burdens.

This pamphlet is about how to extend this revolution from the few to the many. The Government can set the scene. But we need allies in every authority in the country dedicated to the same objectives and ready to take up the struggle.

Responsibility of central government

Some people appear to believe that there was once a 'golden age' for local authorities when they were able to operate largely on their own initiative to provide services free of government controls on spending, borrowing and the formulation of policies. They argue that this is justified by the local mandate which local councillors obtained from their local electorate, and that the object should be to get back that degree of freedom.

This is a misreading of history. And the attempt to obtain that degree of freedom by some local authorities is to pursue an unobtainable and undesirable illusion in which the public are the losers. Parliament must continue to play a role in determining the essential framework in which local authorities operate, and in judging their appropriate share of the national cake. But within that framework the Government is keen to avoid unnecessary and time-wasting bureaucratic controls which frustrate initiative and responsibility at local level.

Going back to the nineteenth century Brian Keith Lucas and Peter Richards in their *History of Local Government in the Twentieth Century* characterised Victorian attitudes to local government thus,

> The Victorian tradition was that local government was a necessary evil; [its] services were essential and the local bodies providing them needed to be kept in check. They should not be allowed to undertake functions other than those approved by Parliament. There should be some element of central scrutiny to see that money was not wasted and in some services to ensure that minimum standards of provision were maintained.

And local authorities were kept in check—by strict *ultra vires* rules which were unpopular with local authorities, reinforced by periodic inspection and the audit of local accounts.

In the 19th century, local government powers could be expanded only by Parliament. There were much stricter controls on borrowing; borrowing powers were commonly obtained through private Bills: controls were strictly imposed on the amounts borrowed and on the period of loans. And in the 19th century, just as now, there were problems over central government grants paid to local authorities. In 1888, central government broke away from the principle that the central taxpayer should be expected to provide a set proportion of whatever local authorities decided to spend. Instead it introduced an 'assigned revenue' system of grants to local authorities which by assigning the proceeds of certain taxes broke the link between expenditure and grants of a percentage grant system. That was not very popular with local government, either.

Throughout the earlier years of this century the number of specific grants, accompanied by detailed rules, increased and covered not only large services like education and health but smaller services like air raid precautions, physical recreation and training, midwifery services and so on. In the 1950s nearly all central government grants came with strings attached, and Whitehall controlled many detailed decisions.

In 1958, however, the pendulum began to swing the other way. In that year a number of specific grants were replaced by a new general grant and a large number of detailed controls were abolished or modified. Further simplification and abolition of controls have followed in successive local government Acts since then.

Central government must, however, continue to play an important role in relation to six key areas,

- the constitutional framework of local government and its practices and procedures;
- determining the main functions of local authorities and the framework within which they should operate;
  - the overall burden of the local authority sector on the economy;
  - the levels of taxation on all the different groups in society;
  - standards of provision for services of a national character; and,
  - value for money in the provision of local authority services.

Local authority practices and procedures: the Widdicombe Report

The framework within which local authorities operate has recently been comprehensively analysed in the Widdicombe Report on the Conduct of Local Government Business. The report stressed the essential part which healthy local government can play in providing the means by which people can participate in public affairs at the local level.

The Committee found much to admire in the way local authorities operate; but they also found some serious weaknesses. They set themselves,

> to make recommendations for the conduct of local authority business which will assist in the development of a way of operating that is stable, locally responsive, widely accepted and attuned both to political reality and to the effective delivery of services.

That objective is exactly right. The Committee made a large number of recommendations about the organisation of council business, the functions of members and of officials, safeguards against abuses, the role of the auditors and the local ombudsman. Some of the improvements needed may best be made by local authorities themselves. But for others there will clearly need to be some legislation. In deciding about this, we must remember that local authorities will soon be working in the changed circumstances which the Community Charge will bring about. Thus the need which Widdicombe identified to help authorities to be more responsive and accountable to their local electorate, to encourage competition, and to reduce the capacity of special interest groups to exert undue influence on decisions is already being tackled. If the accountability, responsiveness and efficiency of local authorities can be improved in this way there will be much less need for central controls and intervention.

Enforcement of national standards

It is not easy to achieve the right balance between central and local government in the organisation and provision of services to the public. There are many individual services in which central government has an interest and for which it is held responsible by the electorate. A substantial proportion of the commitments made in the manifesto of any national party concern services directly provided by local authorities: housing, education, personal social services, public transport, environmental health and so on. At the same time, however, there is widespread agreement that the organisation and management of these services is best undertaken at local level, and that decisions about levels of service or new developments are a proper matter for local political discretion.

For some services the national concern with the standards and methods of operation and functions has always been paramount. The police and fire services are obvious examples. In other services, principally those of a regulatory nature, a tight statutory framework governing the standards and procedures to be applied locally has always been necessary—planning procedures, building regulations, environmental safety standards are good examples. At the other extreme there are services such as the provision of recreation and leisure facilities which are almost entirely a local matter, and in which there is little need for central government involvement.

Education is an example of a service in which there is a very strong national interest, and a growing national political concern with standards. Many people find it unacceptable that simply because of where they live their children should have a different standard of education. They regard education as a service which should have high standards throughout the country. We believe therefore that it is right to set a national core curriculum for education so that parents have some yardstick with which to judge the education that their children are receiving.

What is clear in all this is that the more effectively and efficiently local authorities operate in providing services in an accountable way, responsive to the needs of their local communities and competing effectively with other providers where that is relevant, the less need there is likely to be for central government and detailed control. That is why improvements in the local operation of service and of local authorities are so important. Conversely, where local responsibility breaks down there is inevitably stronger pressure for central intervention. I am determined to recreate the situation in which local solutions to local problems can satisfactorily be found.

Local authority spending and accountability

Our proposals to reform local authority finance were triggered by our concern about the burden of local spending and taxation. Local authority spending accounts for 25% of total public spending, and in spite of the various measures of constraint current spending has risen by 18% in real terms over the past eight years. That is only an average, and the figures conceal wide variations. It is often in those areas which can least afford the burden that overspending and overmanning have reached absurd levels and have had a deleterious effect on the local economy. In order to fulfil national economic objectives, we must exert a downward pressure on local authority spending as well as on national spending.

In the Government's Green Paper *Paying for Local Government* we analysed two alternative ways forward—increasing central control or improving local accountability. We pointed out that increased central control of local government spending might at first sight appear an easy answer to the problem, as its results could be substantial and guaranteed. We rejected the various versions of increased central control, however, because they would all have required government departments to get drawn into detailed financial affairs of local authorities, would have increased central and local manpower, would have led to further dilution of local accountability, and would have exacerbated conflicts between the central and local authorities.

The alternative of improving local accountability must be the better way forward. It guarantees the continued existence of a healthy democratic system of local government. It should reduce the tension between central and local authorities. It should help to ensure that services are provided more efficiently. And it will strengthen the link between the local authority and those who live in the area.

Local accountability depends crucially on the relationship between paying for local services and voting in local elections. Of the 35 million local electors in England only 18 million are liable to pay rates, and about a third of those receive full or partial rebates.

The Victorians interpreted the concept of democratic accountability by limiting voting rights to ratepayers. We intend to widen the liability for local taxation to nearly all voters through our Community Charge proposals. This is a logical step towards greater local authority freedom. It should allow us to stand much further back from local government because the electors will stand much closer.

Our reforms of the grants system will also assist accountability. At present the distribution of the rate support grant is so complicated and varies so much between authorities that sensible planning and accountability is seriously damaged. Rate levels fluctuate from year to year to reflect changes in grant levels that may have little to do with changes in expenditure. So ratepayers do not know whether to hold the authority or the government to account for the changes in the rate levels. Under our new proposals changes in Exchequer grant will be distributed as a single amount related to a simplified needs assessment for each authority, and will not be affected by the authorities' own decisions on expenditure. There will therefore be a direct relationship between each authority's spending level and the Community Charge which it has to levy. And the electorate will be able to make direct comparisons between different authorities on the standards of service they provide and the level of charge they levy.

Efficiency and value for money

Value for money remains a major concern for both central and local government. Successive studies by the Audit Commission have identified the tremendous potential for improvement in local government across the whole range of their services. Many of these reports confirm our view about the importance of the stimulus of competition. Competition has sharpened the operation of many local authorities' direct labour organisations, or led to the transfer of work to more efficient competitors in the private sector. Now we are extending this kind of competition to a much wider range of local authority services.

Local authorities in the future

Local authorities are big business. English authorities spend between them nearly £50 billion a year. They employ nearly two million people, 12% of the total workforce.

During the past eight years the growth of expenditure has been reduced from its rate of increase in the 1970s, but it has recently started to rise again. Overall manpower fell from a high point of 1.975 million in 1979 to 1.887 million in 1982, but it started to climb again in 1985 and is now back to 1.924 million.

Within these overall changes there are interesting differences between services.

Manpower in education has fallen by 58,000 mainly due to falling school rolls, transport by 17,000 (following bus privatisation), refuse collection and disposal by 12,000 (following contracting-out) and construction by 19,000 (due to the effect of competition on direct labour organisations and some reduction in activity). By contrast, social services have increased by 30,000 (following demographic changes and shifts in policy towards more care in the community), housing services by 12,000 and law and order by 20,000.

These figures suggest that although there have been some clear improvements in efficiency and value for money in some services (particularly those where competition has been introduced) the resultant savings have not yet been enough everywhere to secure the Government's objective of restraining the growth of expenditure while enhancing the quality of services. This is confirmed by successive reports from the Audit Commission identifying many areas in which significant improvements in value for money should still be possible.

Looking to the future, what further changes to the pattern of local government activity can we expect as our policies on greater accountability and competition take wider effect, and as other changes come into play? Clearly the answers will be different for different services and functions. For example, in housing, parts of the social services and parts of the transport services, I can foresee a much more diverse pattern of provision in the future by a variety of different agencies working alongside local authorities. The role of the local authority will no longer be that of the universal provider. But it will continue to have a key role in ensuring that there is adequate provision to meet needs, in encouraging the various providers to develop and maintain the necessary services, and where necessary in providing grant support or other assistance to get projects started, and to ensure that services are provided and affordable for the clients concerned.

For other services, principally those of a regulatory kind, there may be less scope for a diversity of providers or for direct competition with the private sector. In these cases the impulse for competition and improved value for money will have to come from within the authority, from the stimulus provided by comparisons with other authorities, and from the investigations of the auditors.

Education

There will inevitably be differences between services as to whether the influence of local accountability or national concern with standards is dominant in bringing about change. In education, for example, there is at present a strongly articulated national political demand for the introduction of national standards of assessment and attainment. The current Education Bill provides the means for bringing these standards into effect. At the same time there is a growing local demand for more local influence over individual schools, and from other educational establishments to have more control over their own destinies. The strengthening of the power of school governors, and the new proposals for allowing individual schools to opt out of local authority control, reflect this demand. As the national standards establish themselves, and as opting out leads to a wider variety of providers of education there will be effectively more competition and more stimulating comparisons between different areas and between schools. All this will put education authorities on their mettle to keep their standards up to scratch, and to achieve an efficient delivery of education.

Social services

In social services there are constant demands for increased provision of services for a variety of clients. The numbers of old people are steadily rising. The trend towards care in the community instead of in institutions needs the development of new support services. But this too is an area where authorities ought not and need not regard themselves as the universal suppliers. There is a whole range of private and voluntary agencies able and willing to play their part as well as to support those who need help. The role of the local authority should be to encourage diversity and alternatives, with some elements of competition between the different providers. The social services are performing an essential role of caring. But it is sentimentality to argue that therefore they should be exempt from the same disciplines of competition and value for money as other parts of the public sector.

Transport—the benefits of competition

Transport and local bus services provide a good example of how competition can improve standards and value for money, following the legislation I brought in in 1985 to open up services to competition.

Throughout the debates on that subject, the Government was accused of attacking local democracy. Councils who had managed their affairs for years by signing the annual cheque to the local bus company, and others who had thought they had planned a complex 'coordinated' and 'integrated' network, strongly objected to the idea that the market—ie consumers—could actually make better choices than the council computer model. What were the results? Between 1975 and 1985, fares had risen by up to 24% in real terms. Between 1975 and 1985 subsidies (not taking into account free bus passes or tokens), had increased from little or nothing to over £500 million. On deregulation day in October 1986, some local authorities reported immediate savings in subsidy of 40% while broadly maintaining levels of service. Between October 1986 and November 1987, bus mileage actually increased by 12% after years of decline. 250 areas now have minibus services and the market share held by private sector operators has increased from 8% to 12%. 83% of services—a much higher figure than anyone predicted—run commercially and without subsidy. Already 47 NBC subsidiaries have been sold, with more to come, although we were assured that privatisation and competition could not proceed together.

In this process, the role of local government in transport provision has been transformed. It hasn't diminished—indeed the job is more challenging—but it has changed. Before the 1985 Act, there was no competition. Local authorities had to substitute their 'guesstimates' of the market place for the reality in negotiation with a monopoly operator. They presided over an opaque system of cross-subsidy from popular to unpopular routes which distorted market forces by pricing people off the popular routes. Now the market—bus operators interpreting passengers' wishes—operates without intervention except in the enforcement of safety standards and requirements of professional competence. The local authority's role is confined to two political decision-making functions, both involving straight value for money considerations: first to provide subsidy directly for tendered services on routes which would not be viable without subsidy, but which the council considers necessary for social reasons; and second to fund fare concessions for particular groups of people whom they feel have a strong social need. In other words, instead of being providers, they are facilitators and enablers. They step in to help where the market does not supply, and use public money to provide services where they feel for social reasons it is necessary.

Surely this is a perfect example of local democracy working as it should? To most people it is largely irrelevant who provides the service, so long as it is there, corresponds with their needs, is good and efficient—and they pay as little as possible for it. It is the market place which is the most efficient mechanism for providing goods and services where there is a demand for them. But where there is not enough demand to make a service viable then it is a proper matter for political discretion as to whether other factors justify the use of taxpayers' and ratepayers' money to provide a service. The function of both national and local government is to reconcile such conflicting interests, but not surely to seek to provide services which would be provided efficiently without their help. What after all is the reason for trying to supplant the market? It is to interfere with choices made by individuals which the market works to satisfy. In transport, the complicated web of cross subsidy which supported the old regulated system meant that potentially profitable routes were overpriced and potential custom driven away so that people were denied the choice which they should have had.

Exactly the same principles can be brought to bear when we examine the role of local government in providing other services: on housing, and education. In housing, council tenants who already have the right to buy will be given a new right to choose a new landlord if they feel dissatisfied with the performance of the local authority as landlord and think they can get a better deal elsewhere.

In education, parents are being given the right to get out of local authority control where they are not satisfied with the service provided by the local education authority.

Housing—ripe for more competition

By the time the right to buy has run its course we estimate that somewhere around 1.5 million council homes in Great Britain will have been sold to their tenants. That would still leave around 5 million homes in local authority ownership. Many of the remaining tenants will not want to buy or may not be able to afford owner occupation. All the more reason for ensuring that their housing is supplied efficiently. To do that we need to break up the local authorities' near-monopoly of rented housing. In our new Housing Bill we are giving council tenants an opportunity to choose an alternative landlord; encouraging a revival of investment by private landlords; encouraging more private finance for housing associations and making plans to set up Housing Action Trusts to improve conditions, diversify tenures, and bring in private sector money and expertise in some of the worst housing areas.

This more pluralist approach should not only be more efficient; it will be much better adapted to today's housing problems which vary so much between one region and another; between inner city, suburb, small town and rural areas; and between different types of tenant.

But there will still be a key role for local authorities. Freed from having to be managers and providers of general housing, with all the day to day problems that that entails, they can concentrate on ensuring that those who are genuinely in need, and unable to get adequate housing on the open market, are properly catered for. To do this they will need to retain a range of clearly defined powers and responsibilities. Many local authorities are themselves coming forward with proposals for disposing of their remaining housing stock. We greatly welcome and are encouraging this trend. The less they have to own or manage directly, the freer they will be to concentrate on their role of facilitator and enabler. They will be able to devote more attention to the tasks of ensuring an adequate supply of sites for housing, for example through planning decisions; for channelling grants and subsidies towards the people and areas in greatest housing need, for carrying out the roles of monitoring and inspection, for instance of fitness and safety regulations; for ensuring that there are adequate arrangements—perhaps through contracts with the providers—for housing the homeless, and vulnerable groups such as those released from institutions for care back into the community.

This is not a minor role. It does not imply a diminution in the importance of local authorities. It means simply that authorities will concentrate on those tasks that only the public sector can do. Freed from other concerns, they will be able to carry out that role more objectively and more efficiently; providing better value for money, and ultimately better housing for those in greatest need.

Competitive tendering

For the services which will be subject to competitive tendering, that process, providing the council sets and monitors performance standards properly, will guarantee the customer value for money. Again, there is no reason whatsoever why the management of these services has to be 'political'. In all these cases the emphasis shifts from the council as monopoly provider and manager to the council as enabler and monitor, and casts the spotlight on its role as the maintainer of high standards. No council which can put its hand on its heart and say that it provides and runs the most efficient and customer-responsive services possible has anything to fear. If it is right, it can expect its workforce to win the contracts and its tenants and the parents of children in its schools to recognise that fact and not wish to opt out of local authority control. But the effect of these pieces of legislation on those who are not quite so confident—and there are many of them—is already apparent. The local authority union NALGO are urging their shop stewards to introduce more efficient working practises so that they can win the contracts when the new legislation comes into effect. A whiff of competition can have a greater effect than years of time-consuming and often fruitless negotiations between employers and employees.

What underlies these policies is the concept that it is for local authorities to organise, secure and monitor the provision of services, without necessarily providing them themselves.

Inner cities

These principles apply to all authorities, but perhaps the greatest opportunity to make them work is provided by the inner cities. The only way that prosperity can be brought back to some of our older industrial areas and inner cities is by getting the private sector to invest in regeneration, and by encouraging those who want to be enterprising to bring employment back to the city by their activity. Local authorities can enable this to happen by their attitudes and their actions, particularly on planning, land assembly and rate levels. What they cannot do is to create and sustain the development themselves. They (or rather their electors) cannot afford to finance it on a sufficient scale, nor will they be able to interpret demand as sensitively as the market. Again they are more likely to succeed as enablers than as providers.

Local authorities' capital programmes

The same principle should surely apply to local authorities' capital programmes. Local authorities in England are spending £6.2 million in aggregate on capital projects this year. This is mainly financed by borrowing or capital receipts which would otherwise be used to repay debt or used by others to invest. So local authorities capital programmes have an immediate effect on public sector indebtedness which in turn is an important element in economic management. Because it is desirable to reduce public sector debt to a minimum (even the Labour party seems to be coming to this view—at least as applied to the US economy!), we should ensure that as much capital expenditure as possible is financed by the private rather than by the public sector.

Local authorities finance new council homes, sports centres, leisure centres, shopping centres, industrial estates as well as many other things. But do such things need to be provided at public expense at all, let alone by public investment? Why not let the private sector provide them—maybe better? Spending public capital resources on buildings which could as easily be built and run by the private sector ties up huge quantities of public resources when there are many competing programmes where public sector capital expenditure is essential. It is perfectly possible for local authorities to provide pump priming finance or subsidies specifically for the people they are trying to help—for example subsidised rents for poor tenants or subsidies to enable the least well off to attend sports or leisure centres, or to use public transport—without necessarily having to own or build or run the facilities themselves. Should it be a function of local government to own retail centres, or factory units? Many councils—and not just Labour controlled councils—think that it is a necessary part of their activities. It may be right to use public money to bring such facilities into existence, but continued ownership does not seem a sensible use of the taxpayers' and the charge-payers' resources.

Local authorities own much that it is necessary for them to run, but too much that is unnecessary. Many local authorities do not even have a handy list in one place of all council houses, arts centres, leisure centres, shopping centres, workshops, and bits of land which they own. And even those authorities which do have lists often have no idea of the price their properties would fetch on the open market.

This Government goes in for private ownership, because assets in *private* hands are cared for and used efficiently, while assets in public hands have too often been allowed to decay and stagnate and become a burden on the community. Our direct holding of land and buildings is minimal and for essential purposes—mainly for Defence and departmental offices. The process of making state-owned businesses more efficient through privatisation has yielded tremendous receipts for the Exchequer. Selling the ownership of 16 major businesses since 1979 has reduced the state-owned sector by more than a third, and has brought in £16 billion. We expect to bring in almost as much again by the end of the financial year 1989/90. This means that our borrowing and national debt are, cumulatively, much lower than they would otherwise have been. This is essential for the productive management of the economy.

Over and above the national privatisation programme, there has been a massive transfer of local council assets to the private sector. Sales of over a million council houses to tenants, mostly under the right to buy, have brought in £5.5 billion. Sales of other local authority assets have raised £3 billion. The sale of New Town assets has raised £1.5 billion. In all, this is another £10 billion so far. All this has contributed to the better management of the economy. And the better care for these assets is visible in fresh paint and improvements on the face of formerly drab and uniform council estates. Efficiency has been served because of the greater pressure in the market place of the private sector to use assets efficiently. What was a burden is now producing real satisfaction and real wealth. The family silver gleams on the family table, it doesn't languish unpolished in the store cupboards of the public sector. And rates and taxes are lower than they would otherwise be.

If we are to have stable sustained growth in the economy there is a limited amount that the government can afford to set aside for public spending on housing. A great advantage of our policy of selling council houses and other assets is that the reduction of what was a burden on the community liberates a proportion of receipts for further spending on housing. Thus, for the financial year of 1988/89 the gross provision for such public spending is just over £3 billion of which £1.9 billion is accounted for by public receipts. The fact that a local authority may be able to spend only 20% of its capital receipts in one year does not prevent these capital receipts being a tremendous help in meeting the cost of our national housing problems.

These massive asset sales are necessary, since local authorities have tended to accumulate so many assets in the past. Imagine how things would have stood if they had not been sold. How many more local authority houses and flats would have been decaying? How many of the buildings now being put to good use, and how much of the land now being developed, would have remained under-used or altogether idle? How much greater would have been the burden on the people who pay through rates and taxes? Had they never accumulated these assets, local authorities would (within the constraints of the management of the national economy) have been freer to invest where investment was needed in the public services and infrastructure; freer to provide pump-printing finance where necessary and more open minded about securing services from effective competition and targeting subsidies on those who need help. Municipal ownership of property, like municipal management of a massive workforce, is a distraction from the proper job. Far too easily it becomes an end in itself. The drive to dispose of assets did not really begin until 1979. The message has been slow to get through. It is a priority for both central and local government to put all their assets to effective use, and that is often better done in the private sector. In doing so, we will reduce these vast debts, symbols of the burden that so much municipal property has proved to be.

There will clearly continue to be a substantial role for local authorities in the 90s and beyond. Those who speak as though we are seeing the end of local government are quite wrong. The functions and services which have been provided by local authorities will be as necessary as ever. But authorities will need to operate in a more pluralist way than in the past, alongside a wide variety of public, private and voluntary agencies. It will be their task to stimulate and assist these other agencies to play their part instead of, or as well as, making provision themselves. Comparison and competition between authorities will bring increasingly potent pressures towards value for money in all services. And greater accountability will mean that the public are increasingly able to insist on high standards.

The role of local authority members

Inside every fat and bloated local authority there is a slim one struggling to get out. It is the role of politicians both nationally and locally to assist in this struggle.

Government's role at the centre is that of the consultant prescribing remedies. For a few of the most overweight authorities our remedies have had to be somewhat severe and painful. We have had to put direct limits on excessive growth through rate limits and grant penalties.

But for the great majority of ordinary authorities a regular pattern of prudent control of expenditure and search for value for money is a much better discipline than external controls and regulations. A few authorities have already made major progress in this direction. But I am concerned at the tendency to middle aged spread in a large number of average authorities of all shades of political opinion. Inefficiency is not, I regret to say, confined to councils run by the Terrible Trots. That is why I want to re-invigorate them with the fresh air of competition and greater accountability.

A central political task for local councillors in the years ahead is to apply these ideas and principles to their authorities. Some unfortunately seem to think that the application of ideas to the practice of administration in this way has a limited role in local government. The use of competition and privatisation as a means to secure better and more cost effective services are seen by many people in local government as having little relevance to them. The idea which we have consistently and successfully pursued at a national level that where the private sector is better at providing goods and services than the Government then it should do so, has not penetrated deeply enough into local government circles. Similarly, there is still a marked preference for the public sector to provide capital assets even when it is perfectly possible for the private sector to provide them and run them profitably (if necessary, with pump-priming finance or specific subsidies from the local authorities). There is a notion that the more massive the ownership, and the more widespread the provision, the more imposing does the council become and the more central in the eyes of the public. The temptation to municipal aggrandisement is strong.

A radical politician trying to direct the actions of a conservative administration or indeed change the perceptions of his political colleagues (supported perhaps by the more go-ahead local authority officers) never has an easy task. There are always many reasons why changing the habits of decades is resisted. It requires determination and conviction—political conviction—to stand up to resistance to change and to push it through. The resistance faced from vested interests by the Conservative administration of Wandsworth Council to their policy of privatisation and competitive tendering required immense political courage to overcome. Anyone wanting to learn the lessons should read Paul Beresford's excellent CPS pamphlet *The Good Council Guide* (Policy Study no 84, April 1987). As a practical lesson in 'best practice', nothing I could say would improve on his account. In Wandsworth the politicians, backed up by able and loyal local government officers won, and the result has consistently shown up in good poll results for the Conservative administration (confirmed again in a recent by-election in November 1987); in an increase in 'front line' services at the lowest local rates in London; and in a considerably slimmed down but better motivated workforce whose initial scepticism was replaced by pride in working for a model administration.

Between 1978, when the Conservatives won control of the council, and 1985, staff numbers were reduced by a third. Every fringe activity was rigorously examined and the number of departments and directorates was reduced. Competition and privatisation were extensively introduced. The council was successful in achieving lower expenditure and a lower rates bill. But they were determined that the quality of core front line services should be maintained and enhanced.

There is no reason to suppose that savings comparable to those realised in Wandsworth could not be achieved by other councils. In 1978 Wandsworth had rate levels similar to those of other inner London boroughs, but its local rate is now one of the lowest in London and its standards of service stand comparison with any.

In political life, councillors are subject to pressures from a variety of different sources: from outside local interest groups demanding this or protesting against that: from the Councils' own workforce and its Unions—very powerful lobbies: from local members of the political party they represent and from their own political colleagues: from the media and of course from the general public. Councillors are elected to serve the general public, but what the general public 'wants' is difficult to judge from a pile of ballot papers, particularly when in local elections only a minority of electors bother to vote; and they tend to vote on national rather than local issues. It can be difficult for the politician on the basis of the representations he gets from the public to assess what is in the public interest. A councillor's ward casework consists largely of people with particular problems: council tenants who want to transfer, or Mrs. Smith angry about her neighbour's proposed extention. At a 'group' level there are lobbies arguing for more resources. In these circumstances it is too easy to respond to problems according to the pressures of who shouts loudest at the time. The council workforce is itself one of the most clamorous interest groups. Fear of conflict and disruption and of being unloved is, I suspect, one of the major reasons why so few councils have put services out to tender.

Most councils still subscribe to the principle of central wage negotiations, which continue to award wage increases above inflation without commensurate productivity strings. Though the difficulties of opting out of such national machinery are very great, very few want to do so. For many local government services, our competitive tendering legislation will exert a pressure on local authorities and unions to take more account of local market conditions when setting wage rates and working practices. Indeed one hopes that many council workers will form companies to compete for contracted out work, and in due course take their companies into the private sector.

What the general public wants of local government is that it should provide good services as efficiently as possible. It is above all the duty of councillors to ensure they achieve it by the application of these principles:

- that while the public sector should set and enforce standards and determine the level of provision, competition is the best way of securing value for money.
- that we should always question whether it is right for the public sector to do a job when private individuals or companies could and would compete to do the job themselves.
- that we are seeking wherever possible to encourage personal responsibility rather than promote the State as universal problem-solver and safety net.
- that the delegation of as much as possible to the private sector enables the local authority to direct resources better to where they

are most needed and provide for them more effectively. It also helps to promote local firms and jobs and entrepreneurs.

We need members and officials who are not wedded to the power base of a large department; who do not believe that success is measured by the number of staff they employ and the amount of money they spend; who are not the prisoners of any pressure group; who are not overinfluenced by the unions or other producer groups. Their task is first and foremost to serve the public, the consumer. If the public can best be served in some area by private sector provision, then the task for the authority is to work out how this can be achieved and to assist and encourage the private sector. If a variety of providers is desirable then the council needs to work out how to encourage diversity and fruitful competition. If regulation is needed then the task is to find how to do this fairly, efficiently and swiftly without stifling initiative and enterprise. We need people who are prepared to test the advice they get against these principles.

The Conservative response to change

I know I have not delivered the CPS request to provide an analysis of the history and present aims of the Conservative Party in local government.* But one thing became clear fairly quickly as I embarked upon the task. An analysis of Labour in local government cannot be paralleled by a paper on Conservatives in local government. Thankfully indeed, one cannot point to ideological 'trends' and 'groupings' in the ranks of Conservative councillors in the same way as one can in the Labour Party, throughout which there permeates the doctrine of 'municipal Socialism'; which has done so much harm to local interests.

Conservatives have always been more pragmatic and locally based in their approach.In the 19th century one could find Tory council groups in cities not so far apart believing quite contradictory things. At the turn of the century, for example, when the debates about municipal spending were essentially between 'improvers' and 'econ-omisers'—those who wished to finance new facilities and those who wished to retrench, the Conservatives were 'economisers' in Man-

*The Local Left; and its national pretensions. David Regan, Centre for Policy Studies, November, 1987.

chester, but 'improvers' in Liverpool. Indeed the improving proclivities of Liverpool Conservatives led them to endorse municipal provision of tramways, electricity and even a zoo in the early years of the 20th century. In my experience there are still enormous variations in the way different Conservative councillors perceive their role. So it is difficult to define coherent political 'trends.'

Conservatives go into local government often for reasons which have little to do with theoretical politics. They might for example have been affected by a council decision and been drawn into politics by the thought that they could do the job better. They might have come in through their involvement in the Party at a local level, an involvement which often has a strong social element. There has been a strong tradition of 'Independent' councillors. Many of these have now become Conservative but still tend to eschew links with the central party organisation and are generally suspicious of party politics as applied to local government.

This is healthy in many ways, but there are dangers in too little politics just as there are dangers in too much. What I have described in this pamphlet is a more sharply defined idea of what it is that local politicians are there to do. It is a Conservative idea but it is also a practical view of the best way to provide good local services which should apply to all local authorities, whatever their political persuasion. It should particularly appeal to Conservative councillors.

The problem is that in the widespread dislike among Conservative councillors of 'politicisation', what is political and desirable sometimes gets confused with what is political and undesirable. We all agree in deploring the 'gesture politics' and dubious political tactics associated with the Labour Left: the extravagant spending on blatantly political aims: the use of local government as a platform to conduct political warfare against central government rather than as the means to provide efficient local services: the autocratic domination of the political caucus overriding individual judgement. But too often the dislike of the 'political' extends to a rejection of policies put forward by a Conservative government which would greatly assist councillors in providing better service to the public: policies like competitive tendering or privatisation. Going on from that, while Conservatives applaud the tremendous achievements of this Government in getting inflation down and setting the economy right, they do not always see how the controls which we have on local government spending, borrowing and use of capital receipts are an essential and integral part of the strategy that made these achievements possible; nor quite see how they can achieve similar success through employing similar policies.

John Gyford in his book *Local Politics in Britain* defined three levels of the councillor's idea of his role.

> 'At one level the councillor might insist that the policy making is the politicians' prerogative and might devote much time along with his political colleagues to devising policies in line with their shared political objectives. Or the councillor may be happy to leave policy initiatives largely to officers concentrating his attention on examining the proposals they bring forward to ensure that they are politically acceptable. Or yet again they may accept quite uncritically whatever policies are put forward by the officers deriving satisfaction not from the content of policy so much as from 'being in the know', 'pushing things through' and 'getting things done'.

In my view, the first definition is a definition of the proper role of a politician—any politician—and we wish to encourage that in local government. So to that extent, I would like to see my colleagues in local government become more politicised. This Government is a radical government with a radical message. It is not prepared to rubber-stamp time-honoured policies and practices which have been responsible for our decline. As it is radical, it hopes to see Conservatives at all levels of administration and government adopting a similarly questioning and innovative approach.

To be effective as a politician as opposed to a manager or administrator, one cannot work in a political vacuum. The essence of politics is the communication and development of ideas between people. Conservatives have a strong localist tradition, but the danger of too much localism is that the Party's voice and through the Party the political interpretation of the Government's voice is not heard. The persuasive arguments in favour of competitive tendering for example may never be given an airing and can be stifled by well briefed vested interests on the other side. At a time when the legislative framework within which local government operates is changing so fundamentally, it is essential that the Party at all levels discusses the implications and how it can best take advantage of the changes. Remember, communication is not all one way either. Many of the most successful government policies which affect local authorities began from initiatives taken by local government which have been promoted in national legislation by central government: council house sales and competitive tendering to mention two.

When the new system of local government finance comes into effect, it will be of paramount importance that Conservatives are well prepared to meet the challenge of the far reaching transformation in the relationship between councillors and voters and the atmosphere of local politics that it will bring.

How do I think the atmosphere will change? In two major ways.

First, if a crude distinction is made between voters who want to see local authorities increase the scope of their services and spending and those who want to keep both to a necessary minimum, the balance will shift markedly to the latter end of the scale because everyone will pay something towards the cost of services and we will no longer have the phenomenon of the voter who pays nothing towards services but benefits from them.

Second, I believe that a clearer system of this sort which enables simple comparisons to be made between the different performances of local authorities will lead to greater interest by voters in what their local authority actually does and how it performs. There will be a move away from national issues as a determinant of people's votes in elections, towards local issues. It will mean that the actions of local politicians will, like those of national politicians, come under close public scrutiny.

These developments will be reinforced by the reforms we are making in the provision of local authority services which I have described, which will make local authorities more responsive to the wishes of the clients of those services.

The result will be to turn the spotlight strongly on local authority activities. We may see more interest in the manifestos of local political parties and greater scope for diverse political groupings, with Independents and charge-payers' representatives coming back as alternatives to the main political parties. Conservative councillors with their belief in prudent and responsible management of local authorities are well placed to take advantage of these changes. But there will be no room for complacency or drift. Conservatives represent a lower spending alternative to Labour, but they may not always represent the most efficient and frugal possible administration in the eyes of local voters. They will have to be careful to ensure they do. Spending decisions will be much more controversial and closely scrutinised than they are now. The level of the Community Charge and the costs of services provided by different councils will be compared and questioned. People will expect more information and involvement in local council issues.

In changing the ways in which things have been done for decades, we are predictably accused of attacking local government. I emphatically reject that charge. Certainly local government's powers in certain respects will be limited, but they will be limited in practice not by the Government but by local people. The style of local government will have to become much more 'interactive'. There are few of any party in national or indeed local government who admit to being happy with the way in which many monopoly council services are provided now. The lack of choice in housing and education, accompanied by what appears to ordinary people to be a remote and insensitive attitude form a consistent feature of political rhetoric, whatever the Party. By giving rights to those who complain about these things, we bring about more democratic participation in local affairs. This should be welcome to Conservatives whose belief in local government is founded on a belief in pluralism and participative democracy.

When people vote in local elections they tend to vote on national issues. This is regrettable—but it is so. They tend to vote according to their perceptions of the aims of a party as expressed and implemented by national politicians. If the local council they vote for, though it may call itself 'Conservative' or 'Labour' does not seem to conform to the national model, people may feel that they are not actually getting what they voted for. Adopting a party label is something which should ideally aid democratic choice. The fact that the Conservative controlled authorities who try hardest to support the aims of the Conservative Government are the ones who do better than average in local elections is no accident. And I believe that a closer attention to the actual performance of the local politician and an assessment of how he matches up to the image which the voter has of the party he represents will be a major feature of the new Community Charge era.

Finally the role I have described for a local politician is not merely one which should promote better local government, it is also one which should make the role of local councillor—partiulcarly a Conservative councillor—more rewarding and fulfilling than it is now. His role will shift from the role of manager to the role of enabler and decider of local priorities, always conscious of what his decisions will cost his charge-payers. As the monopoly position of local authorities in many areas is challenged, so councillors will less and less be in a position where they can be manipulated by the power of monopoly unions. It will be both in their interests and in the interests of the workforce to put high standards and good service to the public above everything else. In that sense the politician's role will be much more political.

Many local Conservative politicians are or have been managers of one sort or another in their own careers. They do not on the whole go into local politics because they want more of the same. They do so because they are aware of something beyond management which is quintessentially 'political'—enabling the local community to have those services which the free market would not provide, which must be provided communally.

We hear constantly of good people leaving local government because of the time being demanded to discuss matters both of a national nature—like South Africa and nuclear policy—and detailed matters of a managerial nature. If the role for councillors described in this pamphlet were substituted for the current role, the job of being a local councillor would, I believe, be more attractive to the leaders of local communities, not less so. It would take less of busy people's time.

It would make for healthier local government too. The growing tendency by certain left wing councils to intervene in day to day management has resulted in a growing volume of complaints by local government officers of political interference in administration. They do this because left wingers see management itself as a tool to be manipulated in favour of particular client groups whose support they hope to buy. This is a very time consuming, and even corrupt, use of political power. It gets away from the idea of politics as serving the public interest to pork-barrel politics—political patronage. The more that is managed outside the council, subject to regulation as well as the pressure of competition, the less this sort of abuse can take place.

There needs to be open debate both in the country and within political parties about the role of local politicians in local government, in the light of various reforms which are now taking place. I hope this pamphlet will start the ball rolling in the Conservative Party, and perhaps beyond.

3

Victorian Values and Twentieth-Century Condescension

Gertrude Himmelfarb

'Manners and morals'—the expression is peculiarly, unmistakably Victorian. Not 'manners' alone: Lord Chesterfield in the eighteenth century was fond of discoursing to his son on the supreme importance of manners, manners as distinct from (if necessary in opposition to) morals. And not 'morals' alone: philosophers had always taken this as their special province, had, indeed, made it so elevated a subject that it had little to do with anything so mundane as manners.

It was the Victorians who combined these words so that they came trippingly off the tongue, as if they were one word. Manners were sanctified and moralised, so to speak, while morals were secularised and domesticated. When Thackeray earlier in the century, or Trollope later, protested that manners were taking precedence over morals, that 'the way we live now' (in the memorable title of one of Trollope's last novels) encouraged the cultivation of manners at the expense of morals, it was because they themselves attached so much importance not only to morals but to the continuum of manners and morals.

Margaret Thatcher has been reported as saying that she would be pleased to restore all Victorian values, with the exception of hypocrisy. If she did say that, she betrayed a serious misunderstanding of Victorian values. Hypocrisy, in the well-known phrase of La Rochefoucauld, is 'the homage that vice pays to virtue'. It is also the homage that manners pay to morals. The Victorians thought it no small virtue to maintain the appearance, the manner, of good conduct even while violating some basic precept of morality.

This was, in fact, what the eminent Victorians did when they felt obliged to commit some transgression. They did not flout conventional morality; on the contrary, they tried to observe at least the manner of it. George Eliot, living with a man whom she could not marry because he could not legally be divorced from his wife, reproduced in their relationship all the forms of propriety. They lived together in a perfectly domestic, monogamous arrangement, quite as if they had been married. Indeed, she called herself, and insisted that others call her, 'Mrs Lewes', and had the great satisfaction of hearing the real Mrs Lewes involuntarily call her that. And when Mr Lewes died, after twenty-four years of this pseudo-marriage (one can hardly call it an affair), she almost immediately took the occasion to enter a real, a legal marriage with John Cross—with all the appurtenances thereof: a proper trousseau, a formal wedding in church, a honeymoon. All of which shocked her friends more than her earlier pseudomarriage because this seemed to them a true misalliance; her new husband was twenty years her junior and much her intellectual inferior.

And so too with other notorious 'irregularities', as the Victorians delicately put it: extra-marital relationships (like that of John Stuart Mill and Harriet Taylor), or marital relationships which were unconsummated (the Carlyles and the Ruskins), or homosexual relationships (such as were presumed to exist in the Oxford Movement). Those caught up in an irregular situation of this kind tried, as far as they possibly could, to 'regularise' it, to contain it within its conventional form, to domesticate it and normalise it. And when they could not do so (or even when they did), they agonized over it in diaries and letters—which they carefully preserved, and which is why we now know so much about these scandals. Like the 'fastidious assassin' in Camus' *The Rebel*, who deliberately gave up his own life when he took the tyrant's life, so the Victorians insisted upon paying for their indiscretions. They tormented themselves, one has the impression, more than they enjoyed themselves.

So, at least, it was until the end of the century, when the moral certitudes began to falter. 'For the Englishman,' Nietzsche wrote in 1889, 'morality is not yet a problem'. Not yet a problem, he thought, because the English still had the illusion that they could sustain morality in the absence of a religion; they did not realise how firmly rooted in Christianity their morality was. When Christianity lost its ascendency, as Nietzche thought it inevitably would, the English would discover how tenuous, how problematic, their morality was.

Nietzche's words were prophetic—not, to be sure, for the English as a whole. But then Nietzche was not talking about the English as a whole—the masses, or 'slave class', as he called them, who mindlessly observed the manners and morals imposed upon them by the 'priestly class'. He was talking about the priestly class itself, the intellectual aristocracy, many of whom were atheists and some of whom came to think of themselves as 'free souls', liberated from both religion and morality.

Nietzche had no sooner made that pronouncement than public confirmation of it began to appear in the *fin-de-siecle* movement celebrated by such 'esthetes' and 'decadents', as they proudly described themselves, as Oscar Wilde and Aubrey Beardsley. It is interesting that from the beginning the movement was known under that French label, as if to suggest how alien it was to England—rather like the 'French flu' or the 'French pox'. A character in a novel of the period remarks, in an execrable accent, 'It's *fang-de-seeacle* that does it, my dear, and education, and reading French'.

The movement was well-named; it did not survive the *siecle*. *The Yellow Book* expired in 1897, Beardsley died the following year, and Wilde died in exile (appropriately in France) in 1900. In his last, and perhaps best, play, *The Importance of Being Earnest*, Wilde delivered himself of one of those witticisms that was possibly truer than the author himself knew. 'I hope,' a young woman says, 'you have not been leading a double life, pretending to be wicked and really being good all the time. That would be hypocrisy.'

It was a nice accident of history that saw Queen Victoria die in January 1901, so that the end of the reign coincided with the start of the new century. The end of the reign and, for an influential group of intellectuals—the new priestly class—the end of Victorianism. The High Priests of Bloomsbury were not hypocritical in pretending to be more wicked than they were; their only hypocrisy, recent scholarship has shown, was in concealing from the public the wickedness they flaunted in private. After the death of Leslie Stephen (the Victorian paterfamilias of Bloomsbury), his children moved from respectable Kensington to what was to become the new Bohemia, Bloomsbury. 'Everything was going to be new' his daughter pronounced. 'Everything was going to be different. Everything was on trial.' Later, Virginia Stephen (Virginia Woolf, as we now know her) assigned a different date to that new era. 'In or about December 1910' she pronounced with remarkable assurance, 'human character changed'. December 1910 was the date of the Post-Impressionist exhibit (organised by another member of the clan, Roger Fry) that so dramatically altered the artistic sensibilities of her generation. It was also, as Virginia Woolf saw it, the time when a new ethic was beginning to emerge to complement the new aesthetic. Just as art now appeared to be autonomous, dependent on no external reality but only on the vision and imagination of the artist, so the character of the artist (or of the writer, or of any other person with superior sensibility) was seen as autonomous, self-contained, not subject to the judgement of others nor bound by any sense of 'obligation to others'. The conventional idea, Virginia Woolf declared, of 'living for others, not for ourselves', was intended for 'timid natures who dare not allow their souls free play'. Bloomsbury was made of sterner stuff. Later, one of its founding fathers described its basic tenet. 'We repudiated entirely', Maynard Keynes wrote, 'customary morals, conventions and traditional wisdom. We were, that is to say, in the strict sense of the term, immoralists.'

'Everything was on trial', Virginia Woolf had said. What was mainly on trial was Victorian morals and manners. Another member of Bloomsbury, its most flamboyant one, had the audacious idea of putting on trial some of the most eminent Victorians—and by implication Victorianism as such. *Eminent Victorians* was published in 1918. A half century earlier that title could have been used and understood in all sincerity. When Lytton Strachey used it, no one could mistake its ironic intent.

Strachey made no secret of his purpose or his method. Ordinary history, he explained in his preface 'proceeded by the direct method of scrupulous narration'. The historian of the Victorian age had to adopt a 'subtler strategy'.

> He will attack his subject in unexpected places; he will fall upon the flank, or the rear; he will shoot a sudden, revealing searchlight into obscure recesses, hitherto undivined. He will row out over that great ocean of material, and lower down into it, here and there, a little bucket, which will bring up into the light of day some characteristic specimen, from those far depths, to be examined with a careful curiosity.

Strachey concluded his preface with the familiar adage 'Je n'impose rien; je ne propose rien; j'expose'.

The eminent Victorians Strachey chose to expose were eminent in different fields. Cardinal Manning was an eminent ecclesiastic; Florence Nightingale an eminent social reformer; Dr Arnold an eminent educator; General Gordon an eminent soldier and patriot. They were all eminences and, more to the point, heroes. Strachey's intention was to belittle and disparage them—demystify them, we say to-day; de-heroise, would be more accurate. In each case what passed as heroism Strachey interpreted as megalomania, a ruthless drive for self-aggrandizement. It is interesting that in seeking out the defects which would belie their heroism—in dipping his bucket into the depths of that murky sea—Strachey never came up with the two 'dirty secrets' that a muck-rating biographer would look for to-day: money and sex. Drunkenness, yes, and vanity, and wilfulness, and irrationality, and physical flaws. But not financial gain and not sexual misconduct. If there was anything sexually scandalous about them, Strachey intimated, it was either their celibacy, as in the case of Manning and Nightingale, or their conspicuous normality, as in the case of Dr Arnold, who fulfilled his marital duties all too faithfully, as the existence of his ten children testified. (It is not surprising that there is no mention of Gordon's reputed homosexuality; that might have required Strachey to have presented him in a more favourable light.)

Apart from their megalomania, the one flaw they had in common was their weakness for religion. They were all religious to a fault. Cardinal Manning might be forgiven for this; it was, after all, his job to be religious, although he went beyond the call of duty by believing what he preached. The others not only professed to believe when they had no obligation to do so; they actually did believe. Strachey's wicked comment about Florence Nightingale is often quoted: 'She felt towards Him [God] as she might have felt towards a glorified sanitary engineer: . . . she seems hardly to distinguish between the Deity and the Drains'. But Strachey was even more distressed by her truly religious feelings, her 'mysterious moods of mysticism', her 'morbid longings' to find peace in God. So too he was contemptuous of Dr Arnold not only because of his vulgar conception of education (the public school as a nursery for English gentlemen) but also because of his habit of communing with the 'invisible world' and his resolve to do battle with the 'wicked one'. Some of Strachey's readers protested that he had maligned General Gordon in the famous scene where the General is found seated at a table 'upon which were an open Bible and an open bottle of brandy'; it was the open bottle of brandy that offended them. But Strachey himself made far more of

the open Bible; the first paragraph of that essay has Gordon wander-
ing in Jerusalem with a Bible under his arm, and the last paragraph
has him 'in some remote Nirvana' fluttering the pages of a 'phantas-
mal Bible'.

To 'expose', as Strachey saw it, the religious proclivities of these
eminent Victorians was to expose, and undermine, the very foundations of their morality. It was also to expose them as frauds—not in
the sense that they were hypocritical about their religion; the trouble
was not that they were hypocritical but that they were true believers.
What was fraudulent, Strachey suggested, was their claim (or the
claim made on their behalf) that they were heroes. Heroes could not
be religious any more than heroines like Florence Nightingale could
be seen—as Strachey depicted her—putting a dog's wounded paw in
a splint.

There were, in fact, no heroes in Strachey's scheme of things,
because the heroic virtues were as suspect as all the other virtues.
And not only heroic virtues but also heroic attitudes—the manners
and morals, as it were, of heroism. For Strachey, religion, public
service, civic education, patriotism were absurd in themselves. But
they were even more absurd in the manner of their pursuit—in the
passionate, extravagant way heroes were wont to pursue them. And
they were more absurd still in the manner of their reception, the
respect accorded them by a credulous and deferential public.

Early in the Queen's reign, another eminent Victorian (not satirized
by Strachey, but he could well have been) wrote the classic defence
of heroism. 'Society' Carlyle wrote, 'is founded on hero-worship . . .
[the] reverence and obedience due to men really great and wise'. Like
Nietzsche anticipating the time when morality would have become 'a
problem' in England, so Carlyle anticipated the time when the heroic
virtues would become problematic. Indeed, he thought that time had
already come. 'Show our critics,' he wrote in 1840, 'a great man, a
Luther for example, they begin to what they call "account" for him;
not to worship him, but to take the dimensions of him—and bring
him out to be a little kind of man!' It is not clear which critics Carlyle
had in mind—perhaps Mill or Bentham, those pettifogging, 'dry-as-
dust' rationalists. But it could easily have been Strachey he was
describing when he wrote:—

> We will always take the liberty to deny altogether that [mot] of the witty
> Frenchman, that no man is a Hero to his valet-de-chambre. Or, if so, it

is not the Hero's blame but the Valet's: that his soul, namely, is a mean *valet*-soul! . . . The Valet does not know a Hero when he sees him! Alas, no, it requires a kind of *Hero* to do that.

This is not to say that Carlyle saw no flaws in his heroes; on the contrary, he expected a hero's flaws, his vices, to be as large, as heroic, as his virtues. When the biographer of Sir Walter Scott was criticised for being indiscreet, for recounting episodes that made Scott appear (so the critics said) unheroic, Carlyle came to the biographer's defence. And he took the occasion to mock the conventional biography. 'How delicate, decent, is the English biography, bless its mealy mouth'.

In deriding the mealy-mouthed biography, Carlyle did not mean to condone the Strachey type of biography which poor-mouths or bad-mouths its subjects, reducing the hero to a 'little kind of man'. Still less would he have condoned the present fashionable genre of history that disdains any type of heroism or eminence, that reads history 'from below', as it is said, celebrating not individual heroes, not great men (or even great women) but rather *le petit peuple*, the 'common men', the 'anonymous masses'.

One of the paradoxes of the new mode of history is that it professes to celebrate the common man while demeaning the virtues usually associated with the common man. If Strachey's *Eminent Victorians* is in disfavour to-day, it is not so much because it is unscholarly history as because it is 'elitist' history. It disparages the manners and morals of eminent Victorians but says nothing about the manners and morals of ordinary Victorians. It is, a Marxist would say, insufficiently 'critical'; it demystifies the heroic virtues and not the bourgeois ones. Like Marx exhorting the philosophers to turn their attention from the 'holy forms' of alienation to the 'unholy forms'—from the illusory world of religion to the real world of exploitation—so the new historian is more interested in exposing the unholy, bourgeois virtues than the more exalted holy, heroic ones.

It is these bourgeois or middle-class virtues that Margaret Thatcher seems set upon restoring; or rather bourgeois 'values', since 'virtues' is too moralistic, indeed too Victorian a word for our enlightened age. These values—thrift, prudence, diligence, temperance, self-reliance—were indeed bourgeois ones. But they were also classical ones; they were hardly unfamiliar to the Greeks. And they were also religious ones; it was, after all, from the Jews and Christians that the Puritans derived them.

They were working-class values, too: ones aspired to (not always successfully, but then all of us fall short of our aspirations) by the 'respectable' Victorian labouring classes.

'Respectable'—there's another Victorian word which makes us uncomfortable, which we can scarcely utter without audible quotation marks. An influential school of historians interprets the idea of respectability, and all the virtues connected with it, as instruments of 'social control'—the means by which the middle class, the ruling class, sought to dominate the working class: a subtle and covert way of conducting the class struggle.

Some early applications of the social-control thesis were plausible. The invention of the modern clock, it has been said, made possible habits such as promptness, regularity, conformity and rationality which were useful for the so-called work-discipline or time-discipline of an industrial, capitalist economy. Even here, however, the thesis has sometimes been stretched to the point where it seems as if the clock had been invented for that very purpose (this a couple of centuries before the emergence of industrialism and capitalism!); as if the rural economy knew no form of work-discipline; and as if nature did not have its own rhythms which can be no less compelling and oppressive.

But there is a more serious flaw at the heart of this social-control thesis. This is the assumption that the Puritan ethic—the values invoked by Margaret Thatcher—was little more than a work-ethic designed to 'moralise' the new industrial proletariat and imbue the workers with middle-class values which would make them more productive members of society. Such alien values, so this argument runs, were imposed upon the workers by a middle class which enjoyed a cultural as well as an economic and political 'hegemony' and were accepted by a working class led astray by 'false consciousness', unable to recognise its own true, indigenous values and interests.

It is not clear what these indigenous values are supposed to have been—communal, presumably, rather than individualistic, and co-operative rather than competitive. One historian has said that it is only through the 'distorting lens of middle-class aspirations to gentility' that the idea of self-help, for example, can be understood. But does this mean that this idea, the value of self-reliance and independence, was alien to Victorian workers, in which case are we to understand that dependency was congenial to them? And what of the other alien, middle-class values supposedly imposed on them? Is it to be assumed that workers were naturally indolent rather than industrious, or profligate rather than frugal, or drunk rather than sober? And if these middle-class values reflected the interests of capitalist society, does it mean that a socialist society would embrace a proletarian set of values—indolence, perhaps, or profligacy, or intemperance?

It must be remembered that the social-control thesis is advanced not by reactionary historians but by radical ones who are avowedly sympathetic to the working class, who, as one put it in an often quoted passage, want to rescue the poor and oppressed from the 'enormous condescension of posterity'. One wonders, however, which is more condescending: to attribute to the Victorian working class a radically different set of values from those professed by the rest of society, or to assume that most workers essentially shared these so-called middle class values, and that if they sometimes failed to abide by them it was because of the difficult circumstances of life or the natural weaknesses of the human condition. Is it more condescending to describe these workers as the victims of 'false consciousness' or to credit them with a true consciousness of their values and interests? False consciousness is a crucial part of the social-control thesis, because the radical historian has to account for the inconvenient fact that a great many workers seemed to view their own lives through that 'distorting lens' of middle-class values. And it was not only the so-called labour aristocracy (as it is sometimes claimed) that suffered from this myopia; lesser skilled and unskilled workers did so as well, perhaps because they had most to lose if they lost their respectability.

These values, moreover, were shared—and consciously so—by the most radical workers. The memoirs of the Chartists provide poignant testimony to their efforts to remain hard-working, sober, frugal, clean, in short, respectable, in spite of all the temptations to the contrary. There were groups among the Chartists who made this their main concern—the Temperance Chartists and Education Chartists, as they were called. Indeed the central tenet of Chartism, universal suffrage, was based on just this claim to respectability. The argument for political equality depended on the argument for natural equality, a common human nature—common values, aspirations and capacities.

As for those middle class reformers, educators—political economists and politicians who encouraged these values among the working classes—how condescending were they? Was it condescending on their part to credit the poor with the values that they prized so highly for themselves—and not only the values but the ability and will to fulfill these values? Were they patronising the poor when they applied to them a single standard of values rather than the double standard that had prevailed so long—a double standard, incidentally, implicit in the social-control thesis? So far from keeping the working classes in a condition of inferiority and subservience, that single standard was an invitation to economic betterment, social advance and, ultimately, political equality. It was also an attempt to bridge the 'two nations' barrier dramatised by Disraeli. A single standard of values was conducive to a single culture, a single society—and a single nation.

To the degree to which Victorians succeeded in 'bourgeoisifying' the ethos, they also democratised it. That ethos was not, to be sure, an exalted or heroic one. Hard work, sobriety, frugality, foresight—these were modest, mundane virtues, even lowly ones. But they were virtues within the capacity of everyone; they did not assume any special breeding, or status, or talent, or valour, or grace—or even money. They were common virtues within the reach of common people. They were, so to speak, democratic virtues.

They were also liberal virtues. By putting a premium on ordinary virtues attainable by ordinary people, the ethos located responsibility within each individual. It was no longer only the exceptional, the heroic individual who was the master of his fate; every individual could be his own master. So far from promoting social control, the ethos had the effect of promoting self-control. This was at the heart of Victorian morality: self-control, self-help, self-reliance, self-discipline. A liberal society, the Victorians believed, depended upon a moral citizenry. The stronger the voluntary exercise of morality on the part of each individual—the more internalised that morality—the weaker need be the external, coercive instruments of the state. For the Victorians, morality served as a substitute for law, just as law was a substitute for force.

And so, in a sense, manners were a substitute for morals. Or perhaps not quite a substitute; that puts it too strongly. The Victorians were no Utopians. They were acutely aware of the frailties of human nature, and thus of the need for whatever inducements or sanctions—social, religious, legal, ultimately physical—might be required to encourage virtue and discourage vice. A better image is that of the continuum. Manners were placed in a continuum with morals, as morals were with laws, and laws, as a last resort, with force. It was that great realist, and moralist, Machiavelli, who said, 'For as laws are necessary that good manners may be preserved, so there is need of good manners that laws may be maintained.' And it was another great realist and moralist, the mentor of so many eminent Victorians, Edmund Burke, who wrote:

> Manners are of more importance than laws. Upon them, in a great measure, the laws depend. The law touches us but here and there, and now and then. Manners are what vex or soothe, corrupt or purify, exalt or debase, barbarise or refine us, by a constant, steady, uniform, insensible operation, like that of the air we breathe in. They give their whole form and colour to our lives. According to their quality, they aid morals, they supply them, or they totally destroy them.

4

Natural Partners: Co-operation and Competition

Michael Ivens

Natural partners of enterprise

It is an irony that many critics of 'Thatcherism' who allege that it has lost its connection with its ancient conservative roots, are precisely those who were complacent at Britain's steady movement into corporatism.

One's Marxism's more helpful metaphors is that of quantity becoming quality (the atoms rearrange themselves and water becomes ice or steam); and Britain's steady advance towards corporatism and unionocracy produced qualitative changes in our society. The only solution was a reforming government. Fortunately we got one.

This has produced a second irony; that of conservatism as a radical, reforming movement. How else was the State society to be dismantled and privatised, half time Britain to be made full time, schools to become educational and de-politicised, local government to lose its corruption, industry to stand on its feet and powerful trade unions to cease as political mafias?

A visual-media society cannot digest too many concepts and one essential word that has done duty for many of the essential reforms is 'competition'.

Politicians, the media and the public have taken 'competition' to heart as explaining the basis of 'Thatcherism'. Politics, however, is many-sided and the projection of one truth is often achieved at the expense of another.

The identification of conservatism mainly with competition has serious drawbacks. The deep attraction of conservatism is related to a strong sense of the desirable continuity and organic nature of society. This is summed up not only by politicians like Burke but also by greater writers such as Shakespeare and Goethe. For the ordinary man or woman, it arises from a sense (even if vague and intuitive) of the essential nature of man. And man's nature is by no means essentially competitive.

I am not rejecting the essential need for competition to be understood as a basic ingredient of success for Britain in the 1980's. As an Aims of Industry man since the 1960s, I am hardly likely to do that. In a hard, competitive world we will sink unless we have it. And our governments since 1979 deserve praise for having brought this to the front of national consciousness. It has been a psychological accompaniment to astonishing successes. We have been some way along the road to a valuable and bloodless revolution.

In stressing the importance of competition, however, we have oversimplified the nature of the achiever. The motives of artists, entrepreneurs, and managers, are often creative rather than competitive. The poet's poem, the entrepreneur's enterprise, the manager's solution, are seen as worthwhile in themselves—not necessarily in relation to the achievement of a rival. That generalisation also applies to the factory operative or the shop assistant; sometimes the motive may be to earn more on piece-rates or commission than other operatives or assistants, but often it is the achievement of the job itself that is valued. The creative drive is generally there. Directors and managers are privileged in being able to practise it to the full. That is why it is necessary to build as much creativity and decision making into the jobs of those at the bottom of the organisational pyramid.

But modern conservatism needs to do more than broaden its concept of competition and of the nature of the achieving drives in men and women. It should also be aware that the identification of conservatives as the party of competition leaves out something of which the public are dimly aware and for which they should be looking to the Conservative party for clarification.

The lives of most men and women are not based on competition. Nor does society function solely on its values. Whether we live in a modern industrialised society or a primitive one, we live through a fantastically complex arrangement of co-operation. That applies whether we work in a vast industrial firm or a small shop, live in a family, and go about our business on the ground, on rail, by sea or in the air. The signals flash, the buttons are pressed, and we survive because of the co-operation of others.

That may sound like a truism—but it does reflect a truth not only about man but also about nature. I believe that conservatism suffers great damage if it is identified with an illiterate pseudo-Darwinism of competitive nature, red in tooth and claw. Conservatism stands for realism (and that includes an understanding of the irrational and super-rational nature and needs of man). It doesn't stand for hardheartedness or romantic brutalism.

Nor does it accept the heresy of subsuming man under the economic framework. That is the Marxist heresy. And naive economic libertarianism is the other side of the coin to Marxism.

It does behove conservatives to be semantically accurate when talking about the 'virtues' of competition and co-operation. These activities are morally neutral: good when used for good purposes and harmful when used, for example, for competitive and co-operative cocaine smuggling. A responsive market economy demands a co-operative society with effective rules on fair competition and the protection of the consumer. And the motives of the successful entrepreneur or manager are more likely than not to be an amalgam of self-achievement, morality and competition.

This is not, however, to argue that conservatives should leave the moral ground to socialists (as some sophisticated people have advocated, on the cynical grounds that the public will vote for efficiency). Such a view of human values, even of voting intentions, is very shallow.

No: the serious task for conservatives is to dispel the illusion that success for one person is always at the expense of another person. This pessimistic puritanism—or sad socialism—is still current; and is accentuated by the radical chic philosophy which adopts this chip-on-the-shoulder pessimism and applies it to a variety of human situations: eg. male happiness is only at the expense of female dolour. Or that success and profit is the child of 'greed'.

The origin of co-operation

One missing ingredient can be found in the major work of that brave and attractive anarchist, Prince Petr Kropotkin's *Mutual Aid*.[1]

Kropotkin was born in Moscow in 1842, and did original work in geography, geology and zoology in Siberia. His work as a zoologist started under the influence of Darwin's *Origin of the Species.*

Kropotkin looked for that bitter struggle for the means of existence among animals belonging to the same species which was considered by most Darwinists (though not always by Darwin himself) as the dominant characteristic of struggle for life, and the main factor of evolution.

What Kropotkin saw with his own eyes gave him a different view which he made public in opposition to T H Huxley's famous manifesto, *The Struggle for Existence: A Programme,* which was published in *The Nineteenth Century.*

Kropotkin countered with *Mutual Aid* in which he drew attention not only to co-operation between animals of different species—but to the abiding role of mutual aid in man: among primitive people, in the medieval city and in the modern world.

Huxley, whose manifesto appealed to a fashionable, romantically brutalist laissez-faire philosophy, never replied to Kropotkin's articles, which later appeared as a book. As Ashley Montagu put it:

> Kropotkin found that the interpretation of 'the struggle for life' in the sense of a war cry of 'Woe to the Weak' raised to the height of a commandment of nature revealed by science, was so deeply rooted in England that it had become almost a matter of religion.[2]

An awareness of mutual aid as a prime factor in life was not the only thing Kropotkin learned from his observations in Siberia. He realised:

> the absolute impossibility of doing anything useful for the mass of people by means of the administrative machinery. With this illusion I parted forever—I lost in Siberia whatever faith in State discipline I had cherished before. I became an anarchist.

Kropotkin stayed an anarchist for the rest of his life—though he abhorred violence and supported the cause of the Allies in 1914–1918 in what he regarded as a defensive war against Germany. Arrested a number of times, he rejected a government post from Kerensky and it can only have been his great reputation which prevented his liquidation by the Bolsheviks (especially when one considers the boldness and courage of his letter to Lenin reprimanding him for the taking of hostages).

If you admit such methods, one can foresee that any day you will use torture as was done in the Middle Ages . . . Nor can you, Vladimir Ilyich, you who want to be the apostle of new truths and the builder of a new State, give your consent to the use of such unacceptable methods . . . What future lies in store for Communism when one of its most important defenders tramples in this way on every honest feeling?

We know the answer to that. Kropotkin ('personally . . . amiable to the point of saintliness and [who] with his red full beard and lovable expression might have been a shepherd from the Delectable Mountains,' said Bernard Shaw) died in 1921. If he had lived a little longer his reputation would no longer have saved him from the firing squad or the gulag.

His *Mutual Aid* should be required reading for any conservative (though not leading to the road of anarchism), along with other essential non-conservative books like Hayek's *Constitution of Liberty* and G K Chesterton's *Man who was Thursday* and *Orthodoxy*.

Kropotkin's evidence for the contribution of mutual aid is overwhelming. He begins with bees, ants, termites and thence to white-tailed eagles who combine for hunting; Brazilian kites who act as a kind of removal gang for heavy prey; co-operative fishing pelicans; lapwings who combine to take on an eagle; wolves and wild dogs who hunt in packs; the patriarchal society of rabbits; elephants and their sentries; and the mass ballet of certain birds.

On he goes through mutual aid in primitive man and the role of parental love; co-operation in mediaeval society; the early protection of the market-place in which no stranger might be slain; the guilds; the unions between cities; the work on the miraculous cathedrals; the mutual work of the crafts.

And then on again to the spoliation of the guilds by the State; the assault on the independence of villages and communal ownership, the growth of trade unions.

Kropotkin, as an anarchist, omits the growth of mutual aid that accompanied the expansion of the church, the industrial revolution and the birth of capitalism which flowered into the complex organisation of the limited liability company[3]. Capitalism's achievements are based on a combination of creativity, competition, the urge for expression, the harnessing of science to the industrial revolution and business organisations which achieve an astonishing degree of co-operation.

The aberration of corporatism

The sense of mutual aid is deep in man and is not met by the edicts of compulsory co-operation under socialism and fascism. Nor by the corporatist arrangements of States to ensure that such co-operation is forthcoming.

The Labour party had a respect for democracy and (many fellow-travelling communists and Trotskyists excepted) still does—and yet its ideas have been anticipated by the corporatism of Marxism and Fascism. To take just one example: it is interesting that the terms of reference under which Labour first set up their State investment organisation are almost word-for-word those of Mussolini's I.R.I. *(Istituto per la Ricostruzione Industriale)*. It is an ironic footnote to history that the great British prophet of State investment in industry, Mr Benn, was anticipated by the Quisling industrialist (there is always one) appointed by Mussolini to run I.R.I.—Signor Benni. History sometimes enjoys puns!

In the days of crawling and galloping socialism in Britain, co-operation was too often used as a semantic disguise for corporatism. The system of trinitarianism—bringing together government, industry and trade unions—was stale fascist theology. It is also well beloved of Latin-American generals and colonels, as I discovered when lecturing on that continent. 'Co-operation' for them, as often for the Labour Party, meant domination.

The catspaws

Another example of the perils of corporatism has been shown by the catspaw role of industry's personnel managers. They and their national organisations, with agreeable frontier relations with the trade unions, connived while Britain moved into unionocracy with debased closed shops, non-Labour trade unionists bullied and deceived into paying the political levy through their wage packets, corrupt ballots, inadequate membership records and restrictive practices. The initiative to break these and attempt to restore trade unions to their proper representative functions came not only from the Government, but also from organisations like Aims of Industry and the Freedom Association. From the personnel managers' organisations there was much initial sorrowing with the trade unions at the harshness of Government legislation.

Socialist 'co-operation'

The danger of confusing co-operation and corporatism in the public's mind is a real one; but is not avoided by saying nothing. There is, as I have indicated, a missing ingredient in the current philosophy of conservatism. At least as it is communicated; for it is by no means missing in conservative plans and actions.

Mr Bryan Gould, the Labour party's Shadow Trade and Industry Secretary, has a keen sense for the music of political time and is putting forward Labour's intention to have closer 'co-operation' between government and industry. Perceptively, Mr Gould anticipates those critics who have seen that Labour's last General Election was stuffed full of corporatism. 'There will of course be those who fear that such a concept of co-operation will merely provide a cloak for corporatism', writes Mr Gould. 'This is certainly a charge to be taken seriously; but the dangers of renouncing this form of co-operation, or of undertaking it with the wrong partners (as is true at present) far outweigh the dangers of preferring mutual incomprehension to dialogue, and in consequence allowing our economic performance to decline, in comparative terms, still further'[4].

You can (to put it vulgarly) say that again! Especially when you scrutinise Mr Gould's proposals more closely. The CBI, he states, is too dominated by financial institutions, importers and those who manufacture abroad. 'An industry which is offered a real role to play,' he states, 'in relation to government will find it necessary and desirable to organise itself rather better than it does at present'.

The message is clear. A Labour-sponsored and approved CBI is to be created with lots of Signori Bennis. It will be back to those days of the 1960s when industrialists beloved by Harold Wilson and passionate about national plans appeared almost nightly on our television sets.

The message is not only corporatist; it is ineffably condescending. Just imagine Mr Gould telling the TUC that it is unrepresentative and needs re-structuring in order to have a 'real role' to play with government.

Mr Gould's recent message to the TUC is, in fact, a very different one: 'The next Labour Government will naturally wish to bring the trade union movement back into the mechanism of decision-making on economic policy.'

Mr Gould knows a trend when he sees it. And so, like it or not, this Government must spell out, clearly, the antithesis between conservative and socialist ideas of co-operation.

Co-operation can be learnt

One of the best ways of displaying conviction is that of example. Government itself very often fails to display the co-operative virtues that it looks for in others. Departments fight their corners with a fierceness and a skill in leaking that makes the arguments in company board rooms look mild indeed.

Most politicians are professional arguers and most Secretaries of State are better at arguing than their humbler colleagues. Government departments are not only competitive for resources: they also face the great power of the Treasury.

Is it possible for Government to learn the skills and arts of co-operation from business?[5] Sir John Hoskyns, a former head of the No 10 Policy Unit and now Director-General of the Institute of Directors, takes the view that Ministers will always have to fight their own corner as long as they are drawn from the ranks of MPs, are career politicians and are backed by life-time career civil servants.

On the other hand, as John Redwood, another former Head of the No 10 Policy Unit, points out, privatisation has shown that if politicians believe that they will be successful by *not* obstinately fighting their own corner, they are happy to carry out a group task (even if, as in this case, it means reducing their empires). The Government should use this *modus operandi* in other areas.

Privatisation, Professor Patrick Minford has observed, has improved government management. And there are lessons which government can learn from industry in promoting co-operation. For example, Nigel Mobbs has made the point that government management is too often concerned with conflict and confrontation, rather than maintaining a constructive partnership between departments. 'They also lack a sense of urgency in their decision-making due to the fact that they are not bound by the normal measurements of performance which would be applicable in the private sector'. Financial accountability and effective communication, as Lord Hanson and Walter Goldsmith indicate, are often lacking in government. Sir Frank Gibb of Taylor Woodrow supports the Ibbs Report which recognised that management of government business had improved through the introduction of private sector disciplines but maintained that further substantial improvements were possible. He, too, believes that privatisation has removed the need for government to interfere in the running of industry and has diminished the habit of government departments fighting their own corners on every budgetary matter.

The possibilities for further privatisation (and thus of allowing the spirit of co-operation to enter in, in its manifold forms) are vast, almost limitless. Valuable experience has been gathered from the large-scale privatisation of the new towns. That exercise must come to an end and it would be a great pity to waste the acquired wisdom.

The rites of co-operation

Governments, national and local, are often responsible for the rites or liturgy of co-operation. By this I mean the events which celebrate and symbolise national occasions, the monuments or statures that express public attitudes, the cultural buildings such as opera houses, galleries and museums, the public glories like the London parks.

All these are, in a sense, offerings by the public (through the Government) to themselves. Walking through Regents Park, one can not only praise the Prince Regent and Nash and the then Government, but also acknowledge the modern presenters of these splendid semi-rural facilities—which include, via one's taxes, oneself.

The justification for acts of privatisation should not blind conservatives to the contrasting justification for preserving communal facilities which enrich our lives. What conservative will argue for privatising the Trooping of the Colour?

One problem in a democracy with public liturgy is that the left often wishes to politicise it, just as it tends to politicise art and literature. One of the ugly developments in the 1960s was the use of Arts Council money to stage left wing propaganda in some of our national theatres.

In the 1970s and 1980s we have witnessed a belief by sexual pressure groups such as so-called gay-rights, that the public should not merely attend propagandist performances, but also subsidise them through taxes and rates.

Because the left is often not conventionally religious, it compensates (for example in the Soviet Union, China, Albania and Cuba as well as in left wing British councils) by *erzatz* religious liturgy. A National Union of Miners' occasion with banners, music and Mr Scargill as mime, prophet, priest and rabble-rouser rolled into one, is a fair illustration.

The left are entitled to their partisan liturgy—but not at the national expense.

The monarchy is one of our greatest liturgies of co-operation. Its existence presents the left leadership, many of whom are republican and anti-monarchist, with an awkward problem, since the monarchy's popularity in Britain transcends party affiliation. This is an issue on which the left dare not speak its mind for fear of losing public support. The blocked political career of the capable Mr Willie Hamilton is a salutary example of what happens to a moderate Labour politician who says aloud what is on the mind of most left wingers.

The NHS is, in many ways, a noble though old-fashioned liturgical monument, one for which the British public has a deep affection. It is right to look at saner ways of paying for it—but we should recognise the depths of feeling involved. As W B Yeats might have said: 'Tread soft when you tread on my NHS dreams'.

The webs of co-operation—at home and abroad

One false and misleading myth is that of the terrible isolation of individuals in our cities and suburbs. This may be true for some of the old and unfortunate; but it is by no means representative. Scratch below the surface of life in cities, suburbs and villages and an intricate web of voluntary groups and societies comes to light. The years of competitive Thatcherism are also years of burgeoning charities. The amount donated to them by industry has approximately doubled in recent years. And individual effort and enterprise are constantly producing new ones.

The desirable twin themes of co-operation and competition—the two faces of enterprise—exist at international level, too. In the Common Market, we see legitimate and fruitful competition between national and multi-national companies; but we also see, and need, co-operation at EEC level. If we are to seize the great opportunities, and surmount the great challenges, which the Common Market will present us in 1992 we need to understand the uses both of co-operation and of competition—as in practice we do in our domestic affairs.

In the world at large, too, we should work for freer trade and competition—but to achieve it we need rules, and some measure of monetary stability as an agreed framework within which to compete (and co-operate).

Lessons for industry

Industry's quest for the alchemy of co-operation has been long and expensive. It has been almost over-receptive to new fashions in industrial sociology and psychology in response to the question,'How do we motivate the worker?'

Taylorism's 'scientific management' did not only appeal to American capitalists; it also produced enthusiam from Lenin and Mussolini.[6] This was succeeded by the participative approach of Mayo and his successors. Mayo placed emphasis on group cohesiveness and social skills in contrast to authoritarian approaches.

In Britain, the development of the National Institute of Industrial Psychology saw a different approach with studies on fatigue, rest-periods, factory conditions, absenteeism, etc.

In the United States, we saw the human relations school, experiments in organisational structure (pyramid and flat structure leading to differing results), and studies on employee satisfaction and efficiency—which suggested, as in the research on the accuracy of bomb aimers in the last war, that unfortunately happiness and efficiency do not always go together; some (though not excessive) tension seems necessary to group success.

In India, the classic research by A K Rice in the Ahmedabad Manufacturing and Printing Company examined a situation in which automatic looms, with workers allocated to each component, produced lower efficiency and morale than the non-automatic method.[7]

The research in which Indian workers were given the kind of social cohesion which they experienced in their villages resulted in satisfactory production.

In different forms, we have seen workers in the US and in Scandinavia achieve excellent results when decision-making has been pushed down, as much as possible, to the shop floor.

One obstacle to fruitful co-operation—and prosperity—in Britain is still the shop steward, who often acts as a bottleneck in communication; also the sense of the foreman or supervisor that he is being by-passed by managers and operatives, who prefer to talk to the shop steward. American managers working in Britain are startled when they find that they are not expected to talk directly to the shop floor, and that operatives approach the shop steward rather than their supervisor.

A second major obstacle is that many Trade Unions still fail to look after the long-term interests of their members. The puritanism that rejects American rewards along with American productivity emerges as a death-wish that eventually (as in the case of the print workers) or suddenly (as in the recent Dundee catastrophe) leads to loss of jobs.

Hence the practical value of co-operation by unions and employers in keeping ahead of conflicts; and in producing stability by means of long-term agreements with one union, or at least a limited number of them—including no-strike agreements.

The American system of a big bust-up after a three-year agreement, which eventually clears the air and leads to positive results, is at least to be preferred to the sporadic testiness of some British labour relations (although, since 1979 wild-cat strikes have greatly diminished).

Joan Woodward and the Tavistock Institute of Human Relations in the UK broadened their research into industrial behaviour to take account of the influence of organisation and technology. Tavistock's important work in the coal mines was, alas, allowed to lapse in Britain, but it led to major research on broadening the responsibilities of shop-floor workers in countries such as Sweden. The current approach is to take in both the organisation and the environment in studies.

The 'Half time Britain' thesis by consultant William Allen, produced partly as a result of his work for Esso which led to the Fawley Agreement, was almost too far ahead of its time. Allen postulated, in the early 1960s, that Britain had too many workers on the machines, had a low standard of rewards, poor education and was the country of excessive overtime. (The last has still not been tackled.) The disease of 'Half-time Britain' has been alleviated by the Thatcher Governments and by ambitious entrepreneurs like Murdoch and Maxwell. An ultimate test for companies is to produce ambitious targets, together with the necessary communication programmes, for management, supervisors, employees and trade unions.

Industrialists are sometimes bemused at being told that British industry suffers from class rigidities, whereas the evidence of David Granick's studies in *The European Executive* and *The Red Executive* showed that we were alone in allowing promotion from the bottom to the top of industrial organisations: one emergent weakness, however, was the lack of qualifications of our socially mobile management[8].

Britain has since the Middle Ages been a notably class mobile society. That is why we have a social ear for class consciousness. It is the result of our mobility—up and down.

What morals can industry draw from the variety of approaches enjoined on it in the last sixty years? There is evidence that effective communication, involving participation in the context of work, can reduce resistance to change. But that is not invariable; workers may sometimes look to their trade unions rather than to management for participation.

'Political' forms of communication such as elected workers on boards obviously present a threat to the enterprise structure of companies. Nor do they really touch on the fundamental problems of communication in the context of the job. So far Britain has resisted co-determination pressures such as putting trade union representatives on the board. We will have to continue to do so.

One major problem for the future is not that of the Marxist thesis: the alienation of the worker from his or her work. It is rather the alienation of the valueless worker from society. Work can provide important satisfactions but not the ultimate human solutions; and it is only too easy for the twentieth century worker to project his inner emptiness and lack of satisfaction onto his work. For the future, Jung and Kropotkin are likely to offer more hints than Marx.

We should turn also, if we can find a copy, to that small classic—the study of conservatism and literature by T S Eliot, *The Literature of Politics*, published by the Conservative Political Centre in 1955. May someone publish it again soon!

After giving his seal of approval to Bolingbroke, Burke, Coleridge, Disraeli, Canon Demant, Christopher Dawson and Reinhold Niebuhr, T S Eliot concluded his essay by emphasising the importance of tapping pre-political thinking which is the earth into which politics sinks its roots.

And my defence of the importance of the pre-political is simply this, that it is the stratum down to which any sound political thinking must push its roots, and from which it must derive its nourishment. It is also, if you don't mind my changing the metaphor so abruptly, the land in which dwell the Gods of the Copy Book Headings; and, abandoning figurative language altogether, it is the domain of ethics—in the end, the domain of theology. For the question of questions, which no political philosophy can escape, and by the right answer to which all political thinking must be judged, is simply this: What is Man? what are his limitations? what is his misery and what his greatness and what, finally, his destiny?[9]

The appeal of a conservative thinker is not that he answers all these questions but that he appears to have reflected upon and been preoccupied with them.

Dr Desmond Morris, author of the *Naked Ape,* points out that, for man, these pre-political roots go very deep indeed:

> Early man is looked down upon as a thug—all *ug ug* and *thump thump.* In fact he was extraordinarily co-operative. We survived only because we achieved the perfect balance between co-operation and achievement[10].

Early man may not have enjoyed a formal Conservative Party but his approach to co-operation and achievement provides an admirable lesson for us to-day.

Notes

1. Petr Kropotkin, *Mutual Aid; a factor of evolution,* Penguin, 1939.

2. Ashley Montagu; *Introduction to Mutual Aid;* Porter Sargent (USA).

3. See Fernand Braudel's *Civilisation and Capitalism;* William Collins, 1984.

4. Bryan Gould, Time to bridge the industrial divide; *Daily Telegraph,* 20 February, 1988.

5. See William C Mitchell; *Government As It Is;* Hobart Paper 109; Institute of Economic Affairs, 1988.

6. C S Maier, *Between Taylorism and Technocracy: European Ideologies and the Vision of Industrial Productivity in the 1920s,* Journal of Contemporary History, 5, 2, 1970, 27–61. Also Michael Rose: *Industrial Behaviour; Theoretical Development since Taylor;* Allen Lane, 1975.

7. A K Rice, *Productivity and Social Organisation: the Ahmedabad Experiment,* Tavistock Publications, 1958.

8. David Granick, *The Red Executive,* Macmillan, 1960; also his *European Executive.*

9. T S Eliot, *The Literature of Politics,* Conservative Political Centre, 1955.

10. At home with the Ape Man, interview with Desmond Morris, *Daily Telegraph,* 26 March 1988.

5

Gentrification or Growth: Cultural Causes of Economic Failure

Sir James Goldsmith

Traditionally there have been two main systems which can lead to prosperity and a vigorous civilisation. One is based on imperial conquest. That is the Roman way and the way proposed by Soviet Russia. Such a system needs discipline and a strict hierarchy. The other is based on freedom. That is the mercantile way. In a mercantile society, all citizens are free to work to improve their position. They can aim as high as their personal vision allows them to see. Their rewards will vary according to their ability, determination and luck. Individually their effort is motivated principally by personal and family ambition. Collectively their effort will build a prosperous community.

In a failing society, which is unable to sustain prosperity, prosperity itself is derided. The élite suggests that somehow it is incompatible with a civilised way of life. In reality it is prosperity which allows many of the most agreeable aspects of civilisation. The cultures of Athens, Florence, Venice, to name only a few, were founded on prosperity from commerce. A prosperous society can take a long view and can invest in such vital projects as protection of the environment, beautification of the cities and countryside, the establishment of centres of learning and of art. Poor communities have to struggle from day to day. Only a prosperous society can offer optimum opportunities for employment. Only a prosperous society can offer proper help to its disabled. As has often been said, the Good Samaritan was a successful merchant.

My purpose this evening is to try to analyse the British experience and why it is that, over the past decades, Britain's relative prosperity has declined dramatically. Not long ago, Britain was among the most prosperous nations of the world. Today, among industrialised countries, it is one of the poorest. British industry has been unable to compete. Since 1948 Britain's share of world trade in manufactured products has dropped from 29% to about 5%.

Why is it that despite the salutary measures taken since 1980 by this Government, the economic recovery has been relatively slow? To be sure there has been a real recovery and it can be measured in terms of job creation, growth in GNP and diminishing rates of inflation. But the recovery seems to be driven by only one cylinder. Why?

I am not going to concentrate on the abuses of Trade Union power nor on the destructive effects of socialism. They are very real but they are well documented. I would like to dig deeper. What is it that has driven so many decent British people to support a Trade Union movement which has devastated one major industry after another destroying employment and prosperity? Why have so many decent people supported socialism despite its proven effects on industry, the economy and personal freedom? This last point has always seemed a particular mystery. At the height of socialist power, under Jim Callaghan, the British people, historically proud and independent, had been willing to accept quite extraordinary constraints on personal liberty. There were wage controls, price controls, exchange controls, closed shops, taxation of up to 98% on income from savings, State control over about 60% of the GNP, as well as the whole apparatus transferring family responsibility to the Welfare State. The average Englishman was no longer free to choose the school to which he sent his children, the doctor who cared for his family, the hospital to which he sought admission. He was no longer free to sell his labour for the best market price, nor to work for a company without first paying obeisance to the Trade Union which, by law, he was forced to join.

The loss of so much personal liberty was partly the result of the desire to transfer to the State many of the traditional responsibilities of the family. Also the State took over the task of fixing, on a nationwide basis, with the Trade Unions and the employers, salaries and terms of employment. The transfer to the State of these extensive responsibilities resulted in a corresponding transfer of power with the inevitable loss of personal freedom. Nonetheless, it is surprising that free men and women were willing to concede so much of their fundamental liberty.

To understand this evolution, I believe that we must start by stepping back and looking at the period following the industrial revolution. At that time a new and successful industrial middle class was emerging. The reaction of the old ruling class, and subsequently of the old Conservative Party, was one of distaste. Later this was fostered by the intellectuals who created the environment for political thought; men such as Arnold Toynbee, Arthur Bryant, G.M. Trevelyan and others, were hostile to industrialisation. They variously described industry as philistine, competition as predatory, commerce as debased and considered the whole thing as rather vulgar. The Conservative Party agreed. Despite being the heir to a successful industrialist, Baldwin disliked liberal capitalism. 'Laissez faire' he said, was as out of date as the slave trade.[1] Later Macmillan stated that 'Toryism has always been a form of paternal Socialism'.[2] Lord Hinchingbrooke, representing the Tory reform committee announced that 'True Conservative opinion is horrified at the damage done to this country by individualist businessmen . . .'.[3] Quintin Hogg, now Lord Hailsham, criticized capitalism as an 'ungodly and rapacious scramble for ill gotten gains . . .'.[4]

In such a climate, businessmen lost their confidence. At the very moment of its triumph, the entrepreneurial class turned its energies to disguising itself in the image of the class it was supplanting. To be accepted, successful businessmen went through an accelerated process of gentrification. They became ashamed of the very virtues that created their and their nation's success.

The hunger for gentrification led to a consolidation of the class system. Progressively there was a mingling of the old landed aristocracy with the new industrial class and the emergence of a gentrified middle class. This middle class sought to distance itself from the working class whose values were uncomfortably reminiscent of those of which, so recently, they had become ashamed.

And so emerged the extraordinary upstairs/downstairs society. Upstairs, admiration was reserved for amateurs, dilettantes and a somewhat effete set of values which were supposed to represent a cultured way of life. Adventurers, risk takers, tough and ambitious professionals were considered rather uncouth and vulgar. To be a good loser was more important than to be a winner.

Downstairs were trapped the old and earthy British virtues of vigour and vitality.

Of course there was some movement on the staircase. But on the whole, those who moved up were expected to adopt, or pretend to adopt, the mores of their betters, including the clothes that they wore and the accent in which they spoke.

It was inevitable that these two nations would one day struggle for supremacy.

To prepare for this struggle, the underclass was offered the Trade Union movement and socialism. By uniting within trade unions and transferring extensive powers to their bureaucracies, they had a weapon with which to fight. By promoting an omnipresent State, they could create a powerful structure, strong enough to humble the upstairs people.

And so Britain found herself with a devitalised overclass ashamed of the values needed to succeed and an underclass no longer willing to accept its pre-ordained position and whose vigour, instead of being used to build a successful community, was alienated and misguided.

It is against this background that a number of significant facts fall into place:

1. The overclass went on the defensive. They were frightened by change. Change would challenge the existing order and jeopardise established privilege. So the rate of change had to be kept as slow as possible. The strategy was to compromise. This was explained to me some years ago, in New York, by Lord Poole. At that time Poole was a prominent merchant banker. After the war, he had been Chairman of the Conservative Party. Poole explained that when the Conservatives lost the General Election in 1945, Harold Macmillan, Rab Butler and he decided to work out a new post-war strategy for the Conservative Party. He explained that, for them, the fundamental question was not whether Britain would be socialist or conservative, but whether a socialist Britain would be better administered by a Conservative Government than by a Labour Government. They had accepted the idea that the tide towards socialism was irreversible and that they should adjust to accommodate it. So successive concessions to socialism were made in the hope that this would slow the anticipated drift to the left.

2. The gentrification of the overclass created an extraordinary opportunity for those who were neither infected with this disease

nor were trapped in the underclass. This explains the success achieved by that relatively tiny band of immigrants from Australia, Canada, South Africa, as well as Jewish and other miscellaneous groups. Is it not extraordinary that this small group of people should have created I.C.I.; Shell; Marks & Spencer; Great Universal Stores; Thomson International; News International; Beaverbrook; Associated British Foods; Thorn; Trusthouse Forte; Tesco; Sears Holdings; Grandmet; Land Securities; S.G. Warburg; and so many other great British companies.

The common denominator was that most of these people came from humble origins, were not trapped in the upstairs/downstairs culture, and had not been devitalised by gentrification.

They were free men who were not prisoners of the British caste system.

Now look at those of Britain's great companies which have been run by people who were indeed prisoners of the system. The directors and management of such companies are seldom capitalists or entrepreneurs. More often they are honourable functionaries. Unfortunately their pay is poor because high pay is culturally unacceptable in Britain. In any case it would be confiscated by inordinately high tax. So profitability and risk-taking became less important than respectability. For them, it is important to avoid controversy and 'rocking the boat'. The ultimate reward consists of the symbols of acceptance by the overclass. I always think of Dunlop, Distillers and the Joint Stock Banks as examples of the many companies that fall into this category. The Savoy Group is another. Compare its record with that of Trusthouse Forte or Grandmet.

3. The far left was also handed an opportunity. They were able to exploit the grievances of the upstairs/downstairs society. They could foster resentment and envy and aggravate the class conflict. Throughout the world, the far left harnesses such genuine causes so as to guide them to Marxist Leninism in the furtherance of their totalitarian ambitions.

4. The recent outcry about the salary increases to 'top people' can be understood in this context. Let me remind you that the sequence of events was that the Government increased salaries of judges, generals, very senior civil servants etc. The socialists reacted by screaming that this was an outrageous example of class privilege. The gentrified overclass reacted by saying that the Government had made a bad psychological mistake and that this was yet another banana skin. What was the reality? In fact, the salaries, after tax, of

these people were absurdly low. They were the equivalent to the amount earned by relatively junior management in competitive international companies and a small fraction of the amount earned by their top people. But the far left was able to exploit the incident because too many of the 'top people' in question are drawn from the overclass. So it could be made to look like class abuse. The gentrified middle class behaved as expected. They were horrified by any firm action, terrified by the outburst from the left and, as usual, started to apologise. It is significant, is it not, that there should be such resentment when 'top people' earn some money but not when 'ordinary people' win pools, or when pop-singers become multi-millionaires, or when Arabs become billionaires. The 'top people' are perceived as being from the overclass, the others are not.

There is no such loss of will in Mrs Thatcher. She still has all her vigour. She could clearly see the ravages of socialism. She understood that Britain had to recover her desire and ability to compete. And that that depended, not on disembodied theories of planning, but on the vitality of the people. She understood that that vitality had to be rekindled by radically cutting back the suffocating powers of the State, returning responsibility to individuals and motivating them by allowing them the possibility of success and rewards. It was strong stuff and that is why the patricians and the trimmers in the Conservative Party, the descendants of Macmillan, Butler and Poole, resented her. As we have seen, for them, triumph consists of losing slowly.

But Mrs Thatcher failed to see the origins and the causes of the disease that she was fighting. To dismantle the swollen powers of the State and the Trade Unions was, of course, right. But it had to be accompanied by a similar dismantlement of the class structure. Otherwise how could the underclass accept such unilateral disarmament? Their principal weapons, the socialist State and the special powers of the Trade Unions, were being taken away and they were being left trapped in a structure which they considered oppressive.

That is why Mrs Thatcher now must convince her Party to lead a great national revolution. She must aim at systematically and radically eliminating every vestige of the class system. She must liberate the vast latent energies of the people. She must convert Britain into a truly meritocratic society firmly based on the reality of freedom and opportunity for all. That is what will create a national renaissance.

The Labour Party cannot do this because it is now Marxist/Leninist.

For them, individual freedom must be sacrificed to an all powerful State assisted by dominant Trade Unions.

The Liberals and Social Democrats cannot because they have already rejected all hard options and have opted for slow and woolly national decline but with a comfortable, do gooder, exclusively middle class, conscience.

Only a Conservative Party, reaching out to the future and no longer pining for the past, can point the way.

Let me make a few suggestions for an initial agenda:

A bi-cameral parliamentary system

Britain needs a credible and strong second chamber. At present the House of Commons has absolute power. There is no constitution and no Supreme Court to restrain that power. There are no checks and no balances. A disciplined majority in the House of Commons, which in the recent past has been obtained with the votes of as little as 29% of the electorate, has total, uncontested dominion over the nation.

The House of Lords, no matter how good or bad its debates, no matter how 'civilised' its environment, is not credible. It is a relic from the past. About 70% of its members are hereditary and represent a miniscule and relatively inactive part of the population. Many of the remainder are there as a mark of respect at the end of their careers.

The present state of the House of Lords has been a cause for satisfaction to successive governments, both Labour and Conservative. An ineffective House of Lords ensures the absolute power of the House of Commons. The socialists have the additional benefit of using the House of Lords as a symbol of the class system. So without outside pressure, the Prime Minister of the day and the House of Commons is happy to protect and perpetuate this impotent anachronism.

The House of Lords must be converted into an effective, powerful and responsible senior chamber—a British Senate. Its electoral term should be longer than that of the Commons so as to ensure a more strategic, rather than tactical, outlook. Its members should be elected in a complementary and not a similar way to membership of the other house.

My preference would be to elect representatives from the regions for staggered seven-year terms. Also I believe that membership of this House should be of particular importance, so there should be substantially fewer members than in the Commons.

Primaries

It is fundamental that selection of parliamentary candidates be made through primary elections in which all party supporters can vote. In Britain, many parliamentary constituencies are historically Labour or Conservative. If selected as Labour candidate for a constituency like Ebbw Vale, even a donkey would have been elected. If selected as Conservative candidate for a constituency like Chichester, even a goat would have been elected. In such constituencies, it is the selection committees which, in effect, appoint the Members of Parliament. The electorate no more than rubber-stamps the choice of these committees.

At present, both Labour and Conservatives have methods of selection which are profoundly anti-democratic. Many Labour selection committees have been captured by the militant left. They select candidates who represent extremist minorities and not the views of Labour supporters as a whole. Conservative selection committees are dominated by the overclass. They represent the values of that class and this makes it extremely difficult for the underclass to feel at home in the Conservative Party. Of course many members of the underclass vote for the Conservatives because they abhor socialism. But the majority of those who do so, do not feel that they, themselves, are natural Tories.

Arbitrary power and the law

This Government has done much, although not yet enough, to curb the abusive powers of the Trade Unions. But it has done nothing to curb the abusive powers of the establishment.

Throughout Britain, in almost every walk of life, in every profession, there are groups of people who wield great and quasi-judicial power. They might be called councils or committees, quangos, qualgos, associations, boards of governors or what have you. In reality they are self-perpetuating oligarchies, usually drawn from the overclass, whose main task is to protect established privilege.

Often these committees have the power to adjudicate on matters of very great importance to those working or wishing to work in the fields of endeavour which they regulate. Often the criteria used by these committees are not whether the individuals concerned have the talents necessary to succeed or the right to try. They are more interested by whether the face fits. That means whether they are part of the overclass or, if not, whether they have paid sufficient homage to it. Have they been willing to adopt or copy their mores, do they wear the right clothes, do they speak in the right voice, are they satisfactory Uncle Toms? If not, invisible barriers are erected. Usually they are erected in secret session and the individuals concerned are not informed why adverse decisions are taken. And they have no right of appeal to the nation's courts. These magic circles are often given special rights and privileges which protect them from legal action by aggrieved individuals. Like the Trade Unions they have been placed above the law.

Even the present radical Government has fallen for the proposition that the magic circles offer self-regulation and that the alternative to self-regulation is bureaucratic regulation. That is not so. When regulation is really necessary, laws can and should be clearly set and the judiciary should be responsible for ensuring that they are respected. The judiciary would do this in a dispassionate way without prejudice or privilege.

In any case can there be a greater inhibitor of energy than a national network of powerful committees devoted to protecting established privilege, blocking change and thwarting people who might 'rock the boat? In Britain today the boat needs to be rocked everywhere.

The magic circles should be stripped of all judicial or quasi-judicial power and all special legal privileges which protect them from the consequences of their actions. Let me quote Edmund Burke, one of the prophets of conservatism, 'Law and arbitrary power' he said, 'are in eternal enmity'.

Education

Education in Britain is a reflection of the diseases that wrack this nation. The private sector consists substantially of students selected from the overclass on the criteria of wealth and birth. As is to be expected, the public sector is a misguided reaction to the private sector. It seems to be based on the idea that streaming according to merit is evil and that it is socially destructive to promote the gifted faster than those who are less so. So you get the worst of all worlds.

What is more, these two parallel streams of education divide the nation at an early age and consolidate the class system.

The streams should be unified. That does not mean destroying the public schools and remaining grammar schools. On the contrary there should be no monopoly or semi-monopolies on education. There should be a great polyculture of schools, all competing one against the other. This would include schools run by religious groups, by teacher co-operatives, by charities, by private enterprise, by local communities, and even if absolutely necessary by the State. And there should be some form of State voucher system which would allow parents to choose. They should be free to use that voucher in any kind of school. They should be free to apply for entry for their children in any school. When the number of applicants to a particular school is greater than its capacity, then the criterion used to pick successful applicants should be personal merit.

You will notice that each of these proposals has a common denominator—their purpose is to increase the rights of individuals. Individuals would be able to elect the members of the senior house of Parliament; individuals would be able to elect their party's parliamentary candidates; individuals would be free to pursue their lives without arbitrary action from magic circles and could take those privileged groups to court; individuals could choose for their children from a variety of schools. That is what needs to be done everywhere in the nation. There must be individual freedom and the Conservative Party must be the guardian of that freedom.

Before concluding, I will make one final point. Some will look at the miners, who during the recent strike, fought brutally and unlawfully and they will look at the football hooligans and they will conclude that these people are just subversives or criminals. I see it differently. My conclusion is that it is a tragedy that all that vigour should be alienated and should be used to destroy rather than to improve. I believe that the question which needs to be asked is how to liberate that energy. My point of view has much in common with the view from the far left. They also can see the energy, the resentment and the anger. They, too, want to harness it. But their purpose is to use it politically to further their totalitarian ambitions. Marxist/ Leninist and Communist politicians are using the vigour and vitality, which are trapped in the underclass, so as to turn them against the nation. That is what is happening throughout the country and more particularly in many Trade Unions and municipal governments.

In a great civilisation people are individually free; they have equality of opportunity; they are united in a common objective. None of these circumstances exist in Britain today. If the nation is to be saved, this must be recognised and put right. And let it not be forgotten that those who are not willing to fight for their freedom deserve to be enslaved.

Notes

1. See Cowling, M. *Impact of Hitler, (Cambridge 1975) page 52*
2. *Beer, Samuel. British Politics in the Collectivist Age,* (New York 1967) page 271
3. Addison. *The Road to 1945* (London 1971), pages 232–33
4. *The Case for Conservatism,* (London 1947) pages 51–52

Part Two

New Thinking on Welfare

6

Beveridge Revisited: New Foundations for Tomorrow's Welfare

Stephen Davies

Introduction

The 'welfare state' is in crisis. This statement, once unthinkable, is now commonplace. Throughout the democratic world, welfare and social security systems, once sacrosanct, are under attack and lack popular support. Books with titles like *Welfare State in Crisis* or *Crisis of the Welfare State* are published without explosions of rage.[1] All this reflects the general opinion that the difficulties and problems now confronting welfare systems in many countries are not temporary or contingent but fundamental and inherent.

Anyone reading the literature published on social policy of late is soon struck by the extent of the consensus both as to the nature and the causes of the crisis. This is surprising, given the wide range of political opinions represented. Agreement however is 'negative' rather than 'positive'; no consensus exists on solutions. (As argued later, the lack of positive agreement has grave political implications.) The trends which have created this gloomy unanimity are the same in every country: the growing cost of the 'welfare state', growing discontent with the practice of state welfare, growing concern about

123

the long term consequences of present policies—particularly the
moral ones.

Moreover the economic and social foundations of the 'welfare state'
are being eroded by changes in social structure, particularly in regard
to the nature of the family, and by the radical alterations in the
economic order which have taken place since about 1965, notably in
patterns of work and employment. Historical precedents exist. Debates over the fundamentals of welfare and poor relief recur because
many of the basic issues are to do with moral philosophy as much as
with administration. Periodically changes in the economic order force
governments and people to reconstruct the welfare system from first
principles, whereupon such questions come to the fore. Many of the
issues now exercising academics, politicians and public are the same
as those argued in the 1940s, 1880s or even the 1830s.

Every social order of any complexity has a welfare system; that is,
a set of rules, institutions and practices which aid the needy and
indigent. In fact there are as many systems of welfare as there are
societies.

Four key questions can be asked about any welfare system, the
possible answers to which lead to a host of different policies.

Firstly, how is poverty relieved? It may be through cash payment,
benefit in kind or institutional care.

Secondly, who is responsible for administering the relief? In some
societies the burden falls mainly upon the state, in others upon public
institutions such as churches, in yet others mutual aid and philan-
thropy predominate. Historically the commonest agency of poor
relief has been the family or kin-group; but for several reasons this
has not been the case in western societies.

Thirdly, what is the fundamental purpose of the system? Two main
answers have been given to this question. For some the goal is the
creation of a 'floor', a minimum basic standard of living which
everyone should have. For others the goal of the system is a state of
greater equality, to be achieved by the redistribution of wealth. In
addition to these declared goals other 'hidden' ones may come into
play, such as the promotion of certain social values, the maintenance
of political stability, the supporting of this or that system of social
relationships.

Finally, the most difficult question to answer is the simplest to
ask—what is poverty/need? How are such terms defined? The idea of
poverty is far from simple or self-evident. By some definitions a

beggar and a monk are both poor. But how comparable are their positions?

Whatever the definition of poverty (to which we shall return), in Western Europe, ever since the shift to a market economy in the sixteenth century, it has ultimately been concerned with lack of money. The main causes are two: lack of income-yielding property and lack of income from work (due either to low pay or to inability to enter the labour market). The latter cause may be outside one's control—old age, sickness, disablement—or may be voluntary: for example, in the case of a young unmarried woman who chooses to have a child.

All four questions raise matters not so much of a technical or administrative nature as of a moral kind. The notion of a welfare system which is morally neutral is a chimera. Every welfare system will in practice reward some kinds of behaviour and penalise others; and in so doing will affect the behaviour of individuals. Implicitly or explicitly the institutions and operation of welfare will reflect and promote certain moral assumptions and values. Thus the nineteenth-century workhouse demonstrated a morality based upon a rigorous idea of personal responsibility, which made most poverty blameworthy. Today the practices of the DHSS often promote values of servility and dependence, together with a disregard of personal responsibility.

In every welfare system two questions of practical policy bring these moral issues to the fore: how to define the concept of need which qualifies a person for welfare and how to help those categorized as needy without harming their own long-term interests or undermining important moral values. In particular, the system while alleviating the state of poverty must avoid penalising effort and relative success. Although general agreement may sometimes be reached on the methods, the moral and philosophical consensus periodically disintegrates under the pressure of events. When this happens, as in the 1830s or 1880s, the nature and intent of welfare policy becomes a matter of fervent debate.

The questions at issue are always the same. What is poverty, i.e. how is eligibility for relief to be defined? What role should the state have? Should the system explicitly promote particular values and if so which ones? Should relief be uniform or differentiated? Should it be universal or targeted on a narrowly defined class of 'needy'? Answering these questions necessarily involves addressing the four basic questions outlined above and facing the moral issues as well. So the debate today over how to respond to the acknowledged crisis of the welfare state must necessarily be a radical one, concerned with fundamentals.

The use of tests: the 1930s and later

Always when welfare policy enters such a rapid flux one of the proposed solutions is universalism, the idea of a basic benefit automatically given to everyone, usually as cash, so ensuring that everybody has a specified minimum income. This idea historically has been rejected on three main grounds. In practical terms it is rejected as too expensive. It is seen as wasteful and inequitable because it gives relief to many who do not need it by any criterion, so leaving less for the truly poor. More seriously the notion of universalism is seen to constitute an unacceptable moral hazard because it involves 'getting something for nothing' on a massive scale; and because such a system would (it is feared) radically erode the incentive to work, with the result that a large number of free-riders would be supported by the industrious. These arguments have been put by people as diverse in their views as Edwin Chadwick, Beveridge and the Webbs.

The alternative is to have some kind of test whereby only those who qualify are given help. This may involve a distinction not only between poor and not-poor but also between two categories of poor, the 'deserving' and the 'undeserving'. (The exact form of the test proposed is varied.) In the last century the workhouse test in principle restricted relief to those physically unable to work. In many present-day systems, for example in Sweden, a work test is imposed whereby if a job is available the claimant must take it or lose entitlement to benefit. And under the original Beveridge scheme the test was to be the payment of contributions.

The most famous, or infamous, example however of a qualifying test in recent British history was the means test operated in the 1930s. This is worth examining in some detail, both because it illustrates the problems associated with the operation of means tests and because it led to many of the welfare steps taken during and after the war— which in turn led to the present position.

State-organized unemployment insurance had been introduced into Great Britain in 1908/9 by the then Liberal government. The scheme introduced by Asquith and Lloyd George was a strictly contributory system: benefits directly linked to contributions. It was administered not immediately by the state but by voluntary organisations, chief among whom were the trades unions.

By the 1920s things had changed. Although the scheme which covered unemployment benefit had been expanded in 1920 the fund was unable to cope with the enormous demands consequent upon the long term unemployment of the inter-war years. By the later 1920s it was technically bankrupt. Meanwhile the state had removed all responsibility for administering the fund from trades unions, who therefore no longer had any direct responsibility for unemployment relief, despite the fact that their own policies played a major part in the genesis and worsening of the problem.

Registered unemployment by December of 1930 had risen to 2,660,000 yet wage rates had fallen by only ½% as compared to 1924.[2] The system of insurance, as then operating, greatly helped to lead to wage rates becoming so rigid. All in all, by the financial crisis of 1931 the position had become insupportable.

In 1931 the relief of unemployment was effectively taken over entire by the Treasury, at least so far as its financing was concerned. At the same time the means test was introduced. This ruled that anyone living in a household whose total assets were above a certain sum should not be eligible for benefit. The legislation, however, allowed local authorities great discretion to determine what this sum should be; and in consequence local disparities were great. In 1934 the Unemployment Act created a fund intended to break even at an unemployment rate of 16¾%, the actual rate for that year. Since that rate was never reached again the fund remained in surplus. The fund was administered by a central body, the Unemployment Assistance Board. At the same time the administration of the means test was made more uniform; but in practice, because of wide variations in interpretation, the new scheme was seen in many areas as an effective cut.

Throughout the 1930s the means test, however administered, was the central feature of the welfare system for many people. This led to acute resentment and moral disquiet. As A J P Taylor put it:[3] "The taxpaying classes were indignant if men received relief from public funds when they possessed resources of their own. The working classes were equally indignant that a man who had the misfortune to be out of work should be penalised because he had been provident or because other members of his family were in work." Six main drawbacks of the test can be identified, as it operated.

1. *The stigmatising effect.*

Those qualifying under the test were marked out not only as needy but also as thriftless, improvident and socially worthless. In its administration the notion of 'desert' entered in. Such a notion, with its moral judgement, was bitterly resented.

2. *The arbitrary administration.*

Because of the imprecision of the concept of 'means' the system was seen as capricious. So much depended upon the judgement of the individual officer and (before 1934) on the attitudes and political sympathies of the local authorities.

3. *The paternalistic relationship between recipients and officers.*

Recipients felt themselves reduced to mere claimants unable to act or judge independently, chattels of the State, their independence forfeited.

4. *The effect of the threshold.*

The threshold penalised thrift and self-help. It was this feature which was resented most of all. To have savings or possessions of any kind was disastrous: past prudence was punished. In previous slumps (e.g. the 1880s) the poor had supplemented their incomes with many kinds of casual labour and small-scale enterprise. Now such jobs were not open to them—unless they were willing to lose benefits, and suffer a reduction in net income. Under the means test it paid to do nothing, to spend rather than save and to have as few permanent belongings as possible.

5. *The moral impact.*

This was very damaging. Its workings encouraged mendacity and furtiveness: these were in effect rewarded, while honesty was penalised.

6. *The creation of dependency.*

By making it difficult for anyone to assist themselves the means test created a class of permanent welfare dependents of the State, unable to change their status. The pattern of unemployment in the 1930s meant that this class was concentrated in the 'assisted areas'.

All this comes across very clearly in works of oral history. Thus one respondent from Manchester remembers his father losing benefit because of his outside earnings and then getting some back by means of a trick. Another from Salford recalled how the test led to families being forced to part with many of their possessions before they could qualify for relief. Yet another feature of the times which many remember was how people would pretend not to be resident in a particular household, so that the unemployed members of their family could continue to draw benefit.[4]

The overwhelming impression is of intense bitterness and resentment, engendered by the working of the test and its demeaning effects. This has become part of the folk memory in many parts of the country. Oral accounts are often criticized by historians as being too much coloured by hindsight and emotional recollection, but in this context that particular objection is irrelevant. What the oral research certainly tells us is the nature of popular conceptions and images and in social policy such subjective factors must be taken into account if only because they influence behaviour.

By 1940 it was widely accepted that the welfare system commanded no support and needed drastic reform—not only of unemployment insurance but also of pensions and other benefits. The response was, of course, the Beveridge Report of 1942, the origin of the system we have today. Developments since 1945 have however so changed the original design that we should retrace what that in fact was, and why Beveridge took the position that he did.

Firstly, his overall strategic aim was the creation of a minimum standard of living below which no person should fall or in his own words 'the abolition of want'. His intention was to create a 'floor', a basic standard of living which would be guaranteed to all. He had *no* intention that the system should be an instrument for the radical redistribution of wealth, or for the creation of greater equality.

Secondly, his plan was to found a scheme based upon insurance: i.e. depending upon a contributory system of finance. Insofar as the contributions of those in work would pay for the benefits given to others, this did involve a—strictly limited—degree of redistribution. But the essential point to remember is that for Beveridge benefits were to be tightly tied to contributions—no contribution meant no benefit (except in special cases such as children).

Thirdly, the means by which poverty was to be relieved was by cash payments to individuals rather than benefits in kind. This would retain the element of individual choice and control. In Beveridge's view the welfare system was to be an 'enabler' rather than a 'provider'.

The fourth point, often overlooked, is that for Beveridge one main aim of his proposals was the relief of poverty among children.

Indeed, he said that this was 'the primary aim' of his system.[5] Care for the old, although important, was not so central.

His fifth plank, the one which has attracted most criticism since, was universality of benefits. (It is here that the shadow of the means test can be seen.) Benefits were to be universal in two related ways. They were to be given to everyone, regardless of means, so the means test was to disappear, leaving only the basic criterion of payment of contributions. They were also to be uniform and automatic with no element of special discriminatory payments and hence no power of choice or judgement between cases for any official. This policy has been criticised recently by authors otherwise sympathetic to Beveridge's scheme; but he was clearly influenced by the disastrous history of the previous decade.[6]

Even less attention has been paid to the sixth part of Beveridge's programme, although for him it was central. This was cooperation between the State and the voluntary sectors. Beveridge made it clear that he saw a most important role for voluntarism in the welfare society. In particular he wanted sickness benefit and all extraordinary aid to be channelled and administered via voluntary organisations. In this way the absence of special discretionary payments would be compensated.[7]

Thus, in a speech at Newcastle upon Tyne in 1944 he declared:[8] "I urged that, with a view to encouraging to the maximum voluntary insurance and voluntary organisations for self-help, the Friendly Societies should be given a responsible place in the national scheme, administering State Sickness Benefit in addition to their own benefits to their own members." Thus, he thought that the role of the state should be limited to coping with those large problems which private initiative could not handle.

Finally, Beveridge made two crucial assumptions without which his scheme would not work. First, he assumed full employment, since otherwise the insurance element would not work. It is quite clear from his speeches and writings that by 'full employment' he meant not only the presence of a limited number of men looking for work, but also the absence of any marked fluctuation or change in the demand for labour. If the labour market were to become too volatile with much casual and short term labour, the central element of insurance would not work.

Secondly, Beveridge assumed the rapid demise of means-tested benefits. True, under the original plan a means-tested benefit called 'national assistance' was to cover the transition period to the full

Beveridge scheme. As this became the origin of supplementary benefit the scale of the deviation from the original plan hardly needs comment!

It is important to stress that the reshaping of welfare policy at this time was influenced in a fundamental way by the experience of the 1930s and of the means test—seen as a terrible warning of the consequences of over-ambitious targeting.

Since 1945 the system has moved a long way indeed from the design of the Beveridge Report. It is now contributory in name only, with no real link at all between contribution and benefit. National Insurance has become for many, if not most, simply another tax. The importance of voluntarism in the administration of the system is minimal. Instead of a clear arrangement of a few basic benefits there is a complex web of separate payments, many of them discretionary. Not least the idea of doing away with means tests is dead and buried—the number of means-tested benefits grows all the time. In fact the present-day British welfare system resembles one of those great overgrown country houses where each generation of occupants has added another wing, until the original plan is completely concealed.

What, though, is the condition of the welfare state in Great Britain, 1986?

The present—a catastrophe in the making

Since 1945 the welfare state in Britain has developed not in accordance with any overall design but in response to the successful importuning of the Government by various pressure groups. The result is a higgledy-piggledy structure which is by universal consent a catastrophe for everyone involved—from the claimants to the almost equally unfortunate ministers and civil servants who have to run and answer for the mess.

The human consequences of the present system are enough to give anyone pause. By general consent, among all shades of the political spectrum, today's welfare state has reached a point where something drastic must be done—but what?

First though, what is the problem? Here there *is* agreement. All commentators from *Marxism Today* to the Institute of Economic Affairs proffer the same diagnosis.[9] From almost the moment when the Beveridge system was inaugurated developments have undermined its basic principles. The shift towards selective benefits has been massive, until by 1984/5 no fewer than 4,590,000 people were drawing Supplementary Benefit, 12,160,000 getting some form of housing benefit and 210,000 in receipt of Family Income Supplement—all at a cost of £10.1 billion.[10]

The contributory element, as has been said, is now a chimera with no clear link between contributions and benefits, qualification conditions which are often arbitrary and perverse and flat-rate benefits which need to be supplemented by means tested ones. The underlying fact is the spuriousness of the 'contributory' element. The state has never used the contributions, as a properly defined provident fund would, to finance future payments via investment; instead, current contributions are used to pay current outgoings. This causes particular problems for the financing of old age pensions; and has led to a shift away from flat-rate to earnings-related benefits, marking yet another departure from a central principle of Beveridge's. The welfare system which results from these movements can be criticized on at least four main grounds—the cost of the system, its organisation, its effects and its failure to adapt constructively to changed circumstances.

Cost

The DHSS is easily the biggest spending department, accounting for about 30% of all government spending. The total cost of benefits is presently about £37 billion with administrative costs of over £1.5 billion. These sums are set to rise relentlessly unless changes are made. For example, as things stand, the State Earnings Related Pensions Scheme alone will cost nearly £30 billion by the start of the next century. Consider the burden of financing such a massive expenditure. At least one historian has argued recently that the cost of the DHSS has played a central part in Britain's post-war decline.[11]

Paradoxically, however, Britain has the lowest level of benefits in Europe. The enormous sums spent are producing poor results.

The organization

Criticisms concentrate on four interlinked elements.

(a) *The system is ineffective on any criterion.*
There are many poor people in Britain, effectively barred from participation in society. The system for relieving poverty is providing only a palliative, at best, for many people. To some extent, this reflects our poor economic performance over the last 100 years. On almost every measure of economic well-being Britain does worse than other European countries.

(b) *Targeting of the system is bad.*
Benefits often fail to reach those most in need or with special needs. Those who need benefit most may not even qualify. The recent work of Julian LeGrand clearly shows that in general the better-off are gaining most from state spending.[12]

(c) *The complexity of the system would be laughable if its effects were not so miserable.*
85,000 people are needed to run it and 10,000 simply to keep National Insurance up to date. There are two methods of collecting finance, National Insurance and taxes; three different types and categories of benefit (contributory, non-contributory and means-tested) and four distinct agencies concerned in its administration (DHSS, Inland Revenue, Department of Employment and Local Authorities). People can qualify for different benefits at the same time on different criteria, can find that qualifying for one benefit excludes them from another—but maybe not always—and often have to undergo different tests at the hands of distinct agencies to obtain various payments. For most people all this is simply incomprehensible.

Collection of means tested benefits is responsible for most, if not all, this complexity. Nobody knows how many of these there are. The Government has admitted to 'over thirty'. In 1977 the National Consumer Council counted forty-five. In fact there are as many means tests as benefits; and several, particularly those which supplement Supplementary Benefit (!!), are in practice discretionary since the rules are too complex and contradictory for objective administration obeying uniform rules. Perhaps the most telling proof of the incomprehensibility is the very modest take-up of many benefits.

(d) *The lack of any defined and agreed goals and methods of operation is responsible for this incoherence.*
The system is in effect a mish-mash arising from the application of many different principles, with no single one predominant.

The effects of the system and failure to adapt

It is here that the often tragic side of the present system is found. The four main effects, acknowledged and much analysed, are:—

(a) *The poverty and unemployment traps.*
For many people the gains from taking employment are almost cancelled out by the loss of benefits, especially means-tested ones. When additional expenses such as transport and working clothes are added into the total they may well find that they are no better-off working: and indeed, may even be worse off. For those on low pay the situation is even more discouraging; gains in income can lead to loss of a whole range of means-tested benefits. Taken together with higher outgoings for tax and National Insurance this means that they may face effective marginal tax rates of over 100%, as high as 110% in some cases. Thus, many people are caged in a state of poverty by the system which is supposed to help them!

(b) *The creation of incentives for behaviour and attitudes which are highly undesirable.*
Effort, initiative and work are penalised; passivity and lack of will are rewarded. Administration of many benefits is highly paternalistic, undermining individual responsibility for, and control of, many aspects of claimants' lives. People can escape the consequences of actions which are by any reasonable definition irresponsible; yet attempts to act in a responsible manner can lead to loss of entitlement to benefit and of income. A 'nanny' syndrome is created in which individuals surrender their autonomy and become dependents of the state which then keeps them, albeit in a very poor condition. This has led some left-wing critics to argue that the covert purpose of the system is to control the poor and prevent their acting in any directed or organised fashion.

(c) *The creation of a class of permanent state dependents excluded from the normal workings of society and existing in a marginal half-world on surreptitious casual work.*
OECD statistics reveal that in Britain 40% of the unemployed have been so for over a year; and that these unfortunates tend to be geographically concentrated in 'communities of welfare'. Often it seems they have little or no hope of escaping from their unemployment traps. Authors hesitate to name this class but there is one old and descriptive word available; paupers. In any case their situation is

desperate. As Bill Jordan puts it in his work *Paupers*[13] "Once a man has taken the dive down into the claiming class, it requires a tremendous leap to get him back into the working class again. If he qualifies for Family Income Supplement, rent rebates, exemptions from prescription charges, free school meals and all the other selective benefits, there is no incentive for him to earn a few pounds—just to lose all these benefits again. If he becomes unemployed, it will take a job with wages several pounds above the one he previously held to tempt him back into work of his own accord again. A family can join the claiming class at the stroke of a Whitehall pen, but nothing but a major increase in its earnings can put it back into the working class again."

Quite apart from the obvious social and political dangers, the waste of talent and degree of unhappiness involved are, quite simply, intolerable. It is clear that several serious errors made by the State have contributed to this human disaster (especially failures in public sector housing and education). At the root of these failures is the creation of a welfare system whose machinery has trapped many individuals in a position where they *cannot* help themselves, and are dependent upon the often capricious workings of an impersonal yet paternalistic state.

(d) *The confusion of public attitudes towards welfare policy and benefits.* The survey undertaken as part of the Government's Green Paper revealed a formidable degree of ignorance. Thus 45% of respondents thought "that more than half of their National Insurance contribution went towards the NHS" (the actual figure is one tenth). Few people knew how means-tested benefits worked; only 27% could identify Supplementary Benefit; only 16% knew that housing benefit was means-tested.[14] Not surprisingly only those who had recently been unemployed had much idea about the rules governing Supplementary Benefit; not surprisingly, too, respondents' attitudes to particular benefits varied according to whether or not they received them themselves. Thus state support to families with children was supported 69% to 29% by those receiving it, but opposed 52% to 39% by retired people.[15]

In contrast, help to the elderly enjoyed strong support amongst all groups. From this and other surveys no clear consensus emerges for any particular kind of welfare system; only some mild, general approval—and there is strong support for individual benefits from the beneficiaries themselves. Taken together with widespread lack of

knowledge about the system, this suggests that opposition to particular changes can be mobilised quickly but that it will be very hard to
create any large coalition for fundamental reform.

That general ignorance, and individual enjoyment, of benefits
constitute a powerful force for inertia cannot be denied. The only
contrary indication is the widespread feeling that the system is too
complicated, and a willingness to give up other desirable features if
this is needed to get greater simplicity.

The failure to adapt

Indiscriminate giving of benefits to large aggregate groups and
sluggishness of decision-taking at the centre has led to a lack of
variety of provision, and a failure to respond to several important
social changes.

(a) *Over the last twenty years the profile of poverty has greatly changed.*
A generation ago its commonest feature was old age, pensioners
being the largest part of the 'low income group'. Now the largest part
of the group are couples with children. In round percentages, in
1971, of the bottom 20% by income, 35% were pensioners, 10% were
single persons of working age and 40% were couples with children.
By 1982 the corresponding figures were 19%, 16% and 47%. The
proportion of poor who fell into the categories of couples without
children and of single-parent families hardly changed, rising from
7.0% to 8.0% and 9% to 10% respectively.[16]

This change in the composition of the poor is not hard to explain.
More pensioners now have some kind of occupational pension, and
more now have considerable capital assets in the form of owned
houses which can be converted into cash or income. The main cause
of low income is now unemployment.

Couples with children are particularly hard hit because their care
costs a lot. In a household with children at least one parent (almost
always the mother) cannot enter the labour market proper and is
confined to low paid work. Only if a job is paid well above average
will the income cover the cost of near full-time child care. If both
parents are unemployed the care of children makes it even more
difficult to earn a high enough income to escape the poverty trap.
The system however has not responded to this change, and old age
pensioners are still taking the biggest slice of the cake. The implica-

tions of SERPS in an unreconstructed form were that this slice would become even larger, barring very large increases in overall spending.

(b) *Another problem to which the system has not responded is that of adolescents, especially young men.*
This is a group of indeterminate status. Nobody is clear whether they are adults responsible for themselves, dependents whose parents or guardians are responsible for them or something in between. What is lacking is one clear age of adulthood: sexual consent comes at 16, voting at 18. Good reasons for this there may be but the absence of established principle has awkward consequences. For demographic reasons the number of adolescents has never been higher than today, posing major problems for employment and training.

The welfare system has worked neither on the basis that these young people should be helped directly as responsible individuals nor on the basis that any aid to them should be channelled via families or guardians. Instead there has been an indeterminate mixture of the two, complicated by the way much employment legislation works in practice (and often design) to shut young people out of the job market.

(c) *Lastly and most seriously, the nature of work has changed, and still is changing, radically.*
Since the mid-1960s the number registered as unemployed has risen throughout the OECD countries in a steady, remorseless fashion. What is happening is not a mere matter of a cyclical 'downwave' nor is it evidence of a mass slump, but rather a fundamental change in the pattern of work and employment, of which the rising rate of registered unemployment is only one part.

Several other phenomena are concomitant with the rise in unemployment—other facets, as it were, of the same complex process. Simplified, this can be seen as a reversion to an older organisation of production at a higher level of technology. Although the amount of work may remain the same or even increase, it is performed in a very different way from that to which we have been used. All Western economies are moving to a much more flexible form of both work and production. This means that more part-time work is done, more work on short term or fixed term contracts, and more casual work. The labour force is being divided into a periphery of casual and part-time workers and a much smaller core of permanent employees, often highly paid. All this goes together with organizational change: a great expansion of subcontracting, and a tendency towards production in smaller, decentralised units, often a household or a small local workshop. Self-employment in all the OECD countries has risen, in Britain faster than elsewhere.

Between 1979 and 1984 the number of self-employed rose by 31% to 2,494,000 or just over 9% of the working population—the highest figure since 1921.[17] More and more people are earning an income which is irregular and fluctuating, unlike conventional wages and salaries. The most obvious sign of these changes is the growth of what is usually called the black economy, its size impossible to measure, but agreed by all to be very large and growing. Estimates range from 2.5% to 10% of the British GNP. It is often argued that this 'off the books' production, distribution and exchange is simply a response to high taxation; but that argument overlooks the nature of most 'black' work which tends to have the features described above.[18]

More probably many of these changes are happening in a furtive, concealed manner because the tax and welfare system is based upon out-of-date assumptions about the nature of work and production. If taxes were lighter they would still happen, but overtly and more efficiently.

Finally, most of the new jobs created in the last three years have been going to women. This important economic change is congruent with the shift to part-time working and domestic production.

The assumptions of most economic policy are that the average worker is male, is employed, has one job, has a permanent job, will have one job for the greater part of his working life and will be paid a regular monthly/weekly salary or wage. The emerging reality is that the average worker will be female as often as male, will have a portfolio of part-time jobs or be self-employed, if unskilled will have casual employment, will have many different occupations in the course of a working life and will have an irregular income—not necessarily a low one. In many ways this is a reversion to an older kind of economy, of the kind historians have come, misleadingly, to call 'proto-industrial'. We must realise that the pattern of work and employment which we take for granted is comparatively recent, becoming general only during the 1880s.

To sum up, implications for the welfare system are far-reaching. A system designed for old patterns of work will have great difficulty handling the economy which is now developing. The clear dividing line between employment and unemployment is becoming blurred with many people in a grey intermediate area of casual and part-time employment. At present their activities, penalised by the system, are driven underground. Several of the changes we have outlined will, for better or worse, greatly affect family relationships and relations between men and women, so undermining many unexamined assumptions on which our present welfare system is based. With increasing numbers not 'employed' in the traditional sense, raising of income tax is going to become harder and harder: this will apply to other kinds of statutory deduction too, such as National Insurance.

Finally, the present system is costly, ineffective, far too complicated, has many damaging side effects, has been unable to respond to changing demand, and is being fundamentally undercut by economic change. So much is agreed—what then needs to be done, what should be done and what can be done?

The Government's response: step-by-step or big bang?

In its second term of office the present Government undertook a total review of welfare provision, resulting in the Green Paper in June 1985 and the White Paper in December of that year. Everyone should be grateful that the Government has had the courage to open and examine this can of worms, and start a serious debate on policy. Much of the Green and White Papers is unexceptionable, some is praiseworthy, but the overall impression gained of the Government's strategy is disturbing, suggesting a state of profound pessimism, even despair, over prospects for radical reform. Yet it is clear that the Government is well aware of the extent and depth of most of the problems.

Some of the measures proposed in the Green and White Papers are undeniably welcome—the proposed reduction in the number of benefits and thereby simplification of the system particularly so. The Government also deserves much credit for trying to tackle the horrendous problem of SERPS, given that the bills for this programme are not going to be presented until the next century. But it is most regrettable that, under pressure from the pensions industry, the Government has drawn back from its initial, radical proposals. Nevertheless, at least a start has been made.

In general, however, the Papers are better at diagnosis than at prescription. The Green Paper contains a wealth of information and sets out most of the problems clearly enough. And it is clear, too, about the overall goals of the exercise—simplification of the system, concentration of help where it is needed, provision of incentives to work. But the changes proposed are too limited and not radical—certainly not in the strict sense of going to the root of the matter.

The papers are not convincing about the methods needed to achieve the goals they set. In particular they do not address the central problem of how to use a means test to direct aid to the 'needy' without producing the consequences experienced in the 1930s (and indeed today). The problem is the likely contradiction in practice between the use of a targeting mechanism on the one hand and the provision of incentives to work on the other. The trouble, as we know, is that if help is concentrated on a specific test-defined group, a person who moves out of the group may find himself no better off.

The White Paper emphasizes the need for cash relief to be given to groups or individuals in special need. There is no doubt that the administering of general benefit (e.g. Supplementary Benefit) through the same part of the system as is used for special payments for particular or short term needs is not satisfactory. The Government's solution, outlined in the fourth part of the White Paper, is the creation of the Social Fund.

As a short to medium term response to the problem, pending more fundamental reform this has superficial attractions; but the long term consequences could be very deleterious and the operation of the fund would introduce a most dangerous principle into the welfare system. Problems involved in running such forms of 'particular' relief through a State bureaucracy are acute and ultimately insoluble. Because it is envisaged that the State would have a near monopoly of this kind of relief, pressure would be overwhelming to define criteria governing its giving. Otherwise the system would be intolerably arbitrary. Yet use of rigid rules is what this proposal seeks to avoid! They are seen to be as undesirable as the exercise of arbitrary judgements. The dilemma, for a state system, seems inescapable.

By contrast, when charities administer aid of this type, as they did for most of the 19th century, an element of choice is introduced both for the recipients and for the donors who are free to decide which specific groups and circumstances they wish to see helped.

The underlying assumptions of the Fund are paternalistic. A class of people is seen to exist who may require to be granted help by a superior authority which can judge whether or not their need is 'real'. In fact this proposal would revive one of the central features of the old Poor Law which was severely criticised in the 1834 report—the use of *ex gratia* payments on a discriminatory basis. The Papers rightly identify a problem but the proposed solution is dangerous.

Another weakness of the Government's proposals is that they do not take likely long-term economic change into account. For example, one of the Fund's roles would be to provide cash to people suffering from problems of cash flow. This would indeed meet a definite need, but, given the new patterns of work outlined above, the demand for such a type of relief could become enormous. The 'normal' type of labour market and organisation of production is taken for granted by the papers. Many of their proposals will be overtaken by events. The need for change in areas such as unemployment relief will soon become acute. As said earlier, it is changes in economic life which are the cause of many of the system's problems. Failure to recognise the inevitability of change will lead to inadequate response.

What, though, *does* the Government envisage? The Papers are reticent about the institutional nature of the 'reformed' system; but reading between the lines we can discern the rough outlines of a model towards which the Government wishes to move. Ultimately, the creation of a three-part system seems to be envisaged, consisting of basic flat rate benefits financed at least nominally by contributions, consolidated means-tested cash benefits to supplement the income of clearly defined groups of 'needy', and the Social Fund to meet special and short-term needs. Earnings related pensions are treated separately.

This kind of model presumes basic policy decisions, most notably:
a) retention of a contributory element; and
b) an attempt to devise a means test to target the main non-contributory benefits.

Why then does the Government not announce something on these lines? And present at least an outline of any 'grand design' which it is forming?

The answer, perhaps, is to be found in the political tactics favoured by the Government which underlie the Green and White Papers; tactics of step-by-step change. This has three elements: to embark upon a series of reforms, none very dramatic in themselves, which when taken together over time amount to a fundamental change of direction; to enact these reforms in such a way as to take advantage of institutional inertia, and make them difficult to reverse; and to create a momentum in a particular direction so that (it is hoped) subsequent administrations will find themselves locked into the gradual process of change. This seems a subtle way of enabling fairly drastic reforms to be put through by a kind of political game of grandmother's footsteps.

Alas, in the area of social policy these tactics are mistaken. Objections are manifold. Fundamentally, the tactics *maximize* opposition to change. It may well seem to a harassed minister that to go for a root-and-branch reform is folly—why provoke all the voters at once? When changes however are made piecemeal each individual change provokes opposition both from those directly affected and from those who fear that their turn will be next. Thus the opposition is long drawn-out, becoming ever more intense. A process of continuous debate exhausts the political will of the ministers and their supporters, and leads to the formation of 'blocking coalitions' of interest groups. In practice a series of concessions to the opposition are made on an essentially *ad hoc* basis; with the result that the powerful have their privileges preserved, and the weak lose out.

Thus, radical reform is made more difficult since to make the process at all manageable so much has to be left untouched. It is very hard to keep the ultimate goal in sight. The effect of pressure from lobbies is so to amend measures that arrows fly wide of their target. The tactics of step-by-step change make it almost impossible to mobilise a majority for any real reform. Yet such reform can be carried through if a large plan is put into public debate, as was done with the Beveridge Report or the Poor Law Report of 1834. A consensus can be reached upon the answers, if fundamental questions are set out at the very start. For it is essential that a consensus be created, no matter how hard this may seem to be. It is a fact of history that no long lasting reforms have been made in welfare policy without one. A consensus *can* be created. In the 1820s there was intense debate over poor law reform, but by the 1840s the New Poor Law of 1834 was accepted.

The tactics of 'big bang', the large one off change, is not lightly to be undertaken. But such tactics do stand a better chance of breaking through the deadlock of interest groups than does the step-by-step approach. Before they can be set afoot, however, a measure of agreement, however vague, must be established on the definition of poverty, and on the overall purpose of the system. At present no such agreement exists. It is this lack which more than anything stands in the way of the necessary radical changes. What then are the elements from which a consensus might be created, and what kind of reformed welfare system is a possible outcome?

The way forward—definitions and proposals

One thing is certain—proposed solutions to the problems of the welfare state are plentiful. These fall into four broad categories which will be looked at separately. But the first step must be to define poverty/need. The ground here is shifting. The once-fashionable tendency to define it in relative terms is losing support.

'Relative deprivation' meant categorising a set proportion of the population as poor. The disadvantages of such a definition are obvious. Barring a state of almost total equality, it would mean the poor must be 'always with us'. There will after all always be some who are 'deprived' relative to others and hence under this definition poor. Assertions which such a definition leads to are ridiculous, such as that a person in a state of relative comfort in a developed nation is poor—while using the same word of someone in Africa who lacks the means of subsistence. To make equivalences of that sort is offensive and intellectually disreputable. The result is to rob the concept of poverty of any objective meaning at all.

Fortunately this definition is losing ground. Another which is still popular calls into aid the term of 'multiple deprivation'. Thus if you have a combination of bad housing, no television, no inside toilet, and inadequate diet and clothing then you qualify as poor. This idea still has two drawbacks. Some of these deprivations may sometimes be voluntary: a few people still choose not to have a television. But should one ever define a term by its effect? People are poor *not* because they live in such bad conditions. They suffer the conditions because they are poor. Poverty in other words means lack of money.

Despite all the ink spilt on this point the best definition is still that given by Rowntree in the 1890s.[19] This involves defining a level of income necessary to maintain a minimum acceptable standard of living. Anyone whose income falls below this level is called poor. Of course the acceptable level will probably rise over time, but the definition is still the most objective available. It also enables us to discover how many poor people there are, and why they are poor, whereas the 'relative' definition will lead to a constant proportion of the population being classed as poor while 'multiple deprivation' will make it impossible to discover why (and if) people are poor in the ordinary sense of the word.

Using Rowntree then as the means of defining poverty the next step is to discover what are the causes of poverty now, and what they are likely to be in the future.

Here we are on much more uncertain ground. It may sound strange, but we do need more research on the causes of poverty in contemporary Britain. True, the work done for the Green and White Papers helps. Low income in modern Britain has four main causes;

old age, formerly the main one but now tending to diminish in importance; long term factors such as chronic illness or disability which exclude a person from paid work; unemployment and low pay. The last two are by far the most important and present trends if continued will make them even more so.

The poor of Britain will probably consist more and more of some elderly, an indeterminate number of those unable to find work, a fairly large number of people on low casual pay and—from time to time—people who, in the more flexible labour market of the future, have a temporary, but perhaps in some cases recurring, shortage of immediate cash. The needs, which the Government has clearly identified, are to provide long term support for the elderly and other groups such as the disabled, to supplement the incomes of those on low pay or earnings and to provide support and help for those facing a temporary crisis. But what should be the goal behind the fulfilment of those needs?

The definition of relative deprivation implies that the goal is to diminish differentials of wealth and income. As said, the signs are that this is being abandoned as the fundamental purpose of the system—even by many on the left. Is it possible (taking the objective definition of poverty as the starting point) to agree that the fundamental goal of a welfare system should be to ensure a minimum standard of living for all, a floor through which no one can fall? And that the next goal should be to give special help to groups particularly in need? And that, all in all, fulfilment of these two goals would be tantamount to the abolition of poverty?

This should be done in a way which makes the most of individual responsibility and choice, and enhances self-determination. Again, this kind of general end should command wide support. A corollary here is that the role of discretionary state power should be minimised. The State must become not a provider or paternalistic protector, but a liberator which gives individuals a capacity to do things and participate in the market economy *but no more*. If they do not take advantage of the floor—of the capacity which the State has ensured— then their failure will not be the responsibility of the public authority. The recent rhetoric of the leader of the Labour Party suggests that he and others in that part of the spectrum are starting to think in this direction.

What specific proposals are put by various bodies and people to achieve these broadly defined goals? As has been said before plenty exist, but the proposed schemes can conveniently be segregated into about four camps; social dividend, income supplement, insurance and the least mentioned yet most promising, mutual aid.

Social dividend

The idea of a social dividend has a long history—it was advocated by J S Mill 150 years ago—but has always been rejected on the ground spelt out earlier. Even so it still has many advocates and does present a truly radical solution to the problems of welfare in modern society. At the same time that the Beveridge Report was being debated in 1943 Lady Rhys-Williams produced a fully-worked-out proposal for such a scheme in her work *New Look at British Economic Policy*. This advocacy has been continued by her son, Sir Brandon Rhys-Williams, most notably in a pamphlet written for the Conservative Political Centre in 1967 entitled *The New Social Contract*. The Liberal party has given much support in recent years for such a policy—for example in a document brought out in 1983 entitled *Each According To . . . The Liberal Plan for Tax and Social Security* by Philip Vince. There is also support on the left for a social dividend with the libertarian socialist author Bill Jordan a long standing advocate, especially notable being his most recent work *The State: Authority and Autonomy*. Support has also come from other groups such as the Claimants Union and the National Council for Voluntary Organisations.

All these propose the payment, without a means test or contributory rule, of a flat rate universal benefit which would replace all existing benefits. The most careful and well worked out proposal is that put forward by Hermione Parker in a publication of the Social Affairs Unit in 1983 entitled *Action on Welfare*. In brief, she outlines a scheme with the following features.[20]

(a) All adults get a basic income, paid weekly and tax free, set at a level sufficient to meet basic needs, housing only being excepted.

(b) Children under the age of 16 get a lower basic income which in all but very exceptional circumstances is paid to the parent(s).

(c) The recipient unit is the individual rather than the household.

(d) All existing benefits are abolished, consolidated into the one single benefit. This comprehends the flat-rate old-age pension, unemployment benefit and sickness benefit and all means-tested benefits including Supplementary Benefit. It also replaces student grants, training allowances and other payments.

(e) The tax system is integrated with the benefit system and radically reformed. All allowances and reliefs are scrapped. The social dividend is an individual tax allowance for taxpayers replacing the old allowances.

(f) All extra income on top of the allowance is taxed. Alternatively there is a small additional allowance so that people can supplement their income to some degree before incurring tax. (This however would make the scheme much more expensive.)

(g) In addition to the basic income extra payments are made to expectant mothers, elderly, infirm and disabled.

(h) Income tax and National Insurance are consolidated into a single tax.

(i) The most awkward question is that of housing costs. Parker, very reluctantly, allows for a means-tested housing benefit which at the basic income level would pay a housing allowance plus rates, rent and water rates. This would be tapered off with extra income. The aim would be eventually to abolish this means-tested element and consolidate the payments into the basic income, but this would require major changes in local government finance and other areas.

In her work Parker outlines three slightly different schemes with varying implications for costs and taxation rates. For example, with a personal basic income of £18.60 a week, £13 a week for each child under 16, an extra £23.65 a week to invalids and over 64s rising to £28.65 for those over 84 plus the means-tested housing component the total cost is about £70 billion, and tax rates start at 40% with rates of 45% at average earnings, and a top rate of 60%.

There are other ways of arranging the scheme. Thus a low personal basic income of £9 per week with the other payments much the same gives a total cost of about £50 billion and starting tax rate of 36%, while a medium personal basic income and a ceiling of three children getting benefit would give an overall cost of about £58 billion, and a starting tax rate of 34%.

Several considerations apply to all such schemes. There is no means test for the social dividend. The contributory principle is abandoned for state welfare. The distinction between employment and unemployment is removed, in fact the very notion of unemployment is abolished. The schemes are individualistic in both their workings and their effects. The crucial ideas are universality and certainty, with the contingent elements of means testing or administrative discretion removed.

A social dividend scheme would enjoy several major advantages—especially in present circumstances.

1. Poverty in its objective sense is abolished. Some individuals may become poor through improvident behaviour or personal failings such as gambling or drunkenness but they are made personally responsible rather than becoming a charge on society at large—since the public liability is discharged via the basic guaranteed income.

2. Paradoxically, in view of the element of universality, such a system can improve targeting to help the most needy. Schemes like Parker's provide automatic aid to the specially deserving and this kind of policy leaves room for extra provision to particular groups or cases (though not perhaps by the State). In particular her scheme would give most assistance to young couples with children whom the Government have identified as the most deserving group.[21]

3. Individual autonomy and self-direction are brought to the fore. As the benefits are all in cash the individual is left to decide how to use it and bears the responsibility for that use. The system does not distinguish between individuals by status (e.g. married or unmarried) and contains no element of moral judgement or social control. These are seen as not being the responsibility of the State, at least not in its welfare role.

4. The social dividend removes the poverty trap and, it can be argued, the unemployment trap as well (see below).

5. The State, having exercised its responsibilities through the basic income guarantee, is free to withdraw from the direct provision of welfare services, thus allowing the much greater efficiency and variety of market provision.

6. A social dividend means that the economy and labour markets in particular can work more effectively and adapt more quickly to the changes outlined earlier. The kind of economy emerging at present is one where the major welfare need is for a secure basic income, given the fluctuating nature of earnings from work. A social dividend achieves this and makes possible a much more flexible use of labour and capital.

7. Consequently, it goes a long way towards eradicating the black economy (an increasingly severe problem for governments) the cost of which is considerable, not least due to the effort of trying to police it. And the existence of the 'underground sector' means that businesses in the 'aboveground sector' are often faced with unfair competition.

8. A social dividend would make the welfare system much simpler and easier to understand; and cut the administrative costs of a system of overlapping and contradictory means-tested benefits.

9. Politically, such a reform could command wide support because it is advocated by people of widely differing political allegiances. Easily understood, it could be 'sold' to a wide section of the public across the political boundaries.

The objections however are essentially those outlined earlier, together with a number of other specific ones. The main objection is cost, the sums involved being very large indeed. Such schemes would however replace all—or nearly all—the existing state benefits and also the whole of the 'middle class welfare state' of tax breaks such as mortgage interest relief, and of subsidies such as those paid to southern commuters. These are expensive, inequitable and harmful even to the recipients. The increase in cost of a social dividend would thus be less than one might suppose.

Another objection is that the scheme would lead to higher taxes. But remember that in 1983 the starting rate of tax when National Insurance was included was 39%. To argue that NI is different is to ignore the total collapse of the 'insurance' element. The tendency has been steady in recent years for the burden of taxes and contributions to fall more heavily on those with lower or average earnings, making the system increasingly regressive. Certainly administrative implications such as the uniting of tax and social security are formidable, but computerisation of PAYE will make them easier. It is true that a social dividend would give money to the better off but they would pay more tax; so that this can simply be accepted as a cost to be traded off against the gains.

But the classic objection is that it would erode work incentives. Some people would choose not to work; though this, too, can be seen as a trade off (even an advantage in some economic circumstances). In any case most people appear to want and need work for non-financial reasons which would still apply.

The one major practical difficulty concerns the level of the basic income; if set too high the cost would be prohibitive but if set too low then some kind of means-tested assistance would become necessary, so defeating the object. The art would be to strike a balance, while using some system other than state benefit to make up any shortfall (see below).

Income supplement

The next major group of proposals are for various kinds of income supplement. They all include the crucial feature of a method for a) supplementing the cash incomes of those whose income falls below a critical level and b) tapering off this supplement as incomes rise. The commonest proposal is a 'negative income tax' where people below a threshold are paid by, rather than pay, the Inland Revenue. Such schemes are often linked to the introduction of rigorous testing in the administration of benefit.

The two most reckonable schemes are those advocated by the Institute for Fiscal Studies in *The Reform of Social Security*, and by Professor Patrick Minford in his recent book *Unemployment: Cause and Cure*. (A similar scheme to his is also suggested by the Adam Smith Institute in the relevant portion of *The Omega File*.[22]) All share the central element, referred to above—that is, the proposal that means tested benefits should be replaced by a negative income tax which pays money to those below an income threshold, with a taper to preserve some incentive. In addition Professor Minford proposes two other measures: a) the imposition of a 'cap' on unemployment benefits so that they do not exceed 70% of average earnings, thus fixing the replacement ratio and creating a strong incentive to take up employment; and b) the creation of a 'workfare' scheme on the lines adopted in parts of the United States whereby after a period of time people are not entitled to benefit unless they take a job from a 'workfare' pool.

Again these proposals have several attractive elements:

1. All people are brought up to a particular minimum income level.

2. As in the case of the social dividend, personal responsibility is enhanced.

3. The cost, while greater than the present system initially (see the Adam Smith Institute's comments) is much less than that of the social dividend.

4. The targeting of relief is much improved by the use of income tax assessment as the single and universal means test. The use of a taper means that the universality of a social dividend is avoided.

5. The unemployment trap is removed, by the 'cap' and the use of 'workfare'. This should lead, in Professor Minford's view, to a substantial fall in the number of unemployed.

6. The system is made much simpler. As with social dividend, the social security and taxation systems are merged. National Insurance is consolidated into taxation with the employer's contribution being abolished.

7. The system would be much easier to administer than the present mess.

The disadvantages, however, are serious. Primarily, it is exceedingly difficult to devise a taper to the income supplement which does not make the problem of the 'poverty trap' even worse. Under a negative income tax, as a person's income rises towards the threshold the income supplement is progressively withdrawn. However, if this is done on a pound for pound basis then extra income from work or higher pay brings no net benefit. All proposals therefore suggest that the supplement should be tapered off more gradually, with only a certain proportion being withdrawn as income rises. The difference provides an 'incentive element'. If this 'incentive element' is too large then the targeting effect of the negative income tax is lost and its cost rises sharply. However, if it's moderate, then, given the hidden costs and disutility of work, there is no effective incentive for those below the threshold to get employment or improve their earnings.

The great danger is that negative income tax would create a class of people with low incomes, dependent upon the supplement and with no incentive to try to raise their incomes above the threshold. This would mean the creation of a *distinct* sub-class of casual workers dependent upon state *support* and effectively unable to escape.

The historical precedents are not encouraging. Cash or other supplements to income were a major feature of the old Poor Law in the last 40 years of its operation before 1834 and the effect then when used in an economy in flux was low wages, rising Poor Rates and the creation of a substantial class of paupers, so provoking the 1834 Report.

Insurance

A third possibility is, in effect, to 'go back to Beveridge' and revive the idea of a strictly contributory system. In particular it might be possible to take up one variant which Beveridge considered but rejected, that used in New Zealand. Here the insurance payment takes the form of a special tax which is used only to fund specific reliefs, notably old age pensions. The special tax is voluntary in the sense that individuals can contract out of it; but if they do, they must take out equivalent private provision. One recent work arguing for a strictly contributory scheme is *The Iron Road to Social Security* by A. Parrott.[23]

Adopting a genuine contributory system would necessitate the following steps. All means-tested benefits would be abolished. In return for contributions, flat-rate benefits would be paid to particular groups, in particular the elderly, the sick and unemployed. A special charge on earnings would be paid into a separate and distinct National Provident Fund to pay for the benefits. This should be self-financing and not topped up from taxation. The Pay As You Go method of finance whereby current payments meet current outgoings (so that the working population directly supports the retired and other groups) would be phased out as rapidly as possible. All other special needs could be met by large scale expansion of private insurance.

This too has advantages over the present system. It is much simpler. It avoids relying upon an array of means tested benefits by having a few general ones. By linking benefit to contribution it shows that 'you can't get something for nothing'. The operation of the system should encourage self-help by promoting provident behaviour. It is easy to understand and to advocate. It would be easy to combine with a benefit 'cap' and a 'workfare' scheme as in Professor Minford's plan, so avoiding the unemployment trap.

Inevitably there are disadvantages as well. It is still hard to see how a contributory scheme, public or private, could cope with prolonged mass unemployment. Sooner or later, as in 1931, help would be required from general taxation. Low pay also presents a problem. If benefits are set too high then the unemployment and poverty traps will stay in place—yet if benefits are too low they will not be enough to take their recipients out of a state of poverty. So the level is critical, and some kind of extra provision is needed. If by the State then we are back where we started. Also the problem remains of those who cannot pay the contributions for whatever reason.

The other great difficulty concerns the behaviour of the State. The political temptation to abandon the reality of the contributory principle while maintaining the appearance is overwhelming (as is the tendency to move to PAYG). The USA social security system provides a salutary warning.

Mutual aid

The strategy which has received the least attention is mutual aid. Indeed no works exist, so far as this writer knows, which advocate a major role for this type of relief in a reformed welfare system. This is odd, since mutual aid was, in the recent past, the major form of relief in our country.

The 19th century was its great age. At one period, almost every working man was involved in some kind of society, whether in great affiliated orders like the Oddfellows or in small local or trade societies, collecting societies, burial societies and provident societies.[24] This feature of 19th century working class life has been sadly—scandalously—neglected by historians. A multitude of works has been written about the workhouses and other aspects of the New Poor Law, yet almost nothing about collective self-help, despite its evident importance in the lives of so many citizens.

In 1892 out of a working population of 7m, 3.86m were members of registered societies and 3m of smaller unregistered societies or collecting societies.[25] These societies provided a wide range of welfare services at low cost—sickness benefit, unemployment insurance, cheap medical care, funeral expenses, help for special cases, help in the shape of grants or interest-free loans given in acute need due to temporary circumstances. They were also active in health care, education, circulating libraries and what was usually called 'conviviality'. In many cases they had very low administration costs.

Many eminent Victorians believed that in time mutual aid, together with philanthrophy, would provide all the poor relief necessary. Gladstone advocated the setting up of a national benevolent society to carry out the functions of the Societies, and the leading feminists of the time, Harriet Martineau and Jessie Boucheret argued for an organised network of them to take over the role of the Poor Law. In fact radicals like Gladstone and Martineau were the strongest supporters of mutual aid, seeing it as an extension of the peoples' power.

The great advantages of mutual aid are easy to state. First and foremost it is controlled by the recipients themselves because they *are* the society or association. Customer sovereignty reigns; a society which was badly run or run on lines of which the members disapproved would—or should—cease to exist. Mutual aid thus locates power and control among the users of the system rather than among the elite or the State. That is why the Victorian élite had mixed feelings about it. It can provide relief which is flexible and varied, allowing for particular circumstances and often utilising local and personal knowledge. Spurs to financial discipline and efficiency exist.

Lastly, it has beneficial moral consequences. It promotes self-help and self-reliance and at the same time encourages sociability, responsibility, charity and concern for one's fellows.

If mutual aid was and is so marvellous then why is it not dominant today? The main historical reason is straightforward. Friendly societies were very good at providing special or short term benefits and services but they could not cope with the problems of long-term support, and in particular with the provision of a basic income. In the 1880s two problem areas emerged; support for long term or large scale unemployment and payment of old age pensions. These led the Liberal government to introduce the state insurance scheme in 1908.

The strengths and weaknesses of mutual aid complement those of the three other strategies. The State is capable of providing a basic income or standard of living whether by social dividend, income support or a contributory scheme, but has great difficulty in 'topping up' its relief or coping with special needs. With mutual aid the reverse is true. The terrible problems which the operation of a means test pose for governments do not apply to mutual aid associations.

What is to be done?

One thing is clear; the status quo is not a sensible option—not even in some amended version. The system needs radical reform. Any of the proposals outlined earlier would be an improvement on the present dogs' breakfast which the unfortunate inhabitants of the Elephant and Castle have to serve. What though would be the best strategy to follow, whether via step-by-step or 'big bang' tactics? Three aims must be set: the provision of a basic income so that a floor is established through which no one can involuntarily fall; the grant of additional help to given groups, and the meeting of special needs. State aid and mutual aid should complement each other, each sector doing what it is best at—the State providing basic support, the voluntary sector providing the rest. Thus all will be protected by the State from actual destitution while special needs will be met by social co-operation and private provision.

The demise of so many contributory systems makes them an unsuitable vehicle for the State to use for its role. Beveridge should be laid to rest. The idea of a negative income tax is certainly attractive but the problem of reconciling targeting, incentives and the abolition of the poverty trap may well prove insuperable.

The wisest policy would be a social dividend with a middling basic-income guarantee. This would replace all existing benefits, including flat-rate State pensions, and would be paid directly to each individual. A lesser payment would be made to people between the ages of fourteen and eighteen while single parents would be paid a supplement for each of the first two children. There would also be supplements for elderly, disabled and sick people, as well as expectant mothers for the last six months of pregnancy. A means-tested housing element could be avoided if reforms were made in the areas of local government finance (i.e. the replacement of rates) and housing law, particularly the abolition of rent control; but otherwise a benefit of some kind would be needed. The social security half of the DHSS would simply be abolished and the Manpower Services Commission wound up. Earnings related pensions would be totally privatized. So too would be such matters as income and mortgage protection, all of which would be provided through private insurance. (Such schemes already exist and provide better value for money than the State 'cover'.)

All income above the basic income would be taxed with a starting rate of 40%. The existing reliefs would all be abolished. So, if this were done every adult of working age would receive weekly from the Government an income of about £22.50. With this the public responsibility for their welfare would be discharged. They would be free to work or not as they chose, to take any kind of work or to take time out for further or higher education. The individual would be responsible for his own life, once having received the basic income.

All this would have far-reaching consequences. In particular such a course would greatly encourage the move to a more flexible form of labour market. The adoption of a limited social dividend would fit in with several other desirable changes and reforms such as the encouragement of self-employment and profit-sharing, more flexibility in adult education and training, reform of taxation and moves towards a wider distribution of property.

The second part of the strategy should be the greatly expanded use of mutual aid. Specifically, the matters covered by the proposed Social Fund should be handed over to the voluntary sector. Initially this could take the form of government funding of the Social Fund expenditures but the actual administration and handling of the money being done by 'recognised' bodies such as friendly societies and trades unions. This would be not unlike the scheme for sickness benefit originally proposed by Beveridge.

In the longer term the State would probably have to require that all adults be registered with a friendly society/mutual aid association or else take out private insurance. The choice of a particular policy package or organisation would be left to the individual. There would clearly be considerable variety in the type and scale of benefits paid but this should be seen as an advantage. People would be able to choose the type and extent of protection which they wanted, given their circumstances and requirements. The State would need only to prevent fraud and to set a basic qualifying minimum of benefit. This could easily be done via the existing machinery of the Registrar of Friendly Societies.

The voluntary sector would provide assistance for unexpected events such as death, funeral expenses, maternity costs, loss of income through unforeseen circumstance, special needs (e.g. special clothing or furniture), easy term loans and so forth. A move in this direction would not be too difficult. Many of the great friendly societies and orders still exist and could rapidly expand. In recent years commercial insurance companies such as Cornhill and Allied Dunbar have already developed cheap policies for income protection and provision of special need. If these were bought in bulk by a mutual aid association the cost per head would become even less. There are indeed many other services which could be provided by mutual aid such as health care, leisure, education and even protection from crime; but these lie outside the strict scope of this paper.

The consequence of these proposals would be a move away from the idea of a welfare State towards that of a welfare society, a social order where people by co-operating together both protect their own interests and help to relieve the distress of others. Such a society would be based upon the twin principles of self-reliance and mutuality, the two being, in truth, supportive of each other, not opposed to each other.

Conclusion: seven policy implications

1. SERPS should be privatized, as originally proposed.
2. Urgent steps should be taken to reform pension law and make all pensions personal and portable.
3. As a first measure National Insurance and income tax should be consolidated, and the employers' contribution abolished.
4. As a medium-term measure the number of benefits should be greatly reduced.
5. The Social Fund should take over most of the remaining means

tested and special benefits. These should however be handed over to the voluntary sector as soon as possible.

6. The aim should be to consolidate all other State benefits into a social dividend by the early 1990s. In practice this means consolidating unemployment benefit, invalidity and care benefit, flat-rate pension, housing benefit, child benefit, FIS and other payments such as student grants and training allowances. The supplementary benefit would disappear: its function of providing a basic income taken over by the social dividend (any special provisions to be met by the voluntary sector).

7. Meanwhile private insurance and mutual aid schemes should be encouraged either by grants or through the use of tax reliefs for a specified period of years (which could be wound down gradually as the social dividend is introduced).

These measures are radical, even revolutionary. It may seem naive to suppose that a modern, democratic British Government could even think of setting off down such a road. Yet, as argued earlier, the evidence of history, from Chadwick to Lloyd George to Beveridge suggests that it is *only* the radical proposals which stand any chance of success, or of gaining support widespread enough to overcome the resistance of vested interests. Creation of a consensus is essential, and must be the outcome of agreement on the moral issues and questions outlined at the start of this paper. The welfare system which we have today is morally corrupting and harms rather than helps the needy. And damages the economy—seriously—too. The idea of a welfare society of free and responsible men and women is not an impossible dream. It is one which we can grasp. Only if we turn it into reality can we as a nation escape from the trap in which we are all, rich and middling and poor, caught alike.

Notes

1. R. Mishra, *The Welfare State in Crisis: Social Thought and Social Change*, London, 1984.

2. W.N. Medlicott, *Contemporary England 1914–1964*, London, 1967, p. 249.

3. A. J. P. Taylor, *English History 1914–1945*, Oxford, 1965, p. 102.

4. N. Gray, *The Worst of Times: An Oral History of the Great Depression in Great Britain*, London, 1985, pp. 15–19, 188–9. See also the large collection of material in Manchester Studies Centre, Manchester Polytechnic.

5. Sir W. Beveridge, *Why I am a Liberal*. London, n.d., p. 74.

6. I. Bradley, *The Strange Rebirth of Liberal Britain*, London, 1985, pp. 95–102.

7. Sir W. Beveridge, *Voluntary Action*, London, 1948.

8. Sir W. Beveridge, *Why I am a Liberal*, p. 24.

9. See, for example, the comments at the start of P. Alcock, 'Welfare State—safety net or poverty trap', in *Marxism Today*, July 1985, pp. 9–15.

10. *Ibid.*, pp. 9–10.

11. C. Barnett, *The Audit of War*, London, 1986.

12. J. LeGrand, *The Strategy of Equality*, London, 1982.

13. B. Jordan, *Paupers: The Making of the New Claiming Class*, London, 1973, p. 71. See also H. Parker, *The Moral Hazard of Social Benefits*, London, 1982.

14. *Reform of Social Security*, volume 3, Background papers, Cmnd 9519, pp. 75–85.

15. *Ibid.*

16. *Ibid.*, pp. 8–10.

17. Report in *Daily Telegraph*, January 2nd, 1986; statistic derived from *Britain 1986*, H.M.S.O.

18. A. Heertje et. al., *The Black Economy*, London, 1982; P. Mattera, *Off the Books*, London, 1985.

19. P. Townsend, *The Concept of Poverty*, London, 1970 and the same author's *Poverty in the United Kingdom*, London, 1979; S. Rowntree, *Poverty: A study of Town Life*, London, 1901.

20. Lady Rhys-Williams, *A New Look at British Economic Policy*, London, 1943; Sir Brandon Rhys-Williams, *The New Social Contract*, London, 1967; P. Vince, *To Each According to . . . The Liberal Plan for Tax and Social Security*, London, 1983; K. Roberts, *Automation, Unemployment and the Distribution of Income*, Maastricht, 1982; B. Jordan, *The State: Authority and Autonomy*, London, 1985; H. Parker, *Action on Welfare*, London, 1983.

21. See *ibid.*, and Jordan, *The State*, pp. 358–9.

22. Institute for Fiscal Studies, *The Reform of Social Security*, London, 1982; P. Minford, *Unemployment: Cause and Cure*, London, 1985; Adam Smith Institute, *The Omega File*, London, 1985, pp. 313–31; C. Clarke, *Poverty Before Politics*, London, 1977.

23. A. Parrott, *The Iron Road to Social Security*, Sussex, 1986.

24. P.H.J.H. Gosden, *The Friendly Societies in England 1815–1875*, Manchester, 1961, and the same author's *Self Help*, London, 1973; D.G. Green, *The Welfare State: For Rich or Poor?*, London, 1982.

25. *Reform of Social Security*, vol. 3, Background papers, Cmnd. 9519, p. 60.

Bibliography

J. Atkinson, 'The Flexible Firm Takes Shape', in the *Guardian*, 18 April, 1984.

Sir W. Beveridge, *Report on Social Security and Allied Services*, Cmnd. 6604, HMSO, 1942.

Sir W. Beveridge, *Voluntary Action*, London, 1948.

Sir W. Beveridge, *Why am I a Liberal?*, London, n.d.

Sir W. Beveridge & A.F. Wells (eds) *The Evidence for Voluntary Action*, London, 1949.

C. Clark, *Poverty Before Politics*, London, 1977.

F. Field, *Inequality in Britain: Freedom, Welfare and The State*, London, 1981.

E. Ginsberg, 'The Jobs Problem', in *Scientific American*, January 1977.

P.H.J.H. Gosden, *The Friendly Societies in England 1815–1875*, Manchester, 1961.

P.H.J.H. Gosden, *Self Help*, London, 1982.

I. Gough, *The Political Economy of the Welfare State*, London, 1979.

D.G. Green, *The Welfare State: For Rich or Poor*, London, 1982.

A. Heertje et al., *The Black Economy*, London, 1982.

J. Higgins, *States of Welfare: Comparative Analysis of Social Policy*, Oxford, 1981.

R. Howell, *Why Work? A Radical Solution*, London, 1981.

C. Huhne, 'Conundrum of Buoyant Growth and Rising Unemployment', in The *Guardian*, 19th April 1984.

Institute for Fiscal Studies, *The Reform of Social Security*, London, 1982.

B. Jordan, *Paupers: The Making of the New Claiming Class*, London, 1973.

B. Jordan, *Freedom and the Welfare State*, London, 1976.

B. Jordan, *The State: Authority and Autonomy*, London, 1985.

B. Jordan, 'The Social Wage: A Right for All', in *New Society*, 2 April, 1984.

J. LeGrand, *The Strategy of Equality*, London, 1982.

P. Mattera, *Off the Books*, London, 1985.

J. E. Meade, 'Poverty in the Welfare State', in *Oxford Economic Papers XXIII*, 1972, pp. 289–326.

P. Minford, *Unemployment: Cause and Cure*, London, 1985.

R. Mishra, *The Welfare State in Crisis*, London, 1984.

C. Offe, *The Crisis of the Welfare State*, London, 1983.

H. Parker, *The Moral Hazard of Social Benefits*, London, 1982.

H. Parker, *Action on Welfare: Reform of Personal Income Taxation and Social Security*, London, 1983.

A.L. Parrott, *The Iron Road to Social Security*, Sussex, 1986.

Lady Rhys-Williams, *A New Look at British Economic Policy*, London, 1943.

Sir Brandon Rhys-Williams, *The New Social Contract*, London, 1967.

K. Roberts, *Automation, Unemployment and the Distribution of Income*, Maastricht, 1982.

J.J. Rosa (ed.) *The World Crisis in Social Security*, London, 1982.

S. Rowntree, *Poverty: A Study in Town Life*, London, 1901.

A. Seldon, *Wither the Welfare State*, London, 1981.

R. Shutt, *The Jobs Crisis: Increasing Unemployment in the Developed World*, Economist Intelligence Unit, 1980.

R. Sugden, *Who Cares?*, London, 1983.

P. Townsend, *The Idea of Poverty*, London, 1970.

P. Townsend, *Poverty in the United Kingdom*, London, 1979.

P. Vince, *To Each According to . . . The Liberal Plan for Tax and Social Security*, London, 1983.

The Reform of Social Security: volume 1, Cmnd 9517; volume 2, Programme for Change, Cmnd 9518; volume 3, Background Papers, Cmnd 9519; Reform of Social Security: Programme for Action, Cmnd 9691 (1985).

7

Pensions and Privileges: How to End the Scandal, Simplify Taxes and Widen Ownership

Philip Chappell

Foreword

It happened inadvertently, it was not premeditated and the consequences were unforeseen—but giving pension funds tax exempt status has led to the greatest shift of ownership from individuals to institutions since the opposite happened at the time of the Dissolution of the Monasteries.

And the process is accelerating. Yet it runs clean contrary to a fundamental principle of Tory philosophy, namely that the diffusion of economic power, and the multiple sources of patronage which flow from it, are prerequisites of a free society.

So the process must be reversed before it is too late. Philip Chappell advocates two steps made possible by the Government's introduction of personal and portable pensions. The first is that any individual should have an annual right to transfer his fair share from an institutionally administered pension fund into a Personal Option Pension. Such a unitisation of funds would, at no extra cost, begin to turn what is now nobody's money back into somebody's money. The institutions would become administrators, not owners.

A good step. But it would not go far enough. At present huge

161

transfers of assets from the working to the non-working are hidden under a panoply of fiscal privilege and cross subsidies that few citizens are aware of. So the paper calls for a new transparency in tax and social security arrangements. It demonstrates that, by removing tax exemption from all future pensions saving, the general levels of tax could drop dramatically: and that most other tax privileges would then become irrelevant. With the consolidation of many minor taxes, and the abolition of all higher rate income tax, the tax law becomes hugely simplified.

From this base, and from an enhanced national old age pension, the individual would be encouraged to save as he pleased. Such a move would have a double benefit. It would lower the desperate social barrier of the poverty trap. And it would relate additional retirement provision to the initiative of personal saving rather than the chance of working history. As an educated citizenry struggles from the bonds of state paternalism, Personal Option Pensions and tax reform would enable everybody to keep a higher proportion of their earnings and develop an understanding of the capital which already (but invisibly) underpins their future.

Because pensions are so complex a subject, their immense influence on our economic and social structure does not secure them the attention they deserve. Philip Chappell, in this pamphlet, 'thinks the unthinkable'. Not for the first time the Centre for Policy Studies, through its Studies and Challenges, is one step ahead of contemporary wisdom.

NIGEL VINSON
Chairman, Wider Ownership Group

The main themes

The number of shareholders in Britain has grown dramatically in the last five years, but the proportion of equities held by individuals continues to decline. British pension funds are continuing to grow, far faster than net personal wealth, and are 'crowding out' the private investor. Pension funds are also far more dominant in Britain than in our major overseas competitors; we need a better balance between structured retirement provision and flexible, personal, thrift.

The solution is to recognise pension funds for what they really are—the property of the workforce; the first key proposal is that each member, including deferred members and pensioners, should then be given an annual opportunity to take their assessed share in their fund. It would be managed by existing institutions, but as a unitised personal and portable asset.

This leads to the second key proposal, a reconsideration of the tax relief for retirement provision, the extent of which has never been widely understood; it is the single privilege whose removal opens the way to wholesale simplification of the tax system. What started as a modest allowance to benefit the long-serving worker (probably not a taxpayer at the time) has become a major tax benefit to all employees, worth as much as 40% of salary for a senior executive.

All resources in existing funds would remain on the present gross fund basis and no-one would forego any entitlements already earned. The full changeover to the new system would take up to 40 years, giving full time for education and understanding of its effects.

All future pension contributions by an employer would be treated as a benefit-in-kind and taxable in the same way as wages; employee contributions would no longer be tax allowable.

The total flow of savings would remain largely unchanged but in due course a three tier level of retirement provision would apply:— basic State, employers' top-up, and personal arrangements.

The tax change broadens the taxable base by £25 billion and allows elimination of the higher rate of income tax. Income tax could be levied at a single flat-rate of 15%, plus 7.5% on all incomes in place of employees' National Insurance Contributions. The next major step would be to eliminate all personal allowances and reliefs, and reduce the flat-rate tax to a 10% income tax, plus a 7.5% social welfare tax. A major reform of taxes on capital is also required to ensure simplicity.

Wider ownership becomes a reality, with over £200 billion allocatable to 16 million individuals. The tax system becomes comprehensible. Those who defend the present system must be challenged with the choice:—do you prefer a panoply of privilege—or the simplicity of neutrality?

Introduction

At first sight, this paper is about pension funds and tax reform and it falls naturally into those two parts: but the underlying theme is determined by a philosophical commitment to wider ownership. Ownership is a fundamental human instinct: one which should be encouraged in any free society whose members believe in their ability to be responsible citizens, capable of making their own decisions. But ownership must be personal; only thus can it give independence to the individual and secure the dispersal of economic power and patronage. *Institutionalised* capitalism is an enemy of the open society.

Yet, apart from the important field of home ownership, post-war Britain has seen a growth in the institutionalisation of wealth: despite the commitment of the present Government to wider share ownership and the huge increase in the *number* of shareholders, the *proportion* of financial assets owned by pension funds and life assurance companies continues to grow (see Chart 1 overleaf). This trend has received too little attention. Most of us postpone thinking about retirement, and saving for retirement; our eyes glaze over; and the complexity of the present system inhibits debate. Policies about pensions have been left to the experts, while popular comment tends rather to focus on the growing proportion of the population above normal retirement age.

The results are plain to see. Most of the capital of British companies is owned by those who at best are no more than trustees. The beneficiaries, the British workforce, are uninvolved and have little understanding of the importance of our industrial success. The nature of capitalism, thrift and wealth are alien concepts to many. Phrases such as 'second-hand ownership', 'nobody's money', 'short-termism', express this criticism of the present system. The institutionalisation of pensions cloaks the reality of ownership. Nearly five years ago (17 September 1983) the *Economist* commented:—'Secure in their tax breaks, the investment philosophy of the new breed of City Barons, the investment managers of the big institutions, mirrors the

Chart I

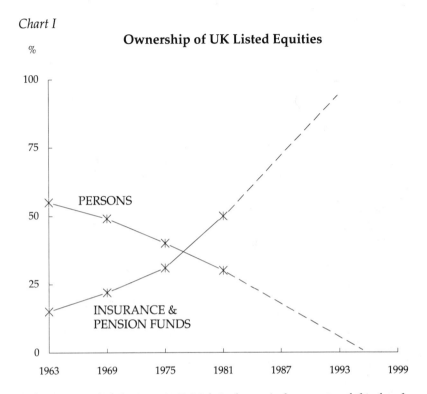

%

Ownership of UK Listed Equities

cautious attitude of many in British industry': the assets of the funds were dubbed 'civil servant assets'.

Nothing has changed in the last five years, except that the barons have extended their feoff; they have become today's equivalent of the landed gentry who resisted the repeal of the Corn Laws in the last century.

The cure does not lie in superficial suggestions to strengthen the role of the institutions as nominal owners; the preferable solution is a radical reform, returning direct ownership of pension funds to individuals. For pension funds belong to the workforce, they are not a City toy, or a tax haven for the employer. The first part of this paper addresses this issue.

The second part calls for radical reform of the tax system as it affects savings. Many people purport to favour a level playing field for all forms of saving; but the major tax privileges still given to retirement provision (and other perks beloved by entrenched interests) distort the structure. Individuals have been shrewd enough to realise these privileges and have voted with their pockets accordingly.

Marginal tax rates on income are probably unintended, and certainly not well understood; many commentators have written about employees' National Insurance Contributions, which are non-deductible and can devastate marginal incomes at the lower levels, one form of the poverty trap: for most people, earning between £105 and £305 a week NICs are now charged at nine per cent if contracted in. But fewer commentators have drawn attention to the proportion of a senior manager's remuneration which comes through employers' pension contributions and other perks on a tax free basis—a recent management consultant's report suggested that up to an additional 45% of salary was packaged in this way.

Following the 1988 Budget, a senior executive may actually pay a lower marginal rate of tax on his earned income than his junior employee. Here is an example:—

A man on average earnings, not contracted-out of the State pension scheme, will pay income tax at 25% and national insurance of 9%, a total of 34%. The marginal tax rate paid by his senior manager in a non contributory occupational pension scheme (even assuming only 20 per cent employers' contribution rate) will be 40 per cent of 120 i.e. 33.33 per cent, calculated as 40 per cent on his actual income and nil on the associated tax free perk of pension contribution.

Marginal tax rates on unearned income are perhaps even more absurd, jumping from nil to 25% with a higher rate of 40% on taxable income from £19,300.

These figures may surprise those unconcerned with fiscal reform. A prime aim of the taxation system advocated in this paper is that it should be simple and equitable, and unbiased as between earned and unearned income.

Many poverty action groups may care to note that taxes on earned income are far less progressive than often assumed. A simple, proportionate, income tax would achieve the same result, wasting nothing on special incentives and reliefs, and avoiding the problems of the so-called poverty trap.

With absurdity comes complexity and an army of advisers concerned to exploit fiscal privileges and minimise the impact of taxes. But the basic truth is that one man's tax privilege is another man's tax burden.

Complex tax systems are the up-market equivalent of providing employment by digging holes in the road and filling them up again.

Undoing the privileges given to retirement provision is the most important key to tax simplification and equity. Public understanding of the privileges given to retirement provision is slight. On one argument they are worth nearly twice mortgage interest reliefs. By removing these privileges for the future (but leaving existing arrangements intact) the way would lie open for a flat-rate income tax. In the process, all other perks and reliefs would be devalued and could be left to wither. Choice between immediate consumption and saving for retirement would no longer be influenced by fiscal privilege. The savings market would be freer. The possession of financial assets would follow the lead set by home ownership—a flexible and personal pattern adapted to the changing needs of the saver.

This paper was designed well before the global stock market realignments of October 1987. But those who sought to argue that stock market changes of this nature destroyed the arguments for personal ownership of retirement provision forgot to observe two trends.

First, the froth of the run-up, and the crash itself, might never have happened if investment policy had been in the hands of millions of individuals rather than on the screens of computers, or in the heads of global fund managers with their eyes fixed on the short-term. Second, even taking into account recent market falls, the assets of pension funds have shown a compounded annual return of about 18% for the past five years, as compared with average annual earnings increases for the period of under 8%. For most people, a Personal Pension would still have provided a far better financial return than an occupational pension based on final salary. It is a portable "pot of gold", transferable from job to job, and a claim on future wealth creation.

These two themes, unitising pensions and ending their fiscal privilege, are of course independent of each other. So the two sections of this paper stand on their own feet. They are linked together as a package to emphasise the development of personal responsibility implicit in both proposals. Wider ownership and major tax reform can win votes; they are also fundamental beliefs of anyone opposed to centralism and bureaucracy.

The 1988 Budget was a great achievement and reinforces the Government's intention to return to the individual as many as possible of the State's powers. But, as many have noticed, it has done little to remove the fiscal distortions in the savings market. Personal Equity

Plans and a diminished BES do little to offset the expensive privileges caused by the favoured status of retirement provision.

Pension funds in Britain have developed 'immoderate greatness', the prime cause (according to Gibbon) of the Decline of the Roman Empire. Further Budgets in this Parliament must tackle the need to disperse this immoderate greatness of theirs, by returning economic and financial power to individuals. Only then can the Tory vision of property owning democracy come about.

A new structure for pension funds

The shambles of retirement provisions

Arrangements for retirement in Britain do not meet reasonable aspirations—and should not require fiscal privilege to support them. Everyone is now prepared to accept that the system built up in the 1970s was inequitable, misunderstood, and inadequate to meet the needs of a more mobile workforce.

The publication in 1983 of *Personal and Portable Pensions—For All*[1] coincided with the determination of this Government radically to revise pension provision. Yet five years later the proposals in that document have been so eroded, both by those seeking to preserve entrenched positions and by the problems of taxation in a minefield of privilege, that a new initiative is urgent. 'The Muddle Over Pensions', 'Myopia About Retirement' were Financial Times headlines, not in 1980 before the present reforms, but in 1986 when the full structure of the new Social Security Act was known.

The proposals in this paper leave intact all the benefits which have accrued to individuals, use the existing structure as far as possible, but create opportunities for reform which can endure. They bring together the recognition of the individual's rights, the acceptance of a responsible employer's duties, and the growing interest (worldwide) in tax reform. Pension reform has to provide a framework which will last the lifetime of today's youngest employee, a planning period of not less than sixty years, looking ahead to social and economic conditions at present unforeseen. It would be remarkable indeed if a structure which still retains much of the feudal paternalism of the 1930s was well adapted to the different conditions of the

Retirement provision

Tomorrow's ideal, to-day's reality

		Analysis	*The Present Shambles*
1	Limit the role of the State	Since the State itself has no money, all it can do is channel resources from one group of citizens to another. In promising retirement benefits many years away, all the State is doing is committing future taxpayers to a transfer of resources: a so-called contributory system is a misnomer. Ideally, State support should be given only to the disadvantaged.	The present State pension, on its own, is inadequate to support the old in an acceptable living standard, so that an array of social security support systems is provided to supplement it. The State does pay pensions to those who may not need it, and even pays an additional pension (SERPS) to the fortunate, those who have been in employment, leaving the unfortunate to exploit the system as best they can.
2	Recognise the responsibility of employers	Private sector provision originated in the best sense of paternalism, i.e., from employers determined that at least their long-serving employees would enjoy a basic standard of living in retirement, better than that which would be available under the State system. They were also concerned to protect the families of employees who died in service. It is less clear how employers came to accept an expected obligation to maintain a standard of living in retirement which matched the income of the workforce while in employment.	The design of final salary schemes inevitably penalises early leavers—no amount of legislation on revaluing deferred benefits can avoid this basic flaw. Employers began to see pension provision as a form of golden handcuffs on their most valued employees. Problems of economic forecasting up to sixty years ahead also makes it inevitable that the actuarial requirement for funding is full of uncertainty, leading to under-funding or, more probably based on caution, over-provision; over-funding in turn leads to under-statement of corporate profitability, with all the ongoing implications for investment decisions, dividend policy, and public perception.

3	Encourage personal savings	The need to develop a wide power base of individuals, enjoying the independence that ownership of financial assets alone can provide, ought to be a prime requirement. Individuals may decide to choose a collective investment vehicle, to spread their risk, enjoy skilled management, and reduce costs; but it should never be imposed on them.	Despite the campaign to encourage personal shareholders, the increasing dominance of pension funds continues and, on all present assumptions will continue to grow. Pension funds in Britain are far more dominant than in our major international competitors (appendix E).
4	Ensure job mobility	The concept of 'career jobs' is increasingly replaced by those who believe in varied job patterns, including the ability to move in and out of the workforce, or to become a part-time employee or enjoy multiple employment. This is especially important for women wishing to leave and re-enter the workforce. Public policy should encourage job mobility.	Employers have, naturally, a vested interest in retaining their workforce, if only on the grounds of retraining costs: but they should achieve this through good employment practice, not fiscal subsidy. Present occupational schemes are well-suited to (and well-supported in public argument) 55 year olds with 35 years service and five years to retirement: only personal provision can meet the needs of mobile employees.
5	Clarify employees' understanding and involvement	If savings are to be made on behalf of an individual, there are two fundamental requirements (a) he must be kept well-informed about the nature and growth of his assets, the investment policy, the quality of any guaranteed benefit (b) he must fully understand his rights in various circumstances of death, retirement and leaving early.	Some progress has at long last been made in requiring occupational pension funds to make annual disclosure to their members of their investment policy: but no information need be given on portfolio performance or on the details of actuarial solvency. More seriously, the ultimate ownership of the fund, and any surplus it is found to contain, remains uncertain: some have argued that it belongs to the employer, as the major contributor and ultimate guarantor, others to

employees, on the basis that all contributions are deferred pay. Individuals can hardly be expected to take an interest in the successful performance of the portfolio, i.e. largely the success of the country if they cannot understand how that stake is calculated.

It is, of course, far preferable that most savings should be the direct property of the individual, so that it is accessible for his varied needs at different stages of a normal lifespan.

6　Provide fiscal neutrality for all forms of saving

An ideal tax system offers no privileges, allowances or concessions, in the full understanding that one man's tax privilege is another man's tax burden, and in the recognition that the State has no role to play in distorting personal decisions by fiscal privilege. In the real world pressure groups do secure concessions for what is seen to be socially desirable: but at the very least such concessions should be transparent, limited in amount, understood by the beneficiary and properly subject to public debate.

The fiscal privileges surrounding retirement provision are the biggest single distortion in the savings market. We suffer from the absurdity that no tax concession is available for the so-called contributory system of basic State provision (which all applaud): but occupational schemes enjoy privileges which have been little understood and are far more generous than is realised: privileges to the self-employed are also available on a less generous basis. The articulate minority are the major beneficiaries, with non taxable contributions being made to occupational schemes which may represent 40% or more of salary. Even if some modest concession might have been appropriate to encourage personal saving and ensure that the old are not a 'burden on the State', it should never have been extended to cover contributions which need only an actuarial certificate to justify their amount. £500 p.a. for all might be justified: an annual £40,000 tax free perk for a senior manager on £100,000 p.a. was surely never intended. Even worse, a senior manager receiving a salary increase in the last year of his service in excess of the actuarial assumptions will need a pension contribution of at least ten times his salary increase to fund the enlarged liability.

7 Avoid cross-subsidisation

There is an inherent objection to all forms of cross-subsidisation, at least unless all the parties fully understand and agree what is happening. In insurance, for example, a group of individuals may club together on a voluntary basis to provide mutual support against the human risk of mortality or loss of property. It is far less acceptable for an employer to impose cross-subsidies on his employees, without their even realising it is happening: in many cases not even the employer appreciates the full extent of pension costs and how they vary with age, thus reducing opportunities for the young to enter the workforce.

Cross-subsidisation is inherent in any final salary scheme and is the fundamental criticism of such a basis. But in this case it is not the strong who help the weak but exactly the opposite: the gainers from final salary schemes are the high-fliers, the married, the long-servers and the female: the losers are the majority of the workforce (there are more plodders than high-fliers), the single, the mobile and the male. It is surprising that organised labour has not yet woken up to the present inequities; in Christopher Fildes' more colourful phrase:—'trade union leaders should have a proper dislike of watering the workers' beer,' an inevitable outcome of occupational pension schemes based on final salary.

middle of the 21st century. Flexibility and personal responsibility are the key requirements of an enduring system.

Most people would probably agree on the main desirable features of retirement provision; they are set out in column 1 of the matrix above. Column 2 analyses how such objectives might be met in an ideal system and column 3 how far our present system falls short of those objectives. Heading by heading, it is a damning indictment of our present short-sightedness.

A new approach to pension provision

On almost every count the present system fails to meet the desirable objectives—and as funds grow yet more dominant, it becomes ever harder to re-construct a system which will meet the future's needs. We have to recognise the variety of expectations that have been established, on the basis of which many personal financial transactions (such as pension mortgages, however inappropriate) depend. It is clearly essential that all existing commitments in respect of employment to date, whether from the State or private sector funds, must be honoured. Criticism can be expected from those who will be calculating their personal position under the new proposals. So it is vital to emphasise that *no-one foregoes any entitlements already earned by past service.*

The State's role

The role of State pension provision is outside the main scope of this paper: on fiscal policy, however, it must be desirable that present National Insurance contributions (nearly half of which are presently dedicated to the payment of State retirement pensions) should be integrated with personal income tax, perhaps under a new title of 'Social Tax'. All earnings, and all other forms of income, would become subject to this tax: the figment of the contribution basis is abandoned, its range is extended to make it fairer, and a major simplification of the tax system, currently collected on two different systems by two different Departments, is achieved.

A fairer formula for the basic State Pension is needed, while recognising that its level must always be a matter for political agreement at the time among the voters of the day; it is they who have to be persuaded to accept the transfer of resources from the economically active workforce to the retired. It should be available to all citizens, regardless of their employment history, and related to average earnings, as a fairer reflection of the relative prosperity of the day. The amount of State pension must remain at a level where there is real incentive for the individual, on his own account or through his employer, to provide additional resource for his retirement: it follows that some level of supplemental support, and machinery to implement it, will always be required to meet the needs of the spendthrift, the disadvantaged and the unlucky.

The debates of 1985 about SERPS would be ended at a stroke by ending SERPS. The Government erred in that debate by allowing the argument to centre round future costs. They failed to take the high ground of political argument by stating clearly that, while it may be the task of the State to help the disadvantaged, it is certainly not its job to add to the advantages of those who have been employed. SERPS is part of the tradition of consensus of the mid 1970s and should be scrapped along with all the other intellectual impedimenta of that decade. It may be expensive, even when diminished through Personal Pensions, but the more effective attack is that it is inequitable, unjustified, and hopelessly complicated.

The proposed solution—Personal Option Pensions

The main structural reform calls for one simple change to pensions provided in the private sector. First it should be agreed that all past contributions to a fund are deferred pay and, therefore, that all monies in it belong exclusively, as of right, to the members. Next units in the fund should be offered to members—an easy transition.

Once-for-all unitisation of pension funds may well have been considered before. But the present proposal envisages that unitisation would be an option exercisable annually. Personal Option Pensions, with their convenient acronym of POPs, signify the opportunity for individual choice. In detail, the proposal would operate as follows:

(a) As a condition of continuing approval by the Superannuation Funds Office, each separate fund would be required to *produce a discontinuance valuation* on at least an annual basis.

(A discontinuance valuation, in outline, calculates the liabilities that would arise if the fund were to be closed at the valuation date, and measures such liabilities against the market value of the assets at that date. With modern technology, and proper pre-planning, a discontinuance valuation can be prepared both cheaply and quickly. It is a much simpler calculation than a projected liabilities valuation, since it uses market value for the assets and does not require any long-term assumptions to be made about income growth, patterns of future earnings, early leavers, or prices: it is these assumptions which cause all the difficulties in long-term pension funding. The details of such a discontinuance valuation should in any event be published, as a matter of good accounting practice, as part of a company's annual balance sheet; such a valuation, and any surplus or deficit revealed thereby, is of considerable interest to anyone assessing the value of a company).

(b) Each member of the fund, including all deferred members and pensioners, would be given *an annual benefit statement* based on this valuation: and this statement would show the individual's percentage share of the fund and its capital value at valuation date. The basis on which the individual shares were calculated would be within guide-lines established by the Government Actuary and agreed by the Trustees: mortality assumptions are the most significant risk. The essential point is that since the whole fund belongs to the members, the aggregate percentage shares must add up to 100, and the aggre-gate capital values so calculated must add up to the total market value of the fund.

(c) *The key element of the proposal is that each member, including deferred members and pensioners, would have an absolute annual right to transfer a specified percentage (not less than 95%) of his share as assessed into a segregated personal fund, in exchange for abandoning his accrued rights.* An employer could require anyone leaving the company, other than on normal retirement arrangements, to accept his assessed share and thereby lose all claim on the fund. The option could be exercised by the employee on each annual valuation, so that he would earn an annual increment to his segregated fund; but, if only for simplicity of administration, the option must be exercised in respect of all past service and the employee should not be able to maintain a partial claim on the fund. The specified percentage would be determined by the trustees, provided it is not less than 95%: the small margin leaves scope for valuation uncertainties, and is designed to allow the Trus-tees of the ongoing fund to have a modicum of uncommitted resource to aid special cases.

(d) Given present tax treatment of retirement provision, the segregated personal fund would be a gross fund, free of income and gains tax: and a pension could be drawn out of it only on normal retirement, or earlier retirement on agreed ill health grounds. But the actual retirement date selected could be flexible, on the same basis as that now available to the self-employed.

The personal funds would, therefore, be like those to be established under the new Personal Pension rules: in that sense this proposal does no more than extend to back service what has now been accepted for future service. The main difference is that, since the employer cannot know which option the employee will select each year, he must continue to contribute on behalf of all members accepted into the scheme. One of the inequities of the new Personal Pension regime is that the employer is not legally required to make any contribution at all to employees who opt out of the occupational scheme in favour of making their own personal provision. But the employer is saved the appropriate contribution to the occupational scheme; and this saving should be reflected in the employee's total remuneration. (A few private sector companies have indicated that they will make a top up payment to employees who opt for personal pensions: it is doubly unfortunate that this Government, so enthusiastic in principle to support personal pensions, has failed to set such an example of good practice in respect of its own employees.)

(e) Though there would be no real justification, the Inland Revenue would probably insist that such segregated funds be administered by an *authorised depository*, existing funds doubtless being authorised so to act. But the individual must be free to choose his depository, and transfer from one to another, provided he bears the costs of doing so. Initially, at least, there would be some constraints on investment flexibility and a minimum quantum for each individual should be held in a limited range of authorised investments (bank deposits, gilts or broadly-based investment vehicles) to ensure, for example, at least a 50% increase over the basic State pension at retirement: but those with substantial segregated funds should enjoy complete freedom of investment policy. While there would be no compulsion, those approaching retirement might choose to place a larger proportion of their portfolio in low-risk gilts or index-linked stocks, to minimise uncertainty at retirement date.

Specifically, there would be no restriction on using funds above the prescribed minimum for investment by the employee in shares of the employer's company, thus opening up huge new opportunities for widening ownership at the place of work. Problems of 'too many eggs in a single basket' cannot apply once the prescribed minimum has been met. It is patronising, and a denial of personal freedom, to say that individuals cannot understand the risks involved and should be forced into the merry-go-round of diversifying investments (an argument sometimes advanced by those whose business derives from recommending such diversification). It ignores the mounting evidence of the success of companies which enjoy a high degree of employee financial participation; there is, therefore, a public interest in encouraging employee ownership. The same principle would apply to unquoted and riskier investments: if an individual chooses to sink part of his retirement provision into his nephew's newly established software business, he should surely be encouraged to do so, not prevented by so-called superior wisdom. Let institutionalised investment be for those who want it; let those who prefer their own judgement be rid of the yoke.

(f) An employer could insist that an employee provided death-in-service, and ill-health, cover for himself or family. Or he might choose to unbundle such provision from the main pension fund, opening the way for more flexible arrangements. It would be also desirable that those faced with redundancy or special hardship, before normal retirement, should have some access to their personal fund's capital value.

(g) On retirement, no one would have to take the whole segregated fund either as an annuity or a capital commutation: an individual could choose to leave his segregated fund as a gross fund, paying income tax only on amounts withdrawn. Provision for spouses would be obligatory and a limit on annual withdrawal would be necessary to ensure that a prescribed minimum level of funds always remained: but any assets remaining at the death of an individual (as of his spouse and dependents) would accrue to his estate. There would be no objection to anyone, at any stage, placing all or part of his funds with an insurance company to spread the mortality risk: insurance companies might offer special policies that recognised the needs of long-term survivors, reversing the present pattern of term policies paying out only on death. Tontine Funds would come back into fashion, providing special protection for the longest survivors.

(h) The proposal would be extended to cover those in *unfunded schemes*, where a definite commitment to a pension accrues for each year in service: this applies mainly to state employees. If their pension right is inflation-proofed their annual benefit statement would be in the form of the right to take index-linked gilts. This has the advantage of formally recognising the cost of the notional liability which has been created, and at the same time increasing the supply of such stocks; they are the most useful measure of the market assessment of the cost of providing inflation-linked pensions, as well as providing governments with a very strong incentive to minimise inflation.

The advantages of POPs

(a) Everyone can develop an understanding about the behaviour of assets held for retirement provision. Everyone will have a direct stake in our society, want it to succeed, and can benefit visibly from the success of his investments. *Employee ownership of the wealth of Britain becomes a reality,* with all the advantages of employees' financial participation in their companies.

(b) All the arguments on early leaver entitlements, premature retirement, inflation protection, and portability become irrelevant: and job mobility is enhanced. Instead of Personal Pensions being restricted to future service, POPs open up over £200 billion to popular capitalism—an average of at least £12,500 per member (though obviously varying widely to reflect age, past service, salary pattern and family circumstances).

(c) POPs eliminate criticism of the role of institutional investors as indirect owners of UK equities; they are seen to be only managers and trustees for their beneficiaries, to whose investment decisions they must respond. (If beneficiaries support merger mania and take short-term gains, that is their business—no blame to the 'City'). Broader investment questions, eg, on ethical arguments or overseas diversification, are left to each of us to decide. If everyone is free to take his segregated funds where he will, then that is his means of criticising the investment policies of managers. Given reasonable investment flexibility for segregated funds, opportunities would emerge for backing small new firms and creating new jobs. No one denies the great support to developing companies above a certain size, given by institutional investors: but it is recognised that a gap still exists at the smallest level, where the need is for local knowledge and costs cannot be carried by a centrally-based investor.

(d) Most money would, of course, remain with the same institutions, either as part of a continuing main fund or as managers of personal segregated funds; costs and administrative saving alone ensure the latter. But at least the monopoly principle would have been broken. The change in property rights would be fundamental. The average employee would have his personal funds managed by his present institutional manager but would enjoy complete freedom to take them elsewhere if he chooses: his financial understanding would therefore be far greater than that of the employee who at present has an ill-defined stake in a remote pension fund. Those who argue that personalising pensions will only re-introduce institutional investment dominance in another guise have not understood this crucial difference; they have only to ask the self-employed, to whom existing money-purchase policies have offered just this realisation. A whole new market for managers of broadly-based investment funds would be opened, with all the advantages of pooled costs. Opportunities for local financial advice from intermediaries, based on the individual's family and other circumstances, become a reality.

(e) The cross-subsidisation inherent in all final salary schemes would be more clearly seen, and better understood. In the past it has hardly been in the interests of the articulate minority, who gain from the system, to explain the detail to the wider majority, who lose. The simple explanation lies in the "aggregate funding rate" (the phrase used for the level of contribution to be made to an occupational pension scheme on the recommendation of its actuary). This is paid, as an equal percentage rate, on behalf of all the active members. It must be obvious that, age for age, a married member of the scheme, with entitlements to spouses' or children's benefits, is likely to cost the scheme more than an unmarried member; it should be equally clear that anyone who enjoys above-average increases in their salaries, most especially in the years approaching retirement, is more expensive to the scheme than a member whose salary progression is limited to the average or is below it. Women live longer in retirement and may retire earlier; they therefore represent a greater drain on the fund's resources than men. The young subsidise the old and early leavers subsidise the long-term career stayers. Everyone may understand that, as personal circumstances change, the claims on the fund continuously vary: what is less often said is that the same principle applies as to tax privileges—*one employee's gain must be matched by another employee's loss*. There may well be a general social argument for the strong, or the lucky, giving some support to the weak or the disadvantaged; the fundamental criticism of final salary schemes is that it is the strong (who are in the minority) who are the gainers, at the expense of the weak.

Those who opted annually for withdrawal would understand much better the true cost of retirement pension depending on age, salary and personal background: (interestingly, it might encourage the young to remain in occupational schemes until marriage, to get credit for back service, albeit unmarried for most of that period). Employers who decided to continue with final salary schemes would continue to make annual contributions, with or without members' contributions, expressed at the aggregate funding rate, in respect of all employees in the scheme.

(f) The administrative problems of pension managers would be reduced: all the snippets of future pensions in respect of past service of mobile employees would be rolled up into one single fund, if the employer exercised his right to require an early leaver to take this segregated fund option. It clarifies the principle that an employer's obligation to early leavers is concluded at the date of his departure.

(g) The debate about pension funds surpluses would be resolved for employers, members and the Inland Revenue. It would be clear that moneys passed over to pension fund trustees were the sole property of the members, with no right of recovery by the employer in any circumstances (the best funds already accept this principle).

(h) All the problems about Inland Revenue limits on the permissible level of pension are eliminated: those who choose Personal Option Pensions effectively possess money purchase schemes and the only limit is on the amount of contributions, not on the size of the fund that can be built up to provide benefits. Far greater flexibility on actual retirement date is available to an individual with a segregated fund, to take account of both personal circumstances and employers' wishes.

(i) Complete protection is available to the employees, and the pensioners, where control of a company changes and the appointment of Trustees (and therewith control of the pension fund), falls into new hands. The predator cannot claw-back if all members have an inalienable right to extract their assessed share: pensioners are no longer at the mercy of their former employer's pension fund.

The criticisms of POPs

All simple proposals have their critics and Personal Option Pensions will find objectors among the paternalists, the technocrats, the vested interests and some employers. The first task is to persuade the critics that more and more people realise that the present position is unjust and untenable: the threat of external interference should induce new strategic thinking. Six main strands of criticism of Personal Option Pensions have been identified: but the answers are straightforward and convincing. They will be found in Appendix A.

The link between personal pensions and tax reform

What is important now is to stress the link between personal pensions and tax reform: a link which could transform attitudes towards diffusion of wealth and the enhancement of liberty. And Personal Option Pensions could be introduced forthwith. By making the annual choice an option, no one is forced into a money-purchase scheme against his will: by making the annual choice available, the criticisms of the ossified structure are eliminated and unitisation offers the prospect of wider ownership—to all the existing members. Personal responsibility for retirement provision becomes much more widely understood and could be progressively implemented over the next generation.

But such a change would still only tinker with the distortions in the savings market: so long as one segment of everybody's expenditure is biased by fiscal privilege toward one form of saving, no-one who believes in free markets can be satisfied. Those who champion wider ownership regret that the form of saving particularly favoured by fiscal privilege enforces institutional ownership and denies to the individual the right to spend his money as he chooses. How patronising that an employer distributes 90% of remuneration to be spent as the employee chooses, but insists on retaining the last 10% to be saved for old age under a sheltered tax umbrella! A free market should facilitate access to savings, rather than insist they be kept for retirement: a good tax system gives everybody the extra wherewithal with which to save, allowing different decisions according to changing needs.

Fiscal privilege is the enemy of the savings market, of the proper transfer of assets from today's workers to the retired, of the financial understanding which should be part of every saver's decisions. Hence the need to associate unitisation of pensions with a review of such privileges.

Fiscal privilege for pensions—or simpler taxes?

Broadening the tax base

Any mention of the tax privileges surrounding retirement provision encounters an instant reaction from entrenched interests. For example, the pensions lobbyists resisted fairer treatment for the Early Leaver (as recently as 1978 there was no compulsion to provide early leavers with any deferred benefit whatever, other than a return of their own contributions); they resisted (and still resist) the provision of Personal Pensions, as diminishing their role as the monopoly provider; and they mounted a major campaign in 1985 to retain tax privileges for retirement saving. What is needed, both at the popular level and by the experts, is a realisation that the present system is inequitable; and must be reformed.

Tax reformers too often argue from an analysis of the existing privileges, rehearsing their costs and discussing the effect of minor modifications. This is to look at our fiscal system through the wrong end of the telescope. The better approach is to consider the tax system as a whole. Everyone is aware of, and frustrated at a personal level by, the complexities of the present system: rather fewer may be willing to recognise that we can simplify the system only by broadening the tax base. The prime requirement must be to eliminate the burden of those many taxes which distort the balance of choice between saving and spending and act as a barrier to personal ownership.

Two stark statistics illustrate the need for change:

(i) Income tax bites too soon: the threshold at which income tax becomes payable, expressed as a percentage of average manual earnings, has fallen from 99.8% in 1950 to 37.5% in 1987: (this figure applies to a married man with two children, but Appendix C of IR Statistics[2] sets out the full data for a wide range of personal circumstances and earnings).

(ii) Taxes on earning are too high: in 1950 the actual amount of PAYE deducted was £499 million out of total pay, plus occupational pensions, of £6.470 billion, giving a "tax percentage" of 7.7%: by 1985 those figures had grown to £30.9 billion and £157.0 billion respectively, so that the tax percentage had grown to 19.7%. On a revenue-neutral basis, the only way of reducing that percentage is to widen the base on which PAYE is levied.

The consequences are clear to anyone concerned with work incentives, and most of all to those concerned with the creation of new jobs, the problems of the poverty trap, and attitudes to taking up employment. National Insurance contributions become an additional burden on lower levels of earned income, so that the marginal rate of tax, including NICs, for an individual earning as little as £100 a week can be 34%, an absurd disincentive. NICs produce their own brand of fiscal distortion and barriers to work: they introduce a higher level of tax on earned as compared with unearned income: and they are based on arbitrary cut-off points in earnings which bear no relation to the starting levels for higher rate income taxes. National Insurance's claim to be a contributory system has always been a charade: the only argument against integrating NICs with income tax is that it exposes marginal tax rates for what they really are (as anyone with a payslip in his hand can instantly see).

Higher rate income taxes

Higher rate tax systems are themselves now open to challenge. Our present tax system, based partly on a flat rate VAT levied on a substantial proportion of personal spending, and partly on progressive taxes on income where 'ability to pay' is used as a criterion, is an obvious confusion of principles. The additional revenue from higher rate income taxes is relatively small: but they produce a demand for ratcheting salaries to take account of tax, coupled with widespread perks and privileges and an army of advisers to minimise the tax impact. It should always be remembered that it was Karl Marx who first proposed progressive taxes on income for his quite specific political motives: and that their introduction to Britain (at the rate of 5%, considered penal at the time) was for the specific semi-hypothecated programmes of national defence.

We now need to state unequivocally that *all forms of progressive taxation are a direct denial of the individual's freedom* to spend his money as he himself chooses. The debate on the 1988 budget shows how few people have understood the need to change public attitudes. Higher rate taxes are an attempt to buck the market, by trying to readjust salaries set by the market; as such they belong to the paraphernalia of Socialist thinking. It is time to challenge that basic set of attitudes. Pride in reducing the top rate to 40% and regarding that as the maximum objective (brave though it seemed at the time), shows that the nonsense of higher rate taxes has not yet been exposed, or that the means of earning income tax-free has not been fully understood.

The political attractions

Radical tax reform can be made politically attractive if it is seen to meet three basic demands.

(a) Does it simplify the tax system to a basis which every individual can understand and calculate for himself?

(b) Does it restore choice, allowing the individual to spend what he properly regards as his money in his order of preference?

(c) Does it widen ownership by removing the distortions which favour institutionalised savings at the expense of creation of personal assets?

Reliefs for retirement provision

The scale of the problem is such that only the removal of retirement provision relief can provide the room for manoeuvre necessary to simplify the system. A summary of these reliefs, which have often been set out in great detail, is given in Appendix B. Enough here to state that the reasons for granting reliefs go back to the very origin of occupational schemes at the beginning of the century, at a time when only a small proportion of the population paid income tax and when pensions were regarded as provision for the thriftless poorer classes, rather than as today one of the major perks of employment. It was also a time of lower interest rates and no capital gains taxes, so that gross fund status was less valuable. (The cumulative effect of gross returns are not widely understood: but after 20 years the tax-exempt owner of money earning 4% is 21% better off than a tax-payer with a basic rate of 25%: but if the total rate of return rises to 12% the exempt owner is as much as 72% better off. (Using a tax rate of 40% the advantage to an exempt fund grows to a benefit of 37% assuming a 4% return, and 139% on a 12% return.)

The arguments for providing these reliefs were perhaps laudable at the time: a specific fiscal encouragement to postpone consumption and provide a nest egg for retirement complemented the policies of paternalist employers. No-one at that time visualised the pension commitments to today's high salary earners, where non-taxable (and non-contributory) contributions to occupational schemes may represent a tax-free increment of 40% or more of salary.

Some have even sought to argue that, since pensions are fully taxed when it comes to payment, "the tax rules under which approved pension funds operate do not put them in a privileged position:"[3]. But the long history of Revenue involvement with closing the more blatant loopholes does imply that retirement provision is encouraged by fiscal privilege, a position which most would accept.

The cost of pension fund reliefs

What is less acceptable is the virtual absence of public discussion about the true costs of these reliefs. Since it is the very small minority on the highest salaries who gain the most from the present basis of final salary schemes, this may not be altogether surprising. The under-privileged and over-taxed majority of average wage earners is being robbed to pay the minority of high fliers.

As recently as 1978, Treasury witnesses to a Select Committee were unable to give the cost of "tax relief on private pension schemes or tax reliefs on lump sum payments under public and private pension schemes, since the information needed was not available". By 1983, IR Statistics put the cost of income tax relief at £1.1 billion: but later in just the same year the Revenue published their first attempt at a detailed statistical analysis.[4]. Their paper offered three separate approaches, costed at between £2.450 billion and £2.9 billion, at a time of higher tax rates than at present: but no-one attached much credence to the figures at the time and there was little public debate. It was a measure of public apathy on the issues that just one year later (see Hansard 9 January 1985 p. 491) one figure (the estimated cost of tax relief for employees in respect of employers' contributions) could be virtually doubled from £1.1 billion to a "particularly tentative" £2.1 billion: even then no-one seemed to question the detailed assumptions or why the figure had changed. A mere £1 billion of tax relief (enough to take 1p off income tax at the time) was not considered news-worthy. By 1986 (see Hansard 3 June 1986, c 532) forward projections of future costs were abandoned and it was argued that it was too expensive to calculate the costs of these reliefs in future years. But promises are being made now which will represent commitments in future years and it is unacceptable to operate a system today which burdens the next generation to an unknown extent. No attempt has been made to measure the cost of gains tax exemption— yet gains tax is possibly the single most important discouragement to wider personal ownership.

It was not until 1984 that the present Chancellor began to remove the first of the fiscal anomalies affecting savings, by ending Life Assurance Premium relief. There was therefore widespread speculation that his 1985 Budget might have wished to raid the "Pot of Gold" that retirement relief represented. In the event the political lobby mounted by the National Association of Pension Funds, described as "unprecedented" at the time, a report "Taxing Pensions" by the Institute for Fiscal Studies, and a general feeling that a run-up to an election period was not the time to propose major changes in savings flows, all combined to persuade the Chancellor to withdraw any ideas for major reform in the last Parliament.

The 1987 Budget did indeed introduce some minor changes to fiscal privilege, but they affected only lump sum commutations of over £150,000 and the accrual period for a full two-thirds final salary entitlement. But it was a signal that the present system was not perfect—and widely interpreted as such. The 1988 Budget brought major changes to the level of tax, but did nothing in the cause of fiscal neutrality in the savings market.

Why change now?

For five main reasons:—

(a) It is becoming clear that the true cost of retirement provision relief may have been substantially understated. The next section outlines a different approach to such a costing exercise.

(b) Interest in major tax reform is growing. We can now aim not just to ape the new American pattern (which still retains many fiscal privileges and distortions) but to leapfrog them. A single flat-rate low-percentage income tax is now accepted to be achievable.

(c) The system does not reflect the changing patterns of work, moving from one job to another, from employment to self-employment, the growth of part-time jobs (especially for women). Why should housewives, children, or the non-employed fund the tax privileges of the employed?

(d) New entrants to the work force should not have to face the disincentive of high marginal tax rates.

(e) Retirement provision relief, in its present form, is a direct fiscal encouragement to institutionalised saving. Employers no longer believe they are getting value for money for their contributions: and the working population has no sense of identification with their savings as represented by these funds, nor with the wealth-creating commercial activity which alone gives value to such funds.

A new approach to costing pension relief

One extreme of calculation would be to assume that all existing reliefs were withdrawn with immediate effect, or even retrospectively, with a devastating impact on the solvency on existing funds and on the legitimate expectations of present and future pensions. Such a calculation would bring into the taxable base not only all future contributions, but also the existing funds and their capital gains as realised; it would add up to £10 billion of investment income and net capital gains of some £20 billion annually to the calculation of a wider taxable base shown below.

Now this is clearly unrealistic. But it is reasonable to assume (at least for demonstrating the true costs) that existing schemes are closed to new contributions: they would continue to operate on the existing gross fund basis, paying out pensions which would themselves be subject to tax, and maintaining commutation rights, however anomalous, as at present. Such an approach *honours all existing promises* and would simplify the introduction of Personal Option Pensions. Another advantage would be that the impact on individual expectations would be gradual. Forty years would pass during which everyone would grow to understand the dynamism of personal saving. But for the future the taxation of retirement provision would be quite different:—

(a) employers could operate new occupational schemes and their contributions, just like wages and salaries, would be allowable as tax deductions in the company's computation: no limit on such contributions need be imposed but no increase in cost to employers would be involved;

(b) such new funds would be subject to income tax (at the single standard rate, since higher rates would have been abolished). Since they would operate on a tax-paying basis, they would lose the benefit of gross fund roll-up; either a higher level of contributions would be needed to maintain benefit levels, or ultimate benefits would be lower. But, following the reduction in tax rates, individuals would be more willing to set aside a higher level of savings on a purely personal basis. New funds would also be subject to gains tax as if the fund was owned by all the individual members so that an annual exemption of a fixed sum per member might be acceptable;

(c) contributions by employees, or by the self-employed, would no longer be deductible. This puts the self-employed in the same position as the employee; although an employer would continue to be able to make contributions which were deductible, the employee and the self-employed would both contribute out of their net after-tax income;

(d) as the most significant change, all contributions by employers would be regarded as employees' emoluments and assessed as a benefit-in-kind on the employee, just as if they were wages or other taxable benefits; and

(e) since the funds would operate on a fully taxed basis, all withdrawals and commutations would be ended by equating any such payments with all others.

Special treatment would be required for unfunded schemes. The grant of a definitive deferred pension right would give rise to a benefit assessment, on a scale to be determined: true ex-gratia grants would be taxable only in the year of receipt, and deductible by the grantor only in the year of actual payment.

An exact calculation of the impact of such a change requires a more detailed statistical base for current levels of contribution. For this analysis it is assumed that contribution levels remain unchanged and that:—

(i) total contributions, by employers and employees, are £17 billion per annum, (they are shown as £15.8 billion for 1983 in the Government Actuary's survey[5], equivalent to over £19 billion in 1988 prices. Lowered contribution rates to reflect the well-publicised problems of surplus, are unlikely to have reduced the total by more than £2 billion);

(ii) contributions by the self-employed are £1.25 billion: as is well known, this is far below the potential figure since many self-employed do not or cannot afford to take advantage of the full reliefs available;

(iii) the grant of rights in unfunded schemes would be valued as equivalent to contributions of £4 billion: over 3 million employees are believed to be covered by unfunded pension arrangements, often on a generous index-linked basis, and one quarter of the contributions paid to funded schemes is a reasonable minimum estimate;

(iv) commutation payments are running at some £3 billion per annum (they were £2.350 billion in 1983 and IR Statistics 1987 put the cost of relief at £1.1 billion, implying taxable payments of around £3 billion).

Adding these four items together demonstrates that such a new approach to taxing pensions would *increase the income tax base by £25 billion per annum.* (And if contribution levels were to fall as a result of the change, taxable profits of companies would be increased, so that the tax take would at worst be unchanged.) Assuming an average tax rate at a little over the standard rate, say 28%, the true cost of income tax relief is put at £7 billion; by contrast mortgage interest relief now has a cost (at current interest rates) of just over £4 billion.

This excludes any additional cost for capital gains tax reliefs. Revenue Statistics have consistently declined to give any figure for the cost of exemption from capital gains tax for approved pension schemes. But it may be assumed that existing funds, with annual sales of securities subject to gains tax of at least £50 billion per annum, would be making capital gains of at least £15 billion per annum: although such gains represent only £1000 per member or deferred member, they represent a major tax shelter for the higher paid. It would be some time before new taxable funds made substantial capital gains but the present yield gap between equities and bonds is an indication of the level of capital growth assumed by the market. A true calculation of gains tax costs depends on the basis of levying capital gains in a reformed tax system.

Arguments against this approach, and counters to them, are to be found in Appendix C.

The prize

This can be very briefly stated. Any politician must see that enlarging the taxable base for income taxes by up to £25 billion per annum provides opportunities for radical reform beyond the normal tinkering of an annual Budget; it could allow the abolition of some of the existing taxes and reliefs which act as barriers to personal owner-ship and tilt the playing field out of level. In an ideal (but possible) fiscal world, saving and spending are treated alike and *this* saving does not attract *that* privilege.

The first charge must be to abolish the higher rate of income tax altogether, if only because the gravest impact of the change in the tax treatment of pension contributions would be on the highest earned incomes—a senior manager might find his taxable income rising by 40% or more on a proper allocation of his employer's contributions. Such a change also opens the way to levy employees' National Insurance contributions on all forms of income, earned and un-earned, and without upper limit. Higher rate income tax will proba-bly raise only about £1.5 billion in 1988; the balance of savings will be available to make a major reduction of income tax, well below the 20% presently set as the target for this administration.

Detailed calculations depend on figures which are not publicly available, so that the following calculations are illustrative only. The total income on which tax could be charged (allowing for the increase in the taxable base arising from the pension changes) is about £350 billion; from this has to be deducted the impact of personal allow-ances (£70 billion), mortgage interest relief (£20 billion) and other, minor allowances (£10 billion). Note that this is the reduction in the taxable base attributable to these allowances; the actual 'cost' is described as a little over the basic rate as a proportion of these gross sums.

Income tax in 1988/89 is estimated to yield £42 billion, employees' NICs about £14 billion; raising £56 billion (ie, on a revenue-neutral basis) from a taxable base reduced to £250 billion requires a total tax rate of 22.5%. This could be described as a 15% income tax, to meet the general needs of law and order, defence, etc and a 7.5% Social Welfare Tax, primarily dedicated to State pension provision. Descrip-tion of such a percentage as a Social tax would bring home to people how much 'free' welfare costs them. Since the reform is revenue-neutral, the nation as a whole is (in budget language) neither a winner nor a loser.

With that reform accepted, the way is opened for the next major reform—*a truly simple tax system with no allowances whatever*; just as VAT is levied on all personal income. The onus would be on the payer to deduct tax on all payments of income, so that avoidance becomes virtually impossible. The absurdities of the poverty trap on marginal incomes are eliminated, there are no PAYE coding notices, no separate treatment of married couples, the Inland Revenue computer becomes largely redundant and its hard-pressed officials better able to devote their time to their proper task of enforcement. The number of man-hours spent on personal tax returns (estimated as up to 100,000 man *years* per annum), and the talents of tax accountants and inspectors, could be devoted to more productive uses. Additional resources would be required to raise the State pension, and the needs of those on very low incomes would be met by specific grants adjusted to their need (a means-tested negative income tax).

At this level of simplicity, the calculations are more straightforward. An extra £20 billion might be added to the taxable base due to the elimination of the black economy—in which case a 10% income tax plus 7.5% Social Tax yields £65 billion on a taxable base of £370 billion, providing an extra £9 billion of government spending to increase State pensions and compensate losers. Simple arithmetic, rather than an army of Inland Revenue officials and accountants, would thereafter determine the necessary level of tax.

Capital taxes

There would still remain the panoply of taxes on capital—a formidable barrier to wider ownership. Stamp duties (yielding £2 billion), Gains tax (even in its allegedly simplified form, yielding £1.9 billion), and Inheritance taxes (yielding £1.0 billion), altogether provide under £5 billion. But they are a maze on which much ingenuity is devoted to minimise their impact. Their effect is diverse. Stamp duty on houses discourages a form of investment which all agree should be encouraged and, through the market-makers' exemption, preserves the monopoly of the Stock Exchange in listed securities. Gains tax is levied now only on real gains, and with an annual exemption, but still requires complex calculations. Inheritance taxes choke the natural instinct to leave a better world to the next generation; and discourage the maintenance of family control of enterprises large and small. A full discussion of capital taxes is outside the scope of this paper; but after the simplification of income taxes, the next target must be taxes on capital. A simple, equitable gains tax at the combined Income and

Social Tax rate of 17.5%, levied on all types of gain realised within a given period, could be designed to yield £5 billion, ie, less than 1% of net financial wealth held by the personal sector.

The boon of fiscal reform

The reforms which this paper proposes give prizes to all. At the tax rates suggested most special tax incentives do not need to be repealed; they simply wither away. Who would mourn for retirement provision relief, or for BES, or for unemployed tax experts, if the alternative were the abolition of all personal taxes on income and capital, except for a low single-rate Income and Social Tax and a genuinely simplified gains tax? What politician could be blind to the appeal of such simplicity? What Party would win the support of the electorate if it threatened to re-instate them?

At least let the choice be clearly presented to the electorate. A Bonfire of Controls was the successful election cry five years after the war. A Bonfire of Butterworths (the tax text books) would be splendid to behold before the next election; and the electors would be full of wonder and approval.

The high road to wider ownership

Pensions and tax reforms are not to be seen as ends in themselves, but only as necessary steps towards the prime political and economic goal of wider ownership. Something must therefore be said in conclusion about the philosophical basis which underlies the specific recommendations in this pamphlet. No doubt the commitment of the author, and of the Group with whom he serves, is apparent. Wider ownership is the key; and without a constant drive towards this goal we shall not preserve our freedom. But what may not be so well known is that, for all this Government's avowed espousal of this cause, and for all the success of its privatisation schemes, the trend is still, and massively, towards indirect ownership. Reversal of this trend would be the principal justification, as it is the principal objective, of this paper. First of all we must ask ourselves:—

(a) Is this trend towards indirect ownership one which the individual really wants?

(b) does it pose threats to acceptance of the most important justification of capitalism, the dispersal of economic power?

(c) is it so biased by fiscal privilege that the tax system can no longer stand the strain?

(d) do these proposals, while retaining the skills and cost efficiencies of professional investment management, at the same time give the individual a greater sense of personal involvement?

For a generation or more the concept of extending the ownership of property (using that word in its widest sense to cover all forms of asset) has been supported in theory, but neglected in practice. Now, with a fresh emphasis on 'the enterprise culture', wealth creation takes the centre of the stage. But wealth creation can be seen as a valid economic process if, and only if, wealth itself is distributed, through direct ownership, in what is perceived to be a fair manner: and it must be widely available, for immediate spending or saving, by individual consumers. Wider ownership offers not only the best opportunities for economic growth, but also the fundamental safeguard of democratic liberties.

However, the transition from acceptance of these basic attitudes to implementation remains surrounded with a variety of barriers. One might have hoped that politicians would have recognised changing attitudes and done all that was possible to eliminate these obstacles.

A study of any primitive society, preoccupied with the ownership of land or animals, or of the acquisitive instincts of a growing child, should have been enough to demonstrate how fundamental is the human aspiration for ownership. As ownership is extended throughout a society, the power of patronage exercised through consumer decision is dispersed and the foundations of an open society are strengthened. In every way, the prospect of ownership offers hope; and it is a prospect not only to the aspiring millionaire on the stock market, but equally to the young entrant to the job market. So ownership must be recognised in its true position as a prospect for all, a key political requirement, a commander of the popular vote.

Not everyone agrees, of course. From Plato to Marx and modern socialism, there have been many who urge the wisdom of allowing a central authority to gather together the individual's pot of wealth and redistribute it according to need. Only such a central authority, it is argued, can develop sufficient wisdom and discretion to perform this task. Put thus crudely its absurdity is obvious and history demonstrates its inadequacy: the task is impossible and history shows that concentrations of power always become unacceptable. But there are variations of this approach, put forward in all integrity by those who normally speak most proudly of the benefits of personal freedom and choice. Consider, for example, the argument of the 'good employer'; since an individual cannot be trusted to provide for his family or his own retirement, it is said that it becomes the positive obligation of the State, or an employer, to set aside such a provision on his behalf. Others argue that the opportunities for fraud and misrepresentation at the personal level are such that regulation and supervision of markets must be imposed, which force the individual into the hands of the expert or the institutional manager. Paternalists, crypto-social-ists and centralists come in many forms: but often enough these statements, appearing to take a high moral view, are merely the basis for protecting an existing position. There is nothing more plausible than arguments of apparent integrity concerned with protecting an entrenched interest. They must always be tested against the main beliefs of those who put them forward and challenged for what they really are, a derogation from the consumer's freedom of choice.

But ownership alone is no longer a sufficient aim. Those who rely on Adam Smith's *Wealth of Nations* for their support of the capitalist system should never forget the thinking in the second part of his trilogy, *Moral Sentiments;*—'there are evidently some principles in man's nature which interest him in the fortunes of others and render their happiness necessary to him'. Unless ownership brings with it a sense of personal responsibility and charitable duty, of using assets with proper regard to their value, the case for dispersing ownership will be imperilled by those who can point to examples of foolishness, profligacy and waste. Yet using such examples is not really an argument against widening ownership, but rather for encouraging it in order to give greater opportunities for developing sense of respon-sibility. Such responsibilities cannot be shrugged off to trustees and institutions. Let us repeat:—

(a) Ownership provides the framework for human dignity and independence: it should be a key objective of the economic system.

(b) Ownership, to be effective, must be diffused as widely as possible, and thus become a central concern of the political process.

(c) Ownership must be as personal and direct as is possible, encouraging both a sense of thrift and duty to society.

(d) Ownership is not in conflict with care. For it provides the stimulus for wealth creation which generates the resources needed for care.

Anyone who agrees with these four themes must now be ready to test how far wider ownership is actually being achieved.

Ownership in Britain—facts and trends

Given the importance of ownership, it is surprising that the information on the personal sector's holdings of assets receives so little attention, (though partly this is because complete data is not accessible). For over three hundred years attempts to measure personal wealth in Britain have been made, culminating in the Diamond Royal Commission and their voluminous reports in the 1970s. These reports had a social aim, being concerned primarily with the re-distribution, not with the creation, of wealth. Even so, different ways of allocating accrued pension rights made a major difference to the calculation. For example, in 1980, the most wealthy 25% of the adult population were estimated to hold over 80% of marketable wealth. But this fell to 58% when accrued pension rights were included. Naturally, the value of pension rights depends on the age of the beneficiary. The distribution of wealth is bound to reflect the human instinct to acquire assets over a lifetime of work, and to provide a decent sum, whether for retirement or to pass on to heirs. The personal sector's wealth can also be gauged by reliance on the Inland Revenue statistics, which use the net capital value of deceased estates as their basis (and are questionable on that account). For recent years, the fullest data is found in CSO's Financial Statistics (Table S.2, published only each February). See Appendix D.

Here are some of the conclusions which study of this Appendix suggests:—

(i) Housing remains the personal sector's most important asset, but has increased by only 4.5 times over the decade; despite the publicity given to prices, housing has not become a very much greater proportion of personal wealth. In round terms, during this period the percentage of owner-occupation rose from 58% to 67%, so that on a truly comparable basis housing is still responsible for 50% of net personal assets.

(ii) Of financial assets, the highest rates of growth come under the heading 'equity in insurance and pension funds': but the actuarial problems of pension fund valuation are such that considerable under-statement is almost certain. In this decade alone, the value of the

equity of the personal sector in pension funds and insurance companies has grown nearly eight-fold, from 41% of net financial assets to
70%, and now represents around 25% of total net wealth. And there
is no evidence to suggest that the dominance of retirement provision
will not continue to increase. The Institute for Fiscal Studies has
projected an annual inflow into funded pension schemes alone of £20
bn per annum, at 1984 prices, for the next 40 years, with no sign of
deceleration of that growth. The IFS comment that "this growth
reflects, in large measure, the fact that the sector is a considerable
way short of maturity"[6]. Something of an understatement? (See Chart
2 on page 48.)

(iii) This evolving pattern of wealth ownership is inevitably mirror-
imaged in the decline in the direct holdings of ordinary shares.
Statistics for holdings of listed equities are documented in the Stock
Exchange's Survey of Share Ownership[7], which examined the distribution of shareholdings in 1963, 1969, 1975 and 1981: the two selected
intervening years confirm the trends shown between the two extreme
years. Between 1963 and 1981 the percentage distribution of shares
held by persons fell from 54% to 28%, (a rate of decline which would
have eliminated the private shareholder by the end of the century).
Their decline was mirrored almost exactly by the rise of shares held
by insurance companies and pension funds (from 16% to 45%).
Within that total the share held by pension funds grew fastest, from
6.4% to 26.7%; their share quadrupled in these 18 years, compared
to a doubling by insurance company holdings. (The market value of
occupational pension funds in 1957 was only £2.1 billion; they then
held under 3% of listed equities, with individuals holding 66% of
listed equities.)

Some will argue that all this has changed thanks to the present
Government's success in its wider ownership campaign, which is
largely based on what is seen to be immediate profits from coupon-
clipping on privatisation issues. And much credit is due to the
Government. The number of direct personal shareholders has increased in this decade from around 2 million in 1980 to over 9 million
today. Of these, up to 2 million have been introduced directly through
employee share schemes, which enjoy a variety of special tax privileges or favourable terms on new issues.

But that success masks other statistics.

(i) In the five years to December 1986, the personal sector was a
net seller of company securities to the tune of £2.25 billion, at a time

when it was a net contributor to life assurance and pension funds of £90 billion. The latest figures for 1987 have just become available (CSO Financial Statistics: Table 9.2); even in the boom year for the Stock Exchange, net new investment by individuals amounted to only £6.2 billion (of which £5.9 billion was invested in the third quarter alone, just before the Crash); this compares with a maintained flow of £20 billion into institutionalised saving, three-quarters of the total.

The proportion of equities held by individuals therefore continues to decline, and is probably below 20% today. Anyone with experience of company share registers will have welcomed the increase in the number of private shareholders, but also seen the inexorable growth of the stake held by the small number of their largest shareholders. The ten largest pension funds (six of them in the public sector) alone now control over £50 billion of assets, one quarter of all assets held by pension funds.

(ii) The new shareholders are capitalists in only a limited sense. Over half the 9 million hold shares in one company only, normally based on a privatisation application or an employee allotment, and only 20% hold six or more different shares, a portfolio whose spread might be thought the minimum desirable for equity risk[8]. On one estimate, the number of private shareholders with a portfolio in ten or more companies has actually fallen in the last seven years. Given the potential profit, what is most surprising is that at least 30 million adults have not been persuaded to try their hand in the stock market.

(iii) About half the sample estimated the total value of their equity holdings at up to £3,000 and the Stock Exchange estimated the average value at under £4,000[9].

A portfolio of one or two privatisation issues is not an ideal basis for wider ownership—but at least it is a platform on which new attitudes to ownership can be built. However, none of the many shareholder surveys which have been so well reported have mentioned the key fact of British ownership, the one which this paper has tackled. Albeit at second-hand, some 16 million members of pension funds own financial assets with a value of over £200 billion. This gives an average holding of £12,500, though the actual figures would range from nil for the newest recruit to over £500,000 for a senior manager nearing retirement.

Giving these 16 million people an opportunity directly to own their assets would give them a real stake in our society. Let us start, now, down the high road towards wider ownership and popular ownership, and make sure that we never turn back.

Chart II

**Market Value of Self-Administered Pension Funds
1957–1987**

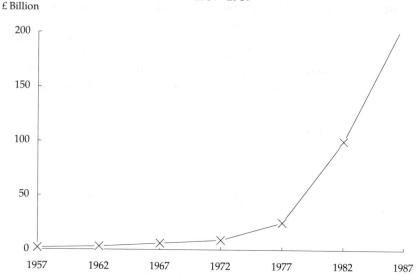

£ Billion

Conclusion

Ownership is important and is the Tory alternative to the centralists, paternalists and socialists. But personal ownership in the UK is
crowded out by the continuing growth of structured retirement
provision: it dominates financial markets and diminishes the understanding of the workforce that the size of the rice bowl which will be
available to support their retirement depends on their efforts, and
those of their children, not on some impersonal Pensions Department. This growth is actively encouraged by fiscal privilege, with the
inevitable result: more and more people may be shareholders, but
they own less and less.

By giving 16 million people the opportunity to own directly the
assets which are truly theirs, retirement provision contributes to an
understanding of how prosperity can be achieved: by removing tax
privileges for pensions in respect of future service, we can enjoy

today a tax system which is fairer, simpler and a beacon to a responsible electorate.

Appendix A.
Objections and counters to POPs

(a) *Actuaries* will argue that it is not technically possible to assess the true share of an existing fund where it has to be split among a wide group of individuals with differing personal circumstances. But it is clear that, in retrospect, liabilities can be calculated, since otherwise a discontinuance valuation would itself become impossible. And since actuarial expertise can agree on the division into appropriate shares of a fund with only a few beneficiaries, modern data management technology can divide a fund with a very large number of members. Provided the basis of valuation was published and it was seen to be broadly acceptable (and calculated annually on the same basis) employees would be satisfied: a ready-reckoner points system, allowing for salary changes, length of service, marital status etc, would adequately assess personal entitlements.

(b) *Fund managers, and pension fund trustees* will argue that pension fund investment policy is dictated by the long term and should not be influenced by possibilities of annual withdrawal. But that argument is ridiculous at a time when City institutions are continuously accused of 'short-termism' and when turnover and activity, in both bonds and equities, is continuously rising. (Precise definitions are difficult but all recent surveys have shown annual stock turnover by pension funds in British equities at least doubling over the present decade, up to around 60%: all other categories, overseas equities, fixed interest and index-linked, are now over 100% per annum). If these statistics do not invalidate the argument, it can readily be met by insisting that the portfolio of those who choose a segregated fund should continue to be managed, on a unitised basis, by the existing Trustees as an adjunct to the main fund for a limited period. A more serious criticism might be that individuals have shown themselves to be more passive investors than institutions, and that the dealing structures and facilities in the City have been built on the expectation of increasing turnover. That argument must be decided elsewhere, with the Inland Revenue as an interested observer of the trading activity of pension funds: but increasing turnover and long-term investment attitudes by definition are irreconcilable. Analysis of equity turnover should start by asking the question—what should be the anticipated retention period, on average, of an investment? Personal holders might suggest an answer of ten years: but on this basis even the lower market turnover levels of early 1988 are far higher than would be consistent with long-termism in portfolio management. Industrialists should welcome wholeheartedly any proposals which give a more stable background to the ownership of listed companies.

(c) *Technocrats* will argue that individuals will not understand that the capital value of their benefits may change, upwards and downwards, on the annual valuation, because a change in the personal circumstances of members alters the attributable proportion of available assets: this argument is no more than saying that transparency in pension fund policies is impossible. On that weakness alone the argument can be rejected: if the mathematics of cross-subsidisation become clearer to employees as a result so much the better. Those who do not like cross-subsidisation may freeze their share by taking their unitised proportion: and the losers from cross-subsidisation will soon emerge as the articulate majority. The long-term aim of changing the vocabulary, from the choice between final salary and money purchase schemes to the choice between defined income benefit and defined asset purchase schemes, will be achieved. Another cause of changes in capital value will, of course, arise from changes in market values: but capitalism does bring with it the penalties of failure, as well as the rewards of success: and so long as employers maintain defined benefit schemes, no-one will be forced into capitalism against their choice. It must be noted, however, that on a discontinuance valuation most schemes still show a very substantial surplus at the present time and will have assets valued at up to twice their liabilities: despite the market re- alignment, perhaps the temptation to choose the present opportunity to become a capitalist will never be greater.

(d) *Centralists* will argue that some holders of segregated funds will be stupid, or unlucky, with their investment policies; and some employers might feel it their duty to protect the unlucky and the foolish. It is, however, assumed that the DHSS would insist on investment policies that protected minimum pensions so that even the unlucky and foolish would not become a "burden on the State". This might be relevant in respect of private sector pension provision of up to half the basic state allowance, putting Social Security demands out of reach of the claimant: but the argument cannot be applied when considering full maintenance of living standards in retirement. It is fundamental to this new approach that a year's allocation to retirement provision, if it is withdrawn into an individual's segregated fund, represents the complete fulfilment of the employer's obligation in respect of that year's service. Transitional restraints on total investment flexibility might be allowable—but only until people are educated to understand what is at stake.

(e) *Paternalists* will also want to argue that it is only final salary schemes which maintain an employee's living standard in retirement and that this has become a cardinal aim. Quite apart from the fact that final salary schemes do not normally guarantee inflation protection during retirement (a period which has become increasingly long as life expectations increase), it is a statistical certainty that most pensioners will enjoy an enhanced retirement income under these proposals, always assuming the level of contributions remains unchanged. In practice, of course, the expectation of "two-thirds salary" on retirement is not often met. Although many schemes operating on the two-thirds salary basis make no deduction for the State pension entitlement (so that a long-serving employee can achieve an aggregate pension in excess of final salary), the overwhelming majority retire on occupational pensions of much less than this. The *average* occupational pension (but including widow's pensions) presently payable is under £2,000, around 20% of average earnings: the boast of "maintaining living standards in retirement" is not yet met by actual pensions.

(f) *Employers* may argue that the proposals represent a confusion of principle between final salary and money purchase schemes; in particular, since employers take the risk of making up any shortfall in the fund required to meet pensions based on final salaries, they should be entitled in full to any surplus. Such an attitude is clearly out of line with modern thinking, particularly among the work force, and fails to take into account the principle of total remuneration costing. If it were to be maintained, it should have been far more clearly presented, and fiscal privilege for such policies would clearly not be justified. It is, however, recognised that specific agreement must be reached in advance as to how any shortfall in a final salary fund would be met by employer or employee contributions.

There is one last group of objectors, whose public criticism will be based on one of the above arguments, but whose true motives rest on their existing interest in keeping pensions complicated. It is a fundamental aim of these proposals that pension provision should be simplified and become comprehensible to the beneficiaries.

Appendix B.
Retirement provision relief

The precise details of retirement relief have often been set out, but many laymen are unaware of their full extent. To summarise them:—

(a) Contributions by employers and employees to an approved fund are exempt from corporation and income taxes respectively, provided an actuarial valuation can be held to justify the level of contribution. It is well known that pressure groups ensured that the contribution rules introduced in the 1986 Budget designed to limit overfunding have been established on a far less stringent basis than that adopted for normal valuations: the problem of over-funding, well documented in various studies, remains.

(b) The self-employed, and soon those who choose Personal Pension provision, also enjoy substantial reliefs, but limited to contributions as a percentage of earnings.

(c) Most importantly, approved funds enjoy gross fund status giving exemption on both income and gains taxes during the accrual period.

(d) Commutation rights give substantial tax-free sums on retirement; however desirable under the present inequitable system, since they provide the first whiff of ownership to many (albeit late in life), these rights are recognised as an anomaly, indeed a 'much-loved anomaly'. They provide the unique double privilege of tax deductibility on entry and tax exemption on payout.

(e) The only effective constraint is the limitation of benefits, to two-thirds of final salary (as may be generously determined) in the case of defined benefit schemes. No such limits are placed on defined contribution schemes.

Unfunded pension commitments do not, of course, have the advantage of gross fund status during the accrual period: but since beneficiaries can obtain a similar scale of ultimate benefits, the effect is broadly similar. Indeed, the origin of many funded occupational schemes was to match the benefits of unfunded civil service pensions.

Curiously, however, National Insurance contributions, designed to contribute towards the basic retirement provision which all applaud, do not enjoy the privilege of tax deductibility: and those contracted into SERPS do not enjoy tax relief on their higher levels of contribution. The effect of high marginal tax rates on lower levels of earned income has already been noted. But perhaps the ultimate absurdity comes from the basis of calculating allowances for additional voluntary contributions, with the result that those in non-contributory occupational schemes effectively enjoy higher levels of deductibility than those in contributory schemes.

Appendix C.
Objections and counters to fiscal proposals

There are four possible arguments against adopting the new fiscal approach which has been outlined:—

(a) It will be said that under the aggregate funding rate used for final salary schemes it is not possible to allocate to each individual a precise amount for the employer's contribution. It would, of course, be quite acceptable that the aggregate funding rate itself should be used as the basis for calculation. Such a device is already used when companies show the pension contributions made for Directors: the Companies Act requires the disclosure of "any contribution paid in respect of him" under any pension scheme and accountants have been happy to approve accounts using the aggregate rate. The basis has already been sanctioned by custom and practice.

The likelier result, however, would be that employees came to understand the effect of cross-subsidisation inherent in a final salary scheme when it became evident in their tax bill: and that they would insist on money purchase arrangements, where the allocation of contributions is straightforward. They would see that pensions were part of salary costs and that there was flexibility in choosing between a company scheme or using the contribution towards personal provision. In due course, far more flexible salary arrangements, on the so-called cafeteria system, would become the norm: it would be all one to the employee whether he accepted wages or pension contributions.

(b) It is also argued that it would be wrong to charge individuals with a tax liability today in respect of a benefit which may be deferred for up to 40 years. But the benefit is received today, in the form of much lower tax rates: and the more that pension costs are seen as part of normal remuneration, the greater the argument for treating the contribution as a taxable emolument. It is on that argument also that the definitive grant of an unfunded pension right is treated as an emolument in the year of grant.

(c) Companies might also tend towards pay-as-you-go pensions on a truly unfunded basis rather than the establishment of separately funded schemes. This makes no difference to the advantages of a wider tax base. The change in fiscal treatment is likely to lead to a reduction in the scale of structured pension funding, accompanied by an increase in personal saving: the obvious choice for companies would be to fund for a modest enhancement of every employee's retirement on an equal basis, leaving the higher paid to make their own provision as they chose. The fiscal change would have triggered the ideal three-tier arrangement, well-supported by the CBI and other employers:—a basic state pension, some enhancement for all employees based solely on length of service, and true flexibility for personal provision.

(d) Those involved in the capital markets may choose to argue that the flow of savings on which new industrial development depends will be changed. This misunderstands the nature of savings flows. The basic assumption is that employers will continue to contribute to pension provision at present contribution rates, and may require employees to match such contributions in line with present arrangements. If this happens, the only change is that the investment income of new funds would be subject to income tax and individuals would need to create personal savings to match this loss: in year one the total involved would be less than £.25 billion, well within normal margins of consumer change. If companies were to reduce pension contributions and not distribute the savings to employees, they would both pay more corporation tax and have higher retained funds for investment.

As noted in c) above, the ideal solution would be for companies to fund a general pension provision giving all employees an equal and modest enhancement of the State pension, regardless of their salary scale, and allow higher-paid employees to fund additional flexible savings out of after-tax income. True fiscal neutrality would have been achieved: a free market does not distort choice between saving and spending and the individual must be educated, over time, to learn the consequences of premature squandering. It must also be emphasised that about half the working population are not presently members of occupational schemes and have needed to rely on this philosophy of thrift for many years past.

Appendix D.
Distribution of personal wealth 1977–1987

Holdings at Year-End (£ billion)

	1977	1982	1985	1987(est)	Compound Growth Rate % 1977–1987
Physical Assets					
Housing	166.3	378.5	559.2	755.0	16
Other	96.3	159.4	190.3	230.0	9
Financial Assets					
Cash, Deposits, etc.	68.4	127.9	177.7	210.0	12
Ordinary Shares	29.3	43.1	65.3	75.0	10
Equity in life assurance and pension funds					
Self-administered	28.7	87.0	157.4	210.0	22
Managed by insurance companies	28.0	68.7	115.2	140.0	17
Other financial assets	37.8	77.5	110.5	130.0	13
Financial Liabilities					
Housing Loans	33.2	76.2	126.1	170.0	18
Other	21.5	50.0	77.8	95.0	16
Net Wealth	400.2	815.9	1171.9	1485.0	14
Life Assurance and Pension Funds as % of					
Net Financial assets	41.3%	56.0%	64.6%	70.0%	
Housing as % of Net Wealth	41.6%	46.4%	47.7%	50.8%	

Source: for 1977, 1982, 1985—CSO Financial Statistics Table S.2; for 1987—extrapolated and estimated

Appendix E.
Overseas comparisons

Comparisons with overseas practice are always dangerous, and any figures quoted are subject to the impact of volatile exchange rates and market conditions. Other countries have different expectations as regards the funding of public sector pensions, or the treatment of pensions in payment as pay-as-you-go obligations. But those who argue for allowing the status quo to continue in Britain must recognise that the extent of dominance of funded retirement provisions is almost unique to Britain. While it is recognised that the figures below are tentative, the main point is clear: *in Britain, pension funds represent a much higher proportion* of personal savings than in other countries. Countless studies could no doubt be mounted to examine the detail and provide fuller analysis, but this would be seen only as a delaying tactic.

The following table estimates the annual growth rate of funded private pensions and the proportion of National Income that existing funding represents:—

	Growth Rate %	Funded Assets as % of National Income
Britain	23	60
USA	14	46
Japan	21	20
Australia	19	16
West Germany	8	7
France	16	5

Source: Economist, 8 November 1986: Survey p 4

This evidence is reinforced in a recent major comparative study on pension funds in industrialised countries[10]. One analysis there shows the proportions of household savings distribution over the years 1966 to 1984, with similar results to the table above.

	Life Insurance & Pensions		Equities		Bank Deposits		Other	
	1966	1984	1966	1984	1966	1984	1966	1984
Britain	23	48	31	12	3 7	38	9	2
USA	20	24	38	24	27	41	15	11
Japan	12	14	12	5	62	62	14	19
West Germany	20	22	6	4	68	58	6	16

It is clearly absurd that Britain's pension funds should be triple the claim on future national income as compared with Japan, a country with a high savings ratio: and there is no obvious benefit to the UK from a stock market which is capitalised at three times that of Germany.

Funding future pensions is, of course, purely a bookkeeping entry and a funded pension right, whatever the assets in which it is said to be invested, is no more than a claim on future wealth creation. That claim can be transferred overseas by the purchase of overseas assets: but the merry-go-round of international diversification by pension funds came to an abrupt halt when it was found, in October 1987, that all markets collapsed together. There was no obvious advantage, except to the commission driven global equity salesman, in British pension funds buying overseas securities if those purchases were matched, in whole or in part, by equivalent purchases of British equities or bonds by overseas funds.

It is a further reflection on the disproportionate scale of British pension funds that their overseas assets are greater in absolute terms than those of US pension funds; they represent about 40% of all global diversification by pension funds. Such international exposure is more properly the role and decision of the personal saver and should not be delegated to the institution responsible for retirement provision.

It is, of course, accepted that all major countries offer tax incentives in varying forms to pensions and other forms of saving. But, since retirement provision is so dominant, Britain is unique in allowing retirement provision tax relief to represent such a major distortion in financial markets. At a time when tax reform is being seen as a necessity (and a vote-winner) Britain has the opportunity to signal a new era.

Notes

1. *Personal and Portable Pensions—For All*, Vinson and Chappell, CPS, 1983
2. *Inland Revenue Statistics*, HMSO, published annually
3. *Myth or Reality*, FR Langham, Pensions World, March 1980
4. *Cost of Tax Reliefs for Pension Schemes*, Inland Revenue study, 1983
5. *Occupational Pension Schemes 1983*, by Government Actuary, HMSO, 1986
6. *Taxing Pensions*, by Fry and others, IFS, 1985
7. *Survey of Share Ownership*, Stock Exchange, 1984
8. NOP Market Research, 1988
9. *Changing Face of Share Ownership*, Stock Exchange 1986
10. *The Challenge of Private Pension Funds*, ed. Gabrielli and Fano, 1986

Part Three

Equity for Everyman

8

Equity for Everyman: New Ways to Widen Ownership

John Redwood

Why widen ownership?

> They love their land because it is their own
> And scorn to give aught other reason why;
> Would shake hands with a king upon his throne
> And think it kindness to his Majesty.
>
> *Fitz-Greene Halleck*

The industrial revolution brought many blessings. It brought greater output. It freed many people from working on the land and brought them new homes, new products, new luxuries. It raised wages and living standards, generated employment and developed new technology for the benefit of everybody. In the United Kingdom, its institutional power house was the Public Limited Company. Private capital was made available through the local community or the national market place and invested in plant, machinery and buildings that could fashion swords and plough-shares, guns and cookers, steam trains and garden tools. Through industry, new families became rich, though then, in the English fashion, they sought to enter the ranks of the landed aristocracy by jostling for position and title and purchasing agricultural estates.

Whilst this process generated new wealth, and made almost everyone richer, it did *not* spread the ownership of the means of production widely in the community. At the turn of the 20th century, ninety per cent of the British people still rented the house in which they lived, went to work in a factory wholly owned by somebody else, or on a farm owned by the local lord of the manor, much as their predecessors had done a hundred years before. We were a nation of free men, free under the law, with all the rights and perquisites of citizenship. But we were still two nations—a tiny concentration of wealth holders on the one hand, and on the other the broad mass of workers who had nothing but their chattels and tools.

It was this state of affairs which produced Marxist thinking in favour of wholesale expropriation of wealth by an all-powerful state. And it also generated the more moderate, but still radical democratic-socialist thinking which proposed taxation and benefit systems designed firmly but gradually to redistribute wealth away from the rich and powerful to the humble and meek.

Some fifty years have now passed, during which socialist reforms and thinking have become deeply embedded in our culture. By democratic means, socialists and even a few Marxists alike have had their chance in power and have helped to shape the climate of ideas and opinions within our country. They have imposed their redistributive taxation and have busily taken over, in the name of the state, large chunks of British industry, commerce and the welfare services. Yet despite this process, many people in industry and commerce still feel distanced from their employer. They still resent the rigid distinction between owner and employee. The experiment with nationalised industries, far from creating a harmonious sense of shared ownership, has instead brought disappointment and that profound sense of alienation which men feel who work in large units in which they have no direct stake.

It is one of the ironies of history that it has fallen to the Conservative Party to adumbrate and carry through those policies which do most to redistribute wealth. Starting from the proposition that this had to be done in a positive way—by the generation of more wealth and through enabling people to purchase their own stake—the Conservative Party has for decades championed policies which promote home ownership. From these modest beginnings at the turn of the century, a combination of tax incentives, the sale of publicly owned houses, reductions in private rented accommodation through restrictive rent legislation, and the development of large financial institutions able to aggregate and distribute funds for house purchase, has seen the proportion of home owners mount from ten per cent to sixty one per cent in some eighty years. This has all been achieved by individuals buying their houses for themselves out of their own incomes and resources. The average man, having had the chance to keep more of his earning power, invested it in an asset which provided a roof over the head of his family and was a source of comfort and of pride in his community. No single strand of policy has done more to broaden the basis of ownership in this country and widen opportunity for everyone.

But policy to spread ownership in industry and commerce has until recently been very much less satisfactory. Industry and commerce was gravely affected by the measures of nationalisation taken after 1945. By 1979, water, coal, electricity, gas, the atomic industry, buses, trains, aeroplanes, airports, telephone systems, The Post Office, a major part of the car industry, the ship building industry, the steel industry, a section of the North Sea oil production industry, the largest lorry company, a collection of engineering businesses including Rolls Royce, British Aerospace and Shorts and a whole host of lesser investments were held in trust by the Government for the taxpayer. This prevented employees and the public at large having any personal stake in a vast range of business activities.

But it did more than that. Far from improving industrial relations in those industries as prophesied, their strike record was bad, and the large units that were created were almost unmanageable. Far from lifting the rate of productivity and efficiency, the managerial and labour relations problems often impeded any swift advance. Far from meaning that all investments would be well-funded and productive, nationalized industries vacillated between large and expensive investment programmes, like that in unwanted steel capacity which never produced a return, and investment famines created by the exigencies of national budget planning, as in the cuts administered following the IMF visit of 1976. Far from making people feel that wealth had been redistributed and the capitalist class defeated, the nationalized industries exacerbated the strains. The former owners were rewarded with compensation. So nationalization did nothing to reduce the divisions in society.

The Government elected in 1979 was determined to arrest the downward trend in the individual ownership of company securities, and to reverse the ever-growing size and influence of the state in matters of industry and commerce. The attack upon lopsided business ownership took many forms. First, a range of policies was put into effect to stimulate self-employment, so that genuine employee-owned businesses could flourish. The Business Expansion Scheme provided tax advantages to an individual paying income tax who financed a small or new business. Up to £40,000 of investment each year can be made out of gross income. An initiative on deregulation sought to free small firms from a host of bureaucratic encumbrances. Small firms corporation tax was lowered to thirty percent. National Insurance contributions were reduced. The Enterprise Allowance was introduced to allow the unemployed to set up on their own with taxpayers' help.

Secondly, a range of tax measures was introduced to encourage employees to own shares in their firms or to participate in the profits. These schemes have grown in popularity so that around one and a half million people now enjoy their benefits.

Thirdly, reform of pension fund arrangements has enabled more people to set up their own personal and portable pensions if they wish—thereby offering them direct control over the assets in their schemes and giving them an immediate interest in the creation of the wealth needed to pay their future pensions.

Fourthly, the selling of large amounts of publicly owned business equity to private owners has led to the wider dispersal of wealth, both through the direct encouragement to employees in those businesses to purchase shares, and through the attractions of some of the shares to the wider investing public.

A climate has thus been created which is favourable to self-employment, enterprise and profit.

But in this story there has been one missed opportunity. Eleven million members of occupational pension schemes have by now saved with their employers some £15,000 worth each on average (a total of £170 billion of assets) to provide for their retirement. Members of the schemes know very little about the management of these enormous funds. Because most of them are tied to final salary promises, pledging a level of benefit payable on retirement, the individual seldom interests himself in the nature of the investments his fund managers make, vital though they are to his future prosperity.

The Government's proposals to allow the transfer of assets from one pension fund to another or to a personal fund when an individual changes his job, is a welcome step towards giving members a clear interest in the wealth that is properly their own. But it would be an easy and equally welcome step to go one stage further and make it clear to every member of every occupational pension scheme what the value of his fund might be at any given date if he chose to make his own provision and set up his own pension fund. In this direct and simple way eleven million people would gain effective access to wealth that has already been saved on their behalf, and be able to choose whether they wished to remain with the final salary pledged scheme of their employer, or instead to exercise control over their own assets. Overnight, up to eleven million people could be turned into owners of stakes in British business and commerce!

Without such a move pension funds remain a no-man's-land between warring factions. Companies are inclined to think of them as their own. In return for agreeing to meet a pledge about future payments the company feels that it can manipulate the figures and use any surpluses that may be created for its own purposes. For their part, the members or their union negotiators often claim that the surpluses should be distributed to them in the form of pledges for ever better benefits in the future—against arguments by the cautious actuary or finance director only too aware that the value of investments may go down and the picture look less rosy.

Politics will undoubtedly soon intrude into all this if things are left unchanged. The large accumulated surpluses in pension funds, now estimated at somewhere between £25,000 million and £70,000 million are too tempting. Better, surely, to give them immediately to those who own them as transfer values, rather than allow them to be nibbled away by avaricious politicians?

Privatization—the British experience

Privatization in Britain has been pragmatic. Each individual sale has had its own characteristics and its own problems. Each one has borrowed and adapted solutions from a variety of sources. Innovation has also had a part to play in the story—it has been a journey of pioneers. For the first time ever a large British company has been bought out by its management and employees. For the first time ever an issue has been sold in the British stock market, with a tender to establish the price. For the first time ever a British stock issue has been made with negotiated underwriting commissions. For the first time ever—anywhere in the world—an issue of over £1,000 million has been attempted.

Three main routes have been followed for the sale of companies. There has been the management buy-out, pioneered on a large scale in the case of the National Freight Corporation. There have been offers for sale to the public, including British Telecom, Cable and Wireless, British Aerospace and Amersham. And there have been sales to individual companies and trade buyers, as with the sale of Sealink Ferries to Sea Container, of the Scott Lithgow rig-building yard to Trafalgar House, and the sale of Alvis Military Vehicles to United Scientific Holdings.

Sometimes, corporations have been sold in their entirety. Cable and Wireless, British Telecom, British Aerospace, Amersham, and National Freight were all sold whole in forms similar to those which they had had in the public sector. But some of the larger conglomerates made little industrial sense, or had too much monopoly power without splitting them up. There have therefore been a series of part sales and disposals. These have included the sale of oilfields from British Gas, formed into a new company called Enterprise Oil; the sale of Jaguar as a separate company from BL; and the sale of the British Rail hotels as separate businesses.

Running through the debates over the privatization of public assets has been the question of the adequacy of customer safeguards and the strength of competitive forces. The debate has been at its liveliest in the cases of British Telecom and British Gas. In order to brake the great monopoly powers of British Telecom, the Government encouraged the establishment of a rival telecommunication cable system in the form of Mercury. It allowed a number of cellular radiophone operators to be licensed, encouraged a liberal regime for new value-added services, and made sure in the license and Oftel regulations that there was reasonable access to the British Telecom system for other providers of telephone services. Finally, a free-for-all was created in the provision of equipment to add to the end of exchange lines, where before British Telecom had had a complete monopoly.

In the case of British Gas, the decision to privatize the Corporation as a whole is coupled with the development of a tough pro-competitive and regulated stance. There has to be more freedom to import and export gas, thus allowing sales by gas producers direct to third parties using British Gas lines as a common carrier, and strong teeth to the Ofgas regulator to ensure that charges are fair and reasonable as between different categories of customer, and in relation to the costs of gas supply and the structure of the corporation.

It is easiest to review privatization progress department by department—as departmental culture is deeply embedded in the Whitehall machine and each act of privatization is seen as a departmental rather than a governmental problem.

Department of Transport

The Department of Transport has made rapid progress in privatizing the ragbag of assets it inherited in 1979, particular speed being made under the latest Secretary of State, Nicholas Ridley, a keen exponent of the powers of competition and private capital. When the Department sold the whole of its largest lorry business in Britain in 1980, there was a sharp improvement in profitability, the use of assets, and the rate of growth of the business as a result of the direct participation through their shareholdings of over half the lorry-drivers and managers in the business. Their story is testimony to the benign effects of the privatization movement seen at its best.

The nationalized bus industry in the shire counties is being opened up to competition, following the success of deregulation of the inter-city coach service market. Early relaxation of the licensing requirements spawned many new businesses, cut fares dramatically, and increased the number of passengers substantially. The same consequences are expected to flow from the deregulation of the shire county stage-carriage bus services. Sale of the individual bus companies themselves, at present owned by the public sector, will follow the successful passage of the bus bill through Parliament. The result should be a felicitous combination of strengthened competitive forces and wider ownership of the bus company assets.

British Airways, the country's largest airline, is scheduled for rapid privatization following a period of several years in which a new management team, using the promise and threat of privatization, has rebuilt its profits and started to improve upon a much-weakened balance sheet. Planes are now more likely to fly on time, services are better, and many employees are looking forward to the day when they can buy a stake in the business themselves through a preferential share scheme. The business was of course already competitive. The British Airports Authority is also scheduled for sale but this is planned as a whole, so monopoly regulation will be essential.

British Rail remains as a state pensioner, although it has been shorn of some of its assets, which are now leading healthier lives in the private sector. Hotels, ferries, and some of the catering services have been returned to private enterprise, and the engineering services, particularly the building of new wagons and locomotives, may follow.

The motorway service areas have been sold on long leases to private contractors; and consideration is now being given to a plan to sell the Dartford Tunnel to a private consortium—a plan linked to a further scheme for an additional cross-Thames facility to be built with private capital. The Ministry of Transport is also being imaginative about the harnessing of private capital to various other facilities like the Docklands light railway link using British Rail tracks. Many new service roads in the country are now financed by housing developers from the gains they make out of the grant of planning permission for housing and commercial building. Finally there is the Channel fixed link, the largest project for transport infrastructure ever undertaken in this country, which will be privately financed.

Department of Energy

The Department under Nigel Lawson made very rapid strides towards privatization of the oil enterprises. The Labour Government's British National Oil Corporation was split into two. Britoil was established, and took over all BNOC's producing assets and prospective exploration acreage. This was sold complete as Britain's third largest oil exploration and production company. Sale of a competitive business in a competitive marketplace enabled the directors and managers to go overseas to diversify their asset-base and, free of the dead hand of the Treasury, to raise cash and develop a corporate strategy. Next to go from Energy was Enterprise Oil, formed out of the oil assets of the British Gas Corporation. A separate trade sale was made of the Wytch Farm oilfield to a consortium of oil investors.

The coal industry has not been privatized despite the rifts caused by the recent strike. True, a few peripheral assets have been sold, like the investments in Associated Heat Services and in the builders' merchants Sankey. One possible course for the future is to sell off the open-cast coal-mining activities. These are profitable and are now undertaken by private contracting firms using TGWU labour. Consideration could be given to returning individual mines or groups of mines to co-operatives of coal miners, if necessary giving them away with a dowry if they are loss-making. Miners' co-operatives may well be able to make a success of them; several private enterprise small drift mines, for example in South Wales, do now work at a profit.

Alternatively, the Nottinghamshire pits could be given to the Nottingham miners who would then enjoy the benefit of the profits through dividends. This could bring about the most dramatic transformation in the mining industry in history.

The Atomic Energy Authority is being turned into a trading fund, but the Government is reluctant to sell it to the private sector given the sensitivity surrounding nuclear power and the problems experienced with nuclear leaks. Peter Walker is championing the sale of British Gas, with a bill going through Parliament in this session to facilitate the public sale of the whole of the Corporation as it is, with a substantial stake for employee shareholders. He is especially keen to see shareholdings in the new Corporation spread very widely. This leaves electricity as the one major public utility for which no privatization plans have yet been developed, a challenge likely to be left until after the next General Election.

Department of Trade and Industry

The Department of Trade and Industry inherited many investments in many different industries. Most of those grouped under the National Enterprise Board have been disposed of. The shareholding in ICL computers was sold to STC at an advantageous price and time. The substantial investment in Inmos was sold to Thorn EMI when it was still profit-making, before a major decline in the silicon chip market. Ferranti was returned to the private sector in an offer for sale and has flourished ever since. Individual investments from within the BL stable have also been sold, including Alvis, Prestcold Refrigeration and Jaguar cars. Unipart should be the next to go.

Graham Day at British Shipbuilders has done a marvellous job returning pieces of an overextended and disappointing industry to private ownership. Scott Lithgow, the rig-building yard, the three warship-building yards and the ship-repairing activities have been sold off to private investors. Only the basic shipbuilding capacity making merchant ships remains in public hands. At British Steel some of the myriads of peripheral investments have been sold including Stanton and Stavely, and part stakes in Phoenix developments in the attempt to bridge public and private ownership of crucial areas of the steel industry. These schemes, however, have often entailed more nationalization than denationalization and a success cannot be claimed until the remaining 50 per cent in public ownership is returned to the private sector.

The telephone system was split off from The Post Office and British Telecom was sold in its entirety. Cable and Wireless and Amersham were both returned to private sector owners. Only the Post Office staff remains untouched. The whole of the aerospace and defence weapons-maker British Aerospace was returned to the public in an offer for sale.

At the Ministry of Defence the Royal Ordnance factories are being put onto a commercial footing ready for sale. Making a great variety of small arms, ammunition and weapon systems, they will be returned to the private sector before the next General Election, when they should become profitable and successful private sector businesses.

The British Columbian experience

In the early 1980's a Conservative administration was returned to power in British Columbia in the wake of a disastrous left-wing experiment. The British Columbian Government, under its new leadership, wished to tackle the problem of the British Columbian Resources and Investment Corporation established by its predecessors, which was in desperate need of new capital—proving to be yet another cash-hungry monolith. The original idea of sale of BCRIC to the British Columbian public fell foul of clever opposition politicking on the slogan of 'Why Buy Something You Already Own?' Plans for the offer for sale were already well advanced and there was considerable political investment in the successful conclusion of the sale. It fell to the lot of the Prime Minister and his closest advisers to find a way of salvaging their scheme of denationalizing BCRIC; and they hit upon the idea of giving shares free to all the adult voting population of the state. At the same time they issued new equity for which individuals had to subscribe six Canadian dollars per share purchased.

The issue was a great success, with a very high proportion of the British Columbian public taking up their free shares—which they had to do by positive application. Very many subscribed for additional shares at the subscription price. The experiment demonstrated that there is so real a hunger for ownership (certainly in the North American continent) that people are prepared to subscribe new capital for likely ventures, and that a government offer for sale coupled with a free share issue can reach individuals who would not otherwise contemplate buying shares on the stock market. The public proved to be wise in their initial purchases, as the shares soon traded up to the nine Canadian dollar mark. There was general agreement that the offer for sale was an attractive one at the pricing decided upon by the professional advisers, whilst the free shares were of course indisputably a good deal! (The subsequent sharp decline in the share price served as a salutary reminder of the hazards of equity investment.)

British Columbia succeeded in solving the registration, dividend and reporting problems which a very large share register can produce, overcame political obstacles by giving people part of what they already owned indirectly as taxpayers, and demonstrated considerable support for this privatization policy. The question naturally arises whether any of this experience can be translated elsewhere, and whether it is desirable so to do.

Where next in Britain?

> Make ye sure to each his own
> That he reap where he hath sown
>
> *Rudyard Kipling*

In order to claim that the objectives which have been set for privatization have been achieved we must be able to demonstrate that ownership has been much more widely dispersed, that competitive forces are being sharpened, that customer service has been improved, that industrial relations are being enhanced and that output and productivity have benefited from the process. In any particular privatization case there will be a balance between the range of objectives set and the different successes achieved. Overall, given the magnitude of privatization, its scope and opportunity, it should be possible to demonstrate that all the objectives have been largely achieved.

There are three areas where the current thrust of policy could be strengthened. These are the involvement of employees in the direct ownership of their businesses, the number of share owners in the public at large and the strengthening of the forces of competition.

The public sector which may remain to be tackled after the 1987/88 election comprises coal, electricity, atomic energy, the railways, part of the car production industry, part of the steel industry, The Post Office and the commercial shipyards.

Some of these businesses are already strongly competitive. There is no lack of challengers in car production, in steel manufacture, in shipbuilding; indeed, the strength of the competition—particularly from overseas—has been a factor in making it hard to maintain profitability and develop new products fast enough. On the other hand the inadequacy of competition in the electricity industry, postal delivery and, to a lesser extent rail transport, causes real problems.

Pro-competitive ways of privatizing public monopolies

Each public monopoly is different, but few are natural. Take the case of electricity. Whilst one can argue that the duplication of the electricity grid would be expensive and unnecessary, there is no such case for a similar monopoly in the provision of electric power to the grid, or in the servicing of individual electricity customers.

The bulk of the investment in electricity goes into the generation of power by large capital-intensive plants, burning a variety of fuels from atomic power through oil and gas to coal. Each one of these large plants is phased in or phased out of production according to the overall level of demand in the system, its use or non-use being determined by its ranking in the unit cost league. The cheapest power—from the nuclear stations—is generated and supplied on a continuous basis to the grid. The dearest power, often supplied by the marginal, older oil-burning stations, is brought into use only at peak times in the winter when loads are especially high.

One pro-competitive approach to privatizing electricity would be to sell off groups of power stations to different owners. The power stations could be grouped geographically or by type of fuel burned, or by baskets of different types to provide a balanced portfolio. For example oil stations could be sold in one lot and the coal stations in two or three lots. Alternatively, a basket of coal, oil, and other power stations could be put together with varying levels of unit cost so that the buyers could always have one or two stations providing the base loads, and one or two stations which could be switched in or out, depending on total demand in the system. It might be necessary to keep nuclear stations in the public sector because people are sensitive about the importance of maintaining safety standards—although it is not necessarily the case that standards would be higher in the public sector. In practice high safety standards are going to be achieved by the setting and adequate policing of government norms, whether the stations are in public or in private ownership.

The grid could continue to be a nationally owned asset and its management by a central buyer of electricity would have to be based on clear rules similar to those presently governing the purchase of power stations by individual electricity boards. The owners of power stations would have the right to supply their power when total demand necessitated switching in their station, and the order of switching for their station would be entirely determined by the unit price at which they were prepared to supply the electricity. The only way in which an individual station's rank in the merit order could therefore change is either by an improvement in its operating efficiency which would produce lower unit costs, or by a commercial decision to lower the margin on the power sold to the grid operator in order to gain more market share. Providing there was a minimum of three or four groups of power stations competitive conditions in the market should prevail. No one owner should be allowed to own a disproportionate number of stations as he would then have excessive market power. Single power station ownership whilst permissible might not be a sensible idea as the downward movement of that individual station in the merit order—for reasons outside its control— could have an overwhelming impact upon the investor. But this would remain a business decision for the company concerned.

The retail and service end of electricity supply can also be broken up. Servicing, installation and maintenance of electrical equipment is not a monopoly anyway, and private sector operators can be relied upon to enter and improve their position in this market-place. Similarly, the sale of new electrical appliances has already been opened up to competition with a consequent check upon prices and an improvement in standards of service supplied through the electricity showrooms. But the sale of electricity to customers, their billing and the maintenance of the mains and mains connections, could remain as a public function together with the grid network. It is difficult to see how enough competition could be introduced into the sale of electricity to domestic users—although there should be free entry to anybody wishing to make connections to the main system whether for supply to industrial or domestic consumers, subject to observation of the necessary safety standards.

To sum up, the main cost of electricity generation lies in erecting, maintaining and fueling the power stations. And this cost can be made subject to competitive pressures. There is no easy way for the mains and the electricity grid to be made subject to competitive pressures. If these were to be privatized it would have to be via a regulated monopoly. So they may just as well stay within the public sector—where, however, stronger regulatory policing is necessary than at present, if the customer is to get a better deal on price and efficiency. It would be a pity if the opportunity to strengthen competitive forces in the electricity market was lost, since this would give credence to the view that the principle purpose of privatization is to raise large sums of money as surrogate sources of revenue rather than to improve economic performance at company level.

The Post Office is already a corporation operating in a semi-privatized state. Although it is responsible for routing the mails around the country in a fleet of vans, and providing services through the 2,000 Crown post offices which it owns, much of the rest of the system is de-centralized and in private hands. The 20,000 sub-post offices are leased operations in private shops, often the village store, sharing overheads with the shop itself and providing a useful but modest source of income for the owner, together with a range of approved services for his customers. Some of the despatch by air and rail is contracted out (using postal staff) to other transport operations, whilst the parcels mail is competitive with private providers. Document exchanges, courier systems within universities, professional groups and businesses, and certain types of high class mail are also in private hands, competing at the margin.

The biggest revolution can come through freer grants of licenses to private stores for the provision of post office facilities, and through the growth of a wider range of counter services for those branches which remain under post office control. The trend of modern retailing in larger branch networks is towards subletting space and creating franchise areas within each store. It would be useful to have more post office branches open during normal Saturday trading hours; useful, too, for other organisations to be given authority to sell stamps, postal orders and the other basic services provided by the system. Conversely, The Post Office could act through its main branches as an agent for various types of financial and other paper transactions, e.g. for share purchase and sale, for certain kinds of insurance activity and the like. The way forward is most likely to rest with such dynamic participation in the financial services revolution, with a blurring of the boundaries between public and private service in using the post office buildings and with sub-contracting and contracted-out functions to other enterprises.

The National Coal Board's monopoly over coal reserves is neither natural nor should it remain unchallenged. It would greatly strengthen the industry, aid productivity and improve working conditions if a variety of providers were introduced. Opencast licences could be granted along with deep mining licences by the Department of Energy direct to contractors who are prepared to bid for them. The existing deep mines under Coal Board control could be split into different operating groups and diversified ownership patterns established. Only under a public monopoly system could so much anguish have been created, and such a fast rate of decline experienced in an industry whose operating environment improved in the '70's and early '80's through the major price increases in the principal competitor fuel, oil.

How can the role of employees be strengthened?

The principal disappointment in the privatization programme to date is that the satisfactory history of the National Freight Corporation has not been more thoroughly exploited. NFC showed that ordinary groups of employees were interested in acquiring a stake in their business: and once they had acquired it attitudes began to change and they felt the excitement and responsibility which shared ownership can bring. It also considerably enhanced their prosperity as share prices went up eleven-fold in the space of some three years. This does not prevent the business having from time to time to lay men off, nor will it guarantee a strike-free future. Jaguar demonstrated that only too well by facing a strike for higher pay shortly after return to the private sector. But wherever significant shareholdings have been built up by employees, attitudes do begin to change, barriers do begin to break down between managers and workers and employees do begin to receive more rights in running their own businesses and more say in how they adapt to changes of market and other circumstances. Surely these are trends which should be welcomed by any democrat?

The most promising way to carry the practice further is to take one or two of the larger loss-making or low-return industries, and to *give* them to their employees. Treasury arithmeticians and the guardians of the public purse and conscience need not be faint-hearted. They could not argue that we are giving away something which is a priceless national asset; for in the case of motor car production, commercial shipbuilding and steel production, the public has received nothing but losses and bills for the last seven or eight years. But what we would be doing would be to give control of *potentially* productive assets to people who might labour day after day to make those assets yield a return.

The financial terms surrounding the gifts of the assets would clearly be hard fought. Those about to receive them would want some reassurance that they would not be saddled with an unrealistic burden of debt, even though the debt had been built up over the years of loss-making in those industries. They might well also wish to feel they would not be disadvantaged in queuing for government support for export contracts or for the usual kinds of subsidies available through DTI for industrial purposes. Reasonable assurances and financial changes should be made to expedite the gift, but it would be a pointless exercise to give away the assets if at the same time clauses were put into the agreement that effectively underwrote any losses which might occur in the natural hurly-burly of business life.

The easiest cases to treat would be individual commercial shipyards, and individual groups of coal mines. These have the advantage of being local and relatively small-size—and hence less complex. They are still units that can produce meaningful quantities of products which have a chance in national and international markets. Steel and cars are a little more difficult because of the scale of the operations but basically can be treated in the same way.

BSC and BL are anyway being reduced in size by disposal of peripheral concerns and by splitting the businesses into their component parts. For example, the truck, bus, and spares activities of British Leyland do not need to be part of the main car-assembly activity. It would also be possible to divorce the high-performance and more expensive cars at the top end of the range which sell under the Rover and Honda marques from the cheaper mass-production cars selling as Austins. In the case of steel, separation of some of the higher value-added processes like tinplating and high-performance steelmaking from the basic process would also permit the introduction of widespread employee capital, in units that made sense of employee management.

Universal sharegiving?

The British Columbian experience is difficult to apply to Britain. Firstly, the population of British Columbia is far smaller. In consequence the problems of registration, dividend payment, report filing, and accounting are not as great for the shareholders' register in British Columbia as they would be for an exercise covering the whole of the British population. Secondly, Britain now has developed methods of privatization which are well-established: switching to a system of 'free' gifts of shares to everyone would be a marked departure from existing practice, which can pose more problems than pioneering a new technique in the first place. Thirdly, the argument that did most to force the Prime Minister's hand in British Columbia towards the free gift of shares, namely the opposition gibes that he was trying to sell to the public something which it already owned, does not apply with the same force in Britain, as few here feel they 'own' the nationalized industries. Fourthly, the British Columbian Investment and Resources Corporation represented a diversified portfolio of investments with profit prospects and without monopoly problems. There is no similar animal in Britain.

However, the idea of a free gift of shares in a large corporation to every member of the British public in order at one stroke to spread the habit of share ownership as widely as possible, *is* extremely attractive. It would give everyone a first experience of owning shares, albeit modest. It would stimulate the growth of financial services, introduce the habit, and spread the responsibility, of ownership. Instead of three million shareholders, we could have thirty-five million.

The problems involved are not insuperable and are certainly less than the obstacles that were overcome when the first privatization measures were put through Parliament. For the idea to be taken seriously we have therefore to consider which industry or industries are the most suitable cases for treatment.

The first criterion to examine is that of size. There is no point in giving people an asset which is worth less than £100. With a 35 million adult voting population, we are therefore looking for an asset worth at least £3,500 million. This cuts out most of the small public corporations and smaller investments held by the British public sector.

It would scarcely be practicable to give a free share in a corporation where shares had already been sold for a substantial value. Existing shareholders would understandably object to the market being deluged by a large number of free shares, some of them passing into loose hands once the specified holding period had elapsed; and one could easily envisage court actions following from aggrieved groups of shareholders. This rules out British Petroleum, British Telecom, and British Gas (the share disposal method for the first part of the latter must be settled by now).

There are therefore two serious runners left. The first is British Rail. As a loss-making business, on profit-and-earnings grounds it does not meet the requirement of large scale. However with the public subsidies paid for specified public service duties, and with the substantial property, rolling stock and rail assets, it is a serious contender, and is certainly a large corporation with considerable potential. It is not a monopoly, in the sense that the transport market is strongly competitive and British Rail has experienced growing competition, even on its inter-city routes from a combination of cheaper-fare airline services and the deregulated inter-city coach services. It is a national network and segregating it into separate rail regions for privatization makes little sense.

One of the great problems of British Rail is the virtual absence of cross-London routes and the perseverance of regional attitudes. If BR is to fight back it must provide a national transport service capable of linking the north to the south and the east to the west so that passengers can travel across the country without too many changes and disruptions. (A start has been made this year with inter-city services from Kensington Olympia.) BR *can* become an extremely attractive business. Its properties are still under-exploited, given the potential revenue that could be drawn from the number of customers passing through the mainline stations, and the redevelopment potential of many of the prime sites which British Rail owns in the centres of many of our principal towns and cities. It is a business where morale and customer service are important—precisely the virtues fostered by a sense of co-ownership through shareholdings.

The gift of shares in British Rail to every adult man and woman on the voting register would not of necessity preclude moves towards greater competition within the railway system itself. Present encouraging efforts to bring in private capital for property redevelopment and for the rail services themselves (as with the docklands light railway) could continue. Joint venture and partnership could become a pronounced feature of the privatized universally-owned corporation, as the management sought novel ways of financing its activities and introducing innovation and better customer service.

The principal obstacles to be overcome would concern price protection (particularly on the commuter services) and the financial framework of government subsidy under which the privatized railways would at least for the time being need to operate. The commuter may well be right to assert that he needs special protection, for although there are competitive modes of travel available, on the buses, by car, and underground, nonetheless many people base their lives upon access to a British Rail station and a daily commuting journey. The experience of life in the public sector has not been favourable to the commuter as his real fares have gone on rising over two decades. In order to offer him some protection a simple price control formula may have to be introduced at the time of any privatization legislation, which would give him a better guarantee than anything he has enjoyed to date under nationalization.

If the system passed into the hands of private shareholders there would certainly need to be an obligation to run rail services rather than simply to close the rail routes and exploit the potential of the property *per se*.

The question of how much money the Government provided to British Rail would also need careful setting out. The railways are not likely to operate in a subsidy-free world. What is important is to limit the subsidy, see that it is concentrated on those routes where the railway has the best chances of success, and provide a firm framework so that on the one hand subsidy is not used to build up unreasonable profits at public expense, and on the other hand is not so skimped that the railways have an impossible task in balancing their books. Designing such a system is not easy.

We must start by defining what the subsidy is trying to buy. The first rule should be that it is concentrated on passengers and not on goods. Goods should have to compete in the open market and make a profit if they can. The second rule is that the subsidy should be limited and do the maximum good for the pounds spent.

This requires some kind of tendered contractual arrangement. The obvious way is to tender per passenger mile on certain kinds of routes. There is, however, the danger that if only one group, namely British Rail, is tendering figures, there is no check, other than an administrative and bureaucratic one, on the costings of overheads between different lines and different types of operation. It may therefore be necessary to encourage other groups to come in and offer transport services over the maintained way. Could we perhaps move towards a system in which all of us through our individual shareholdings owned the fixed way, the stations and the other properties: provided the engineering services and maintained the standards and the timetabling system for the network as a whole: *but* the individual train services were supplied by a range of competitive operators, tendering for so much subsidy to run such and such a route? The board itself would have a five-year plan of subsidy laid out in an expenditure White Paper. There would be incentives to ensure that the amount of travel bought for that subsidy, and the revenue from passengers so generated was maximized. In order to meet the requirements of safety and employment, there should be a rule that in the early years of tendering consortia had to use British Rail staff at British Rail rates of pay in order to run their trains (but they could be free to negotiate their own manning arrangements with the rail unions). But the danger here is that the advantages of this adventurous type of privatization could all too easily be dissipated in the detailed regulations needed, and by unhelpful union response.

The case of electricity

The second candidate for wider ownership by individual share-holders is electricity. As a huge, profitable, cash-generating business it meets the criterion of size. It fails, however, to meet the criterion that it should not be a monopoly. Proposals to turn the generation of electricity into a competitive business have been briefly outlined above. The candidate here for wider ownership by share distribution is that part of the business which has to be regulated and could otherwise remain in the public sector, namely the grid and the electricity boards themselves, not the generating stations.

Under a system where competing power operators supply power to the grid on a basis of unit costs and prices, the behaviour of the grid operator and of the electricity boards would need to be regulated, since competition is difficult if not impossible. But these assets could be passed to individual ownership through free shares. Nor would the Treasury be entirely despondent because it would have raised money from the sale of power stations themselves to bidding commercial consortia. The free gift of shares in the grid and the board system would entitle the regulators to be firm in controlling costs and prices.

Given the need for strong regulation it would not be the most exciting equity issue. This illustrates the dilemma involved in privatizing any monopoly while at the same time wanting shareholders to acquire a successful investment. Their interest in higher profits is too easily at variance with the need to protect customers from predatory pricing.

The technical problems

Is Parliament entitled to give away property which is owned on behalf of the taxpayer by the Treasury or the responsible Department? Certainly there is no reason why a sovereign Parliament cannot enact legislation to give away assets at present in public ownership. True, the Public Accounts Committee and other Parliamentary watchdogs are always on the lookout for unreasonable deals, selling public assets short or misusing them. But this is a different matter from giving them away to *all* the British voters. If an asset has been sold too cheaply, then not only has the public sector lost value but a particular interest in the country has gained value at the expense of the general public. If on the other hand assets are being *given* to the public as a whole, no such impropriety exists.

But would 35 million shareholders be too many for a company to service properly? Under existing company law there could be substantial difficulties. The thought of two million shareholders in British Telecom terrified the registrars of securities, the payers of dividends, and the convenors of the general meetings. But to date it has been manageable and the operation has been conducted with military precision. Still, to go from two million to 35 million is a very large quantum leap. If just one per cent of shareholders wished to be present at the Annual General Meeting a hall would have to be found to take 350,000 people. There is no such hall.

The cost of sending out annual statements and dividends would be very great; and it may therefore require amendments to the stipulations of the Companies Act for this particular operation. Suggested amendments could include: the mailing of a single shortform statement of company performance once a year to all shareholders, or advertisements in every major national newspaper in lieu of a full statement sent to each individual shareholder. Annual rather than biannual dividend payments could be made. Some control could be devised over the attendance of members at meetings; for example every shareholder who wished to attend the Annual General Meeting in person might have to write six weeks in advance saying that he intends to do so, so that the company can decide whether to book Wembley Stadium or the Birmingham Exhibition Centre. Alternatively, consideration might be given to holding regional AGMs which would send on conclusions, recommendations and votes to a national AGM (attendance at which would be limited to representatives appointed by the regional AGMs).

These things look cumbersome and difficult in prospect but in practice, as British Telecom illustrates, they may be more easily soluble than people fear. What *is* required is that detailed thought be given to the likely difficulties before embarking on any such course of action.

For example, would the new shareholders all sell out and create chaos in the market? If you give 35 million people a small bonus in the form of shares and most of them own no other shares, there is indeed a strong possibility that many may do so at the first opportunity. And if vast numbers did sell out it could be argued that the company might just as well have been sold in the normal way— giving everybody a tax rebate based on the proceeds.

To stagger the rate of sale and to encourage as many as possible to remain shareholders a number of tactics might be adopted. The Government could impose a surrender penalty of decreasing severity as the years advanced. It could consider treating sale as a small bonus for old age and limit selling rights to old age pensioners. It could tax sale proceeds as income for the first couple of years. Any of these devices could employ a combination of the tax system and control over registration of transfer in order to slow down the rate of sale. Requiring people to apply for the free shares in the first place could also strengthen commitment to their ownership.

Two promising avenues

This pamphlet has charted the progress of the privatization movement which was effectively pioneered by the United Kingdom and still has considerable momentum. It has shown the wide variety of solutions which have been embraced; although in varying degrees all the solutions point in the direction of more employee participation and motivation, wider share ownership, more competition, better service for the customers and better management. It has shown that the technique of *giving* shares has already been used successfully in the case of British Telecom in order to widen the shareholding public and give the shareholders a substantial stake. But as yet, nowhere in the world save in British Columbia, has a universal issue of free shares been attempted as a deliberate act to involve a whole voting population in the ownership of industry and commerce.

In the lifetime of this and the next Parliament, given a Conservative victory at the polls, it is a feasible target to remove all industry and commerce from nationalized ownership. The task is already advanced and this pamphlet has set out ways in which it can be carried further by tailoring solutions to individual industries.

Two avenues have been explored which deserve particular attention, given the state of present thinking and debate on privatization. The first is the need to take more vigorous steps to segregate businesses in the remaining public sector monopolies and introduce competitive forces. As we have shown, in the test case of electricity it would be possible to split off the generation from grid management and to introduce competitive forces in the operation of power-supply to the integrated national grid. Similarly, in the case of British Rail, although the competitive forces from other ways of travel are already strong, it might be desirable to introduce a further element of competition. This could be done by tendering to manage the service provision itself within the framework of a national railway board whose duty it would be to maintain safety and engineering standards, to develop properties, to see to customer satisfaction and to timetables. As electricity is likely to be privatized it is vital that a pro-competitive solution is adopted. British Rail is a more difficult case in view of the large element of public subsidy involved.

The second avenue involves being less timorous in the approach to businesses which are already competitive but are not performing well. Here the gift of shares to employees is often a good way of transforming a business and reducing taxpayers' risk at the same time. The experience of the management buy-out of National Freight shows what can be done, and the growing trend for management and employee buy-outs throughout the private sector shows just how favourable the climate now is. A bold movement to introduce employee ownership in certain kinds of pit in the coal industry, in steel plants and in car plants could transform motivation and provide the stimulus which is needed. Any visitor to those industries will know that the years have not healed the divide between managers and men, even though managers are themselves no more the owners of the business than the employees over whom they hold sway.

The pamphlet has also examined the British Columbian experience to see how worthwhile it might be to go one stage further and offer free shares in a complete nationalized company. The advantage is obvious. At one fell swoop, ownership of at least one industry in Britain becomes as wide as it possibly can be. The technical objections about the feasibility of a large share register, the holding of meetings and so forth, could be overcome, whilst no serious argument can be mounted to say that Parliament is powerless to give something away which Parliament by other powers has taken in to public ownership.

The major difficulty in debating the idea is to determine how it fits in with the need for competitive forces within the nationalized industries. These problems could be overcome in the case of the electricity grid and area board distribution systems. Shares in the latter would not have the razmatazz that the British Columbian Investment and Resources Corporation had—although that worked both ways! The Boards would remain under some kind of regulatory control because they would retain considerable monopoly powers. The returns to the shareholders would, therefore, be in part determined by the severity of the regulatory framework. The conflict between satisfactory profitability on the one hand and a decent deal to the customers on the other would always be a major factor in considering the worth of the shares and the future policy of the company.

Nevertheless government should consider this as another possible part of its general strategy of rapid widening of ownership and of reducing state power. It could find that an idea which for years had appeared to be too difficult or even silly is now ready to come of age. Certainly, the case of British Telecom shows that there is a hunger for share ownership in this country today, as seen not only in the excellent take-up of the issue itself but also in the decision by a majority of applicants to take the additional bonus shares rather than the rebate on telephone bills. This desire for ownership, fed by the vigorous privatization programme already undertaken and envisaged, will find even greater fulfilment if a far bolder share distribution can be brought to fruition.

Appendix
Privatization achievements

British Aerospace

51.6% of the ordinary shares was sold on 13 February 1981 at 150p per share. The issue raised £148.6m. with sales expenses of £5.6m. £100m. was paid to the company as new capital, leaving net receipts to the Treasury of £43m. 3.6% of the ordinary shares was sold to employees on concessional terms.

On 10 May 1985 the remaining Government holding was sold. At the same time BAE raised new capital from the sale of 50,000,000 shares at £3.75 per share. Foreign ownership is limited to 15% in total and no individual was allowed more than 10% on first allocation. The Government retains a special share which can be used to block takeovers. The receipts from the 1985 sale grossed £363m. of which a small amount will go in expenses.

In the first offering eligible employes were given 33 free shares and were allowed an additional 600 free shares on a one-for-one basis against those for which they had applied at the offer price. In practice a maximum 220 free shares were available because of over subscription. There were also facilities for preferential consideration of applications within a total pool of 5,000,000 ordinary shares. In 1985 employees were given preferential consideration in applications for another 5,000,000 ordinary shares.

Cable and Wireless

Just over 49% of Cable and Wireless was sold on 30 October 1981, including 1.4% to employees. The shares were sold at 168p per share and £225m. gross was raised. £35m. of this took the form of new share capital, leaving the Treasury with £182m. after expenses.

In 1982 the holding was reduced by the sale of a further 27.54% of the equity or 100,000,000 shares after allowing for the 1 for 2 scrip issue. Sold at 275p the issue grossed £275m. but cost £12.15m. In December 1985 the remaining 22.7% was sold at 587p a share.

Employees in October 1981 received 29 free shares and shares up to a value of £250 on a basis of one for every one subscribed for.

There was also a preferential allocation of up to 5% of the total issed share capital for employees.

In December 1983 additional preference was given for employee applications of up to 1,000 shares.

The company has been particularly successful with manpower rising from 10,000 in the last complete financial year before sale to 24,000 as at March 1985. Profits have risen from £62m. to £245m. in the last completed year and turnover shot up from £293m. to £862m. Cable and Wireless have exploited to the full the international opportunities which privatization has offered them.

Amersham International PLC

This company was sold on 18 February 1982 in one go at a price of 142p per share. 3.7% of the equity was bought by employees and the issue raised £65m. for the Government when the VAT and interest on application money is taken into account. The company issued 5.1m. shares at the same time to raise £7.3m. of new capital. Employees received £50 worth of shares free and could acquire one free share for each share purchased up to £500 worth. The company has done well since privatization, manpower rising from 2,049 as at the end of 1981 to 2,346 for the year to March 1985, and profits rose fourfold between 1981 and 1985.

National Maritime

Sold in 1982.

Land Settlement Association

Sold to tenants.

Ordnance Survey

Trading fund established. No known further plans.

British Sugar

24% of shares sold in July 1981, all of HMG's holding.

Motorway Service Areas

Sold during 1979–83 Parliament.

National Freight Consortium

On 19 February 1982 the Company was sold to the management and employees for a gross £53.5m. £48.7m. of this had to be paid to the Pension Fund which was showing a deficiency. £100m. also had to be written off. Between 1981 and 1984 profits rose from £4.3m. to £16.9m. Capital investment is well up and new business has flowed into the company. The company has only lost three afternoons in industrial action in the three years since privatization compared with the difficult record before.

Britoil

51% of the company was sold on 19 November 1982 at 215p per share. The rest of the shares was sold at 185p per share on 18 August 1985. Only .1% was taken up by employees in 1982, which showed considerable wisdom and judgement as 75% of the issue was left with the underwriters and on the first day of trading the shares closed 19p down in their partly paid form. The proceeds from the 1982 sale grossed £639m. and from the 1985 sale £449m.

In 1982 employees were offered free shares worth £58.50, the matching of shares up to £400 bought on a one-for-one basis, a share option scheme, a profit-sharing scheme and preference in allocation for up to 10% of the offer. The disappointing response reflected the market circumstances and press comment of the time. In the 1985 offer 750 Britoil employees applied for 3.4m. shares and these preferential applications were allotted in full. The response was much better as market circumstances were better. In the second year of operation of the company employee participation rose to 50% of the workforce. The Government retains a Golden share.

Associated Ports Holding PLC

51.5% was sold at 112p per share on 9 February 1983. 4.3% was taken up by employees. On 17 April 1984 the rest of the shares were sold at 270p. The two sales combined netted £96m. In February 1983 the employees received £60 of free shares and a one-for-one offer up to £250 worth. There was also a preferential offer for the full price shares.

International Air Radio

Sold on 30 March 1983 for £60m. to STC.

British Rail Hotels

Sales completed by the end of 1984 realising £53m. from 22 hotels.

BGC Wytch Farm

Sold in May 1984 to the Dorset Group for an £85m. down payment and a second payment of £130m.

Enterprise Oil

Sold on 27 June 1984 at 185p per share. The sale netted £380m. and employees were given special preference up to 13,500 shares. The Government retains a Golden share.

Sealink

Sold on 27 July 1984 to British Ferries, a subsidiary of Sea Containers Inc., for £66m.

Jaguar PLC

Privatized on 3 August 1984 by the sale of all the shares at 165p per share. BL grossed £297m. from the sale. Employees received preferential applications for up to 5% of the shares and bought 1.3% of the company at issue. The performance since privatization has been excellent. The Government retains a Golden share.

British Telecom

50% sold on 28 November 1984 at 130p per share. 4.6% was taken up by employees. The sale grossed £3.9 billion. Employees received £70.20 worth of free shares, at a matching offer of two free shares for each one purchased up to 77 shares, and a 10% discount on the offer for sale price on the final instalment for employees who have held up to 1600 shares. Profits and growth have been good since privatization. The Government retains a Golden share.

Scottish Transport Group MacBryne Haulage

Sold to Kildonan Transport Limited July 1985 for £500,000.

BP

In June 1977 66.8m. shares were sold for £564m. On 9 November 1979 80m. shares were sold for £290m. On 13 July 1981 the Government did not subscribe for the one for seven rights and sold its rights at a 17p premium grossing £14m. On 23 September 1983 130m. shares were sold grossing £565m. 31.7% of the shares remain in government ownership.

Remaining Public Sector Investments

49.8% of British Telecom remains. There is a public commitment to retain the present holding until 9 April 1988 in the form of a letter from the Secretary of State to the Chairman of the Company.

BL

There is a stated intention to make more progress towards privatization of the BL Group, and Unipart has been specified as the next target. Other possibilities must include Land-Rover, Truck and Bus.

British Airports Authority

A White Paper was issued on 5 June 1985 outlining that the BAA would be sold as a whole. It was included in the manifesto.

British Airways

Civil Aviation Act 1980 conferred the powers to sell the whole of British Airways. The sale has been delayed by legal difficulties. Press comment indicates that the sale is likely this year of the whole company.

British Gas Corporation

A Gas Bill has been introduced into the House of Commons to enable the sale of the whole of British Gas, possibly late in 1986. It is to be sold by public flotation.

British Nuclear Fuels

A business with £1256m. in net assets, 15,000 employees. No policy decisions have yet been taken. It was turned into a PLC in January 1984.

British Rail Engineering

No decision has been taken, although there has been comment about possible privatization of the engineering business, for new building of locomotives and rolling stock once the rationalisation has been finished by the Chairman of BR.

British Shipbuilders

The warship yards have been largely sold under the 1983 Shipbuilders Act. Similarly the ship repair yards have been sorted out. This leaves the commercial shipyards for which there is no known privatization policy.

British Steel Corporation

Much work remains to be done in identifying business areas within British Steel that are suitable candidates for return to the private sector.

British Technology Group

Inmos was sold to Thorn EMI for £95m. on 6 September 1984. 63.6% of Data Recording Instruments was sold by placing, in September 1984, and the residual share holding remains to be sold. In September 1984 19% of BUE (British Underwater Engineering) was also sold, but a residual shareholding remains. British Robotics Systems Ltd and some smaller companies remain to be sold. ICL, Ferranti and Fairey holdings were sold by the National Enterprise Board in 1979–80.

Civil Aviation Authorities Scottish Airports

The sale of the airports was advertised in the autumn of 1984 but no serious enquiries were received. This is still possible if a buyer could be found.

Covent Garden Markets Authority

No plans have yet been developed.

Crown Agents

No public plans to deal with Crown Agents.

Crown Suppliers

Secretary of State for Environment announced terms of reference for a review on 28 March 1985 and we are awaiting its outcome.

Electricity Supply Industry

Still as in the manifesto with a commitment to: 'Increasing competition in, and attracting private capital into, the Gas and Electricity Industries'. No specific plans.

South of England Electricity Board and North of Scotland Hydro Electric Board

As above for the electricity industry.

Forestry Commission

Modest disposals are continuing year by year.

National Bus Company

Discussions still under way to determine the final structure of the sale but the Bill is going through Parliament and it is known that the bus companies will be returned to the private sector.

National Coal Board's peripherals assets

Associated Heat Services was sold in 1983 and J.S. Sankey & Sons in April 1984, realizing £15m. between them. Other possibilities include National Fuel Distributors, Southern Depot, Stavely chemicals, National Smokeless Fuels, Horizon Exploration etc.

National Giro Bank

No known decisions.

National Seed Organisation

Stated in the House of Lords on 21 May 1984 that HMG was considering privatization. Makes a profit of £700,000 on a turnover of

£7.7m. It promotes and markets seed varieties developed in government-funded institutes.

Rolls Royce

Government is pledged to privatization within this Parliament, and the company is making progress in trying to reduce its losses. It will probably be sold by a public flotation.

Short Brothers Ltd.

On 6 December 1984 the Secretary of State told the House of Commons that Shorts is a candidate for privatization. It is likely to be sold as a whole in a public offer for sale.

Water Industry

Minister of State announced on 7 February 1985 that the Government would be examining possibilities of privatization in the water industry. Awaiting public outcome of that review.

9

Every Adult a Share-Owner: The Case for Universal Share Ownership

Shirley Robin Letwin and William Letwin

Why every adult should be a share-owner

Suppose that every adult in Britain acquired £100 worth of shares in some British company. Suppose that, apart from undertaking not to transfer those shares for five years, each adult enjoyed all the rights of a shareholder. He would receive regular dividend payments. He would be entitled to vote for directors of the company and to question or criticize the management's policies at annual general meetings. He would receive frequent mailings from the company, reporting on its performance, informing him how to interpret such reports, explaining his rights as a shareholder, and inviting him to take advantage of certain privileges. To put every adult in this position is the objective of Universal Share Ownership (USO).

How would USO affect the character of Britain?

USO would, first of all, give every adult a sense of increased independence in relation to his economic environment, a sense at present confined to a few. Unlike a bank deposit or an insurance policy, a share gives its owner a direct stake and active voice in the management of an enterprise of his choice. It gives its owner a definite relationship to a business. A firm that would otherwise be a remote abstraction—a name, a set of buildings seen from the outside if seen at all, an entity enigmatically discussed in the back pages of the newspaper, an organization directed by unknown magnates—becomes instead an operation in which the shareholder has a measurable interest, and which, as an active participant, he comes to see more clearly, closer to the inside. Just as voters in a democracy sense that they exercise some control over how they are governed because they have the power, at the very least, periodically to turn the rascals out, so shareowners acquire an enlarged sense of being in control of their lives. By being a shareowner, a person becomes a freer man.

To value freedom is to hold that every adult ought to have a sense, accurate rather than illusory, of controlling his own life. In the past, certain advocates of free government maintained that nobody could enjoy real political or economic independence unless they owned land. Today, in an industrialized society, this is no longer feasible nor necessary. The ideal of independent proprietor-farmers has yielded to the ideal of a property-owning democracy.

Not all forms of property however can serve that ideal equally well. Title to one's dwelling—which some 60% of British households now possess, thanks partly to the policies of the present Government—is in many ways desirable and commendable. But it does not give one a direct interest in, or what is more important, a right of control over, productive enterprises. In other words, owning one's home does not, like owning shares, involve one in public economic life. Further, the vast majority of British adults own investments in bank accounts, life insurance, unit trusts, and pension funds; and they thereby, though often unknowingly, possess indirect claims on shares owned by such financial intermediaries. But here again, however rewarding such investments are financially, they do not and can not give their owners a sense of enjoying a rightful and potentially active voice in determining the policies of the nation's enterprise. In short, the ideal form of a property-owning democracy in today's world is a share-owning democracy.

Some might question whether a share-owning democracy could be effected by USO, as it would put into the hands of every adult only a miniscule fraction of a company's shares, far too little to lift him even into a back seat, let alone the driver's seat. But if that argument carried any weight, it would also be a fatal objection to political democracy. In fact, although no single voter can by himself determine the outcome of a general election, the majority or even plurality of voters do; and even a relatively small minority of voters can influence the Government's policies. Similarly the majority of shareholders can show out the existing management, and a concerted minority can force it to re-examine its conduct. Groupings arise among shareholders, akin to political parties, that amplify the otherwise feeble voices of isolated individuals. Besides, shareholders dispose of some weapons sharper than those available to electors: they can claim legal redress against malpractice by directors, they can invoke the help of various regulatory agencies to launch official investigations of how their company is being managed, and they can, whenever they choose, withdraw from the company by selling their shares—which, if done by many shareholders at the same time, depresses the share price and thus threatens the existing management. For all these reasons then, USO is a practical step toward a share-owning democracy, one in which all adults enjoy real power to influence directly the business firms of which they are the employees and customers.

As the number of shareholders in Britain increases, the case for universal share-ownership becomes more urgent. As long as hardly anyone owned shares, the vast majority without them could comfortably ignore the difference between those eccentrics and themselves, supposing they even noticed it. But now, when many adults, even if still a minority of the order of one in ten, visibly do own shares, those outside their number are more likely to feel excluded and to resent it. As share-ownership grows more common, and is regarded as normal, to be without shares grows more painful—just as those who today lack refrigerators, television sets, or cars may well regard themselves as relegated to the position of outsiders. Therefore wider share-ownership, desirable as it is, constitutes a powerful argument for universal share ownership.

USO would in yet another way foster the consensus that constitutes the foundation of a property-owning democracy. USO would effectively counteract the opposition to a free society that is fostered by some few declared enemies, and by many others who inadvertently threaten it by demanding massive intervention to iron out inequality. Socialists have patently lost the intellectual argument, as is indicated by the efforts of the Labour Party and TUC to re-clothe socialism in non-collectivist garb, as for instance by giving nationalized industries the new name of 'public enterprise'. Yet old habits of thought and feeling die out slowly, especially among people whose minds are attuned to practicalities and indifferent to theory. It is still habitual for many, when they notice that some are better off than themselves, to conclude that this inequality can only be explained by oppression and injustice, and to respond to it with envy and resentful anger. Preaching against such ideas and emotions does little good. By now, a different method of persuasion is needed, a method that is enticing rather than admonitory. And that is what USO can provide.

If every adult owned shares and thereby possessed a definite stake in a capitalist enterprise, he would have that much less reason to put his trust in agitators and charlatans who picture capitalism as a regime imposed by the few on the many. If every adult owned shares, each one's resistance to such propaganda would be fortified by that of his neighbours, just as their common experience as shareholders would make them less vulnerable to envy and bitterness.

Universal share ownership would thus tend to demolish the 'we-they' myth, the notion that the country is divided into two classes permanently at war. This notion, that capitalists always flourish by making workers always suffer, does not stand up to a number of unmistakable facts. Pay and conditions of work in Britain today are dramatically better than in the past, chiefly because of competition rather than collective bargaining or government regulation. Weekly hours have been reduced within a century or so by half, holidays have lengthened, schooling goes on longer, retirement comes earlier, and the burden of physical exertion has been radically lightened by 'capitalist' machinery. An ever larger fraction of the work-force does white-collar jobs in relatively luxurious settings. Real incomes of employees, both in and out of trade unions, have multiplied; standards of private consumption, of cars, clothing, TV and holiday travel, rise to ever higher levels. Yet in the face of all such evidence the 'we-they' syndrome persists.

It is sustained partly by the view that the interests of workers must clash with those of owners because increased wages must cause diminished profits, a view which, though tautologically correct at any instant, is false over any stretch of time. It refuses to acknowledge that profits help to fuel investment, and that increased investment (in viable enterprises but not in dying ones artificially resuscitated with public grants) leads to increased productivity, which free labour markets translate into increased wages. Workers infected by 'we-they' attitudes are able to see neither that they benefit, as their employers do also, when their company earns a reasonable rate of return on capital, nor that protracted failure to do so will inevitably force any company to shrivel or go into liquidation. They are blind to the consequences of exacting unrealistically high wages: companies facing consumer resistance or stiff international competition will lose sales, diminished profits will dry up the flow of investment and condemn the company to a deteriorating and out-dated plant, or management will replace over-priced jobs with labour-saving machinery. Far from being hypothetical, these consequences are witnessed in the statistics on business failures, industrial output, and unemployment. Despite this, as we have said, the 'we-they' syndrome survives.

It could be dislodged by making every adult a share-owner. What lends credence to the myth of class conflict is not inequality but the qualitative gap between those who recognize themselves as owners of productive capital and those who, because they own none, feel excluded from and by 'the system'. If that division were to disappear, the 'we-they' myth would in time evaporate. Ownership of shares, even of a few, would put the small shareholder on a continuum with the biggest shareholder. Though small ones might well still envy the big, it would no longer be the worst kind of envy—that of the outsider, excluded from a world which is at once alluring and unapproachable. USO would make every adult a capitalist.

A person who sees himself as a capitalist cannot be utterly indifferent to the success of the system in which he takes his place. Like anyone who owns his own house, he would be disposed to look after his property, and would be outraged by any attempt to deface or destroy it. As an employee-capitalist, he would be less inclined to regard his boss as an antagonist, less liable to shirk, cheat, or do malicious damage. In short, his ownership of shares, and the visible stake that they gave him in a capitalist enterprise, would counteract, most simply and effectively, the divisive and destructive attitudes which have over the years been encouraged by the enemies of capitalism.

What would make the shareholder's stake in capitalism visible to him, more than merely the piece of paper that certifies his ownership, are the interests and information connected with ownership. Just as the man who plays the football pools looks eagerly at the game scores, so the shareholder has an incentive to take a serious interest in the progress of his company.

Owning anything also gives one a rational interest in understanding it. Shareholders' desire for understanding is partly satisfied by the managers of any widely-owned company, who have an immediate interest of their own in explaining to shareholders how the company works. Unless they can explain their record cogently and convincingly, they will lose their capacity to raise equity capital, whereupon the company (and with it their own careers) will either decline or be taken out of their control. In other words, the managers of a company have compelling reasons to engage in a constant effort to inform shareholders about the economic situation that their company faces and that they as shareholders accordingly face. Although the effort to inform may sometimes be corrupted into an effort to misinform, that vice is generally held to a tolerable level by the exertions of dissatisfied shareholders, the investigative passion of financial journalists, and official enforcement of company law.

Understanding of one particular company is a spur towards acquiring an understanding of the general economic set-up. The more a shareholder becomes familiar with the workings of a company of which he owns a part, the more he comprehends the workings of other companies, and how the operation of each is related to that of others. Thus he comes to understand important aspects of how a market economy works. Consideration of how a particular company decides to invest a certain amount, and in certain sorts of capital equipment, promotes a generalized recognition of the function of capital in production and the role of profits in providing funds for investment or attracting external finance. In this way, the shareholder also acquires some general understanding of the relation between risk and profits, ignorance of which accounts for some of the most serious misconceptions about capitalism. To the informed shareholder it becomes clear that profit is not a 'rip-off' extorted by a capitalist conspiracy but rather the legitimate reward for putting capital at risk. Other general economic relations impinge on the attention of shareholders, such as, to mention only two, the interplay between changes in the interest rate and fluctuations in share prices, and the ways that the balance of trade can influence the rate of interest.

In short, the shareholder, because he is being regularly informed about his company, tends to acquire an understanding of how capitalist enterprises work. He is no longer an alien in a world whose language he cannot understand. Even if he works on a production line and earns wages toward the bottom of the scale, he no longer feels like an outcast nor is he readily seduced by those who maintain that the sole remedy for all discontents is to destroy 'the system' and replace it with another. USO would thus help to sustain political stability.

The shareholder's personal interest in the value of his shares, and his incentives to understand the various commercial and economic circumstances that affect it, is reinforced by his power to govern his company. That power, stemming from his right to vote for directors and to vote on specific matters of policy as vital, for instance, as takeover bids, makes him aware that he plays an active part in determining the company's conduct. Making every adult a shareholder would thus serve as a specific antidote to the passivity and lassitude that overcome dependents of a welfare state. It would encourage a more active, enterprising attitude to economic affairs.

Shareholders could normally be expected to exert their influence so as to promote the efficiency of their company; that premise underlies USO, just as an analogous premise underlies universal suffrage. But whereas politics exhibits not a few instances of self-serving factions that try to milk the public purse, this disorder (short at least of outright fraud) is less likely to occur in a widely-held company. For instance, a blatant attempt by employee-shareholders to push through a policy of excessive wages or thinly disguised feather-bedding would be resisted by the mass of shareholders who are not employees of that firm. Moreover, informed employee-shareholders could easily recognize, along the lines of the golden goose parable, that they would profit little by destroying the profitability of their company. To the extent that it may be desirable, as some believe, that employees should have some direct representation in management, the safest and most productive way to establish that is by making all workers shareholders.

Resistance of a similar sort should offset any attempt by shareholder-customers to force through a commercially unwarranted reduction in the company's prices. Even if a housewife's interest in cheaper soap powder would in the short run be greater than in her dividened, she and her like could be outvoted by the mass of shareholders who are not among the company's customers, as well as by shareholders whose private interest as customers is outweighed by their interest as receivers of dividends. So again, to the extent that it might be desirable for consumers to exercise some influence over company policy, it would be safer and more productive that such influence be exercised by customers within the body of shareholders (which presence USO would guarantee) rather than by consumers' consultative councils or consumers' pressure groups outside the company.

Overall, the shareholder's pressure on management, after USO was instituted, would be most likely to concentrate, as it does already in widely-held companies, on urging management to strive for higher earnings. And this is as it should be because—leaving aside monopolies, which can sometimes raise their profits simply by raising their prices—increased earnings come about by increased efficiency, that is by turning a given flow of inputs into a more valuable stream of outputs. Increased efficiency thereby benefits shareholders and employees and customers and the public at large.

USO would tend further to improve general economic efficiency by stimulating investment. It would have this effect for the simple reason that people's taste for any particular object of expenditure depends on its being familiar to them; the whole industry of advertising rests on this proposition. Familiarity grows with practice: as people increasingly watched television in their friends' homes, they increasingly wanted it for themselves. The same is likely to happen in the case of share ownership.

As USO went into practice, as the great mass of Britons became for the first time shareholders in their own right, and as they came to recognize the benefits of share-ownership, their taste for acquiring investments should gradually grow. As that taste increased, individuals would be disposed to spend more of their income on investments. Moreover, that expenditure would rise still further as real personal incomes rose. And it would be stimulated even further by the decline in brokers' fees that is fairly certain to follow the deregulation of Britain's financial markets, the so-called 'Big Bang' scheduled for this October.

All in all, USO could be expected to reinforce the foundations of a free society and to enhance the efficiency of the market economy.

How USO would work

Distribution of shares

The privatisation policy of the present Government provides an admirable opportunity for bringing USO into existence. USO would be initiated if the Government offered every adult the opportunity to buy shares that the Government still owns in British Telecom. Its holding is quite large enough, at its present market price, to offer about £100 worth of shares to each of the 40 million or so people in Britain over eighteen years old. In order to induce all adults to become shareholders, £100 worth of shares would be offered at a nominal price of, say, £10. As a condition of the bargain, purchasers would have to hold these shares for at least five years before selling them or giving them away. In the meanwhile, they would receive standard dividends and enjoy all the other rights of ownership.

In order to achieve universal share ownership, and the political and economic benefits flowing from it, similar distributions of shares would have to be made several times. This would be necessary partly because some of those who acquired shares during the first distribution would after the end of five years exercise their option to sell them, and not all of them would use the cash to buy other shares. Further distributions would be necessary also to make USO available on concessionary terms to the million or so people who become adults every year. In order therefore to build up momentum toward universal share ownership, subsequent distributions should take place every few years. This is not to say, however, that distributions need become perpetual or even very numerous. As the policy of USO began to achieve its intended effects, more and more people might acquire the habit of devoting part of their income to the purchase of shares. Eventually USO should become self-sustaining, needing no further stimulation by government.

Reinforcement of share-ownership by education

The habit of owning shares would be reinforced by a flow of information that would naturally reach participants in USO.

In the regular course of business, the management of their company would send them periodic reports about matters bearing on their immediate practical concerns as shareholders. As many of these reports would be accompanied by dividend cheques, it can be predicted with confidence that the envelopes would be opened and their contents examined. During the minimum of five years that the subscriber to USO held his shares, he would receive some ten or more mailings of this sort.

Recognizing that the great majority of the adults who acquired shares during the first USO distribution would be utter newcomers to share-ownership, the managers of the company concerned would have good reason to initiate them into general information about the implications of share ownership. For instance, they would find it worthwhile on their own account to explain to shareholders their rights to elect directors and to question and criticize the management's policies. In keeping with a recent trend toward 'social-impact reporting', the management might be expected to explain how its activities are intended to achieve objectives ancillary to its purely commercial goals. In short, people who under the auspices of USO become shareholders for the first time would receive a regular stream of information from the companies concerned.

It cannot be denied however, as the *Financial Times* recently put it, that much important information in company reports "is tucked away at the back in accountant's jargon that is difficult for outsiders to understand". Many or most recipients of shares under USO would experience some difficulty in understanding the basic format of financial accounts, quite apart from the specialized notes and appendices presented in accountant's jargon.

Accordingly, in order for USO to be as effective an educational device as possible, measures should be taken to help shareholders toward basic financial understanding. As companies may not voluntarily assume a duty in this direction, and could not sensibly be compelled by law to assume it (since managers are not after all experts in spreading abstract knowledge), this desirable function should be carried out by other bodies. One or another of the regulatory agencies being established in connection with the 'Big Bang'—say, the SIB or the Stock Market—might take responsibility for this, perhaps at the Government's expense. Alternatively, the Department of Trade and Industry might commission qualified academics or professionals to do it. Or some private philanthropic organization might undertake the task. In any event, what must be guarded against is anything that could reasonably be dismissed as political propaganda or self-serving advertisement. The aim instead must be to explain in as purely objective a manner as possible, and with the greatest lucidity, what a company's financial reports can tell the shareholder about the present and prospective value of his investment.

In these ways, subscribing to USO would in effect constitute enrolment in a continuous course of education, which apart from reinforcing the habit of share-ownership, would yield the broader advantages, political and economic, discussed above.

Eligibility for USO

The general principle that USO should be offered to any person above the age of 18, like any other broad principle, will need further specification in practice. Obviously it is not intended—to choose an extreme example—that the USO scheme be available to a foreign tourist who luckily happens (or deliberately arranges) to visit Britain on a day when the subscription list is open.

As a first approximation, British citizenship might be set as the qualifying condition. But this seems too narrow, for it would exclude a large number of permanently resident aliens, people who have already lived in Britain for at least five years, who may stay here the rest of their lives, and who may be intending to acquire British citizenship. A further class that may merit inclusion are adults who while not 'ordinarily resident' in Britain are deemed to be resident here for tax purposes; although they are not members of the polity, they do contribute to the public purse. Clearly to be excluded, on the other hand, are aliens admitted for a few years, say as diplomatic personnel or university students, who have no long-term link with British politics or with the economy.

Even among the broad categories of citizens and permanent residents, it might be reasonable to exclude persons certified as insane, incurably senile, or prisoners serving long sentences for serious crimes. Not that such persons do not deserve compassion; rather that the purpose of USO is not to augment the mechanisms of the welfare state.

The suggestions above indicate only a broad outline. More specific rules, and many of them, would have to be worked out by ministers, officials and MPs—but working out such details is beyond the scope of this present study.

Cost of USO

USO would cost the Government surprisingly little. Supposing that in the first distribution, £100 worth of shares were sold at £10 to each of 40 million adults, the Treasury would receive £400 million. Supposing that the Treasury had instead sold those shares at their full market price, it would have received £4 billion. Reckoned in this way, the first tranche of USO would cost the Treasury £3.6 billion. But that calculation is somewhat misleading.

Suppose that the Treasury made up the foregone capital sum of £3.6 billion by borrowing it. Then the carrying charges on that loan would run at something under £360 million per year. Would that be too high a price?

In one sense the question is unanswerable, because it is impossible accurately to assess the monetary value of the political, social, and economic benefits that USO would yield. But the same must be candidly admitted about any number of other public policies that are widely endorsed after having been in place for years. It would be impossible to discover an even remotely accurate figure for the value rendered by having streets swept, or maintaining public parks, or (above all) of keeping up the defense establishment. We rightly do many things that cannot be justified by cost-benefit analysis.

On the other hand, it is in this instance possible to justify the price in broad terms. Recognizing that all adults pay taxes in some form or other (even though only some pay income tax), the annual carrying charge to the Treasury of £360 million would imply an additional average annual tax bill of £9 per adult. In exchange for this, each adult's £90 worth of shares (disregarding, that is, the £10 worth that he paid for) should yield something in the neighbourhood of £9 a year worth of dividends plus capital gains. 'Should yield' is neither optimistic nor pessimistic but neutral. Shares in any given company may, of course, yield more or less than the average of all shares, and will yield less at some times than at others. Nevertheless, in the long term, efficient capital markets will tend to equate the average rate of return on shares with the rate of interest on government loans.

In short, considering USO in its purely financial aspect and disregarding all its contributions to the quality of national life, USO promises to be an excellent bargain to the public at large. What they stand to gain as shareholders would more or less exactly equal the additional burden that they would have to assume as taxpayers.

The long-run future of USO

As we have said, the first USO distribution should probably offer BT shares now owned by the Government. Because a market already exists in BT shares, every adult could ascertain the current market value of the USO offer by consulting his daily newspaper. Instead of being invited to buy a pig in a poke, the prospective subscriber would be offered an asset of established value—and though that value would fluctuate during the minimum five years that he held the shares, it would (in the case of BT) more probably rise than fall precipitously. Another reason for choosing BT shares for the first USO offering is that the government's present block of them is more than large enough to be cut up into 40 million reasonably thick slices.

As we have explained, a series of successive USO offerings would be needed in order firmly to implant the habit of shareholders among practically all adults. If, as a result of USO offerings and ordinary privatization sales (such as the forthcoming disposal of British Gas), the Government had disposed of all nationalized industries, that need not impede further USO distributions. Lacking shares to sell, the government could instead sell 'investment vouchers'.

Investment vouchers, priced as before at say £10, would entitle the purchaser to buy £100 worth of shares listed on the Stock Exchange, but not shares in unit trusts, investment trusts, or in any other indirect form of investment. At each USO distribution, one and only one voucher would be offered to each adult, and the voucher would be valid only for purchase of shares. Companies whose shares were bought in this way would simply present the vouchers to the Treasury for redemption, just as though they were cheques or credit-card sales-slips. USO distributions by vouchers would cost the Treasury, and ultimately the taxpayers, no more than direct distribution of shares. Subscribers would enjoy the advantage of being able to select whichever shares seemed to them most promising, and the effort of choosing among all the shares available would have great educational effect.

Care would have to be taken of course to ensure that investment vouchers could not be traded illegitimately, or perverted into a sort of black-market currency. But this poses no more practical difficulty than is now satisfactorily dealt with by the issuers of manufacturer's coupons, luncheon vouchers, airline tickets, and other non-transferable chits. Arrangements would also have to be made so that stock certificates bought with investment vouchers could not be sold within five years of purchase, but once the proper legal arrangements had been perfected that would call for little more than a simple exercise of printer's art.

If £4 billion worth of investment vouchers were suddenly injected into the stock market, would that cause share prices to sky-rocket, blowing up a sort of South Sea bubble that would burst sooner or later with disastrous effects? Such a fear is quite unfounded. Additional demand of the order of £4 billion, though substantial, would be small relative to the total annual volume of transactions in the stock market. Moreover, it would have no unsettling effect at all if it were matched by new flotations to the extent of £4 billion, as it might well be, since in the stock market, as in other efficient markets, increased demand tends to call forth increased supply. Neither is there reason to fear that speculators could take undue advantage of the knowledge that a block of investment vouchers was about to enlarge demand for shares. Certainly they might hope to profit by buying shares before the vouchers were issued on the expectation that they could sell when share prices rose after and because of the issue. But as they could not foretell which shares, if any, would mount in value as the result of the issue of vouchers, speculators—or at any event shrewd ones operating on a large scale—might well regard any such gamble as unwise. In any event, their efforts could be neutralized by judicious users of the investment vouchers, who would be reluctant to buy those shares whose prices had been speciously bid up by speculators. All this suggests that investment vouchers should be so fashioned that their holders could use them at any time within say a year of receipt. Aside from avoiding an instantaneous surge of demand, it would also give their holders ample time to consider which shares they wished to buy.

Would the issue of investment vouchers tend to dilute the value of existing shares? Nothing of the sort. So far as investment vouchers were spent for previously issued shares, this would represent merely substitution of the buying share-owner for the selling share-owner, without an effect on either the real assets underlying any share or on the voting power attached to each share. If, on the other hand, the issue of investment vouchers did stimulate an increased supply of shares, that in itself would have no tendency to drive down the assets behind each share because each of the new shares would be paid for by cash that swelled the company's asset base. It is true that whenever a company issues new ordinary shares, the relative voting power attached to each share diminishes—but this effect can only be accepted by existing share-holders, who would rationally accept it as a concomitant of bringing additional equity capital into their company. It is in any event no more threatening than the fact that each voter's voice is somewhat diminished as a country's voting population grows.

Aside from their particular suitability for the purposes of USO, investment vouchers would help to demonstrate the general utility of vouchers as a means of deploying ear-marked grants of public funds in a manner most compatible with the individual's freedom of choice.

Justification of the policies required

The case for private ownership

Since USO would initially work by distributing shares in nationalized industries to private owners, the general case for it rests partly on the reasons for preferring private ownership to public ownership.

Public ownership of productive assets is generally defended on grounds of efficiency and expediency rather than of morality. Even if the goals are asserted to rest on moral principles, the means towards them have no independent moral standing.

Take as an illustration the argument for state schooling. It starts from propositions such as that every child ought to have at least a basic education, whether or not his parents are able and willing to pay for it, or, in a stronger version, that all children should attend the same schools, comprehensive state schools, regardless of their parents' incomes, religious affiliations, or educational preferences. Though these propositions are debatable, they are undeniably moral in character, resting as they do, partly at least and however precariously, on such moral imperatives as every individual's claim to self-filfilment or right to equality of opportunity. But when we come to questions of implementation, whether, in particular, universal schooling necessarily entails public ownership of school buildings, moral considerations drop out, to be replaced by pragmatic calculations. It might be cheaper for the state to own school buildings; it might alternatively be cheaper for the state to lease school buildings from private owners. It might be more or less convenient in other ways for school buildings to be publicly owned; it could not however be more or less moral.

Similarly, in the case of other public services. To maintain that no person ought to do without essential medical services for want of ability to pay makes good moral sense—which is not to say that this assertion is indisputable either in principle or, more pertinently, in details such as whether provision of wigs constitutes a medical service or an essential one. But even if the assertion is accepted as valid, it implies nothing about whether the Government should own NHS hospitals (which it does), or all hospitals (which it does not), or the surgeries of NHS doctors (which it does not at all).

Finally, the case of nationalized industries points more clearly still in this direction. Some industries, for example in ship-building, were nationalized to avert closure following the bankruptcy of private owners, because closure would have resulted in job losses. Even if it were asserted that the Government ought to assume responsibility for providing every willing worker with some job, it would not follow that the only or best way to honour that responsibility would be by turning a privately-owned industry over to public ownership; it would, for instance, be morally equivalent to honour the responsibility by giving public subsidies to the private owners. Again, some industries, such as steel, were nationalized on the ground that this would put the Government in charge of "the commanding heights of the economy". In the background there certainly lurks the principle that a Government has a duty to control the economy, though that principle looks more like a practical recipe for economic well-being than a moral imperative. Be that as it may, the corollary that government control of the economy is facilitated by government ownership of certain industries falls entirely within the domain of practical judgement.

All these arguments support the conclusion that public ownership has no claim to be regarded as morally superior in itself to private ownership. The only rational basis for disputing this conclusion would be the belief that communism is the ideal situation of mankind, in other words the belief that common ownership, or government ownership as its surrogate, is right, whereas private property is theft. On this view, public ownership sponsors civic virtue by directing the individual's endeavours toward the public good. A somewhat less stern line of argument is advanced by those who reject the communist ideal but regard government as a great engine for achieving magnificient objectives, whether economic progress, theocratic purity, world revolution, equality, or any combination of such corporate goals. As these latter understand things, intervention by government in private affairs is a *sine qua non* for achieving their objectives, and public ownership is welcomed as one mode of government intervention.

Quite the opposite view is held by those who believe that a Government has only one legitimate purpose, to establish a framework of law that will secure the opportunity of individuals to pursue the different objectives that they map out for themselves. On that view, public ownership is out of place because a Government ought not to operate productive enterprises; its proper role is that of an umpire, not a player.

Because they have held this view of government, various classical exponents of the minimal state, though they have differed about many particulars, have always taken a strong stand in favour of private property. John Locke, for example, insisted that the prime function of government is to protect the individual's property as well as life and liberty. This is essential to the individual's autonomy, he argued, because if a person's property is confiscated by other private persons or by the state, he falls into servitude, even if he does not die of want. Blackstone held private property to be one of the absolute rights guaranteed by English law. Jefferson, following Locke and Montesquieu among others, maintained that a republic—by which he meant a representative democracy—could remain free and stable only if most of its citizens were self-reliant proprietors, independent of plutocratic citizens and, more important, capable of refusing to become clients and thus dependent creatures of their Government. Indeed all classical theories of free government have regarded private ownership of productive assets as an essential safeguard of individual independence.

Because USO would not only effectively diminish public ownership but also extend private ownership, it accords with the principles of free government.

Why shares in nationalized industries should be distributed to every adult

Government ownership of nationalized industries, properly understood, is a trust of which the Government (or, according to refinements of constitutional theory, the state or the Crown) are the trustees and the people at large are the beneficiaries. Whatever the ideas that motivated nationalization of various industries, nobody has dared then or since to proclaim that public ownership ought differentially to benefit any special group within the community, ought to operate in the particular interest of ministers and officials, managers or employees, consumers, taxpayers or others. To be sure the obvious principle, that nationalized industries ought to benefit the public at large, has been radically perverted in practice, so as to confer special benefits on people living in certain regions, or on consumers at the expense of taxpayers, or on employees at the expense of consumers. Indeed this has been done in so many different ways, and has so muddied the economic record and financial reports of nationalized industries, that even experts in the field cannot tell which particular persons have been subsidized, or by how much, or at whose expense. Nevertheless, it remains clear in principle that the public as a whole, and only they, are the proper beneficiaries of public ownership.

It follows that when privatization is undertaken, the Government's holdings should be distributed in such a manner as to benefit the public as a whole. This requirement can be met by the ordinary sort of privatization offering, which prices shares at or near their market value and enables any individual to bid for as many shares as he likes; for the total proceeds of the sale go to the Treasury, to the benefit of all taxpayers, who are the whole public. But the requirement would be more completely satisfied by USO because it would distribute shares to every adult, or more precisely, it would dramatically increase everyone's opportunity to buy shares by taking advantage of the discount inherent in a sale price substantially lower than market value.

However, to maintain that every citizen of a representative democracy has a rightful claim to share in the privatization of publicly-owned assets is not intended to suggest that all subsequent privatization should proceed through USO distributions. Neither should USO become the only way in which individuals can acquire shares of any sort. It is proposed as an important supplement to the familiar present methods of buying and selling shares, not as a replacement for them.

Why every adult should receive an equal subsidy toward buying shares

Even within USO's important though limited scope, the justification for offering every adult an equal subsidy, consisting of the difference between the nominal price asked for the shares and their market values, is that there is no rational ground for a discriminatory distribution of the subsidy. Equality is a suitable rule in this instance because, though not good in itself, it is better than any other option.

The Government acquired its shares in most nationalized industries by buying out previous private owners. Those purchases were funded from tax revenues, or by public borrowing, which must in turn be serviced from tax revenues. Millions of people provided those tax revenues—many of them now dead. It would be quite impossible to identify them: no record exists, for instance, about which individuals have paid excise taxes on liquor, tobacco, or petrol. It would be still less possible to trace the tax payments that ended up in the funds that the Government originally paid over at the moment of nationalization or which financed its vast periodic subventions to nationalized industries. Therefore, whether the Government acquired title from previous private owners, or whether the Government originally set up nationalized industries as public agencies (such as the Post Office), in either case it is impossible to tell which individual taxpayers paid how much toward such enterprises.

In this state of invincible ignorance, it makes good sense for the

Government, having decided to return to the community of taxpaying individuals (which comprehends every adult) something that they as a community paid for, to distribute the bonus element in it equally to each.

Other considerations would come into play if USO were in any degree designed as a redistributive measure. In that case, all the familiar arguments about need and merit would be relevant. But USO is not intended to and would not impinge on the existing system of redistribution. The subsidy element in it is not intended either to equalize wealth or to make it less equal, but rather to stimulate universal ownership of shares, for reasons having nothing to do with egalitarianism. That being the case, it is entirely fitting that each adult be offered an equal subsidy, bonus, bargain, or call it what you will. At the same time it may be noted that the psychological value of the equal bonus will undoubtedly vary from one individual to another. If, as might very roughly be predicted, the bonus were more highly valued by the needy, the young, and the old, that would certainly not tell against the proposal.

Why subscribers to USO should pay a price, though a nominal one, for their shares

The maxim that people generally appreciate most those things that they have had to struggle for does not require elaborate proof, even if like all maxims it admits of exceptions and qualifications. On this ground it might be argued that shares would mean more to people if they had to pay their full price. But to require this would defeat the objective of USO, since until now only some 10% of British adults have been willing to pay the full market price of shares. Universal share ownership can be accomplished only by offering shares far more cheaply than their real worth. Needless to say, it could be accomplished most certainly by giving away shares free of charge. But then the recipients might pay as little attention to them as they do to other unsought hand-outs. All this leads to the conclusion that the price set by USO should be less than the market value of the shares but more than *nil*.

Fine prudential judgement will be needed to estimate how the dual considerations of expensiveness (to the public exchequer) and cheapness (to USO subscribers) should be balanced. Whether the price charged by USO for £100 of shares should be £1, or £10, or more is a question that must be left to the politicians and officials who became responsible for detailed interpretation of USO. They would do well to seek guidance from market research or even from local experiments. Although we can be practically certain that they—like the managers of any stock flotation—will set a price that is marginally too high or too low, such errors of fine tuning would not jeopardize the broad success of a USO policy.

Why subscribers to USO should be required to hold their shares for at least five years

Donors commonly attach conditions to their gifts and the common law has, with the rarest exceptions, upheld this practice. Nobody would regard it as morally questionable that people should destine a bequest exclusively for the education of their grandchildren, or endow a church of their own sect and no other, or give money for research into the behaviour of ghosts and witches. Such qualifications on gifts are recognizably just, on the part of the donor, because they derive from his fundamental right to use property in any way that neither violates the laws nor injures others. They are recognizably just, so far as concerns the designated beneficiary, because they cannot possibly harm him; he can always avoid the constraining conditions by rejecting the gift. As a qualified gift is either worth taking or turning down, it is fruitful at best and innocuous at worst.

USO would offer a conditional gift: you may take title—free of charge—to £90 worth of shares (assuming a market value of £100 offered at a price of £10) provided that you agree not to sell them for five years. There is nothing oppressive or coercive in this offer. Many informed and practiced investors voluntarily buy financial paper to which stringent limitations attach; very many people voluntarily and indeed wisely buy pension rights that they cannot realize, transfer, or hypothecate for upward of thirty years.

Yet it might be objected that although the subsidy element (say £90) of a USO purchase is a gift and as such may properly be qualified, the same is not true of that part of the shareholding's value (say £10) that the subscriber has paid for. Is it proper to deny to the subscriber the right to recover the part of the shares' value that he has paid for by selling at will the appropriate fraction of his holding? The good reason for insisting that USO should not be conducted by outright gift has already been explained. It should be noted further that the normal rate of dividends, at 5% or more, means that the USO subscriber could expect to recover his cash outlay within two years. And finally, any adult who did feel that the five-year period of non-transferability was too onerous could of course decline the whole bargain.

Exceptions from the five-year role would be allowed in special circumstances. Shares could obviously be transferred following the owner's death, or used to satisfy creditors' claims following the owner's bankruptcy. We can all accept that a party to a voluntary agreement ought to be relieved of obligations when performance has been made impossible by events beyond his control.

An exception from the five-year rule might also be made to allow USO subscribers, under certain circumstances, to exchange the shares they originally acquired through USO for shares in other companies. Such an exception would fit in with the spirit of USO, which is intended to foster the habit of owning shares in some company or other, not to lock USO subscribers into owning shares in any particular company. A facility for exchanging shares would be particularly appropriate if the market value of shares in nationalized industries acquired by USO subscribers began to decline disastrously, as might quite conceivably happen to shares in British Coal, British Steel or British Shipbuilders. If in the face of such decline, which foreshadowed bankruptcy of the company and consequent worthlessness of its shares, the five-year restraint against transfer continued in force, it would disillusion many USO subscribers and to say the least discourage the habit of share-owning.

Prudence suggests that some provision be made at the outset to deal with a threatening sharp decline in the fortunes of any presently nationalized company whose shares USO distributed. Leaving such an eventuality to be designated as an emergency and to be resolved by *ad hoc* action would load a burden of discretion on some administrative agency made responsible for invigilating the market value of shares distributed through USO and for conjuring up some scheme of relief. Moreover, it would subject the government to political pressures whenever the prices of such shares faltered. Far sounder, then, to build in arrangements from the outset that would enable USO subscribers to exchange such shares for others.

How could such exchanges best be effected? Barter would be totally unwieldly. Exchange in the normal fashion, by selling one lot of shares for cash and using the cash to buy another lot, would tend to undermine the five-year rule, because some shareholders, after cash-ing in their original shares, would spend the proceeds, and the policing required to prevent this would be costly and intrusive. The best medium of exchange between original shares and replacement shares would accordingly be investment vouchers (see page 259).

Besides its main purpose of fostering the habit of shareownership, the five-year rule would have the auxiliary function of avoiding excessive volatility that would infect share prices if novice shareholders, not yet well informed or inured to short-term fluctuations, panicked in response to rumour. If, then, USO subscribers were authorized to exchange shares for other shares within a five-year period, through the medium of investment vouchers, it might be wise to limit this privilege so that it could be exercised only, say, once a year. Those responsible for working out the detailed practicalities of USO might however judge that no such limitation would be required, inasmuch as brokerage fees would sufficiently brake the USO subscriber's impulse to exchange his shares at the slightest decline in their value.

Conclusion

Many official schemes now exist to encourage investment. These operate chiefly by offering tax relief to persons who invest indirectly through pension plans and assurance schemes or who invest directly in their own houses. An unintended, though not altogether unforeseeable result of such incentives has been to discourage people from making direct investments in shares, dividends on which are taxed without any relief or deferment.

An effort to reverse this tax discouragement to direct investment in shares is the PEP (Personal Equity Plan) scheme advanced in the Chancellor of the Exchequer's latest budget. Under this scheme, capital gains and reinvested dividends realized on PEP investments of up to £2,400 per year would be free of tax. Excellent as this scheme may be in promoting wider shareownership, it would unfortunately afford incentives only to those people whose earnings are above the income-tax threshold. While benefiting them, it would impose a commensurate burden on others, assuming that total government expenditure is unlikely to decline. Tax revenues lost on account of PEP would have to be replaced by increasing other taxes, with the likely effect that concessions to PEP subscribers would be paid for in part by people whose incomes fall below the income-tax threshold.

The same is true of other tax concessions for the sake of stimulating investment, of which there are many varieties.

USO, by contrast, would be far more equitable, inasmuch as the subsidy offered (which is perfectly equivalent to tax relief) would be available to all adults, no matter how low their incomes might be. And it would thereby immeasurably widen the incentive to share-ownership.

Far from being a Utopian proposal, USO merely extends practices that have long been established in Britain as well as in other representative democracies presiding over market economies. The measures needed to implement USO correspond to policies that have long been advocated by many in various political parties and are being actively pursued by the present Government. By broadening the ownership of shares to include every adult, USO would have much the same effect as transforming a restricted franchise into universal suffrage.

There is every reason to expect that such a transformation would enjoy widespread popular approval, lending support to the Party and the Government that instituted it. Apart from that, USO would do much to strengthen a free society by spreading understanding of how it operates, promoting loyalty to it, and encouraging the enterprise that sustains its prosperity.

10

Shares For All: Steps Towards a Share-Owning Society

Sir Nicholas Goodison

A renaissance in share ownership

Share ownership is enjoying something of a renaissance. There are many more people today with a direct share in the risk capital of British industry and commerce than there were five years ago. When I talk about wider share ownership at a Conservative Party committee meeting, I am no longer treated as if I am an apostle of the Unknown God or a preacher of impractical reform. There is a greater understanding of the advantages of wider share ownership, even a touch of religious fervour. Wider share ownership has got onto the agenda.

The change is splendid. I even detect the possibility of a measure of agreement between the political parties, originating from the constructive attitudes of the Alliance. I hope that the spread of share ownership will become, as home ownership has become, a case of the parties vying as the years go by to pinch each others' clothes. But obviously the Conservatives ought to be way out ahead in the new sartorial fashion: and I hope the Centre for Policy Studies, which has contributed much to the Party's initiatives on the subject in the past, will continue to stimulate constructive action.

Why?

There are many answers to this question and you are familiar with them all. Let me briefly mention five:

Investment

The growth of the contractual savings institutions, on the back of the inflation of wages and a biased tax system, has certainly helped to increase the level of savings and to bring some security to peoples' lives. But this has been at the sacrifice of a more direct personal investment in the risks and rewards of industry. We are a commercial nation. When Napoleon called us a 'nation of shopkeepers', he no doubt intended it to imply small-mindedness. But it surely indicates two features of our national temperament. We are traders, and we like a slice of the action. It is surely better, in this competitive last quarter of the twentieth century, to have as many people directly involved in the rewards and risks of our industry and commerce as possible. It is better for the workplace. There is evidence that industry performs better when all employees feel they have a stake in the prosperity of the company. And it is better in the country at large, not only because everyone can have a slice of the action, but because it leads to greater understanding.

Understanding

Greater involvement brings greater understanding—understanding of the prime importance of industry and commerce to the quality of life in this country; understanding therefore of the prime importance of profits in industry and commerce; understanding of the need in industry for top quality management; understanding of the need for inventiveness, for quality of the goods and services produced, for efficient production, for effective marketing and after-sales service, and for co-operation between manager and managed at all levels; understanding of the folly of permitting political dogma to intervene in these fundamental needs; understanding of the need to bury Clause 4 of the Labour Party's constitution with the usual British decency, giving it a finely worded obituary despite the damage it has done to our economy. Direct investment in shares, in short, has a high educational value.

Efficiency

The verdict of history, with a very few exceptions, is that the State is not likely to be an effective manager of industry. Institutional

investors can of course bring pressure to bear on inefficient management. But a large number of directly involved shareholders, both in
the work-place and outside it, is also likely to be a spur to good
management.

Investment

In the case of state industries, too, there is the argument that access
to public capital markets and the absence of bureaucratic or political
restraints are more likely to lead to capital formation and profit.

But there is a broader point here. There is an enormous pool of
personal wealth in the country for industry to tap. No government of
a major industrial nation in any political system can ensure the totally
efficient allocation of resources. But something is surely wrong in a
country which depends fundamentally on the success of its industry
and commerce if personal savings are steered toward unproductive
assets. The country's privately-owned housing stock is said to be
valued at about £420,000,000,000. Building society deposits stand at a
further £91,000,000,000. Both are examples, at least to some extent,
of fiscal steering. Owner-occupied houses have been particularly
favoured by the tax system. The total value of the ordinary shares of
British listed companies in the hands of direct investors is estimated
at only £65,000,000,000. A nation of industrialists? Or a nation of
houseowners? Would resources not be allocated more productively,
if the system was not so biased?

Successful saving

Investment in ordinary shares has been profitable. In a successful
economy it should continue to be so. Of course, in the obligatory
words of unit trust advertising, the prices of shares can go down as
well as up: but the true value of fixed income investments and cash
deposits has done nothing but go down over many years. So let us
not underrate the appeal of well-chosen industrial risk capital to
today's savers, or indeed the fun of direct investment. It is an
absorbing and enjoyable pursuit.

But enough of philosophy. What is the practical reality? How far
have we come? Where do we go next?

Table 1
How People Saved 1981-1985
(in billions)

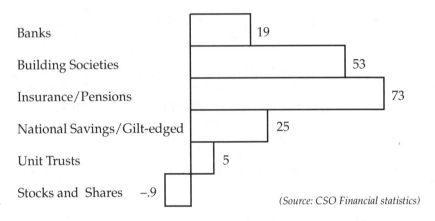

Banks	19
Building Societies	53
Insurance/Pensions	73
National Savings/Gilt-edged	25
Unit Trusts	5
Stocks and Shares	−.9

(Source: CSO Financial statistics)

How far have we come?

Ideas on how to encourage wider share ownership have been about for years. They have included particularly direct tax incentives of various sorts, employees' profit-sharing and savings schemes, and retirement accounts. All have relied on fiscal reform—in other words, either on directly encouraging savings in shares through the tax system or on reducing the discriminatory tax burden levied on direct share ownership.

Britain cannot unfortunately claim to have been in the lead. The Loi-Monory scheme introduced in France in 1978 was hugely successful in bringing the small investor to the Bourse and increasing the amount of equity capital subscribed to French industry—and I must remind you that it was the latter point that was the chief objective of the reform. Between 1977 and 1982 the proportion of French households investing in listed securities rose from 7% to 17%. In modified form the Loi-Monory has been copied by other European countries, most notably Belgium and West Germany. A similar scheme in Sweden has turned one-sixth of the population into investors. In the USA Individual Retirement Accounts (IRAs) and Keogh Accounts offer other lessons. The New York Stock Exchange conducted a survey of share-ownership in 1984 which showed that 45% of all share-owners participate in an IRA or Keogh account. In the face of that evidence there can no longer be any doubt about the positive manner in which people of relatively modest means will respond to fairer tax treatment.

How have things gone in Britain? The first ray of hope came in the closing stages of the last Socialist Government, when the Liberals pushed an unwilling administration into the first-ever tax concessions in the area of employee profit-sharing. It was a significant reform, and reflected the mood in the country against the domination of faceless State industry and powerful centralised unions. It was a blow for the individual and his rightful place in the economic scheme of things.

Now, I do not want to sound churlish, but I found the incoming Conservative Government in 1979 distinctly slow off the mark in furthering the cause of people's capitalism. On a charitable view they were deflected perhaps by all the other very good reforms on which they were engaged. Apart from reductions in income tax and CTT (and I do not underrate the importance of either of those), the first term saw little other than a modest extension of the employee profit-sharing schemes and some tinkering with taxes on saving, such as capital gains tax. Very little was done towards equalising the tax treatments of all types of investment.

In the second term more has been done and the pace has quickened. The change in attitude which I mentioned earlier has taken firmer root. In 1984 the tax privilege attached to life assurance was abandoned. So was the investment income surcharge. At last, transaction taxes, mostly in the form of stamp duty, were reduced. Employee share schemes were given a further boost. There are now over a thousand all-employee share schemes in operation, involving around a million employees. In 1979 there were only 30 such schemes in existence. I think we can agree that the growth is remarkable.

And the Government has used the de-nationalisation of major enterprises as a positive opportunity to promote wider share ownership.

The effects of all this are already apparent. The steady decline in the number of direct shareholders has stopped. The growth of employee share schemes and the de-nationalisation programme particularly have reversed the trend. In recent months, surveys have suggested that rather more people in Britain own shares than we used to think. In a Treasury study conducted in February this year, research indicated that some 14% of the adult population own shares. Two studies made by The Stock Exchange have suggested a slightly higher figure of about 16%. Another survey suggests about 12%. The exact figures vary because of differences in the questions which people in the sample surveys are asked about share owning. All in all, it is a fair assumption to say that at least 12% of the UK adult population own shares, and that is some five million people.

But let us not instantly jump for joy at these crude figures. It is certainly pleasing that the total number of people who own shares directly has risen. It is also pleasing that, according to The Stock Exchange's survey, share ownership is spreading across the social scale and that 58% belong (in the jargon beloved by market research organisations) to the C, D and E socio-economic groups. It is excellent that commentary on stocks and shares can now be found in the pages of the *Daily Mirror* (as it can be, incidentally, in the pages of the leading Communist newspaper in Italy). See Table 2.

But other findings are also significant. The Stock Exchange survey showed, for example, that 51% of shareholders have shares in only one company and that a further 20% do not hold shares in more than three companies.

These figures reflect no doubt the success of profit-sharing schemes (some 35% of shareholders responded that they obtained their shares through a scheme run by their employer) and of the de-nationalisation of British Telecom, which was used as a means of tempting a lot of first-time investors. But with only 29% of shareholders—only one and a half million people—having more than four equity holdings, we have a very, very long way to go before we can say that shareholding has become a habit. And a habit it must become, a habit which

Table 2
Profiles of shareholder groups

	All shareholders	BT Only	Own Company	Shares in BT
Unweighted	483	84	112	237
Base	%	%	%	%
Men	58	52	73	60
Women	42	48	27	40
AB	42	27	34	35
C1	29	31	29	29
C2	16	24	22	19
DE	13	19	16	17

Table 3
Number of companies in which shares are held

Base: all shareholders (483)	%
1	51
2	11
3	9
4–5	10
6–7	4
8–10	4
11–15	4
16–20	1
21–30	1
31–50	*
Over 60	1
Don't know/not stated	4
Average number of companies in which shares are held	4.1

* = less than 0.5

Table 4
How shares are obtained

Base: all shareholders (483)	%
Bought them myself	68
Through an employee scheme	30
Inherited them	18
I was given them	9
Other answers	1

(Some respondents obtained shares in more than one way, so this table adds up to more than 100%.)

people throughout the country will regard as an accepted and desirable part of our way of life.

The signs of further growth are encouraging. Profit-sharing schemes are firmly established and are on the increase. Further denationalisation campaigns are in the pipeline, with British Gas this autumn due to be the largest issue ever. This will surely do still more to encourage first-time buyers to purchase shares and to sustain the interest of shareholders brought in by the British Telecom issue. I hope that the question marks hanging over The Royal Ordnance, British Airways and one or two other candidates can be resolved without delay.

In the field of pensions, reforms are under discussion which will allow all members of existing pension schemes to switch to personal portable pensions should they wish to do so. This would encourage wider share ownership by turning remote collective ownership into direct individual ownership. Schemes already exist enabling self-employed people to invest their retirement accounts directly in shares. An extension of this principle to all savers is a natural extension of the desirable principle of direct involvement.

More recently, the Government has announced its intention to reduce stamp duty further to one half percent from October. This does not go far enough, but it will help to cut the costs of transactions. And, perhaps most significant of all, is the proposed introduction of the Personal Equity Plan, the PEP scheme as it has become known. This will allow any adult citizen to invest up to £2,400 a year in shares with the benefit of tax-free profits and dividends. The PEP concept falls short of the more ambitious incentive schemes like the Loi-Monory and will probably not be as successful in encouraging the same numbers of new investors as in France, Belgium, Sweden and Norway: but it is a significant pointer for the future and was inconceivable at Westminster a few years ago.

Where do we go from here?

Having been late off the mark, the Government needs to act decisively during the rest of this Parliament. The immediate need is to carry through to their logical conclusion many of the steps already taken:

- promote de-nationalisation vigorously;
- get the personal pension reforms worked out in practice;
- abolish stamp duty;
- simplify the hideously complex rules on the indexation for capital gains tax purposes: even abolish capital gains tax;
- promote PEPs vigorously and simplify their administration; and
- open the doors wider on employee share ownership schemes.

We need meanwhile to study whether this programme, which continues on the lines of present policies, is enough. Here surely is fruitful work for the Centre for Policy Studies, and I hope it can be done quickly.

Two lines of enquiry occur to me. The first is the obvious one of fiscal neutrality. Does the PEP plan go far enough? I suspect not. I said earlier that share ownership is a very long way from becoming a habit, and backed that up with figures. To turn it into a habit we need bold and decisive fiscal reforms aimed at making share ownership desirable, something each saving citizen feels he cannot forego. The PEP scheme is a first tentative step, but it will not achieve this aim. I do not want to underestimate the originality or the significance of the proposed reform in the context of our awful tax system, but the fair treatment of savings calls for something more far-reaching.

The second line of enquiry is the idea mooted by several, including John Templeton and now the SDP, of handing over shares in nationalised industries to all adult citizens free of charge rather than going through the offers for sale which have been used as the means of implementing the de-nationalisation plans. I have much personal sympathy with this idea, while recognising that it is administratively very complex and that the Treasury will find it unappealing. But I like the idea of a really massive increase in the number of shareholders and, indeed, of a single company with up to 41 million of them. A nightmare for the Registrar perhaps, but the stuff that the wider share ownership supporter's dreams are made of. There are, after all, nearly 30 million holders of National Savings accounts and about 29 million building society accounts.

But steps taken by the Government of the day may never prove to be decisive—because some of them can be reversed—unless something more fundamental occurs. We need to change attitudes toward risk.

I have heard it said that the real cause for the decline in private share ownership is that the British people are more 'risk averse' than others. I doubt it. Certainly the experience of the bookies and the pools promoters suggests otherwise. It is surely more likely that during the long decades when politicians preached against private wealth, against industrial success and against profit, when the shareholding habit was considered immoral and when The Stock Exchange was described frequently by people who should have known better as a casino, when industrial profits were declining to practically nothing and politicians seemed not to care about it, when taxes on saving in industrial risk were penal . . . it is surely more likely that people avoided shares in response to political leadership and bad policies. Things are different now. So let us set about creating some enthusiasm.

Table 5
Attitudes of shareholders and non-shareholders

	Shareholders	Non-Shareholders
Base:	149	862
I think stocks and shares are an interesting way of saving or investing	3.47	2.85
If I had some spare money to invest I'd consider stocks and shares	3.62	2.66
I follow the Stock Market closely	2.53	1.34

5 = *strong agreement;*
1 = *strong disagreement*

Much of this campaign of education necessarily needs to come from government. But we should all play our part in it.

The Stock Exchange can and will take two major steps. First, we are trying to remove the mystique of share ownership, by spreading the word about how to buy and sell shares. The goal must be to 'de-mystify' The Stock Exchange as an institution, to make more people aware of the way in which an investment of shares is made and business is done. With this objective in mind we launched an advertising campaign in the national newspapers last spring. The second phase of the campaign began a fortnight ago, backed up with the publication of a free 48-page booklet for investors giving them information about how to get started in the market.

Second, we are developing an automatic share execution system which will help make dealing costs more economical for brokers and encourage them to expand their business for direct investors.

The brokers are well aware of the commercial opportunities developing, and it is encouraging how some of the larger ones are catching the enthusiasm of their smaller competitors for the business of direct investors. Their new enthusiasm will I hope infect the investors whom they hope to serve.

The change of attitude to risk is important. The need is to make the change irreversible, to ensure that owning shares is regarded across the political spectrum as desirable as is owning a house. That can be achieved either through education or through making large numbers of voters shareholders, but preferably through both.

Part Four

Sense and Nonsense in Education

11

Aims of Schooling: The Importance of Grounding

Oliver Letwin

Aims of schooling

Since the 1870s English politicians have been worrying about the organisation of schools: Church or State? Local or national? Comprehensive or selective? Large or small? Sixth form or tertiary? These are choices which have become familiar to every politician. The merits and demerits of each possibility have been exhaustively discussed, and a whole new breed of 'educationalists' have come forward to participate, equipped with enough technical jargon to sink a battleship.

It is remarkable that, in all the discussion about systems and organisation, not much has been said about the aims of schooling. Indeed, for many years, the discussion has been carried on—and huge changes have been brought about—with hardly any reference to the school's ultimate purpose.

The time has come to stop talking and acting in such a cavalier way, and to ask instead what schools are for. Why do we force children to attend, day in day out, these delapidated brick and concrete buildings with their smell of stale cabbage and detergent, their strange assortment of teachers and their large quantities of paper and ink? Is it just, in reality, a holding operation—a way of penning up the little dears while their parents get on with their work?

Or is there something more to it, something that is actually meant to be achieved in a school which could not be achieved by leaving a child free to wonder and watch like the children of gypsies and nomads?

Two kinds of answers are usually given to this question. One concentrates on the input—what the pupil is taught. The other concentrates on the output—what the pupil learns. Those who concentrate on the input invest the curriculum with enormous powers. Teach the right things, they say, and all will somehow be well. In this, they find powerful support not only from a long tradition of thought stretching back to Plato—probably the first designer of a 'core curriculum'—but also, more recently, from Matthew Arnold. In his *General Report* of 1880, Arnold made clear that his aim was to ensure a proper input by introducing children to a curriculum that included a wide range of subjects. 'In general', he wrote:

> our schoolchildren, of from eight years to ten, should all be receiving instruction in these eight matters, reading, writing, arithmetic, poetry or poetic literature, grammar, geography, elementary natural science and music.

This is not so much the wrong thing as the wrong kind of thing. By concentrating on what is being taught instead of on what is being learned, the advocates of input (like the people who concern themselves with the organisation of schools without considering the aims of schooling) run the risk of attempting to provide cures without having diagnosed the disease. To say anything sensible about the aim or purpose of a school, one has to concentrate on the output—the end of a pupil's schooldays.

Many teachers would no doubt say that the quest for such a description of the desired effect is fruitless because any given form of schooling will have different effects on different pupils; but this argument is invalid. Of course it is true that every pupil is different from all others; but the proper conclusion to draw is that to have the desired effect each pupil needs to learn different things in a different way, not that the same things should be taught to all pupils regardless of the fact that this will have different effects upon them.

In a relatively clear-cut form of training such as medicine, the point is accepted as obvious. Everybody knows that the aim is to produce doctors who are capable of curing people, and medical training is adapted to meet this commonly agreed goal—with courses and teaching methods following rather than dictating the desired end. In schools, the aim is not so obvious; but the principle ought to be the same: first decide what effect you want to have on your pupils by the time they leave, and then arrange things so that all of them, with their different capacities and inclinations come as close to achieving this as possible.

To advocate this is by no means to advocate that every pupil should, on leaving school, look exactly the same as all other pupils. Nothing could be less desirable. Pupils should be, and will be, as different from one another at the end of their schooling as they were at the beginning—indeed, in a good school, they will be more different (and certainly more interestingly different) from one another at the end than they were at the beginning. But the differences ought to have a common theme. This is true of morality. We all aim to be morally good—but this single aim does not compromise our individuality, and would not do so even if we all fulfilled the aim by becoming morally good, because we would be good in quite different ways. That is the characteristic of a quality like goodness: it is sufficiently general not to constrain individuality.

If schooling is to avoid constraining individuality, its aim must be to produce similarly general qualities in the pupils. What are these qualities, sufficiently general to allow for the particular character of each pupil, but sufficiently specific to establish a school as something with a definite role of its own?

An educated person

The usual answer is that children are sent to school to become educated. This, at least, concentrates on the general quality of the output—what the pupil has learned—rather than on the input. But there is debate and confusion about what 'becoming an educated person' means. At one time, education and eternity were thought to be closely linked. When Dr. Alington, headmaster of Eton, was asked by an anxious mother what he prepared his boys for, his answer was short, unequivocal, and pious: 'Death, madam, death'. More recently, and in other places, secular morality has sometimes taken the place of eschatological ambitions; the American philosopher, John Dewey, wrote that:

> when the school introduces and trains each child of society into membership within . . . a little community, saturating him with the spirit of

service and providing him with the instruments of effective self-direction, we shall have the deepest and best guarantee of a larger society which is worthy, lovely and harmonious.

Others have seen education as a cultivation of the individual. Coleridge, for instance, described it as 'that which draws forth and trains up the germ of free-agency in the individual', and D.H. Lawrence said that it meant 'leading out the individual nature in each man and women to its true fullness'. Others yet, regard education as something intrinsically intellectual: Michael Oakeshott, in a famous essay described it as 'the process of learning, in circumstances of direction and restraint, how to recognise and make something of ourselves'.

The collection of widely differing views about the true nature of being educated, and hence about the aims of schooling, has been enough to dizzy and appal the administrators—particularly when they are also faced with the views of philistines pressing for more practicality, and with the opposing clamour of the Arts lobby who want every child to learn Dante and Caribbean music. The British Civil Service has dealt with this problem in its time-honoured fashion. With absolute sang froid and total lack of discrimination, it has collected every current idea about the purpose of schooling and the nature of education into a grandiloquent but entirely incoherent melange, aptly summarised in Burgess and Adams's account of one Green Paper as the cultivation of 'enquiring minds, respect for people, world understanding, use of language, appreciation of economic controls, mathematical and other skills, and knowledge of cultural achievements'. What are our schools meant to do when they are served up with that kind of administrative pea-soup?

But the trouble is not just that people have unclear ideas about the nature of education. Indeed in practice most of us know how to spot an educated person. We recognise, in practice, that someone can know a lot without being in any sense educated, as is true of many people with PhDs. We recognise a certain scepticism (however deeply buried) which marks out the educated person from other, possibly knowledgeable, but uneducated people: an understanding that no knowledge is complete, that one does not and cannot in any ultimate sense have 'the whole answer' to any complicated question. And we recognise, with this, a certain intellectual tact, a sense of how to approach a new set of ideas, a certain capacity to feel at home in the world of thought.

The real trouble is that this highly desirable condition of being an educated person is not, and could never be, the aim or result of schooling for most people at most schools. It depends too heavily upon fortunate circumstances. Many teachers are not themselves educated people: they may know something or other, but lack any sense of discrimination, intellectual refinement or scepticism. Such teachers may well be able to provide their pupils with something valuable, but they are not able to provide the level of critical self-awareness which will help their pupils to become educated. Moreover, becoming educated is not something which happens automatically to the pupil even if the teacher is himself an educated person and teaches conscientiously, since conscientiousness may fail utterly to produce the spark of inspiration which is required to light the necessary flame of critical self-awareness in the pupil. Becoming educated also requires special qualities on the part of the pupil; he has to be capable of going beyond the mere performance of tasks; he has to be able to abstract from his immediate practical concerns and understand at least to some degree what he himself is doing, and what steps he might take in the future; he has not merely to reach conclusions but also to understand how those conclusions might be qualified and refined. These are not ordinary capacities. There are plenty of pupils, including some who are competent and intelligent in various respects, who may never become educated, no matter how conscientious or how inspired the teaching. Of course, in any school, there may be some teachers who are sufficiently educated and sufficiently gifted, and some pupils who are sufficiently imaginative. Even in the very worst schools, there may be one or two of each: and in such circumstances, there will be some true education going on. But it will only be in a great school, a school with large numbers of superb teachers and of imaginative and highly intelligent pupils, that one can hope to see large numbers of educated people emerging and even then there will certainly be some pupils who go through a great school and bear no marks of it whatsoever, remaining fundamentally uneducated to the end of their days. It is therefore absurd to impose upon every ordinary school an unfulfillable duty to ensure that all their pupils emerge as educated people. Providing an education is something wonderful, but special.

One of the qualities which marks out a great school is the presence within it of a certain intellectual tolerance—a sense of the importance of eccentricity. This is a vital ingredient if a school is to enable large numbers of its pupils to become truly educated; because eccentricity, properly understood, draws attention to possibilities beyond the obvious and entices pupils to take their eyes off the immediate task, so that they become able to see their own intellectual position in relation to other possible (more refined or more profound) positions. In a great school, there will be large numbers of really interesting eccentrics both among the teachers and among the pupils: people so imaginative that they do not conform to any obvious social or intellectual pattern. But in a great school, eccentricity is not merely tolerated and admired, it is also kept rigorously under control. That is the peculiar quality of such a school: the sense of tradition, the deep orderliness of its daily transactions, the prevailing sense of discipline (both intellectual and social) are such that eccentricity can flourish, entice, enlarge the mind of the onlooker, without degenerating into mere absurdity and decadence. In anything other than a great school, this delicate balance is unlikely to be achieved. Either eccentricity will be ruthlessly stamped out—depriving pupils of an incentive to transcend the obvious, to acquire a real sense of self awareness and thereby to start becoming educated—or it will rapidly degenerate into a loose absurdity, inspiring nobody. If an ordinary school, in a too concentrated attempt to avoid mediocrity, attempts to cultivate eccentricity without the necessary underpinning of discipline and orderliness, it is all too likely to end, as many of our schools have ended, by falling into sheer pretentiousness and failing to provide anything of real value.

The sad and paradoxical-sounding, but nonetheless important and unchanging fact is that providing an education in the true, full sense of the word—rendering pupils educated people—is not something that most schools can hope to do for most of their pupils. What, then, is their purpose? What is it the duty of most schools to provide for most pupils?

Grounding comes first

I maintain that the strict duty of every school is to ensure that, by the end of their schooldays, every pupil has what I shall call a grounding. By this, I mean an understanding of those things which it is necessary to understand in order to take a properly independent part in the life of our society. To be such an independent actor, people must be able to read and comprehend information of divers sorts; otherwise, they are unable to make properly independent choices about their jobs, their houses, their everyday purchases, their travel and so forth. They must also be able to make sense of the newspapers, and the spoken words of public life, since how else can they hold independent, informed attitudes about their governors, and the political system? It is essential, too, that people should grasp enough mathematics to see the simple effects of their decisions upon their lives, since otherwise they are constantly at the mercy of others, who will use their ignorance as an opportunity for themselves. And, perhaps most important of all, people must be able to express themselves with sufficient clarity both on paper and in speech, to make themselves fairly understood, since they are otherwise virtually unable to cope with the choices which are the stuff of an independent life in our society, or to be recognised by others as possessors of an independent voice, worthy of being heard in its own right. A person who lacks such a grounding, and is therefore unable to take an independent part in the life of our society, clearly represents a failure on the part of the school or schools which he attended. If we care at all about living in a liberal democracy, in which people are permitted to make choices for themselves, then we are duty-bound to provide everybody with tools which enable them to make and express such choices, on the basis of understanding what is being chosen, rather than as mere arbitrary leaps in the dark. This involves enforcing schooling upon all potential citizens; but it also involves providing, in school, the grounding that validates such compulsion. A person who fails to receive a grounding represents a paradox, because he has been the subject of compulsory schooling which would be justifiable only if the life of our society is somehow dependent upon his having attended school; yet he has not received what would have justified such compulsion.

Grounding involves acquiring both a range of skills and a certain amount of knowledge—at a level where knowledge and skill are almost indistinguishable from one another. Reading and writing, understanding simple mathematics, and expressing oneself clearly, are of course skills: one has to know how to do them instead of merely knowing that something or other is the case about them. But, in the course of learning, one inevitably acquires certain specific items of knowledge. One learns that certain words refer to certain objects and activities, that $2+2=4$, probably also (on the way) that the moon is not made of cheddar cheese, and a number of other items of sheer information. Whether the skills are taught by teaching the information, or whether the information is acquired through teaching the skills, is a matter of teaching practice, rather than of teaching aim—or indeed, simply a matter of luck. But about the aim, the duty, there is no room for disagreement. Every child needs, by whatever method, to have acquired the combination of knowledge and skill which enables him to live in a liberal, democratic society.

The provision of such a grounding is, I believe, the only absolute duty of a school.

Many people concerned with education—and certainly almost all the present educational establishment—would deny this, to the point of finding it outrageous. They would argue that such a concept of schooling is hopelessly narrow, and that any school which provides its pupils with no more than a rudimentary grounding is falling miserably in its duty.

These arguments fail to recognise the extent of the opportunities which are opened up for someone who has a grounding. An individual is, in a most fundamental sense, someone who makes decisions for himself rather than having them made for him by others— someone who has sufficient access to the fruits of civilization to enable him to understand something of what is on offer and to develop real preferences. That is just what a grounding enables a person to do. Like the working man at the Workers' Educational Association, and the audience at the improving lectures of the last century, a person with a grounding can go to the library and read, go to lectures and listen, ask questions and apprehend any answer that is given in clear English. A person with a grounding has what nobody without one can ever have—a basis upon which to build an understanding of the world.

Of course, a grounding is not the crowning achievement of a school in relation to the encouragement of individuality. A school which provides only a grounding has no right to claim that it has done all that could be done for its pupils' capacity to make independent judgments. That would be to suggest that individuality is an open and shut affair—which it most certainly is not. A person is not simply capable of individual judgement or simply incapable of it. Some people are more capable of it than others. As a person's understanding of his world, of the possibilities within that world, becomes larger, his range of choice widens: he becomes aware of possibilities which his imagination was previously unable to furnish. This is a product not of grounding, but of true education. The two aims of schooling, the essential duty to provide a grounding and the larger, hoped-for goal of enabling pupils to become educated both contribute—at different levels—the encouragement of individuality.

Many educational theorists, and amongst them many who count themselves as conservatives of one sort or another, will no doubt argue that it is both wrong and dangerous to describe the aims of schooling in this very general and abstract way. They will complain that these aims make no mention of the teaching of English history, of scripture, of the encouragement of artistic creativity and musical ability, of training for jobs. Above all, they will complain that no mention is made here of the need for schools to teach sound morals to their pupils. But these omissions are intentional. Contrary to the prevailing fashion, it is neither safe nor right to lay down, from the pulpit or from Whitehall, a whole range of specific skills and items of information that should be taught by every school. Beyond a grounding, which is the indispensable prerequisite for playing an independent role in our society, there is no specific skill which needs to be acquired by every pupil: schools which fail to teach their pupils how to conduct physical experiments or how to speak French or how to play the piano may nevertheless be adequate or even very good schools. In some narrowly religious schools, for example, none of these things are taught. But still the pupils receive a grounding and (in some cases) emerge as educated people through their study of sacred texts, the languages of their own community and the traditions which are attached to these languages. On what basis has anyone the right to object if children are, by the choice of their parents, provided with a schooling so manifestly suited to their way of life and so clearly justified by its social results?

The idea that a school's aim is to train people for jobs is equally noxious. Acquiring a grounding is probably as important for most jobs that are now done, as it is for living as a citizen in a liberal democratic society; but there are still many jobs that can be filled adequately without any grounding; and there are many more that can be done well by people who are in no sense educated. This is an utter irrelevance from the point of view of schooling; if both grounding and education were unnecessary for every job in the world, that would not detract in the slightest degree from their importance. Jobs are done to provide those who do them and their customers with economic benefits which have some human value because they contribute to a civilized existence. Schooling, both in providing a grounding and in attempting to yield educated people, is making a direct contribution of its own to the sustenance of a civilised existence. It is therefore on a par with, not subservient to, economic work.

The teaching of sound morals is a much more delicate issue. The instilling of moral principles and practices is a prime aim of a school, in the sense that everything done in a school, not only in the classroom but also on the sports field and in the example set by the teachers should obviously encourage pupils to become better rather than worse people. In the days when it was taken for granted that every school had a duty to provide its children with a grounding, this moral aim could be stressed without danger. When Tom Brown was told that his moral education mattered more than any deep learning he might acquire, that was perfectly sensible, because it was assumed by his father that he would receive a decent grounding as a matter of course. But things are different now. It is not taken by any means for granted that every school will aim to provide a grounding for its pupils by the time that they leave school. Instead, a large number of teachers and 'educationalists' take the view that the provision of a grounding is unimportant so long as the children emerge as nice, compassionate, sensitive, socially progressive people. This is as dangerous as any educational doctrine that has been perpetrated during the last forty years. The pupils who attend schools dominated by this doctrine may emerge with delicate consciences; but they are likely to be so unsuited to play an independent role in society, that they will soon turn into embittered, miserable adults. Moral training is not therefore a substitute for providing a grounding. It is something that ought to go on through, rather than in addition to, the specific activity of teaching and learning.

Some failures

Why all this stress on the provision of a grounding? Is it not something that every British school already does handsomely for all its pupils? Can we not simply assume that a grounding is being provided, and go on to more interesting matters?

Unfortunately, the answer to these questions is a resounding 'no'. For a large number of pupils, many of our schools are failing to provide a grounding.

This appalling fact can be illustrated by many pieces of evidence. I shall take just one: the surveys of reading and writing ability conscientiously undertaken by the Assessment of Performance Unit of the

Department of Education and Science. In his pamphlet on the teaching of English*, Dr. Marenbon has with some justice, made a number of critical observations about the attitude taken towards grammar and syntax by the Assessment of Performance Unit: but, despite such observations, the sheer factual material unearthed by the Unit remains invaluable evidence of what is going on in our schools.

Here is a passage, reproduced in one of the Unit's reports, in which a pupil describes one of 'the three most interesting things . . . learned during the last two weeks':

History
We learnt that poor people suffered very painfully towards illnesses in the 1800's because they couldn't afford to pay for surgery Common deceases in the 1800's Still born—caused by the mother working too hard whilst pregnant. Trophiad Fever—Drinking polluted water

The poor were cramped by having five family's into one house as they couldn't afford anything better One family lived in each room and one lived in the cellar This caused decease to spread very quickly The part of a town around a the factory's are called 'The Slums' Rich people lived farer out into the country. The farer out the richer they were. The rich and the poor mixed very rarely. (SPU: *Language Performance in Schools,* Secondary Survey Report No. 2).

What age was the author of the passage? Eight? Eleven? Thirteen? No, fifteen. After ten years of compulsory schooling, this pupil had achieved no greater mastery of writing than one would expect of a child five years younger. The misspellings, the bizarre capitalisations, the absence of full-stops and of all other punctuation, the neologisms, the misuse of prepositions, the wrong tenses, the inability to organise a sentence with anything other than a single, main verb, the consequent inability to link complex propositions into a coherent sequence—all these tendencies mark out the writer as someone who does not feel at home, and cannot feel at home, in his own language. And this, at the age of fifteen, with just one more year of compulsory schooling and with every chance that the egregious errors will go uncorrected in that final year! The author is likely to have remained in this condition for the rest of his or her life.

An exceptional case? By no means. The script was rated 3 on a scale running from 1 (worst) to 7 (best); no less than 26% of the 15

---

* ENGLISH OUR ENGLISH: the new orthodoxy examined, John Marenbon, CPS, June 1987

year olds tested fell into the same or lower categories. This, in other words, is the best that can be achieved by one pupil in four, a year before leaving school—and that figure of course, excludes pupils in special schools for the handicapped (who were not tested), but includes pupils at grammar and independent schools, who were tested; moreover, it disguises what are no doubt significant regional and local variations. If one were to conduct a similar test in maintained comprehensive schools in certain inner city areas, there is little doubt that the proportion of pupils achieving the same, or lower, standards would be far greater.

For one pupil in ten, nationally, the position is far worse. For those pupils who score a 2 or less (representing over 9% of the population, or over 10% if one includes those who did not even attempt the writing test) the problem is not just one of failing to feel at home in the language: they are constantly on the brink of collapsing into incomprehensibility. Witness this 15 year old, who scored a 2:

> In the last two weeks I went to the R.A.F. for information and I learned a lot from going. like the pay the age the training the signing years and reservered, and what I have to do to get the job. and I have learned about the Coil in physics because I have always wanted to know it. I was interesting to know all the different trades off all discibsion in engerneering and other trades.

What is this young person trying to say? What are 'the signing years and reservered'? Does the author know? Certainly, the reader is in no position to guess.

The trap in which these pupils are caught is unimaginably awful and made no better by being shared with hundreds of thousands of others.

They are about to leave school; some £15,000 (in today's money) has been spent on their so-called 'education'. They will shortly be expected to take their place in the big world, to play an intelligent part in a liberal, democratic society, to express their views, to conduct their affairs in an orderly way. How on earth are they to do it?

Perhaps some commentators will say that this is overstated, and that writing does not matter too much. Do they take the same view of reading?

The sad truth is that a high proportion of pupils leaving secondary schools cannot make their way through a simple story and understand clearly what it is about. The APU's 1979 Secondary Survey

Report contains a straightforward tale about Billy, a lad who arrives in Bath to start a new job, takes lodgings with a landlady and is duly murdered by her. To judge by the number of right answers given to a series of questions, about one pupil in ten was almost completely lost; about one in seven was unable to spot even very simple points, such as the warm and cosy look of the room as seen by Billy from outside; and almost one in two were unable to say either why Billy started off by thinking the landlady dotty (though this is clearly described in the story) or why he later begins to get suspicious (though this, too, is painfully obvious).

This may all sound rather abstract. To put it more concretely: if any ordinary upper middle class parents who sent their children to independent schools were to discover that their fifteen year old son or daughter was at this reading-level, they would conclude that the 'child' was subnormal. And that is the condition in which millions of the sons and daughters of other ordinary, but not so affluent parents are emerging from our schools. It is a catastrophe that can be sustained and tolerated only because of the hopelessly low—and hopelessly wrong—estimation which most schools have of the abilities of most of their pupils.

Conclusion

A really solid grounding—a sure and certain grasp of written texts, an ability to be and feel at home in the written and spoken language, a basic numeracy—these are treasures beyond value that could and should be acquired by every normal British schoolchild. Until and unless that is being universally achieved in our schools, we should be concentrating the entire efforts of our administrators and teachers on that task. Only in those schools where the basic minimum is so well established that it is taken for granted, can there be any excuse for diverting effort to any other task.

The failure to take this approach is in a true sense tragic. It is a case of the best being the enemy of the good. That, indeed, has been the theme of British education for the past forty years: noble but grandiose ambitions to do the impossible resulting in utter failure to achieve the possible. Perhaps in the next forty years British schools will adopt more modest aims and will achieve more as a result, attempting to educate only when they have already provided a thorough grounding and encouraging depth only when they have already given solidity.

Certainly, if they continue with the destructively pretentious aims of the recent past, they will go on providing their pupils with what Lewis Carrol so accurately describes as:- 'the regular course . . . the different branches of Arithmetic . . . Ambition, Distraction, Uglification and Derision'.

12

Diamonds into Glass: The Government and the Universities

Elie Kedourie

A glance backwards

A growing malaise has been afflicting British universities during the last ten to fifteen years, and of late it has intensified. The immediate reason is not far to seek: by far the largest part of the universities' income derives from government; and in common with other institutions paid for from public funds, universities have suffered stringency, the inevitable consequence of severe and continuous budgetary restraints. The ensuing retrenchment has brought out starkly, and has served to make even more pronounced, far-reaching and fundamental changes in the relations between the government and the universities.

Relations between the government and the universities! Should there be such relations? The question seems at first sight disingenuous. Do not Ministers, large numbers of civil servants, and Parliament itself, bend with wise and solicitous care over university education, and do not they go to so much trouble in order to formulate and to execute policies for the welfare of higher education, and tirelessly work to disseminate its benefits widely, not to say universally? And is not the taxpayer, lastly, made to bring his tribute—by the £1000 million—to the sacred altar of learning and scholarship? Yet, not so long ago, in fact within living memory, these things had not even been thought of.

Of course, this is by no means to say that universities have ever been considered as purely private organisations. They were, and are, public institutions, the efficiency and good working of which are subjects of public interest. And this is not necessarily because they may be supported by public funds—as they are today in this country. By virtue of their royal charters, universities have licence to award degrees; and they benefit from charitable endowments, the proper use of which is subject to regulation and supervision. Indeed, the grant of charters to new universities in recent decades, public enquiries by royal commissions into the workings of Oxford and Cambridge, legislation such as that which set up the federal University of London, are so many tokens of their public character. What, until fairly recently, this meant was simply that the public weal required universities to be well-run and able to discharge their duties. These duties are easily specified: to educate the young, to preserve and transmit traditions of learning and civility, and to promote the increase of knowledge. It was also believed—taken for granted—that these ends were achieved, could only be achieved, if universities were self-governing corporations, articulating for themselves the ends for which they existed, and pursuing these ends according to their own inner, self-moving dialectic. Those who remember the university as it used to be, only three or four decades ago, will know that here lies the secret of its extraordinary power to stretch the intellect of those within its portals, and to inspire loyalty and affection as the alma mater who bounteously bestows, on all those who work to possess them, the prodigious riches contained in the Aladdin's Cave of the mind.

The great value of Aladdin's Cave is that its riches are wholly unexpected and uncovenanted. The moment a licensed valuer is sent to make a survey according to ruling market prices, the charm is broken, gold turns to lead, diamonds to glass. Here is a list of books produced over the years by a university faculty: *Averroes' Commentary on Plato's Republic; Neolithic Cattle-Keepers of South India; A Nestorian Collection of Christological Texts; Water Rights and Irrigation Practices in Lahj.* Here is the 1905 volume of the *Annalen der Physik* with a paper on 'A New Determination of Molecular Dimensions'. Which planner could have said beforehand that one or other of these subjects should or should not have been pursued; and which accountant or valuer can say that neolithic cattle-keepers in India are worth more, or less, than Averroes' commentary on Plato's Republic? The paper in the *Annalen,* it is true, is by one Albert Einstein and the valuer will, in retrospect, put a high price on it. But unless he is a physicist, can he say—as valuers are usually required to say—exactly, or even approximately, how much?

While Rector of the Catholic University of Ireland, J H Newman wrote a lecture for the School of Science on 'Christianity and Scientific Investigation'. He told his audience that unless the scientist

> is at liberty to investigate on the basis, and according to the peculiarities of his science, he cannot investigate at all. It is the very law of the human mind in its enquiry after and acquisition of truth to make its advances by a process which consists of many stages, and is circuitous. There are no short cuts to knowledge; nor does the road to it always lie in the direction in which it terminates, nor are we able to see the end on starting. It may often seem to be diverging from a goal into which it will soon run without effort, if we are but patient and resolute in following it out; and, as we are told to gain the mean merely by receding from both extremes, so in scientific researches error may be said, without a paradox, to be in some instances the way to truth, and the only way. Moreover, it is not often the fortune of any one man to live through an investigation; the process is one of not only many stages, but of many minds. What one begins another finishes; and a true conclusion is at length worked out by the co-operation of independent schools and the perseverance of successive generations.[1]

Scientific activity, the characteristics of which Newman so precisely described, forms part of what in his fifth discourse on the idea of a university, Newman called Liberal Education. It is liberal, not servile, because viewed in itself, it is 'simply the cultivation of the intellect, as such, and its object is nothing more or less than intellectual excellence'

> To open the mind [he went on], to correct it, to refine it, to enable it to know, and to digest, master, rule, and use its knowledge, to give it power over its own faculties, application, flexibility, method, critical exactness, sagacity, resource, address, eloquent expression, is an object as intelligible . . . as the cultivation of virtue, while, at the same time, it is absolutely distinct from it.[2]

Newman found it necessary to spell out the character of university education to his Irish audience, because the hierarchy in Ireland manifestly looked to the new foundation to buttress Catholics in the faith and preserve them from harmful and subversive intellectual contagion. Newman was however quite clear that this, like any other utilitarian calculation, would be merely self-defeating. As a catholic, he recognised and acknowledged the sovereign authority of the Church, but this did not mean that a Catholic university was simply its instrument or agent. To make his point he used an illuminating analogy. The Catholic University, he told the science students, 'is ancillary certainly, and of necessity to the Catholic Church; but in the same way that one of the Queen's judges is an officer of the Queen, and nevertheless determines certain legal proceedings between the Queen and her subject'.[3]

Newman saw that the aims of Archbishop Cullen in Dublin were just as inimical to the purposes of a university as the very different ideals of Lord Brougham and the Edinburgh Reviewers. The latter

> insist that Education should be confined to some particular and narrow end, and should issue in some definite work, which can be weighed and measured. They argue as if every thing as well as every person, had its price; and that where there has been a great outlay, they have a right to expect a return in kind. This they call making Education and instruction 'useful', and 'Utility' becomes their watchword. With a fundamental principle of this nature, they very naturally go on to ask, what there is to show for the expense of a University; what is the real worth in the market of the article called a 'Liberal Education', on the supposition that it does not teach us definitely how to advance our manufactures, or to improve our lands, or to better our civil economy; or again, if it does not at once make this man a lawyer, that an engineer, and that a surgeon; or at least if it does not lead to discoveries in chemistry, astronomy, geology, magnetism and science of every kind.[4]

Archbishop Cullen and Lord Brougham are the mirror-image of one another; brothers under the skin.

George Bernard Shaw was yet another brother. In 1894, Sidney Webb received news that a benefactor who was unknown to him had left a large sum of money to set up a trust, of which Webb was to be a trustee, to carry on propaganda on behalf of the Fabian Society and its Socialism, and to forward its other purposes. But Webb sought to find a way of using part of the Hutchinson money to establish a London School of Economics devoted not to the propagation of socialism, but to the impartial study of economics and cognate subjects. Webb took legal advice from Lord Haldane who asked him 'whether he remained a convinced Socialist, and whether he believed that the more that social conditions were studied scientifically and impartially the stronger the case for socialism became?' Webb answered yes to both questions, and Haldane declared that the project could go ahead. Webb believing that 'to know the causes of things'—which became the motto of the School—would ultimately redound to the advantage of Socialism is akin to Newman in his belief that the disinterested pursuit of scientific truth would end by fortifying Catholic truth. At the opposite pole of one another in belief, temperament and cast of mind, yet Newman and Webb believed, both of them, that to harness a university to the promotion of a religious dogma, or a particular kind of social organization would be useless and self-defeating. But Webb had a vehement and noisy antagonist, his fellow-Fabian Bernard Shaw. In a letter to Beatrice Webb he demanded that Hewins (the first Director-elect of the LSE) should be told 'flatly' that he had to 'speak as a Collectivist and make it clear that the School of Economics will have a Collectivist bias'. Again, 'the Collectivist flag must be waved and the Marseillaise played if necessary to attract fresh bequests'. And again, one had 'to avoid shocking the common sense of the public . . . by talking about academic abstraction and impartiality'.[5] If Shaw had had his way, the London School of Economics would have become a sectarian conventicle.

A common crusade

And now we find the present Government making common cause with Archbishop Cullen, Lord Brougham and Bernard Shaw in a tough-minded, no-nonsense crusade for utility as the alpha and omega of university education. In exchanges about government and education which raged, all last spring, in the columns of the *Times Literary Supplement*, Mr Robert Jackson MP intervened at one point. Mr Jackson is now the Parliamentary Under Secretary of State in charge of university education at the Department of Education and Science, and his views have therefore attached to them all the weight of office. Mr Jackson holds up for our inspection—and no doubt discomfort—a picture of universities as cartels of 'producer-interests' sunk in a 'rentier culture of wealth-consumption'—mercilessly battening like harpies on a national economy with an 'increasingly pitiful relative performance'. The 'apparatus and ethos of the self-regarding academic producer-monopoly', proclaims Mr Jackson, 'must be dismantled'. Shooting from the hip he discharges on his cowering targets a stream, a hail, of accusatory questions, to wit, 'Are your students getting from you what you are paid to give them? How good is your research, actually? Are you working hard enough? What attention, if any, do you pay to the real costs of what you are doing? Does anybody outside the secret garden have the remotest interest in what you are doing? . . . What sort of responsibility do you feel to that world outside which pays for your work?'[6]

The academics are of course, no doubt as they are meant to be, struck dumb. Who, then, will answer the question? It is obvious: the Minister himself. He it is who will decide if the third-year undergraduate in engineering at Hull University is getting more, or less, value for money than the second-year undergraduate in Kurdish at London University. The Minister will set up time-and-motion studies to establish whether the Lecturer in Thermodynamics at Strathclyde University is working harder than the Professor of Sanskrit at Oxford University. He will commission market research in order to determine whether the public is more interested in Pharaonic archaeology than in the theory of speech acts. Nor must we think that such aspirations are original to Mr Jackson. For in the last two or three decades such, remarkably, have been the burdens which wise and experienced eminences have, step by step, found themselves tempted to bear. A landmark and watershed in this development was the Committee on Higher Education, headed by Lord Robbins, which was appointed in February 1961 and which reported in September 1963. To follow this development we now have an excellent account of the making of this Report and the working out, over the years, of its consequences.

J P Carswell who published in 1985 *Government and the Universities in Britain: Programme and Performance 1960–1980,* brings to his book the instincts, talents and experience of an accomplished historian who expresses himself lucidly, strikingly and felicitously. Mr Carswell was very well placed to observe unfolding events since during this period he was successively a member of the division of the Treasury concerned with university finance, served as an assessor to the Robbins Committee, desk officer responsible for universities in the department of Education and Science, and Secretary of the University Grants Committee.

The nineteen-sixties saw an enormous expansion in university education. The expansion had indeed been underway before the Robbins Committee reported. The Committee recommended that this should continue, and its Report armed the movement for expansion with a beguiling, a conquering ideology, and gave it a momentum which almost no one in politics, and scarcely anyone in the universities, wanted to, or could resist. Political leaders of all colours, beginning with the Prime Minister, Mr Harold Macmillan, believed that university expansion was a vote-winner, while academics and civil servants provided cast-iron, scientifically attested reasons which proved that expansion was absolutely necessary and wholly beneficial.

Mr Carswell takes us back to that far-away age, and provides many arresting *vignettes* of those strong-minded personalities who gave it its innocent, blessed certainties. There was, first, Sir Keith Murray, Chairman of the UGC: 'In manner large, benevolent, persuasive, in action almost inexhaustible, he was a convinced and consistent expansionist . . . He was a man for the times.' But expansionism, not unexpectedly, also meant restrictionism, for Sir Keith Murray was the creator of the University Central Council for Admissions (UCCA), to which all candidates for admission as undergraduates are compelled to apply, specifying five, and no more than five, universities to whom their particulars would be sent. Mr Carswell admires the invention, declaring that without UCCA a university system on a national scale matched to opportunity would have been grossly inefficient, probably impossible'. It is by no means obvious that he is right, or that such a serious restriction of choice—unique in civilized countries—is necessary for the welfare either of students or universities. The United States, for instance, contains a vast multitude of institutions of higher education. They and their students seem to manage without the benefit of such rationing, with neither chaos nor anarchy ensuing.

Then there was Sir Richard Clarke, (Otto to his familiars), Third Secretary in the Treasury: 'He had some of the characteristics of a high officer on Ludendorff's *Grossgeneralstab:* massive presence, neurotic mannerisms, sparkling intelligence, a rather squeaky voice. A more relentless man I have never met . . . He was essentially a man of ideas, all of which seemed to him unquestionably right so that those who opposed them, once he had explained them, were in his eyes simply lacking in intelligence'. Lord Robbins: 'When I first met him he impressed me as a bland silver lion, all mass and whiteness . . . I have never encountered anyone except Otto who was more confident that he was right. It was a friendly, comforting confidence, and disagreement was tolerated: but made no impression'. Sir Philip Morris, Vice Chancellor of Bristol University: 'the most potent member of the Robbins Committee'; he was 'almost clerkly, precise, unobtrusive and hard as a diamond', 'one of the great men of the Attlee years', 'probably the most powerful man in the West of England'. 'He was at heart', Mr Carswell tells us, 'a unifier, above all in education, which he saw as moving inexorably towards a co-ordinated, if indirectly administered, publicly supported system. No member of the Committee, not even the Chairman himself, had more influence over the final emphasis of the Report: indeed it could almost be said that he was its architect'. Morris was 'a convinced expansionist' and had 'a high regard for the Whitehall establishment as it then was, and for the arrangements it had for financing the universities'. There is one paragraph[7] in the Robbins Committee Report which Mr Carswell says bears the stamp of Morris rather than Robbins. Refusal to 'co-operate in national policies or to meet national emergencies is an unsympathetic attitude' declares the Committee, 'and it would be easy to think of reasons why it should be over-ruled'. But it is better to show forbearance, though the recalcitrant institution 'must not complain if various benefits going to co-operating institutions do not come its way'. The self-assured certainty that national policies as formulated by authority are here by definition infallible, and the tone of polite menace pervading the paragraph are harbingers of much that was to come.

The great theme which these self-confident and categorical men launched upon the country was that of a publicly funded and open-ended commitment to provide a university education to all those qualified to receive it, and desirous of doing so. This splendid vision was rapturously welcomed by those who had authority to speak for universities, and endorsed by the Government—indeed by successive Governments, who undertook to provide large and ever-increasing funds for the purpose. What was even more onerous, though Ministers, gluttons for decision-making as they often are, may not have thought so, was that governments now had to formulate policies and plans for their charges. The 1972 Education White Paper was entitled 'A Framework for Expansion', and the less ambitious Brown Paper of six years later still took it as axiomatic that it was the responsibility of the Government to finance, and also to plan, higher education. Now more than ever, the authorities work in the belief that they must have a policy for the universities, thus increasing the burden of over-government under which they, equally with those who have become their dependants, must labour.

The Robbins Report began by making a novel and controversial point which, however, it obviously thought there was no need to justify. It saw the universities then existing as forming, or having to form, a system which required 'co-ordinating principles' and 'a general conception of objectives'. Indeed, 'the needs of the present and still more of the future demand', no less, 'that there should be a system'.[8] The Committee then went on to specify a variety of objectives the 'system' had to fulfil. It declared, harmlessly enough, that it wished 'to state unequivocally that . . . there is a broad connection between the size of the stock of trained manpower in a community and its level of productivity per head'. It went on, more urgently, to lay it down in one of those sentences which those who draft official reports will deprecate as needlessly giving hostages to fortune that: 'Indeed, unless this country is prepared to expand higher education on something like the scale we recommend, continued economic growth on the scale of the targets set by the National Economic Development Council is in our view, unlikely to be attainable.'[9] The targets set by the National Economic Development Council! What a powerful whiff of nostalgia the words carry! A following paragraph[10] wafts an even headier whiff:

> We are reinforced in our conclusion by recollection of a conversation with the authorities in the Soviet Union. In the Soviet system of planning much reliance is placed upon projections of manpower requirements and these are made on a most ambitious scale. When we indicated difficulties in understanding how, with all the uncertainties as regards invention and the advancement of knowledge generally, reliance could be placed on statistics of requirements for more than a few years ahead, we were met with the reply that in the Soviet Union there would always be use for people who had been trained to the limit of their potential ability.

Manpower planning, as in the Soviet Union, was not the only objective prescribed in the Report. Other kinds of social engineering are also described. We are told, for instance, that it is 'not a good thing that Oxford and Cambridge should attract too high a proportion of the country's best brains', and we must enquire whether their present methods of selection are 'socially just'.[11] The Committee also believed that disparity between the incomes and prospects of persons doing similar work in different universities is 'unjust'.[12]

All these contentions are clearly question-begging. Equally so is the analogy[13] between decisions taken by individual families to spend more of their income on education, and a decision by the Government to do so. The Committee were clearly not willing to see the difference between decisions freely taken by families about the manner in which they wish to spend their income, and official decisions financed by taxation abstracted from private pockets and implemented by ministers and officials according to their lights and in response to the political convenience of the hour. In line with this analogy, the Committee laid it down[14] that there had to be, in the interests of 'national needs' 'a greater degree of survey and co-ordination of higher education than has prevailed in the past'. The Government, all-wise and all-seeing, should preempt all strategic decisions on university education, which individual universities were incapable of taking on their own:

> It is unlikely [the Committee bluntly affirmed] that separate considera-
> tion by independent institutions of their own affairs in their own
> circumstances will always result in a pattern that is comprehensive and
> appropriate in relation to the needs of society and the demands of the
> national economy. There is no guarantee of the emergence of any
> coherent policy. And this being so, it is not reasonable to expect that
> the Government, which is the source of finance, should be content with
> an absence of co-ordination or should be without influence thereon.[15]

This unashamedly *dirigiste* and openly interventionist document received a tumultuous and enthusiastic welcome. The prospect for universities was believed to be of a bonanza hitherto undreamed of. Mr Carswell writes that 'It was contrary to the scheme of things to discuss student numbers in figures of less than a thousand or finance in sums under a million'. No wonder that it became the fashion at the time to put such emphasis on numeracy. I happened in those days—those palmy days—to attend a seminar on university education, addressed by a very high official of the Department of Education and Science. I still vividly remember the nonchalant and assured air, the effortless superiority (said to be the hallmark of the administrative class of the civil service), with which, like an accomplished conjurer, he blithely plucked out of the air marvellous and imposing statistical castles, complete with their projections of student numbers and forecasts of expenditure per capita.

In this, of course, he was only echoing the assumptions and conclusions of the Robbins Report which had quickly become gospel. But the Report did not anticipate the difficulties and tensions likely to be experienced by universities as they competed for the favours of government with a thousand other deserving causes. The ecstasy soon dissipated, as financial incontinence and mismanagement plunged one government after another into successive crises. Ministers, beset by multitudinous demands and pressures, besieged with fiscal embarrassments, were likely, as time went on, to become more and more irritated by perpetually importunate, seemingly idle and useless dependents, even though it was government itself which had created the dependency, which had, like a blundering magician, conjured up those monstrous blocks of concrete and glass, with their daubings and their graffiti, their regiments of clamorous teachers, their hordes of dissatisfied and mutinous students. Listening to Ministers like Mr Jackson and his predecessor in office, Mr George Walden[16], chastising their charges with whips and scorpions (with no hint of a recognition that what they so disliked was the very handiwork of official wisdom and benevolence), no one can doubt that there is nothing more corrosive and demoralizing than the relation between a harassed, grudging benefactor and a helpless, perpetual supplicant. A prudent and reasonable man would have foreseen and tried to avoid such a state of affairs. The Robbins Committee did not. The omission is one more striking peculiarity of the Report, since one of its great themes is that universities are and ought to remain autonomous in their activities. Such an assumption, as might be expected and as events soon proved, is not to be reconciled with dependence on public funds.

Yet another major theme of the Report was that the greater share of the expansion was to go to providing more places in science and technology, to be divided equally between men and women. But this aspiration did not take into account whether girls' schools were really able to produce qualified entrants in the numbers envisaged, or the outlook and wishes of women students, or of their prospective employers in industry. In the upshot there was a very large over-provision of places in science and technology faculties—of the order of 136,000 places, the equivalent, Mr Carswell remarks, of at least a dozen universities the size of Oxford. This large misallocation of resources puts one in mind of so many other grandiose ventures undertaken by government—ventures the archetype of which is the notorious East Africa ground-nuts scheme. Committees, civil servants, ministers are not, after all, endowed ex officio with superior wisdom or second sight. The large undertakings on which they are tempted to embark, perhaps in a fit of hopefulness, or out of gullibility, or in pursuit of momentary advantage, are more likely than not to come a cropper. How can government, brilliant Soviet planning notwithstanding, possibly determine how many doctors or nurses or accountants or linguists or chemists should be trained? And yet time and again we find it engaging in such costly, fruitless and absurd exercises. Medicine is a case in point: a committee decided in the early nineteen-sixties that too many doctors were being produced; a while later, a commission found that there were too few.

Cry cry what shall I cry?

The first thing to do is to form the committees:

The consultative councils, the standing committees, select committees and sub-committees.

(TS Eliot, Difficulties of a Statesman)[17]

Guessing

Government, then, has taken upon itself to determine the quantity of resources to be devoted to higher education, and to articulate the public interest in respect of it. It has assumed the novel, heavy and perilous burden of formulating policies for higher education on the basis of what can be no more than guesses, hunches, gropings in the dark, or those fashionable nostrums which academics themselves invent and persuasively propagate.

Before Robbins, British universities were considered, rightly, to be at the forefront of higher education. They were academic republics—the only genuine republics to subsist in the modern world—well-run, efficient and economical in their teaching methods and in the use of their comparatively modest resources. Those who taught and studied within their precincts, and those who sought the services of their graduates, were better suited, through their successive and cumulative decisions over time, to articulate the public interest which higher education represents. Better suited, because their judgement whether to teach this subject or that, in this or that manner, or to pursue this or that enquiry, or that this university or department was better than that one—such judgements were informed judgements arising out of a living, intimate and lifelong engagement with the matter in hand. These judgements did not issue from the desire—benevolent as it may be—to execute social justice, or in pursuit of the illusion that universities can be made into instruments of social engineering.

The capacity to make such judgements has of course by no means disappeared, but it has lost much of its value and efficacy. Instead, we have haphazard and hasty exercises such as the one which the University Grants Committee conducted recently. The Committee took upon itself, or perhaps had imposed upon it, the task of evaluating the contribution to research of British universities. Using its own private criteria and on the basis of what can have been no more than quick impressions and sketchy information, the Committee proceeded solemnly to bestow on every university department in the land a gold, or a silver, or a bronze star. An impressive exercise in comparative science—a science in which it is inexplicable that the Government has not pressed every university to establish at least one chair.

But this kind of haphazard exercise simply bears no comparison to the more strict, systematic and centralized official planning of academic activity which we have seen in the last two decades or so, and which, if recent official statements are any indication, promises to spread over the whole university field. The Social Science Research Council was set up in the nineteen-sixties. From its inception, the Council operated a system of allocating scholarship quotas among various subjects and universities. Such a rationing system could be nothing but arbitrary. It seems to have rested on extra-academic and essentially misconceived considerations. There seems to have been a desire to maintain a balance between various universities and departments. But the very notion of balancing must militate against the objective of maximum academic excellence. Initiative and innovation in teaching and research, or the value of a particular subject or line of enquiry, cannot be planned for or appraised in advance by a committee however wise and judicious its members. The fruitfulness of a particular teacher's research will appear only in the sequel. A *sine qua non* for the vitality of teaching and research is to let 'a hundred flowers bloom' or, as the case may be, wilt and die. The straitjacket of these quotas was out of place. This *dirigiste* system also meant that the best students in a given year might not receive an award, or that they might not be able to pursue the subject of their choice, or go to the university of their choice, even though they might have otherwise gained admittance. What is true concerning these graduate scholarships would also hold good in relation to research projects to promote which the SSRC had large sums at its disposal. One central body composed of so-called subject committees, made up of academics nominated to them by the SSRC Council, which in turn was nominated by the Secretary of State, and which required a large number of officials to service them—all this meant a high risk of decisions being hidebound by precedent (the necessary lifeblood of bureaucracy) or blinkered by ruling orthodoxies (the blight of teaching and research).

The same hankering for *dirigisme*, presumably in the belief or hope that it would, with the smallest outlay, produce results both unimaginably brilliant and extraordinarily lucrative, is manifest in a recent paper, *A Strategy for the Science Base*, published by the Advisory Board for the Research Councils. The Board, standing at the apex of a pyramid of Committees and Councils, proposes to classify universities into three categories, namely type-R, type-X and type-T. The first are adjudged to be centres for excellence on whom much will be bestowed; the second are half-and-half, good only in some kinds of research; the rest—T presumably standing for mere teaching—are the lowliest, to be deprived of all research facilities. A somewhat similar trisection has been recently effected by a committee which investigated and reviewed economic and social history departments. The eminent persons who have been engaged in these taxonomies are no doubt sound in their judgements, but since in teaching and research the wind bloweth where it listeth, there can be no assurance that the excellent will remain excellent, or that the last shall not, some time, become the first. Such reversals and peripeteias are very common in the annals of universities. In the United States, for instance, it is common knowledge that universities which at one time were not associated with any expertise, let alone excellence, in a particular subject, did manage within a decade or so to turn decisively around. But then, they were not frozen into a type-casting which ineluctably had to govern the flow of funds from the single, unique official source. Such type-casting can, in any case, be no more than an arbitrary judgement based on some idea of a university's past performance.

These successive inquiries, probings, inquisitions acquire their own obsessive momentum, aspiring to a scientific exactitude which, from the circumstances of the case, must be forever unattainable. Thus a Working Group drawn from the Committee of Vice-Chancellors and Principals and the University Grants Committee has now compiled a list of no less than thirty-nine (!) 'performance indicators'. Further precision will most likely increase the number to three times thirty-nine, and the proper comparison between the 'indicators' for successive years supplied by the several universities will no doubt require the services of a powerful computer. And then? Who can digest and master the evidence comprised in such a *grimoire* and reach decisions on its basis? Who? The answer is simple: the new professors of comparative science, who will thus signally demonstrate the ability of their subject, and so prove that they are worth their weight in gold.

There can be no doubt that this busy whirl in search of so-called facts and figures is the outcome of the hasty and injudicious expansion of the nineteen sixties—an expansion dictated by government, which government now finds itself unable or unwilling to fund in the manner to which its dependents had become accustomed. Government has thus to pre-empt those decisions which go to make up the character of a university, and which have slipped out of the hands of those who, in effect, are the university. The funding of a university has now come to be governed by the number of home (and EEC) students admitted and, to control the total UGC budget, the authorities have imposed quotas which a university must not exceed. These quotas and their sum depend, ultimately, on budgetary calculations very remote from, not to say irrelevant to, the interests and welfare of universities and their students. Arbitrariness is inherent in the situation. But the arbitrariness of the restriction is the mirror-image of the previous open-handed arbitrariness of expansion. A recent comparative exercise, for instance, placed Aberdeen university in an unfavourable position. In a letter to *The Times* of 22 June 1987, Professor R V Jones commented on this outcome:

The university [he pointed out] yielded to the temptation of over-rapid expansion in the heady years following the Robbins report of 1963, and in the process lost quality in stuff and students alike. Undergraduate numbers rose from 2,071 in 1961 to 4,573 in 1967. Staff numbers were increased proportionately and to fill the ranks tenure was given to staff who at no other time in university history would have found a place.

All this was amply obvious by 1973, when undergraduate numbers reached 4,833; but, instead of suggesting any restraint on further expansion, the University Grants Committee not only endorsed the university's own proposal to expand to 10,000 by 1981 but asked it to raise this target to 10,500.

On July 31, 1973, the Chairman of the UGC wrote to the Principal of the university: 'Do you think you could possibly plan for another 500 arts students?' And when on August 2 the Principal replied 'I would expect my colleagues to be unwilling to go beyond 10,000 students by 1981–2', the Chairman pressed on August 9 for Aberdeen's agreement, concluding his letter, 'The Committee will be disappointed if it is negative'. The university duly agreed to 10,500.

The small minority who pointed out that such figures were far beyond realism, especially since the UGC had also endorsed the creation of many new universities, have since had the bitter satisfaction of seeing their doubts substantiated by subsequent events.[19]

After two decades of government-sponsored excess and prodigality, we see now abroad a vague but powerful discontent and impatience with the ways of universities, laughably described as ivory towers, a nameless yearning for some formula or recipe—more science perhaps, more information technology, more questionnaires, more monitoring—which will scientifically (or better, magically) prove that they are not wasting their time, which will hook them up with the humming conveyor-belts of industry. Such yearnings radically misunderstand the character of universities, and so are doomed to the same disappointment as the visions of the Robbins Report which began by spreading a manic euphoria, and now inspire gloomy despair.

Official discontent and a restless quest for new and better methods of controlling universities and their activities are amply evident in a clutch of documents which appeared in quick succession during 1987. These were: *a Review of the University Grants Committee* by a committee under the chairmanship of Lord Croham, formerly Head of the Civil Service (Cmd. 81, published in February); a white paper, *Higher Education: Meeting the Challenge* (Cmd. 114, published in April); and two 'notes' by the Department of Education and Science (both published in May) on *Changes in Structure and National Planning for Higher Education*, one dealing with a proposed Universities Funding Council, and the other with Contracts between the Funding Bodies and Higher Education Institutions. The thrust of these documents is unmistakable. They all start from the assumption that universities have to have their goals prescribed by government, and that the realization of these goals is to be closely monitored through a new body employing a new method of control, which the Government is to set up.

Compared with the new *dirigisme*, the Robbins Report is a monument to *laissez-faire*. Higher education, the white paper lays it down, must serve the economy more effectively and have closer links with industry and commerce and promote enterprise[18]. Funds to be made available to universities would now 'properly reward success in developing co-operation with and meeting the needs of industry and commerce'.[19] The Government will investigate by means of an interdepartmental review the 'prospective needs for new graduates by industry, commerce and the public services', and if it is found that 'graduate output' is not 'in line with the economy's needs, the Government will consider whether the planning framework should be adjusted'.[20] Individually and collectively universities 'should do more to reassure the public about the ways in which they control standards', and it is to this end that 'performance indicators are to be developed'.[21]

This particular paragraph is curiously followed by one which seems to adumbrate an opposite line of policy. The paragraph deals with polytechnics and colleges in the public sector whose standards and courses are under the oversight of a chartered body, the Council for National Academic Awards. The work of the Council was investigated by the Lindop Committee which reported in 1985. As the White Paper says, the Lindop Report found that 'quality in higher education was best assured when polytechnics and colleges accepted maximum responsibility for their own standards'. This the White Paper approves of, while universities, as has been seen, are in contrast to be submitted to a finicky system of continuous monitoring. The methods of the Council prior to the Lindop Report were engendering veritable mountains of paper to make sense of which required yet more paper. The new arrangements proposed for universities bid fair to produce similar mountains.

The Croham Report was as *dirigiste* as the White Paper which it preceded. It proposed to replace the University Grants Committee by a University Grants Council with greatly enlarged powers, but which was also directly subordinated to the Secretary of State. The Council's 'principal responsibility' was to 'construct a national strategy for the investment of public funds' and to reconcile the separate strategies of individual universities with 'perceived national needs'. But the Secretary of State was to have 'a reserve power to issue directions to the Council, if need be'[22], the Secretary of State presumably being the judge of such a need. Indeed the Croham Committee is emphatic that the Government should have policy objectives and should state them clearly.[23]

This full-bloodedly interventionist view is a far cry from the objectives originally set for the University Grants Committee. When it was first established by a Treasury Minute in 1919 the Committee was required to enquire into the financial needs of universities and advise the Government on the application of any grants made by Parliament for this purpose. The terms of reference were considerably enlarged in 1946. It was now required, inter alia, 'to assist, in consultation with the Universities and other bodies concerned, the preparation and execution of such plans for the development of Universities as may from time to time be required in order to ensure that they are fully adequate to national needs'. Operating with these enlarged powers, the UGC presided over the expansion of sixties and seventies and now, in a climate of financial stringency, manages whatever contraction of university education is believed to be needed.

But a body with these large powers, or even with the much larger powers proposed by the Croham Report does not seem to satisfy Ministers. They wish, instead, to establish a Universities Funding Council. This new Council will receive from the Government, according to the 'note' published by the Department of Education and Science, 'strategic guidance on the size and broad balance of the university system'[24]; the Secretary of State will 'regularly' offer 'guidance and information' on 'the nation's needs as regards the size and broad balance of the university system' and on 'specific policy developments'. The Secretary of State is also to have a 'reserve power to issue directions to the Council'. The establishment of the Council will be provided for 'in primary legislation'. But 'more detailed statutory provisions' would be 'provided by means of statutory instruments'; the reason for this is said to be 'the difficulty of securing Parliamentary time for amending provisions required in the light of changed circumstances'.[25]

The other 'note' which was published at the same time, on Contracts between the Funding Bodies and Higher Education Institutions describes the novel mode of operation proposed for the Funding Council. There will no longer be either block or earmarked grants to universities. Instead the Council will enter into 'contracts' with universities. This is said to make for 'greater precision in the specification of what is expected of institutions in return for public funding', and for 'closer links between funding and institutions' performance in delivering specified provisions'. This manner of proceeding will also make possible 'periodic renegotiation of contracts'[26]. To enable the Council to judge whether universities are fulfilling their contracts will require 'the introduction of more systematic review and monitoring of what institutions achieve with public funding'. This will require the 'timely' collection and analysis of information about performance.[27]

'Contract' is a legal notion. It assumes at least two parties to a contract who enter freely into specific and mutual obligations, and who make provision for arbitration in case of dispute about the fulfilment of the terms of the contract. Contracts are also, ordinarily, enforceable in the courts. But it turns out that the Secretary of State does not exactly have in mind a contract as commonly understood. In an address to the Committee of Vice-Chancellors and Principals on 30 October 1987, Mr Kenneth Baker declared that he did not intend that these contracts should be 'a narrow set of legal arrangements' or that they should be enforceable in courts of law. It turns out, then, that this talk of contract is simply metaphorical—on a par with the social contract, known to historians of political thought, which was so frequently paraded to rhetorical effect during the Labour administrations of 1974–79. But why have recourse to such a metaphor? It is not clear. In a recent pamphlet, *The Attack on Higher Education*, Professor John Griffith has suggested that 'the use of this device may be to try to avoid the legal complication that might arise if a university resisted the imposition of detailed controls by reference to the purposes and obligations set out in its royal charter'[28]. He may be right.

That detailed controls are in contemplation cannot be doubted. Thus the recently published Education Reform Bill makes provision for compelling universities to end the practice of academic tenure. So intent is the administration on this abolition that it proposes to make it retroactive, by forbidding tenured appointments from the day when the bill was published. Why this drastic and exceptional proceeding which sits ill with constitutional government? It is also proposed that universities should be able to declare a teacher redundant on the grounds, *inter alia*, that the requirements for him 'to carry out work of a particular kind . . . have ceased or diminished or are expected to cease or diminish'. Such requirements will now of course be prescribed in 'contracts' made with the Universities Funding Council—'contracts' which universities will be in no position to reject. The Council, in turn, 'shall comply with any directions given to (it) by the Secretary of State'. And unto the Secretary of State there is none who may say, What doest thou? Is it so sure that academics over whom hangs this perpetual sword of redundancy will be better teachers and scholars? Have the dangers of pressures on teachers to conform to scholarly or even political orthodoxies to which this change opens a door been weighed and considered? All this is paradoxical at a time when the cry is so loud for parental choice in school education, and opting out of local authority control. Why it should be thought right and necessary for universities to be submitted to a regime akin to that of a command economy is quite obscure. Nor is it clear how a

Universities Funding Council, however eminent its chairman, knowledgeable its fifteen members, and energetic its chief executive officer
could possibly have the necessary knowledge to write up-to-date
contracts with fifty-three universities on subjects ranging from aero-
dynamics to zoology. So far, it has to be said, universities have shown
themselves reasonably competent to run their own affairs successfully. Is there reason to think that a Council made up of a chairman,
prince of (part-time) chairmen though he be, supported by fifteen
(part-time) Renaissance men (and women) as they no doubt will be,
and served by a nonpareil among chief executives, would do for
universities what full-time university teachers in daily touch with
their requirements in various subjects have long been accustomed to
do with fair efficiency? It is much to be feared that the outcome of
this activity would be a creeping rigidification of teaching and research. Also an increasing politicisation, since university affairs
would be bound up with who knows what irrelevant considerations
and calculations made within the Sublime Porte at Whitehall, as
when, on a day in 1975, scales of pay for university teachers, already
agreed, were summarily cancelled at the sovereign wish of Mr Jack
Jones, General Secretary of the Transport and General Workers'
Union. Malcolm Bradbury's *History Man* encapsulates all the charm
of the post-Robbins academy. What prodigies, what monsters will
the contract machine of the Universities Funding Council bring forth
from the womb of Time?

Glimpses of freedom

The question which must be asked is whether this surfeit of
contracts and quotas and controls and indicators is really necessary.
Whether, in fact, it is necessary or indeed feasible for government to
have a university policy at all? Or whether one should rather examine,
not so much the ways of making ever more detailed plans for
universities (most or all doomed to frustration), as the ways of
safeguarding the existence of free universities in a free society? The
issue at the outset was financial; and it is financial stringency which
has stimulated this bombination of enquiries and of schemes of
control.

Universities cannot have a claim, as of right, to be maintained by
the taxpayer. Along with everyone else they must take their chance
in a hazardous world where, like everyone else, unless they know

how to swim, they will surely sink. And why not? But for them to be able to do so they must cut free from the anxious leading-reins of government departments, and their benevolent nannying. If it is a public interest that the young should be educated, then let those who have the greatest interest in their welfare, namely their parents, themselves attend to the education. Instead of the state taking the taxpayer's money with one hand and dishing it out in grants and scholarships with the other, let the money be directly spent by those on whose behalf it is now expended. It may be objected that things have gone so far that this is no longer possible.

But there are things which are possible. Discussing the finance of universities, the Robbins report observed that fees then provided no more than eleven per cent of university expenditure. The Committee 'regretted' that the proportion was so low, but refused to concur with those who urged that fees should be raised until they covered if not all, then at least a large percentage of university expenditure. The Committee gave no detailed justification for their refusal, but recommended that fees should rise so as to meet at least twenty per cent of university expenditure[29]. Why, again, this particular figure? No explanation was given. The round figure has the appearance of being one of those which official bodies have a way of plucking from the air. For neither eleven nor twenty percent could remove the disadvantage of the universities' increasing dependence on direct official grants.

About a quarter of a century later, the Croham Committee reverted to the same issue. The eleven per cent of the Robbins Report had now become eight per cent. They, too, have assumed without argument that a major proportion of the Government's support would continue to be through direct grants to universities. 'In the extreme case in which support was entirely through payment to the student rather than to the Institution', they observed, 'there would be little point in having a Grants Committee'.[30] And so? Would not this mean that the Government would then be liberated from the burden of making decisions which ought to be made by universities and by those who attend them?

Another device frequently discussed in recent years both by ministers and by outside observers is that of loans to students—a device which many countries have adopted. It has been observed that university education brings substantial advantages to those who benefit from it, and that loans repayable over a period from the higher incomes which university education makes possible are only equitable. But loans would also have the great advantage of diversifying the income of universities, and of making them alert and directly responsive to the needs of those whom they educate. But, of course, loans will have the disadvantage of loosening official control over universities.

Yet another means of tightening the nexus between universities and their students, and loosening it between them and an interventionist bureaucracy is by allowing expenditure by parents on the university education of their children to count against tax. This of course is an indirect subvention to universities and their students, but the same advantages which attach to loans would also obtain here. An indirect subvention dispensed through tens of thousands of students is preferable to the direct subventions which entail so fearful a burden of central planning and control. And for this reason, if for no other, such allowance is unlikely to be instituted. It may also be objected that tax allowances will not help those whose income is too low to afford to take advantage of them. The objection is cogent, but it cannot be beyond the wit of fiscal experts to make suitable provision for the hard cases. What cannot be sensible is to devise a method of university finance the over-riding objective of which is to cater to hard cases. Hard cases, as is well-known, make bad law.

It is obvious that to function properly, to keep up and improve their fabric and their facilities universities need more than current income to cover current expenditure. Universities need a capital endowment. Two British universities, Oxford and Cambridge, are fortunate enough to enjoy the security and elbow-room which a large endowment confers. But it has become apparent that the existing endowments are by no means adequate to present and prospective needs. Oxford, it has recently been reported, is to launch a £200-million international appeal 'to rescue it from bankruptcy and the clutches of what it sees as a Government determined to undermine its autonomy'.[31] It has to be said that tax law here has not encouraged the private benevolence which makes possible the building up of a large endowment fund. The Royal Commission on the Taxation of Profits and Income, the Final Report of which came out in 1955, had occasion to examine this issue. The assumption from which they started was that 'taxes themselves are raised to be spent in meeting the immediate needs of the whole community'.[32] It is a very surprising statement to have made in an era when unimaginable and delightful vistas of income redistribution, demand management and fine tuning by taxation had opened up for Chancellors of the Exchequer through the scientific sorcery of Hugh Dalton (the songster of progressive taxation) and Maynard Keynes. However, as a matter of 'pure theory', the Commission might have preferred to see the tax concessions to charity given in the form of an allowance to the subscriber rather than to the recipient, as is done in the United States and Canada, but administrative convenience forbade; 'giving a personal relief to each individual taxpayer for sums paid by him to valid charities would be a very considerable addition to the present work of returning tax on covenants to the charities themselves'. 'On the whole', the Royal Commission concluded, 'we do not recommend it'.[33] There the matter has rested, except for a very recent concession allowing taxpayers to recover income tax above the standard rate on their charitable donations. This attitude to private benevolence has reinforced the prevailing assumption that if education and the like are to be promoted, the cost has to come out of taxation.

The Government now spends annually very considerable amounts in direct grants to universities. How then if a capital sum representing the present discounted value of, say, ten or fifteen years' subventions were to be given to each university which would be told that henceforth, given such a handsome dowry (or better, alimony) it would have to fend for itself?

Each one of these measures has probably been proposed and been duly rejected by the powers that be. And no doubt they have pleaded cogent or weighty reasons, administrative and fiscal, to reject them. What is now needed is a turning round of the policies which have been increasingly pursued since Robbins, and which have led to the present situation. It is, one suspects, unwillingness to reconsider existing policies—whether in the DES or in the Treasury—which transforms every administrative difficulty which might conceivably be encountered in implementing any of the proposals sketched above, into a mountain. *Non possumus* is the standing response. But there are pressing reasons why this negative attitude should be abandoned. It is in the public interest that there should be lively, efficient well-run universities. It is not in the public interest, not in the interests of universities and their inmates, that they should be tied to, and dragged behind, the chariot-wheels of the Government.

Notes

1. *The Idea of a University Defined and Illustrated*, new ed. 1891, pp. 474–5.
2. Op. cit. pp. 121–3.

3. Op. cit. p. 459.
4. Op. cit. p. 153.
5. Janet Beveridge, *An Epic of Clare Market*, 1960, pp. 25–28.
6. *Times Literary Supplement*, 8 May, 1987.
7. Robbins Committee Report, Cmd. 2154, 1963, para 715.
8. Ibid. paras 18–20.
9. Ibid. para 192.
10. Ibid. para 194.
11. Ibid. paras 217 & 222.
12. Ibid. para 542.
13. Ibid. para 635.
14. Ibid. para 702.
15. Ibid. para 719.
16. *TLS*, 27 March 1987.
17. TS Eliot, 'Coriolan: II Difficulties of a Statesman', *Collected Poems 1909–1962*.
18. *Higher Education: Meeting the Challenge*, Cmd. 114, April 1987, p. 1V.
19. Ibid. para 4.43.
20. Ibid. para 2.13.
21. Ibid. para 3.7.
22. *A Review of the University Grants Committee*, Cmd. 81, February 1987, paras 5.10 and 5.9.
23. Ibid. para 2.22.
24. ibid. para 22.
25. Ibid. para 39.
26. *Changes in Structure and National Planning for Higher Education*, May 1987, para 8.
27. Ibid. para 21.
28. *The Attack on Higher Education*, October 1987 (obtainable from the author, 2 The Close, Spinfield Lane, Marlow, Bucks), p. 17.
29. The Robbins Report, paras 649–654.
30. *A Review of the University Grants Committee*, op. cit. para 2.30.
31. *The Times*, 9 October 1987.
32. *The Royal Commission on the Taxation of Profits and Income*, Final Report, 1955, Cmd. 9474, para 169.
33. Ibid. paras 182 & 184.

13

Choice in Rotten Apples: Bias in GCSE and Examining Groups

Mervyn Hiskett

Foreword

For the vast majority of schoolchildren, the GCSE is the most important examination of their lives. There can be no doubt that in its setting and marking and modes of assessment, in the laying down of syllabuses and the selection of textbooks, a great deal of the ideas of the 'new orthodoxy', building on the consensus of the 'sixties, has successfully—and disastrously—taken over. Much of the responsibility for this lies at the door of the teacher training colleges, whose practices should be urgently re-examined.

But what else should be done about it? The attitudes of the members of Examining Groups are not going to be changed overnight. The new orthodoxy of many, or perhaps most, teachers and their unions, and of many headmasters too is another fact of life.

In his paper Dr Hiskett does not suggest the exchange of one ideology for another. There should be no place for the political pendulum in the education of our children. But the demand, implicit in his criticisms, for rigour, for strict standards, and for the selection of subjects and textbooks with sound academic credentials should be heard.

It is true that the GCSE 'general criteria' contain firm admonitions against introduction by Examining Boards of any form of political bias; and it is the duty of the SEC to bring to heel those who stray. But they have not done so in the case of many religious, social science and history syllabuses, as Dr. Hiskett clearly shows. The new SEAC, the composition of which has yet to be announced, should be more vigilant.

Their task of supervision would be helped if employers who use examination results, perhaps under the aegis of the CBI and other bodies, set up a committee, the main function of which would be to publish and sell an annual scrutiny of the conduct of the Groups. Given the value of such a review to schools, the operation could hope soon to be self-financing.

Another spur to the work of the Groups should be applied. Governors of schools should reconsider choice of Examining Groups every four years, with a view to change if they were dissatisfied.

Not that the choice is a very real one, for all that the Secretary of State for Education says that he wishes to maintain competition among the independent Groups, and for all the multitude of syllabuses on offer. And the unreality of choice is not just because so many of them show tendencies similar to those which this paper demonstrates. There are other limits to effective competition, too. GCSE examinations remain the preserve of the Groups who used to administer O-levels and GCE; and it seems that the Secretary of State would not award any would-be entrant to the GCSE ranks with any greater mark of approval than 'equivalence' with the existing Groups. Then again, GCSE Examining Groups are not profit-making bodies. These restrictions should be lifted.

For one main objective of any reform to the examination system should be to give schools (and, through them, to give parents) a greater *real* choice of GCSE examinations. If restrictions were removed, a new board might establish itself as the nucleus of a new Group, offering examinations which were simpler and severer, at once in the content of their papers and in the intelligibility of their marking criteria. There might not be many schools who would immediately subject their pupils to GCSE courses and papers which had more rigorous standards; which did not, for example, insist upon coursework or offer the delights of differentiated assessment. But some schools there would be. They might even be prepared to pay more for the higher standards of this or that new Examining Group.

Finally, the case for asking parents to pay GCSE examinations fees should be considered—with suitable safeguards, of course. The principal benefit would lie in the incentive which this would give to parents to interest themselves in the nature of GCSE examinations, and to see that they obtained better value for their money. They could also, with even more justice than now, insist that they were provided with adequate information about the successes and failures of their children (and about the criteria by which they were assessed).

Director of Publications
10 February 1988

Introduction

The changes in the Education Reform Bill will give greater power to individual head teachers, boards of governors and parents, while at the same time reducing that of local education authorities. And this is certainly welcome. But if the Bill was in any way intended to circumscribe ideological indoctrination then the welcome should be muted. For one of the main channels of bias will still lie outside the control of individual head teachers and school governors; and the influence of parents or public opinion is indirect and fragmentary. I refer to the national examination system, which necessarily exerts a powerful formative effect on what is taught in schools, and how it is taught. The purpose of this paper is to examine some of the published GCSE syllabuses in Religious Studies (RS), Social Studies (SS) and History for 1988; to illustrate a bias which is contrary to the spirit of education, which should be sceptical and candid; and to urge that reform of state education must include measures to open the examination system to newcomers and to forces of competition, for the honour of schools, the satisfaction of parents, and the benefit of pupils.

There are four English Examining Groups—Midland Examining Group (MEG), Southern Examining Group (SEG), London and East Anglia Group (LEAG) and Northern Examining Association (NEA). There is also a Welsh Joint Education Committee and a Northern Ireland Schools Examinations Council, neither of which are studied here. Each Group publishes syllabuses for Mode 1 examinations, which set out the content of the subject and, in some cases, offer specimen examination questions with model answers, as well as suggestions for the two-year 'Assignment' or 'Course Work' which, together with the worked papers, will contribute to the final GCSE result. They also include notes on supervision, etc., for the guidance of teachers. In the case of Mode 2 and Mode 3 examinations, the syllabuses are devised by individual schools, though under the strict supervision of the Group for which the school may opt, which will insist that such syllabuses conform to the national criteria (see below).

Martin Luther or
Martin Luther King?

The GCSE Religious Studies syllabuses of all four English Groups provide many examples of how teachers foster ideas and attitudes associated with the Left (especially unilateralist ideas). Candidates are often required to comment on Liberation Theology, Passive Resistance, and the 'just' war—'just' picked out by quotation marks. Bruce Kent, Martin Luther King, Desmond Tutu and other dissident churchmen make frequent appearances and are recommended as exemplars worthy of study.

Still more significant is what these syllabuses leave out. Thus MEG, in a pamphlet entitled *Specimen Papers* has (p. 70):-

(ii)   Name one religious group which teaches pacifism
(iii) Name one statement by a Christian church on peace
(iv)   Name one Christian pacifist and one of his writings.

Where, one may ask, is the candidate given the chance to name eminent Christians who have argued against pacifism, or believed that war may be justified in defence of certain basic moral values? Other current issues of controversy are similarly treated. For instance, on p. 31:-

Name two well-known people in South Africa opposed to apartheid.

Pupils are not encouraged to imagine that there are Christians in South Africa who argue the moral case that apartheid is the lesser of two evils. But is it not part of a good education to study several sides of a question?

There is of course an excellent case to be made that subjects such as liberation theology and apartheid should not form any part of a school's syllabus, on the grounds that there is no respectable corpus of textbooks to study; no tradition of accepted discipline. It would surely be better to study Martin Luther than his twentieth-century namesake Martin Luther King. But MEG *Specimen Papers* (p. 31) include:-

Outline the work of Dr. Martin Luther King concerning Civil Rights.

This is one of a number of references to the Doctor, who would scarcely have gained the approbation of the father of the Reformation

(mentioned so far as I can find only once, and passingly, in any of
the RS syllabuses) who wrote that,

> For no matter how right you are, it is not for a Christian to appeal to
> law, or to fight, but rather to suffer wrong and endure evil; there is no
> other way. . . .[1]

An experienced teacher of RS, who is also the Principal of three
Christian schools, has commented as follows on the GCSE RS syllabuses:

> I run three Independent Christian Schools and have come to the conclu-
> sion that the GCSE Religious Studies syllabus is incompatible with the
> aims of a Christian School. The same is true of the Scottish "O" Grade
> in Religious Studies. Christianity is seen as but one of several world
> religions, each of equal validity. Religion is seen as a human phenome-
> non and if pupils are made aware of the rites and customs of a few
> religions, it will promote good race relation through tolerance, today's
> virtue.
>   The pupils are encouraged to evaluate the minute amount of Biblical
> material prescribed, sixteen chapters of St. Mark's gospel in one Board.
> But the Gospels were not written for the critical appraisal of 16-year-
> olds, but to show them the way, the truth and the life.[2]

In the light of this comment, it is interesting to read the following
from the *Annual Report 1982–83* of the Joint Matriculation Board of
the Universities of Manchester, Liverpool, Sheffield and Birmingham
(JMB):-

> The Subject Committee for Religious Studies has been concerned for
> some time that it is possible for a candidate to gain Grade C in Religious
> Studies (Ordinary) Syllabus A, Christian Responsibility, by following a
> course of study which might more properly be described as Social
> Studies (p. 15).

So it seems that the problem of secular entryism into RS afflicted
GCE as it now afflicts GCSE.

Religious Studies have a place among the Additional Subjects of
The National Curriculum which may be studied for GCSE. This being
so, it is desirable to restore to the subject a more traditional approach.
It seems unlikely that this can be accomplished within the present
GCSE, and this is one of the reasons why an alternative examination

should be created, for adoption either by the existing examining boards or by one of the new boards recommended in the foreword.

Primer for social engineering

The GCSE Social Studies or SS syllabuses provide abundant examples of disguised political propaganda. My first example is taken from the SEG SS syllabus. This has an introductory section (p. 6–13) headed *Subject Content,* intended to define the broad parameters of the two-year course leading up to final GCSE. One first finds *Social Issues* (a) Poverty. The syllabus then goes on, under *Associated Contents* to define poverty under two divisions, absolute and relative. Yet can the examiners not know that many would object to the very concept of 'relative' poverty on the ground that measurement cannot be agreed upon? The concept demands that we regard as impoverished the least advantaged groups in any society regardless of the basic standard of living in that society. Unless we accept egalitarianism as the *summum bonum,* this is an absurdity,—well demonstrated by the leading article in *The Times* of 23 December 1986, 'The Poor at Christmas',

> The term invented to confuse poverty with inequality is, of course, relative poverty. The essentially bogus character of this concept can be seen in this hypothetical example: if a slump were to cut the median income by half but the earnings of the bottom-fifth by only a quarter, the low-paid might be starving but they would be relatively better off.

The SEG examiners can hardly be unaware of such basic criticisms. If, therefore, they wish to introduce this dubious notion, they should at least not assume it as axiomatic but rather pose it as an open question—"Discuss the validity of the concept 'relative poverty' ". This they do not do. Indeed, they go on to ask the question.
Can poverty be reduced?
for which the model answer is given as,

> Social, political and economic initiatives, e.g. the development of the Welfare State; positive discrimination; pressure groups.

But this assumes the self-evident desirability of a state-centralist response to the alleged problem. Neither here nor elsewhere in the syllabus is the candidate invited to discuss the contrary view that minimal or even negative government, reliance on market forces and cooperative voluntarism might offer a better remedy for what is termed poverty than the Welfare State. It is as if Hayek had never lived. The assumption that welfarism and social engineering are the correct responses to social problems is so enmeshed in these sylla-buses that, almost, it may be unreasonable to criticise the examiners on this ground, just as it might be to criticise an examining board of theologians for taking for granted the existence of God.

The presumption of 'relative' poverty raises its head in the follow-ing question (page 28, no 3), this time taken not from SEG but from LEAG GCSE SS syllabus. It starts by rehearsing this passage from the London Weekend television programme, *Breadline Britain*:-

A major survey of poverty when applied to the population of Britain as a whole showed that:

Approximately 3 million people in Britain today cannot afford to heat the living rooms of their homes.

Nearly 3 million people don't have consumable durables such as a carpet, a washing machine or a fridge because of lack of money.

At least 5 million people regularly go without some essential food item, such as a roast joint, once a week.

And so on.

Then follow questions, among which are:

(a) What is meant by the term 'relative poverty'?—certainly better than the previous arbitrary imposition of the term. Then:

(c) What reasons can be suggested for the persistence of poverty in Britain?

The first objection is that a piece of television journalism is used uncritically as an authoritative source. In this instance the media is taken as sound because it supports the egalitarian concept of 'relative poverty'. Yet, on other occasions, the SS examiners frame questions to elicit answers casting doubt on its veracity. It is of course true that the television programme, if it is accurate, does describe considerable hardship (though it gives no indication whether this is short term or long term—most important in evaluating the significance of such statistics). All the same, to imply that a roast joint is an essential food item, to go without which constitutes poverty; or that to be without a carpet or a fridge is poverty, is far fetched except on the assumption that the norm is universal equality. Moreover, (c) is clearly *parti pris*.

It requires acceptance of the statement poverty exists in Britain. But there are those who argue that poverty means less than bare subsistence and that, except in a statistically insignificant number of cases, this is nowhere to be found in present-day Britain. The question would be respectable only if it were framed in some such way as: 'Discuss the view that poverty exists in Britain.' These examiners clearly require the candidate to accept the premiss without further ado.

Many other examples of this attitude to inequality—always seen as a problem, never as a fact of human existence which has social advantages as well as disadvantages—will be found in the MEG SS syllabus. Under the head *Social Inequality* there appears the question,
What causes inequality?
to which the required response is *Economic scarcity; scarcity of talent; power and authority; private property and inheritance; sexual and social divisions of labour.* A second question is:-
What are the major causes of poverty in Britain today? to which the required response is *Age; family size; unemployment; low pay; single parenthood; sickness and disability; the poverty trap.* Trust in the workings of the state is implicit in all this although, apart from the use of the term poverty, not all of it is contentious.

More disturbing is what is left out. Excepting the reference to scarcity of talent no acknowledgement is made of possible differences in human intelligence. Nor is there any recognition of individual lack of motivation, which some may consider to be the outcome of the welfarism that the examiners so favour. And is private property and inheritance amongst the causes of inequality? There is a familiar argument that the ebb and flow of private property sustained by inheritance promotes the social and economic mobility that is the most effective agent of true equality. But there is no hint in this syllabus that such ideas deserve questions and answers.

All the SS syllabuses address the problems of crime and deviance. Once again, their approach suggests that they have taken sides on the way people behave before they have properly considered all the data. Take the SEG syllabus (p. 13 ff.). The initial key question runs,
What are the causes of crime?
to which the required answer is *Cause of crime: social, economic, political, psychological,*—a set of guidelines that omits any reference to moral considerations. The following specimen examination question points clearly to where these guidelines lead in practice,

Read the following interview between Bill, a skinhead gang leader, and his social worker, and then answer the questions which follow:

> Q. "When did you become leader of the gang?"
> A. "Nine months ago."
> Q. "How did you become leader?"
> A. "I beat up Harry (the previous leader). Now the rest of the gang do what I tell them."
> Q. "So, if your friends don't do as they're told, you beat them up?"
> A. "No! We decide together what to do. It's only when someone gets heavy (aggressive) that I have to sort him out—or he leaves the gang. I like to be fair though. I'm not a bully. Some leave the gang because they chicken out."
> Q. "What sort of things do the gang do?"
> A. "Well, we go fighting, nicking and smashing things. The best thing is being chased by the police."

This is followed by two questions, based on the above interview:

(i) Many people would consider that the activities of the gang challenge 'Authority'. Why do you think this is so?

and

(ii) Does Bill have power, or authority, or both, over the gang? Give reasons for your answer.

What are we to make of those questions about authority? Are teenagers likely to regard Bill as an awful warning, or more likely as a hero? The same equivocation seems to lie behind this next question (SEG, page 18):-

(Headline): "Teenage Truants Arrested with Women Rioters at Greenham Common." Why might the behaviour of both the teenagers and the women be considered deviant?

The model answer to this requires that *a good answer should have clearly defined deviance and recognise* [sic] *the social construction (through the media) of deviance and conformity. . . .*

This implies that the roots of deviance and conformity are no more than those suggested to us by the media—a proposition which ignores tradition, moral teaching, parental example and a host of other factors. What the examiners appear to be angling for is the response that both truancy and riot are to be judged relatively, not absolutely; and that both may be justified by reference to the cause for which they are undertaken, in this case that of the women of Greenham Common.

The cultivation of orthodox left-wing attitudes is pursued in these syllabuses in order to draw out the favoured answer, with conviction and tenacity. Model question 7, from SEG (p. 19) is a case in point, trivial in itself but nonetheless instructive. Candidates are told to: Study the photograph of an assembly in a girls' school.

The reproduction is poor, in smudged black and white. The girls, dressed in dowdy gym slips and blouses, sit stiffly upright, hands folded demurely in laps, scarcely a smile among them. Elderly teachers, drab and forbidding, sit at the ends of rows while one stands at the main door, as if to guard against escape. The hall is bare of furnishings save one ancient iron wall radiator and what may be heavy dark curtains over the door. The scene could not be more lugubrious. Candidates are asked to respond to such questions as Explain TWO things which you think this photograph tells us about attitudes to discipline in this school. The model answer calls for comments on *School uniform. Way in which girls appear to be sitting; girls trained to keep hands in lap . . .* etc., and states that,

In fact, it is a photograph for a private school's prospectus.

Clearly, any candidate who arrives at this conclusion should be given credit. The hostility of the examiners to formal school discipline, school uniforms, and private education is patent; and they hope that the candidates will reproduce it. They must have taken some pains to find such an unprepossessing photograph, perhaps from a long-forgotten Edwardian album.

Another way used by the GCSE SS examiners to elicit answers which conform to their ideas is to string together a chain of questions or prompts leading to foregone conclusions. The model answer or marking scheme, as the case may be, instructs teachers how the prompts should be expanded. The following is an example taken from LEAG (p. 23), Question 17: Describe the functions of a jobber on the Stock Exchange. Question 18 is: What are the reasons for nationalisation? As if this sequence of suggestions was inadequate, the marking scheme (p. 34) sets out among the required responses to Question 17 *Deals on the floor of the Stock Exchange with brokers not the public,* and to Question 18 *Political—nation should share profits.* Thus are pupils steered into attitudes and beliefs which are a far cry indeed from anything approaching an enterprise culture.

Similar methods are employed in the following question from SEG (p. 18):

Describe how consumer wants are satisfied within
(i)   a capitalist society
(ii) a communist society

which, in itself, is unexceptionable. But then it is followed by:

Why do some people in the UK have greater income than others? How could a more equal distribution of income and wealth be achieved?

The marking guidelines require the candidate to

differentiate between income and wealth . . . and inherited wealth/ unearned income . . . and to explain the various mechanisms through which redistribution can be achieved (eg capital transfer tax).

The use of unearned income, where the Revenue term has for long been 'investment income' is another straw in the wind.

The protest culture, too, receives more favour than the enterprise culture. Thus in LEAG (p. 24): Describe the methods by which individuals can protest against Central and Local Government policy. How effective do you consider each method to be? And (p. 22) Explain the term 'picket' (p. 29): What is meant by 'a strike'? What is meant by 'working to rule'? And so on. MEG SS syllabus recommends the following partisan studies as suitable for the two-year assignment,

A case study of local political campaign or incident, e.g., an attempt to prevent a school or hospital being closed. A case study of the reporting by a sample of several national newspapers of a particularly controversial incident, e.g. a strike, the activities of the women at Greenham Common.
An analysis of sexism in advertisements in particular magazines over a defined period.

There will be those who defend such questions and projects on the ground that they do no more than prepare young people to take an active part in the workings of a democracy. Such a justification ignores the recurrent negativism in these syllabuses. For instance, instead of dwelling constantly on protest, why not questions such as "In what ways can the individual serve the community in a democratic society?"; "Discuss measures taken in your area to create jobs and assess their results"; "Discuss the role of youth movements and Service cadet corps in reducing juvenile delinquency". In fact, such positive approaches to society and its problems seem few and far between in these syllabuses.

Despite pressure to include them, Social Studies do not have a place in *The National Curriculum.* So far, so good. But the subject may still be offered for GCSE. Parents and school governors should therefore be aware of its nature and ready to question its inclusion in the school curriculum.

The friendly Red Army

The four English Examining Groups each provide a number of History syllabuses. I draw attention to just one or two examples of conspicuous bias, some of them in papers which are, in effect, mandatory. There are many others.

Anti-Americanism and approval of Communist China

NEA syllabus A, p. 18, includes the following instruction to candidates,

4. Use source material by brief quotation . . . to support reconstructions (e.g. 'The attitude of some Americans to the massacre of Indians was "nits breed lice" ').

One might, not unreasonably, class this as an incitement to anti-Americanism.
NEA B, p.6:-

A3 Communist China (b) The Triumph of Communism . . . (iii) The Communist state established Rule of the Party; Economic and Social Policy—Co-operatives, collectives, industrial expansion, *conversion of the people* (my emphasis).

Contrast this with B, The USA in the 1920s and 1930s:-

(b) The 1920s, (i) The prosperous side of America—Mass production—Henry Ford—Hire Purchase—Social effects: (ii) The darker side of America—Klu Klux Klan, Organised Crime, Prohibition.

But did not Communist China have a darker side too?

A similar exercise in partisanship will be found in LEAG Syllabus A, p. 2, Section A. Asia:

Source B (taken from the Rules of the Red Army), 1. Speak politely; 2. Pay for what you buy; 3. Return anything you borrow; 4. Pay for anything you damage; 5. Don't hit or swear at people; 6. Don't damage crops; 7. Don't take liberties with women; 8. Don't ill-treat captives; (b) (ii) How important was the following of these rules in the winning by the Red Army of the support of many Chinese people?

This may be contrasted with p. 7 of the same syllabus, Section North America. The centre of this question sheet, approximately one third of its total area, is taken up by a photograph of a Klu Klux Klan initiation ceremony. Candidates are asked to identify the organisation and to . . . show how its attitudes and actions were dangerous.

It may be doubted whether the Klu Klux Klan deserves so much emphasis.

Still in the land of our principal ally, SEG Syllabus 2, pp. 48–49 has:-

Internal Issues in the USA, 1945–1976: (a) How great was the discrimination faced by blacks in the United States in the years immediately following the Second World War. (b) Describe the tactics of and the success achieved by the Civil Rights movement in the years up to 1970. (c) Why have these successes been achieved?

These are the sole topics relating to internal issues in the USA over the period 1945 to 1976, as far as I can discover.

On the very next page of the SEG syllabus we come face to face with smiling Chinese grouped around a Dazibao, 'big-character' poster. Candidates are asked to

(a) Write a wall poster (in English) in which, in 1966, you support the ideas of the Cultural Revolution . . .

It is true that a second question requires them to write one, in 1968, suggesting reasons for discontinuing the Cultural Revolution. But are there no aspects of China, 1925–1968, worthier of attention?

Anti-White South African sentiment

That South Africa should be a favourite target of the examiners is to be expected. SEG Syllabus 2, World Powers since 1917, p. 37, displays a notice in the original Afrikaans and in English translation, which specifies two separate picnic sites for whites and blacks. This is the subject of several questions obviously designed to elicit answers hostile to apartheid. It may be thought that the inclusion of such an issue as a designated picnic site in a paper with the scope of World Powers since 1917 reveals a curious set of priorities, as well as a failure to understand that the doctrine and practices of apartheid are best discussed in a less superficial manner (all the more so because of the intense passions which it arouses, and sufferings it causes).

LEAG Syllabus A, p. 4 Section B: Africa South of the Sahara devotes three out of its ten questions to apartheid. Of the rest, one concerns the expulsion of Asians from East Africa, one is a multiple choice question requiring the identification of Lumumba, one is on Rhodesian UDI and one requires the candidate to identify an African state in which there is a Cuban presence. Given the vast range of possible topics—the economic and cultural consequences of the decline of the trans-Saharan trade, the development of rail and air links, the discovery of oil, pan-Africanism and pan-Islamism, etc.—most of these questions, weighted towards issues of racialism, are partial to say the least.

The 'shop-steward' syllabus

This is a course of study, which I have styled the 'shop-steward' syllabus, that may start as early as the Chartist Movement, and is pursued down to c. 1980, tracing the history of trade unionism and, almost exclusively, the Labour Party. It appears in the syllabuses of all the four English Groups, often under what seem unsuitable headings. The method of presentation is often openly emotive, as for instance in LEAG C, Paper 1, p. 12, which shows a cartoon figuring Aneurin Bevan as a Dickensian matron dishing out spoonfuls of physic from a bowl labelled 'National Health Service' to a queue of unwilling doctors. The question based on this source reads,

> Write a sentence to explain one reason why doctors disliked the service named on the medicine bowl when it was first introduced

which rather oversimplifies the welcome given to the NHS by the medical profession. Could *one* reason even begin to be adequate for any such complex issue? If the deviser of the syllabus does wish to use this cartoon (which cannot properly be described as source material) he should ask the candidate, "Do you think this cartoon properly represents the way in which the medical profession reacted to the introduction of the NHS?" That is, he should if he wishes to be objective.

The same syllabus, Paper 2, p. 10, Source A shows that emotive pictorial relic of the General Strike, the photograph of a lorry with the bonnet festooned with barbed wire and guarded by an armed soldier—together with Source B, an extract from the May 1926 *British Gazette,* the official Government news sheet of the day. However one may interpret them, these sources are scant evidence on which to base any judgement about the General Strike.

The mandatory parts of this history syllabus are arranged in such a way that candidates will find it difficult to avoid addressing trade-union issues at some point in their studies. For example, SEG 1 requires candidates to answer two questions relating to the following topics:

> 1. The Old Poor Law, 1750–1836; 2. The Corn Laws and its Repeal 1815–1850; 3. Chartism, 1832–1860; 4. Trade Unions 1866–1914; 5. The Welfare State, 1942–1985; 6. Britain and Europe, 1945–1985

of which only number 6 can be said to lie outside trade-union parameters, while SEG 4 lists the following choice of themes for Paper 1:

> 1. Parliament and Political Parties; 2. * Working-class Organisations; 3. Women in Society; 4. Britain's Changing Position in the International Economy; 5. Education in England; 6. * Laissez-faire to the Welfare State; 7. Ireland; 8. The British Empire and the Commonwealth.

But those marked with the asterisk are Nominated Themes, that is, the candidate must study them. Therefore, whether candidates take

Syllabus 1 or Syllabus 4, like Aneurin Bevan's spoonful of physic they are going to have to swallow the 'shop-steward' syllabus, like it or not, one way or the other.

Nobody should object to the history of trade unionism as one of many options in the appropriate history syllabus. But when it occurs time and again in so many syllabuses, often with what amounts to mandatory status, then it becomes a choice in rotten apples.

I have not discussed MEG History syllabuses. This is because, unexpectedly given the bias in this Group's RS and SS syllabuses, at least three of their history syllabuses seem balanced and objective— The Modern World, 1914 to the Present Day; British Social and Economic History; and British and European History. MEG does contain the 'shop- steward' syllabus but it is fairly presented under British Social and Economic History, and has a sub-head Development of the Conservative, Liberal and Labour Parties.

But the significance of these MEG syllabuses does not lie only in their relative intellectual openness. Both they and the less reputable NEA, SEG and LEAG ones were validated by the Secondary Examinations Council. The GCSE 'general criteria' warn against the introduction of political bias into examination materials. So a validating authority capable of passing the latter in the same breath as the former must expect to have its effectiveness questioned. (This point bears on the Secretary of State's intentions as set out on p. 19, (ii) of *The National Curriculum.*).

RS, SS and History are not the only GCSE syllabuses that display ideological bias.[3] This is because the concept upon which the examination is based is flawed at its source as I hope now to explain.

Genesis of bias in GCSE

Professor H B Rogers describes GCSE as "less revolutionary than evolutionary."[4] It is certainly true that GCSE *evolved* out of a constellation of ideas associated with the 1960s—the potential for reform of social engineering, behaviourism, relativism, structuralism, feminism, poststructuralism, etc., as well as the hallowing of political and social protest. Many of these ideas, of course, have much earlier origins. But during the sixties and early seventies they flowered in institutions of higher learning, influencing the development of educational philosophy in teacher training colleges. Indeed, where I read 'bias' others may prefer to read 'the consensus of the Sixties'. Be that as it may, the wholesale adoption of progressive theory and practice by educationalists is largely responsible for the present state of the national examination system. Before embarking on a brief history of GCSE, it may be useful to look at a few salient ideas of this period, to see how they link up with the dogmatics of the new establishment.

For an introduction to the educational ethos of the period the titles in a Penguin Education Specials book list published in 1973 are instructive: Ivan Illich, *Deschooling Society*, Everett Reimer, *School is Dead*, Paulo Freire, *Cultural Action for Freedom* and *Pedagogy of the Oppressed*, Paul Goodman, *Compulsory Miseducation*, Charles Wein-gartner and Neil Postman, *Teaching as a Subversive Activity*, Trevor Pateman, editor, *Counter Course* and so on. The publisher's blurbs sum up the attitudes which inform the works, thus "Schools are for most people . . . 'institutional props for privilege' "; "subjecting young people to institutionalized learning stunts and distorts their natural intellectual development . . ."; "we must offer our children an education which relates truthfully to their individual social environment . . ." and,

> [The authors'] aim is 'to help all students develop built-in, shock-proof crap detectors as basic equipment in their survival kits.'

Enough said.[5]

Among the more influential of the theorists of the period were Paulo Freire and Ivan Illich. The former was a Brazilian who special-ized in adult literacy and,

> He discovered that any adult can begin to read in a matter of forty hours if the first words he deciphers are charged with political meaning.[6]

This text in hand, the new establishment found it easy to justify the politicization of education which is such a feature of the GCSE syllabuses. Here, too, is enshrined the theory, dear to the GCSE, that teaching and examining should be 'issue based'.

Ivan Illich may not have been received quite so uncritically by the new educational establishment if only because, to all intents and purpose an anarchist, he was as opposed to state centralism as he was to formal education. None the less, his views on education, especially on examining, are reflected in the consensus which is so clearly articulated in GCSE. For example,

Neither learning nor justice is promoted by schooling because educators insist on packaging instruction with certification,[7]

and

Certification constitutes a form of market manipulation and is plausible only to a schooled mind,[8]

a view which adumbrates SEC's 'natural justice' and which has contributed to formulating the apologetic of 'Differentiated Assessment' (see below), the underlying purpose of which is to reduce certification to a subjective exercise based on social, not academic criteria. Illich's opinion that,

School pretends to break learning up into subject 'matters', to build into the pupil a curriculum made of these prefabricated blocks, and to gauge the result on an international scale,[9]

is typical of the thinking that led to the emergence of the controversial Integrated Humanities, the effect of which is to break down the traditional disciplinary boundaries. Finally,

A good education system should . . . furnish all who want to present an issue to the public with the opportunity to make their challenge known.[10]

The authentic voice of Social Studies protest!

The emphasis on 'skills' in history teaching, to which Deuchar and many others have drawn attention, is foreshadowed in *THES* where, in 1976, 'techniques of analysis rather than fact' were advocated, an attitude that can very easily be turned into an instrument for indoctrination.[11]

Not, of course, that all teachers subscribe to all these views. The further you get from the centre—that is, from the Information and the Research Officers whose job it properly is to promote GCSE—the more doubts you encounter among the rank and file. But the 'sixties consensus still prevails, and must be challenged.

From Norwood to Cockcroft

The notion of a 'subject' examination, that is one in which candidates can accumulate discrete passes, subject by subject, as opposed to a 'group' examination, where the award of the certificate depends on satisfying the examiners in a mandatory group or core of subjects—English, Maths, Physics-and-Chemistry and one foreign language, for example—has gained ground amongst the 'new establishment' since the publication of the Norwood Commission's Report in 1943, although as GMD Howat observed in his paper *Oxford and Cambridge Schools Examination Board, 1873–1973* drily observes,

> many of the changes which took place in the 1960s and 1970s were not ones which Norwood himself would have envisaged or welcomed (Howat, p. 12).

Prior to the watershed of Norwood, the tone of the schools examination system in Britain is well summed up by Howat, quoting Abbott, that,

> an examination system contained within the structure of the ancient universities was preferable to one imposed by government (Howat, p. 2).

But the strength of radical pressure for a more centralised, subject-based GCE is shown by the comment that,

> On these matters the Oxford and Cambridge Board was consulted far less than it had been before the introduction of the Higher and School Certificate (Howat, p. 12),

and, yet more suggestive of rough-shod haste,

> Indeed, one may judge that much was assumed rather than said by both the Ministry of Education and the various examining Boards in implementing the change from the old Certificate examination to the new General Certificate of Education (Howat, p. 13).

These initiatives led to the replacement in 1951 of the group-based School Certificate by a subject-based O-level GCE, and the Higher School Certificate by A-level GCE. This was closely accompanied by the CSE, designed as a less academic qualification for those thought unable to manage O-levels. Thus the concept of a sound general grounding in literacy and numeracy, humanities and science, was cast aside; and something near to a free-for-all was adopted in its stead. Ironically, the national core curriculum is now to be introduced to make good the deficiencies.

The first major pointer toward GCE's successor GCSE was the Waddell Report of 1978. This set out the broad framework of a common national system—one to get rid of the separation between GCE and CSE—and recommended the regrouping of the then examining Boards into regional Groups. The leviathan of differentiated assessment was about to break the surface.

Waddell was followed in 1982 by a statement of intent from DES and the Welsh Office.[12] The JMB *Annual Report—1983-84* describes the subsequent

> mounting pressures on the Secretary of State to retain the present O-level and CSE systems . . . in a national press which does not normally show great interest in the more fundamental aspects of public examinations (p. 10).

But JMB need not have fretted. There was even more pressure on the Secretary of State from powerful factions in the educational establishment for him to do nothing of the sort. The ardour of the 'new establishment' triumphed, as is illustrated in the following quotations from JMB, which emerges as probably the most radical of all the Boards involved in the making of GCSE.

> For many years frustration built up in the educational world over the inability of successive governments to reach decisions on the reform of public examinations (JMB, 83–84, p. 2)

and

> . . . and that this modest development [an announcement by Sir Keith Joseph in August, 1983 of his intention to announce a decision in 1984] could be regarded as a welcome blaze of light at the end of a very long and tortuous tunnel is an indication of the protracted history of a proposal which was put forward by the Schools Council in 1970 (JMB 82–83, p. 7).

Such claims to unanimity ignore the weight of opinion to which I refer above, which had questioned the wisdom of these developments ever since Norwood.

The final milestone on the way to GCSE is the *Annual Report of the Secondary Examinations Council* (SEC) for 1983–84. Much of this document consists of a correspondence between Sir Wilfred Cockcroft, Chairman and Chief Executive of SEC, the controlling body of the national examination system, and Sir Keith Joseph, the then Secretary of State for Education.

In their essay on Mathematics in North *et al.*, Coldman and Shepherd, referring to the Cockcroft Report, *Mathematics Counts*, remark on Cockcroft's habit of

> stating that something is the case but offering no supporting evidence or argument, merely handing down judgement from on high.[13]

Here is an example of his *ex cathedra* pronouncements,

> Only when techniques of assessment are developed and applied which allow candidates to demonstrate their skills and abilities, their knowledge and competence, in sufficient depth and with sufficient consistency, can statements about their absolute standards be made reliably (SEC 83–84, p. 72),

which begs quite a few questions in the long-standing argument about the validity of both the theory and practice of differentiated assessment.

But in the end the Secretary of State appears to accept the arguments of the Chief Executive—'assertions' though at one point he styles them[14]—and in a crucial letter of 20 June 1984 sets off the process of establishing the GCSE.[15] On the same date, 20 June 1984, Sir Keith Joseph announced in the House of Commons his intention to introduce a single system of examining at 16+, based on national criteria and to be assessed by grade-related criteria (alias differentiated assessment), as soon as practicable.

A wish to intervene . . .

The overweening claim to authority of SEC is well put in the following quotation from its 1983–84 Annual Report,

> Third, I consider it to be the task of the SEC . . . to monitor all examination courses offered to the 14–16 age group (p. 92).

It will be seen that this is a claim not just to administer and set examinations but to monitor all courses—that is to say, SEC believes its writ to run in every classroom in the land. The absoluteness of the SEC's claim to control over the whole of the state system (and indeed of the private sector as well, which assists in the function of providing compulsory education) is further spelt out in SEC 83–84.

> Council was especially mindful of the independent status of the organisations seeking to innovate within the field of pre-vocational education, but nevertheless felt that it must declare an interest, since all members consider that the national criteria are relevant to all concerned with children during their years of compulsory education (p. 77).

SEC and its successor bodies are, of course, responsible for these national criteria and, as even JMB commented in its *Annual Report* for 1982–1983,

> What is emerging from these developments is a general recognition that, if the new single system of examining is eventually brought into effect, it will be subject to a much greater degree of central coordination that any previous public examination. . . . [The Secretary of State's] comments [presumably the statement of intent of August '83] were interpreted as an indication of a wish to intervene in the content of individual subjects and the way in which they are taught . . . (p. 8).

So much for the spirit of an earlier age when "every effort was being made to ensure that university intervention would not be government intervention writ-large",[16] when ". . . Delegates . . . considered themselves bound to consult the wishes and requirements of the existing schools, and to interfere with them as little as possible"[17] and when "latitude in syllabus requirements were all to [the Oxford and Cambridge Board's] credit."[18]

Such central control, which imposes both general and 'subject-specific' criteria, bears on the question of choice. As far as Mode 1 syllabuses are concerned, the right of schools to choose whichever Group they please, of which the literature constantly boasts, is, once again, like offering a man a choice in rotten apples. Mode 2 and Mode 3 syllabuses are alike subject to the criteria. The choice is an empty boast.

Representation—or domination?

How should teachers be represented on Examining Boards? This is a running battle. The Oxford and Cambridge Schools Examination

Board had established a policy as early as 1917 "to bring teachers into touch with examining bodies. . . .",[19] while the Oxford Delegates declared themselves anxious to "give full weight to the views of teachers"[20] and had long-established links with the Secondary Heads Committee, the Assistant Masters and Mistresses Association, the NUT and NAS/UWT.

The Norwood Report of 1943 "involved teachers to a greater extent than hitherto"[21] and controversy about growing teacher involvement is hinted at in the measured comment of the Board that, "The views of the Norwood Committee upon the part which teachers might play in examinations were adopted more cautiously."[22] A comment by Delegacy was rather sharper that

> At such meetings [of the Standing Joint Committee's Subject Committees or Subject Panels] teachers are in the majority. This most valuable link . . . refutes the ill-informed criticism . . . that the conduct of the General Certificate of Education is in the hands of universities and remote from the teachers in schools (*Structure*, p. 3).

The issue of representation had not been fully resolved by 1978. Waddell observes that the forthcoming Examining Groups—that is the present GCSE structure—should have "representation of the appropriate interests without any of these having a majority voice".[23] But Waddell was overtaken. For the *Constitution of the Northern Examining Association*, published in 1987, sums up developments since the Secretary of State's speech in the House of 20 June, 1984 and proclaims that its Subject Committees are 'teacher dominated'[24] and that,

> The separate Boards will also maintain their own subject panels, thus increasing the breadth of teacher influence . . (*Constitution*, p. 6).

It comments elsewhere on its Examination Committee, which "has the primary task of *managing every aspect of the administration of GCSE* (my italics)"[25] that, "At least half of its members (but in practice a much higher proportion) must be teachers."[26] This is a far cry from the careful balance of interests without a majority voice, envisaged by Waddell as late as 1978.

In fact, perusal of the representation on the various committees of the four English Groups and their constituent Boards confirms that not only are teachers in a substantial majority throughout; they are also nominated not by the Groups and Boards, but by NUT, NAS/

UWT and the smaller teaching unions. It is true that subject associations also nominate teachers to these committees but, since at least a proportion of such nominees will also be members of the teaching unions, this does not do much to dilute union influence.

True, business and industry are represented on SEC, and on Groups and Boards. So how does it come about that Social Studies, for instance, displays such a degree of anti-business sentiment? Is it that businessmen prefer to concentrate on broad administrative issues? They may seldom be aware of the content of individual syllabuses. And perhaps too few business organisations nominate representatives with sufficient interest in educational matters.

Also, although business and industry are represented on councils, finance committees, etc., they are thinly represented, if at all, on the subject committees and those dealing with assessment procedures. For instance, the SEC's Grade Criteria Working Parties, responsible for developing the procedures upon which the validity of examination results depends, appear to consist entirely of teachers, lecturers and members of HMI.[27] The latter are not noted for their backwardness in favouring the 'sixties orthodoxy.

Of course there is a strong case for having teachers on these committees. But ought they to 'dominate' (the NEA's word) them? And ought teaching unions, which have avowed political and collectivist objectives, to play such a dominant part in nominating members? Unions' credentials in assessing the ideals of education are slight. Nor are they even major customers for the products of the examination system (though they perhaps should be).

Some change in the balance of power therefore seems worth considering. A greater number of places on all subject committees and the like, should be reserved for non-teaching graduates and postgraduates, drawn from business, the professions and industry, able to meet the teachers on their own ground but probably with different perspectives from those of union members.

The maze of differentiation

'Grade-related criteria', 'pupil profiles', 'differentiated papers', 'differentiation within papers', 'criteria referencing' 'general criteria and subject-specific criteria', 'performance matrices', 'subject domains', 'task-oriented examinations'—the SEC has developed a tangle of terminology in order, it seems, to obscure the ineluctable fact that in any field of learning some succeed and some fail.

Differentiated assessment, of which all these procedures form a part, is defined as follows:

> a differentiated examination is one in which different components are deliberately set at different levels of difficulty to meet the needs of candidates at different levels of ability (SEC 83–84, p. 17).

Graded testing and the practice of using cumulative courses to build up knowledge and skills and testing them periodically is a familiar and uncontroversial technique.[28] Differentiated assessment differs from this in that it can be applied in one single examination, and even within a single paper.

But what is more disturbing is the dichotomy that differentiated assessment seeks to establish between knowledge, often dismissed as 'factual recall', as if it were inconsequential, and the more highly valued 'skills' which are never clearly defined, though they seem to be valued even in the absence of knowledge or understanding. The dilemma this creates is encapsulated in the following from SEC, 85–86,

> . . . mark schemes have not always been constructed so as to facilitate and recognise positive achievement in the full range of objectives. There has been a tendency to overweight recall at the expense of other objectives and therefore to couch mark schemes in terms of 'product' (the facts that will appear in an answer) rather than in terms of 'process' (the skills being demonstrated) (p. 9).

If this is strictly applied in the case of history, it seems that a candidate who produces a clear, three-paragraph essay on the Battle of Hastings, outlining the preceding events, giving the correct date, correctly naming the dramatis personae, describing the terrain and its influence on the battle and summarising what its outcome signified for English history, would receive lukewarm credit for unessential 'factual recall' or 'product'. How he then fares on 'process' will depend on whether or not the examiner considers him to have measured up to one or more of such discrete assessment objectives as 'concepts of cause and consequence', 'the ability to look at events and issues from the perspective of people in the past' etc, etc. (NEA *Assessment Objectives*). How will examiners choose between such discontinuous objectives? There is no telling. It is a cockshy, not an examination.

A second candidate will produce an essay of a sort, describing how King Harold defeated the Vikings at the Battle of Culloden in 1215. Given the lack of approbation of 'the facts that will appear in an answer'—that is, product—which SEC displays, it may well be that this latter candidate, by making a stab at 'concepts of cause and consequence' and the rest of it, would fare better than the former. The inadequacies of factual recall would not weigh heavily in the balance.

A travesty? Yet I see nothing within the practice of differentiated assessment that would prevent it happening. The swirl of confusion that surrounds this issue is exemplified in the following murky pronouncement from SEC 83–84,

> It will likewise be important to ensure that techniques of assessment continue to recognise quality and overall performance (including relative performance) as well as testing for required levels of competence in the 'domains' of a subject (p. 88).

Does this mean that a candidate will receive credit, say, for the 'domain' of comprehensibility even though what he writes in the 'domain' of knowledge is rubbish? Or does it mean nothing at all?

What these examiners are ignoring is the fact that history is a seamless cloak. It cannot be chopped up into distinct, separately assessable entities. The ability, for example, to 'look at events and issues from the perspective of people in the past' is valueless if the facts are wrong. Behind the facade of 'differentiated assessment' lie as many or more subjective judgements of the pupil's performance as there ever were in the traditional method of marking. But the teachers and their pupils are more confused. That is the difference.

Next consider the implications of the statement that "our present examinations tell us more about what pupils cannot do than about what they can" and which advocates,

> a system which will award grades to less able candidates on the strength of good performance in tasks which they can actually do rather than bad performance in tasks to which they are not suited, (SEC 83–84, p. 83)

in support of which is adduced the following remark attributed to Sir Winston Churchill,

The questions which [the examiners] asked were almost invariably those
to which I was unable to suggest a satisfactory answer. I should have
liked to be asked to say what I knew . . . (SEC 83–84, p. 81).

Despite the source, it cannot be unreasonable to insist that a candidate should be able to give a relevant and appropriate answer to any
question within the range of the syllabus he has studied. If asked in
the Zoology paper to describe the avian alimentary tract and its main
features, should Winston Churchill expect the pass mark for an
account of blue tits feeding off a coconut?

The suspicion must be that all these elaborate stratagems to avoid
ever failing candidates stem from social attitudes, not from academic
rigour. Indeed, this is made clear in SEC 86–87 where it is stated that
the educational case for maximising positive achievement must be
reconciled with 'natural justice'.[29] Which means what? The answer is
in SEC Working Paper 5, *Making Ourselves Clearer: Readability in GCSE*.
Referring to the language used in examination questions, the author
writes,

The use of this kind of language in assessment tasks discriminates
against those students with poor general knowledge and/or a home
environment which does not expose them to networks of knowledge
which underpin the various meanings (p. 12).

The author goes on to give the following example from the Chemistry paper,

Which of the following requires a non-aqueous solvent to dissolve it? A
Salt, B Sugar, C Sodium nitrate, D Sulphur (p. 11),

arguing that 'non-aqueous solvent' is unfair to the disadvantaged and
ought to be rephrased to read,

Which one of the following requires a liquid other than water to dissolve
it? . . . (p. 11).

Similar objections are made to the use of 'lateral', 'vertical' etc., in
the Geography paper and circumlocutions are suggested to avoid
them.

But it should be the job of teachers to teach their pupils so that
they can cope with non-aqueous solvents and lateral faces. Mean-

while, this doctoring of examination questions is unfair to the disadvantaged but bright pupil who does have the interest and intelligence to master a basic terminology but is presently denied the opportunity to do so; nor is it 'just' that the employer should take on a trainee laboratory technician only to discover that he cannot understand the simplest technical instruction.

A great deal of research has been thrown up by GCSE. Confidence in its usefulness is shaken by the sheer banality of many of its findings. For example, on the subject of the readability of examination papers, the author of *Working Paper 5* contributes,

> Many research experiments have shown that there is a clear relationship between the readability of written material and the comprehension levels attained by students using it (p. 2).

One recalls Professor G R Elton's comment,

> Like so much else in sociology [for *Working Paper 5* is sociology of a sort], impressive theories, looked at closely, dissolve into pointless glimpses of the obvious.[30]

Again, in *Working Paper 1*, in reference to marking an English essay on 'a personal experience', the author solemnly asks,

> [Is credit] given for worthwhile work at all levels and not merely for 'good', 'middling' and 'poor' versions of an expected response?[31]

To which the answer ought simply to be, 'Since I mark them in a range of 1–10 and some score 7/10 and others 4/10, "Yes!" '. Most startling of all, the GCSE establishment itself seems uncertain how differentiated assessment is to be applied. In 1983 JMB wrote about

> . . . new approaches to assessment . . . whose advantages have yet to be identified and certainly have not been experienced (JMB 82–83, p. 29).

And the SEC itself, as late as 1986, commented that 'in the approvals process it has become apparent that examiners are only slowly coming to terms with these different techniques'.[32]

These doubt and hesitations were excused on the grounds that

> The rapid introduction of the GCSE was not dependent upon the proposed grade-related criteria being in operation from the beginning (JMB 83–84, p. 11).[33]

It is now clear that differentiated assessment will be applied in the 1988 examination (even to history, perhaps the most doubtful candidate of all). For NEA History syllabuses specifically affirm, in each case, that 'Differentiation in the written papers will be determined through 'outcome'.' 'Differentiation by outcome' is an arcanely oblique method of setting and marking papers by 'neutral stimulus' that is discussed but far from made clear in SEC Working Paper 1.39 It may well be that we are about to push blithely ahead with' . . . What nobody is sure about.'

Notes

1. From Luther's *An Admonition to Peace,* quoted in *Steven Ozment, The Age of Reform 1250–1550,* Yale, 1980, p. 281

2. I am grateful to Mr Charles A Oxley, MA, ACP, for his permission to quote from comments made to the seminar on 'Education and Freedom', organised by the Freedom Association, 9 May 1987.

3. *The GCSE: An Examination,* edited by Joanna North, 1987, chapters on specific subjects; also John Marenbon, *English our English,* CPS, 1987 and Alan Beattie, *History in Peril,* CPS, 1987

4. *The Constitution of the Northern Examining Association,* 1987, p. 5

5. The titles and blurbs can all be found at the back of Illich, *Deschooling Society,* Penguin Education Specials, 1973 and in other issues in this series.

6. Illich, op. cit., p. 25

7. ib., 19

8. ib., 122

9. ib., 45

10. ib., 78

11. N Entwistle and D Hounsell, 'How do students learn?', *THES,* 4 June 1986

12. *Examinations at 16-plus: A statement of policy,* November 1982

13. North, p. 76

14. SEC 83–84, p. 71

15. ib., 95

16. Howat, p. 4

17. *Delegacy of Local Examinations,* University of Oxford, p. 5

18. Howat, p. 6

19. Howat, p. 9

20. *The Structure and Examining Procedures of the Delegacy,* University of Oxford, 1983, p. 2

21. Howat, p. 12

22. ib., p. 12

23. *School Examinations,* Part 1 Cmnd 7281–II, 1978, p. 24
24. *NEA Constitution,* p. 6
25. ib., p. 5
26. ib., p. 5
27. SEC 86–87, pp. 36–38
28. B/TEC, for example, employs a form of criterion grading. But as I understand it this does not involve a dichotomy between skills and knowledge and it does apply academic and/or technical rigour, not social considerations, to the assessment process. It is therefore, in my view, essentially different from the GCSE differentiated assessment.
29. p. 3
30. *Reformation Europe,* Fontana edition, 1963, p. 314
31. *Differentiated Assessment in GCSE,* p. 3. Perhaps the key to this opaque question lies in the author's concern that we should reward not only an 'expected' response but also an unexpected one. But since the essay is on 'a personal experience', the nature of which is necessarily unknown to the examiner before he has read the essay, the response is essentially unexpected *ab initio*—unless possibly we are asked to reward an essay written in sign language or a sketch instead of an essay? Loose thinking of this kind peppers the research and makes it hard to attach clear meanings to what the authors have to say.
32. SEC 85–86 p. 10
33. p. 3. The passage states: " 'free-response questions' discriminate well at the upper end of the ability range but should form only part of any scheme intended to discriminate across the whole range". I take this to open up the possibility of having both free-response questions and other types of questions—say multiple choice—within the same paper. But how does one establish an equivalence in intellectual value between a well-written, well-integrated essay on the origins of the Chartist Movement and a multiple choice question requiring simply the identification by tick of Julius Caesar, Cromwell, Lumumba *et al.?* To suggest that each should carry the same weight seems to me to be intellectually irresponsible.

14

English Our English: The New Orthodoxy Examined

John Marenbon

Introduction

When children leave English schools today, few are able to speak and write English correctly; even fewer have a familiarity with the literary heritage of the language. It is not hard to see why. Among those who theorize about English teaching there has developed a new orthodoxy, which regards it as a conceptual error to speak of 'correct' English and which rejects the idea of a literary heritage. The new orthodoxy has now come to influence every aspect of English in schools—from curricula to teaching in the classroom to public examinations. Her Majesty's Inspectorate is among its staunch proponents. The object of this pamphlet is to describe the new orthodoxy; to examine how its views have spread; to consider whether its tenets are convincing, and whether English might be taught better.

What has happened to English

Here is the beginning of an essay which, according to experienced assessors, is of *roughly average quality for a fifteen-year-old:*[1]

Last week after waching an exstreamly intoresting programe on the television investagateing Indian familys I decided to learn even more

353

about arranged marrages so I discussed what I have learnt to a friend at school who herself is Indian and will have her husband chosen for her by her parents, I arsked her: "Dose it not worrie you that the man to whome you will marrie might be crule to you . . .

Is it surprising that there is such concern today at low standards of English? The writer of this passage is obviously intelligent and inquisitive, but his weak grasp of grammar, punctuation and spelling prevents him from writing with clarity or ease. Surveys and official bodies confirm the conclusions which many will have reached independently, from their everyday experience of the way English is spoken and written. For instance, a recent survey of scripts written by averagely able, older teenagers found a profusion of spelling mistakes and errors of grammar and punctuation—including an almost universal inability to punctuate direct speech correctly.[2] 'O' and 'A' Level examiners have observed 'a growing lack of distinction between the spoken and written word', strikingly evident in such spellings as 'terest house', 'bone idol' and 'icesaw'.[3] Even among candidates for admission to the best universities who have specialized in English only a minority can spell with consistent correctness, use punctuation properly and construct complex sentences grammatically.

These complaints are not made only by those involved in academic life. In industry and commerce employers are equally, if not more, disturbed by the quality of school-leavers' English. They find that powers of writing among their recruits are below the level needed for their jobs.[4] School-leavers, they say, exhibit 'very low standards in grammar, spelling, punctuation';[5] they need a firmer grasp of grammar.[6]

Standards in the knowledge of English literature are even lower than those in language. Businessmen educated a generation or two ago are surprised when a literary allusion which they took for common knowledge elicits no response from their young colleagues.[7] And university teachers discover that many undergraduates, who have specialized in English at 'A' level, arrive entirely ignorant of all literature written before this century, except for two or three plays by Shakespeare and a few hundred lines of Chaucer.

Why it has happened: the 'new orthodoxy'

These grammatical and literary failings among young people are evidence that, in most schools today, English is badly taught, and that it used to be taught better. But English teachers themselves would not agree. Nor would the official body responsible for assessing their activities—HMI (Her Majesty's Inspectorate). To HMI, English is flourishing; in many a school it singles out English teachers for special praise, and its criticisms are reserved for those who persist in traditional ways of teaching grammar and comprehension.[8] HMI does not blame schools for producing pupils unable to write standard English grammatically and ignorant of the literary classics, because it subscribes to a set of views about English teaching which developed in the 1960s and have now gained the status of an orthodoxy. This new orthodoxy finds little value in grammatical correctness and has no place for literature as a heritage. It is shared, not only by many English teachers and HMI, but by educationalists, boards of examination and the authors of text-books. Seven tenets characterize the new orthodoxy about teaching the English language:-

- English is not just a subject;
- English teaching should be child-centred;
- It is as important to teach the spoken as the written language;
- Assessment should not concentrate on the pupil's errors;
- Grammar is descriptive not prescriptive;
- No language or dialect is inherently superior to any other;
- Language-use should be judged by its appropriateness.

In order to understand how the English language is now taught—or, at least, how theorists and officials believe that it should be taught—it is necessary to explain how these tenets are both explained and justified by their proponents. (The teaching of English literature will be examined separately; see below, Chapter 6). Here, then, are the most common explanations and justifications.

'English is not just a subject'
'English', announces one of the most influential theoretical books,[9] 'is quicksilver among metals—mobile, living and elusive'. It is not to be seen as a subject concerned with a particular subject-matter (as mathematics, for instance, is concerned with numbers and shapes). Rather, English provides the opportunity 'to enrich and diversify personal growth' by remaining 'alert to all that is challenging, new, uncertain and even painful in experience'.[10] Or it is to be defined by reference to a variety of aims—it should not only develop 'a wide range of communication skills', but also encourage 'tolerance of the views of others', 'independent and critical thinking' and 'maturity in personal relationships'.[11]

'English teaching should be child-centred'
The English teacher's job is neither to impart knowledge nor to teach techniques, but rather to allow each child to develop his own view of the world by active writing and, especially, talking. 'Civilization begins anew in every child', as one (extreme) theorist declares.[12] The child's needs, as he himself perceives them, should dictate the course of his learning. The teacher should emphasize the children's 'key words', not his own.[13]

'It is as important to teach the spoken as the written language'
Traditionally, English teachers were concerned to impart literacy— the ability to read and to write. The need now is for teachers to recognize the equal importance of teaching 'oracy'—competence in speaking and listening. Classroom discussions, in which pupils speak freely and are not dominated by the teacher, are as valuable as written exercises; and the forms of language used in speaking deserve the same respect as those which belong to writing.

'Assessment should not concentrate on the pupil's errors'
Traditionally, English teachers would mark their pupils' work by correcting mistakes in the surface features of the language. Today's teachers should avoid taking such a 'narrow view' of the 'basics'. By concentrating on 'correct spelling, conventional punctuation, Standard English grammar, and polite vocabulary', teachers are led to neglect features such as 'tone, form and realistic detail'.[14] They should bear in mind that 'perfect spelling is not essential to making meaning' and that 'most correct punctuation is an aid, rather than a necessity, to understanding'; and they should not hesitate to take into account such qualities as sincerity and vigour.[15]

'Grammar is descriptive not prescriptive'
The business of the grammarian is not, as it was once thought, to prescribe certain verbal forms and constructions as correct, but to describe the features of language as it is used. 'Correctness' is not a concept which can be applied to grammar. 'If we view grammar as a set of rules which describe how we use language, the rules themselves are not good or bad, though they may be described adequately or inadequately in a description of how the language works'.[16]

'No language or dialect is inherently superior to any other'
'One of the most solid achievements of linguistics in the twentieth century has been to eliminate the idea . . . that some languages or

dialects are inherently "better" than others'.[17] 'All varieties of a language are structured, complex, rule-governed systems which are wholly adequate for the needs of their speakers'.[18] 'Qualities such as logic or precision can be more properly attributed to individual speakers than to the language which they happen to speak'.[19] This principle of linguistic equality applies to dialects and creoles,[20] as well as to standard languages like English and French. Indeed standard English—the type of English which is 'used by most speakers at school who consider themselves to be "educated" ' and is 'normally used in writing and on radio and television'—should be regarded as 'simply one dialect among many',[21] in no way superior in itself to Cockney, Scouse or a West Indian creole. It is mistaken to believe, as many do, that only standard English grammatical forms are right: 'no one dialect of English is any more "right" or "wrong" than any other.'[22] If, therefore, a pupil says 'I done it' or 'I ain't got it', the teacher should not tell him that he has used bad grammar: although he has deviated from the grammar of standard English, he has spoken grammatically within his dialect.

'Language-use should be judged by its appropriateness'
Different circumstances call for different types of language. The grammar and vocabulary used in casual conversation will be different from that required for an interview or public speech; biographical reminiscence or a short story will be written in a different manner from a piece of technical description, a business letter or an advertisement. The English teacher should help children to use the type of language appropriate to each of the various common situations of life; and he should judge each use of language 'in its own context of use, and not by the standards of other uses which it was not intended to satisfy'.[23] It is in this context that he should consider the value of teaching standard English. Linguists recognize that standard English is expected in various formal situations and that the attitudes towards correctness which they condemn none the less have wide currency in society. Most theorists would agree that teachers (at least at the moment) should teach children to *write* standard English—as one form of English appropriate to certain circumstances; although some 'hope for a future in which dialect tolerance will be extended even to the written language' and recommend teachers to work towards this goal by 'showing that there are no taboos about the use of non-standard grammar in written work'.[24]

The spread of the new orthodoxy

The new orthodoxy was the invention of educational theorists. But it did not long remain confined to their narrow circle. It was given official sanction in the Bullock Report of 1975. It has come to dominate the judgements of HMI and to regulate the assessments of the unit at the DES employed to monitor standards in schools. And the thinking behind the new GCSE examinations is based on it.

The new orthodoxy in the Bullock report

Even by the title of its report, *A Language for Life,* Sir Alan Bullock's Committee indicated how fully it had absorbed the new orthodoxy. A brief chapter (remarkable for its confusion, vagueness and ignorant mishandling of the philosophical concepts it employs) offers a 'theoretical foundation' for the report, which is summarized in its concluding sentence: 'to exploit the process of discovery through language in all its uses is the surest means of enabling a child to master his mother tongue'.[25] Noting the close links between the acquisition of language and any sort of learning, the report rejects any notion of English as a distinctive subject, with a body of knowledge and a set of techniques which its teachers should transmit. The teacher's function is, rather, to help children in their 'process of discovery'. The report rejects 'correctness' as a concept to be used in judging speech, preferring 'appropriateness' as the criterion. Linguists, it comments, have long held the view 'that an utterance may be "correct" in one linguistic situation but not in another'. By using the criterion of appropriateness, it suggests, teachers will be operating 'positively rather than negatively': 'the aim is not to alienate the child from a form of language with which he has grown up and which serves him efficiently in the speech community of his neighbourhood'. Although the child should be enabled to 'use standard forms when they are needed . . . the teacher should start where the child is and should accept the language he brings to school'.[26] In written language too the children should begin from the forms most natural to the child: 'the first task of the teacher is one of encouraging vitality and fluency in the expressive writing that is nearest to speech'.[27]

The Bullock report draws from these more abstract discussions a number of specific recommendations about teaching methods:-

• teachers should not dominate the class but rather encourage the active participation of all the pupils;
• great attention should be paid to 'oracy';
• traditional language exercises, designed to teach correct grammar, should in general be avoided;
• in correcting work, teachers should not pay too much attention to 'surface features' (such as spelling and grammar).

The new orthodoxy and Her Majesty's Inspectorate

How deeply HMI has taken the Bullock Committee's recommendations to heart is evident from its comments on English teaching in individual schools. Its approval is reserved for classes where children do the talking and use a variety of styles of language. The inspectors praise schools where 'efforts are made . . . to encourage different kinds of writing and writing for different readers, including their peers . . .'; 'there are examples of marking which make a genuine attempt to establish a dialogue with the pupil'; 'a number of lessons were seen where an attempt was made to develop oral skills through class discussion and group work: one effective discussion led to a cartoon strip representation of a short story . . .'. Their criticisms are directed towards lessons which are 'teacher dominated' and exercises which it perceives as too tightly disciplined. The inspectors berate schools where 'the content [of written work] is narrow and over-directed by the teacher with few opportunities for pupils to use the rich language they exhibit in discussion sessions'; 'oral work . . . was marred by a tendency for discussion to become teacher dominated;' 'there is too much "over formal" language work which is not necessarily related to their [least able pupils'] real needs'.[28]

HMI's most explicit discussion of the English curriculum, *English from 5 to 16*, is unusual in considering that English teachers should, among other things, aim 'to teach pupils *about* language, so that they achieve a working knowledge of its structure'.[29] This idea was misinterpreted by newspaper reports, which viewed the document as an attempt to reintroduce 'traditional lessons on grammar, spelling and punctuation'.[30] But in fact, in *English from 5 to 16* as elsewhere, HMI shares the new orthodoxy's hostility to old-fashioned *prescriptive* grammar; what the booklet suggests—and that only tentatively—is that more *descriptive* grammar should be taught in schools. In general, *English from 5 to 16* advocates the new orthodoxy. Teaching English is not, it explains, just a matter of imparting skills or knowledge: 'in teaching English we are teaching pupils to think clearly, to be self aware, and to be responsible to their experience of the world of people and things about them'.[31] 'Oracy' receives as much emphasis as literacy; and the teacher is to make his start what children 'want or need to say': 'the language children bring with them from their home backgrounds should not be criticised, belittled or proscribed. The aim should be to *extend* their language repertoires'.[32]

Nevertheless, the original version of this booklet *did* place an emphasis on teaching standard English which is not to be found in HMI's other pronouncements, although it attributed this importance merely to the fact that standard English happens to be 'appropriate' in many contexts. This feature of the booklet, along with the rigour and specificity of the objectives it proposed for pupils at different ages, provoked widespread criticism from teachers. In response, HMI produced a second edition of the booklet, with revised recommendations more clearly in line with the new orthodoxy. For instance, in the revised edition the author stresses that non-standard forms are not 'inherently inferior, or limited in their capacity to convey meaning; in some respects indeed they may be "superior";[33] he acknowledges that 'the case for recognising ethnic diversity in English within the framework of commonly agreed objectives has been strengthened by the responses';[34] he removes the rigorous and precise specifications of the original version and replaces them with mere examples of 'the qualities, attitudes and skills which pupils should be seen to be acquiring at the age points given'.[35]

The new orthodoxy and the Assessment of Performance Unit

In the DES there is an Assessment of Performance Unit (APU), which has the task of monitoring schoolchildren's performance. The APU's surveys of 'language performance' deal with the area traditionally regarded as English. Its surveys present information carefully gathered and analyzed in detail, but from the standpoint of the new orthodoxy. Although the skills supposedly tested are reading and writing, little attention is given to the mastery (for comprehension and use) of grammar and vocabulary. Tests of reading merge into tests of general intelligence: how well, the assessors seem to be asking, can children handle information, reclassify it and draw conclusions from it? And the children are usually asked to demonstrate these skills, not in the form of continuous writing, but as answers to multiple-choice questions or as notes. Tests of writing, too, are largely assessed by criteria which have little to do with knowledge of English. For instance, eleven-year olds were set as a written exercise the game in which a different passenger (a farmer, a housewife, a cook, a Prime Minister) each argues why he should not be the one to be thrown from an over-heavy balloon. In their judgements, the assessors allow grammatical and technical propriety to fall into the background. What interests them, rather, is the plausibility of the cases made (and— good civil servants that they are—they appear to be particularly irked by those children who attribute too much importance to the Prime Minister!).[36]

It is true that one of the categories the assessors promise to measure is children's 'knowledge of the grammatical conventions in written English'. But, if the reader should infer from this that the APU is so deviant from the new orthodoxy as to allow *correctness* in standard English as an admissible concept, he will be mistaken. For the assessors make it clear that:-

'Markers were asked not to record as grammatical errors the use of grammatical features that are characteristic of regional variants of standard English, or the use of colloquial expressions, or of slang. If such usage was judged to be inappropriate in a particular context, it was taken account of in relation to the category of style, as was the inappropriate use of non-standard forms such as 'I done it'.[37]

This principle helps to explain aspects of the APU's findings which would otherwise by puzzling. For instance, in a survey of fifteen year olds' writing the APU gave top marks to 28 per cent of the candidates for grammar, and to 26 per cent for punctuation and spelling.[38] Yet in the samples of work reproduced in its report, misspellings, deviations from the grammar of standard English and punctuation which obscures syntax are the rule, and even the best pieces are not free from such errors. But the APU (like other exponents of the new orthodoxy) would regard such failings as minor, and sometimes not even as failings at all.

The new orthodoxy and GCSE

There are eight assessment objectives specified in the National Criteria for GCSE English. Five of them are characterized by their vagueness and generality. Children are expected to 'understand and convey information'; 'understand, order and present facts, ideas and opinions'; 'evaluate information in reading material and in other media, and select what is relevant to specific purposes'; 'articulate experience and express what is felt and what is imagined' and 'recognise implicit meaning and attitudes'. All of these aims are valuable, but they can be achieved only by gaining the particular abilities taught by particular disciplines. A subject which makes such vague and general aims its criteria will become—as exponents of the new orthodoxy wish English to become—no subject at all. One of the three remaining assessment objectives concerns ability in spoken English (oracy). Another seems to demand correctness in written English: it asks candidates to 'exercise control of appropriate grammatical structures, conventions in paragraphing, sentence structure, punctuation and spelling'. But here the word 'appropriate' indicates that the examiners will not demand a mastery of correct standard English, in the traditional sense. And another of the objectives underlines this stress on appropriateness by demanding a 'sense of audience and an awareness of style in both formal and informal situations.'[39] The assessment objectives for English GCSE are founded, then, on three of the tenets of the new orthodoxy: that English is not just a subject; that it is as important to teach the spoken as the written language; and that language-use should be judged by its appropriateness.

The questions set in sample GCSE papers reflect these criteria. They are divided between those which ask candidates to gather and classify factual information, and those which ask them for their own opinions or personal narratives. Although markers are told that they should look for an adequate grasp of conventions of spelling, punctuation and grammar, the papers do not contain questions designed specifically to test these abilities. Moreover, not every candidate for GCSE English will even sit an examination. It will be possible to take GCSE in this subject entirely by assessment of coursework produced outside examination conditions—an arrangement which will make it very hard to measure how well candidates can write standard English unaided by their teacher. In its criteria, type of questions and methods of examination, GCSE English represents the triumph of the new orthodoxy.

What is wrong with the new orthodoxy

No part of this new orthodoxy, now so widespread among theorists, officials and teachers, stands up to scrutiny. Its tenets express, at best, half truths, in which a point of commonsense is exaggerated and distorted; and sometimes not even that.

'English is not just a subject'

This view has a positive aspect (English is more than a subject) and a negative one (English has no specific, definable subject-matter). The positive aspect is misguided, and the negative unnecessary. It is doubtless valuable that children should grow emotionally, that they should learn to tolerate the views of others and to engage in critical thinking. But these—and many of the other ambitious aims often proposed for English—are virtues which are slowly acquired in the course of acquiring particular intellectual skills and areas of knowledge. Time given to a vague and generalized attempt to gain such virtues is time lost to the specific and rigorous studies which alone will foster them. English could be one of these studies, were it to pursue the simple and well-defined aims of teaching children to write and speak standard English correctly, and of initiating their acquaintance with the literary heritage of the language.

'English teaching should be child-centred'

Good teachers have always recognized that effective instruction requires the active participation of the pupil: unless his attention and efforts are engaged, he will learn nothing. But the pupil's interest is merely a necessary condition for his learning: there is no good reason why it should determine *what* he learns. Few would contest this view with regard, for instance, to mathematics. The good mathematics teacher may well gain his pupils' interest by showing how numbers and their relations are relevant to their everyday concerns; but he will base his teaching not on the pupils' view of their needs, but on his own, informed, view of what they need to know in order gradually to achieve a mastery of mathematical techniques. So long as English, too, is recognized as a subject, with definite aims, the same principles should guide its teachers. The grammar of English, its range of vocabulary and styles and its literary heritage exist independently of the child who is learning to use them.

'It is as important to teach the spoken as the written language'

Spoken language is as important—in some respects more important—than written language. But, whereas writing and reading are skills that require specific instruction, children learn to speak and listen just by being present at these activities. The child learns to speak and listen just by being present at these activities. The child learns to speak and listen *better* in three main ways: first, by practice in the course of everyday life; second, by coming to understand more about all the various particular activities which can be the subjects of conversation (the more he knows about—for instance—woodwork, the more easily he can be taught to discuss it); third, by mastering the standard written language and thereby increasing his range of vocabulary, grasp of syntax and ability to chose standard forms correctly.

The fashionable emphasis on 'oracy' is in part a product of the tendency to regard English, not as a subject, but as an opportunity to acquire a haphazard collection of virtues (maturity, tolerance and so on); and in part an attempt to reduce the importance of standard English (which is the most usual form of the written language).

'Assessment should not concentrate on the pupil's errors'

No good teacher sets out to discourage and demoralize his pupils, concentrating on their mistakes to the exclusion of all else. But exponents of the new orthodoxy do not merely wish to insist on this sensible maxim. Their view, that it is 'more important to see what the child can do, rather than what he cannot', sounds tolerant and humane; but, in fact, it condemns those who speak and write badly to go on speaking and writing badly. The dire effects which it has are a simple consequence of other tenets of the new orthodoxy when they are applied to the question of assessment: the belief that English teaching should be child-centred, and the belief that supposed mistakes in speech and writing are, at worst, examples of inappropriate use of language. If these tenets are rejected, then this view of assessment is left without support.

'Grammar is descriptive not prescriptive'

The error of this position is to assume that description must be an *alternative* to prescription. When I see in a French grammar that the imperfect of *je suis* is *j'étais*, I am reading both a description of how people speak in France and a prescription about how I must speak, if I am to speak French. By describing how a certain language is spoken or written, the grammarian prescribes usage for those who wish to speak or write that language. The case is the same for varieties of any given language. A grammar which describes standard English prescribes English usage for those who wish to speak or write it.

Whether the grammarian should phrase his discussion in descriptive or prescriptive terms depends on the purpose of his work. If, for instance, he is writing a monograph for linguists, who know well how to speak and write standard English but who are interested in how its various usages are to be analyzed and classified, he will rightly use a descriptive terminology. But if he is writing so as to teach schoolchildren how to write and speak standard English, it will be proper for him to prescribe. The prescriptive manner of old-fashioned school grammars, usually condemned by modern linguists, was entirely appropriate to their function.

Exponents of the new orthodoxy often use the statement that 'grammar is descriptive not prescriptive' as the slogan for their case against prescriptive teaching of standard English. In this way they manage to suggest that anyone who disagrees with them has simply misunderstood the nature of grammar. But the misunderstanding is theirs. Grammar prescribes by describing.

'No language or dialect is inherently superior to any other'
This principle of linguistic equality can be understood in three different ways. Exponents of the new orthodoxy believe that it is true according to all these three interpretations.

It might be taken merely as a recognition that there is no intrinsic link between communicative adequacy and the particular forms of any given language. By this interpretation, the principle of linguistic equality is almost certainly true. There is no reason why one set of letters or sounds should be intrinsically better than another at standing for a certain sort of object or playing a certain role in sentences: *canis, chien, hund* and *dog* are equally good words for the same thing. Similarly there are all sorts of differences in structure between languages that cannot convincingly be described as better or worse: whether, for instance, the passive is formed by using an auxiliary or by a change of form; or whether verbs are usually placed at the end or at the beginning of subordinate clauses; or whether adjectives precede or follow the nouns they modify.

By another interpretation the principle of linguistic equality means that all languages are equally regular and rule-governed. This position is justified in one important way. Speech in, for instance, Cockney or West Indian Creole is sometimes described as 'ungrammatical'. The linguist is right to object to this description: although Cockney and West Indian Creole do not follow the grammar of standard English, they each have their own implicit rules, which modern grammarians have succeeded in describing. The linguist must, however, qualify this view. Whereas *all* the speech of someone who speaks standard English only will tend, by and large, to bear out the rules with which linguists describe standard English, *all* the speech of a dialect or creole-speaker is unlikely to bear out the rules which describe his dialect or creole. Parts of his speech will follow, not the rules of his own language, but those of the standard language; and, at moments, his usage may reflect rules which belong to neither—for instance, the phenomenon of 'hyperurbanism', where uneducated speakers use constructions such as 'They gave it to my mother and I' in an exaggerated effort at correctness.

By a third interpretation, the principle of linguistic equality means that every language is wholly (and therefore equally) adequate to the needs of the speakers. There is a sense in which this statement is not just true, but truistic. The only measure of a man's linguistic need in a particular area of life is the language he actually uses in that area of life—a language which will therefore be by definition fully adequate, whatever it is. But exponents of the new orthodoxy do not usually take adequacy to need in so limited a way: rather, they assume that the needs of speakers of different languages and dialects are all roughly the same, and that every language and dialect is equally capable of fulfilling them. From these premises they draw the conclusion that no one language is intrinsically more subtle, logical or precise than another; no one language, except by accidental convenience, more apt than another for any particular type of use or activity. This is a remarkable position, and a mistaken one.

Languages develop along with their users' manner of living; their capacity to fulfil functions is slowly gained as their users turn them to those functions. That languages such as standard English, French, German, Italian and Spanish can each be used equally well for such functions as telling a story, describing a scene, rousing a crowd to indignation and putting forward a logical argument is not the reflection of an equality between languages but, rather, of the similarities between English, French, German, Italian and Spanish cultures as they have developed. For an example of languages which have obviously different capacities, it is necessary merely to look at the different languages which English has been at different stages of its development. It was almost impossible to present clearly a complicated, abstract argument in the English of King Alfred's day, and Chaucer's English was still inadequate for this use; but as, in the sixteenth and seventeenth centuries more and more writers tried to use English for such purposes, the language was gradually shaped to fulfil this function, so that Hume had in his native tongue an instrument perfectly adapted for the subtlest speculations. These differences in adequacy did not lie only in vocabulary, but in the possibilities of grammar and syntax. Chaucer's English allowed him to frame a narrative or a description with ease; but it could not accommodate complicated logical relations between concepts and arguments.

The differences in capacity between modern standard English and the modern dialects of English are even more striking than those between Chaucerian and modern English. When a man speaks a language, he draws on the resources of the culture which has produced that language. He enjoys the achievements of the culture and is restricted by its limitations. Standard English is the language of English culture at its highest levels as it has developed over the last centuries: the language, not just of literature, philosophy and scholarship, but of government, science, commerce and industry. Dialects of English reflect the much more limited range of functions for which they have traditionally been used: the exchanges of everyday life, mainly among those unrefined by education. This does not mean that speakers of non-standard English cannot be verbally agile within certain areas of discourse,[40] nor that the topics traditionally discussed in the standard language are *entirely* barred to them. In a celebrated article, the sociolinguist William Labov recounts a conversation about God conducted with a young American Negro in his own dialect.[41] Although Labov exaggerates the logical cogency of the young man's thought, there is no doubt that he was groping towards an interesting argument. But without the resources of Labov's own standard English this argument could not be clearly expressed and so made available for further elaboration and refinement.

Sometimes linguists suggest that, since most dialect-speakers in England also know standard English, they could easily adapt their dialects to cover the range of functions performed by standard English, by borrowing from its vocabulary and syntax. But what gain can there be in using a conglomerate language, which was never before spoken or written, which no one will handle with ease and few will fully understand? And what justification for burdening schoolchildren with the task of inventing it?

'Language-use should be judged by its appropriateness'
One of the criteria for judging the use of language is certainly appropriateness: the man who speaks to his wife as if she were a public meeting, or addresses a scientific congress in the language of the nursery, cannot be said to use language well. But exponents of the new orthodoxy are not content with this commonsensical posi-

tion. Since they advocate the principle of linguistic equality, not only in its first and second, but also in its third interpretations, they believe that appropriateness is the *only* criterion for judging one language or sort of language superior to another. They conclude that, whilst one language might, as a matter of fact, happen to be more convenient or appropriate for a particular sort of occasion, there is no way in which any one language is intrinsically better than another. They allow that French is a better language than Finnish for buying bread in Paris, because most Parisian bakers understand French and few know any Finnish; and that standard English is a better language than Cockney or Scouse for writing a business letter, because most businessmen will receive a letter in standard English more favourably than one in dialect. But they deny that, in itself, any one language is more precise, logical, flexible or subtle than another. These conclusions cannot be upheld, once the third interpretation of the principle of linguistic equality is rejected.

The concept of 'appropriateness' has sometimes been used to defend the teaching of standard English in schools. Standard English, it is argued, should be taught because it happens to be the 'appropriate' sort of language for many activities. This argument is so unburdened by theorizing and apparently commonsensical that advocates of standard English might be reluctant to reject it. But the position it supports—like so many which gain their appeal from their modesty—is a weak one. It lies defenceless against attacks from reformers who wish to change social patterns of language-use in order to remove the pre-eminence of standard English. Those who support standard English solely on grounds of 'appropriateness' can have no principled objection to the substance of the reformers' recommendations. They can object, at most, only to their pace and practicability.

The importance of standard English

At the centre of the new orthodoxy is its devaluation of standard English. From this derives its exponents' hostility to grammatical prescription: *because* they do not think that standard English is superior to dialect, they do not believe that its grammar should be prescribed to children (a position they try to support by mistakenly insisting that grammar cannot ever prescribe); *because* they cannot accept that standard English is superior to dialect, they insist that the language schoolchildren use can be judged only by its 'appropriateness'.

Why is standard English superior to dialect? One important reason has already been suggested. Standard English has been developed over centuries to fulfil a far wider range of functions than any dialect—from technical description to philosophical argument, from analysis of information to fiction and poetry. Only by using another language (such as French) which had been developed similarly, over centuries, by a similar culture, could the speaker enjoy a similar resource.

Standard English gains another advantage over dialect by the very fact of being standard. When a linguist formulates the grammar of a dialect, he is engaged in an exercise which is to a considerable degree artificial. Dialect is always changing: from decade to decade, from village to village, from street to street. Outside the textbooks of sociolinguists, it is never clear exactly which of the constructions that a dialect-speaker is using are grammatical and which are not, because it is never clear exactly which dialect he is speaking, or how consistently he is intending to speak it. Standard languages change too; but very, very slowly. The linguists may be quick to come forward with examples of constructions where usage within modern standard English is undecided (Do we say 'The Cabinet intends' or 'The Cabinet intend'? 'Throw me a lifebelt or I shall drown' or 'Throw me a lifebelt or I will drown'?). But, for the vast majority of constructions, all who know standard English will recognize instantly not only whether they are correct or incorrect, but whether they are usual or unusual in their context. Similarly, all who know standard English can recognize the register to which a given word belongs. Such unanimity in usage makes standard English an excellent vehicle for clear communication, for conveying information and ideas without misunderstanding. It is no accident that standard English, rather than a dialect, has become an international language. Moreover, the existence of clearly recognized norms increases the expressive possibilities of a language. If, for instance, a standard English speaker inverts a construction for rhetorical effect, or uses a word from an unexpected register, he can be sure that other speakers of standard English will notice what he has done and so appreciate his nuance. A speaker who attempted such linguistic subtlety in a dialect could not be sure that his intentions would be grasped, even by someone from the next street.

It is far easier to destroy a standard language than to create one. A standard language requires a body of speakers who have been trained to distinguish correct constructions from incorrect ones, usual forms from those which are unusual and carry with them special implications. Such training is neither short nor easy; and it is unrealistic to expect that English teachers can give it to their pupils if, along with teaching standard English (as one form of the language, appropriate for certain occasions), they are expected to encourage speech and writing in dialect and to attend to the multiplicity of other tasks with which modern educationalists have burdened them. By devaluing standard English, the new orthodoxy is destroying it.

The literary heritage and its enemies

The teaching of English literature is, in one way, more difficult to discuss than the teaching of the English language, because 'language' is a term more clearly and uniformly understood than 'literature'. In order to consider how English literature should be taught in schools, the question 'What is literature?' must be posed. This question seems to call for a definition; to ask, 'What sort of writing constitutes literature?' And theorists have often replied along those lines, saying, for instance, that literature is writing in which words and structures are arranged in a special 'literary' way; or that it is writing which has a special sort of effect on its readers; or that it is any writing which is poetry, prose fiction or drama.

All such answers are deeply misleading. Literature is not some sort of naturally existing category of writing. Rather, the way of looking at writing which recognizes some as literary and some as non-literary developed only after the Middle Ages and belongs peculiarly to European culture and those cultures strongly influenced by it. Literary texts are those texts (including many written before there was a notion of literature) which have come to be considered as literature, and whatever other texts resemble them in the respects which those who are familiar with literary texts recognize. We learn what literature is, and how to read it, by coming to read those works which are recognized as literature, especially those in which the features which are seen as valuable in literature are most evident—the acknowledged literary masterpieces. Coming to know the literary heritage is not, then, an historical exercise remote from the business of learning to value and enjoy literature, but rather the only sure way to that goal.

When, in the sixteenth, seventeenth and eighteenth centuries, the notion of literature was developing, the languages and writings of ancient Greece and Rome were the main subject of study for all in England (and elsewhere in Europe) who received more than the most rudimentary education. The Greek and Latin classics came to be seen as literary classics, and their various forms and styles to indicate much of the range of literary possibility. Englishmen enjoyed a two-fold literary heritage: that of antiquity and that of their own language, the masterpieces of which could be seen as continuing and extending the achievements of the ancients. Until late in the last century, Englishmen received no formal instruction in school (or at university) in the literature of their own language. Their reading of the Latin and Greek classics allowed them to learn what literature is and how it is to be read; and it was left to their own leisure and inclination to become acquainted with literature in English. Such a classical education, complemented by extensive private reading in the vernacular, would still probably be the best way of introducing an Englishman to his literary heritage, if only it were still available. Indeed, without some knowledge of classical literature an Englishman will always be to some extent a stranger to his own culture. Nevertheless, for those who study little or no Greek and Latin, training at school in the classics of English can form a very fair way of learning what literature is and how to read it.

A few decades ago, those who took 'O' and 'A' Levels in English received a good introduction to the heritage of English literature. Those who gave up English before the sixth form would have had the chance to study works by Shakespeare and Milton, eighteenth-century dramatists and essayists, the romantic poets and the nineteenth-century novelists; and English specialists left school with a knowledge of their literary heritage which would shame most graduates in English today (for instance, in 1950 candidates for the Cambridge Board Higher School Certificate, the predecessor of 'A' levels, chose from a syllabus which covered—among other writers—Chaucer, Sidney, Spenser, Marlowe, Shakespeare, Bacon, Jonson, Milton, Bunyan, Pepys, Swift, Gibbon, Fielding, Defoe, Wordsworth, Byron, Shelley, Lamb, Hardy, Browning and Shaw). Nowadays few teachers think it their job to introduce pupils to the heritage of English literature. They emphasize the study of modern works (often of little literary merit) which are presumed to be 'relevant' to their pupils; and they frequently allow even sixth-form specialists to remain ignorant of all writing before the twentieth century, save an isolated text of Chaucer's and a few Shakespearian plays.

This neglect of the literary heritage in schools is the result of three different, and conflicting, attitudes to literature, each of which is popular among schoolteachers: first, the view that literature is not an important part of English teaching; second, the view that literature is an important part of English teaching, but that instruction in it should mainly consist in encouraging the pupil's own imaginative powers and his ability to respond personally to what he reads; third, the view that literature is an important part of English teaching, but that instruction in it should mainly consist in imparting the techniques of practical criticism.

'Literature is not an important part of English teaching'
This is an attitude which is rarely expressed, explicitly and positively, but which a large group of English teachers and educational theorists has adopted, implicitly and by default. When English is considered, not as a subject, but as a training in the skills of speaking, listening, reading and writing, then the study of literature becomes just one of a variety of tasks, easily neglected in the general effort to teach the unteachable. For example, HMI's *English from 5 to 16* includes among its objectives for 16 year olds that they should 'recognise some of the ways in which writers of fiction, poetry and plays achieve their effects . . . have some ability to judge the value and quality of what they read . . . [and] have experienced some literature and drama of high quality, not limited to the twentieth century, including Shakespeare'.[42] But how is the ordinary teacher of pupils of normal abilities to fulfil these admirable objectives when they are just two out of more than fifty?

'Teaching literature consists in encouraging the use of imagination and personal response'
This attitude, now very widespread, has been canonized in the general criteria for GCSE which require candidates to 'communicate a sensitive and informed personal response to what is read'[43]; and one of GCSE Examination Boards even insists that every candidate submit 'at least one piece of work which demonstrates the candidate's own unaided and spontaneous response'[44]. Even in the 'A' level classroom, the teaching which HMI specially advocates is that which promotes 'direct engagement with texts whereby a student finds a voice of his or her own', a voice which will be 'sensitive' and 'individual'.[45]

Advocacy for 'personal', 'unaided' and 'spontaneous' responses is particularly widespread in discussion of the teaching of poetry. For instance, a list of different 'writing functions' prepared by the APU includes the following classification: 'General purpose of writing: to express feelings, Written outcome or product: Response to a given poem'.[46] 'In a sense', a recent booklet on poetry by HMI suggests, 'all writing connected with the experience of poetry is creative'. In discussing poetry, its author believes, 'many pupils have an original contribution to make because of what each uniquely brings to the reading'.[47] 'We must suspend our academically angled ideas of "greatness" . . .', says the writer of a textbook for English teachers, 'The "classics" are Shakespeare, Milton, Pope . . . but for a class finding its feet the best, in the sense of the most effective and accessible may well be Belloc or Causley, riddles or Haiku'. Great poetry, the writer continues, is 'an unlikely stimulus for pupils' own work' and is likely 'to inhibit an honest and personal response and induce apathy as pupils realise that however careful their approach it will be mediocre in comparison with the model'.[48] In line with this attitude is the growing practice in class and in examinations of asking questions about literature designed primarily to exercise the pupil's own imagination. He is asked to write his own poem as a 'response' to one he has read,[49] or is given a question such as this about *Romeo and Juliet*:- 'The Nurse has agreed to be interviewed about the tragedy of Romeo and Juliet. What do you think she would say about her part in the sensational events that have rocked the city? You may write as the nurse if you wish'.[50]

Theorists come to adopt this attitude by failing to realize that regard for literature is in itself a value. They believe that they must explain *why* literature is valuable and imagine that they can do so by presenting it as 'a personal resource' and by making the aim in teaching it to children the promotion of their 'personal and moral growth'.[51] The literary classics are ignored because they are less immediately relevant to the interests of children. Indeed, the very idea of 'classics' is explicitly condemned: ' "Classic" is a status word . . . Classic status has . . . become largely a commercial matter and it is necessary to move beyond such considerations if our judgements 6f books are to be sound'.[52]

'Teaching literature should consist in teaching the techniques of practical criticism'
'Practical criticism' is the name for a special way of reading and writing about literature. The many English teachers who base their classes around its techniques consider themselves defenders of liter-

ature and, although they emphasize the importance of the pupil's 'personal response', they would add that this involves, not just vividness of imagination, but also close, critical attention to the details of the text. Practical criticism may therefore seem to commend itself to those who support rigour in the teaching of English, who distrust appeals to pupils' creativity and who believe in the value of literature. Yet the widespread adoption of practical criticism as the means of teaching literature has been, probably more than any other factor, the cause of schoolchildren's declining knowledge of their literary heritage. The reason for this lies in the way in which practical criticism has developed, especially in the universities.

Practical criticism originated from the anxiety of critics such as I.A. Richards, in the 1920s and 1930s, about the inability of good English graduates to read poetry carefully and to base their judgement of its value rigorously on the text. Richards illustrated these failings by asking a sample group of such students to discuss a series of poems, some of high and some of low quality, which were presented without the names of their authors.[53] The deficiencies which Richards noticed are, no doubt, important failings; and the demand to write in a careful, critical way about an unseen, unattributed text is a method which can help both to manifest and to correct them. Practical criticism, in Richards's version, can be a salutary exercise, although it carries with it the danger of suggesting that texts exist in isolation from a literary tradition, and that reading literature is a special exercise to be performed under laboratory conditions rather than part of the everyday life of a cultivated man. Practical criticism came to be harmful when it began to be used, not as an instructive exercise, but as a method for academics in English departments at universities to write their books and make their careers. Merely to indicate that he had read a work with care could not serve to establish an academic's reputation: he found himself obliged to discover a new and individual interpretation of the text (however well known) which was his subject. The academic critic had to search for all sorts of features of his text which were not obvious to the ordinary reader—patterning of imagery; hidden overtones, ambiguities and word-play; symbolism, ironies and self-parody—in order to produce an entirely new reading which had eluded all the work's readers until then, and would have continued to do so, had it not been for the critic's unusual percipience.

Bright undergraduates, trained by these academics, became English teachers at schools and started to instruct their pupils in the methods they had learnt. They did not—as they might usefully have done—treat practical criticism as a way of sharpening beginners' attention to form and detail in the reading of literature. Rather, every poem became a puzzle; the jargon of literary criticism the means to solve it. A technique which had originally been designed as an instrument for teaching people to read more carefully thus became an end in itself. Instead of learning, slowly and implicitly, to become good readers of literature, pupils were taught an abstruse, mysterious way of writing *about* literature.

Previously, schoolchildren—particularly those who specialized in English—had had the chance to form their taste by reading a wide range of works, from different periods and in different genres. Once teachers began to emphasize the techniques of practical criticism, such breadth of reading was no longer possible. On the one hand, the discovery of hidden meanings and the production of new, individual interpretations took time and so reduced the amount of material that could be studied. On the other hand, many genres of writing in many periods were not suited for practical criticism and so were banished from the classroom. The works which provided plenteous material for a critical essay received the children's, and the teacher's, praise; other material—much of the literary heritage—was depreciated or ignored.

Conclusion

The three main approaches to teaching English literature in schools today all neglect the literary heritage of the language—whether in favour of non-literary works, or of the cultivation of personal response, or of the development of a technique for writing *about* literature. This neglect not merely deprives children of an area of knowledge, but also closes to them a whole field of cultural and intellectual experience. Children can become good readers and good judges of literature only by reading a variety of those works recognized as outstanding by generations of discerning readers. Few English teachers today will give their pupils that opportunity.

How English could be better taught in schools

The good English teacher's aims

A better approach to English teaching in schools would reject every tenet of the new orthodoxy. It would recognize English as a subject—

no more and no less: the subject in which pupils learn to write standard English correctly and thereby to speak it well, and in which they become acquainted with some of the English literary heritage. As such it would contain a distinct body of material which teachers must teach and pupils must learn. English teaching would therefore be 'child-centred' only in the very limited sense that all good teaching is child-centred—that it engages the interest and efforts of the pupils. Improvement in pupils' powers of speaking and listening would be achieved by improving their literacy.

The teacher would not hesitate to prescribe to the children on matters of grammatical correctness. He would recognize the superiority of standard English and see it as his task to make his pupils write it well and thereby gain the ability to speak it fluently. It does not follow from this that he would scorn dialects or their speakers. On the contrary, he would realize that many people use a dialect (or some dialect-forms) in order to identify themselves as belonging to a particular social group. He would not expect his pupils to give up their dialect when talking to their friends or family, but he would recognize that children come to English lessons at school in order to be taught standard English. He would not, however, see it as an important part of his work to instruct his pupils in any specific sort of pronunciation of English (such as Received Pronunciation); but, just as he would try to avoid mistaking regional variations in pronunciation for errors in spoken language, so he would try not to overlook errors in spoken language by mistaking them for regional variations in pronunciation. And he would recognize that some regional accents can make their speakers' English hard to follow, especially to those from outside Britain.

A teacher who followed these tenets would set tasks and exercises for his pupils, not as some inchoate attempt to induce self-criticism, tolerance, maturity or liveliness of imagination, but with the definite object of improving their use of language. He would regard the tasks and exercises proposed both by older textbooks and by newer ones critically but with an open mind. If the old-fashioned text-books and worksheets struck him as dull, he would ask himself whether their dullness was merely an unnecessary obstacle to engaging his pupils' interest or whether it was inevitable in what they sought to teach. He would recognize that the process of learning is often laborious and makes considerable demands on children's self-discipline. If the tasks suggested by modern books on English teaching seemed to him strange, he would nevertheless be willing to set them, so long as he was persuaded that they were the best way of making pupils learn an important aspect of correct speech or writing.

When such a teacher came to assess his pupils' work, he would be guided by the principle that, in English as surely as in Mathematics or Chemistry, there is right and wrong. Like any good teacher, he would mingle encouragement with correction; but he would not let an exaggerated concern to dwell on the pupil's successes distract him from his duty to point out, clearly and firmly, the pupil's mistakes—the instances where writing is ungrammatical, words are misspelt or misused, sentences are mispunctuated. He would know that the apparent kindness which spares children such admonishment is in fact a form of cruelty which denies them the opportunity to learn how to speak and write well.

Whilst such a teacher would not discourage his pupils from writing their own poetry, he would tell them that verse requires both a command of the ordinary tools of language—syntax, vocabulary, punctuation—and also an ability to organize words according to their rhythm and sound. He would insist that his pupils learn to write rhymed and rhythmically regular poetry before venturing—if they wished—into freer forms of verse. And he would not pretend, to his pupils or himself, that their poetry was necessarily of great worth; but he would recognize that practice in this type of formally constrained writing can both help to promote good writing in all areas, and increase ability to read good poetry with taste and understanding.

How much should children and their teachers be taught about language?

Knowing about language is not the same as knowing how to use language. An insistence that children learn to speak and write standard English correctly is not equivalent to an insistence that they learn about grammar. But the teacher who (disregarding the new orthodoxy) sets about making his pupils learn correct standard English, would find his task very difficult if he did not make them familiar with certain grammatical terms; terms with which he can frame rules which describe standard English usage, and so prescribe to those who are learning standard English. His pupils will need to learn to distinguish nouns, verbs, adjectives, adverbs, conjunctions, prepositions and exclamations; to identify subjects, objects and predicates; singulars and plurals; past, present, future; indicative, conditional and imperative; phrases, clauses and sentences. It is sometimes argued that these grammatical categories were originally devised in connection with Latin and Greek, and that they are therefore inappropriate for English. This objection ignores the fact that, as it has developed, standard English has been shaped by Latin usage and by the understanding of grammar involved in a classical education. The traditional, classically-based grammatical categories have themselves influenced the way educated men have spoken and written. It may be that, for the purposes of sophisticated linguistic description, some other set of categories is more precise; and that the professional linguist, writing for other professionals, does well to use them. But the terminology of traditional grammar remains the best instrument for describing the broad features of standard English, and so of prescribing usage to those learning it.

A teacher can impart all the knowledge about grammar necessary to help his children use standard English correctly without himself knowing about more than the traditional classically-based categories. Linguists are fond of saying that specialized knowledge of modern linguistics would make English teachers do their work better.[54] It is hard to see why this should be so. No area of specialized knowledge can, in itself, fail to be of some benefit to teachers. But the demand that teachers learn modern linguistics is often no more than a hidden way of asking that they should be more thoroughly indoctrinated in the new orthodoxy about teaching the English language.

How English literature should be taught

For teachers who, following the new orthodoxy, allow casual speech and non-standard dialects to predominate in their classrooms, it can be difficult to introduce their pupils to literature. The only way open to them is to present literature in the context of the children's own attempts at creative writing; but this approach will still leave most literature other than some modern poetry and some sorts of narrative and drama irrecoverably distant from the pupils. Such difficulties will not trouble the teacher who has rejected the new orthodoxy. From the beginning he will have used literary texts (among others) to illustrate the usages of English, since these texts provide examples of English used at its best. And his pupils' mastery of the grammar of standard English will have removed any barrier, at the level of basic understanding, to the formal writing of the past. Moreover, such a teacher will not have scorned the old-fashioned exercise of 'learning by heart'. He will have realized that, by learning to remember distinguished passages of prose and verse, children not only develop their general capacity to memorize, but also lay down for themselves a valuable stock of literary examples, which they can come to know intimately and which will help to form their taste.

Basing himself on these foundations, the teacher should aim to introduce his pupils to a wide range of their literary heritage. He should not limit even thirteen or fourteen year-olds just to lyric poetry, prose fiction and drama; and he should try to introduce those who specialize in English at 'A' level to a whole range of genres—epic, pastoral, satire, dialogue, didactic poetry, discursive and admonitory prose. He should choose from those works which have been accepted by generations of readers as outstanding. Among poets, for instance, he might turn to Chaucer, Sidney, Spenser, Shakespeare, Donne, Jonson, Milton, Dryden, Pope, Wordsworth, Byron, Keats and Tennyson; among writers mainly of prose to Bacon, Swift, Gibbon, Hume, Richardson, Fielding, Hazlitt, Austen, Dickens and George Eliot. The Authorized Version of the Bible should be given a special place in English courses, since its language echoes through the writing of literature in succeeding centuries.

It is not among the teacher's tasks to make his pupils (even the most advanced ones) into literary historians; but, just in order to become competent readers of literature, they must learn how words change their meanings over the centuries; how literary forms are altered and elaborated; and how works written in times long past, when readers' ideas and expectations were very different from those of anyone today, are vivid and accessible to those familiar with the literary tradition of which these old books have come to be members.

Children learn to read literature as literature only by reading the literary works which are recognized as outstanding, and talking to those who are already competent readers of literature. Beyond care, patience and precision in reading, there are no techniques which can be taught for reading literature. The teacher must try to impart his own competence as a reader of literature by example, and beware of allowing his pupils to substitute for competence in reading an ability to manipulate a critical jargon and produce seemingly impressive essays. He should be sceptical of originality in response to literature because it is most likely to betray a failure of understanding. The competent reader reads a work of literature much as other competent readers read it. His response is 'personal' only in that it is his: his view of the work, just as much as his judgement of it, rightly aspires to receive universal assent.

It may seem to follow from this that examinations in literature are inappropriate. This is indeed the case if they are regarded as ways of testing the competence of candidates as readers of literature. But they are useful for testing whether children have fulfilled the necessary *preconditions* for becoming competent literary readers: that they have read a wide range of outstanding literary works with care and attention to detail. Questions in literature examinations should therefore be simple, designed to test range and precision of reading; they should not—as most questions in 'A' level do now—ask candidates to write literary critical essays.

English and other subjects

There is a chapter in the Bullock Report called 'Language Across the Curriculum'. It suggests that all sorts of other subjects besides English provide opportunities for the teaching of language-use— opportunities which schools should not neglect. 'Language across the curriculum' has now become a slogan of the new orthodoxy, influencing teaching in many subjects in many schools, though not yet so universally as HMI would like. There is no evidence that this policy has succeeded in making children more literate, and its effects on the study of subjects other than English are often regrettable. Pupils are distracted from the business of learning about, for instance, history or mathematics by the teacher's anxiety to develop their linguistics powers. Of course, it is necessary to speak and write well in history and mathematics. But an English course, properly regarded as a training in good English, will provide pupils with the techniques they need to discuss a mathematical problem or compose an historical essay. English is combined and confused with other subjects to its, and their, detriment.

However, there is one subject which, whilst quite distinct from English, has a special connection with it: Latin. The teaching of Latin in schools benefits the English both of those pupils who study it, and those who do not. Standard English has been formed through the centuries by its contact with Latin; and without some knowledge of Latin an Englishman will always remain, to an extent, a stranger to his own culture. But even those children not fortunate enough to be taught Latin, gain by the fact that Latin is taught in school; or—to put it in the form which present circumstances make the more pertinent—will lose if Latin continues to vanish from the school syllabus. That Latin is taught, not just as a specialist discipline like Sanskrit or Japanese, but widely at school-level, affirms that grammatical and lexical correctness are still valued; and, more practically, it ensures a supply of English teachers whose grasp of Latin will make their command of English and its grammar firmer and more explicit.

Conclusion: English, politicians and officials

The preceding sections have put forward certain arguments about how English should, and should not, be taught in schools. They have suggested that it should be regarded as a subject, no more and no less, with two aims: to teach children to speak and write standard English well, and to initiate their acquaintance with the literary heritage of the language. But they have also suggested a conclusion of a different sort. They have shown how a certain set of ideas about English teaching (the 'new orthodoxy'), developed by theorists in the 1960s, have come to be adopted as principles by official bodies, such as the Bullock Commission, HMI and the APU. This conclusion should disturb even those who reject many of the other arguments proposed here.

There is a common tendency for government to look to experts for guidance about specialized matters. It is questionable whether such expert advice can ever be free from fashionable or political bias, even if the subject is apparently scientific or technical. To look in this way to experts for advice about the teaching of a subject such as English is unquestionably to invite confusion. The experts can merely provide theories, and information collected and interpreted in the light of those theories. *They* are not to be blamed for following the theories which have happened to be prevalent in learned circles (although their partiality to every fashionable folly should not, perhaps, go without remark or censure); but rather those who have endorsed their recommendations as if they were readily observable fact or indisputable scientific knowledge.

It is in this context that the activities of HMI are particularly worrying. When the Inspectorate reports on pupil numbers, successes in examinations or the organization of teaching in individual schools, its evidence is rightly regarded as authoritative. But recently—and especially with regard to English—HMI has made reports of quite another sort. Both in its general discussions and in its reports on individual schools, it has recommended how English and other subjects *should* be taught; what should be their aims, and what methods should be used to achieve them. These recommendations largely reflect the tenets of the new orthodoxy; but they have been accepted as authoritative even by politicians whose own explicit, ideological convictions are the very opposite of those on which the new orthodoxy is founded. Ministers of government, preoccupied with the external politics of education, have repeatedly been defeated in the more important internal politics of what is taught and how: defeated by an enemy they do not recognize, in a battle they do not know they are fighting.

It is now being proposed that a national curriculum be established to guide the content of teaching at school. And a committee has already been appointed by the Secretary of State for Education to recommend aims and methods for teaching how the English language works. The motive behind the proposal for a national curriculum is a worthy one: not a desire for uniformity, but an attempt to ensure that no child is denied a solid grounding by the whims of teachers and local authorities beguiled by modish subjects and syllabuses. But the record of official involvement in the English curriculum over the past two decades is not encouraging. In English, at least, there is every danger that a national curriculum will have the very opposite of its intended effect, and that it will succeed only in enforcing principles and practices which its political proponents would be the first to repudiate, if they understood their basis and their implications. It need not be so, if politicians and committees keep strong in their common sense, distrustful of experts and chaste towards fashion. May God grant them sharpness of mind and firmness of resolve, for in the future of its language there lies the future of a nation!

Notes

1. *How Well Can 15 Year Olds Write?*, DES, Stanmore, 1983, sheet 11. The assessors give this piece of work 4 out of 7—the most common mark (gained by 27% of pupils). This survey was produced by the Assessment of Performance Unit, the activities of which are discussed in Chapter 4.

2. The survey was carried out by M. Preston of Garnett College: see the *Daily Telegraph*, 21 February 1987.

3. See the report of the Oxford University Delegacy of Local Examinations, published 3 April 1987, and *The Times,* 4 April 1987.

4. 'English Teaching and the Needs of People in Industry'—report of a working party of employers and teachers set up by the Essex County Council Education Department, in *English, Communication Studies . . . and the Needs of People in Industry,* Careers Research Advisory Centre, Cambridge, 1982, pp. 3–26, esp. p. 9.

5. A. Jamieson, 'Employers' Views of English Teaching and of English Skills required of Young People entering Employment', in *ibid.,* pp. 27–36, esp. p. 36.

6. M. Higham, 'English Communication Skills and Graduates in Industry' in *ibid.,* pp. 43–50, esp. p. 46.

7. *Ibid.,* p. 45.

8. Walton le Dale High School, Preston and Cranford Community School, Hounslow are two examples of schools where English is singled out for special praise (reports published in 1986). See also below, n. 28.

9. J. Dixon, *Growth through English—set in the perspective of the seventies,* NATE, Huddersfield 1975 (original edition 1967), p. 1.

10. *Ibid.,* pp. 12–13.

11. T. Evans, *Teaching English,* London 1982, p. 15.

12. D. Holbrook, 'Creativity in the English Programme' (1969), quoted in D. Allen, *English Teaching since 1965: How much Growth?,* London 1980, p. 18, cf. pp. 15–26.

13. J. Hardcastle, 'Classrooms as Sites for Cultural Making', *English in Education,* 19, 3 (1985), p. 9.

14. A. Stibbs, *Assessing Children's Language. Guidelines for Teachers,* NATE, London, 1979, p. 24.

15. *Ibid.,* pp. 25, 52.

16. G. Leech, M. Deuchar, R. Hogenraad, *English Grammar for Today: A New Introduction,* Houndmills and London 1982, p. 5.

17. R. A. Hudson, *Sociolinguistics,* Cambridge, 1980, p. 191.

18. P. Trudgill, *Sociolinguistics. An introduction to Language and Society,* Harmondsworth, 1974, p. 20.

19. V. Edwards, *Language in Multicultural Classrooms,* London, 1983, pp. 9–10.

20. When two groups of people who do not share a common language need to communicate, sometimes a 'pidgin' is invented—a highly simplified version of one of the group's languages. A creole is a pidgin which has come to be a mother-tongue. Many West Indians speak creoles (based on English), and immigrants to England from the West Indies often continue to use creole.

21. P. Trudgill, *Accent, Dialect and the School,* London 1975, pp. 18, 28.

22. *Ibid.,* p. 38.

23. D. Crystal, *Child language, learning and linguistics,* London 1976, p. 70.

24. Trudgill, op. cit., p. 83.

25. *A Language for Life, Report of the Committee of Inquiry appointed by the Secretary of State for Education and Science under the Chairmanship of Sir Alan Bullock F.B.A.*, HMSO, 1975, p. 50.

26. *Ibid.*, p. 143.

27. *Ibid.*, p. 166.

28. These comments are taken from the following HMI reports on individual schools (all published in 1986): Stanley Comprehensive, p. 12; Fernwood Comprehensive, p. 11; Stanley Comprehensive, p. 11; Allfarthing Primary, p. 6; Hall Green Comprehensive, p. 20; Hertfordshire and Essex High School, p. 11.

29. *English from 5 to 16*, HMSO, 1984, p. 3.

30. *Daily Express*, quoted in *English from 5 to 16. Second Edition (incorporating responses)*, HMSO, 1986, p. 27.

31. *Ibid.*, p. 17 (= unchanged text of first version).

32. *Ibid.*, pp. 16, 15 (= unchanged text of first version).

33. *Ibid.*, p. 36.

34. *Ibid.*, p. 43.

35. *Ibid.*, p. 44.

36. *Language Performance in Schools. Primary Survey Report No. 2*, HMSO, 1982, p. 101.

37. *Language Performance in Schools, Secondary Survey Report No [sic] 2*, HMSO, 1983, p. 62. (An exactly similar statement is made in Primary Survey Report No. 2, p. 97).

38. *How Well Can 15 Year Olds Write.*

39. *GCSE. The National Criteria. English*, HMSO, 1985, p. 1.

40. Cf. Hudson, op. cit., p. 228 (and his general discussion of linguistic and communicative incompetence: pp. 214–30).

41. 'The Logic of Nonstandard English' in W. Labov, *Language in the Inner City. Studies in the Black English Vernacular*, Oxford, 1977, pp. 201–240, esp. pp. 214–8. For discussion and criticism of Labov (from two very different points of view), see M. Stubbs, *Language and Literacy. The Sociolinguistics of Reading and Writing*, London, Boston, Henley, 1980, pp. 139–59 and J. Honey, *The Language Trap: race, class and the 'standard English' issue in British schools*, Kenton, 1983.

42. p. 11.

43. *GCSE. The National Criteria. English*, HMSO, 1985, p. 5.

44. Quoted in P. Scott, *Countdown to GCSE English*, Houndmills and London, 1986, p. 94.

45. *A Survey of the Teaching of 'A' Level English in 20 mixed Sixth Forms in comprehensive Schools*, Dept. of Education and Science, 1986, pp. 10, 20.

46. *Language Performance in Schools. Primary Survey Report No. 2*, p. 91.

47. *Teaching Poetry in the Secondary School. An HMI View*, HMSO, 1987, pp. 24, 18.

48. T. Evans, op. cit., pp. 108, 111.

49. See, for instance, *Teaching Poetry in the Secondary School*, Chapter 5: 'Finding a voice'.

50. Sample question from MEG, quoted in Scott, op. cit., p. 99.

51. *A Language for Life*, p. 125.

52. J. Pearce, *The Heart of English*, Oxford, 1985, pp. 27–8.

53. *Practical Criticism. A Study of Literary Judgement*, London, 1929.

54. See, for example, J. Keen, *Teaching English. A Linguistic Approach*, London, 1978 and M. Stubbs, op. cit.

Part Five

The Years of Privatisation

15

Healthy Competition: How to Improve the NHS

John Peet

Introduction

The National Health Service (NHS) is under attack, perhaps more than at any time since its foundation in 1948. Patients and would-be patients grumble about unresponsive doctors, long waiting lists, dingy hospitals and a lack of choice. Doctors, nurses and health authority managers carp at alleged government parsimony: they see their counterparts abroad or in private hospitals at home freely introducing new medical technology or procedures which the NHS cannot afford. More imaginative critics complain that little or no thought is given to reforming the bits of the NHS, like the family-doctor service or acute hospitals, that are crying out to be improved.

The Government and the new Secretary of State for Social Services, Mr John Moore, are studiously saying as little as possible: indeed, the Conservative manifesto for the June 1987 election omitted any ideas at all for changing the NHS. At the Department of Health and Social Security (DHSS), any proposals for reform that may have been conceived have long since disappeared into endless reviews—of primary care, resource allocation, community care and so on. Despair at the lack of initiative is even leading to some talk of another Royal Commission on the NHS, just eight years after the last—a well-known recipe for continued inactivity.

There is now also the glimmering of a fresh debate about alternative sources of finance for the NHS. This subject was last addressed by the DHSS and the Central Policy Review Staff (the think tank) before the 1983 election, only to be hurriedly dropped as being too sensitive when news of the study leaked out. And, although this time the revived debate looks like continuing outside government (for instance, both the Institute of Health Services Management and the King's Fund Institute have set up inquiries), it is probably safe to bet that no foreseeable administration will feel strong enough politically to incur the odium of discarding the two essential features of the NHS: that it is tax-financed and that it is virtually free at point of use. So the dilemma of limited public resources against unlimited demand, first identified by Mr Enoch Powell in the late 1950s, and expanded on by the British Medical Association's Ivor Jones committee in the late 1960s, will continue.

The present study is not concerned with the probably insoluble question of how to pay for the NHS. But three observations on the growing concern about whether the service has enough cash provide useful points of departure:

(i) The NHS is not alone in being publicly-financed and free to patients. Most western countries apart from the United States finance 80% or more of their health care from the public purse—and even America pays for nearly half its health care this way.[1] Similarly, it is rare in any country for patients to pay directly at point of use. What is different in Britain is that NHS finance comes from the exchequer: most others have some kind of compulsory insurance. This difference is partly responsible for Britain's relatively low spending on health care. International comparisons suggest that health spending correlates with relative prosperity—and that Britain spends about one percentage point less of its national income (in cash terms, around £3½ billion) on health care than countries of comparable prosperity.[2]

(ii) This should not necessarily translate into less health care for Britons. The relative cheapness of the NHS has two main causes: the important role of the general practitioner, or family doctor, as a gatekeeper whom patients must pass before they get to more expensive hospitals (only a tenth of patients actually go through the gate); and lower relative pay (doctors' incomes, for instance, are just 2½ times average earnings in Britain, compared with 3½ times in France and five times in America and West Germany).

(iii) What is peculiar to the NHS is its almost total lack of any incentives to greater efficiency. America, for instance, is adopting health-maintenance organisations which are a powerful force for economy and efficiency. France is experimenting with predetermined cash limits for individual surgical procedures to give hospitals an incentive to carry them out as cheaply as possible. But in Britain, the basic NHS structure, immune from competition and so tending inevitably to inefficiency, is unchallenged: which may partly explain why we have eight hospital beds for every 1,000 people to America's six, why British patients' average length of stay in hospital is 19 days compared with American patients' 10 days, and why the NHS employs over 80 nurses per 10,000 people against America's 50, France's 45 and West Germany's 35.

It is this last observation which provides the principal theme for the present study. Argument about spending (and, probably, about financing too) will always persist—almost certainly never to be resolved. But the pressing need to inject more forces for efficiency into the NHS is widely recognised. In one sense, the amount of cash available for the service may be taken as externally given—it will never be enough to meet all demands. What should not be taken as given is the way that cash is spent: how much health-care is bought with every pound.

How to get better value-for-money, and at the same time make the NHS more responsive to patient demands and needs? The bureaucrat's way is to commission endless audits and press for better management practices. That is how the DHSS's cost-improvement programme has worked. It has been well worth doing: but annual new savings have never risen above 1½% of hospital budgets, and they seem to be falling again. Worse, some of the so-called cost improvements have actually been no more than service cuts, as a National Audit Office study has shown.[3] And efficiency by circular is very slow—and probably not much use in overcoming the health service's appalling multitude of special-interest groups, almost all of them representative of producers not consumers.

Luckily, there is a much simpler and quicker way of increasing pressure within the health service for greater efficiency. It builds on the standard mechanism through which free markets deliver the most efficient outcome at the lowest cost: competition.

Some people believe that competition is not possible in a publicly-financed, charge-free system. Others consider it could be damaging, reducing standards of care or ignoring patient needs in favour of commercial considerations. Still others claim that there are too few alternative providers of services both within and outside the NHS to make greater competition feasible.

This study will demonstrate that all three groups of objectors to the notion of competition are wrong.[4] Competition of some sort has already been introduced in far more areas of the NHS than most people realise. The private health-care industry is growing fast: it is already equivalent, in England, to nearly two Regional Health Authorities—which means that in many places it can and does offer genuine competition. Later in the study, we describe some of the many examples of NHS services being put to tender, and of special contracts being made with private health-care groups. Where the private sector cannot or does not offer enough competition, it is perfectly possible for different providers within the NHS to compete with each other—and be rewarded where they are successful. Again, this model of internal competition is beginning to emerge in practice. As for commercialism threatening standards, no better way has yet been found of judging the extent to which they are met than through open competition—with loss of client or contract the result of not measuring up.

The next few chapters look at places within the NHS where competition, usually in the form of private-sector provision, has successfully been introduced; where there have been obstacles to it; and where there is more scope for it. A number of specific conclusions and recommendations for change flow from the analysis. These are summarised in an appendix.

Acute hospital services

Considering that the NHS is generally looked upon as a universal publicly-provided service, it is remarkable how many contractual arrangements it has with private providers. Many predate its foundation 40 years ago: for instance, Yorkshire and North Western Regional Health Authorities have always had contracts to buy health care for their patients from two different St John of God hospitals. Nor are contracts confined to the charitable sector: for years health (and local) authorities have had contracts with for-profit nursing homes.

The DHSS reckons that some 28,000 NHS patients in England were treated under contracts with private sector bodies in 1985; that around

130 institutions were involved; and that total spending on such contracts amounted to £40 million.[5] And this excludes patients, for example mentally-ill or elderly patients, whose fees at private homes are paid by local authority social services departments.

Types of contractual arrangement

There are three distinct kinds of contractual arrangement which a health authority might enter into with a private supplier:

(i) One-off contracts, for example to carry out a certain number of operations or provide treatments within a budget based on whatever amount of spare cash the authority has available;

(ii) Longer-term contracts, either to care for a particular group of patients (for instance, long-stay geriatric patients) or to provide a specific service (for instance, cervical cytology screening); and

(iii) More substantive long-term arrangements, for example to provide acute services for all patients in a particular area; or to build and operate a district general hospital.

There is some blurring at the edges, for example between (ii) and (iii)—when does a contract to care for a specific group of patients turn into an unlimited contract to provide the care for anyone in the area?—but it is useful to distinguish between the three different types of contract because it helps expose the philosophy behind them.

There has been a burgeoning of contractual deals of the first kind in recent years. Portsmouth health authority, for instance, has more than once bought hip-replacement operations from the King Edward VII hospital at Midhurst. Several other authorities have done the same. In London, Bart's carried out 180 tonsillectomy operations over Easter 1987 from the independent Princess Grace hospital. In Manchester, the health authority has bought 50 urology procedures from the private Alexandra hospital. The waiting-list initiative announced by Mr Norman Fowler, then social services secretary, in February 1987, gave a fillip to these arrangements. Its injections of £25 million in each of 1986–87 and 1987–88 to be used for specific projects aimed at waiting lists provided a good opportunity for contract work.

One or two longer-term deals in the acute sector have also emerged. Some have involved specific pieces of expensive equipment, or costly types of treatment. One example is the lithotripter (a machine which breaks up kidney stones without the need for invasive surgery) at St

Thomas's—one of only three in use in the country—which was bought jointly in 1984 by the health authority and BUPA, and is operated by both. More recently, Bloomsbury health authority has contracted with a private magnetic-resonance imaging centre in Mary-lebone Road to provide MRI as a diagnostic facility for its NHS patients.

Some health authorities have gone to the private sector for help over specific problems. For example, Blackpool health authority used the Fylde Coast hospital run by the Hospital Corporation of America for much of 1986 when it suffered an outbreak of tetanus in its own operating theatres. The authority had previously sent patients to Fylde Coast on an *ad hoc* basis.

A different type of contractual arrangement is seen in the *in vitro* fertilisation unit at Bart's. This was always paid for partly by charitable donations. When it became clear recently that finance was getting tight, Bart's entered into an agreement with the Portland private hospital. The Portland now pays some of the salaries of those operating the unit: its use is shared between their private patients and Bart's NHS patients.

Few of these deals could be said to fall into the third category above—long-term arrangements lasting ten or twenty years. One reason for this is political uncertainty. An independent hospital group is bound to be chary of investing in facilities to sell to the NHS if its contract could suddenly be terminated for political reasons. Yet the older NHS arrangements with charitable hospitals have usually been of this third, long-term kind. For example, Northallerton health authority for many years contracted out to the hospital of St John of God at Scorton the provision of acute services for its patients. Generally, health authorities have not seen these as permanent arrangements: it has rather been a question of temporary expedient pending their own construction of acute hospital facilities. At Scorton, the health authority today contracts only for the provision of psychiatric beds—it now has enough acute facilities of its own.

Some general conclusions can be drawn from this brief but representative list of the different kinds of contract which the NHS has made with private sector groups.

First, it is clear that there is considerable private-sector provision which could be used by the NHS—and, though it has tended to be geographically concentrated in the South-East, it is now spreading to all parts of the country. Work commissioned by the Nuffield Provincial Hospitals Group in 1986 confirms this.[6] Overall, some 6–7% of all acute hospital treatment in England and Wales is now carried out by the private sector (this excludes NHS paybeds). For some cold-surgery treatments, such as hip replacements or varicose vein removal, nearly a quarter of all operations are performed either in private hospitals or in NHS paybeds.

Second, NHS authorities can get a good bargain if they shop around for operations and treatments at the right time. They will often be able to negotiate payment of only the marginal costs of the care, saving on any charges for capital and fixed overheads. They can take advantage of seasonal patterns in demand for private treatment (for instance, there is less demand at weekends or during holiday periods). Indeed, this means that sometimes health authorities may find they can buy in operations for less than it costs to carry them out in their own hospitals.

Third, despite the potential cost advantage, many health authorities are not taking the initiative to explore possible deals with the private sector. The experience of BUPA, the largest independent group, is that private hospitals usually approach health authorities, not the other way round. Moreover, with some exceptions, NHS general managers and health authority members have shown little imagination or willingness to consider unusual solutions to the unmet need of their populations for health-care. Sometimes, they are politically hostile to any involvement between themselves and the private sector: an extraordinary position to take up over services, since the NHS has always (quite uncontroversially) bought most of its goods like drugs, surgical dressings and bandages from private producers. Why should services be any different?

Fourth, even where political hostility can be overcome, the risk of future political interference in a long-term contract could deter private sector groups. If this is a genuine barrier to freer competition and to the achievement of maximum output in terms of patient care from the NHS's limited inputs of cash, it would be sensible to explore ways of getting round it—for instance, allowing health authorities to enter into contracts with penalty clauses for any political decision to break them (this is similar to the sort of contract which both the French and British Governments signed with the Channel Tunnel Group).

Lastly, a prime reason for both hostility towards and misunderstanding about competitive contracting-out is that there are serious difficulties over comparing costs. NHS authorities and hospitals are accustomed to regarding capital as 'free'; so they tend to leave it out of cost estimates. No proper system of capital-asset accounting with depreciation is in use to help determine true long-term costs, though the NHS has talked for some years about the desirability of bringing one in. Even worse, NHS hospitals often do not properly allocate out common service costs. The result is that it can be virtually impossible to compare prices quoted by private groups for hospital treatments with equivalent costs in the NHS.

Internal competition

No doubt there will always be many places where it proves impossible (or where authorities refuse) even to consider contracting out treatments to the private sector. But this need not mean abandoning the idea of competition altogether. NHS hospitals and authorities could easily buy and sell excess capacity from each other: a sort of 'internal' market within the NHS. This idea is often associated with Alain Enthoven, who put it forward in a 1985 study of the health service.[7] But experimenting with it has not really started, despite some powerful advocacy.

One reason for this is, yet again, inadequacies in cost information. Just as for contracting out, it is hard for hospitals to compete against each other if they do not know how much their services cost to provide. A second problem concerns DHSS's resource allocation mechanism, which does not allow for direct cross-charging and movement of cash between regional health authorities. There is some attempt to compensate for cross-boundary flows, but it is crude and works two years in arrears. So a region or district which attracts more patients than its neighbour can, under present rules, find itself losing money. Some teaching hospitals in London have tried to put in place *ad hoc* arrangements to get round this—for instance, Guy's hospital charges other districts within the South East Thames region for cardiac services. An opposite approach has been taken by Bart's: because of inadequate compensation for cross-boundary flows, it has tried to stop doctors referring patients from outside its own district.

Another problem faces the internal market. How can affairs be arranged so that GPs have an incentive to see that their patients are cared for with economic efficiency after they have left their surgery, and arrived at the consultant or hospital to which they have been referred? This is largely uncharted territory. But a start might be made by encouraging GP's to refer to hospitals rather than to individual consultants, and allowing the hospital then to deliver the service to the patient in a competitive way. It would be even better if GPs were given fuller information about the competitive possibilities of different treatments, so that they could interest themselves in how acute care was financed for their patients. As Enthoven himself noted, the best way to see how an internal market might work would be to experiment with it, perhaps in one region with all its districts.

To sum up so far, competition and contracting out in the acute hospital sector have barely started to contribute towards a more efficient NHS. One excellent example of what could be achieved with a little imagination is the story of renal dialysis facilities in Wales.

In 1984, the Welsh Office (which acts effectively as an English health region) belatedly woke up to the inadequacy of renal dialysis in the principality. It decided on a novel approach: to put to tender the construction and operation of two new renal dialysis centres for patients with kidney failure, one in Bangor and one in Carmarthen. The contract was to take the form of estimates for dialysis per patient: a model which drew on United States experience, where renal dialysis costs had been reduced substantially. The contracts were won by two private firms, Community Psychiatric Centres and Travenol, both of whom quoted around £80 per patient against in-house tenders of nearer £120. The CPC centre was commissioned in April 1985, and was operational within six months (one can readily imagine the length of time it would have taken the NHS!).

The savings which CPC and Travenol were able to make arose from four main sources. First, the centres make more efficient use of nurses and other staff, with flexible shift patterns. Usually, staff work three 11-hour shifts a week, which enable more patients to be treated per machine than would be the case with normal 8-hour shifts. Second, nurses also carry out basic technical work, obviating the need to employ expensive full-time technicians. Third, housekeeping and maintenance of the machines are themselves contracted out to third parties. And fourth, the centres re-use dialysers (as happens in most other countries, but not in the NHS). The result is a cheaper service, able to cope with more patients. Every kidney patient in Wales, and every taxpayer too, has benefited from the experiment. Tony Favell MP was so impressed that he introduced a bill into the House of Commons in October 1986 to force all health authorities to put their renal dialysis facilities out to tender. The Government did not adopt this idea.

Hospital support services

To contract out renal dialysis is not, in essence, different to contracting out ancillary hospital services—such as cleaning, catering and laundry—where Mrs Thatcher's Government has, indeed, tried to apply to the NHS the full rigours of competitive market forces (as it is now, belatedly, trying to do for local authorities, too).

The idea of putting support services out to tender was not new to the NHS. But it was only in 1983 that the Government belatedly issued a circular requiring all health authorities to 'test the market' for such services.[8] Interestingly, while the circular made it mandatory for authorities to put out contracts for cleaning, catering and laundries to tender, it also invited them to consider all their other activities for similar treatment.

The first round of competitive tendering in England is now more or less complete (both Scotland and Wales have been much slower). 80% of all services had gone out to tender by the end of June 1987. Annual savings are estimated by DHSS to be a shade under £100 million. Some of the obstacles in the way of private-sector contracting have gone: for instance, VAT which was not chargeable on in-house services can now also be reclaimed on those bought from outside. The rules were further clarified in a circular letter from the NHS Management Board chairman, Mr Victor Paige, in January 1986, in response to pressure from trade associations who reckoned they were not being allowed to compete fairly.

Despite this, a rising proportion of tenders have been won by in-house groups. Of 1,250 contracts so far awarded, 1,050 have gone in-house and only 200 to private groups. Almost all the most recent contracts have gone to in-house groups. This partly reflects a learning curve: the in-house teams are getting better at putting together tenders. Sometimes too few private groups have been interested in or able to offer an alternative service. But even where the service has stayed in-house, appreciable savings have been made. Most NHS managers and authorities agree that competitive tendering has imported much tighter discipline into what had been a thoroughly ramshackle and inefficient area of work.

As with acute hospital services, there have been accounting and costing problems over competitive tendering for support services. The failure to cost out capital properly (a problem which arises notably with kitchens and laundries) has already been mentioned.

There is also the treatment of redundancy costs. In economic terms, the costs of redundancy should not be included in any assessment of tenders: they are one-off transfer payments, which do not affect the long-term need to get the most efficient use out of the money spent on ancillary services. Yet they have to be paid out of health authority budgets. The Government has said that they should be spread over the life of the contract, not 'charged' against the first year alone. But this still means they can influence the decision over the contract. It would be better if redundancy costs were taken out of the comparisons altogether, perhaps by being met centrally.

The objective of such changes would not be to give outside tenderers any advantage, but rather to put the competing service-providers on an equal footing. In time, a periodic change of contractor should come to seem as natural to a health authority as a change of grocer does to a housewife. Better value for money would result.

Benefits of competitive tendering

There are many good examples of the benefits of competitive tendering for support services. Take Mediclean, one of the biggest hospital-cleaning groups in Britain. It has started, with some health authorities, to discuss the possibility of taking on all 'hotel' services—adding things like portering to the usual three support services. At the St Helier hospital in Merton and Sutton, Mediclean does the cleaning, portering and message-delivering. It has saved around 50% compared with previous costs. At the Bristol Royal Infirmary, Mediclean does the food-handling and meal delivery while the hospital itself does the cooking.

The NHS could be more imaginative still if it looked across the Atlantic. In Britain, competitive tendering has often revolved around wages and conditions for staff: those who pay least get the contract. Little stress has been placed on what could be the more important task: staff management.

In America, the largest single hospital-cleaning group is Servicemaster, with roughly 60% of the market. There, it has to clean to a far higher standard than is generally demanded by the NHS. In association with the Shanning group, it has since established itself in the private sector in Britain.

The interesting thing about Servicemaster is that it seldom brings in its own staff. Instead, it takes on existing hospital staff and retrains them—so laying more emphasis on savings through better management and, incidentally, solving the redundancy cost problem. In the United States, it is quite usual for the same staff to stay at a hospital for many years—but with new management each time contracts come up for renewal. This approach has not been tried in the NHS, partly because of the costings/capital problem, but partly also because health authorities are unwilling to contemplate the idea of outside companies coming in and taking on existing NHS staff, which seems to them (correctly) to be a challenge to their own management ability. There is a case for claiming that the NHS has contracted out the wrong bit of ancillary services: the workers not the managers.

But it is the fields other than ancillary services which now offer the greatest opportunities and rewards for competitive tendering. Health authorities and hospitals have pathology laboratories, cervical-cytology screening centres, pharmacies, radiology and radiography departments. Outside the medical field, they employ architects, lawyers, quantity surveyors. Any one of these could easily be made the subject of periodic competition. Yet few have been.

Once again, the NHS should copy from the private secctor. Many private hospitals do not find it cost-effective to run their own pathology laboratories, for instance. They contract with specialist companies like Federal Express or the Jean Shanks Pathology Services group. The Nuffield Provincial Hospitals Trust survey indeed found many private hospitals which used NHS pathology and radiology services. In Portsmouth, the NHS hospital has won the contract to supply the local BUPA hospital with drugs. At a time when the NHS has difficulty recruiting pharmacists, pathologists, radiographers etc, the merits of putting such services out to tender should be doubly obvious.

Nor need this always mean creeping privatisation. In many instances, an NHS hospital or health authority may be the best and most efficient supplier of the service. If it were not, why would so many private hospitals already use them? In a competitive world, it would be quite possible for one or more NHS hospitals to emerge as the best places for pathology, radiology or pharmacy services. This, too, would follow American experience. There, the idea of every hospital having its own pathology laboratory would be laughed out of court. It is cheaper and quicker to send samples for testing to one single specialised centre, which will often handle testing for many hospitals at once—thereby getting economies of scale and building up expertise.

The NHS needs to dismiss the idea that all hospitals and health authorities must be able to provide all facilities themselves. Competition would help to find out what is the most economical and efficient means of providing all these services—and so give patients faster and better health care for their money.

Community care

In many ways, the most obvious place to start the search for more competition between public and private sector providers is in the 'community care' services—the care for and treatment of mentally ill, mentally and physically handicapped and elderly people. There are three reasons for this. First, these are the services which historically have given us the best examples of provision by the private sector but finance from the public. Indeed, in the field of residential care for the elderly, the public sector never ousted the private sector after the creation of the NHS in 1948 in the way it did in most other areas of care—the two have always existed side-by-side. This probably reflects the ability of the private sector to provide a highly cost-effective service. It may also reflect the fact that elderly people in particular have always been able to afford residential care by running down assets accumulated over their working lives, so obviating the need for them to become a burden on tax or ratepayers.

The second reason is that the community care services have always been among the most neglected parts of the NHS. This is well illustrated by the generic term most commonly used for such services: the 'Cinderella' services. In the past decade, successive governments have commendably tried to make the NHS switch resources towards these groups—now officially known as the 'priority' groups. But hospital doctors have never been happy to lose resources from the acute sector; so the Cinderella services have continued to merit their soubriquet. The result of this neglect has not, ironically, been to the advantage of acute hospital services; for a major reason of bed shortages in NHS hospitals is that too many are occupied too long by geriatric patients who might be better cared for outside hospital.

The third justification for re-examining the scope for competition in this sector is of more recent origin. For all three client groups, the trend of the last twenty years has been to move away from care in big institutions towards so-called care in the community. This has not always proved successful, as last year's Audit Commission report vividly showed;[9] now the whole policy is under review by a team led by Sir Roy Griffiths, the DHSS's all-purpose inquirer. One consequence of community care has, however, been a very rapid growth in the claiming of social-security board-and-lodging payments to meet the cost of staying in smaller institutions. The Audit Commission has estimated that these payments—which are a clear example of public finance for a privately-provided service—rose from around £200 million in 1984–85 to £500 million last year.

There are many privately-run nursing homes which are partly or wholly occupied by publicly-financed patients. Some are good, others are not: but it is generally agreed that they are no worse than state-run counterparts. In fact, the most scandalously-run nursing and residential homes for the elderly have often been in the public sector—witness the recent major scandal at a local authority nursing home in Southwark.

All homes in either public or private sector are subject to inspections by public authorities. But several recent studies have shown widely different standards applied between authorities: homes may be more closely examined in one part of the country than in another. More seriously, it has often been the case that publicly-run homes have got away with lower standards than privately-run ones—there are obvious difficulties in the provider inspecting his own premises. (It was notable that, until the recent partial lifting of Crown immunity, NHS hospitals were able to maintain kitchens in a state which would have been condemned in a private hospital).

Co-existence of public and private sectors

The existence of public and private sectors in competition with each other should in the long run be beneficial to both patient and tax and ratepayer. One example of cost-effective provision of care by private sector groups to NHS patients is provided by St Andrew's hospital in Northampton, a charitable institution, which has a contract with the local health authority to care for its psychiatric patients. This is partly because the authority has no facilities, and no plans to construct them. But it is partly also because cost comparisons have shown that St Andrew's can provide the service more economically than equivalent public sector organisations.

In a similar way, a number of health authorities and local authority social services departments contract out the provision of treatment for severely disturbed patients to three psychiatric centres run by American Medical International (AMI), at Kneesworth, Langton and Grafton. Nearly all the patients at these three institutions are publicly-financed. Sometimes, there are contracts to take all severely disturbed patients in a particular authority; on other occasions prices are negotiated case-by-case. What is remarkable about the AMI centres is that they have consistently been shown to be cheaper than the government's own youth treatment centres. There are some grounds for believing that the private sector could make a better job of running the psychiatric prisons at Broadmoor, Park Lane and Rampton too. They should be given the chance to bid.

As so often, there have been grumbles about what some see as the privatisation of NHS psychiatric services. Some have suggested that standards are lower—which should raise hollow laughs from those who remember the innumerable scandals in publicly run psychiatric detention centres since the War. In any case, as with nursing homes, public authorities are charged with the monitoring and regulation of all private-sector bodies.

Another example of private sector involvement in the Cinderella services is in Northallerton. There, the local health authority noted that there were not enough residential-care places for the elderly population. Rather than invest scarce capital in a publicly-financed home, they decided to set up a charitable trust to construct and finance a new home, whose patients will mostly be paid for through the public purse. This first venture of its kind could be a very effective way of attracting extra finance into the NHS, as well as ensuring efficient service delivery.

Whatever conclusions the Griffiths inquiry comes to, it will probably recognise that, though it arose partly by accident, the growth in social-security financed private provision for the elderly, mentally ill and handicapped should be maintained. Indeed, it could be a useful precedent for other parts of the NHS. Properly regulated, such institutions can provide excellent and cheap care to their clients; and in addition give them an element of choice denied them in the old state-run institutions. It could also provide the basis for more experimentation with different ways of looking after community-care groups. For example, so-called social health maintenance organisations (HMOs), which would offer care for the elderly at flat-rate fees, might be a cheaper, more effective and more humane alternative to geriatric care in district general hospitals.

Primary care

In one sense, the primary care sector was the least affected by the advent of the NHS. The mainstay general practitioners (family doctors) even continued to be self-employed—though they must be one of the few self-employed groups in the world who also receive a non-contributory inflation-proofed pension, payable whether they actually retire or not. Since most of the providers are self-employed small businessmen, primary care ought to be tailor-made for competition between them to the benefit of both patients and taxpayers.

Sadly, competition is seldom found in primary care. Except for the requirement of approval from the local medical practices committee (a formality except in the few 'over-doctored' areas), qualified GPs are entitled to a contract with local family practitioner committees (FPCs) irrespective of their merits. And since around half their income is guaranteed whether or not any patients join their lists, they do not even have to make much effort to attract patients by offering a better service than their fellows. Dissatisfied patients have always found it hard to change GPs in practice, however simple it seems in theory. Nor can they anyway find out much about other GPs since advertising is banned by the General Medical Council.

It was partly because there was general dissatisfaction with British primary care services that the Government initiated a review of them in early 1986.[10] Ministers and officials were also conscious—though the British Medical Association will hardly admit to it—that Britain's primary care service was not doing a good job by international standards. For instance, British rates of heart disease, breast cancer and cervical cancer—the incidence of which a well-run primary care service should bring down—are among the worst in the industrialised world. Not that there is much hope of the Government's review leading to radical changes which might improve matters: some of the more radical ideas were excised from the consultative document even before publication, and those that remained have been resolutely opposed by the medical profession. But since the review is not yet concluded, it might be unfair and cynical to denounce its results too quickly.

Competitive primary care

One of the few places where private sector providers of primary care have entered the market in competition with each other is in the provision of deputising services. GPs seldom wish to be on call all the time; so they like to have deputies to cover for them at night or over weekends. Such services are usually provided by private companies, the biggest of which is Aircall, with perhaps 60% of the market. Aircall employs 9,000 general practitioners and doctors on 6 or 12 month contracts at 30 different centres around the country. It contracts either direct with individual practitioners, or with local family practitioner committees, to provide a full deputising service including home visits. Aircall has also moved into other areas of staffing: for instance, it provides hospital locums and pharmacists where hospitals cannot find the people they need themselves.

The reason Aircall and other companies have succeeded in the deputising field is that they have shown themselves capable of providing an efficient and cheap service. Here, perhaps, is a model for primary care in general. Neither Aircall nor any other private company has yet gone so far as to contract with a family practitioner committee to provide GP services in general—though this option, like that of salaried GPs which has been tried, could be one solution to the virtual breakdown of GP services in some inner cities. Indeed, the principle of competitive tendering could be extended to the right to a contract to practise as a general practitioner. If FPCs were to award fixed-term franchises to doctors, that would enable them periodically to check on customer satisfaction, levels of service offered and other factors like hospital referral rates or quantities of drugs prescribed.

The same idea could easily be applied to other primary care services. Dentists, pharmacists and opticians already have to compete harder for customers than doctors do. But only opticians are subjected to the full rigour of the market place, since the Government deregulated their market in 1982–83. Now consumers can buy spectacles wherever they want: opticians have to compete on price and quality to attract them. Those on low incomes who still get help from the taxpayer now receive it in the form of exchangeable vouchers—usually seen as a dirty word in the NHS!—so that they can use their state-provided assistance to best effect, by shopping around for spectacles they like. Here is a practical example which demonstrates that market choice can co-exist with a state-financed service.

Pharmacists, on the other hand, are partly insulated from competition by their new contract with the Government, which came into force in April 1987; this stops rival pharmacies setting up to dispense NHS drugs unless the local FPC reckons there is a need for more services in the area. The object of the new contract was to stop hundreds of high-street chemists proliferating at the partial expense of the taxpayer. But it needs to be supplemented by getting pharmacists periodically to tender against one another for the right to an existing NHS contract. That would ensure that only the most efficient and economical pharmacists got the business. Regular tendering would also make the job of regulating them and assessing quality of service easier. Something similar could be done for dentists.

Opening up primary care services to competition might well be seen by many GPs as giving them an opportunity, rather than threatening their very existence. At the moment, they are constrained in the services they can offer by General Medical Council rules and by the terms of their contracts with FPCs. So enterprising GPs have not had the chance to develop services which their patients might like. For instance, they are unable to charge for private check-ups; nor can they offer them on the NHS unless they have reason to suppose that a patient needs one. So people who want periodic check-ups have been driven to private clinics. Similarly, GPs under present arrangements get little or no encouragement to offer X-rays, cervical-cytology, breast cancer screening or even minor operations, all of which might be more cheaply done outside big hospitals. Nor is there much incentive for GPs to engage in preventive work: indeed, for dentists, the payment system actually discourages this because it ties remuneration so closely to repair work instead of prevention.

One facility which patients might well like to see in the NHS is a modified version of the American health-maintenance organisation. Aircall financed the only British experiment on these lines: the Harrow Health Care Centre, under the medical direction of Dr Michael Goldsmith. Harrow (which now belongs to the AMI hospital group) offered one-stop health care including X-rays, prescriptions (using generic drugs) dispensed on the premises and check-ups to its customers, for little more than the equivalent of the NHS capitation fee which automatically goes to GPs. In a competitive world where GPs or groups of GPs had to tender for the right to an NHS contract, other experiments like Harrow might well evolve—and make NHS primary care services more efficient, more cost-effective and more responsive to patients' needs.

Hospital building

One area in the NHS which could benefit enormously from greater private sector involvement is hospital-building. In a sense, most of it is already done by private firms: the actual building work is usually let out to tender in much the same way as in any large-scale building project. But design specification, management, surveying and architectural work are usually done in-house. The result can be excellent; but all too often NHS hospitals are subject to time and cost overruns, design errors and construction faults. Recent examples include the University Hospital of Wales at Cardiff, which suffered from mosaic cladding detachment and other structural faults; Wonford hospital near Exeter which has severe concrete cancer and is having to be replaced at a cost of £56 million; and the new cardiac wing at Great Ormond Street hospital which had to be repaired at a cost of £13 million even before it opened.

Nor have management contracts, with which the NHS has experimented, proved very good at delivering projects to time and to budget. The Blood Products Laboratory at Elstree, which was constructed under a management contract, was well over budget and also over time—largely because the responsible health authority kept changing the specifications for the design.

There is considerable evidence that private sector groups design, build and equip hospitals both more quickly and more cheaply than does the NHS. For instance, time is generally a key factor in keeping costs down: both AMI and BUPA reckon to be able to complete the whole process from initial design to opening inside two years. NHS projects at best take two or three times longer. Part of the reason for this is that private hospitals generate revenue as soon as they are opened, creating an incentive to early completion. NHS hospitals, though, absorb health authority revenue if they are opened too fast— because it might mean that they treat more patients more quickly. This curiosity of health authority budgeting has the perverse effect of providing an incentive not to treat patients. Competition and cross-charging between authorities might help redress this.

A further feature of private sector hospital construction is that the commissioning company usually 'freezes' the design at an early stage. No doubt this may sometimes prevent them adopting new developments: but it has overwhelming cost advantages, which the NHS all too often denies itself.

Could the NHS entrust chunks of its capital programme to the private sector? Certainly some companies active in hospital-building would be keen to try. For instance, both AMI and BUPA have—so far unsuccessfully—explored the possibilities with a number of health authorities. Similarly, the Shanning group has acquired international expertise in turnkey hospital projects—often going on (as both BUPA and AMI could do) to run the hospitals themselves. There are, however, very few examples so far where private sector groups have broken into the NHS field. One such recent effort foundered on political hostility: a bid by Community Psychiatric Centres to design, build and operate a complete psychiatric facility in the central Birmingham district. The CPC bid met the required specifications in a much smaller area and at much lower cost than the project proposed by the West Midlands regional health authority: in one early version of the project, the difference in cost was £8m (CPC) and £32m (region). Central Birmingham's general manager, Brigadier Freddie Lucas, resigned partly because his authority would not—for political reasons—consider the CPC bid.

This unfortunate case points the way towards a possible model for NHS capital projects. Having decided what they need, health districts could seek a quote from their regional health authorities for the designing and building work; and seek similar quotes from interested private sector groups. They should also make a practice of considering whether the identified need might be met more economically at existing or at proposed private hospitals. Competition between different project managers would enable them to get better value-for-money for their capital investment. To make this work, districts would have to be given their own capital budgets and made to account for them: but that is urgently needed anyway, so as to be able to estimate accurately health authority treatment and operation costs.

Another possibility would cover the financing of hospital-building. At the moment, many worthwhile projects are deferred for lack of capital. Now that the Government has approved the use of private finance both for the planned Dartford bridge and for housing associations, perhaps it might also do so for NHS hospitals—in the interests of better patient care and, conceivably, lower hospital running costs.

Management

From its beginning, the NHS has suffered from inadequate management. This was recognised by the 1982 Griffiths report,[11] which recommended the appointment of general managers at region, district and unit level, together with an NHS management board at the centre. The Griffiths report emphasised that many of the problems of managing the NHS were similar in nature to those faced in big private-sector organisations: the fact that the NHS was seeking simply to deliver a service, not to make a profit, made much less difference to the daily management task than was popularly supposed.

The introduction of general management was a welcome step forward; as are the current efforts to improve NHS information-gathering and the experiments in clinical-budgeting (now renamed resource management). Managers on short-term contracts with performance-related pay should help considerably to improve the NHS's dismal combination of over-administration and under-management. Yet too often the Griffiths general managers have simply been previous district and regional administrators under a different name. And the NHS's very low rates of pay for the management of relatively large organisations have not helped to attract enough outside candidates of the quality needed (indeed, it is a miracle how good many NHS managers are, given the pay!).

One way through this difficulty would be to experiment with competition for the right to manage a hospital or a health authority. Groups like BUPA and AMI could be invited to apply their own management skills to the NHS. Of course, they might not be willing to take this on without being given control over the terms and conditions of service (including pay) of doctors, nurses and other NHS employees; but more flexibility in these (particularly local flexibility to respond to local market needs) is thoroughly desirable at all levels of the NHS in any case.

The Government has flirted with the idea of contracting out the management of hospitals several times. In 1985, the Prime Minister told the House of Commons that there would be no objection in principle to the award of a management contract to private firms—an announcement that led to vociferous scare stories that the Government was planning the 'Americanisation' of the NHS. But no health authority has yet had the courage to go down this road.

An example of how it might work is provided by pay beds. The retention within the NHS of private pay beds is an anachronism, principally intended to satisfy those consultants who find it convenient to treat NHS and private patients in the same hospital. Attempts by the last Labour Government to scrap pay beds were fiercely and successfully resisted by the doctors. To see how anomalous they are, one need only imagine a similar system applied in schools, with state teachers able to take time off to instruct independent sector pupils in the same school building. Nevertheless, pay beds are here to stay—unless and until private hospitals drive them out of business.

And that is the key. Pay beds are one of the few parts of the NHS which unreservedly have to compete. For instance, the pay beds at Guy's have to compete with the neighbouring London Bridge hospital. Understandably, Guy's have decided that this is a good opportunity to see what aggressive management might achieve. They have let out to Hospital Capital Corporation of America a contract to revamp and operate their private paybed wing. The Government, too, has done its bit, by decentralising the task of setting paybed charges (previously, and scandalously, NHS paybeds actually operated at a loss overall). Now health authorities are free to compete and even to make a profit out of doing so. Yet few have been as brave as Guy's. For instance, Oxfordshire district health authority actively considered letting out a contract to AMI or BUPA to construct and operate on the authority's behalf a private patient wing at the John Radcliffe hospital. Political opposition put paid to the idea.

One of the points which the Guy's deal brought out was that it can be statutorily difficult for NHS authorities to make a profit out of any of their activities, including pay beds—because of the terms of the NHS Act 1977. Guy's has got away with it largely because it has special trustees: its ownership is not vested in the Secretary of State. Most other hospitals would be constrained by the terms of the Act not to make profits. This might affect other ideas like commercial exploitation of catering facilities or letting off space to private shops. Clearly, it would be sensible to change the law if it is stopping the new managers exploiting the opportunities which exist to bring in some extra cash to the NHS.

One recent instance which health authorities everywhere might like to copy was provided by Bart's. Its proximity to the City and the worry which many City firms have about the well-being of their expensive employees gave the local district manager the idea of setting up screening and check-up facilities which he could offer to City firms—and which could make a tidy profit for the hospital. As with Guy's, one reason Bart's could get away with this was that it had special trustees.

A significant gesture to encourage managers to go out into the market and compete would be a change in the financing of health authorities. At the moment, the Treasury is keen to apply the usual rigorous public sector rules of annual budgets, no keeping of cash balances and no carry-over facilities. There are good reasons for this caution with taxpayers' money. But, as the Nuffield Provincial Hospitals Trust study last year demonstrated convincingly, the rules can severely curtail health authority managers' ability to compete with the private sector (and with each other). Any such rules which can be shown to be inimical to fair competition should be scrapped. The ultimate objective should, as always, be completely free and open competition between both public and private providers of health care.

Commercial opportunities

The Nuffield study recommended a number of other management changes: appointment of commercial managers to develop NHS revenue-raising activities, separating out the running of pay beds from other activities, encouragement of local management flexibility (though it did not quite get to the logical conclusion of devolving responsibility for pay and conditions of service). These changes should be introduced. The result would be a transformed atmosphere at district health authority level: instead of reacting to cash pressures by closing wards and cancelling operations, managers would develop their own revenue-raising capability.

It is easy to think of examples of what might be done. In 1985, the management consultants Touche Ross prepared a study for Central Manchester health authority. This suggested florists' shops, commercial catering, selling refreshments or books and newspapers to people in waiting rooms, and setting up spectacle shops. An analogy could be drawn with airport lounges, which used to offer few services. Now they are thronging with shops and cafes eager to exploit a captive audience. Why should the NHS not follow suit?

Grounds are another area which might be looked at, especially in some older hospitals: it may not be too hare-brained to imagine children's amusement areas or even miniature golf-courses near some hospitals. And hospitals could exploit their renown: Addenbrooke's, for instance, or the big London teaching hospitals, could issue franchises for other health-care operators who might wish to be associated with one of Britain's better-known health names to set up next to them. The amount of money in question should not be exaggerated: probably less than 1% of turnover. But even this could be a very useful supplement to tight budgets. And it would encourage the spirit of enterprise.

If all these commercial possibilities were exploited, there could even be a danger that too red-blooded an NHS would start driving private sector hospitals out of business. Superficially, that may seem like the rough justice one expects in the market place: those who wish to live by the creed must also be prepared to die by it. But the NHS is in a peculiarly strong position: it has a monopoly on some services like accident & emergency departments, and a near-monopoly elsewhere. An analogy could be drawn with British Telecom and its small rival, Mercury Communications. There, the Government's licence gives Mercury a certain amount of extra protection from BT which it might not get in a free market. That is because, in the long term, both the consumer and BT itself will benefit from the existence of competitors in telecommunications.

This may suggest the need for some protection of the private sector if the consumer is to get all the benefits of competition in health-care delivery. But there is also one area where the public sector NHS needs some protection. This is in the training and educating of staff. At the moment, the private sector makes no contribution to the massive costs of medical and nursing education and training; it relies on the NHS, and then poaches its highly-trained staff. This may be tolerable so long as the private sector is small. But it could mean unfair competition, for instance against the big NHS postgraduate teaching hospitals, whose higher costs within the NHS are recognised in the resource allocation process by special 'service increment for teaching' (SIFT) payments.

To get round this unfairness, some way needs to be found of charging the private sector for the costs of training its staff. One possibility would be to ask private hospitals to make some contribution to SIFT in proportion to their own staffing. Another would be to make them reimburse training costs to the NHS each time they 'poached' NHS staff. Or the staff themselves could be required to pay back the costs of training when they moved into the private sector. The object, whatever arrangement is adopted, would be to put public and private sectors on an equal footing—so as to encourage fair competition.

General conclusions

Few would deny that, as a principle of economic theory, competition in the market place is the best way to allocate resources, to see that customers get what they want and to ensure that providers do not assume a dominant position. Yet the principle is seldom applied to health care (or, indeed, to other public services). Indeed, many belive it cannot be applied, both because consumers are not paying for services, and because there are not enough providers within the system to make a market—there is insufficient spare capacity.

This pamphlet has tried to show that despite these drawbacks (which are anyway exaggerated), competition is possible and desirable in the NHS. It would be based on two simple ideas:

(i) an extension of competitive tendering, to cover not just support services as now but the provision of surgery facilities, primary care services, hospital building and so on. Another way of expressing the same concept is to see health authorities as franchisers: different groups could bid to be awarded the franchise to provide health care facilities for local populations. No part of the NHS should be immune from competition in one form or another.

(ii) quite a lot of competition could be provided by existing private sector groups. And others would no doubt spring up in response. But there is equally no reason why NHS hospitals and authorities should not compete with each other—indeed, an 'internal' market would be an essential component of competition since the NHS is the dominant health-care organisation in the market.

The analysis has shown that there are several specific changes which need to be made to permit and encourage competition. These are listed in the appendix. But the most important change has already been introduced: the appointment of general managers. There is nothing to stop enterprising NHS authorities and their managers from bringing in more competition now, without waiting for administrative or legislative changes, or for competition to be forced on them. Indeed, some have already done so: the preceding chapters have quoted many examples of places where competition for the provision of services has already taken place.

The specific changes which this study has suggested need to be made to foster competition are not particularly new. Most have been identified before. And several—improvement of NHS information, capital asset accounting—are coming in anyway, albeit rather slowly. But what is essential now is some further impetus to competition, which could best come from the top. The Secretary of State for Social Services, Mr John Moore, is himself a convinced believer in the market place and in competition—hence his interest in privatisation. He has so far moved gingerly on the NHS, perhaps fearful of arousing the wrath of its myriad pressure groups. The time has come for him to take his courage in both hands and press hard for a more competitive approach. He would be amazed at how much support there would be within the NHS for such a move.

Appendix
Specific changes recommended

The specific changes needed to encourage a more competitive approach by NHS authorities to the provision of health care services include:

(i) NHS hospitals must adopt proper capital asset accounting, and improve their information generally, so as to enable them to estimate accurately their own costs for comparison with others;

(ii) NHS authorities should compete both with the private sector and with each other. The latter requires proper cross-charging, and so a change in DHSS's method of financing health authorities;

(iii) managers need to be given more financial freedom than is available under present public accounting rules—for instance, in the handling of their own cash, or in the ability to enter into long-term contracts with penalty clauses if they are broken for political reasons;

(iv) where NHS Acts and regulations stand in the way of a more commercial and competitive approach—for instance, by making it hard for hospitals to profit from any of their activities—they should be changed;

(v) where staff pay and conditions inhibit competition, it should be possible to change them. This could, for example, mean some trammelling or adjustment in GPs' freedom to refer patients to consultants of their choice. And it could mean giving managers more local flexibility, including more use of short-term employment contracts;

(vi) for services subject to competitive tendering, redundancy costs should be taken out of the cost comparisons and financed centrally;

(vii) Family Practitioner Committees should be empowered to award and terminate contracts for the provision of primary care services by doctors, dentists and pharmacists;

(viii) hospital authorities should be given more freedom to manage their own capital programmes, including the freedom to instigate the financing of deals with private-sector groups; and

(ix) to ensure fair competition, the private sector should be asked to meet a proper share of the costs of training and educating staff.

Notes

1. See *Financing and delivering health care*, OECD, Paris, July 1987.

2. This is further explained in R. J. Maxwell, *Health and Wealth* (Lexington, Mass, 1981); and in the OECD study op. cit.

3. *Value for money*, National Audit Office, 1986.

4. An early and valuable discussion of this whole approach is in *The Public/Private Mix for Health Care* edited by G. McLachlan and A. Maynard (Nuffield Provincial Hospitals Trust (NPHT), 1982).

5. See Hansard, Written Answers by Mrs Edwina Currie, 12 January 1987 (col 125–128), 14 January 1987 (col 206–210), 16 July 1987 (col 620–623).

6. *Health Services Management: Competition and Co-operation* and *Developing Co-operation between Public and Private Hospitals*, both prepared by Grant Thornton Management Consultants (NPHT, 1986).

7. See *Reflections on the Management of the National Health Service* by Alain Enthoven (NPHT, 1985).

8. *Competitive Tendering for Support Services* (HC (83) 18). DHSS, 1983.

9. *Making a reality of Community Care*, Audit Commission, 1986.

10. The Government published two discussion documents in April 1986: *Primary Care: a Consultative Document* and *Neighbouring Nursing: a report of a review of the Community Nursing Service in England*.

11. *Report of the NHS Management Inquiry*, DHSS, 1982.

16

Privatise Coal: Achieving International Competitiveness

Colin Robinson and Allen Sykes

Why privatise the coal industry?

The nationalised coal industry is now in better shape than it has been for many years. Closure of high cost mines and improved working methods have led to increased productivity and reduced losses. Given these welcome improvements, long held to be unachievable, it may reasonably be asked whether a good case still exists for coal privatisation. It is the purpose of the first part of this paper to demonstrate briefly how privatisation can bring further major benefits, offering the coal industry a secure and profitable future.

In general privatisation schemes can have three principal objectives—increasing efficiency, raising revenue for the Government and widening share ownership. There is potential conflict among these objectives, and in particular between revenue raising and increasing efficiency. In the short term, the Government may see its main interest as being to raise revenue by selling an industry as a monopoly (rather than breaking it up and making it competitive). Potential shareholders may welcome the opportunity to obtain shares in a company subject to few competitive pressures. Moreover, existing management will usually wish to retain its market power but become a lightly-regulated private monopoly rather than a nationalised corporation subject to constant political interference. Finally, financial institutions generally prefer the relatively easy task of bringing well-established monopolies to market.

There are, however, few (if any) benefits to be obtained from transforming public monopolies into private monopolies. There may be some advantage in widening share ownership, but the main national benefits of privatisation come from liberalising the market. By this term we mean introducing competition throughout the industry to ensure that long term costs are minimised and maximum efficiency obtained. In some nationalised industries, it can be argued that there are natural monopoly elements which mean that only parts of the industries concerned can be made genuinely competitive. But that is not the case in the coal industry which is naturally competitive, not naturally monopolistic.

The general objective of coal privatisation should be greatly to reduce the power of monopolistic forces in the industry—British Coal's monopoly of coal production and the mining unions' power to bring pressure to bear on a single producer. Competing sources of coal supply should be established to bring benefits to consumers in terms of lower prices and enhanced security of supply, and to the workforce in terms of more decentralised, less politicised bargaining over pay and other conditions of employment, and better paid and more secure jobs.

Such benefits could not be obtained by simply moving British Coal into the private sector as a monopoly, either with private shareholders (even assuming there were enough takers) or by handing British Coal over to its employees. Nor could they be obtained by leaving British Coal as a nationalised corporation. The competitive pressures would be insufficient, politicians and civil servants would be unable to resist interfering and the management of British Coal would inevitably spend time on political bargaining which, in a competitive market, would be employed in reducing costs. In the past, government attempts to enforce rather easy targets—generally merely to break even—on the nationalised coal industry have never succeeded. There is no reason to suppose they would do so in the future if the industry were to remain nationalised. Its management, in the absence of genuine competitive pressures, would always be tempted to ask for more time and more money from politicians on whom it could continue to exert considerable influence.

When a previously nationalised industry is opened to competition, the role of government is necessarily reduced and the emphasis is changed. Instead of constant interference in the affairs of a nationalised industry, government needs to concentrate on such matters as ensuring that competition is maintained, that the environment is protected, that energy supplies are secure and that safety standards are maintained. These are extremely important functions which are considered later in this paper.

First, however, we set out some of the specific gains which might be expected if the British coal industry is privatised in a form which increases competition in the supply of coal.

Efficiency from competition

One source of efficiency gain (productive efficiency) is the production of goods at lower total costs. To some extent, higher efficiency may be realised by selling assets to private shareholders who put pressure on management to be more efficient so that profits are increased. But liberalisation is needed to force cost reductions on producers, partly because of the pressure of competition and partly because producers concentrate on lowering costs rather than on political lobbying. Competition also ensures a closer alignment of costs and prices (greater allocative efficiency) as cost reductions are passed on to consumers. Finally, in a competitive market, producers become much more interested in satisfying consumer wants by providing a wide variety of price and quality options. The provision of choice for consumers requires competition between suppliers.

Efficiency from private sector involvement

Efficient modern coal industries are highly capital intensive. A privatised, competitive coal industry consisting of entrepreneurial mining companies would have an incentive to make full use of equipment and to experiment with mining techniques which have proved successful in other countries. British Coal is recognised as a world leader in the development of equipment and technology for the longwall system of underground extraction. On average, however, the efficiency with which it uses that equipment compares unfavourably with other countries, even after making due allowance for British geological conditions. Increased competition, more flexible working practices, and the free movement of technical and management personnel aided by transferable pensions, would help to realise more of the potential of high cost capital equipment.

Responsiveness to customers' needs

One argument for public ownership or regulation turns on the presence of 'natural monopolies' which, if privately owned, could exploit customers because of the lack of competitive forces. However, in no sense is the coal industry a natural monopoly. Rather it is naturally competitive, since coal is a variable and geographically dispersed product. No reasonable argument can be made for leaving coal production in Britain in the hands of a single organisation. Even the total dedication of management in a huge monolithic industry, which is the very best British Coal could offer, is a poor substitute for the liberalising forces of a competitive market. To confine competition merely to a national coal monopoly and three other fuels, two of which are also monopolies (gas and electricity) is to throw away an important opportunity for further competition.

Management attitudes within British Coal have not been based upon commercial considerations, since the industry has not seen genuine competition between coal suppliers for 40 years. That is not the fault of British Coal's management, which we recognise is trying to improve the industry's efficiency. It is the fault of governments which first created and then maintained an inappropriate structure for the coal industry in Britain. With nearly all coal supplied from the same organisation, incentive is lacking to expand the most efficient parts of the organisation (e.g. opencast production at the expense of underground production). With only one coal company and imports restricted, neither British Coal's management nor anyone else has proper performance standards against which to measure its acts and achievements. On the other hand, in order to succeed, private mining companies would have to be responsive to market requirements in terms of quality and price.

Reducing political interference, costs and subsidies

As coal mining has been state-owned, there has been continual political interference in the industry. Furthermore, commercial objectives have largely been subordinated to social aims. Production costs of coal in Britain have accordingly remained unnecessarily high and the industry has extracted large subsidies from both the British taxpayer and the electricity consumer. A privatised industry would relieve the taxpayer of most of the substantial capital and operating subsidies which the industry would otherwise continue to require, though payments to relieve the hardship consequent on restructuring the industry would need to continue. Furthermore, unnecessarily high coal prices have led to unnecessarily high electricity and other fuel prices, thus contributing significantly to the decline of British manufacturing industry and to the rise in general unemployment. Retention of a monopoly, either public or private, means continuing these penalties.

Restoration of commercial direction

The large real oil and gas price increases in the 1970s and early 1980s presented British Coal with a windfall opportunity to improve its market position. In fact, far from increasing its market share in these very favourable conditions, it continued to lose share by much more than can be explained by the greater availability of cheap gas. One of the greatest business opportunities since the end of World War II was missed. There were two main reasons. On the supply side, British Coal lacked the commercial imperative which countries operating in competitive markets have; on the demand side, customers (both the electricity boards and industry) were fearful of increasing their dependence upon British Coal because of the monopolistic positions of both British Coal and the National Union of Mineworkers, made all the more powerful by restrictions on imports.

Since 1970, whereas production of coal in both Australia and South Africa has risen by a factor of almost three, in the protected British market it has fallen by about 25 per cent. Privatisation is needed to introduce commercial attitudes towards exploiting substantial but neglected business opportunities.

Enhanced security of supply

Security of coal supply would be greatly enhanced by the diversification of sources of supply, both at home and overseas, which a more competitive market would bring. Given their wide geographical spread, their diverse political systems and the strong competition between them, foreign coal producers would be most unlikely to take concerted action against Britain. Fuel consumers, including the electricity supply industry, would become more willing to invest in coal-fired equipment as they saw coal supplies become more secure as well as cheaper. Accordingly, the market for coal in Britain should expand.

Improved employee benefits and job security

Although, for any given output, fewer people might be employed in coal mining than if privatisation did not occur, they would enjoy much greater opportunities for increased pay and for profit sharing. A diversified, competitive industry would strive for lower costs and higher productivity, taking advantage of market opportunities both at home and abroad, so that eventually total production might well rise. The result should be greater job security, which would be both genuine and deserved because it would be based upon improved efficiency rather than the illusion of security created by taxpayer subsidies and union militancy. In a privatised industry each mine or opencast site would have the incentive to realise its full potential and the workforce would share the rewards from growing efficiency. There might also be some pricing into jobs since bigger pay differentials under more decentralised bargaining might allow some mines which would otherwise be uneconomic to operate profitably.

Opportunities for creativity

The coal industry is not only a mature industry, but one which for nearly two generations has not been subject to commercial pressure. Entrepreneurial flair is needed at all levels of workforce and management. Moreover, local managements and miners ought to be free to introduce systems and methods which are applicable to local conditions and not be constrained as at present by national procedures.

One essential point is that benefits from coal privatisation would be maximised only if the entire British energy sector were to be privatised, and in particular, electricity generation. Similar reasons to those which justify coal privatisation apply. The electricity supply industry normally absorbs nearly 75 per cent of British Coal's production. To maintain it under single ownership would significantly reduce the benefits of coal privatisation. Furthermore, private companies would be much more likely to buy and pay better prices for coal mines and reserves if electricity privatisation were certain to follow. If private coal firms had to face a sole buyer (monopsonist) for power station coal there might be few takers. Similarly if a diversified electricity generation industry had to face a near monopolist it might attract few new investors—see also Chapter 4 below. Because of the importance of electricity privatisation, and the need to link it to coal privatisation we are writing a further CPS paper on this subject to follow up the March 1987 paper entitled *Privatise Power*.

Present state, structure and financing of the industry

Reserves of British coal

Unlike recoverable oil and gas reserves, which are expected to be virtually exhausted some time next century, Britain has recoverable coal reserves sufficient to meet home consumption of coal for several centuries. British coal fields are dispersed across the length and breadth of the country and have widely varying technical characteristics. Though some coal fields are at or near the ends of their working lives, there are opportunities to extend mining into new regions. Two large developments (Selby and Asfordby) by British Coal are opening up new areas. Other coal fields are known to exist but have yet to be exploited.

Restructuring since the strike

British Coal (formerly the National Coal Board) is divided into nine deep mining Areas and the Opencast Executive. Since nationalisation, extensive restructuring has taken place, reducing the number of administrative areas to only 9 in 1986/87*; there were 48 in 1950. Small mines have been closed and new investment has concentrated on

---

* In March 1987 the North Derbyshire and South Midlands Areas were merged reducing the Areas to 9. Statistics for the years up to end 1986 will usually relate to 10 Areas.

Table 1
NATIONAL COAL BOARD/BRITISH COAL FINANCIAL RESULTS, 1980 TO 1986
(YEARS ENDING MARCH)

(£ million)

	1980	1981	1982	1983	1984	1985	1986[e]
Operating profits (losses)							
Collieries	(122)	(107)	(226)	(317)	(595)	(1752)[d]	169[d]
Opencast	110	157	157	192	211	142	343
Other mining activities[a]	6	12	21	23	27	9	27
Non-mining activities[b]	26	17	5	3	(1)	(41)	(4)
Total operating profits (losses)	20	79	(43)	(99)	(358)	(1642)	535
Social costs less grants[c]	(17)	(29)	(61)	(49)	(74)	(78)	(170)
Interest	(184)	(256)	(344)	(364)	(467)	(520)	(437)
Profit after interest	(181)	(206)	(448)	(512)	(899)	(2240)	(72)
Other items	22	(1)	20	27	24	15	22
Overall deficit	(159)	(207)	(428)	(485)	(875)	(2225)	(50)
Deficit grant from government	159	149	428	374	875	2225	50
Surplus (deficit) after payment of deficit grant	0	(58)	0	(111)	0	0	0

(Source: National Coal Board, Annual Reports and Accounts)

Notes (a) Rents, shipping terminals, etc.
(b) Manufacture of coke and smokeless fuel, chemicals, distribution of fuel and appliances, estates and land, engineering, computer services and income from related companies and partnerships.
(c) British Coal's share of the costs incurred as a result of closing uneconomic capacity and the transfer or redundancy of employees.
(d) After crediting £340 million for strike recovery costs which substantially overstated 1986 operating profits. The 1984/85 operating loss would be similarly overstated. Auditors accordingly qualified the accounts in both years.
(e) The provisional unaudited results announced in the 26 May 1987 British Coal press release are stated on a different basis to the 1986 results. The 1986 and 1987 results are listed in Table 1a.

large ones which permit the use of heavy duty machines at the coal face (the favoured method being that of longwall mining). Closures of less productive mines and faces have gathered pace since the 1984–85 strike ended and the number of active coal faces is planned to fall further. The new management style has increased production and improved financial performance.

Coal production and other activities of British Coal

For a variety of reasons, British coal production has fallen steeply from over 200 million tonnes a year in the mid-1950s. During the year ended March 1986 (the first financial year of normal operations since the strike) coal production from deep mines was 88.2 million tonnes and from opencast operations 14.1 million tonnes, a total of just over 102 million tonnes; in the 1986/87 financial year just ended, deep mined output was 87.8 million tonnes and opencast 13.3 million tonnes, a total of just over 101 million tonnes.

Deep mining: despite radical reorganisation and the closure of many unprofitable mines (the number of operating mines has fallen from 200 in 1981/82 to 133 in 1985/86 and fell further to 110 during 1986/87), the underground mining sector of British Coal has continued to return losses except for the last two quarters of both 1985/86 and 1986/87. These underground operating losses before interest and restructuring costs totalled £108 million in 1985/86 (see Table 1a), representing an average loss of £1.22 per tonne of deep mined coal. Preliminary figures for 1986/87 show an underground operating profit of £39 million or £0.44 per tonne.

Opencast mining: this sector, small in comparison with underground mining, is highly profitable. Mining operations are carried out by private contractors, subject to competitive tendering, and in recent years the operating profits of the Opencast Executive of British Coal have been £211 million (1983/84), £142 million (1984/85), £343 million (1985/86) and provisionally £243 million in 1986/87. The 1986/87 provisional results represented an operating profit of £18.3 per tonne, by far the most profitable part of British Coal's activity—and likely to remain so.

Other British Coal activities: these include coal processing into coke and smokeless fuel, distribution services, and consultancy. These activities are small and earn modest profits.

Table 1a
BRITISH COAL FINANCIAL RESULTS RESTATED
(£ million)

Operating Results	1985	1986	1986 Restated	1987 Unaudited
Mines				
Operating profit (loss)	(1,333)	(108)	(108)	39
Strike recovery costs	(340)	(340)	—	—
Writedowns	(79)	(63)	—	—
	(1,752)	169	(108)	39
Opencast	142	343	343	243
Other activities	(32)	23*	43	76
Operating profit (all activities)	(1,642)	535	278	358
Interest	(520)	(437)	(437)	(386)
Trading profit/loss (after interest)	(2,162)	98	(159)	(28)
Net restructuring cost	(78)	(170)	(170)	(262)
Writedowns	—	—	(63)	—
Other income	15	22	—	—
Overall deficit	(2,225)	(50)	(392)	(290)
Write-back of provision for strike recovery	—	—	342	—
Deficit before payment of deficit grant	(2,225)	(50)	(50)	(290)

* Includes provision for and write-back of £2 million of strike recovery costs

(Source: derived from 26 May 1987 Press Statement and National Coal Board 1985/86 Report and Accounts.)

Reported profits

During the 1986/87 financial year (see Table 1a), British Coal reported an operating loss of £28 million after payment of interest charges. Net restructuring costs were £262 million, resulting in a total loss for the year of £290 million. The full results of the previous seven years are set out in Table 1. In considering British Coal's accounts, it must be borne in mind that most capital expenditure and nearly all redundancy costs, interest payments, deficit grants, etc. are attributable to the underground mines. These have nearly always reported an operating loss until the very small operating profit of 1986/87.

It should be noted that for years the Annual Report and Accounts of British Coal have been selective, obscure and difficult to follow, a matter complained of by some professional accountants and by the

Select Committee on Energy in its Report of January 1987. For a nationalised industry accountable to Parliament this is regrettable and should be promptly remedied. Accordingly if we and other commentators make some errors in interpreting British Coal's figures it should not be a matter for surprise, particularly in our attempts to calculate the total cost to the nation of both British Coal and its past and present employees (many of whom are paid separately by the Government).

Present financial structure

British Coal is supported by a variety of government grants. More-over, it has always had an easier financial target to meet than most other nationalised industries. At present it is charged only with breaking even after interest payments and receipt of government social grants (to cover premature pensions, mine closures, concessionary coal and deficiencies in the mineworkers' pension scheme). British Coal's Chairman has confirmed that the break-even target date (1987–88) set in the 1985 Coal Industry Act has had to be put back to 1988–89.

British Coal and British Rail have by far the largest External Financing Limits (i.e. government approved borrowings and grants from external sources, mainly the Government) of all the nationalised industries. Each has an EFL of over £700 million both in 1986/87 and in 1987/88: the sum of the EFLs for all other nationalised industries is only £690 million, including industries such as electricity supply which are net contributors to the Exchequer.

Government financial support for the industry is discussed more fully later in this chapter.

Private sector production

An active, generally profitable, but highly constrained, private coal mining sector is at work in Britain producing about 4 per cent of total national output from about 160 very small underground mines, 60 very small opencast sites and several small-scale discard tips belonging to British Coal. These fringe operations receive no subsidies.

The Coal Industry Nationalisation Act (1946) limits the size of mines in the private sector and allows the nationalised coal corporation to control the number of private operations by requiring those operators to hold a license issued by British Coal, to pay royalties to British Coal, and to accept selling prices imposed upon them by British Coal.

A further activity, the recovery of coal from old mine tips, has been restrained by British Coal and yet coal from tips can be as cheap as, or on occasions even cheaper than, opencast coal. As coal tip removal both creates jobs in areas where coal mining has ceased to be a major source of employment and improves the environment, it ought to be encouraged.

British Coal can thus decide how much competition it will allow and nominate its competitors, acting as both judge and jury over the private sector. For example, the recent Joint Understanding negotiated between British Coal and the CEGB appears to have halved, without any discussion, the quota for some of the cheapest coal available in Britain as supplied by the private mining sector. Collusion between two large public sector monopolies consequently reduced the electric power generation market for this private sector coal from 3 to about 1½ million tonnes per year. Despite having the smallest reserves (which British Coal has no interest in working itself), the smallest production units, and no subsidies, this has been a consistently profitable sector of the industry in contrast to British Coal which has nearly always been unprofitable. Its record indicates the benefits which should be obtainable from privatisation and liberalisation.

Markets

While 1985/86 was untypical in some respects (there was destocking from mines and restocking by consumers) it is the latest year for which full statistics are available. The supply of and demand for coal in Britain in the financial year 1985/86 and our estimates for 1986/87 are as set out in Table 2 overleaf.

The English and Scottish generating boards buy almost all their coal from British Coal. They are by far British Coal's largest customers. Because successive governments have acted to protect the coal industry, the CEGB has been prevented from diversifying its supplies (for instance by importing much coal). Given the domestic protection which it enjoys, British Coal has had no incentive to consider the export of coal in significant quantity. Its costs of production (with no

Table 2
THE SUPPLY OF AND DEMAND FOR COAL IN BRITAIN

	1985/86 million tonnes	%	1986/87 million tonnes	%
Sources of supply				
BC production				
Deep mines	88	68	88	77
Opencast	14	11	13	11
	102		101	
Private licensed mines and tip coal	2	2	2	2
Total BC and licensed production	104		103	
BC stock reduction (increase)	11	8	(2)	(2)
Total BC sales	115		101	
Private non-vested production	3	2	3	3
Imports	12	9	10	9
Total coal supplied	130	100	114	100
Analysis of demand				
Consumption				
CEGB	79) 86	61) 66	82	72
SSEB	7)	5)		
Coke ovens				
(mainly BSC)	11	9	13	11
Industry	10	8	8	7
Domestic	8	6	8	7
Other markets	3	2	3	3
Total domestic consumption	118		114	
Stockpiling				
CEGB	8) 9	6) 7	(2)	(2)
SSEB	1)	1)		
Exports	3	2	2	2
Total coal demand	130	100	114	100

(Source: derived from British Coal Annual Report and Accounts, press statements and *Energy Trends.)*

compelling incentive to reduce them) have for many years been well above the prices of internationally traded coal.

The Nationalisation Act

Chapter 1(1) of the Coal Industry Nationalisation Act 1946 charges British Coal with three general duties—

(1) the duty of working and getting the coal in Great Britain, to the exclusion of any other person. There are only two exceptions to this clause:

(a) coal necessary to be dug and carried away in the course of activities other than mine activities; and

(b) the getting of coal in accordance with the terms of a licence issued by British Coal (that is, private mining).

(2) the duty of securing the efficient development of the coal mining industry; and

(3) the duty of making supplies of coal available, of such quality and sizes, in such quantities and at such prices, as may seem to British Coal best calculated to further the public interest in all respects, including the avoidance of any undue or unreasonable preference or advantage.

The three clauses give British Coal extremely strong powers and clearly defined duties. The use of the powers is evident: the fulfilment of the public duties is not. The British coal industry has not seen efficient development since nationalisation, nor has the public interest been furthered.

By means of its extremely strong powers, British Coal can frustrate attempts by third parties to improve the industry (and has done so). We have already explained that potential private competitors are kept out of the industry so that real competition is limited. Another example of the pressure which British Coal can indirectly exert is the fate of the recommendation made by the Monopolies and Mergers Commission in June 1983 that the statutory limit on the size of opencast reserves worked privately should be raised to 100,000 tonnes. Even that modest proposal has been ignored by the Government.

It is not surprising that British Coal suppresses competition and frustrates external proposals for change since it was established as a monopoly by government forty years ago and has been maintained as a monopoly ever since. The habits and practices of forty years are hard to overcome.

Existing subsidies

Earlier in this chapter, in particular in Tables 1 and 1a, we touched briefly upon the 1985/86 government support for British Coal. It is helpful to consider that support more fully and over a longer period, interpreting British Coal's none too helpful Annual Reports and Accounts, and government statistics as accurately as outsiders can.

The Government's financial support is both direct and indirect. Direct support takes the form of grants made to cover losses, social costs, and redundancies. For the latest five financial years for which full data are available, these have been running at an average level of over £1 billion per year as set out in Table 3 below. 'Deficit' grants cover financial losses as they occur in each financial year. 'Social' grants cover premature pensions, social expenditures consequent on mine closures, concessionary (free) coal to miners and deficiencies in the miners' pension scheme. Redundancy payments are straightforwardly what they purport to be.

Until the end of March 1987, the Government gave particularly generous terms to cover the very large redundancies between April 1985 and March 1987. These amounted to:-

(i) a lump sum of £1000 for each year worked in the industry to those aged 21–49; and

(ii) a smaller lump sum to those over 50 plus a pension payable for life.

These very generous terms secured a reduction (primarily through voluntary early retirement and voluntary redundancy) of 63,600 mine workers, 10,500 other industrial workers and 5,400 staff between the end of the strike in March 1985 and March 1987. The total manpower reduction was thus nearly 80,000. This government funded scheme has now been replaced by a less generous British Coal scheme, the main provisions of which are as follows:-

Table 3
GOVERNMENT DIRECT SUPPORT
(£ million)

	1981/2	1982/3	1983/4	1984/5	1985/6	1986/87 Estimate
Deficit grants	455	386	875	2225	50	290
Social grants	93	134	270	189	513	n.a.
Redundancy payments†	48	81	192	202	566	540*
	596	601	1337	2616	1129	830 +

† *Payments made by government directly which do not pass through British Coal's Accounts.*

* *Government Expenditure Plans, January 1987.*

(Source: Energy Committee January 1987 and British Coal Annual Reports.)

(i) £700 for each year of service from the age of 30, with lesser amounts for each year served below the age of 30; and

(ii) no weekly payments, only lump sum payments. The normal miners' pension scheme applies.

COMPARISON OF LUMP SUM REDUNDANCY PAYMENTS

| | £ payable on redundancy | |
Age at redundancy	New scheme	Old scheme
35–49	9,650	17,000
45–49	16,200	26,000
50–54	19,250	74,600*

* Includes continuing pension payments.

The total sums spent under this scheme are included in Table 3 above.

The total of these deficit, social grant and redundancy payments amounted to £6,279 million over the five years 1982–1986, representing an annual average of £1,256 million—or approximately £6,630 per worker employed over the same period, a sum equivalent to over 75% of the total wage bill.

We do not, of course, argue that subsidies are never justified. The subsidies to British Coal, however, have by any standard been very large, and it is for the proponents of such subsidies to justify them.

There are also hidden subsidies and protective devices (such as the tax on fuel oil of nearly £8 per tonne, preference for coal in the public sector, and restrictions on imports) which have the effect of raising coal, electricity and other fuel prices as we explain more fully below.

These direct and hidden subsidies have imposed a considerable burden on the rest of the nation. They have been paid for in lower net of tax income and higher costs, and consequently higher unemployment elsewhere in Britain. It is difficult to argue that they should be continued at anything like these levels given that there is the alternative of privatisation with liberalisation, including the freedom to import coal when it is genuinely cheaper.

Government finance

Let us now identify the government payments to the coal industry in recent years, together with the capital outlays involved. The Treasury makes payments as British Coal's cash needs arise, rather than when the liabilities occur. (These cash payments are not additional to those in Table 3 above but their timing is slightly different.)

Actual cash payments, including those forecast early this year for 1986/87, are as shown below:

				Forecast
1982/3	*1983/4*	*1984/5*	*1985/6*	*1986/7*
		(£ million)		
773	922	1740	1473	1270
				Total over five years: 6,178

(Source: Energy Committee, 1987)

British Coal makes significant capital expenditures as it develops new mines and re-equips existing ones. These outlays and the total loans (mainly from government) for the last four years, plus the forecast capital expenditure for 1986–87 are as follows:

					Forecast
	1982/3	*1983/4*	*1984/5*	*1985/6*	*1986/7*
			(£ million)		
Mining capital expenditure	826	691	354	645	650
Outstanding loans under the Coal Industry Acts	3710	4179	4343	3868	4070*
Change in loans on previous years	282	469	164	− 475	202*

(Source: Energy Committee, 1987)
* *(Our estimates)*

Excessive capital expenditure?

Before turning to the subject of indirect support one should consider the very large capital expenditure incurred by British Coal in recent years, and planned for future years. Too little detail is available to permit thorough examination but the levels are high by international mining standards, and it seems possible that British Coal's labour productivity improvements are in part being achieved by uneconomically high capital expenditure. Grounds exist for believing that at least part of the expenditure is uneconomic, in that the auditors qualified the 1985/86 accounts by questioning whether or not the high capital expenditures of recent years had produced assets of the value shown (fixed assets of about £4,000 million at March 1986), given that British Coal is a loss making industry and nearly always has been. We believe it is unlikely that the industry could be sold at anything like the value of its currently employed capital of around £5,400 million. We find it difficult, therefore, to see the justification for adding capital at the rate of £650 million a year. Finally, the big new mines being brought on have, by international standards, high expenditures for their planned output (Selby £1500 million for 10 million tonnes per annum, perhaps more, and Asfordby £400 million for 3 million tonnes per annum, etc.).

We doubt if a liberalised and privatised industry with international expertise would need to spend such large sums to achieve an output comparable to that of British Coal. This topic is further explored below.

Indirect support

In addition to direct grants to British Coal the Treasury has provided indirect support via a scheme (now drawing to a close) to give incentives to larger consumers to convert from other fuels to coal. Payments have been as follows:

1982/3	1983/4	1984/5	1985/6	1986/7
		(£ million)		
2	4	10	12	18

(Source: Energy Committee, 1987)

The potential gains from privatisation with liberalisation

We begin by discussing coal imports, since increased competition in the coal market implies freer imports, and then discuss the necessary improvements to the efficiency of British coal mines.

The potential for coal imports

It is sometimes assumed that, even if significant cost reductions were achieved in British mines, domestic production would still be largely displaced by imports of cheap foreign coal (as has happened in parts of Western Europe). Were this to be true it would need careful evaluation to determine how best, how far and how fast to switch to such cheaper imports to the net national advantage. But most national production would not be displaced, since British coal enjoys considerable natural protection against imports.

Coal imports were 12.1 million tonnes in 1985/86 and 10.1 million in 1986/87. Much of this was speciality coking coal imported by BSC. The CEGB at present imports only 1–2 million tonnes per annum. It was not able, or did not choose, to import extra coal during the 1984/85 strike. Other consumers had no such inhibitions. Given, however, that large coal supplies are available at apparently much lower prices than domestic coal, what limits imports to the domestic market?

The CEGB, under pressure from both Conservative and Labour governments, has confined itself to taking coal almost exclusively (currently at least 95%) from British Coal, at prices which at first sight seem well above those at which imports could be obtained. To preserve some bargaining power the Government has allowed the CEGB to have token imports, typically of a few million tonnes a year. They have been delivered to its Thameside power stations which have appropriate docking facilities, usually from the three main North West European ports of Amsterdam, Rotterdam and Antwerp (the so-called ARA ports). These three ports have large modern coal handling facilities to receive bulk coal from the main overseas suppliers (Australia, South Africa, the United States and Poland), Western Europe being the main market for internationally traded steam coal. From the ARA ports coal can be trans-shipped into smaller ships capable of entering British ports. CEGB imports have been limited not only by government imposed policy, but also by the lack of appropriate, modern coal terminals.

The steel industry (BSC) consumes 6 million tonnes a year of the higher grade coking coals, most of which it imports. It has the facilities to do so near its main blast furnaces in the Clyde (Hunterston), Teeside (Redcar) and South Wales (Port Talbot).

Other British customers, being free to import (to the extent that they are not subject to any undue commercial pressures from British Coal), took in about 4 million tonnes in 1985/86, about a quarter of their total requirements, and this proportion may well rise. Their coal imports, being modest, can be handled in numerous small ports around Britain.

What of the future? Substantial imports of coal into Britain are presently limited by the lack of large scale modern port facilities. Although such ports do exist to handle iron ore and coking coal for the steel industry, they cannot handle the volumes which would be necessary were steam coal to be imported on any large scale, particularly for electricity generation. In addition, the steel industry ports are not in general suitably located to supply the power stations. Competitiveness of imports cannot therefore be judged solely from the spot price in the ARA ports—which in mid 1987 is just below £22 a tonne. Coal must first be transferred into smaller ships before it can be landed in Britain, and must then incur extra inland transport costs. Except for Thameside, most of the large coal-burning power stations are inland, close to the coalfields. Rail or road costs to these stations further increase the cost of imported coal. Total costs added by transport from the ARA ports to inland power stations are between £5 per tonne for a few coastal stations to over £13 for nearly all others, compared with just under £5 per tonne average delivery costs for British Coal. Except for the coastal stations home-produced coal thus presently enjoys a transport cost advantage of about £8 per tonne over imports.

Thus, even if the CEGB and the South of Scotland Electricity Board were given complete freedom to import coal, major capital investments in coal terminals would be needed before they could substantially increase imports. Allowing for sites to be chosen, planning enquiries, design and construction, at least five years would pass before even one large scale coal import terminal could be built. It is also likely that increased British demand for internationally traded coal would push up the world price for such coal. World seaborne steam coal trade is at present just under 150 million tonnes a year. Increased annual British demand of, say, 15 million tonnes would represent an increase of about 10% in total world demand for such exported coal and could well cause prices to rise. An increase of 30 million tonnes (which the CEGB suggested as a possibility to the Select Committee on Energy) would certainly raise prices.

Although international coal prices are at present very low, a number of special factors are at work. Much of the growth in coal exports in the last 10 years has come from Australia and South Africa, both of which countries have until recently had depreciating currencies. Moreover, ocean freight rates have fallen because of overcapacity in shipping. A reversal of either trend would weaken the ability of the major overseas suppliers to export coal profitably. Indeed, the recent strengthening in exchange rates of Australia and South Africa has already put financial strain on some coal exporters.

In demonstrating that large volumes of imports could not penetrate the British coal market in the short term, we are not suggesting that import restrictions do not matter. We think that such controls should be removed immediately. If they were, however, the physical and price limitations we have explained above would constrain the increase in imports for a few years. But some significant changes would start to occur. For example, the CEGB might well begin work on a large import terminal; it has investigated the economics of such a venture in the past, but who would seriously consider going ahead if the Government would not allow imports for power stations to increase substantially? As an illustration of the costs of such a facility, the Hampton Roads (Virginia) coal complex in the USA was developed in 1982 at a cost of $120m, say $150m now or around £100m, with an annual capacity of 12 million tonnes. Cheaper facilities may be possible if offshore floating coal terminals are feasible. The question of installing a modern coal terminal is explored further below.

Such a terminal would provide a useful bargaining counter in negotiations with home coal producers, whatever the actual size of imports and would probably be a justifiable investment on those grounds alone. There might also be a change in the previous CEGB power station siting policy, with more coal-fired power stations on coastal sites; indeed, this is now being considered. Thus British coal suppliers, though they would have a breathing space of a few years, would in the longer term need to aim at matching the price at which imports could be delivered into the relevant areas of the British coal market.

Comparing the CEGB coal purchasing contract with available imports

It is worth looking in more detail at the CEGB-British Coal agreement which restricts coal imports and private sector coal supplies. Set out in Figure 1 is a cumulative cost curve per tonne of British Coal's production for the first quarter of 1986, derived from published data in the 1987 Committee on Energy report. It includes opencast mines which comprise most but not all the lower cost production. Superimposed upon it are the three coal prices the CEGB is currently paying to British Coal of approximately £30, £34 and £46.88 a tonne under a 5 year agreement signed in early 1986, called a Joint Understanding, which has provision for annual reviews. All of these are on a mine-mouth basis.

Costs of delivery to power stations are just under £5 on average. If

Figure 1
TOTAL BRITISH COAL
1986 FIRST QUARTER

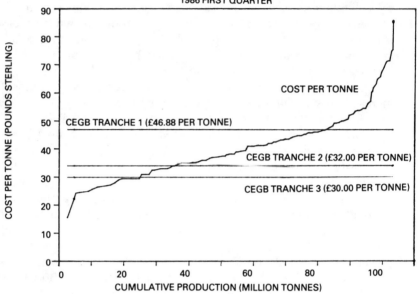

Figure 2
CEGB CONTRACT PRICE & PRODUCTION COSTS
(1986)

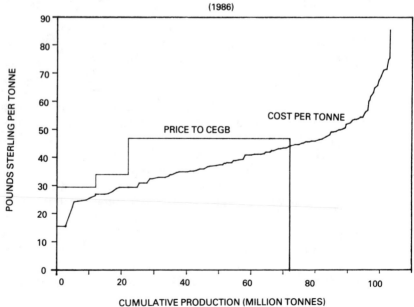

either of the lower prices truly represented the achievable long term delivered costs of imports, and if the 1986 cost curve could not be much improved, then the long term future for domestic coal production in Britain would be bleak indeed. Neither of the conditions, however, is likely to apply. The cost curve, discussed later, can be lowered and, as just explained, coal imports could not be increased substantially in the short run.

Reasoning along these lines presumably underlies the government-condoned Joint Understanding between the CEGB and British Coal. This will be evident from Figure 2 which sets out the same information as in Figure 1 but with the annual volumes given for each tranche, that is 12 million tonnes at £30, a further 10 million tonnes at £34, and the rest (50 million tonnes) at £46.88, giving an average price of £42.28 per tonne for 72 million tonnes a year. In no way do we endorse such inflexible agreements which give no genuine choice of supplier and tend to stop the investment in terminals and changes in power station location which would occur without import restrictions. Nevertheless, if the volume and costs of the two lower tranches reasonably reflect the end-1985 cost and availability of deliverable imports—and they do not look too far out—then in 1986 the CEGB may not have had much scope to purchase its coal supplies more cheaply. The international trade in coal, however, can be expected to grow and to become increasingly competitive and import prices could even fall further. The CEGB (or its successors) needs to be able to adjust its activities, without being hampered by import restrictions, so as to take advantage of that growing trade. Hence, the cost of British coal must be reduced considerably for it to remain competitive. Fortunately, there is considerable scope for such reductions under a liberal scheme of privatisation which would provide competitive pressures to bring down the costs of producing coal in Britain to the level of future available supplies of overseas coal. Nothing less should be acceptable to consumers and the Government.

The scope for improved efficiency

In its *New Strategy for Coal* published in October 1985 British Coal emphasised the need to achieve competitive costs. It expressed its cost targets in a more sophisticated unit than cost per average tonne since that measure took no account of the heat value of the coal:

instead it used the cost per Giga Joule (GJ)*. Mines operating at above £1.65 per GJ (about £41.25 a tonne) were judged unlikely to have a long term future, and to warrant investment other mines had to have a reasonable prospect of their long term costs being £1.5 per GJ (£37.50 a tonne) or less. These and all subsequent costs and prices in this section are expressed in real terms in 1987 pounds. No indication was given of the cost level necessary to meet long term import competition (if indeed that was the aim of British Coal). Given our arguments about imports, however, it appears to us that domestic coal, if it is to be competitive, must cost at most £1.4 per GJ (£35 a tonne) within 4 to 5 years, and for real long term security no more than £1.2 per GJ (£30 a tonne). A definition of relevant economic costs is given below. (Throughout we assume that it would never be government policy to allow Britain to become a dumping ground for coal imports subsidised by foreign producers).

These targets may appear difficult, but there are good reasons to believe they are achievable. As we have shown above, they do not have to be met overnight. Coal imports cannot be stepped up appreciably in the short term, perhaps not for 4 to 5 years. Although some British coal capacity may well not be profitable in the medium to long term, a reprieve is justifiable because it is physically impossible to replace the output (where destined for power stations) by imports unless and until one or more new, modern coal terminals are built.

There is, in our view, considerable scope for further raising the efficiency of coal production and for lowering costs in Britain's underground mines. Also, opencast production could be increased significantly from the present level of 14 or so million tonnes a year—perhaps towards 20 million tonnes a year. With costs already of only about £1 per GJ (£25 a tonne), opencast operations are a particularly important source of domestic coal which can withstand import competition in foreseeable conditions. Like most mining activities, opencast mining has environmental consequences, but disturbance is often short lived. Completed sites, quite rightly, have to be restored after mining to a state at least equivalent to their previous condition and in the process many are improved. Nevertheless, there is for a time considerable disturbance to local people who would be more prepared to accept mining were they given appropriate compensation. The profits from opencast mining are sufficiently large to be the source of such compensation.

---

* For the average quality of coal produced £1.00 per GJ is about £25 a tonne.

The heart of the matter, however, is the scope for reducing costs in underground mines which at present are capable of supplying about 90 million tonnes of coal a year. Figures 1 and 2 show cumulative cost curves for early 1986 which are fairly flat over most of their ranges; the implication is that the amount of coal which can be produced to meet a given competitive price is rather sensitive to cost changes of about £5 per tonne (£0.2 per GJ). In the light of what we have said about import prices, considerable improvements in efficiency must be achieved before most existing and planned mines can look forward to a secure long run future.

Can underground mining costs be reduced to the figure of £1.4 per GJ (£35 per tonne) which we have suggested as a necessary interim 4 to 5 year target? Let us begin with British Coal's immediate target cut-off cost of £1.65 per GJ (£41.25 per tonne), expressed in terms of colliery costs, which include depreciation but not all overheads. Only the 14 million tonnes of opencast output and 50 million tonnes of deep-mined production were produced at costs at or below that level in 1985/86. There was a further 20 million tonnes below the top price charged to the CEGB (£46.88 a tonne) but above the cut-off point, and a further 20 million tonnes beyond that. If these costs are accurate, then the highest cost tranche of 20 million tonnes is unlikely to have a long term future. The potentially profitable *existing* underground tonnage is around 70 million tonnes (i.e. the 50 million tonnes plus the 20 million tonnes). This is the quantity to keep in mind when considering future possibilities. How much of this 70 million tonnes of underground capacity can expect to achieve cost levels, by the early 1990s, of £1.4 a GJ (£35 a tonne), or less?

During 1986/87 British Coal achieved considerable improvements in productivity which just outweighed the estimated 10% (£4.60 per tonne) fall in its average selling price. Unit costs, which averaged £1.78 per GJ in 1985/86, fell to £1.60 in 1986/87 (a fall of 10%) and to £1.52 and £1.44 respectively for the last two quarters, although this may have been partly seasonal. For the year as a whole the underground mines made a small operating profit, before interest, redundancy costs, etc., of £39 million compared with a loss of £108 million in the previous year. Productivity, measured as output per man shift, increased from 2.72 tonnes in 1985/86 to 3.29 tonnes in 1986/87 (21%) and to 3.54 tonnes by the first quarter of 1987. According to British Coal, over half of the 21% improvement in 1986/87 productivity was due to greater use of the expensive, heavy duty coal face equipment and only 5 percentage points to closing down uneconomic mines.

During the year the number of heavy duty faces increased from 88 (23%) to 119 (39%). Over the next four years this equipment is to be installed on most coal faces.

We do not wish to be unfair to British Coal's management and staff who have accomplished a great deal since the strike, but in interpreting these improvements it needs to be remembered that during 1986/87 British Coal shed nearly 38,000 workers, or 21% of its employees. If they could be shed while output was maintained, then it tells us a great deal about the inefficiencies of previous years.

In sum 1986/87 was a year of considerable productivity improvement for British Coal, but at his end May 1987 press conference the Chairman warned that the last year's progress was unusual and future annual productivity gains could be expected to settle at between 8% and 10%. This is in line with what he has been urging for sometime. If a 10% annual improvement could be maintained it would imply doubling in 7 years from the average 3.29 tonnes per man shift for the year ended March 1987 to around 6½ tonnes. However, in the forty years since nationalisation the industry has achieved productivity growth of only about 3% a year on average. To require the industry in its present structure to make a 10% productivity gain each year may accordingly be unrealistic.

Given that more higher cost mines will need to be closed (the 20 million tonnes of capacity with costs above £46.88 a tonne), and given the forecast rise in productivity in the remainder, further major reductions in manning are inescapable. They will occur whether British Coal is privatised or not, just as they have done over the past 40 years. The only question is whether inevitable change is recognized and acted upon positively, or whether it is opposed and eventually becomes more harsh than is necessary. We argue later that man power reductions should be achieved by voluntary redundancy with generous compensation for those leaving the industry. For our part we believe the coal industry is capable of making all the necessary adaptations, but only if there is a sensible privatisation scheme. Then its future can be a secure and attractive one. The industry must be on a smaller scale, at least initially, than at present, but not so drastically reduced as is commonly imagined.

Before setting out the basis for estimates of cost reductions and efficiency improvements which privatisation could bring a comparison of underground coal mining productivity in Britain and the United States will give a useful perspective. Set out in Table 4 below is the underground output per employee of British Coal in 1985/86 and 1986/87 and similar figures for underground coal mining in the United States for 1985, the latest year for which information is available.

Only broad conclusions can be drawn from such a table because American underground mines generally have more favourable conditions than those in Britain. They are younger mines, often with thicker and geologically less disturbed seams, and are normally nearer the surface. Nevertheless, the latest productivity levels in British underground mines, measured by annual output per employee, are only one fifth of those in the United States. Clearly, the scope for improvement in Britain is very considerable. If, as we shall discuss, the improvements brought about by privatisation were to show by the early 1990s, annual output per employee in British underground mining would by then double to over 1200 tonnes. This would still be only 40% of the 1985 American level. Because of the less favourable underground mining conditions in Britain, there is little chance of equalling United States levels of productivity. Nevertheless, privatisation should bring substantial productivity gains in the next few years, and continuing gains thereafter.

To try to determine by how much costs might be reduced in the next few years in a competitive coal market, we have examined estimates of possible productivity improvements (both by British Coal and other experts); we have considered the efficiencies achieved in overseas coal mines, making what allowance we can for geological and other differences; and we have assessed the efficiency gains which only privatisation should make possible. Our conclusion is that a lowering of costs of some 25% to 35% in real terms (that is, about £9 to £12½ per tonne) within four to five years should be achievable given the kind of privatisation proposal we put forward

Table 4
BRITISH AND AMERICAN UNDERGROUND COAL MINING PRODUCTIVITY

	British Coal		USA
	1985/86	*1986/87*	*1985*
Production—million tonnes	88.5	87.8	316.1
Total employees—thousands	179.5*	141.5*	107.0
Annual output per employee—tonnes	493	620	2,955

* *On an end year basis rather than on average during the year*

(Source: British Coal Annual Report and Accounts, and The Coal Exporters' Association of the United States, Inc.)

below. We would not expect the gains to stop there. Costs should fall
further in the medium to long term; and the greater part of the British
coal industry could be competitive in 4 to 5 years at prices of no more
than £35 a tonne at the mine mouth, and at no more than £30 a tonne
a few years later—which are the prices which we have suggested are
necessary to match potential imports.

Turning now to the probable size of the industry on various cost
and price assumptions, there are serious difficulties in making such
an estimate from outside British Coal. British Coal's accounts are not
very helpful and only occasionally do bodies such as the Monopolies
Commission or the Committee on Energy manage to extract detailed
cost information from British Coal. We have, therefore, had to piece
together such information as has been published and apply both
judgement and analysis.

In reaching our conclusions that by 1992 the greater part of the
British coal industry can survive at £35 a tonne mine-mouth prices
(for average grade coal) we have used the following procedure. We
begin with the cost curve for the first quarter of 1986 derived from
published data in the 1987 Report of the Committee on Energy,
assuming that since British Coal supplied the data to the Committee
it is both accurate and representative. The curve relates to colliery
operating costs, and excludes central overheads.

In determining the viable level of output the only relevant costs are
avoidable costs. Thus all British Coal's historic cost depreciation is
irrelevant representing as it does sunk costs. The relevant cost that is
to be included is the continuing essential capital spending necessary
to maintain output and cost levels. This we estimate at £6 a tonne.
British Coal is currently spending £650 million per year, nearly all of
it on its underground mines. Assuming that the expenditure is
concentrated on the lower-cost mines (whose capacity totals around
65 million tonnes per annum), this represents £10 per tonne per year.
Capital expenditure on underground coal mines in the USA is below
£4 per tonne per year. Accordingly, we anticipate that an expenditure
of £6 per tonne will be a reasonable estimate for a privatised industry,
given the geological and other differences between the USA and
Britain.

All British Coal's central overheads have also been excluded since
it is evidently detrimental to close any mine that is contributing to
such overheads. For the same reason the price the new owners will
have paid is excluded as irrelevant to determining the optimal output.

To update the operating costs we then lowered the curve by the ratio of £1.78 per gigajoule (the 1985/86 unit cost for underground coal) to £1.5, the unit costs achieved by British Coal by the end of 1986/87; the cost reduction is almost 16%, although a greater reduction might have been justified if we had used the first quarter 1987 figures. This gives us as up to date an estimate of British Coal's cost curve as outsiders can make. This 1987 derived cost curve was then modified to give an estimated cost curve for 1992. It includes the 10 million tonnes per annum of new capacity presently under construction, and excludes those mines whose production costs are unlikely to be reduced to below £1.5 per GJ by 1992, or within an acceptable period thereafter. These estimates also assume higher utilisation of capital equipment at most mines which will require a major change towards six day working (though fewer shifts per miner per year). Without this change a significant part of underground capacity would be uneconomic. Taken together these factors give a cost reduction of at least £11 a tonne for the economic mines. All this assumes the form of privatisation set out below, and beginning in mid 1988.

It is important to appreciate that private owners making the relevant comparisons of marginal cost to marginal revenue might well keep mines open which British Coal would have closed. No one outside the industry can be sure what information British Coal uses in deciding on mine closures, but it has been criticised for its use of average (rather than marginal) costs and revenues.

Before turning to the longer term implications of these cost estimates under privatisation we first consider the estimated supply and demand position in 1992.

The table is based on the assumption that there are no additional major import facilities by 1992, although they could be in place shortly thereafter if an early decision is taken—see below.

It can be seen from the table that this import constraint and the estimated requirement of the home market for 116 million tonnes to 120 million tonnes requires 107 to 104 million tonnes to be produced in Britain in 1992. Expansion of the opencast and existing private sector, combined with 10 million tonnes per annum of new capacity should provide a total of 32 million to 34 million tonnes of low cost production by 1992. This would leave a requirement from already existing underground mines of 70 million to 75 million tonnes.

The 20 million tonnes of highest cost capacity will not be competitive. Production from some 55 million tonnes of capacity (made up of the lowest cost 50 million tonnes identified by British Coal in 1985/86 plus 5 million tonnes from the intermediate cost category of 20 million

Table 5

COAL SUPPLY, 1986 (ACTUAL) AND 1992 (ESTIMATED)

(million tonnes)

	1986 (actual)	1992 (estimated)
Opencast	14	17–18
Existing private mines	4	5–6
Planned new mines	—	10
Total of above	18	32–34
Underground mines with no likely future	20	—
Underground mines with possible future:		
Higher intermediate cost	15	15–5
Lower intermediate cost	5⎱	60–65
Lowest cost	50⎰	
Home supply	108	107–104
Net imports (assuming 3 million tonnes export)	8	9–16
Total home supply and net imports	116	116–120

tonnes) can probably be increased by 10% to 20% to give a further viable tonnage of between 55 million and 60 million tonnes per annum. The remaining 15 million tonnes of the intermediate category would require an average cost reduction of only about 10% from its estimated 1992 position to compete with imported coal, when further imports become possible, which as already noted might be by 1993. We believe that there is a reasonable chance for realising such further productivity improvement for most of this capacity within 3 to 5 years after 1992.

On the demand side (see the totals in Table 5) we have assumed no change or only a small increase compared with 1986; in the longer term we would expect demand for British coal to expand under private ownership, though by how much it increases will depend on economic growth and prices of other fuels.

We conclude that total coal production in Britain in the early post-privatisation period might be in the range 104 to 107 million tonnes a year, not a great deal less than in 1986 when output was about 108 million tonnes. Of this total only between 5 million tonnes and 15 million tonnes would be under threat of displacement by imports, and then only if costs of production of that tonnage could not soon be reduced by a further 10%.

Obviously, no one can be sure exactly how production would change. But our principal point is that, given the considerable potential for cost reductions, it is unlikely that, following privatisation,

British coal production would be drastically reduced and replaced by massive imports. Indeed, for the reasons we have given elsewhere (the cheaper coal and the greater diversity and security of supply under privatisation), from the mid to late 1990s onwards demand for coal by British coal consumers may well expand.

Table 5 has been compiled on the basis that the British coal industry would need to be competitive at mine-mouth selling prices of no more than £1.4 per GJ, or £35 a tonne, in real 1987 pounds. While this price level is the appropriate target there is some chance, depending primarily on long distance sea freight rates and currency exchange rates, that British mines would have to meet a £1.2 per GJ (£30 a tonne) target price by 1992 to remain competitive. If this were to occur many more of the higher cost mines (representing possibly 20 million tonnes per year) would have at least temporarily higher cash costs than this, and would be candidates for earlier closure. (No mine need be closed just because its cash costs exceed selling prices provided the costs can be sufficiently reduced to competitive levels within a few years.) The shortfall which could result from any further closures of what would be a larger category of uneconomic mines might be partly met by expanding opencast production and the small existing private mines. The remaining shortfall, however, would best be met by increased imports, assuming that such imports were physically possible. In the case of power station coal increased imports would necessitate new coal import terminal facilities, a subject developed further in Chapter 4.

Safety and environmental considerations

It is sometimes argued that, under private ownership, costs would be lowered at the expense of safety standards, which would be prejudiced by practices used (say) in America. But whether coal is in the public or private sector should make no difference to safety standards. The health and safety regulations under which the British coal industry must operate provide the highest standards in the world. The regulations are encompassed in the Mines and Quarries Act and already apply to all extractive operations throughout Britain, whether in the public or private sector. Parliament has the responsibility to ensure that appropriate changes are introduced to keep pace with new technical developments, respond to fresh practical experience, and to act as final arbiter of the rules.

The Health and Safety Executive employs Mines Inspectors who enforce the rules by regular mine visits and discussions with all levels of supervision and management. These inspectors are professional engineers with years of experience in the mining industry. The employment, training and independence of these inspectors would not be altered by privatisation. In addition all mine managers and other supervisors must, by law, pass examinations to prove their knowledge of the health and safety regulations. Privatisation of the mines would not alter these fundamental requirements.

Thus the case for rejecting privatisation for fear of falling safety standards is groundless. Well run mining companies should find that rising productivity is accompanied by improved safety, a common experience in North America.

There may also be fears that the environment would not be sufficiently protected if the coal industry were privatised. Production, transportation and consumption of coal all have impacts on the environment which are not fully incorporated in market prices and which ideally should be a charge on the producer so that the costs used in decision making are the full costs to society. But environmental safeguards are a governmental responsibility which can and should be enforced whether an industry is in public or private ownership.

Estimating the benefits

We can now draw the threads together to make a broad estimate of the overall prize which sensible privatisation might achieve. We divide the benefits of a privatised coal market into three categories. The first consists of the efficiency and associated benefits (primarily gains to consumers) which economists would normally expect to be the result of liberalising a market which had been monopolised. Secondly, there are likely to be benefits to taxpayers who, through the agency of the government, have for years been subsidising the British coal industry. Neither type of benefit is easy to quantify, and there is some overlap between the two. We consider them separately below and indicate the likely order of magnitude of each in 1987 money values. Thirdly, there are the intangible benefits, which in the case of the privatisation of British Coal could be very substantial. The analysis assumes privatisation by mid 1988 (see below). If it is deferred, so too would be the benefits.

Efficiency benefits

As explained above, efficiency should improve provided privatisation makes the coal market more competitive. These improvements would exceed anything British Coal is likely to achieve either in its present form as a state monopoly or even if it were transformed into a private monopoly. So long as the market is monopolised, costs and prices are likely to be unnecessarily high and capital expenditure wasteful, no matter how well-intentioned the management of the industry.

Accepted economic theory shows that monopoly results in deadweight losses to society (losses to consumers, not all of which flow to producers) because of the tendency for prices to be higher and output to be lower under monopoly as compared with competition. In addition to the benefit which would arise from eliminating these deadweight losses, there would be a decline in costs which inevitably tend to be excessive when competitive pressures are absent. When monopolised markets become more competitive there are at least three sorts of cost-reducing influences. Firstly, the presence of competitors makes management and workers alike much more aware of the need to seek lower costs. Secondly, in the case of a market which had previously been in the hands of a state monopoly, reduced politicisation of the market allows management more time to spend on the search for cost savings and to waste less time on bargaining with politicians and civil servants. Thirdly, competition tends to stimulate well-directed research and development efforts which result in faster technical progress (and therefore lower costs) in the long run. In a truly competitive market, most of the cost savings are passed on to the customers of the competing private firms.

We presented above some estimates of likely production cost savings over the next few years if the coal industry were privatised to as to establish competition in coal supply. The reduction in average costs by the early 1990s, according to those figures, would approach 25 to 35 per cent (approximately £9 to £12½ per tonne in 1987 prices). Some improvements will occur under the present management, either as a state or a private monopoly, but we would not expect these, on the basis of the handicaps to efficiency of a public monopoly compared with a liberalised privatised industry, to be any more than some £5 per tonne. Thus we would argue that the short term cost reduction arising from privatisation would be of the order of £4–7½ per tonne in 1987 prices. That would be equivalent to £400–£750 million a year in cost savings over an annual coal output of around 100 million tonnes. In addition, there would be other significant gains of the sort explained above which are rather difficult to quantify, but could well be worth £100 million a year by 1992.

There would be another very valuable benefit of a more competitive coal market. For many years competition in the British energy market as a whole has been limited because of the edifice of protection which governments have erected around British Coal. With removal of that edifice, the *whole* energy market would become much more competitive. Since coal accounts for less than half British energy consumption (excluding transport fuels) spillover effects into the energy market as a whole could be quite significant. Although, even outside the transport market, there are constraints on consumers' ability to substitute one fuel for another (especially in the short run because consumers are locked-in to existing fuel burning equipment), the direct benefits from lower coal costs and prices would be multiplied by such spillover effects, resulting in lower costs and prices in all the energy industries. Clearly, if electricity generation is also made competitive and if genuine competition appears in the gas market there would be still greater effects. We estimate that by 1992 these further benefits would be a minimum of £100 million to £125 million a year. Thereafter, these benefits would rise very substantially.

Taxpayer benefits

Estimating the direct benefits to taxpayers which could be expected from the type of liberal privatisation scheme set out below is not straightforward. It is necessary to postulate the likely costs to the taxpayer if British Coal continues as a public monopoly, which in turn means postulating its efficiencies, the number of workers it will make redundant and so on. These estimates must in turn be compared with the subsidies and other taxpayer costs which will continue for many years even under privatisation, since commitments to redundant and retired workers must obviously continue. There is the further difficulty that comparisons of benefits for any single future year will differ since the industry will be changing whether it is privatised or not. It is important, however, to attempt to estimate the likely changing burden on taxpayers. We therefore give some broad estimates on a conservative basis using such information as is available to the public.

In what follows, as previously mentioned, and for reasons set out below, we assume the industry will be privatised in about mid 1988. For a continued nationalised industry we assume annual voluntary redundancies of around 10,000 for 5 or more years. British Coal have understandably made no statements on this subject, but their productivity targets imply these sorts of numbers. For the privatised industry we assume a further 5,000 a year, also voluntary. In both cases we assume that the Government continues to finance redundancies. Neither of us would wish to be associated with a scheme which skimped on the payments necessary to offset the hardship which inevitably results from the transition of an old-established and regionally concentrated industry such as British Coal.

Whether under continued nationalisation or under privatisation we assume that the Government continues to fund the majority of existing and past commitments to those who have retired early, or taken redundancy. The forecast redundancies of 10,000 a year under nationalisation and the additional 5,000 a year under privatisation are not small but together they are slightly fewer in five years than those achieved *voluntarily* in the last two years. Provided that the redundancy provisions are properly generous; that the admirable job promotion scheme under British Coal Enterprise continues (it has created 16,000 new job opportunities in the last two years and is planning 15,000 in each of the next two years) and that retraining measures also remain in place, then the transition of the industry to one that needs no government subsidies and no import protection, should be acceptable to all involved. It is, after all, the normal condition of most other industries in Britain.

As will become clearer below when we discuss our recommended privatisation scheme, we urge that the Government remains the channel for financing redundancies in the early years of privatisation. This is to ensure equality of treatment and the confidence of all who are affected.

What differences would arise in government funding under continued nationalised *versus* privatisation? In deducing the potential benefits to the taxpayer we have made the following assumptions:

i) under nationalisation, capital expenditures will continue at the present annual level of £650 million;

ii) under privatisation, capital expenditure will be lower;

iii) privatisation will produce both greater and faster efficiency gains;

iv) demand will be broadly level from the electricity supply industry and other customers (although under privatisation it could well rise); and

v) on privatisation, the Government will receive an initial capital sum and further staged payments (see below) which would help to offset outstanding loans to British Coal of about £4,000 million, primarily from the Government.

It should be appreciated that the existing loans are larger than any likely saleable value for the industry; so some capital write-off would be necessary.

If privatisation is effected in 1988 changes are unlikely to occur before 1989. Rather than give year by year estimates we group the four years 1989–1992 and give the expected annual average, and then give a 1995 estimate also. We accept the hope of British Coal that by 1989 it will break-even although we are sceptical about the prospects for significant profitability in later years, given long term trends in world coal prices. We also expect that the high rate of capital expenditure will need continued government financing over and above internally generated cash.

Some government payments will not differ whether the industry is privatised or not; in particular the payments which are a direct government commitment to cover previous redundancies, and other commitments made by British Coal. These combined payments are estimated to average £325 million a year over the period 1989–92, falling to under £200 million in 1995 as prematurely retired miners qualify for a normal pension payable from the normal retiring age.

We arrive at the following estimated annual costs and benefits to the Government (i.e. the taxpayer) from privatisation.

	Annual Average 1989–92	1995
Additional redundancy costs	−£100m to −£125m	Government savings from redundancies in earlier years.
Reductions in investment funding (savings in the PSBR)*	£130m to £160m	Quite possibly continuing.
Tax revenue on the profits of private coal companies	?	Substantial and probably rising.
Net government/taxpayer benefits	£30m to £35m	Significant and probably rising.

* This benefit is not a direct saving comparable with cost savings.

Thus, we expect some increase in redundancy costs in the short term which would be rather more than offset by savings in the external finance which British Coal would otherwise have needed. There would also be tax revenues from the profits of private mining companies, but these we cannot quantify. In sum, there should be a small saving to the taxpayer. Small—because we propose that the social costs of a declining workforce should continue to be met by the taxpayer. In the longer term, net benefits should increase. Privatisation would bring forward redundancies rather than increase them; thus, under continued nationalisation, redundancy payments would probably be *higher* than under privatisation. At the same time, PSBR savings would continue and there would be corporation tax payments by private coal companies.

In addition to the annual net benefits which arise from privatisation it is also necessary to consider the net capital benefits. In selling British Coal, the Government will be foregoing the net cash flow each year equal to:

Interest received + profits distributed − capital contribution for capital expenditure.

While capital contribution appears here and also in the table above, no double counting is involved since net capital gains and savings in PSBR are different categories of benefit. Thus, even where there are no net capital gains, there could still be very large savings in the PSBR from the reduced capital funding demands made upon the Government.

In drawing up the benefit tables so far we have assumed that British Coal would break even by 1989 and make modest profits thereafter. We doubt if this cash flow stream is of significant value since it presumes improvements in efficiencies at rates seldom achieved by British Coal. For example, it presumes no significant set-backs, strikes, etc. Realistically, the expected future income stream under continued nationalisation could easily become negative again as it has been for most of the last 15 years. Continuing capital expenditure will also be required and is most unlikely ever to be fully recovered. If the Government attempted to sell the right to this future cash flow stream while retaining the present structure of control and management, the sum it would realise would be nominal if not negative (i.e. investors would need to be paid to assume the obligation). In contrast, if British Coal is privatised under a liberal scheme of the type recommended below, the Government could receive in excess of £1½ billion, and possibly considerably more in some circumstances.

Hence privatisation, by increasing the value of the industry to the Government from a negligible and possibly negative sum to £1½ billion or more, creates a clear and very substantial *net* capital gain to the Government and taxpayer.

Certainly privatisation would compel the Government to write-off the difference between the capital proceeds of sale and the outstanding loans to British Coal at the time of privatisation (perhaps £4½ billion by 1988). But this is merely to recognise that much of the capital employed in British Coal, as set out in the annual accounts, is irrecoverable.

In sum, giving British Coal the benefits of any doubts about the value of its future income stream, the direct annual savings to the Government and thus taxpayers may be no more than £30 million to £35 million over the next few years, but would rise significantly thereafter. In addition there is the net capital gain of £1½ billion or more from the sales proceeds of privatisation.

Intangible benefits

There would also be important intangible benefits arising from coal privatisation.

i) A major reduction of monopolistic forces in the British coal industry leading to the gains suggested above.

ii) Although there would probaly be some further reduction in direct employment in the coal industry in the short to medium term, the rest of the British economy should become more competitive and the rise in national employment should more than offset the reduction in coal industry employment.

iii) There would be welcome depoliticisation of an unhappy industry, and an enhancement of morale, prosperity, and security of employment for the remaining workforce and management as another major British industry became able to face international competition without subsidy or protection.

iv) The market for coal in Britain should expand as it becomes cheaper and supplies become more diverse and more secure. Consumers would be more willing to convert to coal as the monopoly power of management and unions diminished.

v) The economic case for nuclear power would weaken.

vi) Exports, presently only 3 million tonnes annually, might increase.

vii) The simultaneous privatisation of electricity will be facilitated. This is an enormous prize. Without it, investors in a private electricity industry might be hard to find, if they were left naked to the power of a monopoly supplier, with all the distortions and extortions which that might entail. For example, a 5% improvement in the value of electricity assets, worth maybe £10 billion–£15 billion would add £500 million–£750 million to the sales proceeds.

Aggregate benefits

Our broad estimates of the aggregate direct benefits from privatising British Coal are summarised below. Since these are annual averages they are lower than the figures given earlier in the text for 1992.

These conservatively estimated benefits fully justify the liberal privatisation scheme which we propose.

How and when to privatise

In order to obtain the substantial benefits which privatisation offers, three stages are needed. First, a preparatory stage during which a scheme is formulated. This should overlap a second stage in

Table 6
SUMMARY OF ESTIMATED AGGREGATE BENEFITS
FROM 1988 PRIVATISATION
(in 1987 prices)

	Annual average 1989–1992	1995
1 Annual benefits		
Efficiency benefits		
Lower prices to consumers, etc.	£350m–£500m	£700m plus and rising.
Lower prices of other fuels	£80m–£100m	£250m plus and rising.
Net government (taxpayer) benefits	£30m–£35m	significant and rising.
Approximate total	£460m–£635m	£950m plus and rising.

2 Net capital benefits to government: £1½ billion plus further payments over 5 to 7 years (see below).

3 Plus very substantial intangible benefits.

which the small private coal sector is liberalised, as recently recommended by the Select Committee on Energy. The final stage would be full privatisation with the sale of British Coal assets to the private sector. The second and third stages would require changes to the 1946 Nationalisation Act. Liberalisation would require that the phrase *to the exclusion of any other person* be deleted from Chapter 1(1) of the Act and that changes be made to the clauses restricting the sizes of labour forces and coal reserves. Full privatisation would require that the 1946 Act be repealed.

Preparatory stage 1

The privatisation of British Coal in order to promote maximum competition and to involve entrepreneurial skills over a wide range and size of units, poses problems not encountered on such a scale in earlier privatisation schemes. For that reason the Department of Energy would benefit from the assistance of specialists from many backgrounds, including some with experience of successful co-operatives, management buyouts, finance and venture capital, company law and good industrial relations practice. Some, of course, would need to have special knowledge of the coal industry, both in Britain and overseas, to advise on the numerous technical questions which would arise.

The Department of Energy would have three specific tasks:

(i) supervising certain immediate liberalisation measures;

(ii) planning the packaging and disposal by privatisation of all the assets of British Coal; and

(iii) setting up a new entity, for which an appropriate title might be the Crown Coal Commission, which would have the tasks of holding and allocating coal reserves for future exploration and mining (similar to the pre-Second World War Coal Commission); of administering any residual social and environmental requirements of British Coal; and of promoting competition.

After privatisation, no price regulatory body would be needed since coal prices would be determined by market forces, though if electricity generation remained a monopoly then a regulatory regime would be required to prevent the abuse of power by the CEGB in the purchase of coal. The Crown Coal Commission, however, or some similar body, should be given an overriding duty of establishing and maintaining competition in the supply of coal in Britain, including imports. The Commission would need to exist, at least in embryo form, when privatisation is being planned.

The continued running of British Coal during the transitional period while its operations are being sold poses special but not insuperable problems. One particular task deserving the attention of the specialist advisers referred to above would concern the motivation and reward of management and staff in British Coal during the privatisation planning and handover periods.

Initial liberalisation stage 2

During the initial liberalisation stage the small existing private sector should be encouraged by removing the constraints placed upon it by the Nationalisation Act, and by British Coal's interpretation of that Act. Legal restrictions should be lifted and individuals, co-operatives and private sector firms should be allowed to purchase and operate any mines planned for closure.

Removing legal constraints on the private mining sector

The constraints to be removed may be summarised as follows:

(i) The labour force in underground mines cannot exceed or greatly exceed 30 men (although a little flexibility is sometimes allowed by British Coal). By contrast the average underground workforce in British Coal's mines was 855 at the end of 1985/86.

(ii) In the case of private opencast mines, reserves cannot exceed 35,000 tonnes of coal, or—in the case of adjacent sites—50,000 tonnes. These reserves are very small relative to those of British Coal's opencast operations.

(iii) Private mines are required to pay wage rates similar to those agreed upon between British Coal and the mining unions, thus inhibiting employment and mining activity.

(iv) Private mines receive only discounted prices from the CEGB. Moreover, under the Joint Understanding between British Coal and the CEGB, the latter can take only 5% of its coal (including imports) from sources other than British Coal. Thus one monopoly has a comfortable but clearly undesirable competition-restraining arrangement with another.

(v) Underground private mines pay a royalty of £1 per tonne to British Coal. Privately owned opencast mines pay a punitive £13.50 per tonne. Incumbent British Coal pays no royalty to anyone.

In general the private sector works reserves or remnants which are very small (or for other reasons are of no interest to British Coal) but which still make a valuable contribution to the exploitation of the country's coal reserves. Despite its severe handicaps, this small private sector has been consistently profitable. It is undesirable for it to be so constrained, as the Select Committee on Energy has recently pointed out. The Federation of Small Mines of Great Britain has also commented in its evidence to the Select Committee on Energy that the Joint Understanding between British Coal and the CEGB may be in breach of the 1951 European Coal and Steel Treaty (Articles 65 and 66). It is unwise to be at odds with EEC requirements which have the desirable aim of increasing competition.

Contract mining

During the planning period groups of workers (acting as companies or co-operatives) should be given the opportunity to mine coal at those mines which British Coal has closed or is considering closing, and at mines of a size too small to bear the overheads of British Coal. Such groups would contract to supply a given tonnage to British Coal over (say) five years at an independently determined price; and any such contracts would be binding on the privatised successors. British Coal would supply technical services and lease mining equipment to the miners at a price reflecting the costs of such support. Where mines facing closure do not interest miners or co-operatives, they should be offered by tender to private sector mining firms.

Besides helping towards full exploitation of the country's coal reserves, this method of working would offer employment for miners in areas of mine closures. When a coal company in the United States closes an uneconomic but unexhausted mine, small entrepreneurial teams of local miners welcome it. They see the closure as an opportunity to lease the seam from the company to work themselves. There is every reason to hope that British miners might wish to do likewise once a fair and reasonable scheme is devised.

The case against joint ventures

Joint venturing between British Coal and private sector companies has sometimes been put forward as a sensible interim step. Although new ideas about production, distribution and marketing could be introduced into the mining industry via joint ventures, it is doubtful whether any such arrangements would be satisfactory. British Coal, which has had a monopoly for so long, would probably show no more enthusiasm than have British Gas or the CEGB for sharing their facilities with private sector companies (despite their being required to co-operate by statute). Private investment would almost certainly be inhibited by the continued existence of a nationalised corporation, which would be seen as a subsidised competitor, and as a reluctant joint venture partner, subject to continual government interference.

Furthermore, if joint venturing were restricted to new ventures (which seems to be in the mind of most of its advocates, since they see it as a way of introducing external expertise) the short-term impact would be minimal, since it takes ten to fifteen years to plan and construct underground mines of any consequence. If, however, joint venturing is to include existing mines it could be only as an alternative to full privatisation.

Establishing joint ventures with a nationalised corporation which might soon be privatised is not attractive. Finally, any resulting friction between British Coal and private joint venturing companies could well delay or even frustrate privatisation. In sum, joint venturing may look plausible superficially but in practice would be a mistake.

Privatisation stage 3

Given the aim of achieving competition in coal supply, four features of a liberal privatisation scheme are absolutely essential. The scheme must:

i) provide for generous profit participation for those who remain in the industry, and adequate compensation for redundant management and employees who leave it;

ii) attract enough of the best national and international mining expertise without which full efficiencies cannot be achieved nor the necessary, substantial capital attracted;

iii) be compatible with a liberal form of electricity privatisation; and
iv) be accomplished expeditiously and embrace the whole industry.

i) *Generous treatment of management and workers*
It is unlikely that necessary levels of efficiency can be obtained without productivity improvements of the type outlined above. Thus privatisation would be accompanied for a time by a declining labour force in mining. That decline has been in progress for the last thirty years, during which the number of miners has dropped from over 700,000 to only about 110,000; it has been particularly marked over the last two years (since the strike) during which period the total workforce has dropped by around 80,000.

Redundancies there will be whether British Coal continues in its present shape or whether private sector firms succeed it, since costs cannot otherwise be reduced to competitive levels. The scale of these further redundancies, however, will not be as large as is commonly expected for the reasons set out above, where we estimated total redundancies over the next five years as 75,000, two-thirds of which will probably occur if British Coal continues as a nationalised industry. It is desirable that redundancies should remain voluntary and be generously compensated. We strongly recommend the reinstatement of a government-funded redundancy scheme along the lines of that which stopped at the end of March 1987. Other government-funded measures to alleviate the social impact of closures and the reduction in the labour force should be continued along present lines; for example, generous retraining facilities, measures to introduce new employment in coal mining districts and help with relocation. Equally, those who stay with the industry should be given the opportunity to share in its profitability. The prospective direct gains to coal customers, electricity customers, taxpayers, and the other indirect national gains (most notably in national employment prospects) fully justify such measures.

ii) *Attract the best national and international mining expertise*
To improve productivity rapidly and provide the substantial capital which rationalisation will require, the terms of privatisation must attract sufficient participation of experienced firms in the private sector. For an industry whose production and capital requirements are very diverse, varied forms of ownership are more appropriate than centralisation under either a state corporation or a private monopoly. Some smaller mines might best be run by workers' co-

operatives; there could sensibly be management/staff buyouts for small to medium-size operations; but the largest mines should be owned and operated by experienced mining companies, if only because of the large capital sums and the technical and commercial knowledge required. For these mines it is best to attract four or five major private sector groupings.

iii) *Compatibility with electricity privatisation*
Competition in electricity *generation* (which, like coal, is not a natural monopoly) is highly desirable. Our general assumption in this paper is that electricity generation will be liberalised as well as privatised. If, however, the government mistakenly chooses to preserve the CEGB or a successor private monopoly, special measures will be needed. A private monopoly in electricity supply would dominate a coal industry with competing suppliers. In these circumstances a regulatory body for electricity supply would be needed to see fair play for coal suppliers before potential investors would be willing to bid for coal mines, but this would be a very poor second best for potential coal investors.

iv) *Expeditious and comprehensive accomplishment*
Privatisation should be carried out expeditiously to avoid a long period of uncertainty for management, employees and customers which would inhibit future planning. It should also embrace the whole industry and not leave a rump of the least efficient mines in public ownership.

The timing of state 3 privatisation

Some people who accept the case for privatisation wish to postpone it. Leaving aside those who urge such postponement in the hope of eventual abandonment of the idea, what of those who genuinely believe that a few more years of progress under present arrangements are justified as a desirable precursor to any form of privatisation, on the grounds that it may be better to sell an industry only when it has returned to profit? This is a seductive argument with undoubted political appeal. It is, however, seriously mistaken.

Only if there were a case for privatising it whole (for instance, because it was held to be a natural monopoly, which it is not), would the profitability of the industry as a whole be relevant to the timing of privatisation. In contrast to British Gas, it is certain that higher capital sums would be raised by breaking the industry into a number of companies, rather than by privatising it as a whole (though capital raising should never be the main objective of privatisation). Indeed few might subscribe for shares even in a private monopoly if, as would be all too likely, it persisted in the non-commercial practices of British Coal.

Delay should be avoided for two other compelling reasons. First, the process of privatisation to introduce competition in coal supply and to incorporate the best technical and commercial knowledge from the worldwide mining industry would both enhance and bring forward the gains arising from increased efficiency. Second, once a major change is identified as desirable there are strong arguments against postponing it. A long period of uncertainty would be very hard on British Coal's existing management and workers. It is for these reasons that we urge privatisation as quickly as possible, and assume mid-1988 in our analyses in this paper.

Desirable features in acceptable schemes

In addition to meeting the essential requirements set out previously, any privatisation scheme should incorporate several further desirable features.

i) The fewer the long term subsidies granted the better. Those permitted should be only for social or environmental reasons (and, possibly, to enhance security of supply).

ii) Any subsidies should be for specific purposes and for a strictly defined period, after which they would be subject to review.

iii) Because of the industry's financial state, special terms may be required to ensure that the Government receives fair payment. Capital payments for coal mines could, for example, take the form of an initial sum followed by staged payments, which could be profit-related, over (say) 5 to 7 years. Such a period would allow electricity privatisation to take place and for longer term import trends to become apparent. It would also give management and workforces every incentive to maximise efficiency if a significant part of their pay and incentives were profit-related—see iv) below. If profit-related purchase schemes are considered too difficult to administer, revenue-related ones would be a possible alternative. The Government could also consider the simpler option of retaining minority shareholdings in the larger privatised companies in the expectation of capital appreciation and future sale.

iv) Management and workers, as a condition of sale, should be offered generous participation in privatised mines by some appropriate combination of profit-sharing bonuses and shares (or the equivalent of shares). The terms should ensure that private firms have an interest in buying the mines and running them efficiently in the long term, and that workforces have appropriate incentives, combined with long term job stability.

v) The coal industry pension scheme should be kept in existence to retain the confidence of all in the industry, and to ensure that pensions are portable between the privatised companies. Portability— widely demanded in all occupations—is necessary to ensure management and labour mobility within the diversified coal industry. At the time of privatisation it is also essential that the pension scheme is fully funded, albeit with the right of the Government to recapture any overfunding which can be shown to exist say 7 to 10 years later. The proposed Crown Coal Commission could be charged with overseeing the pension scheme.

vi) The Government, perhaps through this Commission, should own and allocate coal reserves. Access by all parties to such coal reserves should be free and equal. No firms of any size, from miners' co-operatives upwards, should suffer discrimination. Allocation should be on clearly-defined criteria which could include some form of competitive bidding, and commitment to given production levels, or work programmes. Economic rent should be extracted through normal corporate profit taxes, rather than through revenue-related levies such as royalties which tend to increase mine operating costs and create a bias in favour of imports.

Desirable complementary features in electricity privatisation

It is not possible to discuss and recommend coal privatisation schemes without taking into account the privatisation of electricity generation, which—like coal—should be turned into a competitive industry. Generation, unlike transmission and local distribution, is not a monopoly activity. One scheme would be to have say five to ten regional generating groups making use of a common carrier central grid (which would preferably be privately owned and regulated), and five to ten regional distribution boards (again preferably in the private sector and regulated). The regional distribution boards would be the customers of generating groups and at the time of privatisation long term power contracts would be created for most of the output of the generating stations, encouraging competition between them in supplying the remaining needs of the Area distribution companies, with increasing competition over time.

Detailed consideration will be given to these and other possibilities in our forthcoming paper on electricity privatisation. But the essence of what we propose is, on the one hand, stable long-term power contracts to justify a proper price being paid for generating assets; and, on the other hand, the ensuring of sufficient and increasing competition to promote efficiency. Any scheme with these broad characteristics and involving competition between generating companies to buy coal supplies would make it worthwhile for any mining firms confident of their technical and commercial abilities to invest in privatised coal.

There is one more important matter to consider. This is whether there is a case for a modern coal terminal.

The case for a modern coal terminal

In Table 5 above we set out the estimated coal supply position for Britain in 1992 assuming privatisation and the need to sell coal at no more than £35 a tonne at the mine-mouth. The suggested imports might be 12–19 million tonnes, assuming exports of 3 million tonnes. If the level of competitive prices were to fall to £30 a tonne, the need for import capacity could rise to 20 to 25 million tonnes a year. In the light of these potential requirements it is appropriate to reconsider the case for a large modern coal terminal. It is clear that the British coal industry, made up as it is in large part of deep multi-seam mines, many of which are more than 25 years old, and some very much more, is unlikely to be capable of supplying the whole British market economically. Imports are therefore an essential element in a liberalised market, particularly if the demand for coal expands. Accordingly, we believe that the case exists now for the CEGB together with the SSEB to plan a new coal terminal of say 15 million tonnes per annum capacity. For the reasons set out previously it might be four years or more before such a terminal could be operational but it may well be needed by the early 1990s.

Commencing to plan and build a new terminal now would have

several purposes. It would make clear to both the British coal industry and the electricity supply industry that the interests of coal and electricity consumers were henceforth to be paramount. Second, it would sharpen the concentration of all involved in the British coal industry to have to meet international competition without operational subsidies (social subsidies are a different matter) within four to five years. Third, even if the coal terminal is not fully utilised when first built—or even after many years, depending on the efficiency of the British coal industry—it would be an invaluable insurance policy for the CEGB (or its private sector successors). At a cost of say £100 million to £150 million (or cheaper, if a floating terminal is feasible) it would be a sensible investment to ensure keener prices on an annual coal purchase outlay of several billion pounds. Fourth, it would enhance security of supply by protecting against a future oil crisis, a nuclear shutdown or a future coal strike in Britain.

For all these reasons, most of which apply whether or not coal is privatised, we consider the Government should lift restrictions on CEGB and SSEB coal imports and ensure that they plan and construct a large new coal terminal.

The choice of schemes

Three forms of privatisation merit examination:

i) privatising British Coal as a monolith;
ii) offering all mines, both opencast and underground, for sale on an individual basis, subject to tender; and
iii) offering the existing British Coal Areas for sale by tender.

The advantages and disadvantages of these methods need to be considered against the list of essential and desirable features set out earlier in this chapter.

i) *Privatising British Coal as a monolith*
This scheme is the simplest form of privatisation and might be expected to meet least internal resistance from managers and employees; it would bring the fewest pressures for uncomfortable change. The disadvantages are so many, however, that it is very debatable whether it would be any better than leaving British Coal in the public sector.

It would merely mean replacement of an unnecessary public monopoly of coal production by an unnecessary private monopoly. The scheme would be against the interests of customers and taxpayers; it would not enhance national employment prospects, and it would prevent the rapid injection of private sector technical, commercial and management expertise. Above all, it would fail to add a competitive spur to the industry. Moreover, the privatisation of electricity would be handicapped, since the scope for lowering electricity costs and for increasing the security of coal supplies would be reduced.

There are still further drawbacks. If coal were to be privatised in its entirety, there might well be no public interest in buying shares in a company which in recent years has almost always lost money, which would have an unchanged management and workforce, very large capital requirements, and no certainty of long term profitability. Individual shareholders are hardly likely to be interested, nor could they be advised to invest, particularly as they would have little control of management. These objections would also apply to corporate investors since a consortium of companies would need to be involved, and it is hard to see the attractions of joining such a consortium. Any attempt to sell off British Coal as a monolith would either attract too few takers, or result in an unreasonably low price for the Government. For all these reasons privatising British Coal as a monolith should be firmly rejected as a serious option.

A variant of this scheme, which has been suggested, is the selling of British Coal in its entirety to its existing management and workers—the so-called 'co-partnership scheme'. This has superficial attractions because, it is argued, it would create higher morale amongst managers and workers, or at least cause less resentment and fewer difficulties than other schemes. While this might be true initially, it is unlikely that the reaction would be lasting because it achieves so few of the essential and desirable points listed previously. From the Government's viewpoint it is very unlikely that any significant capital sum could be raised from the co-partnership approach; the industry would probably have to be given away. This in itself is not sufficient reason for rejecting the scheme if it could meet all the other criteria of successful privatisation. But it does not. There would be only minimum pressure to rationalise the industry either quickly or thoroughly. There would be no input of the external management and the technical and commercial expertise which the industry so badly needs.

Subsidies might have to continue, perhaps indefinitely unless overtaken by other forms of privatisation. Without competition within the industry, without improvement in the diversity and security of supply, demand for coal would continue to decline. The industry thus privatised might have great difficulty in raising the large capital sums needed for rationalisation and new mines. The Selby mining complex, for instance, has a capital cost of £1,500 million for 10 million tonnes per annum of capacity while Asfordby will cost £400 million for 3 million tonnes per annum. Further, a monolithic, co-partnership privatisation scheme would largely negate the gains to be expected from complementary electricity privatisation. That is a particularly serious drawback.

Co-partnership raises other basic problems, and in particular how the worker ownership is to be inaugurated and how it is to be provided with the financial stability to survive. Presumably, the proposal would require that each working miner would be offered a share and corresponding voting rights in either British Coal as a whole or his particular Area Board. With the latter, basic problems would arise in that the miners in the high cost areas (who face the most insecure future) would be given low value shares, whilst those in the low cost areas facing a secure future would be given shares that were highly valuable.

Under either option the decision taking would be dominated by caucuses of miners and unions with little or no experience of commercial management and caught between their desire for job security (based on continuing cross-subsidisation) on the one hand, and on the other hand their need to come to terms with losses, and with the necessity for commercial viability. Such complications would be incompatible with the decisive and strong management essential if the industry is to survive without subsidies and in competition with imports—the tests which privatisation must meet to be justified.

We conclude that if the industry were privatised as a monolith the outcome would inevitably be a flight of both management and finance from the industry leading either to collapse or to restoration of public ownership. If privatised under co-partnership but on an Area rather than national basis, the initial gross inequities referred to above would be compounded by a rapid flight of management and capital from the weaker Area boards leading to their early insolvency.

In summary we believe co-partnership to be one of the least sensible forms of privatisation. It would appear to be unfeasible both managerially and financially. It would probably fail and require rescue. It is hard to see that it is better than leaving British Coal in the public sector in its present form.

ii) *Privatisation of individual mines*

This scheme has much more in its favour. It would ensure great pressure to achieve efficiencies, and would be of interest to a wide range of firms and existing managers and workers. It could lead to major improvements in efficiency and would have some significant attractions for customers and taxpayers.

The difficulties of privatisation on an individual mine basis, however, are formidable. The technical and legal problems involved in drawing up prospectuses for 100 or more mines and other businesses would be a huge task resulting in such long delays that its accomplishment would always be in doubt, bringing uncertainty, and causing dissension within the industry. Fears of job losses would be increased. Subsequent problems of industry rationalisation by the amalgamation of groups of mines to achieve optimal exploitation of reserves would be considerable. This kind of scheme would not attract, and might well deter, the involvement of the national and international private sector, so vital to achieving efficiency and securing the long term prospects of the industry. Efficient world-scale coal mining companies are usually much larger than all but the very largest of British mines. If a mining group or consortium were interested only in a substantial investment (in, say, 10 to 15 million tonnes per year of capacity) it might be discouraged by the trouble and expense of bidding for say 20 to 30 different mining units in order to achieve a sufficiently interesting and viable set of say 10 to 15 mines. Clearly, then, this route could lead to the failure to sell a large number of mines despite their reasonable long term prospects, leaving them on the Government's hands. For these and other reasons, the Government might fail to realise a proper capital sum from the exercise and, worse still, fail to establish the industry in its most economic long term form. In sum, although this approach has advantages over privatising the industry as a monolith, its drawbacks loom so large that it can hardly be considered a serious option.

iii) *Area board privatisation*

There is some advantage in working, as far as possible, with existing organisations. The last two years have seen increasing devolution to Area management in the coal industry with encouraging results. There already exists a complete or near-complete management team in each area charged with putting it, as far as is possible, on a commercial stand-alone footing. It is, therefore, sensible to build upon this organisation and loyalty by privatising British Coal initially on an area basis. Subsequently, there would be further reorganisation leading to the variety of producing units which, as explained earlier, should be the eventual aim of coal privatisation.

Of all the approaches to privatisation, initial privatisation by area is the most likely to provide the necessary motivation and to maintain morale among existing managers and employees. It would give them the prospect of remaining, in the first place, in a structure similar to the one in which they were already working and would provide the best chance of continued employment with increased security and attractive profit incentives. Managers and employees would be less opposed to rationalising or closing unprofitable mines since they would automatically be considered for transfer to other mines within the area.

It would be much easier to produce the nine or so prospectuses which would be involved in the offer of Areas for sale than the scores of prospectuses which would be required for individual mines, since legal problems involved in defining the precise limits of individual mines and their associated reserves would be avoided. By privatising initially on an area basis, the units would be of a size which could be expected to attract large, experienced companies able, certainly for medium and larger mines, to achieve the necessary levels of efficiency. As mentioned, most modern coal companies are of a size much closer to existing areas than to individual mines. Under this scheme each area would, in the first place, be formed into a 100% owned operating subsidiary of British Coal. Employment contracts would be transferred to these subsidiaries with no diminution in rights, terms of employment, or entitlements to pension.

One relevant question is whether the opencast mines should remain as a unit or be dispersed amongst the areas in which they lie. The case for keeping them together and privatising them as a unit is strong. The opencast sector is certainly the most profitable part of British Coal and could be expected to find ready purchasers. On the other hand, it would reduce the attractions of many areas if they did not contain opencast operations. Many coal companies in other countries operate both underground and opencast mines. Since it is desirable to make it possible for all areas to be privatised speedily and to hold out the prospect of profitability for each one of them (without which private sector participation would not occur), it would appear sensible to allocate opencast operations to the relevant areas in the first phase of the privatisation exercise, and to study the question of management integration. Set out in Table 7 are the area operating profits (losses) for the financial year to end March 1986, calculated on the basis that opencast mines are distributed to the areas in which they lie. The table shows that six of the then ten areas (South Midlands has now amalgamated with North Derbyshire) would have been profitable in the financial year 1985–86 with opencast mines included, as opposed to two which were profitable with deep mine operations only.

It is of considerable importance that the management and employees in all areas have equal and compelling financial incentives to support privatisation. The provision of such incentives (investment opportunities, profit sharing etc) should indeed be one of the conditions for bidding. While this will reduce the sales proceeds of all areas, particularly in the more marginal ones, it is both equitable and essential.

If some areas appeared to involve disproportionate risks or levels of management effort before they could become viable they might prove unsaleable in isolation. It may therefore be necessary to consider making it a condition of sale that these are acquired by bidders purchasing the more strongly viable areas. This would provide greater opportunities for job relocation. These are matters for careful investigation during the privatisation planning period.

Area management, with the help of British Coal headquarters, would provide for the Department of Energy (or directly for the proposed Crown Coal Commission) both technical and cost information on individual mines during the preparatory stage of privatisation. Provision of this information would give potential investors reasonable time to judge how much to bid for areas; payment, as we have explained, could be made under some kind of staged scheme. Where mines seemed to have little hope of a profitable future they might have to be put under a commitment to close before privatisation—in other words, they would be excluded from the areas for which bids would be asked.

To provide continuity and to give a minimum revenue to attract investors, it would probably be necessary to keep in being for a limited period existing arrangements under which areas supply power stations (the CEGB and SSEB) at certain guaranteed volumes and prices; there could, for instance, be a tapering provision (both volume and price would taper) which would reduce over a defined period the proportion of an area's output which was sold in this way.

Table 7

AREA OPERATING PROFITS (LOSSES), YEAR ENDED 31.03.86
Including re-distribution of opencast profits to deep-mine Areas

AREA	Underground tonnes produced	Profit/(Loss) (£ millions)	Opencast tonnes produced	Profit/(Loss) (£ millions)	Total tonnes produced	Profit/(Loss) (£ millions)	Profit/(Loss) (£ per tonne)
Scottish	4.3	(46)	2.6	56	6.9	10	1.4
North East	9.5	(34)	2.8	88	12.3	54	4.4
North Yorkshire	13.9	(61)	0.0	0	13.9	(61)	(4.4)
South Yorkshire	12.5	11	1.5	31	14.0	42	3.0
North Derbyshire	6.2	(26)	1.4	28	7.6	2	0.3
Nottinghamshire	18.7	97	0.0	0	18.7	97	5.2
S. Midlands	6.2	(17)	2.7	71	8.9	54	6.1
Western	9.4	(27)	1.0	12	10.4	(15)	(1.4)
South Wales	6.6	(65)	2.1	57	8.7	(8)	(0.9)
Kent	0.5	(3)	0.0	0	0.5	(3)	(6.0)
TOTALS	87.8	(171)*	14.1	343	101.9	172	1.7

* before strike recovery costs—see Tables 1 and 1a

(Source: National Coal Board Report and Accounts)

As this tapering period drew on, more and more competition would be introduced into the sale of coal. Full competition would exist from the beginning in the supply of coal to consumers other than the CEGB and SSEB, i.e. a quarter of all coal produced in Britain.

During the bidding procedure, the Crown Coal Commission or the Department of Energy would need to guard against collusion and to ensure that the basis for a genuinely competitive industry was established. There would probably need to be limits placed on the number of areas for which a company or a consortium could bid. A general prohibition on owning more than one area would probably be unnecessary; nevertheless the ownership of two of the larger areas might be regarded as competition-restricting. It would be for the Commission or the Department to judge the merits of each situation on the basis of the bids they received.

Privatising on an Area basis would be only an initial (though an important) step which should not be allowed to preclude a wider spread of ownership of mining operations of different sizes. Once the areas were in private ownership, further changes in the structure of the industry would be desirable leading to the diversified structure which would be the objective of privatising individual mines (see ii above). These changes would quite probably come about naturally as the new owners decided that some of their operations should be sold off—for instance, to managers wishing to buy out, to other firms in the private sector, or to groups of miners wishing to set up co-operatives. Were such changes not to occur, it might seem appropriate for the Coal Commission or the Department of Energy to step in to encourage some divestment in the interests of developing competition in an industry where operations of many different sizes should be able to flourish. We would not rule out some combined ownership of power stations and associated coal mines during this second phase, assuming that electricity generation was being privatised and liberalised at about the same time as coal, subject to the provision that there should be no significant diminution of competition.

To sum up, although there are several ways in which privatisation could be achieved, no road towards a fully liberalised coal market will be easy after forty years of nationalisation. However, the approach outlined above (and it is only an outline) seems to us a reasonable basis for discussion since it appears capable of bringing about the major benefits inherent in a much more efficient British coal industry, providing secure jobs and holding out the prospect of long term expansion in output.

Probable sales proceeds from privatisation

One final matter of importance remaining to be discussed is the potential sales proceeds from privatisation. It is not possible to be precise on this matter because it depends on so many factors, but it is important for us to indicate the likely range of sales proceeds. We do this under the following assumptions:

i) British Coal is privatised in mid 1988 by initial Area by Area (including opencast sites) sale to private sector companies.

ii) The privatised coal industry would need to be competitive with imports at the equivalent of £35 a tonne at the mine-mouth (in 1987 real terms) by 1992, and will be producing the 1992 output set out in Table 5 above. This assumes achieving the efficiency improvements which underlie the Table 5 estimates.

iii) The electricity generating industry is privatised on a competitive basis so that the CEGB and SSEB are no longer the sole purchasers of power station coal.

iv) There are tapering coal contracts in price and volume terms (as set out earlier in this section) between the areas and the CEGB and SSEB, and those coal contracts would be assumed by any private sector successors to these entities.

v) Redundancy payments post-privatisation would be funded by the Government.

vi) Managers and employees would be given generous profit participation incentives in the privatised companies on an equitable basis to encourage acceptance of the new industrial structure.

vii) Purchase prices would consist of an initial capital sum and further profit or revenue related payments over the subsequent five to seven years.

Given the conditions noted above we would expect the aggregate initial capital payment to be around £1,500 million, possibly more, and the subsequent annual profit related payments over five to seven years to be in the range of £150 million to £300 million.

Clearly the initial proceeds will depend on the area prospectuses, the enthusiasm of the management and employees of British Coal, and the perceptions of potential private sector purchasers. The further staged annual payments will also depend upon productivity achievements, and the price and availability of imports. We hope, however, to have indicated the orders of magnitude which could be involved.

It is hardly necessary to add that these purchase price estimates, and indeed the whole future of the industry, turn upon the industry establishing reasonably harmonious industrial relations.

This in turn requires a generous profit participation scheme for those who remain in the industry and who could, therefore, expect a more prosperous and secure future. Those who leave the industry must, as we have consistently urged, be treated generously to secure voluntary redundancy. In addition, full support must continue to be given to the creation of new jobs and retraining in those areas affected.

Summary and conclusions

Objectives of privatisation

In this paper we have set out to show the benefits to the nation from coal privatisation on a competitive basis, and how and when this should be done. The main aim of privatisation should be to make the British coal industry internationally competitive within five years. This vitally important objective is achievable only under an efficient privatisation scheme of the form outlined in this paper.

The record of nationalisation

The British coal industry has not realised its potential. Since nationalisation in 1947, when British Coal was given the almost exclusive right to mine coal in Britain, it has been a monopoly high-cost producer, from which the electricity industry has been required (by successive governments) to purchase virtually all its coal supplies. As a consequence, electricity costs in Britain have been unnecessarily high, contributing to the decline in manufacturing industries and thus to the rise in national unemployment. Despite oil price rises during the 1970s and early 1980s, British coal production dropped and market share was lost to other fuels. Only a small, restricted, but nonetheless efficient and consistently profitable private sector is permitted to operate on remnants of coal and the recovery of coal from colliery tips. Its achievements point to what privatisation could achieve.

Despite a captive market and supported prices, British Coal has made losses for much of its history and has required large subsidies fromm the taxpayer. Between 1981 and 1986, government financial support has totalled £6.3 billion, i.e. over £1.25 billion a year on average—a sum equivalent to over three-quarters of British Coal's average wage bill. The net effect of this is an industry which, despite the considerable and praiseworthy improvements of the two years since the strike, has in its present form no serious prospect of viability—i.e. of supplying coal at internationally competitive prices. This condition is not the fault of British Coal's management and employees: it is inherent in its public monopoly structure which causes all major policy and investment decisions to be politicised by management, employees, unions, and government, with minimal long-term accountability or the need to meet the critical tests of commercial reality. Accordingly, in its present form, it will not achieve anything approaching its full potential. The same will be true if it is privatised as a monopoly: it will remain an economic drain on the nation, and the value of its future contribution is likely to be negligible, it not negative. The introduction of competition under a sensible scheme of privatisation would offer a far superior alternative to all involved.

Criteria for privatisation

Coal production is not a natural monopoly and the introduction of competition within the industry will ensure that coal is supplied both as efficiently and as cheaply as possible. However, to reverse the decline of the industry and to ensure competition, fundamental changes to the structure of the industry will be required. These changes must ensure a permanent improvement in the industry's efficiency, and this should be a primary aim of privatisation rather than maximising the sales proceeds to the government, as has been the case with some other major privatisations (e.g. British Gas). In fact, privatising the coal industry on a diversified rather than a monolithic basis will also realise the maximum sales proceeds since the industry will be much more marketable on this basis, and accordingly investors will pay greater sums.

An effective privatisation scheme has certain essential require-ments. These are that the scheme must:

i) realise the identified major benefits;

ii) provide both for generous and attractive profit participation for all who remain, pension arrangements at least as good as the present ones (with full transferability within the industry), and generous compensation for redundant employees with continued job creation and generous compensation for redundant employees with contin-ued job creation and retraining schemes;

iii) attract sufficient of the best national and international mining expertise needed to raise efficiency, and also attract the necessarily large sums of capital required in this capital-intensive industry;

iv) be compatible with a liberal form of privatisation of electricity generation; and

v) be accomplished expeditiously and embrace the whole industry.

All these critical points are fully developed in the main body of this paper but a few important observations are worth repeating. Privatis-ation can and must be made attractive to present and future manage-ment and employees. We estimate that if British Coal is to achieve its stated productivity targets of 8% to 10% improvement a year, some 10,000 voluntary redundancies and retirements will be required in each of the next five years. To reach the higher efficiency targets which are required for the industry to be internationally competitive within five years, a further 5,000 voluntary redundancies a year would be required over the same period, a total of 75,000 over five years. This needs to be compared with the 80,000 reduction in manpower achieved voluntarily in the last two years. If the redun-dancy arrangements remain as generous as those of the past two years (one of our most important recommendations), we believe that those extra redundancies will be achievable without demoralisation or hardship.

We also stress the need to link coal privatisation to electricity privatisation. The electricity industry purchases over 95% of its coal requirements from British Coal (equivalent to over 75% of British Coal's annual output). Accordingly, to privatise electricity generation on a competitive basis, (which is the only way to maximise efficiency) but to leave it to the mercies of a high cost monopoly coal supplier, will greatly lessen its attraction for investors. Conversely, if coal is privatised on a diversified competitive basis it will attract few if any investors if 75% of its output is bought by two customers who are the monopoly suppliers of electricity. Accordingly, the privatisation of the two industries should be planned simultaneously and executed as near to the same time as possible. These are points which we shall cover fully in our forthcoming CPS paper on electricity privatisation.

Favourable impact of privatisation

It is often feared that the impact of privatisation and the consequent need to be internationally competitive would result in a massive closure programme and consequent redundancies. Our estimates, based on our researches into the achievable efficiencies of the British coal industry under privatisation (which probably requires mine-mouth selling prices of £35 a tonne in 1987 money values to be internationally competitive), give a very different picture. By 1992, the output from existing underground mines (now 90 million tonnes per annum) is likely to be in the range 70–75 million tonnes per annum plus a further 10 million tonnes per annum from new capacity due on stream in the next five years. If the total British market for coal remains static at today's level of around 115 million tonnes per annum (though indeed with the lower prices and greater diversity and security of supply under privatisation the market could well expand) imports will amount only to around 12–19 million tonnes per annum compared with 10–11 million tonnes per annum today.

Due to the lack of modern coal terminals it would be physically very difficult to import more coal by 1992, however economic such imports might be. For this and other reasons we urge that the Government should encourage the CEGB and SSEB to build a 15 million tonnes per annum coal facility which could be in place within four to five years. In addition to demonstrating that the interests of coal and electricity consumers are henceforth to be paramount, such a terminal would enhance the security of supply of Britain's energy by protecting against a further oil crisis, a nuclear shutdown, or a future coal strike. In short it is needed primarily as an insurance policy. While it would permit a near doubling of imports from (say) 1993 onwards, the 15 million tonnes per annum of underground capacity which would be displaced by such imports would need only to reduce its 1992 production costs by just over 10% to remain competitive at coal prices of £35 a tonne. Such a cost reduction could well be achievable under privatisation in a further few years beyond 1992.

Benefits of privatisation

Much of our paper is devoted to the critical issue of estimating the net benefits to be derived from privatisation as compared with continuing British Coal as a monopoly. These benefits turn upon the comparison between the performance of the industry under privatisation and monopoly. We believe our estimates are realistic but conservative, and sufficient for basic decision-making. Assuming early privatisation, the benefits (see Table 6) can be set out under three categories:

a) the tangible annual benefits to consumers and taxpayers, after financing generous redundancy payments (net benefits of around £450 million to £650 million in the years to 1992, rising to at least £950 million by 1995, and more thereafter);

b) the net capital receipts from privatisation (estimated to be at least £1,500 million as an initial down payment and a further £150 million–£300 million per annum on a profit related basis over the next five to seven years); and

c) the very substantial intangible benefits which may be summarised as follows:

i) A major reduction of monopolistic forces in the British coal industry leading to the gains suggested above.

ii) The gains to the rest of the British economy, plus the rise in national employment prospects resulting from cheaper coal and electricity, should more than offset the further modest reductions in direct coal industry employment.

iii) There would be welcome depoliticisation of an unhappy industry, and an enhancement of morale and prosperity, together with security of employment for the continuing workforce and management, as another major British industry became able to face international competition without subsidy or protection.

iv) The market for coal in Britain should expand as supplies become cheaper, more diverse and more secure. Consumers would be more willing to convert to coal as the monopoly power of management and unions diminished.

v) The economic case for nuclear power would weaken.

vi) Exports, presently over 3 million tonnes annually, might increase.

vii) Finally, there is the substantial prize of facilitating the simultaneous privatisation of electricity.

How best to privatise

Three main schemes with some variants have been examined:

a) privatising British Coal as a monolith;
b) offering all mines for sale on an individual basis; and
c) a two phase privatisation, first of the existing areas including opencast activities, and second by further rationalisation once privatised, leading to a competitive diversified coal industry.

The first objection to privatising British Coal as a monolith is that privatisation would have to be delayed until British Coal is seen to be earning sustainable profits such that its heavy capital expenditures (presently £650 million a year) would be acceptable to its new owners. It could be years before this happened, if it ever did. There are other serious objections.

Monolithic privatisation is not viable since without introducing some new senior management—possessing great commercial and financial expertise—the industry would almost certainly be unsaleable to private investors. It would be unable to secure the major financial resources which rationalisation requires. Sale of the industry to the existing workforce (the so called co-partnership scheme) would be even less viable since the latter would be even less capable of securing access to financial resources. The management structure would be weakened so as to preclude the essential rationalisation which the industry must achieve if it is to survive.

Joint ventures between British Coal and private sector companies are similarly unattractive and cannot be recommended.

Privatisation of mines on an individual basis is more attractive since it would be of interest to a wide range of firms, existing managers and employees and should introduce major efficiency improvements. It poses, however, formidable legal and technical problems in drawing up prospectuses for over 100 different mines and the delays could run into years, demoralising the industry in the process. Equally seriously, it might result in too many small companies which would reduce its attraction to the international mining companies whose experience, management and financial resources are vital to rationalisation. It could also result in many mines finding no purchasers, leaving the Government with an unprofitable and demoralised rump of the industry. For all these reasons it is not a serious option.

This leaves the third scheme: privatisation on an Area-by-Area basis with tapering, medium term contracts between the Area Boards and the CEGB and SSEB or their successors. This offers the best prospects for speedy privatisation, and the sale of the whole industry in units of viable size. This would achieve the maximum gains in efficiency by attracting sufficient technical, managerial and financial resources. It would hold out the best employment and profit sharing prospects for management and employees, and obtain by far the highest sales proceeds for the Government. For all these reasons, we believe that Area-by-Area privatisation is the best option. Indeed, it is the *only* worthwhile one.

The timing of privatisation

The best time for privatisation deserves careful consideration. Many who favour privatisation in principle wish to postpone it in practice. Partly this stems from fear of management, employee and union opposition which should be dealt with by generous compensation to all who are made redundant (a much smaller number than has commonly been feared). There is also the argument for awaiting the arrival of profitability. We consider, however, that there is no need to wait until British Coal achieves long term viability, if it ever does, because that is a requirement only if it is to be privatised as a monolith, an approach which we reject as undesirable, indeed unworkable.

Delay should be avoided for two other compelling reasons. Firstly, the process of privatisation to introduce competition in coal supply and to incorporate the best technical and commercial knowledge from the worldwide mining industry would both enhance and bring forward the gains arising from increased efficiency. Secondly, once a major change is identified as desirable there are strong arguments against postponing it. A long period of uncertainty would be very hard on British Coal's existing management and workers. It is for these reasons that we urge privatisation as quickly as possible, and have assumed mid-1988 in our analyses in this paper.

The ultimate justification for privatisation

The ultimate justification for privatising the British coal industry is that it offers the early prospect of a strong and viable industry at a level of output similar to that of today. In contrast, continued nationalisation holds out the prospect of the industry dwindling to a fraction of its present size over the next decade while continuing to need large and probably increasing subsidies. In such conditions the livelihoods of both management and employees would be under continuous threat, as would be the security of coal supply to the nation. The demand for coal would accordingly fall.

It follows that privatisation with competition is in the interest of both the nation and those employed in the industry. Privatisation would increase efficiency, lower costs to the point where the industry could compete internationally without subsidies or protection and, by enhancing the security of supply, should expand the market for coal in Britain. It should be seen not as the destroyer of the British coal industry, but as its saviour.

Glossary

Longwall mining	the method by which most coal is mined in British underground mines. A cutter-loader travels along the coal face (or wall) delivering coal onto an armoured face conveyor for subsequent transfer to the mine's main coal transport system.
Giga Joule (GJ)	a measure of the energy content of coal. Coal of average quality contains about 25 Giga Joules per tonne.
Mine-mouth price	the price of coal at the mine, excluding any transport charges to the consumer.
BSC	British Steel Corporation.
CEGB	Central Electricity Generating Board.
SSEB	South of Scotland Electricity Board.
ESI	Electricity Supply Industry.
ARA Ports	the ports of Amsterdam, Rotterdam and Antwerp.
Steam coal	coal destined for steam raising; most British coal is of this type.
Coking coal	coal destined for conversion to coke.
Deep mines	underground mines.
Opencast mines	surface mines.
EFL	external financing limit.
Liberalisation	the introduction of competition throughout the British coal mining industry to reduce long-term costs and increase efficiency.
Joint venture	a suggestion frequently made that coal mines should be jointly owned by both British Coal and private-sector companies.

17

Privatise Power: Restructuring the Electricity Supply Industry

Alex Henney

Preface

Britain's Electricity Supply Industry is on the verge of a programme of heavy capital expenditure, to fill a supply gap forecast to widen rapidly in the early years of the next decade. This gap is a consequence partly of vigorous growth in the economy and partly of the forthcoming retirement of generating plant constructed in the extraordinary round of activity in the late 1950s and 1960s. The onset of this programme will be marked by the closure of the nine Magnox nuclear stations during the 1990s.

Belief that the ESI should be restructured will command general assent—if only because there is no good reason why the enormous expenditure which is planned should be a claim on the public purse. The way in which it is restructured, and the extent to which the industry will be exposed to market forces, will profoundly affect the efficiency of the new system which must serve our economy in the first quarter of the next century. The stakes are high. The net assets of the ESI are some £36 billion; well over twice those of British Gas. Electricity demand has been growing at a vigorous 2.5% a year since the economic recovery began in 1981. An economy which is likely to be orientated more and more towards service and high-technology industries may well become more and more greedy for electricity.

(And the environmental questions are as difficult as the economic ones: what should we do about nuclear waste, nuclear safety, acid rain from coal-fired power stations, the growing concern of scientists about the 'greenhouse effect' caused by the combustion of fossil fuels?)

It is, then, timely to propose policies for restructuring the ESI which will encourage enterprise, competition, efficiency. For too long it has been taken for granted that in our densely-populated island the advantages of a large-scale, integrated system—of a monolithic ESI—are overwhelming. But *is* the ideal model of an efficient system one which comprises a small number of very large power stations, linked by a national grid, and operated in accordance with an 'economic merit order'? Or can there be some other solution, or set of solutions?

Alex Henney is proposing a scheme whereby about ten generating companies, heirs of the CEGB, would be in genuine competition with one another. Genuine, because they would all start from the same point, each possessing a mixed bag of oil, gas and coal-fired plant, geographically dispersed to avoid any dangers of creating regional monopolies. Electricity distribution, on the other hand, may be that awkward and rare animal—a natural monopoly. Alex Henney's scheme of subjecting distribution companies (based on the present area boards) to a strict regime which gives them an interest, as well as a duty, to buy from generating companies as cheaply as possible, deserves careful scrutiny.

These companies would mutually own a new transmission and control company, responsible for developing and maintaining the national grid, and acting as a common carrier. Finally an Electricity Commission, learning from the American experience, would insist upon competition, provide a framework for a forward market in power, and rule upon matters of public interest.

The criticism which in the first part of the pamphlet the author makes of the various sectors of the electricity supply industry reflect his belief that the temptation is irresistible for any monopoly to make life as secure and comfortable as possible for itself. Had there been competitive forces at work in the industry over the past decades, would prices of electricity have remained about a fifth higher than they need have been? And, had power been cheaper, how many benefits would have flowed for all British industry—and domestic consumers? It is for these reasons only that the author has thought it worth while to identify the shortcomings of the ESI. The costs of the inefficiency of nationalised concerns—which British industry has directly to bear—are very high indeed. The price of coal paid by the ESI, a subject to which the Centre hopes to return, is a case in point. Here is inefficiency piled upon inefficiency, cost upon cost. If the consumers are to benefit fully from the restructuring of the ESI, the opportunity must be taken to introduce, wherever possible, the tonic disciplines of the market-place.

DIRECTOR OF PUBLICATIONS

Introduction

The present Government has succeeded in privatising two major utilities, British Telecom and British Gas—but only as largely integrated monopolies. There was doubt whether such large flotations could be achieved, and it was thought there was no time to restructure them in a way which would open them to competition.

The case for so restructuring the electricity supply industry of England and Wales (ESI) might, perhaps, be less powerful if it was operating efficiently. It is shown below that it is not. The Central Electricity Generating Board (CEGB) is forced to buy expensive British coal. Its policies for the ordering of plant seem to be dictated not by commercial considerations but by the political interplay of vested interests. Enormous overruns in time and cost have been incurred in the construction of both nuclear and fossil-fueled installations. Area boards have performed patchily; scope for improving efficiency and reducing costs is evident both in their main business of electricity distribution, and in their retailing operations. Although the South of Scotland Electricity Board (SSEB) performs marginally better than the rest of the ESI many of the same shortcomings are evident.

Overall the performance of the ESI compares poorly with that of British Gas and very poorly with electricity industries in other parts of the world, notably in Germany, France, US and Japan. Indeed productivity in the Japanese industry appears to be *twice* that of ours. Concomitantly, the pay of employees of the ESI is higher than the national average of workers in manufacturing industry. All this suggests that the industry is run not with an eye to net consumer benefit, but in accordance with its own interests which it pursues with little accountability and great secrecy.

This study rehearses the lessons to be gained from the experience of West Germany, Sweden and the United States, in all of which countries electricity supply is fragmented, with varying degrees of private ownership. The German industry which is about a quarter as large again as the ESI, comprises some 940 separate undertakings (300 in generating and transmission, 640 in distribution). Yet their industry is more efficient than ours and, save for the compulsion to buy German coal, is less politically manipulated.

The Swedish industry, which is about one third of the size of the ESI, is very diverse. A State power company generates half the total power and owns the transmission grid. Other companies are owned municipally, others privately. Although the system is coordinated by central despatch of generating plant a market operates in long term and spot power, in transmission capacity, in the assets of generation facilities and in the assets and franchises of distribution companies. Government involvement in the industry is not large.

The industry in the United States is ten times larger than the ESI—and is also very diverse. Private utilities, regulated by public service commissions, predominate. Much thought is now being given to developing the ideas for promotion of competitive power, and wholesale power markets are now emerging in some parts of the country (for example, in California and Texas some 7,000 MW capacity in Combined Heat and Power schemes (CHP) has been brought on line this decade). Conscious of the uncertainty of demand and of fuel prices, and of the financial problems inherent in constructing large power stations, utilities are adopting a flexible and 'portfolio' approach to providing their generating capability. New technologies are being tried in large-scale plants, and an emphasis is being laid on a modular approach—that is, ordering plant which can be built in three or four years and added in smaller increments than is possible for large nuclear and fossil-fuel plants.

Evidence in this report shows that customers are getting a poor financial deal from the ESI. Electricity prices are about a fifth more than they should be. Much of this is due to uncompetitive purchasing of fuel, plant and other services; much due to overmanning and overpayment of employees.

In considering how to restructure the ESI, we should leave to one side the historical reasons *why* the industry has been organised in the way that it has been. Once, electricity companies needed to be integrated monopolies if they were to aggregate demand in order to build up loads to support large and efficient generating plant and to gain the benefits of 'system economies'. These benefits can now be achieved through the national control centre and the national grid which allows the despatch of the sets in economic merit order. It can be argued that distribution and transmission are more or less natural monopolies. But generation? Experience shows that size no longer equates with efficiency. Just as computing in the 1970s moved away from monster main-frame machines to dispersed networks of smaller machines, and just as in the 1980s new printing technology has allowed new newspapers to flourish, so in the 1990s electric power systems should cease to be wholly dependent upon large, centralised generating sets owned by large, integrated utilities.

The overriding aim must be to improve the industry's efficiency and its responsiveness to the customers' needs, in order to help British industry to improve its competitiveness in world markets and to provide domestic customers with the cheapest power possible. This can be done if we:—

• introduce private capital so that the industry is less at the mercy of political and bureaucratic influences;
• make generation competitive by encouraging diverse ownership; and
• create distribution companies as a countervailing force to generating companies, a relationship analogous to that between supermarkets and food manufacturers.

The second and third objectives will be lost if the industry is either privatised intact or as separate regional power boards. A group of medium-sized monopolies with broadly similar interests is much the same animal as a large national monopoly. Both such courses would (in the words of the 1983 Conservative Party manifesto) 'merely replace a State monopoly with a private one, and would waste an historic opportunity to ensure that it did not exploit its position to the detriment of customers'. Rather, the industry should be restructured and privatised by creating:—

• (say) 10 generating companies each owning a portfolio of coal, oil and gas generating capacity with generators of roughly equal fuel type, age and size. If competition is to be effective it is of the first importance that such companies should be geographically dispersed and balanced. They should enter into long, medium and short term contracts with
• distribution companies based on the present Area Boards. These might be sold either in a form similar to the private statutory water companies, or as plcs. They should be subject to a price regime which provides an incentive both to reduce their added costs, and to buy power competitively.
• A transmission and control company (TRANCON) which would be owned on a mutual basis by the distribution companies. TRANCON would own the grid, despatch control and the two large pumped storage plants. It would despatch the sets in merit order, implement a spot market in power, schedule maintenance and develop the transmission system.
• An Electricity Commission which would regulate the distribution

companies and TRANCON, promote competition wherever possible and (like Lloyd's and the Stock Exchange) create and regulate a physical commodity market in power—and possibly a futures market, too.

• A nuclear rump (*sic*). This might well have to remain in 'public ownership' for the present. But some plants might in the future be offered for sale by private treaty or management buyout.

• The South of Scotland Electricity Board (SSEB) should be privatised as a power board together with regulatory checks to ensure that it does not abuse its monopoly position. Given sufficient information available from England on competitive power prices and comparative distribution costs this should not prove too difficult.

These proposals are based on experience, open for all to examine, in the USA and elsewhere. Separate generation and distribution companies; a diversity of fully integrated power pools which despatch units, schedule their maintenance and generally provide a measure of coordinated planning for the companies; long and short term contracts for power—all these *modi operandi* exist in the USA. Already, too, there exist or are emerging markets in spot and long term power.

Now is the time to restructure the ESI in order to make it the most efficient electricity supply industry in the world. This study suggests how this should be done and considers the inadequacies of the present arrangements.

Operational efficiency

The operating cost structure of the ESI in 1985/86 was as follows[1]

	£m	%
Generation and transmission fuel and purchase of electricity	4734	48.7
salaries and related costs	764	7.9
depreciation	958	9.9
rates	179	1.8
other purchases and services	759	7.8
TOTAL GENERATION AND TRANSMISSION COSTS	7394	76.1
Distribution		
salaries and related costs	699	7.2
depreciation	498	5.1
rates	183	1.9
other purchases and services	385	3.9
TOTAL DISTRIBUTION COSTS	1765	18.1
TOTAL TRADING COSTS	9159	94.2

interest and monetary working capital
adjustment   559   5.8
TOTAL COSTS   9718   100.0

These figures illustrate the dominance of generation costs—82% of the total (if adjustments are made for interest and monetary working capital). Within generation they show the importance of fuel costs, comprising about 50% of the total.

This section first examines fuel costs, then the CEGB's plant construction performance which accounts for the major part of the depreciation and interest costs amounting to 15% of total cost. Next it looks at the CEGB's labour productivity. Finally it scrutinises the performance of Area Boards, the Electricity Council and the SSEB.

Coal has always been the major source of energy for generation. It remains so. In 1985/86 generators driven by coal supplied about 80% of the CEGB's output, by nuclear about 17% and by oil and gas about 4%. The cost of coal (£3,681m in 1985/86) represents 40% of the industry's trading costs and 37% of the final price of electricity.[2] In recent years the price paid for coal by the CEGB has been based upon a 'Joint Understanding', originally agreed in October 1979, which committed the CEGB to take not less than 95% of its annual tonnage from British Coal. According to the Monopolies and Mergers Commission, the delivered cost of coal imports in the summer of 1980 was only two thirds of that from British Coal.[3] And during the winter of 1985/86 the price which the SSEB paid for coal from British Coal was a third more than the price paid either for coal mined privately in Scotland or imported.[4] In 1985/86 the average delivered cost of coal to the CEGB was £47 per tonne and the pure energy cost for coal-fired electricity averaged about 2.08p kWh. In comparison, in September 1986, the average cost of coal of similar calorific value delivered to the Virginia Electric and Power Company (VEPCO) was $32.4 (say £22.3 per tonne—at £1 equals $1.45) and the pure energy cost per kWh for coal-fired electricity averaged 1.68 cents—equivalent to about 1.16p. That is almost half the CEGB's cost. Certainly, VEPCO is fortunate to be close to a source of cheap coal. But the difference between the price that it pays and the world market one is not so great as to justify these figures.

In recent evidence to the Select Committee on Energy[5] the CEGB claimed that over the period 1982–85 coal from British Coal 'has cost the Board between £5 and £16 per tonne on average more than the published international price. Put another way, imported coal has offered potential savings of between 12% and 38% percent against the average price of coal from British Coal . . . each £1 per tonne change in the average price is equivalent to almost 1% change in the average price of electricity'. As the CEGB commented 'British Coal has for many years benefited from the protection by successive governments reflected in the levels of subsidy paid by the Exchequer and in other measures such as government policies with regard to the import of coal . . . British Coal has assumed in crude terms that the market would absorb all the coal it wishes to produce, and that the CEGB as by far the largest customer will by one means or another be forced to take most of whatever coal cannot be disposed of elsewhere.[5] The CEGB claimed that it was subsidising British Coal by £1bn annually and that some £550m annually could be saved by importing 30 million tonnes of coal. In June 1986 the 'Joint Understanding' was revised into a three tranche price structure. The pithead price for the first fifty million tonnes is £46.8 per tonne; the price for the second tranche of 12 million tonnes at £33 per tonne is aligned to oil prices; and the price of the third tranche, supposedly aligned to the price of spot coal landed at the Thames was set at £29.50 per tonne. This agreement has reduced the price the CEGB pays for coal by £300 million* per annum initially and will reduce it by a further £140 million annually by the end of five years.

How does this square with the CEGB's statement that it has a 'firm intention of buying supplies at internationally competitive prices'?[6] By no stretch of language is the relationship between the CEGB and British Coal on a 'straightforward commercial basis'. No strict commercial organisation would commit itself to buying 95% of its coal at an average price of £43 per tonne when the spot market price is about $35, or about £23–£25. The CEGB should be buying at an average of £30–£33 per tonne; in effect it has left £7–£900 million on the table.

The CEGB has similar relaxed and non-commercial relationships with British Rail, which moves two thirds of its coal, equivalent to about a third of BR's total freight tonnage. In 1976 the board signed an agreement with BR whereby it undertook to 'forgo the use of road support for coal supplies from rail-connected sources to rail-connected power stations'. It agreed charges linked to inflation which

---

*To offset British Coal's loss of £300m income the Government increased the amount it wanted from the ESI by the same amount. It tightened the negative EFL, the cash limit on the industry, from £1128 in 1985/86 to £1406m in 1986/87, a change which was coincidentally about £300m.

did not allow any productivity improvement by BR to be shared by the CEGB. During the miners' strike the CEGB used road transport heavily and found that it was 'about 30% cheaper.'[5] (Fortunately this agreement has recently been modified.) In a similar way the agreement between the CEGB and BNFL to reprocess Magnox fuel allows a public monopoly supplier to pass on cost to a public monopsonist purchaser. The MMC found the CEGB did not know the basis of these costs; did not know why they had risen threefold in real terms between 1975 and 1980; and did not know why they were forecast to increase a further threefold by 1987.[3]

Construction of plant

The Herbert Enquiry in 1956 was the first, among a series of reports which spanned a quarter of a century, to draw attention to the poor performance of the CEGB in constructing plant. The National Board for Prices and Incomes examined delays in commissioning plant in 1968 and was followed in 1969 by a Committee of Inquiry into commissioning CEGB power stations. In 1970 the National Economic Development Office (NEDO) working party on large industrial sites reported unfavourably on problems of power stations. So did the 1976 NEDO working party on engineering construction performance. Foreign construction, NEDO found, was cheaper and quicker.

Then the Plowden Committee in 1976[7] criticised construction performance, and the Price Commission followed suit in 1979. It found that the delays and cost increases were continuing. The reasons were familiar. Industrial relations on site were bad, productivity was low, and equipment was being redesigned in the course of construction.

In 1981 both the Select Committee on Energy[8] and the MMC were similarly critical. The Select Committee examined the problems of low productivity and industrial conflict in the building of the Isle of Grain oil-fired power station, which was a third over budget and four years behind time schedule. The Committee concluded that 'the CEGB must, in our view, be blamed for their reluctance and inability for so long to assert firm management and to promote and increase productivity.' At the same time the MMC concluded that 'in recent years the backlog of commissioning appears to have been getting worse in relative, as well as absolute, terms'. The five conventional stations then under construction were expected to be delayed from two to three years (which has subsequently increased from three to six years) and to overrun costs in real terms by 19%. The MMC further found that the average overrun of costs on CEGB's advanced gas-cooled reactor stations was just over 100% in real terms; and that compared with planned completion of six years the forecast times were by then fifteen years. These have subsequently increased to nearly twenty years. In real terms Dungeness B cost at least two and a half times the original estimate and generates electricity at 4.66p per kWh, compared with about 2.5p for the first half of Drax, a recently commissioned coal station.

It is fair to add that plant construction has lately improved. Completion of the 1200 MW AGR Heysham 2 is forecast within eight years—half the time its predecessor took to construct—while the 2000 MW Drax B coal-fired station *was* completed in under eight years. None the less these improved performances are still modest. According to an OECD expert group[9] it takes five to six years to build a large coal station in the rest of Europe at a cost of $500–600 per kW as against $950 per kW in Britain. Although it may be argued that some of the continental figures are optimistic and that the CEGB's are based on an outdated design, it remains to be seen whether its claims that future plant will be more competitive are valid.

For at least one decade (if not two) the CEGB's record in its plant ordering strategy has been poor. The MMC held that its forecasting was consistently over-optimistic, and, because plant was ordered to support loads which did not materialise, led to increased costs. Indeed the plant margin (that is, the capacity of the plant available over and above the maximum demand for power) peaked at 42% in 1975, almost double the operational requirement, and would have reached over 60% had the plant been completed on time. Three of the unnecessary stations were estimated to cost £2,500m. To make matters worse, in January 1978, the Government ordered ahead of requirement the 2,000 MW coal-fired Drax plant, then an advanced gas-cooled reactor (AGR) for the CEGB at Heysham, and another for the SSEB at Torness. The MMC considered that the CEGB's investment appraisal was based on optimistic assumptions, and did not pay proper regard to factors of risk and uncertainty. They said that its evaluation of the need to invest in plant 'represents a seriously inadequate treatment of problems of great magnitude and falls short of what one might expect to find . . . material on the planning background is potentially confusing . . . if the Board's costs are to be minimised, it is important that future projects should be assessed on more reliable economic grounds'.[3]

We now turn to management (or rather mismanagement) of the British nuclear power programme. In 1965, under political pressure from the United Kingdom Atomic Energy Authority(UKAEA) and the then British nuclear power consortia, the CEGB conducted an enquiry which purported to show that the UKAEA's AGR design would produce electricity 7% more cheaply than the American Pressurised Water Rector (PWR). The CEGB then ordered four AGRs (and the SSEB one). All ran over time and budget. In the 1970s the estimated requirement for nuclear plant fluctuated wildly, and the choice of system was altered three times. In August 1972 the then Chairman of the CEGB stated that the Board would need to order only two reactors by 1980 and at most eight afterwards. Sixteen months later in December 1973 he stated that the CEGB would like to order eighteen reactors by 1980, and a further eighteen thereafter. In 1979 (by which time the CEGB had actually ordered two) the Board persuaded the Government that it 'would need to order at least one new nuclear power station a year in the decade from 1982'.[8] Only seven years later was an order placed. In 1974 the preferred choice of reactor system was changed from the AGR to the Steam Generating Heavy Water Reactor (SGHWR). But this preference lasted no more than two years, and in January 1978 development was abandoned and £145m of taxpayers' money was written off. Now some combination of AGRs and PWRs were thought to offer greater economic benefits. Subsequently the CEGB has backed the PWR, while the SSEB (whose former Chairman had once supported the SGHWR in favour of the AGR) has argued that the AGR is more efficient than the PWR.

The MMC observed that 'a large programme of investment in nuclear power stations is proposed on the basis of investment appraisals which are seriously defective and liable to mislead. We conclude that the Board's course of conduct in this regard operates against the public interest'[3]. In plain language the board was juggling with the figures because it wanted to build nuclear power stations. Nuclear policy in Britain has never been founded on commercial logic and the interests of electricity customers. It has been dictated at various times by the pressures of the UKAEA; of the plant nuclear consortia (notably the General Electric Company); of nationalism versus Westinghouse; and of the Government wishing to find a counter to the power of the National Union of Mineworkers. The shifting policies have been the result of lack of competent direction *within* the industry and the Department of Energy, and the vacillation of politicians.

Over thirty years the civil nuclear programme has produced nine Magnox reactors which the CEGB stopped building on the grounds of expense; lost several billion pounds on research, development and construction of the AGRs; lost about £300 million—today's prices—on the SGHWR; and spent about £3 billion—today's prices—on research into the fast breeeder reactor which still shows no signs of commercial development.

Since its creation the CEGB has shown no wish to give serious consideration to alternatives to building very large generating sets owned by itself. It believes that big is beautiful and that bigger is more beautiful. In its evidence to the Sizewell Inquiry it ruled out smaller plant as uneconomic (an attitude which has resulted in British boards owning 57% of all the fossil fuelled generating sets of over 500 MW in the EC). It is of course true that larger sets do provide economies of scale, but only *provided that they operate to a full capacity and do not contribute to creating uneconomic plant surplus.* These provisos have not always been met. The large coal sets have operated erratically: the large oil sets have scarcely been used. And consequent over-capacity has incurred great costs over the last decade—which have been passed on to the customer.

In an uncertain world, where fuel prices fluctuate and electricity demand cannot be accurately predicted in the medium term (let alone the long term) a strategy of building only large units, which might result in lowest costs under *known* future conditions, is not necessarily the most economical policy. An approach which allows for uncertainty can be cheaper. This implies building a number of smaller plants which are quicker to construct, thereby reducing the risk of over-ordering on the one hand and plant shortage on the other. This is known in the United States as a modular approach

Combined Heat and Power schemes, and some new technologies

The two principal traditional alternatives to building large new plant are modernising old plant, and Combined Heat and Power schemes (CHP) linked either with district heating for housing or with industrial processes. In its evidence to the Sizewell Inquiry the CEGB claimed that modernising small old plant was not economically viable. Yet this is a business which thrives in the United States. Although modernised plant may not quite match the thermal efficiency of a large new one, the savings in infrastructure and in time can often justify the exercise. The CEGB admits that CHP may be viable, yet a succession of reports over the last decade (including the Plowden Committee Report and two reports by the Select Committee on Energy) have shown how such competition to the CEGB's own supplies have been quashed. Before the Energy Act 1983 the ESI charged unduly low prices for the purchase of electricity. (The Chairman of the Yorkshire Electricity Board recently admitted to the Energy Committee [10] that the price offered to independent generators was a third lower than that now offered.) The passing of the Act left the ESI able to set the terms of trade offered to private generators. It made no provision for independent arbitration on general tariffs. Examination of the recent report by the Select Committee on Energy[10] 'Combined Heat and Power: Lead City Schemes' shows how:

• the structure of the Bulk Supply Tariff (BST) has been altered to reduce the purchase tariffs which the Area Boards have to pay to private generators under the Act;
• Area Boards have claimed that they are unable to sign long term contracts which include price provisions—an inability which undermines the financing of new schemes; and
• no information on system costs have been provided which would enable outsiders to judge the fairness in the terms of trade which they are offered.

The Committee concluded that 'the Energy Act has largely failed to stimulate the growth of CHP . . . if anything the industry has done less since 1983 than it achieved before'.

In its 1982 evidence to the Sizewell Inquiry 'On Alternative Methods of Generation' the CEGB dismissed technological alternatives to generating power other than CHP as either unproven or uneconomic, or at best belonging to tomorrow. For example it said of fluidised bed systems 'a first full-scale plant could be operating somewhere in the world during the early 1990s'. (A fluidised bed boiler comprises coal ground into small particles which are suspended in a vertical air flow. The particles form a bed or layer which is then ignited.) In fact, one commercial sized pilot unit of 125 MW started operating last year in the US, and two more are due to commence in 1987 and 1988.

Also the Stockholm Energy Company is installing one in a CHP plant.

Productivity

From 1965 to 1985 CEGB output (as measured by GWh supplied per employee) increased by 114%. But this figure cannot be taken at face value as representing an equivalent increase in labour productivity. Much of the improvement is due to an improvement in the quality of capital stock, notably the introduction of larger generating sets and phasing out of smaller, older sets. Over the last decade the CEGB reduced the number of generating sets by 44% and halved the number of power stations, but the number of employees has been reduced only by 25%. A recent OECD report[9] shows that plant manning is still much higher than in foreign utilities.

Comparative power station manning

	Manning for a 1200 MW PWR nuclear station	Manning for a 2000 MW coal station
UK	555	844
Belgium	240	380
Canada	—	320
France	280	505
Germany	330	630
Italy	—	495
Japan	200	215
Netherlands	330	580
Sweden	330	500
US	401	490

Although these figures are not directly comparable because maintenance practices vary from country to country, the SSEB confirms that "manning levels in North American stations are significantly lower . . . the significant factor was the lower maintenance requirement of North American plant . . . a number of local understandings and working practices had developed within the Board's central maintenance team which have increased costs or inhibited flexibility . . . such as the refusal of employees to carry tools and other equipment in their private vehicles'.[4]

The MMC commented[8] in 1981 that 'in recent years the rate of improvement [of the CEGB's performance] has slowed appreciably, while at the same time the CEGB's labour costs have been rising more rapidly than the national average. Over the period 1970/71 to 1979/80 while CEGB output per head grew by 13%, labour costs increased by 46% in real terms[3].

The MMC commented 'we detect some evidence of over grading and some obstructive attitudes to change'. They instanced that negotiations for the introduction of job evaluation had been going on for six years with no conclusion. Subsequently the CEGB did improve output per head by 35% over the five years 1980/1981 to 1985/1986. But the trend of increased labour costs is continuing.

Area Board Performance

Although staffing was reduced by 12% over the last five years the real added cost per customer of the area boards, which is the best indicator of their performance, has increased by 3%. The table[1] below shows how varied is the Board's cost performance.

Costs of distribution depend upon customer density. The higher the density the lower the costs should be. What reasons can be given why the Midlands, North West and above all the Yorkshire and London boards, which are four of the five most dense ones, should have such high distribution costs? If all boards reduced their costs to those of the Eastern and Southern boards, both of which serve substantial areas of London, some £40m would be saved annually on distribution.

Nor does there seem any good reason for the wide variations in the customer-related costs. In 1982 Deloitte Haskins & Sells studied these costs in three boards (Eastern, North Western, and Midlands) and concluded that £31m annually would be saved in the latter two if they achieved the same level of efficiency as the Eastern Board, which has long been recognised as the top performer.[11]

Added costs/customer and employees/customer of the Area Boards

	Added costs/ customer in 1985/86 £	Reduction in employees/ customer 1981/82 to 1985/86 %	Employees/ 1000 customers in 1985/86	Distribution Costs/ customer	Density of customers/ sq.km	Customer related costs/ customer £
Eastern	60.6	4	2.68	42.2	136(6)	18.3
Southern	70.9	20	2.78	42.6	137(7)	21.0
South Eastern	71.5	12	2.86	40.4	244(2)	21.5

East Midlands	72.7	7	3.00	45.2	122(8)	23.5
North Western	77.5	14	3.23	48.0	161(4)	23.7
North Eastern	79.1	18	3.12	49.4	92(10)	25.10
Midlands	83.1	17	3.37	47.2	152(5)	24.9
Merseyside & North Wales	83.1	12	3.36	48.8	105(9)	25.5
Yorkshire	83.5	8	3.44	55.2	178(3)	24.1
South Western	89.4	15	3.84	53.6	80(11)	28.4
South Wales	90.5	13	3.78	56.9	73(12)	26.8
London	97.7	22	3.63	56.0	2748(1)	36.0
All Board Average	78.1	14	3.18	47.8		24.3

To evaluate the significance of this table it is necessary to consider:—

• distribution costs related to density of customers
• customer-related costs of meter-reading, money-collecting, and general administration.

An MMC study identified many ways in which costs of meter-reading, billing and collection could be significantly reduced by improving procedures.[12] Another possibility is that savings might be made by employing housewives part time to read meters (as is done in Japan) and by discouraging payment through board shops, which is far the most expensive way of paying bills (the SSEB's collection cost per £100 payment is 10p by direct debit, 14p by standing order, 37p by payment through giro and post offices and 59p through board shops[4]).

More radically, costs can be reduced by introducing 'smart meters' which communicate—and so can be read—via the telephone line or power line direct to the board. Such automated reading could be coupled with electronic transfer of funds. By these means the South Eastern Electricity Board estimates potential annual savings of the order of £150m. On the principle that there is no need to be other than best, then if all boards reduced their costs to those of the Eastern Board, there would be an annual saving of £120m in administration, consumer service and meter-reading.

The Plowden Committee considered that one major weakness of the Area Boards was their inability to challenge the CEGB on the Bulk Supply Tariff (BST) which comprises 80% of their costs. That situation is unchanged today. In January 1985 the London Electricity Board (LEB) refused a request by the London Electricity Consultative Council that it should scrutinise the BST. This relaxed, uncommercial attitude—so different from the relationship between a supermarket and its suppliers—is one fundamental weakness of the ESI, undermining incentives. To quote from an MMC study of the Yorkshire Electricity Board, because the major part of costs are bought in from the CEGB, then 'it follows that quite large increments to or savings in those costs which it can control can have only a minimal effect on its charges or on the rate of return which it achieves . . . in the circumstances it would not be surprising if YEB's approach to control costs was less rigorous than might be desired.'[14]

The industry has never done well in retailing. The Herbert Committee made the criticism that the boards undercosted their retailing activities in order to disguise their poor performance. In 1982 the Office of Fair Trading and in 1983 the MMC showed how the LEB had lost money on retailing for ten years. Similarly the SSEB lost money on retailing for nine years, troughing at a loss of 12.5% of turnover and 35% on capital in 1981/82. To take one example of retailing inefficiency, the LEB appeared to employ too many staff and pay them at ESI union rates, which are much higher than retailing wages.

The Electricity Council

The Electricity Council has a statutory duty under the 1957 Electricity Act to advise the Minister on questions affecting the industry and to 'promote and assist the maintenance and development by the boards of an efficient, co-ordinated and economical system of supply'. In addition to these advisory and co-ordinating roles it performs a number of executive functions such as acting as the ESI's banker, preparing consolidated accounts and tax returns, undertaking research, running the industry's pension fund, negotiating salaries and wages, and looking after the national advertising programme. All this cost £61m in 1985/86 (an increase in real terms of 45% since 1970/71). The Council's costs are recovered by a levy on the boards.

The Council's record in fulfilling these executive roles is not distinguished. For example, the industry pension fund has lost over £100m in abortive property ventures. And its record on pay negotiations do not suggest that it acts in the interest of its customers. Between 1975 and 1985 wages of employees in the ESI relative to those in manufacturing increased markedly. (Nor do the figures below take into account the additional benefit of ESI index-linked pensions.[14])

	Average gross weekly earnings/ hour of full time men (1985 £s)		Increase (%) over/decade
	1975	1985	
Manual ESI	3.85	4.71	22
Manual in manufacturing	3.52	3.87	10
Non manual ESI	5.11	6.69	30
Non manual in manufacturing	4.71	5.90	25

According to figures in the ESI, in 1981/82 in the ESI electricians were paid an average of £5.52 an hour, in private companies £3.97 to £4.62 an hour. A member of the Electrical Power Engineers' Association, opposing privatisation, recently wrote to the Union magazine '. . . no private industry management will continue to support the generous working arrangements that staff currently enjoy.'[15] The industry's wage rates reflect its centralised bargaining structure and the employee's monopoly power to turn off the lights. Its industrial relations have been bought at a cost to the customer.

Nor does the Electricity Council adequately fulfil its duty of arbitrating statutory representations by individual customers and Consultative Councils against Area Boards. The Council's procedures for hearing representations do not meet the requirements normally expected of tribunals. Members of the Council, of whom two thirds are Area Board chairmen, judge complaints against their own members. From nationalisation up to 1984 the Council upheld only two of the thirty-one representations by customers against an Area Board. Such achievement of near perfection does not ring very true.

The critical responsibility which the Herbert Committee conceived for a central authority was that of scrutinising the performance of the Boards. This it has not done. Otherwise it would surely have explained at least why crude comparisons of the performance of the ESI with that of other countries indicate that it is so inefficient compared with the industries of Japan, France, Germany and the USA e.g.:—

• the electricity supply industry in Japan employs 13% more people than the ESI here to serve almost three times as many customers with almost two and a half times as much power. Thus labour productivity is about twice as high.

• In aggregate, the investor-owned utilities in the US employ four times as many people as the ESI; and sell nine times the power to four times the number of customers. They are at least a quarter more productive. Electricité de France is over a fifth more productive.

Ten years ago the Plowden Committee accused the Council of being a consensus body that often had to function to the lowest common denominator. In 1979, despite the perdeominance of Area Board members on the Council and the concern which they are meant to have in the cost of wholesale power, the Council endorsed the CEGB's ill-conceived proposals to build fifteen nuclear power stations in a decade. The Council has never properly checked the CEGB's performance because as Mr R. Orson, an independent Council member, observed at the LEB 'the members of the Electricity Council who are chairmen of Area Boards do not press to scrutinise the CEGB because they in turn resist scrutiny of their own Boards'. Equally it has never checked Area Boards' performances. In the author's view the Council has failed because the Herbert Committee's recommendation that its members should be independent of the Boards was not followed.

The SSEB

Although the SSEB provides electricity 2% more cheaply than the ESI and enjoys a better record in constructing plant than the CEGB, it suffers from many of the same shortcomings. Like the CEGB it pays too much for coal and rail transport, and to an even greater extent than the CEGB it has suffered from political pressure to build power stations of an unwarranted size. Even before Torness (which has a capacity of 1250 MW) comes on line the SSEB has plant capacity of 7,400 MW to meet a maximum demand of only 4,500 MW. The average thermal efficiency of its fossil-fuel stations (33.8%) is slightly less than that of the CEGB (34.7%).

It also overmans its stations and suffers from restrictive practices. Its productivity is comparable to that of the ESI, with distribution rather more efficient than the ESI's (3.0 GWh sales per employee against 2.5 GWh), and its generation rather less efficient (4.4 GWh per employee against 4.7 GWh). The MMC criticised the Board for failing to reduce its manpower as vigorously as it should have done.

The SSEB's retailing performance has been deplorable. The cost of its meter reading, billing and collection is 50% more than the average costs of the Area Boards.

Pricing and financial controls

The real price of electricity declined to an all time low in 1973/4 of 3.7p/kWh (at 1985/86 prices) but subsequently increased to 4.8p/kWh. Tariffs in the following two years increased sharply after the increases in oil prices—and in coal prices due to higher wages paid to the miners (and ESI employees) after the 1974 strike. They then increased sharply over the period 1980/82. (This was due to a change to current cost accounting and the introduction of new financial controls.) They peaked at 5.1p/kWh in 1981/82 and subsequently declined to 4.5p/ kWh in 1985/86.

The Government and the industry proclaim that electricity tariffs follow the principle of 'economic prices' and are based upon long-run marginal costs and the 'continuing costs of remaining in business'. Supposedly prices are similar to what they would be in a free market. This is no place for a detailed analysis of the technical issues involved nor for an explanation why long-run marginal cost-based pricing is an inappropriate principle, nor for an explanation how and why the applied economics of electricity pricing has stagnated in Britain while it has made considerable advances in the 1980s in America. That must wait for a further paper, as must the Treasury's use (until 1983) of the industry to raise a surrogate tax. Nonetheless, the ESI still overprices by 5%.

Finally we must examine the nature of control upon investment. The 1978 White Paper Cmnd 7131 defines the required rate of return which 'industries would be expected to achieve on their new investment as a whole', and which is deemed to represent the opportunity cost of capital. The Government defined this figure as 5% in real terms before tax which it claimed was largely based on 'the pre-tax real returns which have been achieved by private companies and the likely trend on return on private investment'. The figure is low. It was based on the *ex post* returns of private industry at a time when these were in a historic trough—having fallen from 11% in 1965 to 9% in 1973 (and plummeting to 4% in 1975). By 1977 they had recovered to 7%*; so even then the assertion that 5% represented the pre-tax real returns was incorrect. In recent years returns have increased to better levels, averaging about 9% real over the years 1981–85.[16] (It may be noted that the Director General of the Office of Telecommunications has said that British Telecom's return of 11% in 1985 was acceptable).

---

* The figure is for all industrial and commercial companies including North Sea Oil.

No private firm invests in risky projects like nuclear plant in anticipation of the low return of 5%. British Gas (when publicly owned) and British Coal both use 10% real rate for revenue earning projects; Electricité de France uses 9%; the State of New York believes that a rate of 7%–8% is appropriate, and the Severn Tidal Power Group advised that a return of 10% would be necessary to raise private finance for a barrage to generate electricity.[17]

By using the low 5% rate of return, investment is biased in favour of electricity supply rather than conservation; capital intensive plant, notably nuclear, rather than coal-fired plant; and publicly owned rather than independent and private generation.

Public control for the public interest?

The statutory grant of a monopoly franchise to an organisation to serve the public with an essential service is a privilege. The monopolist is spared many of the normal financial risks attendant on business ventures, and can raise money easily in capital markets. The *quid pro quo* for the privilege is that the organisation should operate for the public benefit, and be seen to do so. Those who exercise the privilege should be publicly accountable both on fundamental democratic grounds, and because the discipline of public scrutiny generally improves performance. Herbert Morrison said that 'it is important that from the beginning the public corporation should be regarded by all, and should regard itself, as a public concern. Its first business is the competent conduct of the undertaking committed to its charge in the public interest'.[18] This view still holds good. How far does the ESI respect it?

Customers first?

The previous chapter has shown how the customers' interests in cheap electricity takes third place after the interests of the employees of the ESI and of British Coal. Symptoms of disregard for customers' interests abound. For example the marketing plans of the LEB are based not upon what the customers require of the Board (about which the Board knows little) but rather on what the Board wants of its customers—which is that they should buy more electricity. Little mention is made in the ESI's 1986 Corporate Plan of monitoring the quality of service or of improving the handling of complaints.[19] In contrast leading United States power companies regularly monitor customers' opinions about their performance—Pacific Gas and Electric Company has done so for twenty years. As the Electrical Power Engineers Association discovered, utilities in the United States 'have a consumer responsiveness greater than in Great Britain . . . and the consumers' voice does not go unheeded'.[20]

On occasions the ESI has obstructed improvements in consumer service. For example in 1981 the Policy Studies Institute published research-backed proposals into better ways of dealing with customers who were late in paying their bills. The ESI objected, alleging that the recommendations would cost £61m in revenue expenditure and £145m in capital expenditure.[21] These figures were shown to be inaccurate. But the recommendations were accepted only after a year's delay.

Area boards, being statutory corporations, cannot be contracted for statutory services such as connexion of supply. So they cannot be sued for late supply. Connexion to new developments can be and are delayed to suit the convenience of an area board rather than that of the customer. Furthermore, statutory corporations are not subject to the doctrine of estoppel so that when, for example, they make billing errors and subsequently correct them, customers have no redress. To quote a government report which is still lying idle 'not only do many customers feel powerless in their dealings with nationalised industries, they may actually have more limited rights of redress than in their dealings with private firms.'[22]

Under the 1947 Electricity Act, Consultative Councils are charged with the duty of 'considering any matter affecting the distribution of electricity in the area'. In the debate leading to the nationalisation of the industry a government spokesman said that they would 'participate in the planning of the electricity supply for the whole area'.[23] They have not done so. They have been slow to use even the modest powers at their disposal. Even when they have tried to represent the interests of the customers (as when the London Electricity Consultative Council tried to stop the LEB setting an excessive and possibly illegal tariff) they were shown to lack the resources to seek a judicial review.[24]

The public interest and public policies

It is in the national interest that electricity should be both produced and used efficiently. We have so far demonstrated that the ESI falls short of the first objective. Nor, according to the OECD's International Energy Agency, is the second objective being achieved. Britain consumes 0.73 tonnes of oil per $1000 of gross domestic product, which is more than any other European nation. Germany consumes only 0.53 tonnes.[25] No less than 23% of Britain's primary energy consumption vanishes from the power stations straight into the atmosphere and rivers. Yet the ESI consistently opposes the introduction of CHP schemes. Too many of the ESI's actions seem to be against the wider public interest of our country today and in favour of sectional interests. For example, both the Comptroller and Auditor General and the Audit Commissioner for Local Government have drawn attention to the significant waste of energy in publicly owned buildings such as hospitals and hard-to-heat council estates. And the Government spends £2.5 billion annually on heating support for low-income householders. Well and good—but manifestly the public interest is to ensure that energy is used *efficiently* in public buildings, and by people in receipt of public support.

At the root of the above criticisms lies a confusion about the nature of the 'public interest'. The presumption is that boards should act 'commercially'. But the word 'commercial' has many meanings. Some denote desirable characteristics such as that they should be efficient, should not be redistributive welfare organisations, should make decisions on economic rather than political grounds. But what happens when 'commercial' is equated with sales and profits in a manner inappropriate for a publicly owned monopoly? Monopoly profits are no indication of operational efficiency nor, within limits, of allocative efficiency. Management and unions in the industry proclaim that they should be left alone to run it, but in whose interest—in their own or in that of the customer and the general public? Should not the proper aim of a monopoly be to maxmise 'net consumer benefit'?

Accountability

A campaign to avoid the public scrutiny of nationalised industries was instigated by Lord Citrine, Chairman of the British Electricity Authority, as soon as they were brought into being.[23] In 1950, concerned about their poor performance, Herbert Morrison advocated setting up an efficiency unit or a parliamentary committee, but the nationalised industry chairmen opposed the idea.[23] Twenty five years later NEDO observed that 'Boards of the nationalised industries sometimes seemed to aspire to a freedom from public scrutiny that is at odds with their status as publicly owned enterprises'.[26] Not until the 1980 Competition Act, thirty years after Morrison had first identified the need, was provision made for management audits.

The CEGB is secretive. It did not provide a copy of its Annual Development Plan to the Department of Energy until 1981; it was slow in providing information to the Energy Committee in 1981; it allows nobody (not even the Electricity Council) access to its system model. The Electricity Council conducts its proceedings in secret, declining to provide any formal account of them either to part time members of the area boards or to the Electricity Consumer Council. It has kept the results of consumer research studies confidential, and even classifies an annual report which compares the *published* tariffs of the area boards. Together with the CEGB it refuses to supply more information to the Electricity Consumers' Council about the basis of the BST.

Area boards are reticent with information, too. Minutes for the LEB board meeting of 26 June 1984 state that 'one member remained concerned about the way . . . the Consultative Council Chairman made it clear that he would give detailed reports to the Consultative Council. Debate in the Board would be less open and effective if it were being reported elsewhere . . . other members shared this concern, and wished to emphasise the strong view that individual members' views should never be quoted outside the Board'. What were they considering which the public, the owners and customers of the business, should not know? What were they bold enough to say in private that they declined to say in public? Very little, perhaps. But the minute is characteristic of the attitude of many members and officials. Why such secrecy? To disguise poor performance, and the way the industry is manipulated by the Government for fiscal and political purposes? The Energy Committee recently observed 'as a State owned monopoly there is no strong case for the ESI to have complete control over access to information on its operation and financing'.[10] It is far easier for the public to find out about the operation of privately owned utilities in the US than about a system in Britain which the public nominally owns. Is not that an indictment?

Lack of checks and balances

Many shortcomings in the industry stem from a lack of countervailing checks and balances. In theory the first check is supposed to be provided by the board members themselves whom Morrison envisaged as being the 'high custodians of the public interest'.[18] In practice they seem rarely to act as an independent check on the executive. The Board of the LEB failed for many years to tackle the shortcomings of its shops and contracting; failed to deal with its perennial problem of high costs; failed to demand monthly operating accounts; failed to demand enough information to enable them to check that they were fulfilling their statutory duty to set non-discriminatory tariffs. The MMC has criticised the members of some area boards for their acceptance of management's relaxed attitudes, for failing to lay down objectives and monitor achievement and for 'not examining problems deeply'.[12] As NEDO observed 'it is often difficult to see the contribution which non-executive members can make to corporations in present circumstances. Their low remuneration . . . reflects the comparatively limited contributions which they are in reality able to be allowed to make'.[26]

The Electricity Council has been loth to scrutinise the performance of the industry. The Consultative Councils are ineffectual. And the Department of Energy, the industry's sponsor, is a perfect example of 'agency capture'. True, the MMC investigations under the 1980 Competition Act are welcome. But the Commission's audits are occasional, and are running well behind the schedule. Its terms of reference, prescribed by the Department of Trade & Industry, are often limited—perhaps for political reasons. The House of Commons Select Committee on Energy produces good reports, but has neither time nor resources for dealing with all the issues which merit consideration. Nor does it have power to compel attendance of witnesses and disclosure of papers.

Thus there is no effective forum for the regular examination of performance and of public policy issues relating to the ESI.

Foreign lessons

West Germany

The most striking feature of the German supply industry is the diversity of size and ownership of the various undertakings. About 300 companies are concerned with generating and transmission (of which the twelve largest generate 94% of all power sold by the public supply system): and 640 are concerned with distribution. Many companies, however, supply not only electricity but gas and also heat from CHP schemes (which in 1984 produced heat equivalent to about 10% of total electricity output, against less than 1% in Britain). About a fifth of the electricity companies are in private ownership; about three fifths are owned by public authorities; and the remaining fifth, which owns over 80% of the generation and supplies 63% of the sales, have a mixture of public and private capital.

By and large, regulation is the responsibility of the Ministries of Economic Affairs in the individual Lander; the Federal Government has a limited role in the industry. There is no 'official' central authority, nor any central union bargaining. Pay awards are negotiated on a company basis. Productivity is an eighth higher than in the ESI.

Sweden[28]

The industry has great diversity and mix. The Swedish State Power Board, Vattenfall, produces just over half the supply, distributes about a fifth, and owns and operates the 220 kv and 400 kv grid. Another 10 undertakings—with large elements of private ownership—generate most of the rest of the power. Of the 322 distribution undertakings, 79 are privately owned, 79 are cooperatives and 164 are municipally owned. Reflecting the municipal involvement, half the oil-fired capacity is generated in CHP schemes, which in 1984 produced 1.3 TWh of electricity and 3.7 TWh of heat.

Generation and supply have many elements of competition, with markets in transmission capacity on the grid; in contracted deliveries of power between utilities; in short term spot power; and in the assets of utilities. The large utilities are organised in a Power Exchange Group which co-ordinates the system to ensure adequate capacity, stability and provision of emergency power. The Exchange Group also operates the spot market both between its own members and internationally. It despatches generating facilities in merit order (i.e. in ascending order of operational cost in the way in which the CEGB despatches plant), splits the savings between companies' marginal costs and bills the resultant exchanges.

The Government has let the structure be, because although in theory it is somewhat inefficient the variety of ownership has distinct advantages. Different styles and attitudes compete, and 'peer pressure' operates in the many organisations carrying out similar functions. There appears to be more pressure to perform than in monopolies.

United States

The US industry comprises some 3,200 electricity undertakings, and sells ten times the output of the British boards. The 8% of the undertakings which are privately owned generate and supply nearly four fifths of the power. The industry evolved higgledy piggledy, roughly based on local franchises; but takeovers in some areas have created large integrated generating and supply companies, and utilities have more and more banded into 'power pools'. These are groups of generating utilities which operate—with by no means uniform success—a by and large integrated system that controls power station output, in a similar manner to the CEGB's 'merit order' operation. For example, all the major power stations in New York State are scheduled from one computer every five minutes.

Role and operation of State Commissions[29]

When Franklin D. Roosevelt was governing New York State in 1930 he defined the Public Service Commission's role of 'people's counsel', stating 'it is not, and never has been, merely a court. It is rather intended to represent the public interest in connexion with various industries of a semi-public character subjected to its jurisdiction . . . the Public Service Commission is the representative of the legislature and, back of the legislature, of the people . . . it has the sole function not of choosing between the people and the public utilities, but—as a representative of the people of this State—to see to it that the utilities do two things: first, give service, and secondly, charge a reasonable rate'.

The tenet underlying the American system is that in return for a monopoly franchise and the opportunity of earning a 'fair' rate of return for its shareholders, a company is bound to supply all customers who want service, and to charge reasonable and non-discriminatory tariffs as determined by a regulatory commission. The commission's role is to guard against exploitation of customers and to ensure that the company operates in the public interest.

Public service commissions are essentially specialised tribunals for dealing with the complex issues involved in regulating public services. They are quasi-judicial bodies. They can subpoena people and papers; demand any information they want from the utilities they regulate; impose forms of accounts on them; and require them to have management audits. They can also make regulations under powers delegated to them by State legislatures analogous to those which our Parliament delegates to ministers. They operate within a framework of public service law, part provided by federal legislation, part by State legislation and part by case law. The 1978 Public Utilities Regulatory Policies Act (PURPA) governs features of the operation of both commissions and utilities. The Act requires *inter alia* open and reasoned decision-making by public service commissions; gives the public a right to make representations to them; requires non-discriminatory tariffs which reflect costs; and lays down codes of procedure for connexion and disconnexion. The commissions' decisions can be challenged in State courts and on some issues in Federal courts, but contrary to a misconception in Britain, commissions do not spend a great deal of money on litigation.

The shortcomings of regulation are counterbalanced by many strengths. Good commissions provide a forum for examining and resolving hosts of complex issues in a decentralised and fairly depoliticised, objective, and rigorous framework. They make utilities publicly accountable for their performance, and redress the imbalance of power between the individual customer and large utilities. They provide an independent forum for arbitrating complaints of customers, and for considering issues of public interest such as terms of trade between utilities and CHP system operators. They make for a more open and forthright style of public administration than we enjoy. Commissions may not be as effective as the disciplines of the market place, but the best ones are better at requiring efficient performance and customer responsiveness from electricity undertakings than are the centralised, slow and secretive British arrangements for controlling the industry.

Trends towards competitive generation

Several studies of liberalisation have been made by the US Department of Energy, and some of the leading regulatory commissions, academics and industrialists. The practical move towards competitive generation was initiated by PURPA which liberalised CHP systems, requiring utilities to buy power at a cost equal to that which it would have cost the utilities to generate. PURPA was 'viewed by Congress as a means of reducing the monopoly power of the utility and providing the independent generator with an assured market for its output on reasonable terms and conditions'.[30] Independent generators have grown substantially in recent years. By the end of 1986 generating plant totalling 7,000 MW capacity was on line in Texas and California.

The Texas Commission requires CHP operators to bid competitively to supply power and 'by mid 1984 it became apparent that the utility would be able to obtain real price competition among the cogenerators'. If a utility wants to build a new power station it must estimate at what cost it will generate power, and before receiving authorisation to build must offer the capacity to competitive tender. In New York and New England there is a surplus of generation capacity, and also Ontario Hydro is exporting power to the region. In California there is competition both from CHP operators within the State and from utilities on the Pacific North West coast and in Arizona and Utah. Recently the Virginia Electric and Power Company invited 22 tenders for 900 MW of capacity and accepted one offer of 500 MW and another of 400 MW from companies in West Virginia and Indiana.

Diversity

Long cash-flow drains from construction projects have weakened utility finances. Major disasters have led to major write-offs of bonds and disallowance of imprudent expenditure (which has been borne by the shareholders). For example the New York Public Service Commission has disallowed $1.4 bn of the $4.2 bn cost of the Shoreham nuclear power plant. Utilities are beginning to rely less on large centralised stations, and more upon a diversity and flexibility of supply in order to meet an uncertain future. For example the Electric Power Research Institute's report 'Electricity Outlook' observes that 'the future is uncertain and the consequences of pursuing an approach with long lead times that misses actual future outcomes are severe. Too much capacity raises customer costs in paying for unneeded capacity; insufficient capacity can lead to costs because of power outages . . . flexible technologies, those that can be added to the system quickly and in small increments, will allow utilities to respond to a wide range of events without excessive costs . . . the uncertainties utilities face require a portfolio of future generation options.'[31] In consequence utilities are seizing the occasion to modernise old and small plants and develop CHP systems and combined cycle plants. They are beginning to exploit new technologies, too. Fluidised bed and coal gasification systems, built in smaller units, bid fair to reduce costs below those of conventional fossil-fuel sets. One market estimate forecast that up to the end of the century (apart from plant already under construction) 100 GW of generation capacity will be upgraded and 56 GW of new capacity will be built, of which only 3 GW will be new, large coal plants.

Restructuring the ESI

The evidence in this report leads to the conclusion that the customer is getting a poor deal from the ESI in England and Wales; electricity costs about a fifth more than it should. The ESI:-

• pays too much for fuel: commercial purchasing of coal could reduce tariffs by 8%;
• pays too much for generating plant: competitive purchasing could reduce electricity costs by 4% in the long term;
• pays too much for goods and services: it should be possible to reduce these costs by 20%; thus reducing total electricity costs by 2%; and
• pays too many employees too much: electricity costs could be reduced by 4% on this count alone.
• overprices by 5%.

Evidence from overseas demonstrates that there is nothing special about electricity which requires public ownership. Nowadays the historic arguments for integrated distribution and generating monopolies, necessary for the linking of demand in order to build up loads and gain the benefits of large generating sets and system economies, no longer apply. The national grid provides the linking, and it is no longer true that the most economical way to generate depends upon an exclusive reliance on very large generating sets.

Supply of bulk power has many of the characteristics of an ordinary commodity market. True, an electricity system has some unique features. Electrical energy cannot be stored as such long-term (but capacity can). The system must be balanced from second to second, or it will fail. But on the whole bulk electric power is little different from, say, bulk wheat or bulk oil. In place of statutory monopoly and State bureaucracy, economically and legally contestable markets would provide more diversity, more flexibility, more efficient use of resources and better value for money.

Proposals for reform

The three ways to privatise and restructure the ESI are (i) as a whole; (ii) as regional power boards modelled on the SSEB; and (iii) as independent regional distribution companies based on the present area boards, splitting the CEGB into competing generation companies.

The first of these—outright privatisation as an integrated monopoly—would, to borrow words from the 1983 Conservative Party Manifesto, 'merely replace a State monopoly by a private one and would waste a historic opportunity to ensure it did not exploit its position to the detriment of customers'.

Privatisation as regional power boards would be a little—but not much—better: it would merely replace a national monopoly with a set of regional ones, all with a similar lack of competitive incentives. Furthermore there is a considerable mismatch of generation capacity and consumption between different regions which renders this solution infeasible. For example, the maximum demands in 1985/86 of the London and South Western Boards were 3906 MW and 2324 MW respectively, while the capacities of plant within their areas were 976 MW and 431 MW respectively.

If we are to secure the industry from political interference and open it to pressures which will make it more efficient we must:-

• introduce private capital into the industry, distancing it from Whitehall;

• make generation competitive. This is the fundamental prerequisite to improving performance. Competitive generators would perforce buy their fuel in competitive markets. Competitive generators would seek to construct and operate plant as economically and efficiently as possible. Diverse ownership would encourage diverse technologies and commercial views to flourish; and

• create distribution companies as a countervailing power to the generators (as supermarkets are to food suppliers), with a clear interest in buying cheaply.

Generation

The CEGB should be broken up into nine or ten separate generating companies, all of similar capacities of about 4–5000MW and assets of the order of £1.5 billion. As far as possible each company would have a similar portfolio of generating plant, balanced between large modern coal stations, older small coal stations, oil stations and gas turbines, which they would either own outright or in part (as is common in the US). Thus they would all start from the same competitive point and face identical hazards of fuel price changes etc. Most importantly, in order to maximise competition, the generating capacity should not be geographically concentrated, but be dispersed throughout the country. These well-scattered generating companies would contract directly with the distribution companies (see below), and with anyone who wished to make a forward market in electric power. They would also sell on the spot market through TRANCON (see below). No one company would be allowed to supply more than a fifth of the total requirements of the area boards.

Nuclear generation presents a problem. The eight old Magnox reactors will soon have to be decommissioned at a substantial (if uncertain) cost. They are clearly unsaleable and will have to remain in public ownership. Post-Chernobyl, the five AGRs scarcely seem an attractive investment; and it might well be difficult—if not impossible—to write a prospectus for their flotation unless the Government were to insure them against disaster. They could, however, be offered for sale to a consortium of the private companies who built them, who should have the skills to run what they have built, and who lobby so energetically in favour of nuclear power. Alternatively they might be offered as a management buyout (perhaps funded in part by the ESI's pension fund). Failing these courses they would have to be retained together with the Magnox reactors in a Board which might be combined with British Nuclear Fuel. This Board would not be empowered to build new plant—any such plant should be built with new money—and any investment it undertook would aim to achieve a pre-tax target discount rate of 9% real.

The generating companies can be publicly floated or sold by private treaty. Given that the CEGB's accounts are satisfactory in historic cost terms, then its division into parts should present no difficulties. In order to provide some initial stability of earnings and costs while introducing competition, each company should have a like portfolio of contracts made with distribution companies which would meet, say, 90% of the latter's forecast demand for the first year of operation (leaving 10% to be met by the spot market). These contracts would taper by perhaps 7.5% annually—i.e. the initial ones would fall to 60% after four years and so on. The generating companies would have similar tapering arrangements to take fuel from British Coal on a mix of contracts: some fixed price, some related to world price.

Once the companies were operating they, or anyone else who wishes to enter the market, would be free to develop new generation facilities (without any special licensing except in the case of nuclear installations). A developer who wanted to promote a scheme might offer options for sale, or he might put together contingent contracts for some or all of the output in the same way that property developers put together pre-lets. To preclude disruption should a company go into liquidation, the liquidator of a generating company or of an electricity distribution company would, like the liquidator of a private water company have a duty to continue its operation to the extent required by TRANCON.

Electricity distribution companies

The area boards should be privatised in their present form, as electricity distribution companies. They should retain their obligation to serve customers who take less than (say) a quarter of a million kWh annually, and who thus comprise the 'tariff market'. Customers taking more than this could bargain for contracts in a structure similar to that obtaining in the gas market; and could bypass the distribution companies by using the distribution network direct as a common carrier—as indeed could independent generators themselves. On the other hand distribution companies would be under no obligation to serve such customers.

The companies would be subject to the same requirement of non-discrimination as at present. They would be free to buy electricity from anyone who chose to sell. But in general they would not be allowed to own generating capacity or another electricity distribution company—although they would be allowed to own or have a part in district heating and industrial CHP schemes. In addition, statutory provisions should impose clear duties on them to promote CHP schemes, to use energy efficiently, and to purchase competitively. 'Sweetheart' deals with favoured generators would be a criminal offence.

The electricity distribution companies would be regulated by the Electricity Commission (see below) on the basis of a licence incorporating the price formula RPI minus X plus Y plus Z, set for five years. X would be a factor based on an estimate of the companies' scope for reducing controllable costs; Y would be the local authority rate levy; Z would be an index of the average cost of the companies' purchased power weighted for the load factor. The consequent prices would be adjusted annually. At the end of five years the formula itself would be revised and X would be reset, taking into account *inter alia* the average performance of the distribution companies in reducing their costs over the period. But the new prices would not simply reflect the new cost level for each company. Companies would be entitled to keep a portion of the sums they had saved—over and above beating the bogey of 'X' (see appendix A). Such a system would ensure that although electricity distribution companies would not have to compete for their load, they would have to compete for favour in the capital markets. Above all they would have a clear incentive both to reduce their controllable costs and to purchase electricity efficiently.

The transmission and control company

A transmission and control company—TRANCON—should be set up, owned on a mutual basis by the distribution companies. TRANCON would:-

• own the national grid (which by law would be a common carrier), the Dinorwig and Ffestiniog pumped hydro systems and despatch control;

• have a statutory duty not to discriminate against any generator or distribution company;

• set rules (subject to the agreement of the Commission) requiring distribution companies to meet standards, in particular ensuring that their supply capacity was adequate. TRANCON would also set rules for generators who wished to obtain maximum payment by providing power, especially when it was most needed. Namely, such generators would have to agree to TRANCON despatching units, taking such measures as were necessary to ensure the stability of the system, and scheduling maintenance;

• despatch generating sets in merit order based upon price offers of marginal operating costs, and without paying regard to contracts between generating and distribution companies. Resultant savings would be split between the generators and distribution companies;

• implement the spot market and bill the generating and distribution companies for the interchanges;

• have a duty to develop the transmission system. To that end TRANCON would be empowered to raise funds on the strength of its ability to recover its costs from the distribution companies.

TRANCON would be run like a transparent non-profit trust, in the public interest.

The Electricity Commission

The present Electricity Council would become an Electricity Commission, modelled on the best US practice. That is, five commissioners would be appointed for staggered terms of five years each. Their duties would be laid down in statute. It would operate openly and by due process, and its decisions would be subject to judicial review. Its role vis-a-vis the electricity distribution companies would be to:-

• ensure they fulfil the terms of their licenses, and their statutory duties;

• set the terms of price control every five years (see above) to ensure that customers paid a 'reasonable price' and obtained a share of any productivity improvement; that investors had the opportunity of earning a 'fair' return comparable with investment in stocks of similar risks; and that management had an incentive to improve performance;

• arbitrate complaints by customers (to this end the Commission would run a regional network of small offices);

• arbitrate terms of trade between the distribution companies and independent generating companies;

• ensure fair trading by distribution retail shops and contracting;

• regulate the accounting;

• scrutinise (but not regulate or be responsible for) forecasts and capacity plans made by distribution companies.

In addition it would ensure that TRANCON fulfilled its duties. The Commission would also be given limited powers over the generating companies, to ensure that they did not collude with each other or with distribution companies (collusion would be a criminal offence for which the Commission would have a duty to prosecute). It would promote competition and diversity in the development of generation, and be empowered to rule on general issues of public interest. They hardly do that.

One major responsibility of the Commission (similar to that of the Stock Exchange) would be to provide a framework within which generation companies, distribution companies, energy dealers and energy brokers could operate both a secondary forward market in power and (if feasible) a futures market, in an open and regulated manner with posted prices. Distribution companies would enter into long term contracts to purchase power to the extent that they considered it in their economic interest. If they expected a decline in costs, say through a technological advance, they would wish to provide for some of their needs in the short term market; conversely, if they expected costs to rise they would seek to buy long. The ability to buy and sell contracts for different periods and terms would enable them to manage a portfolio of capacity and energy, so as to satisfy their estimates about future changes in their own demand and in relative fuel prices. Similarly a generating company might wish to withhold from long term sale a portion of a new unit, and want to hedge by selling short-term capacity forward. If demand for long-term contracts exceeded the capacity on offer, the prices of options and of contracts would be bid up; and the high profits realised would lead to new proposals for additional capacity. The Commission's responsibility for operating the power market is central to this proposed restructuring.

The SSEB

The SSEB should be privatised as a power board regulated by the Electricity Commission. Enough performance data would be available from the system in England and Wales to ensure that it did not exploit its monopoly. A duty would be placed on it to buy power competitively (i.e. not just from its own plant, if supplies from England were available at lower cost). Further study is needed on how best to treat the North of Scotland Hydro Board.

Notes

1. *Indicators of Electricity Supply Industry Performance 1985/86.* The Electricity Council, 1986.

2. Central Electricity Generating Board Annual Report and Accounts, 1985/86.

3. *Central Electricity Generating Board: A Report of the operation of the Board of its system for the generation and supply of electricity in bulk.* The Monopolies and Mergers Commission, HC 315, HMSO, 20 May 1981.

4. *South of Scotland Electricity Board. A report on the efficiency and costs of the Board.* Cmnd 9868, HMSO, August 1986.

5. *The Coal Industry: Memorandum 9.* Submitted by the Central Electricity Generating Board, Energy Committee, Session 1985–86, HC 1961, HMSO, 29 January 1986.

6. CEGB's new 5-year Agreement on Coal, CEGB Press Information 5 June 1986.

7. *The Structure of the Electricity Supply Industry in England and Wales.* Report of the Committee of Inquiry, Cmnd 6388, HMSO, January 1976.

8. *The Government's Statement on the New Nuclear Power Programme.* Select Committee on Energy, Volume 1, Session 1980/81, HC 114-1, HMSO, 1981.

9. *Projected costs of generating electricity from nuclear and coal-fired power stations for commissioning in 1995.* A report by an Expert Group, Nuclear Energy Agency, Organisation for Economic Cooperation and Development, 1985.

10. *Combined Heat and Power: Lead City Schemes.* Sixth Report from the Energy Committee, Session 1985–86, HC 488, HMSO, 3 December 1986.

11. *Report on a Review of Standing Charges for the Electricity Council, Part II,* Deloitte, Haskins and Sells, 1983.

12. *The Revenue Collection Systems of Four Area Electricity Boards.* The Monopolies and Mergers Commission, Cmnd 9427, HMSO, January 1985.

13. *Yorkshire Electricity Board: a report on the efficiency and costs of the Board.* Monopolies and Mergers Commission, Cmnd 9014, HMSO, September 1983.

14. *Handbook of Electricity Supply Statistics.* The Electricity Council 1986.

15. Letter by G. L. Cooper to the *Electrical Power Engineer,* February 1987.

16. *Company profitability and finance.* Bank of England Quarterly Bulletin, June 1986.

17. *Tidal Power from the Severn Report.* The Severn Todal Power Group, 1986.

18. *Socialisation and Transport,* Herbert Morrison, Constable 1933.

19. *Medium Term Development Plan 1986–93, the Electricity Supply Industry in England and Wales.* The Electricity Council, September 1986.

20. *Public or Private Electricity?—the American Experience.* The Electrical Power Engineers' Association, July 1986.

21. *Fuel debt, disconnections and hardship.* Annexe by the Electricity Council on the Evaluation of costs of implementing recommendations by the Policy Studies Institute. The Electricity Council, 1982.

22. *Consumer's interests and the nationalised industries: A consultative document.* Department of Trade, 1981.

23. *The Nationalisation of British Industry 1945 to 1951.* Norman Chester, HMSO, 1975.

24. *Speaking out for London Customers: a report on the policies and activities of the London Electricity Consultative Council for the period 1981–85*. LECC, 1985.

25. *Energy policies and programmes of IEA Countries, 1984*, IEA/OECD, Paris, 1985.

26. *A study of UK nationalised industries: their role in the economy and control in the future*. National Economic Development Office, HMSO, 1976.

27. *Efficiency of Nationalised Industries: References to the Monopolies and Mergers Commission*. Fourth Report from the Committee of Public Accounts, Sessison 1986–87, 16 February 1987.

28. Based largely on a personal communication from Mr J. Boshier, Ministry of Energy, New Zealand.

29. *Regulating public and privatised monopolies*. Alex Henney, Policy Journals for the Public Finance Foundation, 1986.

30. *Combined Heat and Power: Memorandum 27*. The role of the public service commissions in facilitating the development of combined heat and power generation in the US, submitted by the Institute for Fiscal Studies. Alex Henney and David Thompson.

31. *Electricity Outlook: the Foundation for EPRI R and D Planning*, Electric Power Research Institute, Palo Alto, California, December 1985.

Glossary

AGR	Advanced gas cooled reactor.
BNFL	British Nuclear Fuels Limited.
BR	British Rail.
BST	The CEGB's Bulk Supply Tariff.
CEGB	The Central Electricity Generating Board.
CHP	Combined Heat and Power system that produces both electricity and heat for either district heating or industrial process heating.
EFL	External Financing Limit, the Treasury cash limit within which nationalised industries have to operate.
ESI	The Electricity Supply Industry of England and Wales comprising the Electricity Council, the CEGB and 12 Area Electricity Boards.
GW(h)	Gigawatt (hour) = 1000MW (hour) = 1,000,000kW (h).
kW(h)	Kilowatt (hour).
LEB	London Electricity Board.
MMC	Monopolies and Mergers Commission.
MW(h)	Megawatt (hour) = 1000kW (hour).
NEDO	The National Economic Development Office.
PURPA	Public Utilities Regulatory Policies Act, passed by the US Congress in 1978.
PWR	Pressurised Water Reactor.
SSEB	South of Scotland Electricity Board.
TRANCON	Transmission and Control Company, a part of the proposals for reorganising the ESI, comprising the national grid, the despatch control and the two large pumped storage stations.
TW(h)	Terrawatt (hour) = 1000GW (hour).
UKAEA	United Kingdom Atomic Energy Authority.
VEPCo	Virginia Electric and Power Company.
YEB	Yorkshire Electricity Board.

Present structure of electricity supply in Britain

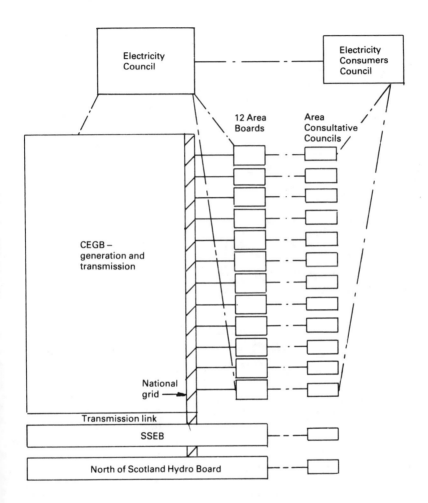

Electricity Council

Electricity Consumers Council

12 Area Boards

Area Consultative Councils

CEGB – generation and transmission

National grid

Transmission link

SSEB

North of Scotland Hydro Board

Proposed structure of electricity supply in Britain

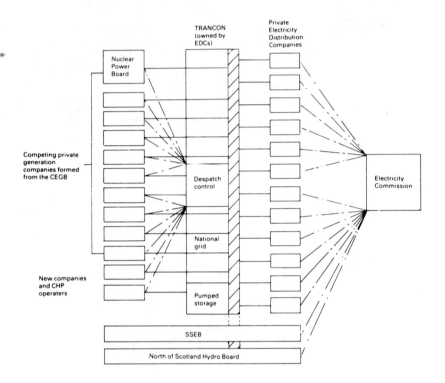

Appendix A
Incentive price control mechanism with shared benefits

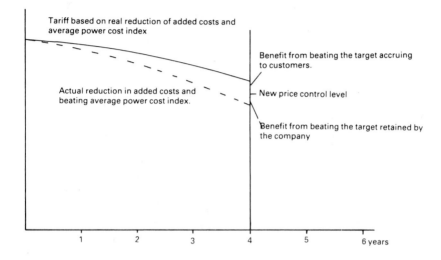

Tariff based on real reduction of added costs and average power cost index

Benefit from beating the target accruing to customers.

Actual reduction in added costs and beating average power cost index.

New price control level

Benefit from beating the target retained by the company

1   2   3   4   5   6 years

18

Current Choices: Good Ways and Bad to Privatise Electricity

Allen Sykes and Colin Robinson

Foreword

The present government's privatisation programme represents the most important initiative in industrial policy in recent times. If properly executed, such a programme could significantly improve the performance of the British economy, lower industrial costs, reduce prices for the benefit of consumers and provide secure employment opportunities.

Nowhere is privatisation more needed than in the energy market where intra-industry competition exists only in oil; and decisions are seriously distorted by the presence and influence of two nationalised corporations. The coal, gas and electricity monopolies have been dominated by producer interests, decision-making has been highly politicised and consumer interests have been given low priority.

In the few months since the Government won a third term of office, privatisation of the electricity supply industry (ESI) has been firmly on the agenda. Widespread public debate is concentrating on the advantages and disadvantages of various options. Both the Electricity Council and the CEGB have retained financial and public relations advisers to help them conduct forceful public and private campaigns to influence the Government's imminent decision. Given all that may be at stake for its senior management this effort, well funded and evidently influential, is not hard to understand. No comparable co-ordinated effort can be mounted by the private sector since those who will be most affected (in particular consumers and potential corporate investors) are too numerous and dispersed to partake with one voice in the public debate and the equally crucial private discussions with government. Accordingly the Government may take disproportionate account of the ESI's views which are likely to favour lightly regulated monopoly (perhaps with token competition as in the case of British Gas and British Telecom). If ESI privatisation is not to follow the unhappy precedent of gas and telecommunications then the Government must show courage, vision and singleness of purpose. Otherwise, an opportunity to introduce competition into the electricity supply industry, and with it into the coal industry, will be lost for at least the remainder of this century.

Objectives of ESI privatisation

The principal objectives

Privatisation schemes can have three principal objectives, between which there are potential conflicts. They are to:—

- increase efficiency
- raise revenue for government
- widen share ownership

The second and third objectives have clearly been predominant in the government's privatisation programme so far. Revenues raised from privatisation of state corporations were about £11 billion from 1979 to 1986 and they are likely to average at least £4 billion a year over the rest of this Parliament. The number of shareholders has much increased in recent years, largely as a consequence of privatisation—according to an NOP Market Research[1] survey from about three million in 1979 to about 8 million (nearly 20 per cent of the adult population) early in 1987. Increasing efficiency, however, seems to have had a very low priority, certainly in the case of British Gas and other recent privatisations.

Improvements in efficiency can take several forms. First, goods and services may be produced at lower cost (increased productive efficiency); second, there may be a closer alignment of prices and costs (greater allocative efficiency); and third, producers may become more responsive to consumers' requirements. In general, the principal means of realising these gains is through liberalisation (the introduction of more competition). Liberalisation measures can be applied to markets for products (the markets into which a firm sells) and to markets for inputs (labour, capital and the materials and services which a firm uses).

Some gains in productive efficiency may be achieved by selling the assets of previously nationalised corporations to private shareholders; but only provided that these shareholders form a more effective pressure group for managerial efficiency than the Government—if, in other words, they introduce stronger capital market discipline. But to realise the full potential for both productive and other types of efficiency gains it is necessary not only to sell the assets but also to liberalise markets. Liberalised markets force producers to reduce costs, partly because of the pressure of competition and partly because they no longer find political lobbying so advantageous. Monopolised markets can, by definition, provide no genuine performance standards for managers, since they lack close competitors with whom to make comparisons. Downward pressures on costs are bound to be weak and ineffective, because the system cannot provide the relevant signals.

Similarly, liberalised markets for inputs will also reduce costs. And so, as cost savings from various sources accrue, the force of competition ensures that the bulk of such savings are passed on to consumers. Thus prices and costs are more closely aligned than in monopolised markets; and allocative efficiency improves. Greater competitive pressures also normally offer consumers a wider variety of price/quality options since producers have to be more responsive to their demands than they are under monopoly.

From the viewpoint of public interest, privatisation is primarily a means of liberalising markets. There may well be political, economic and social advantages in widening share ownership, thus giving people a stake in the success of their own organisations and of the economic system as a whole. There may be legitimate reasons for the Government to raise revenues through privatisation, provided it realises adequate amounts for the assets it sells. (If it does undervalue industries on sale it will impose costs on society similar to those which are incurred when a government borrows at an excessively high interest rate). But in our view privatisation should be directed principally at improving efficiency via injecting competition into previously monopolised industries.

A serious practical problem is posed by the strong vested interests which naturally oppose liberalisation. Employees of nationalised industries understandably wish to retain the advantages they derived from working for monopolies. Financial institutions and potential shareholders may also see illiberal forms of privatisation as being in their short term interests since they are allowed to participate in the profits of a monopoly. The Government may believe that more money will be raised by selling a corporation whole rather than by splitting it into competing parts. All these pressures seem to have operated in the case of British Gas and, regrettably, appear to have been the principal determinants of the form of privatisation.

For the benefit of readers unfamiliar with the somewhat unusual structure of British electricity supply we start with an outline description of the industry.[2]

England and Wales

In England and Wales, the ESI reports to the Department of Energy (except for the Scottish boards, which report to the Scottish Office). It consists of the CEGB and Area Boards and the Electricity Council on which both are represented.

The Electricity Council is the statutory body '. . . responsible for policy formulation and co-ordination . . .' of the industry. It has responsibilities for a number of industry-wide functions such as finance, sales forecasting, generic advertising, investment planning, monitoring tariff proposals, pensions and industrial relations. Despite its overall responsibility the Council has to rely primarily on persuasion in its relations with the CEGB and Area Boards. None of the various proposals to turn it into a strong central body for the industry (for example, in the 1976 Plowden Report) has been implemented.

The Central Electricity Generating Board (CEGB) is, by common consent, the strongest of the nationalised corporations in the ESI (in management, economic and political terms). It is one of the world's largest electrical utilities, owning and operating the bulk of the ESI's assets and carrying responsibility for both generation and long distance transmission of electricity. Power is sold via bulk supply points to the Area Boards.

Twelve *Area Electricity Boards* distribute electricity locally to all categories of consumer. These Boards vary considerably in terms of density of their network and of their mix of domestic and industrial consumers. Area Boards are the customers' main point of contact with the industry.

Scotland

In Scotland, the structure of the ESI is different. There are two integrated power boards which operate both the generation and the transmission and distribution systems. Southern Scotland, the more densely populated region, is served by the South of Scotland Electricity Board (SSEB). One of its distinguishing features is its relatively high proportion of nuclear generating capacity (responsible for over 40% of electricity supplied). The north is served by the North of Scotland Hydro Electric Board which, as the name implies, has a large number of hydro stations, as well as some oil capacity.

The CEGB

Because of the importance of the CEGB, we give below some more details of its operations.

The CEGB, like other power generating authorities, operates a 'merit order' system which allows it to choose the stations which have the lowest operating costs—at present nuclear followed by coal—for base load demand; and thereafter to bring in those which have higher operating costs for intermediate and peak loads. Thus the operating costs of the system (which are mainly fuel) are minimised. When a new power station is built, it will usually have low operating costs relative to other stations and so initially will be high in the merit order and supply base load power. As it ages, its position in the merit order will fall and in the end it may operate only on standby before being retired.

Nearly 80 per cent of electricity is supplied by coal stations, and another 16 per cent by nuclear power (Table 1.1). Although oil-fired stations have high thermal efficiencies, the cost of fuel oil has in recent years precluded their use even for intermediate loads. If oil prices were to stay low for a prolonged period, oil-fired stations might begin to supply intermediate or base load again. They were used

Table 1
ELECTRICITY SUPPLIED, NUMBER OF STATIONS AND FUEL
CONSUMED: ENGLAND AND WALES 1986–87

Fuel Type	Electricity supplied % of total	No. of stations	Fuel consumed million tonnes coal equivalent
Coal	78.2	41*	77.0
Oil	5.6	7	6.8
Gas (for peak power only)	—	11	—
Nuclear	16.4	10	16.2
Hydro, pumped storage	(0.2)+	9	—
	100	78	100.0

* including 4 dual-fired
+ output from hydro stations less net energy used in pumped storage
Source: *CEGB Annual Report and Accounts, 1986–87*

extensively during the coal strike when many mothballed plants were reactivated to ensure continuity of supply. Their use increased again in 1986 when oil prices fell.

Two pumped storage systems, used to even out the daily demand curve, make an important contribution to the efficiency of the system by storing surplus intermediate power and releasing it at peak periods.

Power stations have tended to be located near their sources of fuel. Thus the large coal-fired stations are concentrated in North Yorkshire, the Trent Valley, and the Central Midlands though there are a few stations in the Thames estuary. Nuclear stations, because of their extensive need for cooling water, are usually located on or near the coast but are not concentrated in any one region.

Long distance transmission, via the National Grid, is also operated by the CEGB. The grid has to handle flows of power from regions with surplus generating capacity such as the North of England and the Midlands, to the South and South East where demand is high relative to local capacity. It is linked to Scotland and France, allowing for exchange of electricity in each direction although, in practice, the CEGB is a modest net importer of electricity from both countries. The under-Channel link completed in 1986 has a capacity of 2000 MW, equivalent to one large power station. France has low marginal costs of producing electricity as a result of its surplus nuclear capacity, and exports to other European countries as well as to Britain.

Employment, industrial relations and organisation

In March 1987 the industry employed nearly 147,000 people in England, Scotland and Wales, of which 48,000 were employed by the CEGB, 83,000 by the Area Boards and 16,000 in Scotland. Employment of 'industrial staff' in England and Wales has declined from about 131,000 in 1964 to about 69,000 in 1987, a fall of 47%. Numbers employed in other categories have also fallen significantly. These reductions in manpower have been achieved without compulsory redundancy and the bitter disputes which have characterised other nationalised industries when required to shed labour. When major power cuts have occurred they have usually been caused by serious disruption to fuel supplies.

The ESI has enjoyed good industrial relations and has been virtually strike-free for many years. In its report on the transmission system published in June 1987 the Monopolies and Mergers Commission[3] commended the achievements of the industry and unions in improving industrial relations. The main unions in the industry—the EEPTU, NALGO, GMBATU and the Electrical Power Engineers' Association (part of the Engineers' and Managers' Association) have 'moderate' tendencies. Their enormous industrial power has not been abused.

The CEGB has recently altered the structure of responsibility from a series of self-contained local regions carrying out all activities, to a system whereby operations are divided into four categories, each run by a different operating division. Evidently it wished to streamline both non-technical and technical support now that power production is concentrated in fewer large units, and to strengthen the corporate management and the decision-making of the business as a whole.

Plan of the Paper

The rest of this paper shows how the privatisation principles set out above can be applied to the complex industry whose structure has just been outlined. This study brings out a number of specific issues which need to be addressed in injecting competition into the ESI; describes the particular problems of nuclear power; discusses the very important relationships between the ESI and the coal industry; draws useful lessons from overseas; and deals with the gains which may be expected from privatisation. Then we turn to the main questions which have to be answered—what criteria should be used in assessing privatisation plans and how do the various options stand up to such an assessment? Finally the main points and the conclusions we reach are summarised.

Competition, regulation and some special issues

If electricity supply is to be privatised in a form which will bring substantial benefits, competition is essential for the reasons given already.

Liberalising electricity supply, however, is not straightforward. Some of the difficulties are inherent in all efforts to denationalise industries which have been in state hands for tens of years and have developed the habits which go with state ownership. But there are special problems identified below which practical schemes for electricity supply privatisation must resolve. Some of them have been raised as obstacles to privatisation by those who support continued nationalisation. They are discussed briefly below, together with a list of issues which need further discussion.

The scope for competition in electricity supply

Parts of the present electricity supply industry are 'natural monopolies'. That is, they are activities which can more efficiently be organised under single ownership than under competition. Local distribution is one such activity where competition in digging up roads, laying cables and supplying electricity to small (mainly household) consumers would be unlikely to be efficient. Possibly, changes in distribution technology may eventually allow such competition to develop but at present the arguments seem to be against it. Similarly, a long distance transmission network for transporting electricity is, with existing technology, a natural monopoly. If natural monopolies are privatised, some form of supervision is normally required to avoid the abuse of monopoly power.

Apart from distribution and transmission, the rest of the present electricity supply industry is potentially competitive and could, therefore, be liberalised to reap the benefits summarised above. Peripheral areas of activity of the present industry, such as sales of appliances and electrical contracting, are already in competition with the private sector. Much more important, the generation of electricity (amounting to 70% of all ESI costs) is not naturally monopolistic. There could and should be competition in such generation, in order to give lower prices and a choice of sources of supply to larger customers and to local distributors of electricity.

In privatising and liberalising electricity supply, therefore, the aim should be to:

a) introduce competition into generation;

b) separate long distance transmission from generation so that there is an independent 'common carrier' network useable by competing generators, including manufacturing companies with surplus power to sell. (An independent transmission network, open to all potential users on identical terms, is vital if a competitive generating industry is to develop); and

c) separate local distribution from both generation and transmission.

The industry would therefore consist of competing generators, a long distance transmission network and a number of local distributors of electricity. The latter activities would need regulating.

Gains from competition?

The general case for competition is stated above. What gains would be likely to arise if electricity generation became competitive? Let us start from the apparently plausible case, frequently made by employees of the ESI, that the existing structure already minimises costs by its use of a 'merit order'. Thus, they contend, competition can bring no improvements and might indeed be wasteful.

Such arguments embody a common and basic misconception—that centralised management and size can be equated with efficiency. The merit order used by the CEGB, a system similar to many used elsewhere in the world, will come close to minimising current operating costs. But fuel costs (about half generating costs) are determined to a large extent by a competition-restricting agreement to purchase British coal. Labour costs (over 10% of generating costs) are determined primarily by long-term agreement with unions with considerable monopoly power. In other words, operating costs of individual stations are the outcome of a monopolised regime, as also are the capital costs of existing power stations (nearly 25% of generating costs, including return on capital). Capital costs are irrelevant in operating the merit order, since they are sunk and so unavoidable: but they are a major determinant of total costs. There is too little incentive to spend capital wisely in monopolistic conditions.

Often the main charge which can be levelled against monopolies is not that they directly exploit consumers by making large profits but rather that they are inefficient because they lack the incentives to cut costs. Inefficiency is particularly likely when the monopolies are in state hands, and decisions highly politicised. If electricity generation became a competitive industry, its costs would be reduced compared with those of its monopolistic past, and the bulk of any reductions would be passed on to consumers because of the force of competition. Larger consumers would benefit directly, since they would have a choice of supplier and prices should therefore fall. Lower electricity costs for industry would have beneficial effects throughout the economy. But smaller consumers should also gain more directly, provided regulation of distributors is so designed as to ensure that lower generation costs are passed on.

In suggesting that there are considerable inefficiencies in the ESI which could be greatly reduced by a liberal form of privatisation, we are not blaming the management and other employees of the industry. Present cost levels are products of the environment in which the industry exists, for which successive governments are primarily responsible. If the environment is non-competitive, management has insufficient incentive to spend time seeking cost reductions. If it is both non-competitive and politicised the problem is much worse; it may well be more rewarding to keep on the right side of influential politicians and civil servants rather than to be determined minimisers of costs.

Introducing competition into such an industry and reducing politicisation would be bound to give a new impetus and new incentives to existing management, as well as attracting new managers into it. Instead of arbitrary performance standards being imposed by civil servants, real performance standards would be set by competitors. Thus management would be much more efficient. And liberalisation in the product market would spill over into the markets for the ESI's inputs. It seems very unlikely, for instance, that the 'Buy British' policies for plant and equipment which have existed in the past and have inflated capital costs would survive the introduction of competition in power generation. No doubt manning levels would decline also. As a recent OECD study has pointed out[4], both costs of power station construction and levels of manning appear to be substantially higher in Britain than in other countries. And, of particular importance, there would be downward pressure on the price of the ESI's principal input—coal, which accounts for about one third of the ESI's costs—where a 'Buy British' policy has also been in operation. The Joint Understanding which supports the British coal industry by imposing extra costs on electricity consumers, would not be tolerated by generating companies in competition with each other. It is, indeed, at last coming under scrutiny by the CEGB in the light of criticism of its cost levels. We comment further below on the relationship between the ESI and the coal industry; and attempt to quantify some of the gains from injecting competition into electricity generation.

Regulation

In the cases of both long distance transmission and distribution, but not in competitive generation, some form of regulation would be required to avoid the abuse of the monopoly power inherent in these two activities. Regulation could take several forms. One would be public ownership so that the goverment, as now, acted as the regulatory authority; or there could be regulatory bodies established specifically to supervise private transmission and distribution companies; or local authorities could own or regulate distributors; or there could be a system of franchising companies to operate the transmission network or local distribution for specified periods after which the franchise could be renewed or changed.

Experience in other parts of the world suggests that regulation is seldom very satisfactory. However, the present situation is much worse since, in effect, it involves regulating (by nationalisation) the whole of an industry, only 30% of which as measured by costs is naturally monopolistic. Regulation should be minimised by confining it strictly to those activities where there seems no alternative. An advantage of privatising electricity using the principles outlined above is that the scope of regulation would be considerably reduced compared with the present regime. The regulatory problem would be brought out into the open.

Because of the presence of natural monopolies within the ESI, we devote some attention below to an appropriate method of regulation. We believe that Britain should avoid the excesses of the US method, which is increasingly questioned in the US itself. We believe also that apparently simple formulae—such as the RPI − X + Y used to determine maximum prices for smaller gas consumers after privatisation—should be avoided. The gas formula has already led to a dispute between British Gas and its regulator, Ofgas. In a more complex industry, such as the ESI, the results would probably be even worse. We therefore make suggestions for a regulatory regime which should avoid the worst effects of cost-plus mechanisms, and provide management with incentives to improve efficiency.

Safety, environmental protection and other functions of government

Supporters of nationalisation sometimes claim that public corporations are necessary guardians of the public interest in such matters as safety and environmental protection. In practice, there is little evidence that nationalised industries have a better record in such matters than private companies. There are certainly many complaints about the effects of their activities on the environment and on people. It is also likely that imposition of 'public service' functions on nationalised corporations causes confusion of management objectives.

In any case, in a liberalised market guardianship of the public interest is clearly a matter for government. One advantage of liberalisation is that it would bring into the open certain matters with which government should be concerned, but where at present the responsibilities between nationalised corporations and central government departments are ill-defined and split. Controlling the effects of air pollution from power stations and minimising the unsightliness of large buildings are obvious examples. Dealing with such 'external costs'—for example, by ensuring that the polluters pay for their actions—is properly a function of elected government, and would clearly need to be so in a liberalised market.

Other functions which government would need to perform in such a liberalised market include the maintenance of safety standards (which need not be diminished in any way), and establishment of the regulatory bodies needed to supervise the non-competitive parts of the ESI. A particularly important function of government would be to ensure that the industry did not revert to a monopolised structure.

Thus, in a liberalised electricity supply market the functions of government would change. No longer would there be constant interference in the running of the industry, but in this freer market government would have the vital and more traditional role of protecting the public and the natural environment.

Nuclear power

The existence of a considerable nuclear capacity is a much-quoted obstacle to privatisation. Nuclear power provides nearly 20% of the electricity generated in Britain (though over 40% in Scotland). Ten nuclear power stations are operated by the CEGB and two by the SSEB. Nine are relatively small and ageing Magnox reactors: the other three are Advanced Gas Cooled Reactors (AGRs). Both Magnox and AGR are British designs. Five new AGRs are in various stages of construction or commissioning, and should be in operation by 1988. Considerable technical problems and construction delays have been experienced with the AGRs, and there have also been technical difficulties with the Magnox reactors which will probably begin the process of decommissioning in the 1990s. Permission has recently been given for the construction of Britain's first PWR reactor at Sizewell B and the CEGB is contemplating a second PWR at Hinkley Point.

Security of fuel supplies

Electricity supply is a very large consumer of fuel as well as a supplier of energy to consumers. Disruption of fuel supply is therefore a danger against which it must guard. Would that danger be greater after privatisation?

In practice, the security of the ESI's fuel supplies should be better than it has been in recent years. Successive governments have forced the ESI to depend on British Coal, thus denying it the opportunity to increase security by diversifying its sources of supply (which is the relatively cheap way of enhancing security which a commerical organisation would normally adopt). The industry has therefore had to take extremely costly action—such as building up very large stocks of coal and other materials when it feared coal strikes in Britain, and running oil-fired power stations during strikes. Because of this forced dependence, the monopoly powers of British Coal and its workforce have been strengthened. Thus strikes and threats of strikes have almost certainly been more frequent than they would otherwise have been and their consequences have been more feared[5].

Government policy has had another curious effect. Because of the monopoly power of the coal industry—which governments themselves acted to increase—nuclear power has been seen as a means of diversifying the ESI's fuel supplies. Thus governments supported an expansion of nuclear power in Britain which, though not as rapid as in extreme pro-nuclear countries such as France, was almost certainly faster than the private sector would have been prepared to finance. Whether nuclear power is, in reality, a means of improving security of supply is highly debatable. It does provide another source of fuel for the ESI which, given recent policies of coal support, may have seemed desirable. But nuclear power suffers (rightly or wrongly) from serious problems of public acceptability. Consequently, there is an ever-present danger that existing nuclear stations in Britain might have to be de-rated or even shut down and that new building might cease because of an accident in another country, possibly with an unrelated type of reactor. Thus, a high proportion of nuclear power in an electricity supply system can make for insecurity rather than security. In any case, an obvious alternative is to change the coal support policies which have been the prime cause of such insecurity in Britain.

A privatised ESI, with competition in generation, would have a strong incentive to provide its own security of fuel supply, primarily by a policy of diversification. There is a case, which would apply whether the industry is nationalised or privatised, for some additional government provision by comparatively low cost means, such as holding excess stocks of coal and oil, to meet emergencies. Government might also want to support some nuclear power generation beyond what private generating companies would be willing to install, but whether such action would promote security or insecurity is an open question.

Size of the industry

The size of the ESI is sometimes regarded as an obstacle to privatisation. The assets of the industry (in the whole of Great Britain) on a current cost basis are around £45 billion. However, most commentators assume that the market value of those assets is substantially less—between £10 and £20 billion seems to be a common guess. In principle, we reckon that the market value is well below current cost, since the absence of competitive pressures has almost certainly resulted in over-investment. The very low rates of return in the ESI compared with the private sector lead us to the same conclusion; the target for the ESI is a annual return of 2.75 per cent on net current cost assets and it achieved a return in 1986–87 of just below 3.2%. It may be that these apparently low rates of return are a consequence of an artificially high value placed on the assets of the industry. However, there are such potential inconsistencies among the various financial targets which the ESI is supposed to meet (the ex post required discounted rate of return of 5 per cent on its investment programme, its external financing limit and its annual return on net assets) that firm conclusions are very difficult to draw. What one can say for certain is that electricity privatisation would ask the capital markets to provide a very large sum indeed. Handling needs to be more judicious than in previous privatisation schemes.

Problems of transition

A common and much-neglected problem in proposals for radical reforms is that of transition to the ultimate structure. The present state of affairs may be clear enough; it may also be possible to see where one would eventually like to be. It is tempting simply to argue that the industry should be broken up and competition introduced into generation. But to sell the ESI at its proper price and to introduce the degree of competition which is eventually desirable cannot be done at one stroke of the pen. How to move to that more desirable state is a problem which deserves close attention. We are here dealing with an industry which, like coal, has been nationalised for forty years and was under various forms of government supervision before that. The ESI is very large, and very complex in the sense that it is a mixture of natural monopolies and naturally competitive activities. Consequently, some space here is devoted to practical suggestions for an intermediate stage so that the industry can progress towards full competition without serious disruption.

Coal and the ESI

As shown above, coal is the ESI's biggest input. The two industries are very closely linked. The CEGB takes 95% of its coal from British

Coal and over 70 per cent of British Coal's sales are to power stations. To some extent, these high proportions are a function of collusive agreements such as the Joint Understanding. Nevertheless, even without such arrangements, the ESI is likely to take the bulk of its coal from British sources in the foreseeable future as we explained in *Privatise Coal*. Given the degree of interdependence between British Coal and the ESI, one issue which cannot be shirked is whether it is desirable to privatise one industry without the other.

Scotland

The privatisation of the two integrated Scottish utilities (NSHEB and SSEB) can of course be handled quite separately from that of the ESI in England and Wales, the former being the responsibility of the Scottish Office and the latter of the Department of Energy. It is always open to the Government, however, to have a single privatisation plan for the whole of Britain (including of course Northern Ireland, which this paper does not cover). We have not attempted to take into account such political considerations.

Whichever option in England and Wales is adopted it would be quite possible to maintain the separate existence of the two Scottish Boards. Different treatment for Scotland would not cause significant distortion. If, however, any of the options for England and Wales, particularly those which introduce competition, would give Scotland benefits unobtainable under the present structure, then Scottish consumers are likely to prefer such a scheme. In any case it is desirable that any regulatory arrangements encourage free trade in electricity between all the utilities in Britain. It is also desirable to have similar regulatory regimes where possible. Finally, if special arrangements are needed for nuclear power, the position of the nuclear power stations of the SSEB needs to be considered. If they were taken away for inclusion in a British nuclear power grouping the SSEB would be very short of generating capacity.

Conclusions

This review of the issues in privatising electricity supply suggests that many of the arguments of those who oppose privatisation are ill-founded. Safety standards should be unaffected and environmental protection standards should, if anything, improve. The security of the ESI's fuel supplies should also improve. It is perfectly possible to achieve efficiency gains through competition in generation, even though the rest of the industry would need to be subject to some form of regulation.

Nevertheless, there clearly are several issues which need further discussion. In particular:–

How should nuclear power generation be organised and how should decisions be made about the need for new capacity?

What should be the relationship between the ESI and the British coal industry? Should both be privatised?

What lessons can be learned from overseas?

What would be the gains from privatisation?

What criteria should be used to evaluate alternative privatisation schemes?

How should one judge schemes which privatise the ESI as a monopoly?

Given the objective of more competition in generation, how can a smooth transition be arranged?

These matters are discussed in the rest of the paper.

Problems of nuclear power

Three major problems about nuclear power must be faced. The first is that private companies might be unwilling to buy the Magnox stations and the original, ill-fated English AGRs, though they might be prepared to invest in the Scottish AGRs whose operating experience has been better. If it is, incidentally, true that existing nuclear plants are virtually unsaleable, it is a serious indictment of past nuclear programmes and questions the claim that centralised planning of generating capacity is best. The second problem, related to the first, is that private companies might not be willing to build new nuclear capacity. Finally, would public opinion tolerate private ownership of nuclear power stations? Each of these matters is considered below.

Ownership carries with it enormous obligations in the event of an accident or failure. Furthermore, decommissioning costs which will soon fall due on the old Magnox reactors are likely to be very large (though also very uncertain, since there is little comparable experience). According to Press reports,[6] CEGB estimates the future cost of operation and decommissioning at £6 billion against projected revenue over the remainder of their working lives of £7.5 billion! Most of these costs are likely to relate to decommissioning; and, these costs being so uncertain, it is not impossible that the Magnox stations would be worth nothing at all to a potential purchaser, and indeed might well be deemed a liability.

Construction of new nuclear power stations also presents major problems. The record of building AGRs in Britain has been little short of disastrous. Budgeted costs and construction periods have often been vastly exceeded. The Dungeness B station is still not fully operational 21 years after construction begun, whilst according to the Monopolies Commission the average cost overrun on AGRs has been over 100% in real terms.

Although it is possible that the private sector could improve on this performance, it is by no means clear that future nuclear power stations would be regarded as economic propositions. If the Sizewell Inquiry's comparison of conventional and nuclear power generation costs is reworked with the prevailing, lower world coal prices, and a more realistic, higher discount rate, then the nuclear option no longer appears to be cheaper than coal.[7]

It is almost inconceivable that any private sector organisation could or would assume the risks of building or operating a nuclear power station in Britain. However, the May 1987 Conservative manifesto incorporated the twin aims of a privatised electricity industry and the development of abundant, low cost nuclear generated electricity. These two objectives appear to be inconsistent. If the government is serious in its intention to transfer the ownership and management of the industry to the private sector then it should be prepared to accept the private sector's commercial judgement, even if this results in no more nuclear construction for the present time.

If for reasons such as national security the Government still wishes to ensure further nuclear development it is likely to have to assume full financial responsibility. No matter what form of privatisation is adopted, from monopoly to maximum competition, it is improbable that any new nuclear power stations would, for the time being, be built on commercial grounds.

Despite its manifesto endorsement of nuclear power, the Government should ask itself whether the national security argument still holds good. When first put forward in its first term of office, oil prices were high and rising, while British coal was expensive and at risk from industrial action by the miners. Now oil is cheap and plentiful and coal much cheaper. Privatising coal on liberalised lines would lower costs much further, increase security of supply and, even with generous redundancy payments to displaced miners, would be cheaper for Government than a nuclear power programme. Moreover, as explained above, it is very uncertain whether a high proportion of nuclear capacity in an electricity supply system really does increase security of energy supplies. A privatised electricity supply industry would have a strong incentive to ensure the security of its fuel supplies by diversifying sources of supply—for instance by building coal import facilities, buying natural gas and probably by increasing imports of electricity from France.

Because their operating costs are so much lower, nuclear power stations, once built, will always be able to undercut fossil fuel power stations. Thus they will be employed on continuous base load operations all their lives, regardless of whether they are publicly or privately owned. Consequently, if for security or other reasons the Government decides that more nuclear power stations should be built, albeit at much greater capital cost than fossil fuel stations, the profitability of privatised, non-nuclear electricity companies would be reduced. The Government needs to think further about the evident conflict between its objectives of privatising electricity supply and promoting nuclear power.

The final issue is whether public opinion would allow nuclear power to be in private hands. That is a question on which it is difficult to comment since the answer must depend on the regulatory and safety regime. If the private sector *were* willing to manage and build nuclear stations, no doubt it would be possible to devise the necessary safeguards. There is in general no reason to believe that public corporations are better guardians of the public interest than are private companies.

Relations with the coal industry

For many years, governments have interfered with the fuel purchasing decisions of the ESI. As one of the main benefits from liberalising the industry will come from the liberalisation of the market for its fuel inputs, we begin by describing the present situation.

Government policy

The CEGB has long been required to buy almost all its coal from British coal (formerly the National Coal Board) and the policy of successive governments has been to favour domestic coal as the principal fuel for power generation. Under the terms of the present Joint Understanding with British Coal, the CEGB is allowed to use only small amounts of imported coal and of coal from the tiny and heavily restricted private sector. The tax on fuel oil and severe limitations on the use of natural gas for electricity generation on the grounds that it is a 'premium fuel' have also favoured the domestic coal industry. The government's use of the ESI as a backdoor means of pursuing energy policy and social objectives has clearly increased electricity prices to consumers.

Governments have condoned the Joint Understanding, which is a competition-restricting agreement between the CEGB and British Coal on which we commented in *Privatise Coal*. This agreement attempts to introduce indirect import competition to offset the effects of the CEGB's inability to purchase coal in the cheapest market. Another scheme which tries to offset these effects is QUICS. The two schemes are described briefly below.

The 'Joint Understanding' with British Coal

The original Joint Understanding covered the five year period up to March 1985 and provided that the CEGB would use its best endeavours to take from the (then) NCB 'all suitable coal up to a total of 75 million tonnes a year' provided NCB prices rose at no more than the rate of retail price inflation. It has subsequently been changed several times but the general intent is the same.[8] In its latest version, it provides for the CEGB to take 95 per cent of its coal (at least 70 million tonnes a year) from British Coal. The agreement is not published but it is known that there are three price tranches. In March 1987 the basis was 50 million tonnes a year at a price of £46.88 per tonne, 12 million tonnes at a lower price related to the cost of imported coal (£29.50 per tonne) and another 10 million tonnes related to the prevailing price of oil. The aim is to introduce indirect import competition by relating the lower price tranches to the prices of imported coal and oil.

Over the life of the agreement (four years) the proportion of coal in the highest priced tranche is due to reduce progressively to 40 million tonnes and the middle tranche will increase to 20 million tonnes. The agreement is subject to periodic renegotiation.

QUICS

In response to complaints about high industrial electricity prices, in October 1986 the Qualifying Industrial Consumers' Scheme (QUICS) was introduced to encourage the consumption of coal-generated electricity by high load factor industrial users. Four million tonnes of coal a year is being provided by British Coal—according to the CEGB 'at prices close to those on the world market'—and used to give rebates to companies on average of about 6 per cent.[9]

Privatising and liberalising coal

The Joint Understanding and QUICS are open acknowledgements that British electricity consumers are disadvantaged by the policy of limiting CEGB coal purchases almost entirely to British Coal. Arrangements such as the Joint Understanding give no genuine choice of supplier and they distort decisions about fuel use and about where to site power stations. They are no substitute for real competition.

We argued in *Privatise Coal* that two actions should be urgently taken to benefit coal and electricity consumers. The first is for the CEGB to start construction of a large coal import terminal, to be taken on by its privatised successors. No legislation would be required so there need be no delay. Competitive pressure on British Coal would then significantly increase. Whether or not there was a large increase in coal imports, British Coal would be forced to behave as one competitior in a wider market. Coal costs and prices would be reduced to the benefit of coal and electricity consumers.

The second desirable action is to privatise the coal industry, establishing competition among different sources of British coal supply. In *Privatise Coal* we made detailed proposals on how this might be done and estimated the likely gains. The bulk of these (possibly amounting to £1 billion a year by the mid-1990s) consist of lower prices to consumers. Since such a high proportion of coal is sold to the ESI, electricity consumers stand to gain a great deal from coal privatisation. Similarly, if coal is not privatised a large part of the potential gains from electricity privatisation will not be realised. Electricity customers should benefit from better management and reductions in equipment costs and labour costs under any scheme of electricity privatisation; but they might well forego the reductions in the price of the ESI's major input which coal privatisation would stimulate. Possibly coal prices for power generation would be significantly lowered simply by abolition of the Joint Understanding (which, as we have said, may not be able to survive electricity privatisation). But, to realise the full benefits from liberalisation of the ESI, coal must be liberalised too by means of privatisation.

Another cogent argument in favour of privatisation of coal is that otherwise the ESI may be under-valued on its privatisation. Potential investors in a privatised ESI will inevitably form expectations about the future structure of the coal industry; because of the close relationship between the two industries, this is essential in order to place a value on the ESI. If the Government does not express an intent to privatise coal, investors may guess that a state coal monopoly, supported by the ESI, will remain. If that is their view, they will without doubt look askance at investing in the ESI, with the result that the industry will be unnecessarily undervalued. If the Government believes that it is not possible to embark on coal privatisation at the same time as ESI privatisation, at least some firm statement of intent outlining the form and the timing of coal privatisation, should be made so that potential investors in the ESI are well-informed.

Lessons of foreign experience

Different countries have adopted different ESI structures. These range from the monolithic publicly owned systems of Britain and France, through the diversified public and privately owned systems of Germany and Sweden, to the predominantly privately owned systems of the US and Japan. Systems of regulation of electricity prices are similarly diversified and range from control by government fiat in France, detailed legal regulation in the US, to diverse informal methods of regulation in Germany.

All these systems have the common characteristic of providing widespread access to an assured supply of electricity. This is hardly surprising given that these countries have also conferred extensive if not total monopoly powers on the industry, either nationally or regionally, thus providing a basis for virtually unlimited funding of investment. The comparative efficiency of the various structures in other respects is very difficult to determine given the dependence of such comparisons on exchange rates and the extent to which, in such countries as France and Britain, government has incurred great costs in supporting nuclear power and, in the case of Britain, supporting the coal industry, too. One other single characteristic, however, appears common to them all. It is what might have been expected from an industry in which production predominates and on which such extensive powers of funding have been conferred—endemic overinvestment and excess capacity.

The US system, as one which has been established for over half a century on a predominantly private basis, is one which could be considered for Britain. In what follows, therefore, we briefly review the systems obtaining in other countries before looking at it. The broad conclusion which emerges is that none of the existing models of private power supply would appear either practicable or—in the case of the US system—desirable as the basis for privatisation in Britain. The German and Swedish mixed public and private systems have evolved over time within a general political consensus in a manner that could not be duplicated by a breakup of the British ESI in a far more polarised political context. The Japanese system is dependent on the unusual Japanese corporatist culture. The US system, however, is fundamentally that of regional monopolies operating within an extremely costly and politically contentious regulatory framework which results in a 'cost plus' basis of supply.

Public ownership and centralised control: France and Italy

France and Italy have dominant utilities accounting for nearly all electricity supply, production and distribution. If the CEGB and Area Boards were privatised either as one company or in their present forms, they would remain similar in structure to the French and Italian industries. The new power generation company would, however, in either case be the largest privately owned utility in the world and be unique in having a private monopoly covering an entire country. Other large private utilities with local monopolies, e.g. in the USA and Japan, operate in a heavily regulated regime where no one company has control over the whole country.

Mixed ownership and decentralised control: Germany and Sweden

Examples of countries that operate their ESIs in a decentralised manner include Germany and Sweden. Both have a variety of types of power utility and mixed public and private ownership.

Germany's electricity industry is decentralised, even though the degree of public ownership and influence is still large. There are many electricity utilities ranging from large, integrated systems engaged in all activities to simple distribution companies which buy in all their power. Most of the generation and distribution, however, is in the hands of the twelve largest companies. Many of the enterprises have mixed capital where there is a majority public sector stake and the remainder is private capital. It is, in effect, a disaggregated public sector industry organised along regional lines. Although there is interchange of power between these regions, there is no nationally coordinated transmission grid.

There is a strong element of local and federal government involvement throughout the industry, particularly in regulatory control. The Lander (regional governments) and local councils both partly own and regulate the industry in their regions. Regulation is quite light. All domestic tariffs are in principle free from state restrictions but are subject to the Cartel Law.

A regional system based on the Area Boards would be possible in Britain, but would require strict and detailed regulation. While many European ESIs are organised on regional lines, it is common for local government to be involved in ownership and monitoring of the industry. The levels of local government in Britain do not have the same status and authority as those in other European countries, and the present Government is unlikely to wish to increase their power. Another drawback of the regional system is that it seriously curtails the possibilities for introducing competition.

The industry in Sweden has many features of interest in the context of privatisation. The system is an intermediate stage between full public and largely private ownership. About half of the electricity is supplied by the state utility, Vattenfall; 20 per cent comes from municipal utilities and 30 per cent is generated by the private sector.

Vattenfall buys power from a variety of private generators but, in addition, these companies may rent capacity on the trunk line system which is then used as a common carrier. Thus, the state retains control of the national grid (which has natural monopoly characteristics, and would otherwise need to be closely regulated) and a significant portion of the generating capacity, but preserves many of the efficiencies and benefits that are available from market-led systems.

Both Vattenfall (though state-owned) and the local authority companies are expected to operate like private companies and to compete with the private sector, earning a return on their investment. Because other companies enjoy full access to the grid, a genuine market in power can operate, both for short term and longer term sales. Domestic and industrial tariffs are not directly regulated; but disputes about tariffs can be referred to cartel offices which can instruct a utility to alter them. A mixture of competition and co-operation keeps prices low.

US private utility model

Some 85 per cent of the electrical power of the US is produced by privately owned utilities which hold local monopolies on the production and distribution of power. Let us consider this option and what lessons can be learned from the US experience.

In outline, the utilities are subject to detailed state, county or municipal legislation covering every aspect of their operations—tariffs, investment, profitability. These regulations are enforced by a process of public hearings before local Public Utilities Boards (PUBs) which typically consist of political appointees. The PUBs are empowered to force the utilities to absorb costs deemed to result from inadequate diligence and prudence, but, subject to this, the utilities are allowed to recover all their costs, including a return of around 15 per cent net of tax on their equity, on an historic cost basis.

The advantages of this model are, first, that it limits the exploitation of the monopoly power it confers, by preventing the monopolies from making a return greater than 15% on their equity. It has, however, historically often been ineffective in limiting the exploitation of the monopoly by means of overinvestment to increase total profits. Second, the system does check some of the grosser and more evident exploitations of monopoly in order to support unwarranted levels of costs or salaries.

The US system, however, has very serious political and economic disadvantages:

i) The frequent, lengthy and highly publicised PUB hearings are a convenient forum for all sorts of radical agitation (anti-private sector, environmentalist, etc). This, in a self re-inforcing process, has led to ever tighter regulation and extreme politicisation.

ii) The quasi-judicial form of regulation is extremely costly, with the consumers paying the costs incurred both by the utility and by the regulatory bodies.

iii) The net economic benefit of the system is small because of the inherent ineffectiveness of the judicial review process when applied to highly complex economic issues; the politicisation which some-times works unjustifiably in favour of politically powerful utilities; and the fear that refusal to meet the utilities' demand for rate increases will lead to these critically important local monopolies being cut off from the capital markets. In consequence, the utilities effec-tively operate on a 'cost plus' basis. The major exception is investment in nuclear power stations where a combination of the utilities' poor management and pressure from anti-nuclear lobbies has forced the utilities to absorb substantial costs.

iv) The US system does not encourage or reward efficiency. The predominant impact of regulation is on investment. Until the 1980s the main impact was to ensure that generating facilities were being provided to meet customer requirements and avoid energy shortages. As a result of excess capacity and cost overruns, price increases caused regulators to allocate part of the enormous cost to the inves-tors. The investors had not built such costs and risks into their rate of return. This seems to have been a major factor in the overinvest-ment in nuclear power in the '60s and '70s. The regulatory process does not now encourage new investment of capital because the risk and reward levels are out of balance in the US. In the 1980s the main effect of the regulatory system has been to impede new investment in response both to pressure groups which oppose almost any form of investment, and to consumer groups who oppose new investments as likely to inflate the cost of power. Therefore almost no new large scale plants are being ordered.

It must be expected that all these problems would arise if Britain adopted the US system. They might well be exacerbated by transitional problems (e.g. variations in power rates, deficiencies in service) and the publicity arising from the novelty of the proceedings.

Prizes of privatisation

This chapter illustrates (so far as an outside observer can) the benefits to the economy and sales proceeds to the Government from the privatisation of the ESI. It draws a great deal on the excellent examination of the efficiency of the ESI by Alex Henney in his CPS paper *Privatise Power*. Our estimates cannot be precise; they can only indicate the orders of magnitude of benefits and sales proceeds.

Privatisation schemes differ considerably in their ability to realise economic gains. In particular, the more monopolistic the system and the less the competitive pressures, the smaller the gains which are likely. For purposes of the analysis, competition—without which the benefits outlined below will not be realised—is assumed to be introduced very soon, so that by the end of five years a number of benefits will have materialised.

Economic benefits

The cost structure of generation
Let us first examine the generating industry's cost structure to establish a base from which gains can be achieved. Table 2 is an estimate

Table 2
CEGB'S ESTIMATED COSTS 1987/8
£million

Coal	3300
Other fuels	1000
Total fuels	4300
Staff	880
Materials and services	850
Rents, rates, etc.	250
Total operating costs	6280
Current cost depreciation	1120
Current cost profit before interest and tax	800
	8200

Source: derived from *CEGB Report and Accounts, 1986–87*

of the CEGB's costs for 1987/8, assuming no change from 1986/7 in the amount of electricity generated. This incorporates a reduction in coal prices from the average of £44.6 per tonne in 1986/7 to £42.5 per tonne, as seems likely under the current terms of the Joint Understanding.

Because the industry is so capital-intensive, depreciation and profits account for nearly one-quarter of the total annual costs of the CEGB. Fuel accounts for two-thirds of the costs of generation (excluding depreciation and profits), with coal alone at over fifty per cent.

Coal Costs

By far the largest gains are likely to come from a reduction in fuel costs. As shown in *Privatise Coal,* the sharp reduction in costs possible if coal is privatised and competitive is unlikely to be realised unless the ESI is privatised in a way which gives rise to a number of competitive generation companies. If the coal industry still faced a dominant buyer (the CEGB) the future of privatised coal would be very difficult indeed. If the average price of coal supplied to the CEGB by a privatised British coal industry could be reduced to £35 per tonne (18% less in real terms than now) with further reductions subsequently, the cost saving would be at least £600 million a year.

It might appear unnecessary to privatise British Coal; enough merely to remove import restrictions and to build import facilities. But any attempt to increase British imports very much would probably cause a considerable increase in the price of traded coal, thus reducing the potential gains. Moreover the replacement of British-produced coal by imports might entail large offsetting costs of support for the British coal industry and its workers. Privatisation of electricity on a basis which allowed the privatisation of coal would enable the £600 million to be realised by reducing the costs of British coal to the level of imports (without too much of this gain being lost through these consequential effects).

Nuclear and other fuel costs.

For the purposes of this evaluation we have not assumed that the costs associated with nuclear energy can be reduced, should the nuclear stations be privatised (although cost benefits might well be achieved from opening up these activities to commercial pressure). Nor have we assumed any change in the price of oil supplied to power stations.

Labour costs

Manpower accounts for 13–14 per cent of operating costs. Though numbers have been cut in recent years, manning levels are considerably higher than in most comparable industries overseas[10].

For a 2000MW coal station, a recent OECD report[11] suggests that CEGB manning levels may be nearly double the average, and 25 per cent higher than the next highest. It should certainly be possible to run a privatised industry with much greater labour efficiency. Our assumption—that manning levels could be reduced by one quarter without any adverse effect on efficiency—is probably conservative. Even so, this would save £200–250 million a year.

At present the CEGB's generating activity employs roughly 44,000 people. A reduction of one quarter in their numbers would require 10,000–12,000 redundancies or early retirements over the next few years (say, 3,000–4,000 a year) of which natural wastage should account for a large proportion. At worst, even if the full reduction could only be achieved by redundancy with generous compensation, the sums involved would be comparatively small. If, for example, the average redundancy compensation was £20,000 the total cost would be £200–250 million spread over several years. Set against potential proceeds from flotation of £16 billion or more, this sum would be easily affordable.

Materials and services
This category also accounts for 13–14 per cent of operating costs. More efficient use of materials and services (together with a more commercial approach to purchasing) should enable a 20 per cent cut in their cost to be achieved. Rent and rates, the other remaining costs, is a small amount which should be little affected by privatisation.

Capital cost savings
The OECD study previously cited indicates that the cost of building power stations in Britain is nearly two-thirds higher than in other Western European countries. One of the major sources of cost reduction in the long term would be the more efficient use of capital. At present no less than 23% of the wholesale price of electricity is accounted for by capital charges in the form of depreciation and profit (Table 2 above). Given adoption of a more commercial and cost effective approach to power station building, both the amount of capital required and the costs of servicing it would be much reduced.

The size of these cost savings is, however, difficult to estimate since it requires a forecast of the CEGB's capital spending into the far future. A conservative order of magnitude can be arrived at as follows. The capital spending of the CEGB is currently around £800 million a year. Let us assume that this remains constant in real terms (rather than substantially increasing with the major construction programme now getting under way), and that a 25% greater efficiency could be achieved. This would constitute a cost saving of £200 million a year. The present value of these savings over the long term future would be £2.5 billion, assuming an 8% real discount rate.

Total economic benefits
In England and Wales, competition should reduce operating and capital costs by around £1,200 million per annum within say five years of its introduction (see Table 3). This represents a long term saving in present value terms of around £13 billion at an 8% real discount rate. This includes the associated benefits to the ESI deriving from the privatisation of the coal industry. It should be noted that this is based on the conservative assumption that there are no savings to be made in distribution. Over and above these, the privatisation of coal might well produce further benefits for non-ESI coal consumers equivalent to a net value of about £4 billion. These benefits are additional to those included in the table below. There will also be savings in Scotland, but these will be small due to high dependence on nuclear and hydro power.

Government receipts from sale of the ESI

The benefits outlined above are those which should accrue to the British economy as a whole. Over and above this, the Government will receive sales proceeds to compensate it for the right to the future net cash flows which it would be giving up.

The sales price of the ESI is primarily dependent on the profits which the privatised industry would expect to make. Also to a degree it will depend on the predictability of the regulatory arrangements.

Table 3
CASH SAVINGS ESTIMATED £MILLION

	1987/8 (Estimated)	1992/3	% Change
Coal	3300	2700	− 18
Other fuels	1000	1000	—
Staff	880	650	− 26
Materials and services	850	680	− 20
Rent & rates	250	250	—
Capital spending	800	600	− 25
Operating costs plus capital expenditure	7080	5880	− 17

In general the Government has a clear choice between maximising the sales price and lowering the price of electricity. The higher the price the less the potential for privatisation to reduce electricity prices. Indeed if it attempted to set that price too high no reduction in electricity prices might be forthcoming at all.

Let us assume however, that the government policy will be to sell the ESI for a sum consistent with there being no increase in the price of electricity in the immediate future. In previous privatisations, British Telecom was sold on a price/earnings multiple of 9.4 and British Gas on one of 9.7. Supposing that the price earnings ratio for the ESI including Scotland was similar, Table 4 shows the possible proceeds based on a range of P/E ratios for the year ending March 1987. Note that we are assuming that all the CEGB's generating assets are privatised both nuclear and non-nuclear. No account has been taken of the decommissioning costs of the Magnox nuclear stations, nor of any separation of the grid from the generation assets.

On these assumptions the total value from the sale of the ESI (England and Wales) would range from £13.5 billion to £18 billion. In addition, there will be a sum realised from the sale of the Scottish boards.

Impact of privatisation on the cost of power

It has been frequently claimed by the opponents of privatisation that, because private investors require a higher rate of return on investment, the cost of electricity will be higher. This is erroneous both in logic and in fact.

The error of logic lies in the failure to recognise that the higher rate of return looked for by private investors arises from their absorbing some of the risks—such as those arising from poor investment decisions and excess capacity—which would otherwise be borne by consumers. It would, indeed, be perfectly possible to raise private finance for the privatised ESI as 100% debt finance at the Government's borrowing rate, if the ESI customers were obliged as at present

Table 4
POSSIBLE SALES PROCEEDS ENGLAND AND WALES
£million

P/E ratio	9	10	11	12
Total	13,500	15,000	16,500	18,000

to meet all the risks by simply paying more for power as these risks materialised. In other words, the higher return required by the private sector must be offset against the gains to consumers arising from the private investor taking some of the risk after privatisation; so the chance of future price increases as a result of cost overruns, etc., is correspondingly reduced.

The error of fact is to suppose that the costs of power from the existing ESI system would go up if privatisation produced no cost savings. This is not so, because the assets will almost certainly be sold at such a price as to give the investor a commercial rate of return if the price of electricity stays as it is. The Government will probably choose to set the sale price of the existing system at a level which ensures no increase in electricity prices, any other policy being politically unacceptable. If this is so whatever scheme is chosen, then holding power costs at their current levels will set an upper limit on the maximum proceeds the Government can obtain. Nevertheless there should be a considerable reduction in costs after privatisation.

Additions to the existing generating system are another matter. These assets would have to be acquired by the privatised company at their full current cost of construction. Even so, construction costs should be substantially reduced compared with those which would have been incurred by the CEGB. This, combined with savings in operating costs, should more than offset the higher rate of return being sought, even if one disregards the offsetting gains from the sharing of risks by the investor.

In sum, while many real problems do confront electricity privatisation, higher priced electricity is not one of them.

Criteria; economic and political, essential and desirable

The Manifesto commitments

Privatisation has been a major achievement of the present Conservative Government, and is being widely copied abroad. Its general merits—the application of economic and commercial pressures for efficiency, the depoliticisation of decision taking, the elimination of the burden on public sector financing, and the enhancement of consumer and investor interests at the expense of unreasonably comfortable arrangements for those who work in the industry—are set out above. Indeed the general merits of privatisation may appear too well known to require elaboration. Unfortunately it is not true that any form of privatisation will secure most of the possible benefits, nor that particular forms differ but little from one another in desirability. With the unsatisfactory experiences of privatising British Gas and British Telecom, as lightly regulated, private sector monopolies, it is apparent that the form in which an industry is privatised is crucial. Some forms of privatisation may indeed be inferior to public ownership, and poorly planned and executed privatisation schemes may become serious economic and political liabilities.

Agreement is therefore necessary on the criteria for privatising the ESI. Unfortunately, the main source document, the Conservative election manifesto 'The Next Moves Forward' is almost silent on the reasons for electricity privatisation. The single sentence on the subject states 'Following the success of gas privatisation, with the benefits it brought to employees and millions of consumers, we will bring forward proposals for privatising the electricity industry subject to proper regulation.' The benefits of electricity privatisation seem to be regarded as self-evident. The only clue about criteria may be inferred from the subsequent paragraph urging the general merits of competition for the economy as a whole, where it is stated 'Competition forces the economy to respond to the needs of the consumer. It promotes efficiency, holds down costs, drives companies to innovate and ensures that customers get the best possible value for money.' Presumably this forceful justification of the merits of competition is meant to apply, inter alia, to electricity privatisation.

The manifesto also revealed, however, that not all the important decisions on electricity supply would be left to a privatised ESI. It supports nuclear energy as supplier of low-cost electricity, stating that to depend on coal alone '. . . would be short-sighted and irresponsible' and that it is the Government's intention '. . . to go on playing a leading role in the task of developing abundant, low-cost supplies of nuclear energy. . .' . In short, privatisation of the ESI would be circumscribed by a continued Government commitment to further 'abundant' supplies of nuclear generated electricity.

As the Government has not yet set out its reasons for electricity privatisation save in the briefest and most general terms, and has referred only to the criteria of introducing more competition and to its commitment to 'abundant' nuclear energy, we here set out our own views on essential criteria. Otherwise no evaluations of and comparisons between privatisation schemes can sensibly be made.

Making the criteria explicit

We have previously discussed the broad objectives of privatisation schemes and potential conflicts between them. In assessing the various privatisation proposals, however, explicit and more detailed criteria are needed.

There are many different interest groups who will be affected by electricity privatisation: for example, the Government, senior ESI management, other staff of the industry, its unions, power plant manufacturers, the construction industry, the coal industry, the nuclear industry and potential investors. The criteria used and the weight assigned to each criterion will vary according to the group concerned (and within a particular group, too).

There are also two very large dispersed groups—taxpayers and electricity consumers—almost identical in membership but not necessarily with the same interests in privatisation; since an individual may have one view about a privatisation proposal in his role of taxpayer, and another in his role of electricity consumer.

In the light of this diversity of interests, the criteria which could be used are very numerous. The ones which we take—necessarily a personal selection—include some 'political' criteria which the Government is likely to have in mind. We have chosen economic criteria on the basis of national interest rather than those of appeal to particular lobbies. Not everyone will agree with our criteria, partly because not everyone stands to gain from ESI privatisation (though the gains should be sufficient to compensate any potential losers). By making the criteria explicit, however, it is possible for readers to see how our conclusions have been derived. Sectional interests who press for particular forms of privatisation would do well to follow this example.

Essential and desirable criteria

There are six essential political criteria which we believe the Government is likely to use in assessing ESI privatisation schemes; five essential economic criteria if it is to be demonstrably in the national interest and to appeal to consumers and investors; and several desirable criteria by which options should also be judged.

Any acceptable option must meet all of them—or at least preserve the possibility of their eventual satisfaction. This latter point is most important. For once a formerly nationalised industry is privatised it is almost impossible to alter its structure for many years. Prospectuses on which huge sums have been raised can be written only if rules are clearly written in advance, and designed to be scrupulously adhered to. A government which breaks such agreements lays itself open to legal action, and undermines public support for subsequent privatisation issues. In practice a government has to live with the consequences of any large act of privatisation for a very long time indeed. That is why, if for whatever reason the Government cannot privatise the ESI satisfactorily this term, it is better to defer the measure until such time as completion is possible within the lifetime of a single Parliament.

Essential political criteria

Absence of serious disruption
No government could contemplate changing the structure of so basic an industry as electricity if significant disruption in the supply of power seemed likely to ensue. None of the serious privatisation options is, however, likely to fail this test. The problem of providing reliable electricity supplies is daily met and daily overcome in every major Western country as a matter of routine. Yet the belief is voiced in Government circles and by some private individuals that real danger of disruption exists unless the industry either continues in public ownership, or is privatised as a monopoly. Independent British and international technical opinion lends no support to such an idea. The Government should put just one question to the ESI on this critical matter: 'Can the ESI suggest adequate technical arrangements to avoid disruption for each of the most likely privatisation alternatives?'

If the answer is yes, the 'problem' disappears. If the answer is no, then the Government should take advice from British and international power engineering consultants of repute. They will be reassured.

Assured privatisation within the lifetime of a Parliament
Privatisation of the ESI requires government vision, courage and energy. It is not a measure which a government would like to introduce in the second half of any political term, particularly as the benefits may not be immediately forthcoming. For these and other reasons we assume that the Government hopes to pass the necessary

legislation during the first half of its present term. Further, it will wish to do so in a form which minimises the chances of subsequent renationalisation (for instance by dividing the industry into parts and involving a large number of investors on terms which they would not like to be reversed by a subsequent government). Thus there is pressure on the Government to proceed immediately with ESI privatisation. Speed, however, may be the enemy of choosing the best scheme which may require more time for evaluation and implementation. In practice we assume that the Government's choice is either to complete electricity privatisation well before the run up to the next general election or else to postpone it to a subsequent term.

Minimum risk of electoral unpopularity
Privatisation schemes which neglect the interests of consumers can do serious political damage. If consumers came to resent the prices or service of previously nationalised industries, privatisation would become an electoral albatross. After the experience of British Telecom, the Government will be advised to seek measures which minimise this risk.

Generous profit participation and redundancy arrangements
The Government will want the support of management, workers and unions. Those who leave the industry through redundancy or early retirement must be treated generously to secure their support and to meet the understandable loyalty to ex-colleagues of the majority staying with the industry. Equally those who stay in the industry will need to look forward to a more attractive future than they would have had under continued nationalisation (for instance, by means of profit and capital incentives—although pay increases will need to be earned through increased productivity).

No foreign control or domination of the ESI
The capital sums which the Government can expect to raise from the ESI are huge—certainly more than from any other industry which has been or may be privatised. Any scheme must be within the capabilities of capital markets. Without special measures there is always the possibility that one or more parts of the ESI might come under foreign domination. This is not necessarily a matter for regret, since new management expertise is needed to realise the industry's potential. But in political terms the Government is unlikely to welcome foreign control. The sensible compromise, to the extent that corporate investors are involved in the industry (which we judge to

be likely and indeed essential under the more attractive privatisation options) is to allow consortia with strong minority foreign representation. This, rather than the banning of foreign corporate investors, would assist the Government to realise the highest achievable proceeds from the industry consistent with the other essential criteria.

No undervaluation of assets
The Government will clearly wish to achieve the highest price it can for the assets it sells, subject to other criteria and aims—e.g. no increase in the price of electricity. That price will, however, depend on the form of privatisation (see below).

Essential economic criteria

The distinction between political and economic criteria is in part artificial. What is certain, however, is that unless the essential economic criteria are met investors and business will not make ESI privatisation a success. One of the worst outcomes for the Government would be to choose a scheme of privatisation on political grounds only to find that it failed through insufficient attraction to investors.

Introduction of maximum competition
This is particularly important since it is to competition that we must look for the major efficiency gains in a privatised ESI. Any option which fails to introduce competition where appropriate will fail to satisfy consumers in the medium to long term, and may well seriously damage the Government's credibility. Virtually all independent commentators urge the need for significant injections of competition if privatisation schemes are to bring economic gains. It is also the only criterion made explicit in the 1987 Conservative Election manifesto.

Compatibility with competitive coal privatisation
The interdependence of the ESI and British Coal has been explained above. Unless both industries are privatised, both with the introduction of maximum competition, then the cost reductions which we suggest should be the paramount purpose of privatisation, cannot be achieved. Investors will be deterred from investing in privatised coal unless there is real competition in the buying of coal for electricity generation. Similarly, investors will be less interested in electricity privatisation if an unreformed coal monopolist provides all but a

token amount of coal requirements. Indeed, investor interest could be so reduced as to force the Government to abandon ESI privatisation.

Need for new management and corporate shareholders
New, commercially oriented management is essential if privatisation is to achieve its potential economic benefits, and not prove an economic liability. In practice this requires new corporate shareholders. This requirement arises for the following reasons. First, while the public is accustomed to accept the shortcomings of nationalised industries with resignation, it is less tolerant of a newly privatised industry, particularly if it seems that inferior service is being offered in order to reap higher profits. Second, the managerial requirements of a newly privatised industry are much more exacting because of the formidable problems of transition to competition and maintenance of standards of service within strict cost limits.

The process of competition should ultimately provide higher management standards. But it may take too long, given the immediate demand by the public for better service and the risk of failure in any attempt by existing management to secure the transition to competition.

Simple but effective regulation of monopoly activities
Transmission and distribution are natural monopolies which will need to be regulated. Generation will not need regulation provided sufficient competition is introduced. But long distance transmission must become a common carrier system open to all generators of electric power, existing or prospective, whatever their size. It is also essential that any distributing company or bulk customer should be able to buy electricity from nearly any British power station without penalty. This *does* require regulation, which should however be as simple as possible.

Attractiveness to individual and corporate investors
ESI privatisation must be attractive to enough British individual and corporate investors. This implies a well designed privatisation scheme with a clearly specified form of regulation having a predictable impact on earnings. The transitional and the long term structure will be equally important. Schemes which secure the co-operation of managers, workers and unions will also enhance the attractiveness of the ESI to potential investors. Finally, it will be necessary to promise enough stability of transitional earnings for investors to be ready to

pay appropriate values for what they are buying. All these matters are addressed subsequently when discussing the individual options.

Desirable criteria

Over and above the six essential political criteria and the five essential economic criteria, several further *desirable* criteria deserve attention.

Minimising the pre-privatisation planning period

The period of planning uncertainty before privatisation should be as short as possible, for the benefit of management, staff and suppliers to the industry. Not, of course, that it is desirable to reduce the planning period to the point where an inferior privatisation option is chosen. Certainly, the period of uncertainty will exist up to the point where legislation is introduced (commonly expected to be October 1988); and even beyond as the ESI privatisation bill passes through Parliament).

Minimum period of structural change

In moving from its present nationalised state to a competitive industry a period of transition is needed. Management and workers will have to be assigned to the different parts of the new structure. The assets and, of course, the liabilities and contingent liabilities of the restructured parts, will have to be identified and allocated in order to permit prospectuses and other legal documentation to be drawn up. This said, it is highly desirable that the period of structural change (that between privatisation and the ESI settling down in its permanent form) should be kept to a minimum.

Retention of the industry pension scheme

Some pension arrangements have serious effects on management and labour mobility. The ESI pension scheme should probably be kept in existence to retain the confidence of all in the industry and to ensure that pensions are portable between the privatised companies. At the time of privatisation the pension scheme should be fully funded, albeit with the right of the Government to recapture any overfunding which can be shown to exist after say 7 to 10 years. The proposed Electricity Standards and Regulatory Commission (see below) could be charged with overseeing the scheme, which is one of the largest in Britain.

Evaluating the ESI privatisation options

In the next two sections the major options for privatisation are identified and analysed against the essential political and economic criteria and the desirable criteria outlined here. The results are summarised in Table 5. The various monopoly options, the competitive options and the case for 'doing nothing yet' to the ESI are considered.

Options for privatising as a monopoly

There are four serious options to consider, each of which has superficial attractions; one in particular is backed by the formidable publicity apparatus of the CEGB, and one by the Electricity Council.

i) Privatisation as a monolith, supported by the CEGB.

ii) Initial privatisation as a monolith with new power stations open to private ownership.

iii) Establishment of a distribution monopoly competing with the new CEGB in new generation, supported by the Electricity Council.

iv) Establishment of integrated regional utilities.

In each case regulation (whether of the rigid U.S. method or of the more discretionary British method) would be needed to prevent abuse of monopoly power. Only the best variant of each option is evaluated.

(i) The monolithic option

The first variant of this option is to privatise the present ESI in England and Wales as a single unit. The second variant is to privatise the CEGB (including the national grid) and the distribution utilities (the Area Boards) separately, to produce a monolithic generation and transmission utility and a monolithic distribution utility. In economic terms there is little difference between these variants. A monopoly distribution utility would be virtually the sole customer for the CEGB (excluding only a few bulk supply contracts to major users such as British Rail) and the CEGB would be the only supplier of consequence to the distributing monopoly. So let us consider only privatisation as a single unit (the 'monolith'). This would create a unified ESI for the first time. The present structure has 12 independent Area Boards and the independent CEGB, all loosely co-ordinated by the Electricity Council. The CEGB would inevitably dominate the new 'British Electricity'; and the private monopoly would if anything be even more dominant than the present ESI.

The third variant of monolithic privatisation is to privatise separately each of the 12 existing Area Boards, and also the CEGB. This would merely perpetuate the present dominance of the CEGB; yet generation is the one area of the ESI where real competition is possible. This third variant has no advantages compared with the other two. It will not be considered further.

Monolith with regulation in the style of British Gas
This option of privatising the ESI in essentially its present form would need a government agency to exercise discretionary control over the price structure to avoid abuse of monopoly power. Such control might adopt a formula similar to that for British Gas, where the total cost of gas purchased is passed on to consumers, while other costs can be increased in line with the retail price index subject to a discretionary deduction—the 'x' factor—for what the government or its agency deems to 'reflect improvements in efficiency'. The 'x' factor (which obviously gives wide discretionary powers) was initially set at 2% a year in the case of British Gas.

This option has some clear advantages. It would be easy to understand, to describe in a prospectus, and fairly easy to finance. If financed in one single operation then, at say £13.5 billion to £18 billion (for England and Wales alone), it would impose a serious strain on capital markets. But finance could easily be raised in tranches over 4 to 5 years, without undue risk of foreign control or domination of the ESI.

Privatisation as a monopoly could also be completed more quickly than most other options, and certainly within the first half of the present parliamentary term. The proposal also has the advantages of precedent, and acceptability, or the chance of it, by the industry's unions and management. Thus with token concessions to competition (as outlined below) it may be regarded favourably by decision makers who take the short term view.

A possible final advantage of monolithic privatisation in some eyes is that the Government might sidestep many of the difficulties of handling present and future nuclear power stations. The present senior CEGB management, committed as they are to building PWR reactors, could use the financial strength of the monolith to continue this programme regardless of its economic merits, as in the past. Thus it might be possible to honour the election manifesto commitment to provide 'abundant', if not cheap, nuclear power.

But the disadvantages of monolithic privatisation outweigh the advantages. In particular it does nothing to bring about the possible economic benefits of privatisation. No competition would be introduced at all. Futhermore, there would be little if any introduction of new senior management. For reasons explained below the method of regulation, while superficially simple, would be ineffective. In essence, this option would attempt to achieve by a limited form of regulation what the virtually unlimited powers vested in direct public ownership have failed to achieve in almost half a century, namely to establish competitive standards of cost effectiveness. And it would require regulation of the whole industry, instead of only parts of it.

It may be argued that any form of privatisation is better than a nationalised structure in that it enables government to subject the privatised industry to pressure for greater efficiency from its shareholders, which could be increased by use of its discretionary control over the price structure in order to restrict profits. For many reasons such pressure would not work.

First, such a huge industry would have widely dispersed shareholding and thus be virtually immune to direct shareholder pressure. It would also be immune from takeover. It may be objected that it would be little bigger than BP, with a present market capitalisation of around £20 billion, which is widely regarded as a well run company. Size, therefore, need be no barrier to shareholder pressure for efficiency. The point is valid if the company concerned is subject to effective competition. The international oil industry is competitive, but a monolithic ESI would face no direct competition. Moreover, ESI shareholders, if past privatisations are any guide, would mainly comprise:—

i) a huge number of individuals with relatively small stakes (purchasing on the attractive terms usually offered to household customers); and

ii) a wide spread of institutional shareholders who would, in total, probably have half or more of the shares.

Neither of these groups would be able and willing to exert significant shareholder pressure. In practice, the new ESI board would be almost autonomous.

Second, the complexities of an industry in which a high proportion of costs is governed by investment decisions mean that standards of efficiency are not readily ascertainable. Any management could contend that higher standards were simply not attainable.

Third, since security of supply depends on huge and continued investment, the privatised ESI could exert great political leverage by claiming that its required levels of profit were essential for the maintenance of such investment.

A government agency would need quite extraordinary determination if it tried to reduce profitablity through control of the price structure, thereby risking a slow-down in investment. These considerations would have even more force if the privatised industry were saddled with the multi-billion pound investment requirements of the nuclear power programme. Nor can it be expected that any future Labour Government, with its likely dependence on the ESI unions, would try seriously to use its discretionary control over prices in order to impose higher standards of efficiency.

Past privatisations have been based on minimal regulation using simple formulae. But this would not remain the basis of regulation for the ESI for very long. Over 20% of present generating costs are accounted for by capital charges (depreciation, interest and profit), costs which all vary greatly with the rate of capital investment and inflation. The regulators would find themselves confronted with a dilemma familiar to their U.S. counterparts. On the one hand, refusal to allow such charges to be passed on to consumers risks inadequate capital investment; on the other hand, automatic acceptance of such charges produces over-investment in order to justify greater profits. Ultimately the Government might be driven to impose U.S. style regulation with all the economic and political difficulties outlined previously.

Undervaluation is an undoubted hazard. Almost all the twelve privatisations to date which created new publicly quoted companies have opened at a premium to the offer price after the first day of trading—only Britoil and Enterprise Oil failing to do so. For example, British Telecom and British Gas traded at premia of 33% and 9% respectively to the fully-paid price. The premia to the partly-paid price were much larger (86% and 25% respectively). Other privatisation issues have also been at substantial discounts. If only from the sheer size of an ESI issue—up to perhaps £20 billion, even if phased in over 4 to 5 years—a large undervaluation seems probable.

Many uncertainties would stem from any discretionary element in the system of regulation, giving rise to longer term losses to the Exchequer. The extent to which the monopoly attempted to exploit its market power, and the counter extent to which successive governments and regulators succeeded in preventing it, would determine the return to investors, who would consequently look for a risk premium higher than that which would obtain with the more formalised regulated systems in the U.S. This would certainly be true of sophisticated institutional investors who are likely to be in the majority.

But one of the worst disadvantages of monolithic privatisation is that it would be incompatible with privatising the coal industry on a competitive basis. Thus the greatest opportunity to reduce ESI costs would be missed, and two of the largest British energy industries would remain unreformed and inefficient.

To sum up, monolithic privatisation in this form would freeze Britain's largest company (in terms of British sales and assets), into a form which was non-competitive and non-accountable; a corporatist structure which would combine shareholder and union support in resistance to change. The consumer would not be pleased.

Monopoly with US style regulation
The US private regulated utility system, as described above, is essentially a cost-plus system. The system is well defined legally, and clearly understood in the financial markets (though obviously far better in the US than in Britain). Thus, uncertainty about its operation, so marked in the discretionary regulatory systems described above, would be lessened: which should remove one possible source of undervaluation.

In other respects, however, this option would fail all the criteria for efficient privatisation. It would not inject competition. No new management would be introduced, and the system would effectively operate on a cost-plus basis and then only by means of very costly regulatory procedures. Existing levels of costs would tend to be frozen, and there would be the additional costs of regulation.

It would also be almost impossible to prevent the regulatory process becoming—as in the US—an arena for endless enquiry and debate on every aspect of power generation, specifically on the need for and type of new generation capacity. By adopting this scheme the Government would create a publicly-funded forum for radical agitation, against private sector enterprise and for the wilder forms of environmentalism. Dissatisfaction among consumers with monolithic privatisation (already experienced under British style regulation), would almost certainly find a loud and continuous voice.

This variant would therefore fail all the essential economic privatisation criteria and most of the essential political criteria.

(ii) Initial privatisation as a monolith—but with competitive new generation.

There is strong opposition to privatising the ESI as a monolith, not least because it would stand in the way of the development of competitive sources of new generation. Hence the ESI and its political supporters have canvassed a variant on monolithic privatisation which holds out the prospect of the gradual introduction of competition in power generation. Given the Government's desire to continue with a nuclear programme, the shortness of time before it chooses a privatisation scheme, and the appearance of introducing competition which it has, this scheme is no doubt being seriously considered.

The proposal purports to address a major problem of any ESI privatisation—transition from monopoly to competition in electricity generation. The interim 'solution'[12] which has been suggested is to privatise the existing generation system as a single unit but to introduce competition in stages by permitting private companies to compete to construct and own power stations, and to sell power from the 12,000–13,000 MW or so of new capacity (about 20 percent of existing installed ESI capacity) which may be started before the end of the century. Private companies would presumably enjoy access on fair terms to the transmission network, and be able to sell their power to the public. If the Area Boards were sold as separate companies, these and bulk commercial consumers would constitute their market.

This scheme has many features in common with the previous option; so our comments are limited to evaluating the differences. Advantages are few; and disadvantages are shared with the previous monolithic option, with the exception that there is some prospect of competitive generation. But is this prospect realisable or significant? And can it overcome the otherwise unacceptable drawbacks of monolithic privatisation?

This scheme at least gives the CEGB a political opportunity to welcome talks about new private power generation which it has hitherto discouraged; and talks are reported to be in progress with several private promoters whose combined schemes could generate

1500 MW[13]. Sources of power are said to include imported and low grade, waste tip coal. Efficient combined cycle systems are also proposed. This appears to be a prudent change of heart by the CEGB. Further, the CEGB now may be willing to contemplate some independence for the national grid whereby the latter can arbitrate between the CEGB and any private producers (including presumably the SSEB with its surplus generating capacity which it seems it was discouraged from selling to the CEGB before the miners' strike)[14]. Could this be another major change of stance? Hitherto the CEGB has insisted on being the sole guardian of the national grid. Under the threat of being broken up it may be willing to sacrifice the lesser part of itself to try to preserve the greater. Therefore, we assume, in evaluating this proposal, that there would be an independent transmission system (probably regulated as a natural monopoly). There would be little prospect of effective competition if the transmission network remained in the hands of the CEGB, who could charge over the odds for access. This has been the experience under the 1983 Energy Act. New generation, and of course replacement generation, could be provided either by allowing the CEGB to compete with private promoters (assuredly CEGB's preference), or by allowing private companies exclusively to quote for all new generating capacity. Under either choice the CEGB could be left responsible for new nuclear capacity.

Like monolithic privatisation, this scheme could proceed quickly, involve minimal transitional problems and avoid risk of foreign domination. Moreover, it should not upset management and unions. It has the further, delusively attractive advantage of offering some competition and immediate business prospects for the SSEB, France and private power promoters, lobbies which the CEGB must prefer to have on their side.

In some industries provision of free entry might quite quickly introduce genuine competition. By this means a state monopoly might be undermined without privatisation. If, for example, new capacity could quickly be brought into operation and the original monopoly had no special advantages vis-a-vis new entrants, liberalisation without privatisation might well work. In electricity supply, however, neither condition is fulfilled; so it is improbable that this proposal would introduce any competition worth the name in electricity generation. To be effective new entrants must be able to offer a balanced, flexible supply of power, backed up by reserve capacity. This means they must come in with a spread of power stations, not on a single station-by-station basis. The long time lags in planning and building new power stations (7 years or more) would postpone the emergence of any competition. Moreover, the incumbent would have overwhelming advantages—for example, its size and its relationships with the power plant manufacturers which it has supported.

The new generation planned by the CEGB for the rest of this century is shown below.

Stations	MW	Type
Fawley	1800	Coal
Plymouth	1800	Coal
West Burton	1800	Coal
Killingholme	1800	Coal
Thames Side	1800	Coal
Sub-total—coal capacity	9000	
Sizewell B	1175	Nuclear
Hinkley C	1175	Nuclear
Other PWR	1175	Nuclear
Sub-total—nuclear capacity	3525	
TOTAL	12525	

Source: CEGB Annual Report and Accounts 1986/87 plus our estimates.

These huge stations (costing about £1.5 billion each at 1987 prices) would be economic only if operated on base load.

Before a plant is built in this environment, any new investor would need a long term power contract from customers—on most exacting terms given the very heavy market risks (on top of the risks deriving from all the cost uncertainties) which have surrounded the building of generating plant in Britain.

The CEGB will have to be privatised at a very large discount on the current replacement cost of its assets (not much more than historic costs) if privatised power is not to be more expensive than at present. This would evidently give the new CEGB a major advantage over any investors in new generating facilities who would be paying current costs for their power stations. Also the new CEGB could accommodate any pattern of demand, provide security of supply and require far less stringent contract terms, since it could supply power from a system which enjoyed a greater diversity of customers. Even without recourse to overt cross subsidisation, the new CEGB would be at an overwhelming advantage in the very limited market for large industrial loads. In theory, this advantage could be redressed by making the new CEGB play the part of customer, and requiring it to sell the new power as part of its output. The trouble is that this process could easily result in the provision of merely token competition, as the new CEGB would be determined to preserve its effective monopoly. As with US regulated utilities, such potential competition is easily negated by the purchaser (i.e. the new CEGB) imposing conditions of availability of power, security of supply and price which only it, using its huge system of diversified plant and fuel sources, can afford to meet. Also, implementation of the power contract over the years would be dependent on the purchaser's exercising fairness and goodwill. Would this be forthcoming? That is another formidable risk.

Finally the new CEGB could use its immense powers of cross-subsidisation whenever it chose to bid for any new power station. Formal bars to this practice would be unenforceable. Bidding relates to the cost of power several years ahead; there are no objective means of determining that a successful bidder had quoted unrealistic costs which would require subsidising. Even with very strong regulation along US lines, cross subsidisation could only be proved by expensive enquiry when stations were operational many years later—and could not possibly be checked by the light forms of regulation so far practised in Britain.

If, therefore, competition was to be at all genuine the CEGB could not be allowed to bid to build power stations. Even so competition would only advance at the slow pace of new non-nuclear construction. (The difficulties of private sector capital being used for new nuclear stations are dealt with below.) Thus, on the best of interpretations, and assuming that the policy was rigorously upheld by the 2–3 successor governments which will be in office up to the turn of the century, at most 10% of installed capacity would be in new private hands by the year 2000. Most of this could, as we have shown, only function as a tame supplier for the new CEGB. Even with Scottish and French imports the monopoly would be effectively intact. Few of the potential economic benefits would be realised. And, above all, the continuing domination of the British coal market by the new CEGB would preclude coal privatisation. This option is surely unacceptable.

(iii)   Monopoly distributor competing with the CEGB in generation

This is an option recently proposed by the Electricity Council.[15] A single integrated distribution company would comprise all the present Area Boards under a holding company—presumably the former Electricity Council, though the Area Boards would prefer complete independence. There would also be a single generating company, the new CEGB. The generating company would sell power to customers as the Area Boards do at present; and in addition would have the right to build power stations. It would also control the National Grid. This option would appear to relegate the CEGB to a subordinate position of a supplier of power. In other words it purports to introduce countervailing power against the new CEGB, and at the same time to bring competition into generation.

These advantages are illusory. A distributing monopoly could not, in the foreseeable future, be other than overwhelmingly dependent on the new CEGB: obliged to pay whatever price the regulatory system permitted. Even if all non-nuclear stations were built by other organisations, the CEGB would still in fifteen years' time be responsible for over 90% of power. The distributing monopoly would, therefore, be powerless to challenge the CEGB's terms or to impose upon it higher standards of efficiency.

Only if the distributing monopoly built and operated stations more efficiently than the new CEGB (thereby inducing the latter to adopt higher standards) could 'competition' in the building of new power stations be of economic benefit. But the distributing monopoly and the new CEGB are sister organisations in their managerial origins. With no new management and operating from positions of unassailable monopoly strength, why should they be more efficient than the existing ESI?

The regulatory problems would be even more intractable since the regulator would have to adjudicate on the rival claims of the two organisations to build the new non-nuclear stations. Electorally, this option might well be a greater liability than the single monopoly. The unwieldiness of this structure, and the additional layers of costs would soon lead to public dissatisfaction and hasten the date at which both were subject to US style regulation.

In defence of this proposal stress has been laid on the grid being privatised as a separate company. This is certainly desirable in the context of a competitive generation system. But it is of minimal importance in a system where the grid serves power generation without real competition.

(iv)   Establishment of integrated regional utilities

Under this option a number of vertically integrated regional utilities (henceforth called IRUs) would be created which would combine ownership of both power stations and distribution, a structure similar to the South of Scotland Electricity Board, which is widely judged to be more responsive to consumers then the ESI in England and Wales. The IRUs would effectively be regional monopolies since, apart from a few bulk customers, all other consumers, and particularly households, would depend entirely on the IRU of their region.

Common to all the IRU variants is the need to have the national grid as a separate, independent and regulated entity. It could remain in public ownership. But it would be more responsive to consumer demand and to the needs of power supply if privatised and regulated. It would be a common carrier with fixed terms and act as the common link between the IRUs and bulk consumers. It would have a statutory duty not to discriminate between any users. Its independence would ensure that electricity was traded efficiently between the IRUs, thus preserving a measure of generating competition and allowing reserve capacity to be shared. Indeed, it could and should have full powers to run a merit order system much like the present one. With some £4 billion of assets, consisting for the most part of transmission lines, and an assured income, the national grid would not be hard to sell.

The IRUs could take a number of shapes. They could be based on the existing Area Boards in England and Wales. Or new regions could be formed. In practical terms the existing Area Boards could be used as building blocks, in order to speed the planning period, and to avoid disruption. But there is nothing sacred about the present number of twelve Area Boards. Eventually, it might well be better to amalgamate them into five or six boards of broadly comparable size, if thereby economies of scale in power generation would be achieved.

One problem in setting up the IRUs would be how to break up the CEGB and allocate the existing power stations so that each IRU had enough generating capacity for its own needs (a practical problem on which we comment below). Another difficulty is that existing nuclear power stations cannot easily be incoporated in this regional structure. Few IRUs would want to adopt the existing ones, and even fewer would be likely to want to build new ones. Thus the present nuclear stations would have to stay within the public sector, with the resultant base load power sold on equitable terms to the IRUs. Future nuclear stations, unless subsidised, would be unlikely to be built, except possibly under co-ownership schemes. Problems of nuclear stations are treated more fully below, though most of the comments apply equally to the IRU option.

The IRU option has some advantages. It could lead to more responsiveness to consumers than the present ESI. It would also decentralise generation, and be financed in stages, either by selling IRUs in sequence or, better, by selling them all at once but with staged payments. This should be within the capacity of financial markets and thus avoid foreign control or domination. By creating a number of potential purchasers for coal, it would also permit the privatisation of coal.

This scheme, however, would fail even more of the criteria for efficient privatisation than the other monopoly options. First, it is extremely unlikely that it could be completed within the term of the present Government. Allocating the generating assets to the IRUs would be an extremely complex and technical task which could be accomplished only with the wholehearted co-operation of management and unions. CEGB management would certainly oppose the option, and union agreement to the transfer of the members to new companies would occur, if at all, only after very lengthy negotiations and very substantial improvements in pay and conditions.

Reorganisation would be very expensive; and there would be no offsetting efficiency gains from the introduction of competition. No simple regulation of the British Gas type could be used for the IRUs; since the economics of each would vary depending on the amount of generation for which they were responsible and the extent of the new construction which they would have to undertake. As in the US the utilities would have to be allowed enough profit to finance their building programmes. This in turn would raise all the problems which have arisen with this system in the US; for example, precisely what rate of profit should they be allowed, what conditions of efficiency must be fulfilled, and (most important of all) how could the utilities be prevented from over-investing in order to secure the investment-related profit? And this in turn raises the problem of how to allocate the new building programme between utilities, each anxious for the additional profit and scale of activity which such building would bring.

Almost certainly under this option governments would be driven towards the US system of regulation, despite its high cost, ineffectiveness and political contentiousness.

A final disadvantage is that the IRU option not only fails to meet most of the essential political and economic criteria, but also creates so many new monopolies that it stands even less chance than the other monopoly options of any later restructuring in order to meet those criteria (that is if a government were later to want to inject more competition).

In conclusion, it is evident that none of the monopoly options or their variants can be recommended. All fail too many of the essential criteria. If privatisation is to be effective it must introduce adequate competition.

Options for competitive privatisation

The options so far considered suffer from disadvantages so serious that it would be a grave mistake for the Government to adopt any of them. The Government should either choose a scheme which introduces early competition, or else use this Parliamentary term to study the problems more thoroughly and prepare for competitive privatisation later. This section assesses schemes to introduce competition, and the option to 'do nothing yet'.

The first competitive option was outlined in *Privatise Coal* and has been urged by others (including Alex Henney in *Privatise Power*). It keeps generation and distribution separate, and breaks up the CEGB into units which compete to supply regional distribution utilities (which we will henceforth call RDUs). This is the 'competitive generation' option, or 'CG'. The second option is original to this paper; it was created and developed by A J Merrett. It has the same aim as the first option but would be introduced over a transitional period with safeguards built in to ensure competitive generation. At the start RDUs would own the new CEGB in partnership. Over the years they would sell off blocks of power stations to form a number of balanced, independent generating companies in competition with one another. The National Grid would be independent from the beginning of privatisation. We have called this second option the 'Privatised transition to competition' (PTC).

Let us discuss the CG option first in its most satisfactory version.

(i) The CG system and variants

The CG system recognises that generation is inherently competitive, and that distribution and transmission are naturally monopolistic, needing to be regulated to prevent abuse of power. But distribution, although it is a monopoly activity whether at local, regional or national levels must be in multiple ownership. Otherwise the competing generating companies would be facing a monopsonist (sole buyer), rendering them unattractive to private investors. And distribution must be in private ownership, too. If the RDUs were publicly owned, generating companies would believe that they were facing a *de facto* monopsonist.

Finally, the National Grid would be independent of both generating companies and RDUs. It would link generating companies and other power sources (e.g. France) to all electricity customers, and be open freely to all users on equal terms. Like the RDUs, it should be regulated; unlike them, it could either remain in public ownership (albeit strictly regulated by an independent regulatory agency), or be privately owned. The case for preferring private ownership is that it could function at least as well in the private sector, and might attract a higher quality management, some of whom might with advantage have international experience of large transmission systems.

The regulatory body

All the competitive privatisation options would need a regulatory body which we will call the 'Electricity Standards and Regulatory Commission' (ESRC). The functions of the ESRC are further considered in the context of the PTC option below.

Limits of regulation

Under the CG option it would be unnecessary to regulate generation, since prices and profits would be determined by competition. RDUs could be permitted to pass on (with certain exceptions) all operating costs and capital charges. In practice the RDUs would have only limited discretion over their levels of capital spending. American experience suggests that regulatory procedures which attempt to adjudicate how much of these costs should be passed on would be expensive and ineffective. The RDUs would, however, under their charter be required to spend capital in the most efficient manner possible.

The operating costs which the RDUs could pass on, however, would be limited to those incurred immediately prior to privatisation, subject to agreed indices of inflation. Such operating costs might best be expressed as an amount per user so that more costs in total might be passed on, as the number of users increased.

Regulation of the National Grid would essentially be on the 'cost of service' model established in the US, under which the owning company receives a regulatory rate of return on its investment—15% in

America on the equity after tax, together with all interest charges. The National Grid would be required to give fair access to all generating companies wishing to use the grid on a non-discriminating tariff.

The activities of the RDUs and of the National Grid would be subject to scrutiny by the Electricity Standards and Regulatory Commission described in the context of the PTC option below.

Evaluation

Tested against the essential political and economic criteria, the CG option achieves a score very much higher than any of the monopoly options. It ensures maximum competition and incentives to efficiency. It is the system most commonly urged by businessmen and economists who favour competition. The doubts which exist about it are mainly about the means of creating it in an effective and timely way. By introducing full competition in generating, and an independently controlled National Grid, consumers could look forward to lower power costs. Provided the ESI sales proceeds were paid for in stages over, say, 5 to 7 years (both debt and equity) the strain on the capital markets should not be great; and so risk of undervalued asset sales or of foreign domination and control would be negligible. Corporate investors with controlling shareholdings would need to be attracted to both the newly formed RDUs and the new generating companies (with perhaps 25% equity in both types of companies), in order to introduce enough new senior management to achieve the gains identified above. Regulation of a relatively straightforward kind would be needed only for transmission and distribution.

Finally, this option is fully compatible with coal privatisation on a competitive basis. The major new coal terminal, which the Government should put in hand immediately, could be co-operatively owned by the new generating companies in whose interest it would be to seek the best value in coal purchases.

Further, retention of the ESI pension scheme would present no problems. The list of advantages is formidable.

Problems of timing

The ESI could not, however, be restructured in this way during the present Government's term of office. First, there is the complex technical task of devising a generation system based on five or more independent, viable generation companies each with an efficient mix of generation capacity. Even if adequate CEGB co-operation could be secured in drawing up a plan for its own demise, completion and political ratification could not take less than a year. Only then could the extensive legal and organisational negotiations be begun, and staff recruited. Negotiation, too, with the industry's powerful unions would be necessary, who might well be slow to co-operate at all in the formation of a competitive system. In so far as they did, they would, understandably, demand the most exacting terms for their members' new contracts of employment and operational practices. No one can say how long this could take.

The new companies would also need to establish contractual relationships with the RDUs for the offtake of power. This task would be extremely complex since the load of each RDU would need to be determined by reference to the other RDUs, the generation capacity of all five companies and the efficient working of the system. The CEGB, which alone has the familiarity with the system and the necessary staff would have to undertake all these tasks. It is hard to see how they could be completed in less than three years. Thereafter the final task of floating 10 companies (say 5 RDUs and 5 generating companies) could proceed.

Generating companies with no profit record, and an untried structure and management, could probably not be floated successfully, unless reputable corporate investors were prepared to assume controlling interests. Negotiations to this end would take many months, and by no means all would succeed. The magnitude of the shareholding, the price, the future structure of the industry (e.g. the rules to protect competition), the regulatory regime, and safeguards against subsequent unfavourable legislation would all need to be negotiated in detail before corporate investors contemplated the £500 million or so required for a controlling investment. (The total sales proceeds per generating company would be say £2–£2½ billion, but a majority could be debt.) Cross reference to negotiations by other investors in the other new generating companies would also be required, so that investors could be sure that they were receiving at least equally favourable terms. Complex safeguards would also be needed against the possibility that, if investor interest was inadequate, a very few private companies might find themselves competing against a still formidable state-owned generating corporation.

In short, this option fails on the essential political criterion that privatisation be sure of completion this term. It is indeed improbable that such a restructuring could be accomplished without new commercial management and within the constraints of public ownership. Any attempt to do so could present an opportunity for prevarication and delay designed to postpone privatisation indefinitely. Another route towards the same desirable end must be found. To this we now turn.

ii)   The privatised transition to competition (PTC) option

The PTC scheme aims to build an initial structure which will lead within a reasonable time to competitive generation.

Generation, under control of the CEGB, at present dominates the ESI. The PTC option reverses this. It places the new CEGB under the control of a number of (say, at least five) privatised regional distributing utilities (RDUs) charged with introducing competition after privatisation. In order that these RDUs have new commercial managements able to assume such a responsibility, a controlling interest (say 25%) in each one would be offered to corporate investors on the same terms as the shares are offered to the public. Such corporate investors would need to show proven capabilities in the management of comparable industries, and should, where possible, also have regional associations. It would be desirable to include overseas companies with relevant ESI experience in each consortium of corporate investors, in order to ensure a breadth of ideas, experience and technical knowledge.

These privately owned RDUs would be allowed by the regulatory agency to pass on all costs incurred in their purchases of power. Their remuneration, however, would be along the lines described under the CG option; that is, flow-through (with certain exceptions of capital costs) with operating cost increases being allowed only in line with relevant indices of inflation and increases in the number of consumers.

RDUs would, however, be under a statutory obligation to minimise all power costs consistent with maintaining established standards of service. Discharge of these functions would be monitored by the Electricity Standards and Regulatory Commission described below.

The new CEGB (embodying the generation and transmission functions) would initially be a wholly owned joint venture subsidiary of all the RDUs, and be 100% debt-financed, the debt owned by the Treasury. This debt would be partially redeemed as power stations were sold off, with the remainder reflecting the value of the nuclear stations which would still be owned by the generating company (see below). Some residual guarantees might be required, however, in respect of the nuclear risks associated with the nuclear power stations. The company would operate on a cost-of-service basis; that is, it would have the right to pass on all its costs in the form of cost of power to the RDUs, which in their turn would have the right to pass these costs on to their consumers.

The rationale of this structure is as follows. First, any substantial equity stake by the RDUs in generation creates the problem which has bedevilled the US private utility system. American utilities have a vested interest in increasing their capital investment in order to secure greater profits from the (effectively guaranteed) returns which they are permitted on their equity investments. This, in its turn, requires detailed regulation even to attempt to check abuse. If the investment is 100% debt financed and remunerated solely on cost of service no such incentive to overinvestment exists. Second, it would in any case be extremely difficult to create an equity investment in a generation system which, as outlined below, would be a transitional privatised structure, soon leading on to one which was designed to maximise competition.

Achieving competition in generation
The RDUs would, at the appropriate stage, (specified at the time of privatisation to take realistic account of the time needed to prepare for power stations sales) oblige the new CEGB to offer for sale say five or six representative blocks of its existing stations. Each block would have a mix of type and age of station which could be geographically dispersed. The nuclear units would be treated differently, as discussed below. The new CEGB would then buy back power from the owners on competitive long term contracts; the blocks of power stations would be sold, and the power contract awarded to whichever potential owner offered the most favourable terms. The new owners would have complete freedom in their purchase of fuels. This should greatly encourage companies in the fuel and coal industries to bid for fuel supply contracts, and so should ensure much more competition in the supply of fuels for power generation than there is now. All new power stations other than nuclear (whether for replacement or expansion of capacity) would also be thrown open to competitive bidding on the same lines.

Long term power contracts would also provide the basis for financing the purchase of the power stations largely by debt, with relatively small equity investment. In this way the number of potential corporate investors would be enlarged, as may be essential if political and economic policy restrict the extent of foreign ownership. The long term contract basis has another advantage. It is immune from the risks of subsequent regulatory impositions, leaving bidders free to pitch their bids at levels representing their perceptions of the profit and risk opportunities. This structure would also permit the new CEGB to continue to operate a merit order system.

As well as making the introduction of competition a fundamental charter requirement, the RDUs should also be given the incentive of a direct share in the resulting savings.

Progression towards competition to supply the RDUs
With independent companies owning stations and supplying power on a financially viable basis, it would become possible to progress towards direct competition in the supply of power to the RDUs (rather than via the new CEGB). This could develop step-by-step with the companies supplying power on long term contract to the new CEGB (owning by now only nuclear stations and acting as purchase and despatch agency for the RDUs). The companies would allocate part of their capacity to the supply of power on a competitive basis to the RDUs or direct to large consumers on whatever terms they could negotiate. This, however, could not occur until the companies were established with diversity of supply and capital base sufficient to give them material advantages over the centralised purchase system. This the sale of stations and long term power contracts would provide.

A powerful driving force would be required to ensure that the new CEGB was not obstructive, but conducted the power contract tendering objectively and promptly. This force would be provided by the RDUs and, in particular by their controlling corporate shareholders. The latter would have no vested interest in maintaining the existing CEGB structure; indeed they would be given a strong financial incentive to break it up whereupon they would receive an agreed share of lower power costs, to increase their profits. There would be time for the complex technical and negotiating processes involved in the competitive system to be achieved with the minimum disruption and with privatisation already a *fait accompli*.

Flotation of the PTC structure within the term of the present Government should also be simpler than flotation of any other possible structure. Equity investment would be confined to the RDUs and perhaps be less than a quarter of the equity required to float the monolith structure described above. The whole of the generating system would be debt financed and the bonds representing this debt would be held by the Government to be redeemed as the blocks of power stations are sold off. Consequently costs arising from possible undervaluation of the otherwise immense equity issues would be reduced. The well-defined regulatory structure should also eliminate uncertainties which would otherwise be a source of undervaluation. Finally the much smaller equity investment would diminish the risk that a downturn in equity markets would cause the whole programme of electricity privatisation to be postponed to another term (if not indefinitely). This avoids a major risk inherent in all the other options.

Political advantages are also significant. Risk of disruption through attempting to force the CEGB into break-up as a preliminary to privatisation is avoided. The CEGB would retain a valuable role and scope for its expertise in its continuing control of the nuclear sector, and, in the medium term, the functions of central power purchasing, system planning and operation. Moreover, under this structure the CEGB would initially be privatised as an integral structure, albeit under the stronger and more commercially orientated management of the RDUs and their controlling corporate investors. This should reduce the risk of union militancy sabotaging a privatisation flotation based on break-up of the generation system.

The National Grid
During the planning period the CEGB would be required to separate the assets, management and staff of the National Grid so that it could be hived off as an independent entity, private but regulated, at the time of privatisation. Thus any competitive sources of electricity would be available to the RDUs and bulk customers from the beginning. Then, as blocks of power stations were sold off their power would be freely available to all power customers, a vital requirement for investors in generating companies. Regulation would be as explained under the PTC option.

The nuclear sector
This is an exceptional category of investment, and necessitates exceptional measures—concerning, first, the terms on which any private sector financing might be available for the existing nuclear power stations. Ownership of these stations carries apparently very large, although incalculable, obligations which relate to their operation, possible modification and decommissioning. Their operation involves liability for nuclear accident—a risk all but uninsurable in the commerical markets. If higher safety standards were imposed, the stations could be closed down. In the future they will have to be

decommissioned. The costs are likely to be huge and most uncertain—they depend on the environmental and safety requirements prevailing at the time.

What private sector investor could or would assume these risks? Almost everywhere in the world they are borne either by governments, or by the nuclear generating companies which can pass the costs on in full to their consumers. In the United States they are borne partly by the Federal Government and partly by consumers through the tariffs imposed by the US private utilities.

The nuclear sector also has special problems of power station construction. Cost, long lead times and the many unpredictabilities make it almost inconceivable that nuclear power stations could be built unless these risks are assumed by the Government (as in Britain at present) or in part by the consumer (as in the US). In the United States the construction of nuclear stations is in large measure a cost plus operation since, provided that a utility acts prudently and diligently, it is practically sure to recover its investment through the tariffs which it is allowed to impose.

Options, then for the privatisation of the nuclear sector are as follows:

i) *The US system of regulated private utilities*
It was pointed out above that in the US private financing is secured only at the expense of extensive regulation which generally results in a cost-plus non-competitive system of operation. It is doubtful whether gains in the form of reduction in the public sector borrowing requirement would warrant the very high cost of setting up such a system of regulation.

ii) *Retention within the public sector*
This would mean that the public sector would continue to bear the burden of financing; but that the need for a separate regulatory body would be obviated. But if nuclear power generation is to fit within a merit order system, it would constitute base load capacity (since its operating costs are relatively low). Provision would have to be made so that distributing companies were obliged to accept this power as part of their base load.

This, however, should not pose significant difficulties since a) the nuclear capacity is already operated as base load—hence no change in the operating regime is involved and b) pre-emption of about 20% of the load by nuclear would still leave 80% of power requirements to be met by the private sector.

iii) *Ownership by RDUs as 100% debt-financed subsidiary (the PTC option)*

Under this option the nuclear sector would be owned in partnership by all the RDUs. This nuclear power company would be 100% debt financed (private debt replacing Treasury debt) by firm 'take or pay' contracts from the RDUs. These contracts (commonly employed in the US) require payment of the cost of service irrespective of the amount of power taken. They are essentially a basis for financing. Such contracts in effect already exist since the CEGB charges the consumer whatever the cost of power is from these stations. The new nuclear power company would effectively be given taxing powers. Given the unqualified right of the RDUs to pass these costs on to consumers, the risk of default by the nuclear company would be minimal. Nevertheless, the Government would probably have to provide supplementary undertakings including the assumption of full nuclear accident liability, deficit guarantees in the event of widespread nuclear shutdown and residual financing responsibility if the nuclear programme required more funding than could be obtained from the commercial markets. Since in practice the Government already has the obligations, formalising them in this manner should be acceptable.

In the past governments have reserved for themselves control over nuclear power policy and will presumably do so in the future. This could be provided for (and be seen as a quid pro quo for the undertakings referred to above) by a 'golden share' giving it such policy powers.

The nominal equity of the nuclear company would be owned by the RDUs under the structure described above, which charges these utilities with the responsibility to ensure minimum cost of power consistent with security of supply. This function as it relates to the nuclear company would be limited by the Government's power of intervention on policy. Nevertheless, the distributing utilities would provide a countervailing force reflecting the consumer interest, one with considerable resources, standing—and above all independence. Given also that their reputation with the public would depend to a large extent on containing power cost increases, they would be likely to exercise their powers fully.

There is no way (short of extensive regulation) by which the RDUs could directly benefit from their stewardship over the nuclear company—the cost of service structure effectively involves a flow-through of its costs including the debt service by which it is financed. There would, however, be some advantage in ensuring that these utilities are not influenced in the extremely costly investment decisions of the nuclear company by the prospect of direct financial benefit. As noted above such motivation has had some most adverse consequences in the US.

This option is certainly the 'least worst' and offers significant benefits (private financing and powerful representation of consumer interest) compared with retaining the nuclear industry within the public sector. Nevertheless, it is a pity that no genuinely competitive solution with private risk capital seems possible. The Government should consider whether the alleged economic benefits of nuclear power fully justify the support of a technology which by its sheer scale of financial and technological risk precludes such private sector investment.

Electricity Standards and Regulatory Commission

Under the PTC option, as indeed with all options, an Electricity Standards and Regulatory Commission would be appointed with Government, ESI and consumer representation. For the PTC option, it would:—

i) ensure that historical standards of service were maintained by the RDUs and, where any significant variation was judged in the consumer interest, that the consumer shared appropriately in the benefits;

ii) supervise the regulatory process as it applied to the RDUs and ensure compliance;

iii) ensure that capacity in generation and transmission was adequate to secure reliability. (If it foresaw any inadequacy, it would instruct the RDUs to invite competitive tenders for new stations. Capacity could not fall short unless demand was underestimated—which is a risk to which any system is equally exposed);

iv) ensure that if there were any serious breaches of the charter, the corporate shareholders in the RDUs would be obliged to surrender their shareholdings (on an appropriate non-profit basis) to other corporate investors deemed more suitable;

v) maintain competition in generation, and free entry to the industry by ensuring that all generators of power had access on fair terms to the transmission system and hence to all possible purchasers, and that there was no collusion between generating companies; and

vi) adjudicate on representations that tariff levels were unfair between one category of customer and another. In the event of finding the tariff unfair it could require the RDUs to put forward alternative tariffs.

To sum up, the ESRC would act as regulatory agency for distribution and transmission, and would ensure that power generation remained competitive.

Conclusion on PTC option

The PTC option thus meets all the essential criteria. In particular, it would inject genuine competition, introduce new management, establish effective but simple regulation and provide a path to complete privatisation within the life of the present Government. Not least it also provides a basis on which the large financial burdens of the nuclear sector could be financed from the private capital markets.

And it is flexible and relatively free of risk. At the very worst it might not prove possible—for a considerable time—to reach agreement with the ESI unions on implementing the competitive generation system. If so, then that would apply equally to any other option involving comparable competitiveness. Under the PTC option, however, it would at least be possible to defer the issue and return to it at a later date. This would still leave the new, 100% debt financed CEGB free from the very serious regulatory problems bound to arise if it was substantially equity financed. Sumilarly, the RDUs, having no equity investment in the new CEGB, would have no vested interest in maintaining the status quo, or in opposing subsequent moves towards greater competition. Indeed, they would have a sharp spur to achieve greater efficiency; with financial incentives, they would wish to sell power stations to reliable purchasers as soon as possible. With strong corporate shareholders, they would be a strong countervailing force acting in the interest of consumers, in an industry which has been traditionally dominated by the CEGB. On these grounds we hold that the PTC option (or some variant of it) is superior to any other privatisation option so far proposed.

iii) Privatisation deferred to a later term

No one should assume that all forms of privatisation are superior to maintaining the status quo, least of all those forms with unnecessary or badly regulated monopoly activities. Even sensible forms of privatisation might be worse than deferral if they were inadequately thought-out or poorly designed through lack of time. Given therefore that the Government has not spent undue time planning ESI privatisation, and that margins for error are considerable, the privatisation options should be compared with maintenance of the status quo (or at least with deferment of privatisation to a later term). We have no wish to join the chorus of vested interests urging caution and delay. All the same the case for deferral must be examined.

The clearest gain is that it gives the Government the chance to do the job properly, provided that it wins the next election. But if it does not, the chance for privatisation may not recur this century. Then there is the advantage that risk of disruption to the system is nil; but this risk is slight for any privatisation option.

Consumers might well be dissatisfied with deferral; in particular industrial consumers who would be at a disadvantage compared with their international competitors. GNP and employment would suffer accordingly. Individual consumers would also be hurt, though they might be less aware of it. But since ultimate government control would remain, consumers would not be as badly off as under monopoly privatisation accompanied by unsatisfactory forms of regulation (and unsatisfactory regulation is a real possibility given the lack of British experience in this field). For management and staff redundancies would be fewer, but equally pay would be lower; and there would be no profit incentives and no chance of building up capital. Then, there would be no risk of foreign ownership or domination of the ESI. Finally, since there would be no sale, there would be no problem of undervaluation. But the tendency to overinvestment would continue.

Deferral would fail all the essential economic criteria. Competition would not be introduced (past attempts to permit private power stations have largely failed, and could reasonably be expected to fail in future); there would be a probably fatal incompatibility with a liberal form of coal privatisation; much needed new management would not be introduced; the existing unsatisfactory form of political and bureaucratic regulation on a largely unaccountable basis would continue unchanged; and finally no opportunities would be created for individual and corporate investors. This is a damning economic score, but no worse than for most of the monopoly forms of privatisation. On the other hand, since the status quo preserves the vital option of later privatisation in a liberal form (assuming that the

Government has such a scheme ready for early implementation in a fourth term) we judge that it should be ranked higher than the irreversible monopoly options.

Summary and conclusions

A summary guide to the four basic ESI monopoly privatisation options and the two competitive options is appended at the end of this paper. In this final section we concentrate on the salient points which must be considered if the ESI is to be privatised effectively, that is to meet the essential political and economic criteria. The results of all the analyses in the paper are set out in Tables 1, 2 and 3 below.

The objectives

The manifesto on which the Government won its third term promised privatisation of the ESI. Given the vigorous exposition of the virtues of competition in the manifesto, the principal aim of this privatisation should be the introduction of genuine competition to ensure maximum efficiency. Not that this has been the guiding objective in earlier large privatisation schemes. Raising funds, wider share ownership and the reduction of government involvement in business decision-taking have been given pride of place. But growing consumer dissatisfaction with British Telecom, and more recently with British Gas, puts the electoral popularity of the privatisation programme at risk. To introduce competition, improve efficiency and reduce the cost of electricity should now be the essential aims.

The achievable benefits

The annual cost reductions from an effective privatisation of the electricity supply industry on competitive lines should be a minimum of £1200 million a year within five years, rising thereafter. Half these benefits, £600 million, presume the privatisation of British Coal on the competitive basis set out in *Privatise coal—achieving international competitiveness*, i.e., by reducing British coal costs to import levels.*

---

*Reductions in costs of coal will be speeded if the Government shows its determination to put the interests of consumers first by requiring the CEGB immediately to start building a new coal terminal.

The total present value of these long term savings to Britain from ESI privatisation would be a minimum of £13 billion, plus a further *net £4* billion from British Coal. These represent substantial potential benefits for the nation, but they depend upon *competitive* privatisation of both the coal and electricity industries. In addition, the Sales proceeds from ESI privatisation are estimated for England and Wales at £13½ billion to £18 billion (perhaps a further £2½ billion from Scotland), with a further £1½ billion to £3½ billion from coal privatisation.

Given the magnitude of the potential gains, we argue that it would be better to defer privatisation than to adopt a scheme which involves foregoing these benefits—since a government gets, at best, one chance in a decade to alter the structure of a basic industry. If it makes a mistake the political and economic consequences are incalculable.

CEGB breakup: essential

It is agreed by most people, apart from those serving the vested interests of the CEGB and the power unions, that benefits from privatising the ESI depend upon breaking up the CEGB into say five or six competing generating companies. Nothing less will provide genuine and lasting competition in generating, the non monopoly part of the ESI which accounts for over 70% of the total costs. The CEGB needs to be broken up in this way to provide companies with a broadly equal and balanced spread of power stations, all acquired at comparable costs, such that they can offer reliable, competitive, *variable load,* power to all customers, in particular to the regional distribution utilities (RDUs). Effective competition cannot be introduced into the ESI on a station-by-station piecemeal basis in competition with a continuing CEGB—a massive system of 78 power stations acquired at a major discount to current costs which could use its resources tactically to overwhelm small emergent companies bidding to supply power.

It is a serious delusion to believe that viable new competitors can emerge, paying current costs, and building a mere one or two stations at a time. There is *no* staff option for introducing effective competition.

The only way of creating viable competition is to break up the massive CEBG, already the largest generating company in the Western world. Nor can the marginal import of power from France and

Scotland provide sufficient competition to the continuing CEBG, welcome though the use of these relatively neglected power sources would be. Finally, only a breakup of the CEGB will permit coal privatisation on a competitive basis, since few if any private companies would invest in coal on any terms acceptable to the Government if they faced a near-monopoly buyer.

In other words, there is no easy option whereby effective competition can be introduced into the ESI without breaking up the CEGB. But without competition in generation, privatisation is pointless.

The existing nuclear power stations, and the Government's intention of having many more in future, pose special problems which have been considered at length in this paper. Because of their large risks of operations, the immense costs and uncertainties involved in their construction, and their doubtful profitability if coal is privatised effectively, neither the ownership of existing (or shortly to be completed) nuclear power stations nor the building of new ones, is likely to attract the private sector on a risk capital basis. The Government should consider the analysis and questions posed in this paper and rethink the case for its present nuclear power policy. It is still wishes to have a major nuclear power programme then it must accept either the provision of large subsidies or else special arrangements of the kind we have identified. Nuclear power could be privatised under the PTC option on a private sector financing basis.

Practical implementation—the PTC scheme

While the desirable goal for ESI privatisation is clear the route to achieving it is not. In default of identifying any such route, the Government may seek initially to privatise only the distributing utilities (the present Area Boards) and maintain the CEGB intact while examining further the problems of privatising it effectively. Such an outcome, with no certainty of achieving any of the substantial benefits from electricity and coal privatisation, and which would preclude the effective privatisation of power stations under effective new corporate management, must be deplored. Fortunately, it is unnecessary because there is a scheme identified in the paper—the 'Privatised Transition to Competition' Scheme (PTC)—which can be made to realise *all* the benefits identified, meeting as it does the essential political and economic criteria by which privatisation should be judged.

The PTC scheme introduces corporate investors with the means, experience, management and incentive to transform the CEGB into 5 independent generating companies within 2 to 5 years of privatisation. It avoids the main weakness of all the other privatisation schemes which either maintain the CEGB intact and thus fail to realise the potential efficiency benefits, or which require the CEGB to break itself up, which would be unlikely to happen without the involvement of new entities or new management.

The privatisation options compared

It is impossible to judge the six serious privatisation options which we have considered in this paper (four monopoly ones and two competitive ones) without agreement on the essential criteria. In another section we evaluated six such essential political criteria and five such essential economic criteria. Summary tables follow, with a quick recapitulation of the options in the appendix.

From these tables, and particularly the final summary evaluation column it is seen that the PTC option is the only one to pass all the essential criteria, making it the preferred choice. The CG option fails one essential criterion, but comes second. The 'do nothing yet' or deferral option comes next, because while failing many of the political criteria and all of the economic criteria, it is nevertheless superior to all of the monopoly options. Of the monopoly options, the IRU is somewhat better than the two monolithic options, but none of them scores at all well, and there is little to choose between them.

Conclusion

The PTC is the only competitive privatisation scheme so far identified which meets the Government's criterion of possible accomplishment in its present term of office, without risk of either serious disruption or eventual consumer dissatisfaction. It further ensures maximum efficiency and lower electricity prices by introducing genuine and *sustainable* competition by means of a structure which would attract powerful corporate investors and new senior management, and yet involve minimal regulations.

Thus there *is* a realistic route to effective electricity privatisation for the Government to follow.

Table 1
ESSENTIAL POLITICAL CRITERIA

Options	1 Absence of Serious Disruption	2 Assured ESI Privatisation This Term	3 Minimum Risk of Consumer Dissatisfaction	4 Generous Profit Participation /Redundancy Arrangements	5 No Foreign Control/ Domination of ESI	6 No Unacceptable Undervaluation of Assets
A. Monolith:						
i) US Style Regulation	√	√	X	—	√	X?
ii) UK Discretionary Style Regulation	√	√	X	—	√	√?
B. Initial Generating Monolith—Competitive New Generation:						
i) CEGB Competes for New Capacity	√	√	X	—	√	√
ii) CEGB Prevented From Competing:						
a) In New Capacity	√	√	X	—	√	?
b) In New Capacity Plus Replacement Capacity	√	√	X	—	√	X?
C. Electricity Council Proposal	√	√	X	—	√	?
D. Integrated Regional Monopolies:						
i) US Style Regulation	√	X?	X	√	√	X
ii) UK Discretionary Style Regulation	√	X?	X	√	√	?√
E. Competitive Generation Sale of Asset Blocs with Transitional Power Contracts	√	X	√	√	√	√
F. Privatised Transition to Competition (PTC)	√	√	√	√	√	√
G. Do Nothing Yet	√	—	?X	—	√	√

Key   √ Acceptable   — Neutral or Not Applicable   X Unacceptable   ? Uncertain

Table 2

ESSENTIAL ECONOMIC CRITERIA

Options	1 Introduction of Maximum Competition	2 Compatible with Competitive Coal Privatisation	3 Introduction of New Senior Management	4 Simple But Effective Regulation of Monopoly Activities	5 Attractive to UK Individual and Corporate Investors
A. Monolith:					
i) US Style Regulation	x	x	x	x	√?
ii) UK Discretionary Style Regulation	x	x	x	x	?√
B. Initial Generating Monolith—Competitive New Generation:					
i) CEGB Competes for New Capacity	x	x	x	x	?√
ii) CEGB Prevented from Competing:					
a) In New Capacity	x	x	x?	x	?
b) In New Capacity Plus Replacement Capacity	x?	x	x?	x	x?
C. Electricity Council Proposal	x	x	x	x	√?
D. Integrated Regional Monopolies:					
i) US Style Regulation	x	√	?	x	√?
ii) UK Discretionary Style Regulation	x	√	?	?x	√?
E. Competitive Generation Sale of Asset Blocs with Transitional Power Contracts	√	√	√	√	√
F. Privatised Transition to Competition (PTC)	√	√	√	√	√
G. Do Nothing Yet	x	x	x	x	-

Key   √ Acceptable   - Neutral or not Applicable   x Unacceptable   ? Uncertain

Table 3
DESIRABLE FURTHER CRITERIA

	1	2	3
Options	*Minimum Period of Planning Uncertainty*	*Minimum Period of Structural Change*	*Retention of Industry Pension Scheme*
A. Monolith:			
i) US Style Regulation	2	2	3
ii) UK Discretionary Style Regulation	3	3	3
B. Initial Generating Monolith—Competitive New Generation:			
i) CEGB Competes for New Capacity	2	3	3
ii) CEGB Prevented from Competing:			
a) In New Capacity	2	1	3
b) In New Capacity Plus Replacement Capacity	2	1	3
C. Electricity Council Proposal	3	3	3
D. Integrated Regional Monopolies:			
i) US Style Regulation	1	2	3
ii) UK Discretionary Style Regulation	1	3	3
E. Competitive Generation: Sale of Asset Blocs with Transitional Power Contracts	1	3	3
F. Privatised Transition to Competition (PTC)	3	3	3
G. Do Nothing Yet	-	-	3

Key   1 Is Worst   3 Is Best

A Summary guide to the options

Monolithic privatisation with British style regulation

This option, urged by the CEGB is to privatise the whole ESI as a single entity, subject to minimal regulation as with British Gas. Absence of competition and the ineffectiveness of this type of regu-

Table 4
SUMMARY EVALUATION

		Final Rank
Essential Criteria	_Desirable Criteria_	
Passes Out of 11	_Score Out of 9_	
4 4	7 9	5/6/7
3 3	8 6	5/6/7
4	9	5/6/7
5 5	6 7	4
10	7	2
11	9	1
3 Pass 3 Neutral	3	3

lation would make this option fail all the essential economic criteria. Consumers would be likely soon to be dissatisfied; so it fails some essential political criteria, too.

Monolithic privatisation with competition in new generation

This is to privatise the ESI in its present form, subject to the discretionary type of regulation imposed on British Gas—but to allow competition in new generation. Private companies could compete to build new power stations to supply the new CEGB, distributors and possibly bulk customers direct. In practice few if any would do so, since the need for balanced supply contracts requires that the viable competitive unit has a _spread_ of different types of power stations.

Few economic benefits would flow from this option. Competition with the new CEGB would in practice be minimal, since it could occur only in the building and operation of the non nuclear stations. Even if every new non nuclear station were built by private investors, 10% at most of generating capacity installed at the end of the century would be in private hands. Even this may well be a gross overestimate. The new non-nuclear stations proposed by the CEGB are 1800 MW coal stations costing around £1.5 billion, each with a seven year or more lead time to completion. Few investors would contemplate investments of this magnitude and lead time in order to enter into competition with the massively entrenched new CEGB.

Such a scheme would also continue to confront the coal industry with a dominant buyer, and thus preclude the privatisation of coal with all its potential economic benefits.

Finally, if the type of regulation is as minimal as it is with British Gas, the scheme would probably not produce any improvements in efficiency. Such regulation would most likely prove grossly inadequate, so the governments would be obliged to impose the expensive, politically contentious but still largely ineffectual forms of regulation which pervade the US private utility industry.

Monopoly distribution and transmission with competition in new generation (the Electricity Council scheme)

This, the Electricity Council proposal, combines all the disadvantages of the single monopoly with additional regulatory problems. It would create two separate monopolies (one of generation, one of distribution). The distribution monopoly would be allowed to compete in new generation, but in practice competition would be minimal. All the expertise in building and operating power stations would remain with the new CEGB. And even assuming that the new distribution monopoly were to build all new non-nuclear power stations required by the end of the century, the CEGB would still supply 90 percent of power in England and Wales. Competition would be token. There would be no new corporate investors; and therefore unlikely to be any new senior management. So cost reductions would be improbable. Regulators would face all but insurmountable difficulties in dealing with two such huge monopolies. The proposal fails half the essential political criteria, and almost all the essential economic criteria. It is clearly inferior to the status quo.

Integrated regional utilities (IRUs)

This, the fourth monopoly option, involves the creation of a number of regional 'power boards' having local monopolies of distribution, and generating most of their own power. Because it would be natural for the 'power boards' to favour their own generating sources, they would have considerable incentives to over-invest, so that this system would need US style regulation. That means extensive semijudical review of costs, investments and prices; and adjudication on the need for and type of future additions to generating capacity.

Based on American experience, this would be both costly and ineffectual. Effective competition—and improvements in efficiency—would be minimal. It is indeed more likely that additional layers of costs would be created in forming these companies and meeting union demands. The main benefits which could accrue from this option would be indirect, in that it would create several buyers of power station coal in place of one, permitting the privatisation of coal. Even so, it fails most of the essential political and economic criteria.

Competitive generation with regulated distribution (CG)

This option involves dividing the CEGB into five or so privatised generating companies serving some five Regional Distribution Utilities (RDU's) formed by amalgamating the 12 Area Boards. If it could be achieved within the term of the present government, it would fulfil all the essential criteria. Competition would produce pressure for efficiency, no regulation would be required in generation (70% of total power cost); and the scheme would create the diversified market which would enable coal privatisation to proceed. But it fails the criterion of being achievable within the term of the present Government. It would first require the CEGB to produce a technically viable plan for its own demise, an unlikely outcome. Second, it would require the establishment of some ten new companies—the five generating ones without any previous commercial management, staffing, sales contracts or profit record. Although such deficiencies could be remedied over time, much more than a parliamentary term would be required. So a mechanism is needed which will overcome the transitional difficulties in an acceptably short period.

Privatised transition to competition (PTC)

An intermediate stage of privatisation is required, so structured as to guarantee to bring about the competitive option—but over a more realistic period. The PTC model could achieve this as follows:—

i) amalgamate the existing Area Boards into, say, 5 RDUs and give qualified corporate investors a controlling interest (say 25%) on the same terms as the balance of the shares sold to the public;

ii) establish the National Grid on a regulated independent basis, open to all existing or potential power sources on equal terms to guarantee free access to all RDU and bulk customers;

iii) make the new CEGB a wholly owned subsidiary of these RDUs with the latter given the specific charter requirement to introduce competition in generation as soon as is practical. Since cost reductions would be shared, the RDUs would also be given a strong financial incentive to introduce generating competition. Simultaneously new controlling management should be brought in to provide a basis for quick progress to a fully competitive system;

iv) establish the new CEGB as 100% debt financed, the debt being held initially by the Treasury with all the costs of operation flowed through to the consumer (via the RDUs, effectively as the CEGB's costs now are). Debt financing is to provide for the subsequent sale of part of the assets to private companies, very difficult if the new CEGB was financed by equity (since at the time of privatisation the terms and conditions of its future sale would be unforeseeable); and

v) post privatisation give the RDUs the duty, the power and the incentive to establish competitive generation in an orderly manner. Deriving no profit from the 100% debt financed CEGB they would have no vested interest in sustaining its existence in its then form; indeed, they would be given a strong financial incentive to introduce more efficient and competitive generation. Their task would be to make the CEGB sell off viable blocks of power stations to the private sector; and then buy back the power on long term contracts based on competitive tendering by intending purchasers of the stations. These contracts would constitute a basis on which substantial debt financing could be secured. When enough independent generating capacity had been established in this manner, the new generating companies could then deal directly with the RDUs on a competitive basis, thus realising the desired CG option.

The new CEGB (retaining the nuclear sector on the basis of 100% debt flow-through of costs) could remain a subsidiary of the RDUs. This would provide the financing for the nuclear programme from the private sector and impose further degree of supervision by the RDUs, acting in accordance with prescribed government policy.

The RDUs could be remunerated on the basis of permitting them to flow through capital charges to consumers—but limiting the operating costs which they might charge to those incurred prior to privatisation; subject to increases for relevant inflation and adjustments for the number of users.

Breaking up a monopoly—non-commercial, integrated and unionised—into a number of commercial companies requires new management of very high calibre indeed. Only experienced, corporate investors can supply such management, which must be a feature of any proposal designed to secure the economic benefits and to avoid serious dissatisfaction among consumers. This is what the PTC option, and only the PTC option, provides.

Privatisation deferred

Although it is the Government's proclaimed intention to privatise the ESI in its present term, some forms of privatisation are inferior to maintaining the status quo (which at least leaves it open to privatise on a competitive basis at a later date). In our judgement, *all* the monopoly options are inferior to deferral.

Notes

1. Reported in the *Financial Times*, 19 March 1987.
2. More detailed descriptions are in the annual reports of the nationalised electricity corporations and in *Electricity Supply in the United Kingdom: Organisation and Development*, Electricity Council, 1980.
3. Monopolies and Mergers Commission, *Central Electricity Generating Board*, HMSO, June 1987.
4. *Nuclear Energy Agency, project costs of generating electricity from nuclear and coal-fired power stations for commissioning in 1995*, OECD 1985.
5. See *Can Coal be Saved?* Colin Robinson and Eileen Marshall, Institute of Economic Affairs, Hobart Paper No 105, 1985.
6. Electricity price controls may halt nuclear stations. *The Times*, 3 September 1987.
7. A number of economists have made this point. See, for example, *Privatising Electricity Generation*. Richard Pryke, Fiscal Studies, August 1987.
8. See Robinson and Marshall, op. cit.
9. *CEGB Annual Report of Accounts*, 1986–87. paras 6 and 41–43
10. See Henney, *Privatise Power*, Centre for Policy Studies, 1987.
11. Nuclear Energy Agency, op. cit.

12. On the starting grid but in need of a boost, the *Financial Times*, 7 August 1987.

13. See, for example, CEGB in talks to set up private power stations, the *Financial Times*, 27 August 1987 and CEGB talks on private power stations, *The Times*, 28 August 1987.

14. Private power stations, *The Times*, 28 August 1987.

15. Cabinet to discuss power sell-off, the *Financial Times*, 7 September 1987.

Glossary

AGR	Advanced gas cooled reactor. A British designed nuclear reactor which was the successor to Magnox
CCA	Current cost accounting
CEGB	Central Electricity Generating Board
EEPTU	Electrical, Electronic, Telecommunications and Plumbing Trades union
EPEA	Electrical Power Engineers Association
ESI	Electricity Supply Industry
ESRC	Electricity Standards and Regulatory Commission—a proposed regulatory body
GMBATU	General, Municipal, Boilermakers and Allied Trades Union
GW	Gigawatt—a unit of power. 1 gigawatt = 1000 megawatts
Joint Understanding	A pricing agreement between the CEGB and British Coal
Magnox	Early British designed nuclear reactor
MW	Megawatt—a unit of power. One megawatt = 1 million watts
NALGO	National and Local Government Officers Association
NHSEB	North of Scotland Hydro-Electric Board
PWR	Pressurised Water Reactor. A U.S. designed reactor exported to many parts of the world. The first PWR (adapted to British conditions) to be built in this country will be at Sizewell in Suffolk.
QUICS	Qualifying Industrial Consumers Scheme—a mechanism for providing low cost power to some large industrial users
$RPI - X + Y$	Gas price formula, where RPI is the retail price index, X is a factor set by the Government to reflect scope for improved efficiency and Y is increase in fuel costs
SSEB	South of Scotland Electricity Board